SMITHSONIAN INSTITUTION
BUREAU OF AMERICAN ETHNOLOGY
BULLETIN 175

MOHAVE ETHNOPSYCHIATRY: THE PSYCHIC DISTURBANCES OF AN INDIAN TRIBE

MOHAVE ETHNOPSYCHIATRY: THE PSYCHIC DISTURBANCES OF AN INDIAN TRIBE

By GEORGE DEVEREUX

SMITHSONIAN INSTITUTION PRESS

CITY OF WASHINGTON

Dedicated to

ERIC ROBERTSON DODDS, F.B.A.

Regius Professor of Greek, Emeritus, Oxford University

Ὅστις δὲ πλοῦτον ἢ cθένος μᾶλλον φίλων
ἀγαθῶν πεπᾶcθαι βούλεται, κακῶc φρονεῖ.
Euripides, *Herakles* 1425–26

Originally published 1961

Reprinted 1969

Distributed by Random House, Inc., in the
United States and Canada

Library of Congress catalog card number 73–84180

American Standard Book Number 87474–083–5

Distributed in the United Kingdom and Europe by
David & Charles (Publishers), Ltd., South Devon House,
Newton Abbot, Devon, England

CONTENTS

PREFACE TO THE REPRINT EDITION

The reprinting of this work has permitted me to make several additions and corrections. The most important of these is a sketch of Mohave culture, written at the suggestion of Geoffrey Gorer, who felt that it would be useful to readers unfamiliar with Yuman river cultures. I hope, however, that my discussion of Mohave supernaturalism will prove especially useful to the Mohave expert and to the scholar interested in the relationship between myth and ritual.

The new addenda contain some details accidentally omitted from the first edition, as well as a few supplementary cross-references and comments. An English translation of Latin passages in the text has been added, as well as a case index; both should facilitate the perusal of this work. The corrigenda rectify some misprints and slips of the pen.

Plates 3–10, which show only certain persons and sites mentioned in the text and a few typical landscapes, have been omitted from this edition. Plate 1, discussed in connection with Case 64, now faces p. 282; Plate 2, indispensable for an understanding of Case 78, faces p. 283.

The reprinting of this book also permits me to clear up two misunderstandings found in an exceptionally scholarly, thoughtful, favorable, and, in every other respect, meticulously accurate review:

1. Far from asserting that "psychic normality is relative, i.e., culture bound," I reject this preposterous theory as completely as the reviewer rejects it. I have combatted it already in my first two ethnopsychiatric papers (1939 c, d), have returned to the charge in several of my subsequent publications (1940 a, 1951 a, 1952 a, 1953 b, 1954 a, 1956 a, d, 1958 b, c, etc.) and criticize it also in this work (p. 147, n. 52, etc.). I deem it logically inadmissible to equate adjustment (a sociological state) with normality (a psychological state). On another level I view diagnostic cultural relativism as a symptom of ethical nihilism, alienation from reality, and supine conformism. In short, my conception of normality—like that of the reviewer—is not relativistic and culture bound but absolutistic and culturally neutral, i.e., psychoanalytic.

2. Like the reviewer, I do not believe that "a truly permissive upbringing of children would result in neurosis-free individuals," nor could I possibly have advocated such a view in a book which describes precisely the psychological disturbances of the very leniently brought up Mohave Indians. I have criticized this simplistic thesis both in this work (p. 220, n. 56) and in various other publications (1956 a, etc.). I hold, and my Mohave data show, that even in an "easy" culture, a rational, supportive, lenient, and flexible upbringing—whose theoretical

justification I outlined elsewhere (1956 a, etc.)—does not automatically produce a neurosis-free population; it only diminishes the incidence and, above all, the severity of psychological disorders. It is my belief that this reviewer would find it possible to concur with so conservatively formulated a statement.

I deemed it necessary to clear up these two problems precisely because they were raised by a reviewer whose ethnopsychiatric competence, scrupulousness, and impartiality are unquestionable. By contrast, I consider it otiose to answer here once more the only two reviews which are both captious and also unconscionably inaccurate on the factual level.* I simply note that no other reviewer detected in this book the "flaws" these two reviewers profess to have found in it.

I owe a great debt of gratitude to all those who made the publication of this edition possible and contributed, directly or indirectly, to its improvement. The Smithsonian Institution Press not only did me the honor of selecting this book to be among the first in their new reprint program but also permitted me to make numerous additions to it. The favorable reception accorded to this long and complex book by the many scholars who took great pains to review it both thoughtfully and accurately, materially influenced the Smithsonian Institution Press' decision to reprint it.

The idea of writing a sketch of Mohave culture was, as said before, suggested to me by Geoffrey Gorer in a review so insightful, accurate, and favorable that I wish it might have been reprinted as a preface to this edition.

My wife compiled the case index, edited the new preface, the sketch of Mohave culture, and the English translation of the Latin passages, and collected and organized the slips on which, over the years, I had jotted down various additions and corrections. Without her unflagging and skillful help these additions and corrections could not have been completed in the short time at my disposal.

GEORGE DEVEREUX
February 1969

---

* G. Devereux, Rejoinder, *Transcultural Psychiatric Research*, vol. 1 (1964), pp. 167–169.

A SKETCH OF MOHAVE CULTURE

The Mohave, a tribe of less than 1,000 individuals in aboriginal times, belong linguistically to the Yuman group of the Hokan family. Their culture, in some respects transitional between the cultures of the Southwest and the cultures of California, is the most distinctive of the Yuman river cultures.

The Mohave conquered one of the great valleys of the Colorado River sufficiently long ago to have evolved major myths inspired by certain striking features of their present habitat, such as Avi Kwame: Mountain, the Colorado River, Incest Rock, and so forth. They live on both banks of the Colorado River, whose Nile-like annual floods made alluvial agriculture possible. The country to the east and to the west is desert.

The Mohave consider the Fort Mohave area to be the heartland of their country, though in the course of the last 70 years or so most of the population was clustered around Needles, California, and Parker, Arizona. Living on scattered farms, in square, one-room adobe houses, and having no villages, the Mohave had no localized units and no parochial loyalties. Though their mythology occasionally mentions the occupation of a certain area by a gens, in practice the gentes were not localized. A Mohave could and did live and feel at home anywhere in Mohave country.

The Mohave were close allies of the kindred Yuma to the south and friendly with the Yuman Yavapai and with the western Apache to the east. Their traditional enemies were the Yuman Cocopa who lived to the south of the Yuma, the various Yuman tribes of the Gila River valley to the east, and the latter's allies, the Pima and the Papago. They also clashed occasionally with the neighboring Shoshonean Chemehuevi and with Paiute marauders.

The Political Organization of the Mohave in aboriginal times is poorly understood. The word designating the—conceivably post-Spanish—hereditary chief, *hanidhala,* is derived from the Spanish word for general. The *kohota* was a kind of entertainment chief who presided over certain collective undertakings. A kind of hereditary "nobility," for whose deceased members a memorial rite was performed, was apparently made up of great warriors and their descendants. Other leading personages were shamans, singers, and funeral orators. What held the tribe together and turned the highly individualistic Mohave into a spontaneously disciplined member of the Mohave battle array was the Mohave's intense nationalism, his sense of distinctness from—and cultural, military, ethical, and characterological superiority to—aliens, and, above all, the friendly relationship he entertained with a great many members of his tribe (see below).

Social Organization. The Mohave had 22 named patrilineal, exogamous, and nonlocalized gentes, whose main function was to insure exogamy. The name of the gens was transmitted by the men but was borne by the women (pp. 549ff.). Kinship was bifurcate collateral in the first ascending and descending generation. The extended family existed only in the sense that, in principle, one was expected to avoid incest with both paternal and maternal relatives and relied on their help in situations of need or stress. Many one-room family houses also sheltered one or more temporarily homeless relatives or friends. The basic small unit was the nuclear family, whose membership, owing to the instability of marriages, tended to change from time to time. In theory as well as in practice, any Mohave could count upon the friendly good will and generous help of any other Mohave; lasting in-group enmities were exceptional, an indiscriminate but genuine friendliness the rule. Intratribal aggression, other than witchcraft, witch killings, and relatively harmless boundary disputes, was practically nonexistent.

Marriage. Polygyny was very rare. Most Mohave practiced serial monogamy, often tempered by casual adultery. Only the convenience of the couple determined whether the marriage was patrilocal, matrilocal, or neolocal. Marriage rites and divorce proceedings did not exist. A couple living together was married; a couple which ceased to live together was divorced. Only "incestuous" marriages began with a kind of preparatory ritual and they alone were, in principle, expected to be permanent (pp. 356ff.). In divorce the children usually remained with their mother and were tenderly fostered by whoever happened to be their current stepfather. It was probably the instability of marriages which led to the socially useful belief that the prolonged cohabitation of a man with an already pregnant woman modified the foetus' biological and social identity. This belief enabled an already pregnant woman's current mate to claim the baby as his own and to transmit to it membership in his own gens.

Land was owned individually and could be sold, or otherwise transferred, abandoned, and inherited. A dead man's land was either left fallow for a while by his natural heirs or else was taken over by a nonrelative. Boundary disputes were settled by vigorous but nonfatal collective stick fights (pp. 368ff.).

Economics and Technology. The Mohave planted maize, beans, squash, and certain native foodplants on the overflow of the Colorado River, and also collected wild plant-products, fished, and hunted. They made almost no use of skins and bones, but did utilize stone, wood, clay, and vegetable fibers such as bark. They manufactured crude coiled pottery, painted with yellow ochre, and very simple baskets. In historical times they also made fine beadwork, using imported glass beads. Tools were made of split stones and wood. Their "four" weapons were the unbacked willow bow, arrows, "potato-masher" clubs (wielded with an upward stroke), and straight clubs. The men wore breechclouts and the women skirts made of bark. (Piercing of ears and the nasal septum, and painting and tattooing of the face were common.) Their shell jewelry could also be used as currency. The only aboriginal domestic animal, the dog, was considered to be a "person," in the sense in which human beings and the animals figuring in myths are "persons." Cruelty to animals was abhorred. Industriousness in the production of goods was highly approved, while the retention or hoarding of goods was strongly condemned. "A man can be rich only if he refuses to help the needy." The cremation of all of the deceased's property also made the accumulation of capital impossible. Boundless generosity was a cardinal virtue; stinginess was loathed to such an extent that people gave help freely even to known loafers and to despised habitual parasites.

Warfare was waged for defense against raiders, for glory, and for conquest. At times the Mohave even "declared war," challenging the foe to meet the dreaded Mohave battle array in combat. More or less in the spirit of a safari, the Mohave occasionally even raided tribes living hundreds of miles from their territory. They also traveled far for sightseeing purposes but, except for trips to the Gulf in order to obtain salt or shells, did not engage in trading expeditions. The Mohave fought as infantry, in serried and highly cohesive ranks. When hard pressed, they formed a defensive circle or square and often fought to the last man. When victorious, they scalped the fallen foe and took captives whom they did not abuse; they simply avoided close contact with their captives, for fear of contracting the dread "foreign disease" (pp. 128ff.). During the victory feast old women and male transvestites hazed stay-at-home men, calling them "alyha:" (=transvestite=coward). Though the Mohave feared no living foe and often fought for sport, they were sufficiently ambivalent about aggression to believe that scalpers —and even hunters—were likely to become afflicted with a sui generis kind of insanity (pp. 42ff.).

Sexual Activity was limited solely by the incest taboo, which only witches were prone to violate. The only conspicuously absent sexual practices were cunnilingus, fetichism, and sado-masochism. Though sexual activity as such was felt to be an enjoyable and humorous sport, even the most casual coitus implied, by definition, also an involvement of the "soul": body cohabiting with body and soul with soul. Both male and femal transvestitism were institutionalized, and transvestite shamans were held to be exceptionally powerful. By contrast, reproductive processes—male and female puberty, menstruation, pregnancy, childbirth, lactation, etc.—were deemed to be serious matters and were hedged about with fairly numerous, though neither onerous nor overly meticulous, taboos and observances. Many children cohabited with each other and even with adults long before puberty; the latency period was conspicuous by its absence.

Children were much loved, brought up permissively, and looked after at once generously and lackadaisically. An orphan was fostered quite as lovingly as a child living with its parents. Nursing and cradling were prolonged, weaning usually spontaneous, and toilet training both late and lenient. As late as the 1930s the older Mohave deemed it monstrous to strike a child. In aboriginal times abortion was probably quite rare; it became more prevalent under Reservation conditions, when young girls began to abort in order to conceal their sexual activities from puritanical white officials. Except in myth, infanticide was limited to the killing of gens-less halfbreeds, who could "infect" the Mohave with the "foreign disease." The supervision of children was minimal. Most children roamed around in small bands, played, swam, indulged in sexual games and in intercourse, felt free to take melons from anyone's fields, and were sure to find a welcome and a meal everywhere. As a result, and also because of the instability of marriages, the Mohave child soon learned to like and trust everyone, and therefore did not develop over-intense and exclusive emotional attachments to anyone. This explains why the adult Mohave is so highly "available," both sexually and for friendship. The only exceptions to this rule seem to be twins, whom Mohave culture singles out for great if ambivalent attention (pp. 348ff.).

Leisure, Sports, and Arts. The principal Mohave leisure-time activities were coitus, swimming, certain competitive sports for both male and female teams, gambling (including guessing games), group dancing and singing, listening to singers, orators, and tellers of myths and tales, visiting, chatting, verbal and practical joking, and, in recent times, drinking. Shamanistic curing performances, funerals, and other ritual and quasi-ritual gatherings were well attended. Though backward in the plastic and decorative arts, the Mohave had a rich mythology, great "historical" prose epics, many legends and folk tales, elaborate song cycles "learned" in dream, and a rather beautiful music. The production and performance of the temporal arts was an important social activity.

Crimes and Misdeeds, other than bewitchings and witch killings, simply did not exist. Brawls were almost unheard of and theft unimaginable. Probably all troubles, including witchcraft, were settled privately and, except for witch killings and boundary disputes, without violence. I doubt that in aboriginal times a Mohave would have fully understood what modern man—or even a Sedang Moi—means by "law"; the Mohave language has no word meaning "punishment."

Supernaturalism is rich in myths and poor in ritual. The Mohave gods died in mythical times. The divine culture hero Mastamho turned into a demented fish eagle and no longer intervenes in human affairs (pp. 50ff.). Sky and Earth were active "persons" only in early mythical times; in "historical" times they were simply features of the real world. The shadowy, though immortal, "heavenly beings" become relevant only if they visit the earth as twins. Whether Night and Day, which are "persons" and send dreams, and various minor supernatural beings or "monsters" still exist in the *genuine* present, in the sense in which the supernatural hikwi:r snakes still exist, is debatable. In mythical times coyote, deer, etc., were "persons"; post-mythical, "historical" animals, other than dogs, are not thought to be "persons." The only "supernatural" beings manifestly existing in "historical" times are a few, quite shadowy creatures and the ghosts of the deceased.

The gods and other "persons" of the mythical age, though "dead" (nonexistent) within the dimension of "real" (historical) time, continue to "exist," preserved within an immutable, *permanent* "past" to which certain individuals gain access in dream. Thus, a shaman can obtain "power" either from the gods—who are dead—or else from the ancestors, though after a few metamorphoses the human soul ceases to exist. The future shaman's dream in a sense transports him back into the mythical time of creation and permits him to "witness" the precedent setting first curing of the illness he will be able to treat. Other shamans claim, however, that in their dreams the (dead!) gods "repeated" for their benefit the "first" curing of the illness which they can cure. They therefore say: "I was there—I saw it." Though in practice the future shaman learns the healing songs and techniques by watching the performances of established shamans, it is this dream (re-)learning that counts, because only dream learning can infuse "power" into his performance. Since all budding shamans do not "witness" and "learn" exactly the same ritual and theory "in dream," their theories and techniques are not identical. As a result, shaman A may resent the fact that shaman B's ideas and techniques differ from his and may retaliate by bewitching B. Yet, the latent structure of the ideas and practices of A and B tends to be the same: Hivsu: Tupo:ma's earthy theory of the hikwi:r disease simply reflects the latent content of Ahma: Huma:re's more symbolically formulated theory of that illness (pp. 116ff.).

The crucial datum is that the Creation myth contains, in principle, a precedent for everything that can happen in life. Hence, when firearms appeared, a shaman promptly dreamed that he witnessed the first curing of bullet wounds, *at the time of creation*. The Creation myth is therefore periodically brought up to date in dream in the light of new experiences. It is as though, soon after Papin discovered the steam engine, an archaeologist discovered a papyrus describing Hero's experiments. In the realm of "medicine," a mythical precedent was set not only for the ideal state of health and for ways of preserving it, but also for the prototypal causation of illness and death, and for the curing of disease. Shamanistic healing consists mainly in singing— or, if the songs are forgotten, in telling—in the presence of the patient that part of the Creation myth which describes the precedent setting illness, treatment, and recovery (state of healthiness) which the patient's illness and recovery replicate.

The Mohave, whose gods are dead and whose culture hero is now a totally inactive, psychotic fish eagle, have no "cult": they do not worship, pray, or sacrifice. Their few rituals are man- not god-oriented; they do not "benefit" the gods in any way. Rituals, taboos, etc., simply replicate mythical precedents, but so do mishaps, illnesses, and failures to observe taboos or to perform rites. The capacity to perform— superlatively or disastrously—anything whatever is obtained in dream. The success or failure of a warrior, the fertility or sterility of a woman, etc., are "caused" by good or bad dreams ultimately rooted in a mythical precedent.

Mohave supernaturalism does not therefore substantiate the widely accepted general theory that myth is derived from ritual. Not only is Mohave ritual negligible and Mohave mythology rich and varied; the most important "ritual" is simply or mainly the *telling* of a myth. What matters most is that living, breathing, eating, etc., too, replicate a mythical precedent *in exactly the same sense* in which a puberty, a curing, or a funeral rite replicate it. In that sense the mere act of living, eating, or walking is quite as much a "ritual" replicating a mythical precedent as a puberty or funeral "rite" is simply a particular activity of living. The logical difficulty here is that the prototype-replicating healing rite consists in the narrating of its mythical precedent, which could not have involved the narrating of an even earlier, pre-Creation precedent. This constitutes an Epimenides-type paradox.

Man, like the gods, is, moreover, not immortal. Matavilye's death set a precedent for dying. For four days the ghost of the deceased revisits his old haunts; the surviving spouse may cohabit with the ghost in dream; the deceased may be reminisced about and mentioned by name. After four days the ghost proceeds to the land of the dead and relives a happier version of his life on earth; his name becomes taboo and all contact with his ghost harmful. After some metamorphoses into owls (?) and (or?) insects, even his ghost ceases to exist.

It has not been noted how truly paradoxical, in terms of the obligation to sever all contacts with the dead and to forget them after four days, is the "memorial rite" performed for an important personage a year after his death, and it is doubtful that any Mohave now living could explain this paradox. Perhaps the Mohave felt that the ghost of an important personage, more attached to the world than that of a lesser man, hung about not for four days but for a year and had to be forcibly speeded on his way to the land of the dead by means of a special memorial rite. This explanation is admittedly speculative, but it fits both the fact that important people are harder to forget than unimportant ones and the belief that the witch can delay the transition of his victims' ghosts to the land of the dead until he, himself, dies or is killed (pp. 394ff.).

The Cardinal Values are generosity, hospitableness, kindness, emotional spontaneity, a healthy sensuality, dignity but also humor, absolute honesty, productive industry, national pride, boundless but disciplined courage, and—in theory at least—also marital fidelity. Most Mohave implement these values in daily life as a matter of course and therefore feel that they are both culturally and characterologically superior to all other groups known to them.

Acculturation on the material level was facilitated by the Mohave belief that there was a mythical precedent even for the shooting of rifles or for the driving of automobiles. The Mohave farmer, efficient already in aboriginal times, is today about as productive and modern a farmer as any American. The gallant warrior of yore today volunteers for military service in wartime, preferably in combat units. The $8,000,000 resort development deal made by the Tribal Council benefits the Mohave nation as a whole. Though the modern Mohave is forgetting his language and customs, his ethnic character and value system remain unchanged: aggressiveness within the group is as intolerable to the most acculturated young Mohave as it was for Tcatc, who was born more than a hundred years ago.* Apparently the modern Mohave feels almost as comfortable within his environment and his skin as he did in aboriginal times.

Conclusion: My account of the Mohave would be incomplete if I failed to say that I felt more at home amongst them than anywhere else on earth. The objectivity of my account is that which only a love great enough not to fear confrontation with reality can inspire: the flaws and foibles of the Mohave seem to me part of their humanity and trouble me no more than the smoke of a great and luminous flame.

---

*S. A. and R. S. Freed, A Comparison of the Reactions of Washo and Mohave Respondents to an Objective Technique (Role Profile Test) for Measuring Role Behavior, *Transactions of the New York Academy of Sciences*, series II, vol. 27 (1965), pp. 959–969; *idem*, Mohave and Washo Role Behavior, *American Museum Novitates*, no. 2330, 19 July 1968.

MOHAVE ETHNOPSYCHIATRY:
THE PSYCHIC DISTURBANCES OF
AN INDIAN TRIBE

By George Devereux*

INTRODUCTION

The present monograph is the first systematic study of the psychiatric theories and practices of a primitive tribe.[1] Its primary focus is, thus, the exploration of that portion of Mohave culture that pertains to mental derangements, as understood by the Mohave. In this sense the present work is comparable in its orientation to monographs entitled, e. g., "Ethnobotany" or "Ethnogeography" that deal, respectively, with the botanical or geographical ideas, beliefs, and practices of some aboriginal group, but are primarily contributions to anthropology rather than to botany or to geography. In simplest terms, the present study is a kind of "Mohave textbook of psychiatry," dictated by Mohave "psychiatrists" to the anthropological fieldworker.

The second focus is the recording of all obtainable information on psychiatric illnesses in the Mohave tribe and an analysis of their social and culture setting. In this sense this work is a contribution to the study of "culture and the abnormal personality," or, as this field of inquiry is presently called, ethnopsychiatry.

The primary objective would not have permitted this work to be entitled "Ethnopsychiatry," since this term has come to denote primarily the science of the relationship between culture and mental disorder—i. e., that branch of "culture and personality studies" that deals with the abnormal personality. However, since the secondary objective of this work was to collect data on mental disorders in Mohave society and to interpret them in terms of Mohave culture and society, the title, "Mohave Ethnopsychiatry" is correctly used in both of the senses that the term "ethnopsychiatry" now possesses.

Although this work is addressed primarily to anthropologists, it is hoped that it will prove of interest also to psychiatrists and to the

*Professor of research in ethnopsychiatry, Temple University School of Medicine, and lecturer in anthropology, Columbia University School of General Studies.

[1] Laubscher (1937) dealt primarily with the psychiatric *illnesses* of the Tembu and discussed their psychiatric *knowledge* only incidentally.

historians of psychiatry. For this reason each section contains not only the relevant field data, but also some psychiatric comments and explanations, which the anthropologist who is not interested in such considerations can easily identify and skip. The psychiatrically interested anthropologist will, on the other hand, find these discussions and explanations sufficiently explicit to help him understand the psychiatric significance of the material.

Every work that is addressed to two different groups of specialists must use and explain two sets of basic concepts that are almost truisms for the representatives of one discipline, but are likely to be unknown to the specialists in the other field. The anthropologist who finds certain passages elementary will, one hopes, bear in mind that these explanations may be useful to the psychiatric reader, and vice versa, of course.

The present monograph has, thus, three major objectives:

(1) *Anthropology.*—To describe that segment of Mohave ethnography that deals with primitive science and its practitioners, and to show the articulation of this set of data with the Mohave culture pattern in order to increase our understanding of that pattern (sociology of knowledge).

(2) *History of psychiatry (a branch of culture history).*—To provide exhaustive information about one early system of psychiatry.

(3) *Theoretical and clinical psychiatry.*—To provide practice in thinking through familiar data and problems within a different frame of reference, in the hope that this "exercise" will stimulate the evolving of new insights into various aspects of mental disorder (e. g., pt. 2, pp. 56–71 in regard to the pathogenic effects of the inhibition of abilities and functions.) This seems possible, since Mohave psychiatric theories do fit the clinical realities obtaining in that tribe rather well. (See pt. 8, passim.)

The data on which this monograph is based were collected in the course of three extended field seasons (1932–33, 1936, 1938). Several brief visits, lasting only a few days each (1935, 1947, 1949, 1950), served to fill in small gaps and to clarify minor obscure points. Probably 99 percent of the data were obtained in the course of the three extended field seasons, mostly at Parker, Ariz., with three brief excursions to Needles, Calif., to visit informants Nyahwe: ra, Harav He: ya, and Apen Ismalyk.

The exact date of these field trips is of some importance, since the far-reaching congruence between Mohave psychiatric theories and psychoanalytic views may suggest to some that my questions may have influenced my informants. During my first and second regular field seasons the bias, if any, was frankly antianalytic, while during the third and last prolonged field season my bias, if any, was one of serious skepticism. Thus, some 99 percent of my data were collected in a distinctly antianalytic frame of mind.   In addition, I was at that time so ignorant of psychoanalysis that, to take a concrete example, I could not possibly have suggested to my Mohave informants their theory of convulsions, for the simple reason that I did not even know at that time that there existed a similar psychoanalytic theory of such seizures. In brief, not only did I not seek to "prove" psychoanalysis by means of tendentiously gathered field data, but would have been incapable of doing so, because of my ignorance of psychoanalysis. Thus, the congruence of my Mohave data with psychoanalysis is not the result of a preexisting bias. On the contrary, it was my dawning awareness of this congruence that caused me to become interested in psychoanalysis in the first place.

Having shown the lack of a systematic (psychoanalytic) bias in the fieldwork technique, I should say a few words about the inherent validity of the data themselves.

The most important factor which vouches for the validity of the data was the attitude of the Mohave themselves. All major informants and interpreters were not only devoted coworkers, but also close friends. Many casual informants refused to accept pay for whatever bit of information they provided, while regular informants sometimes spent their evenings tracking down further sources of information or clarifying moot points by consulting various experts. When I commented on their cooperativeness, Hama: Utce: seemed quite surprised that I thought this matter worth mentioning: "And why shouldn't we cooperate with you? You are our friend. With other anthropologists we work. With you we visit." In fact, the only relatively unwilling informant was the witch Hikye: t, who, like all witches, was afraid to talk too openly and who may have agreed to see me only because he thought that his refusal would make him even more suspect of witchcraft than he already was. I think it is reasonable to assume that such devoted coworkers would give only information that they sincerely believed to be correct.

The second factor guaranteeing the validity of the data is their high degree of intrinsic plausibility. Their anthropological plausibility is shown by the fact that practically every single new trait mentioned in this work could be readily correlated either with the findings of other Mohave experts or with data that I had obtained in different contexts. As regards the psychiatric plausibility of the data, special pains were taken to indicate, e. g., that the "hearsay" dream of a woman suffering from nyevedhi: taha: na (Case 47) could not possibly have been invented even by a psychoanalytic expert on depressions, and that this dream satisfied all cultural expectations regarding "typical" nyevedhi: taha: na dreams, which further increases its psychological plausibility, since cultural expectations are known to influence the structure and content of dreams (Devereux, 1951 a). In addition, it is possible to show that many of the data are at once psychiatrically too correct and logically too weird to have been invented on the spot for the benefit of the anthropologist. It suffices to mention the spontaneous references of informants to the phantom phallus, to the globus hystericus, to anorexia following dreams of eating ghost food or of contact with "nauseating" secretions, etc., to prove that the Mohave are good "clinical" observers, and that they reproduce the information available to them with a minimum of distortion. Otherwise stated, the fact that extremely "peculiar" symptoms—well known to psychiatrists but almost unimaginable to people who have had no chance to observe psychotics or neurotics—were mentioned by a variety of informants, is a practically irrefutable proof of the psychological plausibility, and therefore also of the authenticity of the data, especially since in 1938, when most of the data were obtained, I did not even know of the existence of many of the more peculiar symptoms spontaneously mentioned by my Mohave informants.

In brief, the compatibility of the data with what we know of Mohave culture, and the fact that some of them, which simply could not have been invented, fit perfectly what psychiatrists know about psychodynamics and symptomatology, indicate that even data that are, strictly speaking, "hearsay" can possess a high degree of authenticity. This striking fact will also be discussed in the section which examines the objective validity of Mohave psychiatric knowledge (pt. 8, pp. 485–504).

ACKNOWLEDGMENTS

It is a privilege to acknowledge the help of the following organizations and individuals:

The Mohave tribe as a whole, the individual informants and interpreters named in this work, as well as many chance-met individuals, provided the warmest welcome and the kind of dedicated help and friendly cooperation that money cannot repay, nor words adequately acknowledge.

The officials of the Colorado River Agency, and especially the late Mary Anna Israel Nettle, M. D. (pl. 7, a), and James L. Troupin, M. D., reservation physicians, were extremely kind and helpful in every respect.

Prof. A. L. Kroeber, of the University of California, was responsible for my first contact with the Mohave and helped me to understand many aspects of their culture.

Prof. George H. Fathauer, of Miami University, kindly clarified an obscure point of Mohave ethnography in which I was especially interested.

Ellis Devereux, M. D., and Martin H. Stein, M. D., psychoanalysts, discussed with me various problems that arose in the course of the preparation of this work.

Dr. Harry C. Schnur, of Brooklyn College, kindly translated certain passages into Latin.

Mr. C. E. Prince, Jr., a psychologist, helped me cull from my field notes all passages dealing with alcohol, provided me with abstracts from and cogent comments about the literature pertaining to alcohol addiction, and discussed with me various possible ways of interpreting the function of alcohol in Mohave society.

Dr. Matthew W. Stirling, former director, and Dr. Frank H. H. Roberts, Jr., present director, of the Bureau of American Ethnology, encouraged me to prepare my data for publication.

Mrs. Eloise B. Edelen, editor of the Bureau of American Ethnology, with the assistance of Mrs. Phyllis W. Prescott, labored with patience and effectiveness over a difficult manuscript. Mr. Albert L. Ruffin, editor, evolved an index which illuminated various facets of this monograph even for the author himself.

The editors and publishers of the Bulletin of the History of Medicine, of the British Journal of Medical Psychology, and of the Quarterly Journal of Studies on Alcohol permitted me to republish here, in a revised form, four of my previously published papers (which are now pt. 3, pp. 91–106; pt. 4, pp. 202–212; pt. 7, pp. 431–459; and the Appendix).

INFORMANTS AND INTERPRETERS

Hivsu: Tupo: ma was, when I first knew him, a shaman in his middle fifties, and remained my principal informant and close friend until his death. He was a huge and powerful man (pl. 9, a), a voracious eater, and a truly Rabelaisian character. He was believed to be exclusively a healer, but he confessed to me that he had bewitched several persons.

Tcatc, a very old widow, granddaughter of the last independent Mohave chief, was a small, birdlike and lively person (pl. 9, b and c), noted for her wit, warmheartedness, and quick temper. She was one of my subsidiary informants until Hivsu: Tupo: ma's death and thereafter became my main informant; she often referred to me as her favorite grandson.

Ahma Huma: re, a good-natured elderly shaman, who was Hivsu: Tupo: ma's rival in love as well as in some other ways, was an able and conscientious informant. After watching his wife die in labor, he obtained obstetrical powers in dream. He was thought to be a healer, not a witch.

Hilyera Anyay, a very old and blind shaman, believed to be only a healer but not a witch, was a helpful and meticulous, but somewhat slow, informant.

Mrs. Hilyera Anyay, wife of the former, was a good informant about her own experiences.

Hikye:t was generally believed to be more of a witch than a healer. He was an elderly man, rather suspicious, distinctly peculiar and neurotic in some ways and—judging by his statements—considerably more autistic than other Mohave shamans I have known and worked with.

Hama: Utce:, a mixbreed woman approximately 32 years of age when I first met her, was—and perhaps still is—the best educated Mohave. She is an alert, witty, extremely intelligent, moody, quick-tempered and warmhearted person, who was my principal inter-preter, occasionally also my informant, and at all times one of the best and most loyal friends I have ever had (pl. 10, a).

Hitcu:y Kutask(w)elvà, who is Hama: Utce:'s son, I have watched grow from a charming and intelligent, though tempera-mental, small boy of about 6, into a kindly and intelligent young man, generally liked and respected by all. He was, in his early teens, an outstandingly able interpreter in my work with children, and has always been a good friend to me (pl. 9, d).

Sumuràmurà, now deceased, was Hama: Utce:'s husband, and Hitcu:y Kutàsk(w)elvà's stepfather. He was a good friend and the perfect incarnation of everything a good, patient, industrious, sweet-tempered, humorous, and generous man should be. He acted as interpreter on one occasion, and furnished supplementary information on a variety of topics (pl. 10, b).

Pulyi:k, a nearly blind old man, was an excellent linguistic in-formant, highly skilled in unraveling the meaning of condensed Mo-have names and ritual texts.

E. S. is a well-educated young Mohave man, who was a reliable and skillful interpreter and valued friend during one of my field trips.

Countless other Mohave friends and acquaintances provided valu-able bits of information on a variety of topics and sometimes also about themselves.

NAMES

In most cases I give each person's real and principal Mohave name, usually followed by its English translation (e.g., Hivsu: Tupo:ma=burned raw). In a few instances it was found expedient to list all of a person's old and new names; in such cases, however, the person is always referred to in other passages only by his prin-cipal name. In at least one instance I have, for reasons of tact, decided to use not the principal, but the subsidiary or discarded name of a person. One boy, whose Mohave name is not known to me, is referred to simply as Case 78.   One person is designated by the fictitious English name "John Smith," and some very minor personages are designated by obviously fictitious initials, such as "X. Y."

Whenever possible, Mohave names are cited in their complete form, e.g., Hispan Tàruuly, though this person is usually called "Pantàràu: ly." Most of the time, though not always, the designation of a male person by a name consisting of a single word only suggests that it is a colloquial, condensed form of a more complex name, which could not be reconstructed.

Female names consist, in principle, of a gens name only, all women of the Nyoltc gens being called Nyoltc, etc., though sometimes a second word is appended to the basic gens name, as in the case of Nyoltc Hukthar (Nyoltc coyote=crazy Nyoltc).   Women who, being halfbreeds, have no gens name, are mentioned by their self-chosen name, e.g., Hama: Utce:.

The women of three gentes change their names slightly if they happen to lose a child. I refer to a woman as "Nyortc" if, at the time the reported events took place, she had already lost a child and had therefore already changed her name from "Nyoltc" to "Nyortc." If, however, she lost a child only after the event referred to had already occurred, she is designated in the text as "Nyoltc," which is the name by which she was known at that time, instead of as "Nyortc," as she was called subsequently.

The fact that all women of a given gens have the same basic name, made it necessary to devise some means of differentiating between, e.g., my informant Tcatc and some other woman also named Tcatc, who, like my informant, did not have a more personalized second name.   In such a case I give the other woman's gens name, followed by the initial of her English given or family name in parentheses: Tcatc (N).   In some instances, where I have to refer to several sisters, all of whom belong to the same gens, have the same English family name, and have given names beginning with the same letter (such as Mary and Minnie Smith), I differentiate between these sisters by calling them either "Mah (Ma)" and "Mah (Mi)," or else simply "Ma." and Mi."

The same policy was adopted also in regard to two men called Pi:it.   They are designated in the text as Pi:it (I) and Pi:it (II).

G. D. are the author's initials.

ABBREVIATIONS AND SYMBOLS

Words or passages in *parentheses*, even when they occur in a direct quotation of an informant, represent explanatory comments or translations provided by the writer. They never represent "asides" of the informant himself.

Words or passages in *brackets*, which occur in a direct quotation of an informant, represent:

(1) Nonverbal activities of the informant, e.g., [pause] or [mimicks].

(2) Verbal or nonverbal activities of persons other than the main narrator.

(3) Questions and remarks of the interviewing anthropologist.

(Q) and [Q] symbolize a question asked by the anthropologist, where the nature of the question can be unequivocally inferred from the answer given by the informant. For example: "(Q) Of course I went," stands for: "*Anthropologist.*—Did you go? *Informant.*—Of course I went."

Fine print.—On the whole, all passages in fine print are either direct quotations of informants or of printed sources, or else are explanatory remarks and comments pertaining to these direct quotations.

Quotation marks.—Certain technical terms with which some anthropological readers may perhaps not be familiar ("primary process"), certain newly coined expressions ("signal symptom"), a few colloquial expressions which may puzzle foreign readers, and some significant expressions used by an informant (e.g., "he," when referring to a female transvestite claiming male status) are usually placed in quotation marks.

PHONETIC SYSTEM

a as in park
à approximately as the u in but
e as in get
è as in French tiède
i as in pit
o as in rock
u as in put
c as the sh in shoe
dh as the th in the
h is a true h, but with some friction, as the ch in German Rache
kh is a front velar
k(w) is a labiovelar, somewhat as the qu in quest
ly is a palatalized l, somewhat as in lure
ny is a palatalized n, as in Spanish cañon
q a back velar
s as in son
tc as the ch in chew
th as in thought
ts as the z in German Zeit
: indicates that the preceding vowel is long [i:=continental i as in machine]
' a very slight glottal stop
Consonants in parentheses are barely audible, see above: k(w)
å occurs not in Mohave, but in Sedang, and is pronounced as the vowel in raw

PART I. FUNDAMENTALS OF MOHAVE PSYCHIATRY

ETIOLOGICAL THEORIES

The Mohave do not possess a general etiological theory of mental diseases, presumably because each shaman seeks to make his own specialty the cornerstone of Mohave medicine. This tendency is clearly revealed by the attempt of Hikye: t—a shaman also reputed to be a witch—to bring mental disorders within the scope of his own specialty, which was "internal medicine." His account of the "foundations of psychiatry" is, in its own way, as grotesque as are certain modern attempts to bring even the functional neuroses entirely within the scope of neurology, or even of internal medicine. In fact, it is quite probable that Hikye: t's account sounds confusing not only because this suspicious witch may have wished to confuse me, but chiefly because he tried to force the neuroses and psychoses into the procrustean pattern of Mohave organic medicine.

Be that as it may, my efforts to integrate the etiological views of my various informants into a coherent whole having ended in a signal failure, I asked Ahma Huma: re to discuss the matter in my presence with the old blind shaman Hilyera Anyay and with Tcatc. I pointed out that since neither of these two was a witch, differences of opinion would not invite magical retaliation, and also promised that I would not invite to the conference such known witches as Hikye: t or Kwathany Hi:wa, who might bewitch him. In response to my request, Ahma Huma:re embarked upon a long, agitated, and rambling monolog, in broken English, whose gist was not always clear to me. In the course of this monolog he mentioned the late Hivsu: Tupo: ma, as well as the alleged witch Hikye: t, and once more enumerated various diseases. Then, speaking quite calmly once more, he stated that he did not object to the proposed conference.

If you were asking something about those people's suma: tc (dream powers), I could not attend the meeting. But since we are supposed to talk only about insane people, that is different. Your late friend Hivsu: Tupo:ma could tell you things about his power, but he could not have done so in my presence (since I, too, am a shaman). However, when it comes to insanity caused by illness, what I already told you about that topic it is probably just what the others will say, since it is simply a matter of telling you what we ourselves have seen.[3]

---

[3] Extraneous circumstances unfortunately prevented me from arranging such a discussion.

9

The lack of any general etiological theory is tellingly reflected in Hikye:t's chaotic attempt to formulate one.

Hikye: t's statement.—Most insanity begins very early in life. It has its basis in the stomach. As boys or girls grow older, in some cases they must fast every now and then, so that their blood may be kept pure. If these acts are not performed, they (?) come back on the person, in the form of pains of the heart and of the body. As time goes on, the person may feel the cold of the wind and the heat in his body and in his mind. When he inhales and feels either of these in his stomach, he will feel that they cause him very sharp pain. Naturally, he would then want some heavy food.

Our food, as it was given to us in the beginning, is, of course, different from what we now have. The food that we now have is something like (i. e. in accordance with) a prophecy made in the old times, which told us that our food would change from time to time. Such a prophecy I call ku : na : v nyevedhi :. This is something that has never been told before, and the term I use here means the same as what we—or rather what the lay people—call ahwe: (alien). [Is that the same as ahwe: nyevedhi: (alien ghost)?] No, it is not. And so the sickness from the stomach, which may be a gaseous condition, comes up to the heart. Such pains may drive a person to what we call insanity. What people say when the patient becomes insane, is that the hikwi : r (supernatural snake) is in his stomach. His illness may also involve the symptoms of hu: the: rv (cold). This, then, is the hikwi : r illness.

Also, a girl may have sexual relations before she begins to menstruate,[3] and therefore, later on, while menstruating, she may still have this semen in her, which has entered her blood. This is known as hiku: pk (venereal disease). It should be understood, of course, that such a girl has not done any fasting at all. Therefore this blood of hers is rather impure, and is circulating all over her body, and up to her head. This seems to rob her of her sanity.

This whole thing I just told you is not known to the laymen; it is suma: tc (dreamed knowledge). As I said before, what I am telling you now is sort of a prophecy made for the purpose of telling what might happen physically, and in the mind, and in the soul. That is why I told about ku: na: v nyevedhi :. When a person has begun to know and to practice sexual intercourse, if he should be of more than pure blood (i. e. if he is a halfbreed)—well, today we have so many mixed bloods—the sickness I told you about in the beginning is (will be) important. When a boy or a girl has sexual intercourse with a mixed blood (halfbreed) and they happen to kiss (Kroeber, 1948), this causes the "germ"(?) to go down into the stomach of either one of them. Then the original sickness, which I mentioned before, looks upon the germ coming in as an enemy. This causes the sickness known as ahwe:. This "original" disease is ku: na: v nyevedhi :, and one does not even know that one has it.

In the beginning of a person, or of a life, that person comes into the world as a sick person. Thus, his sexual intercourse makes it so that (happens in such a way that) it finally causes hiku: pk. The blood is impure. It is like a smoke within the cavity where the kidneys, the liver, the stomach, and the bladder are found. Diseases like gonorrhea and syphilis are in the impure blood. The blood is circulated down to the feet and, from there, there seems to be a slow upward movement of the blood. This causes what we call hiku: pk tcȧki: tck. This illness is more like rheumatism, or like the sharp pains one feels when one makes an effort to walk, or to use one's feet.

---

[3] Presumably not the menarche, but the monthly period is meant.

This (form of ?) hiku: pk is a disease that is relatively unknown to the
Indians. And this (type of ?) ahwe: disease is also unknown. But today,
because of that ku: na: v nyevedhi:, many of us are of mixed blood. Ku: na: v
nyevedhi: is, however, a prophecy, not a sickness. Ku: na: v means "something
told" and nyevedhi: means "ghost." It is not a material thing. Our blood is
mixed, and we know that the blood of the white man and of the Japanese and
Chinese is stronger than ours (Devereux, 1949 c.). In some of the halfbreeds
we find the strength of this blood working against ours, which is supposed to be
weak. That is the general cause of the sickness called ahwe:. All this was
told in the beginning, and before man knew earthly life.

What we term "hikwi: r," and the sickness that causes insanity, occur on
this terrain, which is the general basis of sickness. By "basis" I mean the
stomach trouble, and the weakness of the blood.

[At this point a brief conference with the interpreter disclosed that neither
of us could understand the general drift of Hikye: t's remarks; I therefore
read back to him all recorded material. When he stated that his remarks had
been correctly transcribed, it was decided to eliminate one intermediate step
that might possibly add to the confusion. I yielded my place at the typewriter
to the interpreter, who, from then on, recorded directly his translation of all
of Hikye: t's subsequent remarks, my own task being limited to questioning him.]

[What, precisely, is the "original" disease?] That is not known. The impurity
of the blood is the original disease. It is known as hiku: pk. A person who has
this disease does not know it. If, during sexual intercourse, he secretes semen,
this sort of forms a puslike matter within the person. If that person is
doctored in time, he may get well. But if he isn't treated, then he is keeping
this pain within himself. It may feel as though it (?) were going out, but,
because of the pains, he will keep it in. When this disease circulates all over
the body, then that person may go insane. This happens when the impure blood
goes into the head and the heart. This condition is then known as ahwe:, which
is the name by which ordinary people know it. It is also known as ku: na: v
nyevedhi:.

[What is hahnok?] It is when, because of disease, the impure blood has
gone to the head, or to the heart. (Hahnok=contamination.)

[What is ahwe:?] It is a disease caused by our mingling with different
bloods (aliens), and by the eating of foreign foods. (Ahwe:=alien.)

[What is hikwi: r?] In this disease the inhalation of cold and hot air is
mixing with the sputum which one swallows and which finds no passage out
of the body. This causes stomach cramps and severe pains of the heart. These
pains become unbearable and the patient becomes insane. (Hikwi: r=magical
snake.)

[What is the relation of all this to Tcatc's account of a type of insanity caused
by snakes?] When these symptoms have occurred, patients see in their dreams
people, and these people are supposed to be the hikwi: r.

[Who can cure insanity at present?] There is no one left who can cure
insanity.

[Then what do they do if someone becomes insane?] There are not very many
cases of that kind. They just take them to the hospital. Some are dying from
what white people call double pneumonia and pneumonia.

It would be unprofitable to seek to read into these rambling data
anything resembling a general etiology of mental disease, especially
since, despite occasional references to well-established beliefs, their

overall patterning, if any, is primarily a product of Hikye: t's private intellectual and emotional world. Indeed, it suffices to compare this chaotic account, which treats a given entity now as a cause and now as an effect, with any of the other accounts cited in this work, to realize the extent to which Hikye: t's views are autistic.[4] In fact, Hikye: t's statement is so similar to the ruminations of certain types of hospitalized psychotics, that it provides support for the thesis that the shaman, no matter how "well adjusted and socially effective" he may be, is, in the last resort, a psychotic in partial remission (Devereux, 1956 b).

Yet, it is obvious that Hikye: t did wrestle with some of the major unsolved problems of Mohave psychiatric and medical theory. His failure to "make sense" is, however, due less to the fact that this essentially supernaturalistically oriented body of beliefs is simply not susceptible of being organized into a rational whole, than to his intellectual limitations and fundamental autism. His case seems to fit perfectly the Mohave belief that people may become mentally disturbed if lyelyedhu: tc hi: wa hakwi: lyk (their knowledge exceeds their heart) which, colloquially expressed, means simply that they "bit off more than they can chew."[5] As Hikye: t himself put it on another occasion: "One cause of insanity is that sometimes a man's knowledge exceeds his heart" (ego functions). (See Case 4.)

These limitations notwithstanding, Hikye: t's account does have the merit of stressing the keystone of the Mohave's world view in relation to the etiology of mental disease. It is a basic principle of the Mohave philosophy of life that everything on earth happens in accordance with rules and precedents dating back to the time of creation. This Mohave axiom underlies that portion of Hikye: t's account which emphasizes the etiological import of these rules and precedents (ku: na: v nyevedhi:=that which has been prophesied or ordained by ghosts). In addition, Hikye: t also mentioned most of the key concepts of Mohave etiology, such as:

(1) Hahnok, which is the principle of contamination or causation (ahwe: hahnok, foreign contamination).

---

[4] It may be of some interest to mention that, in the course of years of fieldwork, I obtained only one other equally disorganized statement. It was the account of a minor Sedang Moi shaman of Tea Ha, Indochina, who, according to the members of that village, had "power" but was, at the same time, "without ear"—i. e., devoid of reason and thought to be practically insane.

[5] This explanation is precisely the one which the Sedang of Tea Ha applied, to the confusion of the shaman mentioned in the preceding footnote. The same phenomenon can also be observed in severely disturbed morons, whose desperate attempts to transcend their limitations are movingly characterized by Lajos Zilahy (1949) in his novel "The Dukays": "The dark eaglewings of a senseless spirit flapped frantically in an effort to achieve the most magnificent heights of sense." Goethe, too, refers to this phenomenon, when he causes Faust to speak of his father as a man who "reflected conscientiously, though with twisted obsessiveness, about Nature and her holy realms."

(2) The role of aliens and of ghosts in the causation of insanity.

(3) Pathogenic dreams.

(4) Saliva and other bodily secretions, which the Mastamho myth (Kroeber, 1948) also views as vehicles of contamination.

(5) The notion that organic illness may cause psychiatric symptoms.

(6) The struggle between health and sickness, and the struggle between several illnesses within the patient's body, etc.

Since a well-informed shaman like Hikye: t was unable to formulate a general etiological theory of insanity, it would be hazardous to try to evolve inductively a comprehensive theory of Mohave psychiatric etiology. One can, however, elucidate at least some of the implicit connections between the various etiological explanations of the several mental disorders known to the Mohave.

One such basic etiological principle appears to be the concept of *disorganized power or force*, which may be either an external or an internal one.

Thus, the Mohave explicitly state that aliens can cause the Mohave to become insane, because their blood is more powerful than that of the Mohave. The same "excess of power" may also be ascribed to ghosts, since, on the basis of altogether different considerations, Fathauer (1951) suggested that aliens and ghosts are more or less identified with each other in Mohave thought. Insanity caused by witchcraft also appears to belong to the category of disorders caused by the impact of some external and supernatural power, since it is practically the prototype of exogenous illnesses. The most important evidence in support of this assumption is, interestingly enough, a misstatement, made in all good faith by Pulyi: k, who is not a shaman. He declared that there are three types of illnesses: sores (hisa: hk), "straight" illnesses (itc hira: vtaha: na), and "not straight" illnesses, which he definitely designated as matadha: uk, although this word means witchcraft, and nothing else. In order to explore this strange assertion further, without alerting the informant, he was asked to describe the manner in which "not straight" illnesses (which I deliberately referred to only in English) were treated by shamans.

His account ran as follows: "When a shaman is treating a "not straight" illness the patient faces south, because his soul was taken away by a witch and the shaman must bring it back." This statement can pertain only to illness caused by soul loss and to the recovery of the soul from the land of the dead, which lies to the south and under the bed of the Colorado River (Devereux, 1937 a). This also happens to be the place where the ghosts take the souls of those of their relatives whom they persuaded to join them in the beyond.

These statements show that Pulyi: k, being a layman, simply viewed witchcraft as the prototype of all "not straight" diseases, even though it is believed that "not straight" diseases can also be caused by ghosts and other supernatural forces, which superimpose a supernatural or magical illness upon a more "natural" sort of illness. In fact, Pulyi : k's account absolutely fails to differentiate even between the abduction of the patient's soul by a witch and its abduction by the ghost of a relative in nyevedhi : taha : na and in other ghost-illnesses.

The "dreadful" illnesses and mental disorders caused by charms are also closely related to sicknesses caused by ghosts, aliens, and witches. Indeed, these charms are essentially "alien" substances, which do not "belong" to the Mohave, but to certain other tribes. Hence, prolonged contact with them is quite as harmful to the Mohave as intimate association with aliens. Last, but not least, the manner in which the power of these charms eventually turns against their owners is very similar to the way in which a shaman's powers may ultimately turn against him. (Pt. 2, p. 56.)

In brief, illnesses caused by ghosts, witches, aliens, and charms have, by and large, the same basic etiology.

The individual's own supernatural powers can also get out of hand and cause disturbances of thought, mood, and behavior. Thus, the nonactualized powers of the potential shaman, who refuses to become a practicing one, can drive him insane, while the powers of a healing shaman sometimes turn against him and cause him to become a suicidal witch.

Natural human powers may also become disorganized to the point where they cause insanity.

Disturbances of the sexual instinct are believed to cause a whole series of disorders, which are sharply differentiated from mere perversions. Disturbances related to uncontrolled aggressive impulses— and to conflicts over the actualization of aggression [6]—likewise account for the genesis of a whole group of neuroses. Conspicuous or excessive activity can, in the end, also cause certain psychiatric disorders.

Even disorders which are seemingly due to external precipitating situations and represent primarily a reaction to trauma are, in a very genuine sense, largely caused by the disorganization of internal forces, drives or impulses. The prototype of such disorders is the so-called heartbreak syndrome (hi : wa itck) which affects chiefly an old husband deserted by his young wife. Superficially speaking, the Mohave seem to view this illness simply as a reactive depression. If we

---

[6] It is seldom recognized that warlike tribes often have deep-seated conflicts related to guilt over aggression. Hence, the Mohave Indians' notorious blood phobia, which is a symptom of many types of mental disorders known to them, is by no means unique even in the Southwest. Thus, according to Hrdlička (1908) a "White Mountain Apache . . . had a boy who, from nervousness, could not eat the red-fleshed pitahaya ; 'it looked to him too much like blood.' "

recall, however, that old Mohave husbands are said to be excessively attached to their young spouses, and if we bear in mind the Mohave belief that "being very much in love" is a ridiculous kind of madness, it immediately becomes apparent that the young wife's desertion is nothing more than a "precipitating situation," which simply provides an opportunity for the actualization of the preexisting, though latent, neurosis of old men whose sexual impulse is already sufficiently deranged to cause them to be (by Mohave standard) excessively in love with a wholly inappropriate (i. e., far too young) woman.

While the preceding considerations emphasize chiefly the etiological role of "power" or "actuating force"—which may be supernatural or natural, and external or internal—it is quite clear that the mere presence of a force of some kind is not necessarily a cause of illness or of insanity. Psychiatric disorders are caused not simply by the presence of some power or drive but, specifically, by some derangement or disorganization of that force. This disorganization may result from a clash between that force and some other entity, as in the case of the deliberate inhibition of one's shamanistic powers; from the presence of unspecified factors inhibiting the free manifestation of a natural force, as in the case of persons who have convulsions because they are incapable of experiencing a real orgasm; from the struggle of a patient's "health" component against the pathogenic power impinging upon him, as in witchcraft; from the loss of a previously available channel for the normal manifestation of a drive, as in hi: wa itck, etc. In brief, the basic, albeit implicit, keystone of Mohave etiological theory appears to be the idea that insanity is caused by some disorganized power or force, whose disorganization is due to some sort of "conflict." This, in turn, means that even the psychiatric symptoms of persons suffering from organic illness may, in a sense, be viewed as products of a struggle between man's preordained "health," which was explicitly mentioned by Ahma Huma: re (pt. 4, pp. 150–175), and some sort of pathogenic force or principle.

The notion—reported from many cultures (Clements, 1932; Hultkrantz, 1953)—that psychosis is caused by "soul loss" is represented in Mohave psychiatry by the belief that the dreamer's soul may be enticed to the land of ghosts by the ghost of a beloved kinsman or spouse who visits the dreamer. The person who lost his soul in this manner becomes both ill and psychotic and, if not treated by a shaman, dies. This seemingly simple etiological theory is, however, far more sophisticated and complex than one may think. Indeed, in dream the "absent" soul behaves as abnormally as does the body deserted by its soul. Thus, since the bodyless soul behaves (in dream) quite as psychotically as does the soulless body (while awake), the theory that soul loss causes psychosis is a gross oversimplification. Apparently, neither of these two entities can behave normally when the other is absent, sanity being a product of the simultaneous presence of both soul and body and of the proper interaction between the two. This, in turn, implies that "insane" behavior occurs when body and soul are separated. The disembodied soul behaves "crazily" in dream and the soulless body behaves "crazily" while awake. This formulation fits not only basic Mohave psychiatric theory, but also every other primitive soul loss theory of psychosis known to me.[7]

The last pattern to be clarified here is the nexus between psychosis and suicide. The data presented in part 7 suggest that suicide is fairly often a substitute for—and possibly also an escape from—the psychosis that is caused by isolation: schizophrenia. It is therefore possible to suggest, at least tentatively, that the absence of schizophrenia among true primitives (Devereux, 1939 d) may be *partly* due to the primitive's flight from an incipient schizophrenia into suicide.

It would be hazardous to try to elaborate further the latent pattern which seems to underlie the etiological explanations of the various neuroses and psychoses known to the Mohave, lest we impute to them a more developed latent pattern than they actually possess.

The preceding paragraphs had a very limited objective. They tried to indicate that the lack of an authentically indigenous and explicitly formulated general etiological theory does not necessarily imply a total lack of coherence and interdependence between the separate explanations of the various neuroses and psychoses. The demonstration of such a coherence does not require the construction of a comprehensive general theory of Mohave psychiatric etiology. It is quite sufficient to show that the various discrete etiological theories have at least one element in common, namely the thesis that a force, disorganized by a conflict, is a major factor in the causation of all mental disorders.

It is, of course, quite possible that, by exerting oneself to the utmost, one could construct inductively a general etiological theory based on genuinely Mohave data and in harmony with the Mohave culture pattern. However, such an undertaking would be simply a display of ingeniousness, devoid of all anthropological significance. Indeed, the culturally most significant aspect of Mohave psychiatric thought is precisely the fact that, despite its implicit internal coherence, it has never been systematized into a general theory, the way theories of dreaming or shamanism have been systematized by the Mohave themselves. The fact that one area of knowledge or interest

---

[7] The fact that the soul behaves abnormally in dream is self-evident, since dreams result from the interplay of repressed wishes and "primitive" intrapsychic controls. Anyone who behaves in waking life as though he were dreaming is schizophrenic.

has been systematized by a tribe, while some other field of knowledge or interest has not, is, from the point of view of the historian of science, as well as from that of the anthropological functionalist, of great significance, since it reveals not only the hierarchization of interests and preoccupations in a given tribe, but also serves as a reminder that culture, like any other living thing, is never a fully completed system at any moment of its history. In addition, the presence of relatively unsystematized but factually rich areas of knowledge may, perhaps, also indicate the channels into which, and the objectives toward which, future cultural efforts may be directed.[8]

NOSOLOGY

In principle, the study of native nosological categories can be approached in two ways:

(1) By asking the names of various mental derangements.

(2) By describing the various clinical entities known to Western psychiatry and asking to what native illnesses they correspond.

Anthropologically, the first type of inquiry is certainly more relevant than is the second. Its sole drawback is that the native list of names of diseases which one obtains may not be complete.

The second approach also has certain drawbacks:

(1) The risk of putting ideas into the informants' heads by asking leading questions.

(2) The risk of seducing them into identifying what was described to them with some native disease category. This risk is not wholly obviated by asking afterward the native names of the salient symptoms, since an intelligent informant can always make up in good faith a suitable descriptive term.

The one real merit of the second approach is that it jogs the memory of one's informants, enabling one to obtain a compendious set of data on mental disorders in the society under study.

On the other hand, the technique of asking leading questions also has definite advantages. Thus, it was found that, by describing certain classical clinical entities and/or by mimicking abnormal behavior and/or by narrating a concrete case history, one could obtain data that might not have been forthcoming otherwise. This is best shown by the fact that after I briefly described to Tcatc and to the interpreter E. S. an attack of hysterical laughter (but, intentionally, *not of crying*), E. S. promptly recalled having seen a Pueblo school girl laugh *and cry* hysterically (Case 62). This, in turn, reminded Tcatc of a Mohave case that she had witnessed and that involved a childhood friend of hers (Case 61). Both E. S.'s and Tcatc's accounts were

---

[8] Thus, the availability of large amounts of disconnected data about animals and plants represented a challenge to occidental students of natural history and eventually led to Linnaeus' partially still valid systematization of that knowledge.

so much more detailed than my leading question and fitted the classical picture of hysterical laughing and crying so perfectly, that their correctness is beyond question. This, in turn, serves to justify the method of leading questions, especially when investigating a little-known problem.

A further, and possibly even more important, advantage of the technique of asking leading questions is that it enables one to ascertain which types of mental disorders are characteristically absent in a given society. Thus, without a long and elaborate description of obsessive-compulsive symptomatology, it is quite certain that the striking absence of this neurosis could not have been discovered.

Naturally, this dual approach makes the presentation of one's nosological data in a rational sequence quite difficult in the end. For example, a given clinical entity, as defined by modern psychiatry, may be split up by native informants into two or more separate diseases of the mind. Conversely, they may assign to a single native diagnostic category several kinds of disorders that, in terms of modern psychiatric knowledge, are not interrelated in any way.

There are several reasons for the extremely limited overlap between Mohave and modern clinical entities.

(1) The systematic classification of Mohave neuroses and psychoses in modern psychiatric terms is an extremely hazardous undertaking. In fact, comparisons between Mohave and Western nosological categories are often practically useless, particularly because the latter are so precise. In other words, the clinical and theoretical data provided by native informants are seldom accurate enough to permit an exact differentiation between, let us say, anxiety hysteria and anxiety neurosis. In addition, shamanistic specialists, nonspecialist shamans, and laymen sometimes describe the symptoms of a given illness in a variety of ways and sometimes also mention altogether different, or seemingly different, etiologies (pt. 4, pp. 117–128).

Generally speaking, it is quite possible that native categories may occasionally fit the psychiatric realities of the tribe better than do the categories of modern psychiatry, which were formulated so as to fit patients belonging to our culture. This is not at all surprising, provided one realizes that the mental disorders found in a given society are the products of the characteristic strains of the tribal culture pattern, which in turn underlies all native psychiatric theories, views, and therapeutic techniques. For example, one and the same culture—that of the Malays—is responsible both for the occurrence of cases of amok and for the cultural formulation of the concept of amok. This means that the term "amok" is, even from the viewpoint of scientific psychiatry, probably a better label for that type of behavior than is "paranoid schizophrenia," because running amok can also occur, e.g., in the course of a delirium resulting from some toxic or infectious condition (van Wulfften-Palthe, 1936).

(2) As regards specifically the noncorrespondence of occidental and Mohave nosological categories, it is partly due to the fact that some of the theories underlying these two systems differ quite radically. Modern nosological categories were originally derived from descriptive, nondynamic psychiatry. For example, the cornerstone of Kraepelin's (1919) concept of schizophrenia was the belief that this disorder was incurable. Hence, at one time any permanent and not obviously organically determined mental disorder was almost automatically diagnosed as schizophrenia, or as a condition close to it. If a seemingly genuine schizophrenic did recover, this was often deemed prima facie evidence that his illness had been misdiagnosed. A lingering survival of this view is the distinction made by some contemporary psychiatrists between incurable "process schizophrenia" or "nuclear schizophrenia" on the one hand, and curable "schizophrenic reaction types" on the other hand. By contrast, those recent psychiatric nosologies that are formulated in terms of the psychoanalytic frame of reference are based essentially on a classification of the underlying psychodynamics, rather than on symptomatology or prognosis.

As regards Mohave nosological categories, they, like psychoanalytic nosologies, are essentially derived from the distinctive etiology imputed to each illness. Moreover, the informants' descriptions of Mohave clinical entities often seem rather coherent, although one must, of course, envisage the possibility that this coherence may be the accidental product of several factors that may now be listed:

(*a*) The patient's knowledge of what disease he is supposed to be suffering from, and his knowledge of what is expected to occur in such an illness, may produce a kind of unconscious "malingering" of the expected set of culturally prepatterned symptoms. The basic dynamics of this unconscious adjustment to the expected or prescribed "pattern of misconduct" (Linton, 1936) (i. e., illness) were discussed elsewhere (Devereux, 1956 b) and need not be repeated in this context.

(*b*) There may occur an automatic imputation of expected symptoms to a patient suffering from a disorder that "must have been" caused by a given "pathogenic" entity, as defined by the Mohave. Thus, it is permissible to suspect that a person who did not heed warnings to avoid a lake believed to be full of hikwi :r snakes, would, no matter what illness he may finally contract, be diagnosed as a case of hikwi :r hahnok, and a description of his condition would then be quite likely to include not only the symptoms that he did, in fact, have, but also the symptoms that, given the nature of his diagnosis, he should have had.

(c) It is conceivable that the Mohave may have developed the concept of a certain new disease entity on the basis of a single case, which did not fit any other native diagnostic pigeonhole.

On the whole, the first of these factors—i. e., the patient's unconscious compliance in developing the expected symptoms—is likely to be both psychiatrically and anthropologically the most important of the three. Indeed, on the basis of the considerations set forth under (b) and (c), one would expect an appreciable lack of truly convincing internal psychological coherence, both in the formal description of the characteristic disease pictures and in the supporting case histories. However, it is precisely this genuine internal coherence of both the characteristic disease pictures and many of the case histories that is perhaps the most striking aspect of the data under consideration. In fact, as regards the one reported case of nyevedhi: taha: na, it was found necessary to stress that this absolutely convincing case history could not possibly have been "concocted" even by a highly sophisticated psychoanalytic expert on psychogenic depression. The same demonstration of "internal plausibility" could have been made also in connection with most of our remaining case histories and descriptions of "characteristic symptomatologies."

The hypothetical tendency of Mohave patients to "conform" to the clinical picture that is expected from them, is indirectly proved also by the frequent effectiveness of the cures performed by a properly chosen shaman, who specializes in the treatment of the disorder from which the patient is supposedly suffering. To take the example of the scalper's psychosis, if a scalper happens to become ill for any reason whatsoever, and/or is under great psychic tension, the very fact that he is expected to have the illness "proper to his occupation" would channel his "choice of symptoms" into the prescribed or expected pattern. This view is compatible with modern psychiatric theories regarding the "choice of neurosis," since the choice of symptoms is but a variety of the choice of neurosis. In fact, this hypothesis simply completes the theory in question, by suggesting that the choice of neurosis may be affected also by cultural expectations (Devereux, 1956 b).

The preceding considerations explain why the problem of arranging the data in some rational sequence was such an arduous one. After considerable hesitation, it was decided to use as the main basis of classification not our modern categories, but the clinical entities of Mohave folk psychiatry, because, in the last resort, the principal purpose of this monograph is to make a contribution to the branch of anthropology that studies primitive science. Once this decision was reached, it became obvious what the individual section headings would have to be. It also became mandatory, with minor exceptions, to group together those diseases whose descriptive labels had one key word in common. Thus, I grouped together ahwe: hahnok and ahwe: nyevedhi:; hiwey lak, hiwey lak nyevedhi:, and (for reasons to be explained in the proper place) nyevedhi: taha: na; and, likewise, the various illnesses supposedly involving the heart (hi: wa).

While this simplified the task at hand to a certain extent, the arranging of these broader groups into a rational sequence and their possible integration with data obtained—without a native diagnostic label—in response to questions concerning the various disorders known to modern psychiatry, still had to be solved in some manner.

Now, although the Mohave developed an elaborate psychiatric nosology, with a more or less distinctive etiology and clinical picture corresponding to each listed syndrome, they did not explicitly systematize this nosological inventory, except by differentiating between "straight" and "not-straight" disorders, as explained in the first section on etiology. A further implicit grouping of syndromes was inferred from the fact that, e. g., two nosological terms contain the word "ahwe:"=alien and/or enemy; two others, the word "nyevedhi:" =ghost; two, the term "hiwey lak"=anus pain; and four, the word "hi: wa"=heart. Yet, even though this form of grouping together various syndromes appears genuine enough in terms of Mohave culture, it must be understood that what connects ahwe: hahnok with ahwe: nyevedhi: culturally is an explicit Mohave etiological theory (pathological effects of contact with aliens); what connects hiwey lak with hiwey lak nyevedhi: culturally is a major symptom (anus pain); while it is my personal impression that the common element in the various diseases whose name includes the term hi: wa (heart) is that the chief characteristic of these illnesses is a psychic distress so intense as to cause temporarily a partial disorientation.

A problem of considerable theoretical import is created by the fact that the term "nyevedhi:" (ghost) occurs in three diagnostic labels—ahwe: nyevedhi:, hiwey lak nyevedhi:, and nyevedhi: taha: na. One must therefore decide whether, e.g., ahwe: nyevedhi: should be grouped with ahwe: hahnok (because, in a way, both illnesses are due to contact with aliens and/or enemies) or with hiwey lak nyevedhi: and nyevedhi: taha: na (because all three of these disease entities involve some type of contact with ghosts). This problem in the classification of diseases can be tackled on four separate levels, and it is of considerable significance for an understanding of the latent, internal coherence of certain segments of Mohave nosological theory, that each and every one of these four attempts to solve the problem yield the same conclusion.

(1) *"Straight"* vs. *"not straight"* *illnesses*—The Mohave postulate that a simple ("straight") illness of some kind can become a "not

straight" (multiple) illness if it is complicated by the ghost factor or by the witchcraft factor. Thus, a quite ordinary illness which, if it just happens, is a "straight" disease, has to be viewed as a "not straight" disease if it is caused by witchcraft. In brief, the ghost or witchcraft factors, which turned a "straight" illness into a "not straight" one, are the Mohave equivalents of modern medicine's "complications" or "secondary invaders." Hence, ahwe nyevedhi: is, according to the Mohave themselves, an aggravated ("not straight") form of ahwe: hahnok, while hiwey lak nyevedhi: is an aggravated ("not straight") form of hiwey lak. This necessarily implies that ahwe: nyevedhi: must be grouped with ahwe: hahnok and hiwey lak nyevedhi: with hiwey lak. By contrast, nyevedhi: taha: na must be treated as a distinct disease entity which, like a simon-pure witchcraft disease (pt. 4, pp. 195–202), can occur not only as a "complication" or as a "secondary invader" in some other illness, but also by itself, as a disease sui generis. (In the same sense, certain microorganisms which tend to attack a patient already weakened by a virus illness, can invade the organism also in the absence of any preexisting virus illness.)

(2) *Active vs. passive*—According to the Mohave themselves, certain ailments resulting from aggressive contact with aliens do not cause "not straight" illnesses. For example, when discussing the psychiatric disorders of scalpers, the Mohave systematically emphasized the patient's own aggressive activities rather than the influence exerted upon him by the scalped foe. Moreover, they explicitly called this ailment a "straight" illness. The same is also true of magical courtship (pt. 1, pp. 83–87), where witchcraft simply mobilizes and amplifies the victim's own sexual impulses. This explains why disorders in which the ailing person's own activities caused his illness, and in which, e.g., the slain and scalped foe played a more or less passive role, being object rather than subject or actor, are discussed in part 1, which is devoted to the study of the disorders of impulses and drives. Specifically, it explains why the god Mastamho's own psychosis, which was due to his hyperactivity as a culture hero, is discussed in part 1, while the psychiatric illness of those who dream of the insane Mastamho is discussed in part 4, which is devoted to "exogenous" psychiatric illnesses.

(3) *Aliens=ghosts.*—Fathauer (1951) and I independently concluded that, on the affective level, the Mohave equate aliens with ghosts and, especially, with the ghosts of deceased relatives. Moreover, it will be shown in part 4 (pp. 128–186) that the equation "aliens=ghosts" can actually be extended as follows: "aliens=ghosts=ghosts of relatives=actual memories of deceased relatives=witches=magic substances and narcotics." Most of these equivalen-

ces are especially obvious in the case of twins. According to one Mohave theory (Devereux, 1941, and pt. 7, pp. 348–356), twins are not immortal visitors from heaven, but the acquisitive ghosts of the dead, whose property-mindedness closely resembles that displayed by some old woman who hoards property for her own funeral (Kroeber, 1925 a) and also the property-mindedness which the Mohave impute to the recently deceased (pt. 7, pp. 431–459). Moreover, the Mohave hold that twins who become shamans are, as a rule, exceptionally powerful ones (Devereux, 1937 c, 1941). These considerations imply that there is a basic affinity between the "primary" and the "secondary" invaders both in ahwe:nyevedhi: (where enemy+/=ghost) and in hiwey lak nyevedhi: (where actual memories of deceased persons+/=ghosts).

(4) *Endogenous vs. exogenous disorders*—Ahwe: hahnok, ahwe: nyevedhi:, hiwey lak, hiwey lak nyevedhi:, and nyevedhi: taha:na are, both culturally and psychoanalytically, closely related to a number of other exogenous diseases of the psyche. Indeed, the list of beings causing exogenous psychiatric disorders includes not only aliens and ghosts (and memories of the deceased) but also the insane deity (=father figure) Mastamho (pt. 4, pp. 116–117), hikwi:r snakes (=paternal phallus and also both parents in the "primal scene") (pt. 4, pp. 117–128), relatives whom one still mourns (pt. 4, pp. 128–186), the dead who are being cremated (pt. 4, pp. 186–195), witches (=incestuous parent figures), and magical substances and narcotics (whose power closely resembles the powers of shamans who are turning into witches) (pt. 4, pp. 195–212).

In brief, the preceding considerations justify:

(1) The separation of certain "straight" diseases, in which, e.g., enemies do play a role, but only as objects, rather than as subjects or actors, from disorders in which enemies, aliens, ghosts, and the like are active causes of psychiatric illness.

(2) The policy of treating ahwe: nyevedhi: as a form of ahwe: hahnok with complications, and hiwey lak nyevedhi: as a form of hiwey lak with complications, and also the policy of treating nyevedhi: taha:na as a psychiatric disorder sui generis.

As an aside, it seems appropriate to note here, at least in passing, that it would probably have been impossible to unravel the basic pattern of Mohave nosological thought, as it pertains to the problem under discussion, without some psychoanalytic understanding of the unconscious meaning of certain cultural data, which had to be analyzed in order to clarify the structure of Mohave nosological theories.

The material is presented in the following sequence:

1. Fundamentals of Mohave psychiatry
2. Disorders of the instincts
    a. Disorders related to aggression and guilt over aggression
    b. Disorders of the sexual impulse
3. Mood disturbances
4. Disorders caused by external beings: aliens, ghosts, etc.
5. Data obtained in response to questions about occidental disease categories and their Mohave equivalents, if any
6. Psychiatric disorders of childhood
7. Suicide
8. Conclusions
Appendix.   The Function of Alcohol

One thing is certain: The one existing broad Mohave system of classification, which differentiates "straight" from "not straight" disorders, could not, by itself, provide a basis for the arrangement of the data into a halfway meaningful sequence, since straight and not straight diseases are not illnesses of different kinds, but merely simple illnesses as contrasted with illnesses with additional complications or multiple illnesses.

The classification of mental disorders here adopted seeks to combine Mohave ideas about the causation of the various disorders, with modern psychiatric insight into the real dynamics of the classical clinical pictures obtained from Mohave informants.   While not necessarily perfect, nor perhaps the best possible, the proposed broad classification is the one which seems to come nearest to doing justice both to Mohave psychiatric thought and to modern psychodynamic theory.   However, in the last resort, I used this particular system of classification simply because I could not think of a better one.

DIAGNOSIS AND TREATMENT

The Mohave psychiatric patient has a definite tendency to develop also organic symptoms, many of which appear to be the result of tension and anxiety.   Conversely, physical illness is so threatening to the Mohave, that the ailing person invariably manifests an appreciable degree of anxiety and may also have extremely disturbing dreams.   These facts more or less explain why the Mohave do not differentiate too precisely, even in terms of their own nosology, between psychiatric, psychosomatic, and organic illnesses.

Broadly speaking, Mohave diagnostic and therapeutic procedures are relatively uniform, regardless of whether the patient has a psychiatric, a psychosomatic, or an organic illness.   Hence, the diagnostic procedures and criteria that are described are used in all cases where a person feels that something is the matter with him.   In fact, it is possible to show (pt. 4, pp. 150–175) that Ahma Huma:re did not feel impelled to discuss the psychiatric aspects of hiwey lak until, in 1938, he was specifically asked to describe all diseases that have a psychiatric aspect or component.

These findings are true not only of the Mohave, but of primitives in general, all of whom view practically every form of malaise, be it physical or psychic, as an illness that the shaman is qualified to diagnose and to treat. In fact, one is almost tempted to suggest that, especially in tribes that had no effective pharmacopoeia to speak of, the shaman treated primarily the psychic components of every illness, and was capable of alleviating physical ailment only by reducing the patient's anxiety and by increasing his will to live. Otherwise expressed, the most ancient tool in the primitive "physician's" therapeutic armamentarium was probably a kind of magically tinged "bedside manner," rather than even ineffective drugs or other "positive" therapeutic maneuvers. Historically expressed, the first medical practice was presumably a strictly phychiatric one, so that, as in modern education (Devereux, 1956 a), the most recent therapeutic philosophies actually represent a naturalistically oriented return to the most primitive of all medical philosophies.

It is now proposed to describe the major diagnostic procedures of the Mohave Indians, it being understood that the same diagnostic techniques and criteria are utilized in all forms of illness, be they psychic, psychosomatic, or purely somatic.

Difficulties of diagnosis.—Mohave diagnoses are sometimes very hard to make, because a patient's illness may include the salient sympatons of several major disease entities. For instance, if a woman dreams about snakes, this usually suggests that she suffers from hikwi: r. If she also has menstrual disturbances, and dreams of her childhood as well, these symptoms may suggest hiwey lak nyevedhi:. Finally, if she also had an affair with an alien, this will make the Mohave shaman suspect that she has the ahwe: hahnok ailment. Such etiological complications led Mohave diagnosticians to differentiate between "straight" (simple) diseases and "diseases that are not straight" (mixed conditions), usually involving witchcraft.

A second major diagnostic difficulty is that a shaman who refuses to treat an insistent prospective patient, perhaps because he feels he is not qualified to treat that particular disorder or has been consulted too late (McNichols, 1944), runs the risk of having his refusal viewed as prima facie evidence that he, himself, had caused his prospective patient's illness (see pt. 7, pp. 387–426). He may therefore make the diagnosis that the patient demands from him and may undertake the treatment, hoping for the best.

Last, but not least, there are sometimes also theoretical differences between two shamans regarding the etiology of a given disorder, although in such cases it is usually possible to show that, at least on the level of latent meaning, these seemingly irreconcilable explanations of a given disease actually have the same meaning (pt. 1, p. 11; pt. 4, pp. 117–128).

Factors facilitating diagnosis.—Although several aboriginal medical specialties are today entirely obsolete and forgotten, it is interesting to note that one rarely hears of a patient who had a disease that no one was any longer qualified to cure, perhaps because shamans only diagnose illnesses that one or the other of them has the power to treat effectively.

Diagnostic criteria.—The single most important diagnostic procedure is the study of the patient's dreams, which supposedly reveal the etiology and nature of his condition. This is a far from senseless procedure, since already Aristotle (n. d.) knew that in sleep one may be more sensitive to inner stimuli—indicative of the onset of a physical illness—than one is in a waking state (cf. Bartemeier, 1950). It is psychologically legitimate to suggest that, given the general knowledge of the type of dreams one is supposed to have if one has, e. g., hiwey lak, the patient's unconscious may comply with these cultural expectations and produce a suitable type of dream.[9]

In other instances it is the physical symptom that provides clues to the nature of the illness and causes the shaman to ask whether the patient had the kind of dreams that should, in principle, accompany his physical symptom. Given the fact that, even in the absence of leading questions, all dreams are modified—by means of a secondary elaboration—in the act of remembering and retelling them, it is extremely probable that a patient, who is being insistently questioned by a shaman, will "recall" having had the expected type of dreams. Such retroactive falsifications are presumably especially common in cases where the diagnostician suspects witchcraft and therefore insists that the patient cannot be helped unless and until he reveals the name of the person who bewitched him. This supposition is greatly strengthened by the fact that retroactive falsifications of dreams occur both when one seeks to deceive oneself (Freud, 1950) and when one must comply with social expectations (Devereux, 1951 a).

In brief, given the tendency of primitives to differentiate less sharply than we do between reality and dream (Kroeber, 1952), and given also their suggestibility (Stoll, 1904), it is extremely probable that, when pressured by an inquisitive diagnostician, the primitive patient will "recall" having had the kind of dreams he is *supposed* to have had, or else will produce the desired dream the very next night.[10] In this context it is noteworthy that, according to Toffelmier and Luomala (1936), the Diegueño boy, whose dream does not fit the

---

[9] The cultural patterning of Plains Indian visions tends to confirm this hypothesis (Devereux, 1951 a).

[10] A Plains Indian patient was systematically induced by me to "dream out" his conflicts, in order to achieve a cure (Devereux, 1951 a).

expected pattern, is told what he should have dreamed, and is then instructed to dream the prescribed kind of dream as soon as possible.

Life history data are also important diagnostic facts. Thus, when a Mohave, known to have repeatedly taken shampoo mud from a bewitched lake, became ill, his ailment was immediately attributed to the hikwi: r, which are said to live in that lake (Case 30).

On the other hand, unlike many other primitives (Hallowell, 1939), the Mohave do not use the confession of sins either as a diagnostic or as a therapeutic procedure. The nearest thing to a therapeutic use of confession is the obligation of a victim of witchcraft to disclose the name of the witch and to report his dreams as accurately as possible. This procedure resembles the confession of sins only because the victim of witchcraft is often a willing victim, and is therefore reluctant to disclose the identity of his "assailant." On the other hand, no confession of sins, in the strict sense, is demanded either for diagnostic or for therapeutic purposes, even though certain trespasses, such as incestuous marriages, are believed to wipe out whole families (Devereux, 1939 a).

In brief, the diagnostician is expected to find out everything relevant about the patient's life history. His clues range from objective statements such as: "I was kicked by a horse," "I associated with aliens," or, "I was threatened by a certain shaman," to more esoteric kinds of experiences or occurrences.

In addition to determining the nature of the illness, the shaman may look for data indicative of the severity of the illness, i. e., for data bearing upon prognosis. Thus, a diagnostician is bound to be interested, e. g., in the information that an owl, a harbinger of death, repeatedly hooted near the patient's domicile.

An important diagnostic factor of another order is the shaman's own field of specialization and his wish to be consulted and paid by as many patients as possible—something not unheard of even outside Mohave society. This temptation is fostered by the possibility of saying, if the treatment fails to effect a real recovery, that the diagnosed illness was only one component of a complex of diseases, the remainder of which must be cured by other specialists. On the other hand, the "ambulance chasing" proclivities of the shaman are inhibited by the knowledge that, if he loses too many patients, he will, later, be accused of witchcraft (Hrdlička, 1908; Kroeber, 1925 a).

Roughly speaking, we may visualize a Mohave diagnosis as the resultant of many vectors: the patient's own preliminary diagnosis, reflected in his decision to consult, e. g., a hiwey lak rather than an ahwe: hahnok specialist; the patient's dreams; his physical symptoms; his life history; and, finally, the shaman's wish to treat him for a variety of subjective reasons, which he sums up in the formula: "I feel I can help him." This expression suggests that a Mohave diagnosis represents, in the last resort, a kind of hunch, whose entire basis is by no means always conscious. In this respect the Mohave diagnostician operates much like any great Western diagnostician who is credited with an "uncanny clinical-diagnostic flair," i. e., with an exceptional inductive capacity. He differs from the great Occidental diagnostician only in that his basic diagnostic scheme is fundamentally more or less arbitrary and non-reality-oriented, since the data, or pseudo-data, that his hunches synthesize are not wholly empirical.

A further difference between great Occidental diagnosticians and the Mohave shamans is that the former always seek to evolve hunches which are naturalistic, while Mohave diagnostic hunches are often supernaturalistic in their orientation (pt. 8, passim).

These findings lead to a generalized distinction between scientists and nonscientists. Psychologically, both types perform their creative work preconsciously, or even unconsciously, by means of what Kris (1952) called "regression in the service of the ego." [11] Even the layman may deliberately use this process; when faced with a perplexing problem, he may decide to "sleep on it." However, unlike the nonscientist, the scientist utilizes only known empirical data, or else known data plus imagined ones which are, however, naturalistically conceived.[12] This is a decisive difference since, as Poincaré expresses it, "method consists precisely in the choice of one's data" (Poincaré, 1946). Last, but not least, the scientist pursues naturalistic objectives, while the shaman does not (pt. 8, passim).

The preceding considerations clearly imply that being a scientist implies primarily a particular orientation, rather than simply objectively valid results. Indeed, it is a logical axiom that correct judgments may be based on false premises exploited illogically. This principle is usually stated in the following form: The correctness of the noema is sometimes independent of the correctness of the noesis. (Thus, I may decide that John Doe is an objectionable person because he wears a green necktie. Now, John Doe may, indeed, be an objectionable person, though not because he wears a green tie. In this case the noema is correct, while the noesis is not.)

Stages in the formulation of a diagnosis.—It is proposed to attempt a characterization of the ideal procedure whereby a final and complete diagnosis is reached. In actual instances one or more of the steps to be discussed may be omitted, depending partly on external cir-

---

[11] It is known that Descartes' philosophy was decisively influenced by certain of his dreams (Lewin, 1958), that Kekulé laid the foundations of modern organic chemistry after visualizing the benzene ring in dream, and that Henri Poincaré solved a difficult mathematical problem in his sleep (Poincaré, 1946).

[12] The classical example is the evolving of the "imaginary datum" *atom* by Ionian philosophers, some two thousand years before atoms became empirical data.

cumstances and partly on the nature and development of the illness itself.

(*1*) *I may be ill.*—The first diagnostic step is the patient's self-definition as a sick person. A given individual may sustain an injury, such as a horse kick; he may notice an unequivocal sign of illness, such as a urethral discharge, indicative of hiku: pk (i. e., in this instance, gonorrhea) ; he may experience malaise and a digestive disorder of an ambiguous character (i. e., suggesting hiwey lak, ahwe: hahnok or some other illness) ; he may have a distinctly pathogenic dream of a well-defined type (e. g., a dream of cohabiting with a dead relative) ; or else he may simply remember a highly disturbing anxiety dream of a relatively nonspecific nature. At this point the Mohave begins to wonder whether or not he is ill.

(*2*) *Am I ill?*—The patient's first action is to consult members of his own family, who usually agree with his estimate that he is, in fact, ill. Sometimes, however, they urge him to consult a shaman whom they happen to know, in order to ascertain whether or not, e. g., his disturbing dream is actually a sign of illness. In such instances the patient does not appear to consult a particular shaman on the grounds that he specializes in the treatment of a certain disorder, but simply visits any shaman he happens to know, in order to find out whether or not he is, in fact, ill.

(*3*) *I may have a particular illness.*—In some instances, where the first symptoms are unequivocal as in hiku: pk, or else strongly suggest that the illness may be, e. g., hikwi: r, the patient, usually acting with the knowledge and upon the advice of his kin, consults a particular shaman, who specializes in the treatment of the illness which the patient thinks he has; i. e., just as an American with a broken leg consults an orthopedist and not an internist, so a supposedly nonpregnant Mohave woman who has certain dreams and also certain symptoms of pregnancy (Cases 45 and 46) consults a hiwey lak nyevedhi: specialist and not, e.g., an expert on hiku: pk. (See also item 7, below.)

(*4*) *You probably have a particular illness.*—The shaman whom the patient consults either in order to ascertain that he is, in fact, ill or about to become ill, or else because he thinks he has a certain illness which that shaman is qualified to cure, may tentatively agree that the patient does probably have some particular illness. In such instances, if the shaman happens to specialize in the cure of that illness, he agrees to try to treat the patient for that illness. In other instances he decides that the patient probably suffers from an illness which he is not qualified to treat, and refers him to a suitable specialist. In still other instances, the shaman may declare that there is nothing wrong with the patient. Thus, Ahma Huma: re, as well as Kwathany Hi: wa, correctly decided that their respective patients, who consulted them because they thought they had hiwey lak nyevedhi :, were actually simply pregnant (Cases 45 and 46). (Cf. also McNichols, 1944).

(*5*) *I will ascertain whether you do, in fact, have this illness, by treating you.*— At first, the shaman usually makes only a tentative diagnosis, to be confirmed by the effectiveness of the treatment. If the therapy is fully effective, the diagnosis is automatically confirmed. If it utterly fails, it is held that the patient waited too long before consulting a shaman (McNichols, 1944), or that (in cases of witchcraft) the patient did not cooperate sufficiently with his therapist, or that the witch is more powerful than the therapist, or, finally, that the initial diagnosis was incorrect. In the first and second instances, the diagnosis is held to be correct, and the patient is taken to another practitioner of the same specialty—or, nowadays, sometimes to the hospital—in order to try a second course of treatment. In the third instance, the witch himself may be asked to undertake the treatment of his victim. (See item 7, below.) In the fourth case, the initial diagnosis is discarded, and the therapist suggests that the patient consult a different kind of specialist, qualified to treat the patient's real illness.

(6) *The diagnosis was basically correct but incomplete.*—If the treatment results in improvement, but not in a real cure, the initial diagnostician-therapist declares that he cured that part of the illness that he is qualified to treat and suggests that the remaining component of the patient's obviously "not straight" illness be treated by another kind of specialist. This procedure may be repeated several times, since some cases of "not straight" illnesses are said to have several distinct components, each coming within the scope of a different shaman's powers.

(7) *We know you bewitched the patient; now you must treat him, and you had better cure him . . . or else!*—When, either immediately, or else because other forms of treatment proved unsuccessful, a Mohave is thought to have been bewitched by a particular shaman, the patient's relatives may put pressure on the witch to cure his victim. Strictly speaking, they only express the hope that the witch's better nature (hi: wantc kinyaim=heart says) will induce him to cure his victim, but behind this politely worded hope is always the threat that, should the alleged witch fail to cure his victim, he would be killed. Such consultations, in which a "layman's diagnosis" is practically forced upon a shaman, must be quite awkward for all concerned. Thus, whenever Kwathany Hi: wa was accused of having bewitched one of his relatives and was asked to treat him, he invariably burst into tears. Hivsu: Tupo: ma was, likewise, deeply hurt when, while trying to treat his "nephew" Sudhu: râ (Case 44), the latter accused him of having bewitched him. Other accused witches became defiant (McNichols, 1944). In principle, if a witch does undertake to treat one of his alleged victims, he usually does his best for his patient. If his treatment is successful, the diagnosis of witchcraft is held to have been correct. However, the repentant witch, who made amends by curing his victim, is not penalized in any way and is paid like any other therapist, even though he simply cured an illness that he himself had caused.

(8) *Maybe we had better try a physician.*—Whenever the patient's condition is desperate, and at least one attempt at shamanistic treatment did not effect any improvement, the patient is taken to the hospital for diagnosis and treatment. However, even though the Mohave may learn the scientific name of the patient's illness, the hospital diagnosis does not appear to replace in their thinking the Mohave diagnosis that may have been made. Thus, only a very few, exceptionally well-educated and sophisticated, persons, like Hama: Utce:, say that so-and-so had spinal meningitis or tuberculosis; the rest of the tribe continues to affirm that the patient suffered from whatever native disease entity he was thought to have had in the first place. Finally, should the patient fail to improve in the hospital, he is usually withdrawn against medical advice, partly in order to try a shaman once more and partly in order to let him die in familiar surroundings (Case 4).

In brief, the Mohave diagnostic procedure usually involves several steps, the initial, tentative diagnosis being made by the patient and his family. Further diagnoses are based on the success or failure of such treatments as may have been attempted.

Validation of diagnosis.—In principle, the conclusive test of a diagnosis is a cure.

CASE 1 (Informant: Ahma Huma:re):

Sudhu:râ was discharged from the reservation hospital as an incurable case of tuberculosis. He was then treated by Hivsu:Tupo:ma, who attributed the patient's illness to an old horse kick. The failure of his treatment proved that the illness had been misdiagnosed, whereupon the patient was referred to me. I treated him for ghost possession (hiwey lak nyevedhi:) and his condition improved so much that everyone agreed that he had the hiwey lak nyevedhi: illness.

The Mohave react differently to shamans who lose several patients in a row and shamans who simply misdiagnose a patient. The former are believed to be witches (Hrdlička, 1908; Kroeber, 1925 a) and are sometimes killed (Devereux, 1937 c), while the latter are not blamed for their failure to cure their patients, especially if they specify in advance that their diagnosis is a tentative one and if, after failing to cure the patient, they refer him to another kind of specialist. It is hardly necessary to add that no shaman ever refers a patient whom he failed to cure to another representative of his own specialty, since such a referral either would imply an admission that his powers are inferior to those of the shaman to whom he referred the case or else would suggest that he is a witch, who deliberately mismanaged the treatment. This may explain why most shamanistic diagnoses tend to be tentative ones.

The Mohave know, of course, that even a correctly diagnosed and appropriately treated patient may die. In such cases they say that the patient failed to cooperate with the therapist (e. g., by not revealing to him the name of the person who bewitched him), or that the witch was more powerful than the therapist, or else that the patient failed to consult a shaman before his illness became incurable. The notion that any illness, if diagnosed and treated in time by a truly powerful shaman, may be incurable, seems to be alien to the Mohave.

This being said, there is no record of shamans accused of having misdiagnosed a patient either in order to harm him or else in order to earn money illegitimately, even though a fretful patient sometimes unjustly accuses his therapist of having bewitched him (Case 44). Indeed, it would be extremely risky for a shaman to pretend that his patient has an illness that he is qualified to cure, since the utter failure of his treatment would expose him to accusations of witchcraft. It is also noteworthy that when an abnormally acquisitive shaman wishes to recruit patients, he causes precisely the type of epidemic that he is qualified to cure and, when consulted by his victims, does his best to cure them, so as to get further patients (Devereux, 1937 c). In fact, the family of a bewitched person may put pressure upon the witch to treat his victim, with the expectation that the bewitcher's "better nature" or fear of consequences—and presumably also the prospect of a fee—would induce him to effect a cure.

While the Mohave were always lenient toward shamans who simply misdiagnosed a case, their leniency in this respect appears to be even greater nowadays than it was in aboriginal times. This impression is based upon the repeated statements of both shamans and laymen that nowadays the Mohave seldom suffer from uncomplicated ("straight") diseases. They mostly have illnesses which are "not straight," in that they involve certain complications, such as witchcraft, or else contact with aliens and with alien food. Hence, it is not always possible for a shaman to make a complete initial diagnosis. Indeed, the fact that the patient's illness is not straight may become apparent only when the first course of treatment brings about an improvement, but not a complete cure. In such cases the first therapist simply declares that he had done his part and had cured that portion of the illness that came within the scope of his special powers, and then refers the patient to a specialist qualified to treat the remaining component of the illness.

It is therefore tentatively suggested that the current prevalence of allegedly not straight illnesses may be responsible for the Mohave belief that modern shamans are less powerful than those who plied their trade in aboriginal times. On the other hand, the Mohave themselves realize that contact with aliens led to the introduction of genuinely new diseases. This insight is reflected not only by their insistence that the chief cause of insanity is miscegenation and contact with aliens (pt. 4, pp. 128–150) but, above all, by the revealing belief that some time elapsed before shamans already qualified to cure arrow wounds also acquired the power to treat bullet wounds.

Summing up, Mohave diagnostic theory has at its roots the axiom that "the proof of the pudding is in the eating" and that the effectiveness or failure of the therapy is the most conclusive of all diagnostic criteria. This touchstone of Mohave diagnostic science is, in many ways, also used by modern medical scientists. Thus, according to Kraepelin (1919), the crucial diagnostic criterion of schizophrenia is its supposed chronicity and incurability. [13]

---

[13] It should be noted that the discarding of this admittedly extreme point of view led to the deleterious tendency to diagnose as schizophrenia a great many "transitory confusional states" and forced nosologists to apply to the "classical" chronic schizophrenias the term "nuclear" or "process" schizophrenia.

The diagnosis: yamomk (insanity).—In theory, though not always in actual practice, the Mohave do differentiate between "insanity" (neurosis and psychosis) on the one hand and "organic illness" on the other hand, even though a few shamans specializing in the cure of organic ailments usually confuse the two, simply because the panic, pain, or toxicity of organic illnesses sometimes produces epiphenomenal mental disturbances. The tendency of such prejudiced native organicists to think of mental disorders solely as symptoms of physical ailments is made evident not only by Hikye:t's confused account of the etiology of mental disorders, but is also echoed by Ahma Huma:re's explicit assertion that hi:wa itck (pt. 3, pp. 91–106), which is caused by a specific and recent psychic trauma, is not a "true insanity." By contrast, more broadminded "organicists," like the shaman Hivsu:Tupo:ma and some others, as well as many intelligent laymen, spontaneously insisted that hi:wa itck is a true psychosis. Furthermore, in contradistinction to confirmed organicists, they tended to view the physical symptoms of certain disorders in which mental disturbances were also present, either as part of the total disease picture, or else, in some very interesting instances, as signs of "organic compliance" (organisches Entgegenkommen) in the strictly Freudian sense of this term.

The Mohave also differentiate between perversion and neurosis—witness Tcatc's assertion that the zoophilia of persons whose insanity is due to witchcraft is entirely different from the zoophilia of shamans, which is a sign of their "devilishness" (perversion). Mohave theory and psychoanalytic theory are in agreement on this point.

It is, however, not always easy to ascertain precisely what critical symptom is used by the Mohave to differentiate, e. g., between mental disorder, muteness, perversion, and organic illness. According to the organically minded shaman Ahma Huma:re, neuroses, psychoses, and muteness should all be labeled "yamomk" (insanity), apparently because, in his opinion, the crucial symptom of "yamomk" is a very broadly defined "speech disturbance," called yavoo:k, which he defined as "they talk, but do not know what they are talking about." Since he specifically stated that the relatives of mute persons could interpret their inarticulate sounds and other attempts at communication, it is obvious that he equated the inarticulate sounds emitted by mutes with the chaotic content of the speech of psychotics.

Thus, even if one is mindful of these special opinions, resulting from idiosyncratic professional interests, it is fairly safe to say that, on the whole, the Mohave differentiate rather appropriately between organic illness and mental disorder. On the other hand, their differential diagnosis of the several forms of yamomk known to them is based on criteria that are sometimes obscure and not wholly satisfactory ones.[14]

The diagnosis of particular disorders is determined by a combination of all the factors mentioned in this chapter and is subject to modification or expansion in the manner described in the subsection "Stages in the formulation of a diagnosis." On the whole, there is usually complete diagnostic unanimity whenever the clinical picture is a relatively simple one and the precipitating event is generally known. Thus, there was complete unanimity about the diagnosis of all cases of hi: wa itck, which is a straight and relatively benign mental disorder. Where the clinical picture is more complex, diagnostic differences usually pertain to whether the basic disorder is or is not complicated by ghostly influences or by witchcraft, i. e., whether it is a straight or not straight disorder.

As the preceding pages indicate, the problem of a final diagnosis is, among the Mohave, closely related to the effectiveness or failure of therapy.

Treatment.—The Mohave treatment of mental diseases is, roughly, of two kinds.

Genuine supportive psychotherapy is administered not only by shamans, but also by laymen, though usually only in such minor ailments as hi: wa itck. This treatment consists in reasoning with the patient and in giving him such moral support as he may need. Tcatc's attempt to comfort me and to reason with me at a time when I was thought to have hi: wa itck (pt. 3, pp. 91–106) is a good example of genuine Mohave psychotherapy. Supportive psychotherapy and reasoning with the patient is also resorted to in combination with more magical methods in persuading certain individuals, who wish to die, to give up their spiteful and vindictive intentions. Thus, sucklings who make themselves ill because they are jealous of unborn siblings (Devereux, 1947 a), future shamans who do not wish to be born (Devereux, 1937 c and 1948 e), and twins who refuse to remain on earth (Devereux, 1941) are urged by shamans to behave rationally and to stay alive.

Serious mental disorders are, on the other hand, treated in the usual shamanistic way: by singing songs or, if the traditional songs are no longer remembered, by reciting the appropriate portion of the Creation myth (Devereaux, 1957 b); by massage; by blowing upon the patient; by the use of saliva; by food taboos and baths; and by other magical means. This type of treatment is described, e. g., in

---

[14] Psychiatrists who, in the course of their work, had to wrestle with official nomenclatures of disease, will, perhaps, sympathize with the difficulties the Mohave experience in this respect.

Harav He: ya's and Ahma Huma: re's accounts of their respective therapies of hiwey lak and hiwey lak nyevedhi: (pt. 4, pp. 150–175).

The initial treatment is almost always administered by a shaman. Only if shamanistic treatments conspicuously fail to help the patient is the sufferer hospitalized. Any attempt to short-circuit this round-about way of getting modern medical treatment is usually frowned upon by the more conservative members of the tribe. The only exceptions are extremely serious surgical emergencies, such as accidents and attempted suicides. Thus, when "Mrs. Smith's" son became temporarily acutely psychotic, she was severely blamed by her relatives for hospitalizing her son without first trying to have him treated by a shaman (Case 64).

In addition, as already stated, patients in extremis are usually withdrawn from the hospital against medical advice, partly in order to try shamanistic treatment once more and partly in order to allow the patient to die in familiar surroundings.

The near-identity of the shamanistic method of treating psychiatric (or, rather, psychosomatic) illnesses with the one used to cure organic ailments not only proves the fundamental homogeneity of all Mohave medical techniques, but also reflects the Mohave shaman's essential failure to differentiate in a fundamental way between psychiatric and organic illness. This is due not only to a lack of sophistication but, presumably, also to the fact that, as among all primitives, organic illness invariably elicits psychic responses of some magnitude, and vice versa, of course.

THE POSITION OF THE INSANE IN MOHAVE SOCIETY

Before the age of witch hunts, Roman law summed up the prevailing sensible attitude toward the insane in the sentence "furiosus satis ipso furore punitur" (the madman is already sufficiently punished by his madness) (Krafft-Ebing, 1875). This humane view was probably due to the fact that these legislators believed insanity to be a natural phenomenon rather than a consequence of personal sin.

The Mohave attitude toward psychotics is somewhat similar. They do not condemn the insane, just as they do not criticize those kinds of suicide which, in their opinion, are determined by the nature of the individual involved. ("It is their nature. They can't help it.") On the other hand, the Mohave condemn, e. g., voluntary suicide, incest (Devereux, 1939 a), and alcoholism (Devereux, 1948 i) because, in their estimation, such actions are not characterologically determined. On the whole, the Mohave are not only lenient toward the insane but are mildly amused by their odd behavior. Thus, while narrating a certain case history (Case 21) both my informant and my interpreter burst out laughing, but when the laughter subsided, my informant remarked rather wistfully, "It sounds funny now, but it wasn't funny at all at that time."

The overall attitude toward the insane was described by Tcatc as follows:

[Did the Mohave ever kill the insane?] No, they took very good care of them. They used to watch them even at night. [Among the Moi of Indochina, when an insane person becomes obstreperous, they tie him up, throw him into a cave and let him starve to death.] That is horrible. People who do such things must be crazy themselves. [Not so very long ago, the white people kept the insane in horrible bedlams. They beat them, tied them up with chains and charged entrance fees to people who wanted to watch and tease the insane.] That is all the whites ever think about—money! [When a French doctor called Pinel released the insane from their chains, they called him insane and locked him up too.] All whites are bad. [Sometimes I think that we have more to be ashamed of than any other race in the world.] Yes.

Throughout this conversation Tcatc's tone of voice and facial expression reflected intense disgust and indignation.

An almost identical point of view was presented by E.S.:

Even if a person was insane, people still took care of him because, despite his insanity, he was their relative. Thus, even though everyone says that O: otc is a kamalo: y, (Devereux 1948 f) and is believed to have helped her husband kill a witch, her relatives are, nonetheless, nice to her when she is around, precisely because she is a relation of theirs (Case 104).

There are, however, quite definite limits to what even the Mohave will tolerate from a person who, like a kamalo: y, is not definitely insane. Thus, when, after an interview with me, O: otc hinted that I had made advances to her, she was severely reprimanded by her indignant relatives, who told her point blank that they did not believe her accusations since, unlike her, I enjoyed a spotless reputation. In fact, if a married kamalo: y became too obnoxious, her husband's friends sometimes raped and clitoridectomized her at the request of her own husband (Devereux, 1948 f).

A distinction is also made between a person whose misconduct is felt to be caused by the budding of his shamanistic powers, and one who simply misbehaves. The behavior of the former is criticized but tolerated, whereas the conduct of the latter is condemned.

The Mohave also behave differently toward persons supposedly able to control their obnoxious behavior and those who are obviously unable to do so. They ridicule the antics of transvestites and of persons suffering from hi: wa itck, though, in the latter case, they laugh only in retrospect since, as stated above, Tcatc stressed that even though the behavior of a certain hi: wa itck patient seemed laughable in retrospect, "it was not at all funny" when it happened. They are also critical of women who ostentatiously throw themselves on the funeral pyre of a deceased husband and then remarry almost at once (Devereux, 1942 a) (pt. 7, pp. 431–450). Finally, even though suicides are pitied, they are also criticized for being weak, especially if they kill themselves over a woman (pt. 7, pp. 308–327).

As regards the genuinely insane, they are treated just like other sick persons. An attempt is made to cure them by shamanistic means, and only if this treatment fails do the Mohave have recourse to American medicine. A progressive family was criticized for hospitalizing one of its members before a shaman had a chance to treat him; and a woman who thought that her daughter would be taken to a mental hospital kept watch over her with a gun (Case 31). Lunacy hearings are attended by tribal deputations (Case 4) and hospitalized psychotics are visited to make sure that they are well treated (Case 4). The failure of a distant hospital to advise the tribe that a neurosyphilitic Mohave patient had died, and the fact that her corpse was put in a morgue instead of being shipped back for cremation, aroused a storm of indignation (Case 75). Should occidental treatment also fail, the patient (especially if he is about to die) is withdrawn from the hospital, against medical advice, and is taken home, partly in order to give shamanistic treatment another try and partly in order to permit the patient to die in familiar surroundings.

A good example of the social *utilization* of the abnormal person is the fact that, even though the shaman is considered more or less crazy, he is called upon to perform important services. By contrast, the *exploitation* of the abnormal individual is relatively minimal in Mohave society. A transvestite may be encouraged to make a show of herself by "fighting for her spouse" (Devereux, 1937 b); the compulsive promiscuousness of an otherwise decent woman may be taken advantage of by men looking for adventure (Case 14); and people may laugh at the antics of some psychotic who is not believed to suffer from a serious mental illness. On the other hand, the Mohave do not systematically exploit or take advantage of the deviant or the abnormal; do not habitually incite him to scurrilous activities; do not abuse him in any way; and, above all, do not kill him, unless he happens to be a self-proclaimed witch. Also, no odium appears to be attached to being, or having been, insane. Mental disease is viewed like any other illness, its occurrence is not concealed and the patient in remission is not personally or socially handicapped in any way.

In brief, the generally humane and tolerant attitude of the Mohave Indians also extends to the insane, conceivably because, due to their constant preoccupation with dreams and other autistic processes of their own psyche, they have a certain ability to empathize with the mental processes of disturbed persons and are therefore able to consider them quite as human as themselves and entitled to the same love, care, and consideration as others.[15]

It may be worth mentioning that McNichols (1944), in an ethnographically accurate (Kroeber, 1944) novel about the Mohave, makes repeated references to the occasional appearance in Mohave territory of homicidal maniacs expelled from other tribes. McNichols describes in some detail the manner in which such a psychotic Paiute was hunted down by a Mohave youth, who was "name traveling" with a youthful white friend; the slaying of this Paiute was accepted by all, save only the oldest members of the tribe, as a suitable climax to name traveling. When this young Mohave was persuaded that he had been bewitched by contact with the insane Paiute's magical objects, which, apart from being inherently dangerous, also carried foreign contamination, he went into a near psychotic panic, but promptly pulled out of his seemingly catatonic condition when a matter-of-fact Mohave shaman told him that his fears were unfounded. This temporary collapse did not diminish in any way the value of this young man's feat in getting rid of the psychotic Paiute witch.

---

[15] The above considerations imply that brutality toward the insane and the failure of early psychiatrists to tackle the problem of mental disorder with insight and empathy are closely related phenomena.

PART 2. DISORDERS OF THE INSTINCTS

AGGRESSION AND GUILT

Aggressivity, as well as feelings of guilt over real or imaginary acts of aggression, play a decisive role in the etiology of mental disorders. In fact, even manifestly sexual derangements are due primarily to a contamination of sexuality by aggression. Hence, in a broadly theoretical sense, it is not really legitimate to single out certain psychiatric disorders as being caused by conflicts related to aggressivity, since problems related to aggressivity are present, to a variable extent, also in every other psychiatric illness.

On the other hand, the Mohave themselves seem dimly aware of the fact that certain mental disorders are especially likely to affect persons who engage in certain aggressive activities, or fear retribution for real, magical, or unconscious acts of aggression, or seek to inhibit, but not sublimate, their aggressive impulses. Suicide also results from aggression, which is first directed at others and then, self-punitively, at oneself. However, for reasons of expository convenience, occurrences which the Mohave define as suicide will not be discussed in this section, but in part 7, and will therefore not be included in the following classification of disorders related to problems of aggression.

Neuroses and psychoses related primarily to aggression may be classified as follows:

A. Pathological outbursts of homicidal rage:
    (1) Pi-ipa : teeva : ràm : People scarcity
B. Pathological sequelae of socially approved aggression:
    (1) Against game: Hunter's neurosis
    (2) Against the outgroup: Scalper's psychosis
    (3) Against antisocial members of the ingroup: Witchkiller's psychosis
C. Pathological sequelae of hyperactivity, which is apparently equated with aggression:
    (1) An illness of ordinary active persons
    (2) The god Mastamho's psychosis
    (3) The psychopathology of singers
    (4) The corruption of shamanistic powers
D. Pathological sequelae of inhibited aggressivity or power:
    (1) Heartbreak (=jealousy) : Hi : wa itck.   (See also pt. 3, pp. 91–106)
    (2) Psychoses resulting from the inhibition of magical powers
E. Pathological sequelae of imagined counteraggression on the part of hated aliens (a paranoid mechanism) (pt. 4, pp. 128–150):
    (1) Disease from aliens: Ahwe: hahnok
    (2) Disease from enemy ghosts: Ahwe: nyevedhi:

The role of aggression in the etiology of various types of suicide is discussed only in part 7. Inhibited jealousy, as exemplified by hi: wa itck, will be described in connection with other disorders of mood (="heart"). In a more remote way, psychopathological phenomena connected with funeral rites (pt. 4, pp. 186–195) and with the ghosts of the dead (pt. 4, pp. 175–184) are also related to aggression, and, specifically, to fears of counter aggression, but, for reasons of expository convenience, are discussed in separate sections.

PATHOLOGICAL OUTBURSTS OF HOMICIDAL RAGE

PI-IPA: TCEVA: RAM (PEOPLE SCARCITY), DUE TO PREMATURE DEATH

Homicide is extremely rare among the Mohave Indians. The only recorded instances involve the killing of witches, discussed in part 7, one homicide committed while the murderer was intoxicated (Appendix, pp. 505–548), and some assaults followed by suicide (pt. 7, pp. 459–484).

The occurrence of amok-running and of impulsive mass-murders was denied by Tcatc, as well as by Hilyera Anyay.

According to Tcatc:

There is another kind of insanity which is caused neither by suma: tc (dream), nor by ahwe: hahnok (foreign disease), nor by hi: wa itck (heartbreak). A person suffering from this illness just dreams that he killed someone, or is being killed by someone. Then he goes crazy. He acts exactly as though he had ahwe: nyevedhi: (foreign ghost). He awakens from his dream and runs. It takes a good while before he gets sane again. Such people are very nervous, even when they are among their own relatives. People say that such persons are suma: tc itcem (dream bad or miss) or pi-ipa: tceva: râm (people scarcity). The shaman who has the power to doctor ahwe: nyevedhi: (foreign ghost) or hikwi: r sama: nyevedhi: (snake? ghost), which resembles the ahwe: illness, or matkodha: u (bewitching), all of which resemble this disease, can also cure this illness.

CASE 2 (Informant: Tcatc):

There was a case of such an insanity at Needles, Calif., which was not treated by any American physician. A certain man would get sudden fits of rage, take a stick and beat up people. He lived apart from others. The Mohave tried to cure him, and a shaman, who specialized in the treatment of colds and pneumonia, was called in to sing for him. He sat down, at a little distance from the patient, and sang for him, but the sick man immediately went away. Eventually this man's mother discovered him dead from cold and exposure.

Comment

Tentative diagnosis.—The case history suggests a fuguelike state, which may have been either psychogenic, or an epilepsy equivalent, or else—less probably—a fugue while the patient was delirious as a result of some toxic or infectious disease. By contrast, the formal description of this illness suggests primarily either a severe anxiety state or an agitated depression. The interplay between aggression and guilt (punishment) is clearly shown by the fact that both dreams of killing someone and dreams of being killed by someone cause the same illness (see pt. 2, pp. 43–45).

Cannibalistic and murderous fantasies:

(1) *Windigo psychosis* of the Canadian Indians (Teicher, 1960). Tcatc never heard of such an illness.

(2) *Sharpened Leg, and Ice- or Stone-Skinned Giants.* Myths and beliefs about these aggressive supernaturals, which occur among Plains Indians and Canadian Indians, respectively, are, according to Tcatc, absent among the Mohave.

(3) *Cannibalism*, except in folklore (Devereux, 1948 h; Kroeber, 1948), was denied by all informants. Tcatc reacted with genuine horror to my account of a Yavapai case of cannibalism (Gifford, 1932, 1936). (But cf. pt. 4, pp. 150–175.)

(4) *Zoanthropy.*—According to Tcatc, lycanthropy does not exist among the Mohave. My interpreter, E. S., added, however, that he had heard of such beliefs among the Pueblo Indians. When I mentioned some of the were-tiger stories current among the Naga (Hutton, 1921 a, 1921 b), the narrative did not jog the informants' memory and merely elicited surprise. According to Tcatc:

One may see a bull or a giant in one's dream and these beings might fight with the dreamer, but the bull is the only animal that the Mohave see in their dreams. In almost all cases they see in their dreams the bull turns out to be simply a certain shaman. These dreams come when that shaman is thinking about the dreamer, or the dreamer about the shaman. [Do you mean that the shaman thinks of him in some special way?] No. [Tcatc then remarked that some of the events narrated in the hukthar (coyote) stories (Kroeber, 1948; Devereux, 1948 h) may or may not have actually happened.]

The information on zoanthropy, elicited by means of direct questions, has two significant implications:

(*a*) The erroneous statement that the only animal seen in dreams is the bull is revealing, since the Mohave seem to castrate all bull calves and rely on Agency bulls for the servicing of their cows. They seem to experience considerable guilt, especially over the castration of bull calves, since they specify that newly castrated calves bellow with pain much longer than do castrated horses or pigs (Devereux, 1948 g).

(*b*) The transformation of the bull into a shaman in the dream itself shows that the shaman is an image of the dangerous, ogrelike oedipal father of the small child's fantasy world.

On the whole, both the data about the pi-ipa: tceva: rǎm illness itself and about dream zoanthropy reflect a paranoid tendency to ascribe aggressivity to the powerful object of one's unconscious hostilities. Since the occurrence of true paranoid persecution complexes was denied by Tcatc as well as by other informants, one is inclined to suggest that Mohave society managed to socialize and culturalize the persecutory attitude, by institutionalizing both witchcraft and fear of witchcraft, and by granting cultural recognition and status to dangerous dream personages, identified either with ghosts or with witches.

PATHOLOGICAL SEQUELAE OF SOCIALLY APPROVED AGGRESSION

AGAINST GAME: HUNTER'S NEUROSIS

(1) While discussing dietary rules, Hivsu: Tupo: ma stated in 1932–33 that a man who eats his own kill becomes insane.[16] In 1950, when I was seeking to obtain additional information on this topic, Pulyi: k first stated that such a hunter does not necessarily become mad; he will be primarily ill. However, in the very next breath he mentioned that such a hunter has hallucinations; he sees game everywhere.

(2) When I cited K. M. Stewart's report (1947 a) that, when a person first ate squirrel, he placed his sandal on his head, to protect himself against loss of memory, Pulyi: k replied that loss of memory was perhaps too strong a term. Instead, he suggested that ·without this precaution such a person would become quite "absentminded" (=nyayu: vomopet'à).

Comment

Pacifying or honoring one's kill, while especially conspicuous among certain Canadian Indians, also occurs in the Southwest, e. g., among the Hopi (Devereux, 1946).[17] These precautionary measures clearly reflect that guilt ·and anxiety over the killing of game occur even in hunting tribes (Devereux, 1957 a), and are directly related to scalping ceremonies, which seek to pacify the scalp and to protect the scalper from insanity (see pt. 2, pp. 43–45.) Once more, the interplay between aggression and guilt is in evidence, though, due to a lesser identification with mere animals, it appears to be dealt with by repression (loss of memory) and/or absentmindedness, rather than by more explosive defense mechanisms leading to serious psychiatric symptoms; in addition, the hunter is not permitted to benefit from his kill. Renouncing the eating of one's own kill is perhaps comparable to the fact that only old men, who no longer went to war, would, or could, marry female prisoners of war, whose proximity was believed capable of causing the foreign psychosis (pt. 4, pp. 128–150). The socially beneficial effects of giving one's kill to others are, on the other hand, too well known to require discussion in this context.

---

[16] According to Kroeber (1925 a) the hunter's infant child may also contract diarrhea.

[17] The ritual art of cutting up a stag in a manner befitting the rules of noble hunting—which is mentioned, e. g., in the legend of Tristan—may well have the same conciliatory significance.

AGAINST THE OUTGROUP: AHWE: MA:N, SCALPER'S PSYCHOSIS

According to K. M. Stewart (1947 a), and to Fathauer (1954), only people who had power derived from enemy dreams (ahwe: sumatc) could scalp foes and purify new scalps.   However, like other members of the war party, they too were subject to the nefarious influence of scalps, prisoners, and aliens, and could contract the dread enemy illness, if they were not properly purified.   This illness consisted in fainting and crazy behavior (Fathauer, 1954) or even in insanity accompanied by hollering in the night (Stewart, 1947 c).   Significantly, the scalpers were also the shamans who cured the enemy illness (pt. 4, pp. 128–150), while Pulyi:k even asserted that the scalper's psychosis was the lethal ahwe: hahnok pure and simple.

Both the existence of purification rites and the fact that, on the way back from a war party, the men deprived themselves in many ways, hardly sleeping at all, fasting, and drinking very little water (Stewart, 1947 c), indicate guilt over the killing and scalping of foes.

It is therefore clear that the scalper's insanity is felt to be due to his guilt feelings over the killing and scalping of foes.   However, between the last aboriginal Mohave battle and World War I ahwe: ma:n could apparently be caused also by mere dreams, since, until 1917, the Mohave did no military service.   Then, when the Mohave began to serve in the United States Armed Forces, it was felt that even if they had not been in actual combat, they were likely to contract ahwe: ma:n.   Thus, when "John Smith" (Case 64) returned to the Reservation after serving in the United States Armed Forces, his mother's cousin urged the family to take him for purification to the Yuma shaman whose name, "as pronounced by the Mohave (sic!)," is Mat-ha: Kuhamaly (mud white), since no Mohave shaman then living had power over the ahwe: ma:n illness.   Since this advice was not followed, when John Smith later on had a psychotic episode, his illness was diagnosed as ahwe: ma:n.   The informant who so diagnosed John Smith's illness also specified that not only scalpers, but all members of a war party, and especially those who were hurt or wounded, were likely to develop ahwe: ma:n, because they kept on dreaming of their military experiences.   This Mohave theory dovetails with the well-known fact that combat dreams tend to be recurrent dream experiences even among Occidentals (Kubie, 1943).

It is probable that the Mohave tendency to postulate that any member of the Mohave war party or of the United States Armed Forces, even if he did not see actual combat, is likely to develop ahwe: ma:n is but an extension of the more ancient view that the contaminating force resided chiefly in the scalps.   Thus, according to Tcatc: "There is also the matter of scalps taken in victory. They are bathed and fixed up with white clay,[18] as though they were living. The person who took a scalp dreamed of it. He dreams that he is taking the scalp and it will prey on his mind. The insanity of scalpers is not unlike that of witch-killing braves. (See pt. 2, p. 45.)

Comment

Tentative diagnosis.—War neurosis. Acute anxiety reaction actuated by guilt. Tcatc's description of ahwe: ma:n resembles her account of pi-ipa: tceva:ràm (see above), which is also preceded by dreams of killing or being killed. Moreover, Tcatc spontaneously compared the symptoms of the scalper's psychosis(?) to the symptoms of the foreign ghost psychosis (pt. 4, pp. 128–150), but without specifically identifying ahwe: ma:n with ahwe: hahnok and ahwe: nyevedhi:, as Pulyi: k did. As for pi-ipa: tceva: ràm, it differs from ahwe: ma:n in that in the former illness actual aggression follows dreams of killing, thus representing the "acting out" of dreams (Devereux, 1953 a), whereas in ahwe: ma:n the killing precedes the dreams of killing. Of course, from the Mohave point of view, this distinction is only a technicality, since, to the Mohave, dream is a genuine part of reality (Kroeber, 1925 a; Wallace, 1947; Devereux, 1956 c). It is tentatively suggested that actual aggression is a symptom of pi-ipa: tceva: ràm, because a dream killing is less cathartic than is actual battle.

K. M. Stewart's (1947 c) statement that scalpers are hollering in the night and Tcatc's and other informants' specification that the scalper's dreams repeat the (anxiety arousing) aggressive act, suggest that scalping was an experience which the scalper's ego was unable to master at once. This inference is greatly strengthened by Tcatc's remark that it takes time to recover from this illness. In addition, her comment and the statements of other informants, such as Anya Hama: rà (day earn, earned daily) and Thinyea: k Hu: say (women to serve them, to show respect to women) of the Vi: mak gens, that such dreams are recurrent ones, suggest that their function is to master the war trauma in dream. This interpretation is strongly supported by the fact that during World War II one standard method of treating guilt-ridden psychiatric casualties was to induce an artificially prolonged sleep, which enabled the patient to dream of the trauma again and again, until he mastered it in dream by means of distortions (happy ending) amounting to a radical reinterpretation of the facts (Kubie, 1943).[19]

---

[18] The Yuma ahwe: ma:n specialist's name is "white mud."

[19] Needless to say, this therapy does not effect a genuine cure. It is purely palliative and effects a social and military recovery, by mobilizing somewhat less incapacitating neurotic defense mechanisms: denial, and others.

The diagnosing of modern war neuroses as ahwe : ma : n is more than passive acculturation, since the Mohave believe that the coming of the whites and of their ways was predicted already in the age of creation, during which whites were referred to as tinyam kuhuya (night flying), which some Mohave, who speak English well, ironically translate as "fly-by-nights."

AGAINST ANTISOCIAL MEMBERS OF THE INGROUP: WITCH KILLER'S PSYCHOSIS

Tcatc described this psychosis as follows:

In those olden days, when a person who had the power to do so caused an epidemic, the braves (kwanámi : hye) used to get rid of him (Kroeber, 1925 a, 1925 b; Devereux, 1937 c, 1948 f). According to the law of the white man, that was murder and was not approved of among the Indians [i. e., the whites did not approve of braves killing the witches (McNichols, 1944)]. Because of this, there is no one nowadays to rid us of shamans who cause epidemics. Hence, the Indians, or at least some of them, are now dying off from epidemics caused by witchcraft, and the shamans have become very bold in threatening the Indians. Anyay Ha :m (light passing) was one of those witches who kill off their own folks, and was going to get rid of some other people as well. So poor Huau Husek' (fly whip) is now in jail for killing that witch (Devereux, 1948 f).

Well, there is also another side to this matter of killing witches. A few braves eventually died because they had killed shamans. They saw in their dreams the blood of their victim; it was someplace on their bodies. At other times they thought that they had killed some animals, and saw the blood all around them, or somewhere near them. This blood plays a role in their dreams because they have killed someone, and eventually they go crazy from it (hahnok). Even if a shaman promises to cure such an insane brave, if it is the (dead?) shaman's will that he should die, he will die.

This type of insanity resembles the madness of scalpers. (See pt. 2, p. 43–75.) [20]

The role of feelings of guilt over an act of aggression in the etiology of the witch-killing brave's psychosis is conclusively demonstrated by the fact that such witch-killing braves are themselves often also witches, who, thus, seem to punish others for the very misdeed of which they themselves are guilty.

Comment

Tentative diagnosis.—Severe anxiety reaction caused by guilt.

The preceding data, which are very similar to those obtained by K. M. Stewart (1947 c), and by Fathauer (1954), clearly show the nexus between the derangement of witch killers, of scalpers, and of hunters who eat their kill. In addition, the data concerning scalpers and witch killers emphasize the Mohave Indian's fear of blood, which manifests itself not only in connection with actual killings and in the belief that the foreign sickness is caused by the "strong blood" of

---

[20] Pulyi : k was alone in doubting that witch killers became insane.

the alien that hits the "weaker blood" of the Mohave (Devereux, 1937 d, 1949 c; Stewart, 1947 c), but also in connection with defloration, menstruation, and bleeding during childbirth (Devereux, 1950 g).

It should also be stressed that the witch killer, like the scalper, is always a brave (kwanámi: hye). This is significant, because braves and shamans, as well as witches, have a number of traits in common: Misbehavior in childhood, dreams of power (Stewart, 1947 c), a more or less explicit desire not to live long (Kroeber, 1925 a, Devereux, 1937 c), a tendency to commit incest (Devereux, 1937 c, 1939 a), and, in the case of scalpers and shamans only, an ability to cure. It should also be added that, by being ostentatiously threatening, the witch seeks to induce someone to kill him (Kroeber, 1925 a; Devereux, 1937 c; see also pt. 7, pp. 387–426).

It is noteworthy that, unlike the hunter's neurosis or the scalper's psychosis, the witch killer's psychosis may actually end in death. This statement, which may or may not correspond to facts, tends to suggest that killing a fellow Mohave, even if he is a witch, arouses more anxiety than does the killing of animals, or the scalping of foes. The fact that witch killers only dream of killing, but, unlike hunters and scalpers, do not seem to dream of being killed, also supports this inference and suggests that so heinous an act as murder, even though it is socially approved, is too traumatic to be mastered simply by dreaming it out of one's system. It is also the only instance in which the sinner dreams that he is practically bathed in blood. This dream imagery may be compared to pathogenic dreams of being covered with the secretions of one's wife (pt. 4, pp. 150–175).

The witch killer's dreams, more dramatic and more gruesome than those which occur in related derangements, show that even where aggression is socially sanctioned and defined as useful, man retains a certain degree of independence in his evaluation of good and evil. When his internal moral code is at odds with the social norm, he may comply with the latter, but will experience at the same time considerable intrapsychic conflict and anguish. This fact alone casts doubt on the usefulness of social adjustment as a baseline for differentiating between normal and abnormal (Ackerknecht, 1943), which is also questionable on many other grounds (Devereux, 1956 b).

PATHOLOGICAL SEQUELAE OF HYPERACTIVITY

The Mohave believe that intensive and significant activity, when engaged in for a long time, may cause insanity and/or psychosomatic illness, especially if such an activity externalizes magical powers ("Nyayu: hudhu: tc takavekám"=Then his-power comes-back-on-him). Yet, the hyperactivity which eventually turns against a person need not be either magical or incompatible with a person's condition. It is normal and desirable for a Mohave to be a good farmer; yet Hilyera Anyay felt certain that he became ill because he farmed successfully for many years (Case 3). Likewise, though it is appropriate for a culture hero to do great deeds, Mastamho became psychotic in the end (Kroeber, 1925 a, 1948) "because he did so many things." [21] In fact, Mastamho's psychosis is not even comparable to the deleterious consequences of having shamanistic powers, since, unlike shamans, Mastamho did not acquire in dream the supernatural power of functioning as a culture hero. The power he had was as natural a part of him as a human being's maleness or femaleness, sight or hearing, intellectual potential or simple muscle power are inherent parts of that person. As for the owners of gambling charms, while they admittedly acquired these charms as a result of appropriate dreams, their power to gamble successfully resided not within them (in the sense in which the Mohave shaman's healing power is within him, rather than in some charm, or Plains Indian type "medicine bundle") but in the material charm itself. Thus, it is not their own, internal power that turns against them; it is the power of the external charm.[22]

It may be objected that the distinction between: (1) the psychiatric sequelae of divine and human hyperactivity; (2) the psychosomatic sequelae of association with power-laden charms; and (3) the harm resulting from the possession of supernaturalistic powers, is an artificial one, in view of the fact that, according to Mohave belief, even such workaday powers as the capacity to bear children, or to be a successful farmer or hunter, etc., are obtained in dream (Devereux, 1956 c). Were one to stress this point of similarity, one would also be obliged to lump together the pathological sequelae of "lay" hyperactivity with the deleterious consequences of the possession of supernaturalistic powers.

While this point of view is not without merit, it is felt that the Mohave themselves differentiate rather sharply between lay powers and magical powers. Indeed, whereas the Mohave specify that a person who obtained shamanistic powers, but refuses to exercise these powers, becomes psychotic (see pt. 1, pp. 57-71), no one mentioned people who had received the power to hunt or to farm successfully and then went insane because of their refusal to hunt or to farm. In fact,

---

[21] The psychotic episodes of legendary Greek heroes—and especially the homicidal rages of Herakles and Ajax Telamonides—may have similar cultural implications.

[22] Needless to say, from the psychological point of view the purely internal power of the shaman and the power of the gambler's charm are closely related. It is, however, hard to decide which of these two types of power is, in the last resort, psychologically more infantile.

there is no evidence that anyone ever refuses to implement the simple, lay powers needed in order to function effectively in the workaday world.

This fact has three important implications:

(1) In contradistinction to supernaturalistic powers, lay powers are never felt to threaten the integrity and equilibrium of the ego. They are not ego-dystonic and therefore no one rejects the call to be a good farmer, the way the Sedang Moi, who feels shamanistic powers budding in him, may seek to reject these powers (Devereux, MS., 1933–34). The essentially ego-dystonic, and even culture-dystonic, quality of shamanistic powers is discussed in part 2, pages 57–71.

(2) It is probable that the idea that power is received in dream was extended from supernaturalistic activities to ordinary, workaday activities as well, partly in order to make them seem more respectable, and partly in order to reaffirm in every possible way that Mohave culture is, indeed, a dream culture (Kroeber, 1925 a).[23] The forcing of essentially extraneous items into the procrustean bed of some leading cultural theme may be denoted by the term "establishment of artificial compendences." The number of essentially extraneous traits that are forcibly subordinated to some leading theme or institution may well be a fairly reliable measure of the importance of that theme or institution in a given society (Devereux, 1957 a). It is suggested that the explanation of success in ordinary activities in terms of dream power represents the establishment of an artificial compendence between ordinary activities and supernaturalistic ones. The artificiality of this compendence is revealed by the fact that, unlike people who refuse to exercise their supernatural powers, those, if any, who refuse—and do not simply fail—to exercise their workaday powers are not expected to become psychotic.

(3) The belief that the intensive implementation of magical powers, and even intensive lay activities, can produce pathological sequelae sharply contrasts with the belief that the nonimplementation of supernatural powers may cause psychosis. These two, seemingly contradictory, sets of beliefs apparently represent a cultural implementation of man's basic ambivalence over all problems of activity. The Pueblo Indians solved this problem by condemning all that is outstanding in the individual (Ellis, 1951). The Mohave attitude seems to be, roughly speaking: "You are damned if you do, and damned if you don't."

---

[23] Likewise, the fiction that feudalism and chivalry still exist in England is maintained by knighting, or by elevating to the peerage, persons whose profession (business, acting) or ideology (socialism) is inherently incompatible with the traditions of feudal society.

AN ILLNESS OF ORDINARILY ACTIVE PERSONS

The first clue to the belief that even ordinary types of activity, when engaged in continuously and intensively, may have deleterious consequences was obtained accidentally, in reply to a question about hysterical peripheral anaesthesias. Tcatc's answer was worded in such a manner that a question about paralysis seemed to be called for. The data she provided were relatively simple and, taken by themselves, did not seem to be related to any specific native belief. Their true meaning did not become apparent until Hilyera Anyay was questioned about flexibilitas cerea (waxy flexibility) that occurs in a certain form of schizophrenia. In reply to these questions, he described a specific form of paralysis, which was clearly neither hysterical nor syphilitić in origin,[24] and which he attributed to prolonged strenuous activity in one's youth. The gradual manner in which this information was obtained shows how difficult it is to investigate relatively marginal and previously unreported beliefs.

A. Informants Tcatc and E. S.:

[Do you know anything about peripheral anaesthesias?] It must be the blood that is not circulating right. They can use their feet all right, although they move them very slowly. Yet, you can pinch their skin, or stick something into it, and they do not feel it. [You mean that their legs are almost paralyzed?] This condition does usually lead to paralysis.

B. Informants Hilyera Anyay and E. S.:

[Do you know of flexibilitas cerea?] In his youth a person may perform some kind of heavy work and feel no strain whatever. However, on reaching old age, it seems that his muscles, which were formerly very strong, can no longer do the heavy work they used to be able to do.[25] This person's arms, or else his feet and legs, are in such a state that he cannot move them normally [i. e., voluntarily]. If he wishes to move such a paralyzed limb, he must take hold of his arm or leg and must place it in the desired position.[26] This condition is called either nyayu: hudhu: tc takavekàm (then his-power comes-back-on-him) or hithu: ly.

C. At about the same time, though in a different context, Hilyera Anyay related a dream that suggests, at least by juxtaposition, a nexus between outstanding performance as a runner in one's youth,[27] and rheumatism in old age.

---

[24] According to M. A. I. Nettle, M. D., who had been the physician of the Colorado River Indian Reservation for 22 years, the Mohave did not suffer from paralysis of syphilitic origin at that time (approx. 1910–32). (Personal communication, 1933.)

[25] All weaknesses of old age, including loss of erectile potency (Devereux, 1950 a), tend to be attributed to muscular weakness.

[26] It is this passive movement which most nearly recalls flexibilitas cerea, though, needless to say, the similarity is a purely external and fortuitous one.

[27] The Mohave were quite outstanding long distance runners. Once Hivsu: Tupo: ma cited as a "typical" example of the degeneration of contemporary Mohave runners a feat of long distance running which was quite startling by Occidental standards: His half-brother needed 24 hours to run from Parker to Needles and back, because, on his way back, he slept a few hours. The distance covered in these 24 hours was approximately 80 miles as the crow flies—most of it through rocky desert country (Devereux, 1949 a).

CASE 3 (Informant: Hilyera Anyay):

I dreamed I was doing some planting on the sandhills. I remember that, in my dream, I was planting corn and, when I got so far, I turned around, looked back and saw that the corn had already sprouted and was about a foot high.

Associations.—These dreams seemed to have occurred just before my arms began to ache. Some people who plant crops year after year have suma: tc itcem (=bad dreams) in their old age, and these bad dreams seem to bring rheumatisms with them. A man who has died since gave me sallyi: tc (=moxa) therapy; he took a piece of arrowweed, thrust its tip into hot coals and, when the stick began to glow, he slightly burned my joints with it. Then he applied some liniment to me. As a result of this treatment I feel much better now. [White people who have rheumatism sometimes heat their aching joints with warm bricks.] I too have seen people do that, and might give it a try the next time I have pains in my joints.

Comment

In aboriginal times the Mohave did not plant on sandhills, but on the overflow of the Colorado River (Kroeber, 1925 a). At present they plant in an artificially irrigated valley. An abnormally rapid growth of the crops is mentioned in several myths, and especially in the myth that describes how the invention of agriculture made infanticide unnecessary (Devereux, 1948 d).

THE GOD MASTAMHO'S PSYCHOSIS

In 1938, when investigating mental disorders among the Mohave, the following myth fragment, dealing with a case of divine insanity, was read to the Mohave:

Then, meditating as to his [Mastamho's] own end, he stretched out his arms, grew into Saksak the fish eagle, and flew off, without power or recollection, ignorant and infested with vermin. [Kroeber, 1925 a.]

When asked to comment on this incident, all informants agreed that it was correctly reported. In explanation, they stated that Mastamho became insane "because he had done so much in the course of his life." This spontaneous explanation is very significant, since, unlike the subsequently published, full text of this episode (Kroeber, 1948), the condensed version read to the Mohave did not even hint at the causes of Mastamho's psychic decompensation.

Before discussing the implications of this episode, it is desirable to cite in full the unabridged version of this episode (Kroeber, 1948). The incidents about to be described occurred just after Mastamho told Thrasher and Mockingbird to teach play and sex to the Mohave, and specifically mentioned venereal diseases, loose women, and ugly, but sexually successful, men. He then informed Thrasher and Mockingbird, who up to then were "people," that, on completing their teaching assignments, they would turn into birds.[28]

---

[28] Once their tasks or adventures are completed, many Mohave mythical personages become birds or even rocks (Devereux, 1939 a; 1948 h).

The myth then continues as follows:

Mastamho was standing at Avi-kutaparve. Now he proceeded to leave (change) his body. That is why the little mountain there is now white in one place. Mastamho was looking to the north, standing close by the river. He wanted to have wings and flap them. He moved his arms four times to make them into wings. Then he said: "See, I shall be a bird. Not everyone will know me when I am a bird. My name will be Saksak." [29] Then he turned around twice from right to left, facing south, and then north, then south and north again, and lay down on his back in the middle of the river. Four times he moved his arms in the water. Thus he reached Hokusave. Then he had wings and feathers, and rose from the water.[30] He flew low above the water so that his wings touched it. He flew southward, looking for a place to sit. He settled on a sandbar. But he thought: "It is not good: I will not sit here"; and he went on again. He sat on a log, but thought again: "No, I do not like this," and went on. He sat on a bank, but thought: "No, it is not good," and went on. So he went far down to the sea where the river emptied into it. There he stayed, and lived near the river eating fish. Now he was crazy [yamomk] and full of lice and nits.[31] *Now when he had told everything* [my italics] *and was a bird, he forgot all that he had known.* He did not even know any longer how to catch fish. Sometimes other birds kill fish and leave part of them. Then Saksak eats them, not knowing any better. He is alone, not with other birds, and sits looking down at the water: he is crazy.[32]

This strange and moving account of the final deterioration of a great culture hero deserves to be commented on in some detail.

The most striking feature of the narrative is its complete clinical accuracy. Mastamho regresses from person to bird and realizes that not everyone will recognize him in this new guise. Not only does he withdraw from his earlier habitat, removing himself to the distant sea (land of the dead?), but, once he is there, he avoids the other birds; he sits alone, staring at the water. He deteriorates completely, forgetting everything he ever knew and becoming filthy, smelly, and verminous. Finally, he is parasitical in his passivity: He does not even catch his own fish, but eats the leavings of other birds. Bourke (1889) also mentions the transformation, but minimizes Mastamho's psychic

---

[29] Kroeber (1948) suggests that this may be either the bald or white-headed eagle, or else the fish-diving osprey. The latter is more probable, since "saksak" may be an onomatopoea for the osprey's cry.

[30] According to the full length, and hitherto unpublished, version of the Yellak Hi: ha song cycle (Kroeber, MS.), certain birds turned into human beings after acquiring land and a name. In the present myth we see persons, whose human task is completed, turn into birds.

[31] Kroeber (1948) translates hatšilye=louse excrement, as "nits" and explains that, according to the Mohave, when a fish eagle is killed, he is always lousy and smells of fish. It is not easy to decide what, if anything, should be made of the fact that there exist two Mohave names "Winged vagina" (Devereux, 1951 c) and "Vagina full of fleas (or verminous)" and that a man was in the habit of insulting women by saying that they smelled like fish (Devereux, 1950 a). Psychoanalysts will probably feel that these data shed light upon the latent content of Mastamho's transformation into a passive, verminous bird smelling of fish, while some anthropologists may feel that these data are irrelevant for an understanding of this episode.

[32] A footnote by Kroeber (1948) specifies that anyone dreaming of Mastamho as a crazy saksak will become insane. This belief will be discussed separately (pt. 4, pp. 116–117).

deterioration.   On the other hand he states that Mastamho, in the shape of a fish eagle, sometimes visits the Mohave.

If one disregards the miraculous features of this account, the factual description of Mastamho's behavior, after turning into Saksak, lists all the classical symptoms of catatonic schizophrenia.[33]   However, the very accuracy of this mythical characterization of catatonia raises certain important questions regarding the alleged occurrence of schizophrenia in those primitive cultures that were not subjected to the violent impact of a more complex conquering culture (Devereux, 1939 d).

It is suggested that the clinically accurate description of Mastamho's terminal condition was based not on the observation of genuine catatonias, but of certain spectacular transitory confusional or stuporous states.   It is of special significance that such sudden decompensations and recompensations occur frequently in a variety of primitive societies and may represent a "forme fruste" of true schizophrenia. It is also interesting to note that the diagnostic label "transitory confusional states" had practically disappeared from American, though not from French, nosologies, until World War II.   At that time, some military psychiatrists reintroduced this term and applied it to so-called "three-day battlefield schizophrenias."   Such transitory confusions seem to represent a reaction to sudden stress; they have a markedly rapid onset, the first symptom being usually a confused, oneiric hyperactivity, followed by a sudden catatonia-like regression. The whole process ends as suddenly as it began, with a more or less complete restitution of all ego functions.   As suggested elsewhere (Devereux, 1956 b), the fugues of persons about to become shamans may also be of this type.

In brief, since so accurate and complete a characterization of a catatonia-like state cannot be the chance product of a primitive mythmaker's imagination, we must assume that this mythical episode was inspired by the observation of actual transitory confusional states, which, in turn, would prove the antiquity of such mental derangements, at least among the Mohave Indians.[34]

The significance of Mastamho's psychosis for an understanding of the Mohave belief that even ordinary intensive activity may have de-

---

[33] The absence of agitated depression excludes the diagnosis of involutional melancholia.   The absence of foolishness makes the diagnosis of hebephrenia inappropriate, just as the degree of regression precludes the diagnosis of paranoid schizophrenia.   The diagnosis "simple schizophrenia" is incompatible with Mastamho's previous level of activity, as well as with the sudden onset of his psychosis in adult life.

[34] Similarly, Homer, in comparing Hector's flight from Achilles to dreams in which one runs without making progress, establishes the extreme antiquity of such dreams, which are also commonly dreamed by contemporary children and adolescents.   By contrast, some Homeric dreams have a distinctly contrived quality, which marks them as "literary dreams" (Hundt, 1935).

leterious aftereffects lies in the fact that, strictly speaking, Mastamho's creative activity was natural, rather than magical. It was activity befitting a deity, exactly as agriculture, hunting, or childbearing are activities befitting human beings, and was not a manifestation of some supernatural power acquired in dream, in the sense in which the shaman's power is a supernatural one. If this interpretation is valid, then Mastamho's psychosis sheds light upon beliefs concerning the deleterious aftereffects of ordinary hyperactivity, rather than upon the "spoiling" of truly magical powers. Finally, and at the lowest estimate, it provides the mythical precedent for insanity, in accordance with the Mohave principle that every human activity must have a mythical precedent.[35]

From the strictly cultural point of view, the most important aspect of the legend of Mastamho's insanity is the notion that supernatural beings can become psychotic. While psychotic deities are not common in Mohave mythology, Kroeber (1948) states that Coyote stole Matavilye's heart because he knew nothing and therefore did not behave like a proper mourner. Mastamho therefore let him go and refused to instruct him.

I do not want to tell him what I know: I want him to be foolish and know nothing: I do not want him to hear what I say. I will let him go. He will be the only one like that, the one I call Coyote. He will not know his own home: he will want to run about the desert and do what is bad. If someone is not at home, Coyote will go there; but if a person is in his house, he will not come; and if anyone sees him, he will run off. (Kroeber, 1948.)

This passage explains why the term "hukthar" (=coyote) also means "crazy" (Case 79). The syndrome described closely resembles the type of hebephrenia sometimes found among hoboes and the Mohave narrative clearly represents Coyote as the hobo of the desert. It is probably also significant that Hipahipa, the ancestor of the Hi:pa gens, whose "totemic" animal is, precisely, the coyote, is described in a Mohave historical epic (Kroeber, 1951 b) as an, apparently hebephrenic, hermit hobo of the desert.

Harrington (1908) makes it clear that psychotic deities also occur in the mythology of the Yuma.

The problem of psychologically disturbed deities is an extremely complex subject, which transcends the limitations of the present work. The only point which needs to be made is that psychotic gods also occur in other mythologies. Thus, Herodotus states that the god Triton was seized by prophetic frenzy, while a variety of Greek sources describe the almost psychotic depression of Demeter when her daughter Persephone married Hades. Other Greek gods, quasi-gods,

---

[35] The Yuma also know of insane supernatural beings (Harrington, 1908). Cf. in Greek mythology Demeter's depression, the psychosis of Herakles, etc.

and divine heroes (such as Herakles) are also said to have had psychotic or near psychotic episodes. Belief in such divine psychic disturbances probably reflects the child's inability to comprehend the behavior of adults (Devereux, 1955 b), as well as certain other early conflicts whose analysis is beyond the scope of the present study.

THE PSYCHOPATHOLOGY OF SINGERS

A special form of the corruption of powers affects the singers of certain major song cycles. According to Kroeber (1925 a), those who receive the power to sing certain semishamanistic song cycles tend to become doctors when they grow old. If we accept the thesis that being a shaman is a neurotic defense against certain intensive intrapsychic conflicts (pt. 2, pp. 57—71, and Devereux, 1956 b), the evolution of such singers into shamans is a special form of the corruption of powers. Two factors favor such an interpretation.

In the first place, several of the song cycles that Kroeber calls "semishamanistic" are, in fact, directly related to various illnesses and to their cure. These cycles include *wellaka* (hiwey lak, anus pain, pt. 4, pp. 150–175), *hiku: pk* (venereal disease), *hayakwira* (hikwi: r, supernatural snake, pt. 4, pp. 117–128), *apena* (apen, beaver, perhaps related to the foreign illness, since beaver is a nickname for whites, pt. 4, pp. 128–150), *ichulyuye* (related to apen), *humahnana* (related to the cure of both the ichudhauva illness caused by eating birds wounded by hawks, and the ichiekanyamasava (pale) diarrhea of infants whose fathers ate their own kill), *ipam imicha* (related to the same illnesses and also to the foreign illness, pt. 4, pp. 128–150), and *yaroyara* (likewise related to the foreign illness).[36] Thus, it is hard to see why such song cycles should be called semishamanistic, rather than shamanistic, since all shamans first acquire their powers, and the songs related to them, in dream, and then, later on, begin to engage overtly in therapeutic activities. Since these song cycles describe the origin and nature of certain illnesses, and, when sung with therapeutic intent, can cure them, they are, figuratively speaking, no more semishamanistic than a textbook of medicine, studied by a medical student not yet engaged in the actual treatment of disease, is semimedical.

The second point is that my informants more or less implied that the singers of such cycles not only turn into shamans in due time, but,

---

[36] The differences between Kroeber's spelling and mine do not necessarily imply that one of us misrecorded these names. They simply reflect the Mohave tendency to condense or compress lengthy technical terms or personal names into a single word, or to abbreviate a technical term by an elision of the first and/or last syllable(s). Thus, in 1933, 1 recorded hiwey lak (Kroeber's wellaka) as weylak. Further differences in spelling are due to an idiosyncratic tendency of linguistic informants, who, when asked to pronounce words carefully, tend to tack terminal vowels onto words, or to insert vowels into the word itself, so as to separate two consecutive consonants.

like some other shamans, may end up by becoming witches, whose self-destructiveness is notorious (Kroeber, 1925 a; Devereux, 1937 c).

On the other hand, certain other semishamanistic cycles cited by Kroeber, such as *Halykupa* (Halyeku: p, grebe), *Halypuka* (Halyepu: k, loon), *Ahakwa'ilya* (dragonfly larva, which may or may not be shamanistic, and *Sampulyka* (mosquito), may not be related to illnesses and may therefore fit Kroeber's concept of semishamanistic song cycles better than do the previously listed song cycles. However, even in this context a certain amount of caution is in order, since Kroeber (1925 a) specifies that (*a*) the singers of halyeku: p shout like birds at memorial rites, and (*b*) are said not to live long. The first specification possibly suggests that halyeku: p may be known only to funeral ritualists, who are, by definition, also scalpers and shamans qualified to cure the foreign sickness (pt. 4, pp. 128–150). The second specification has very distinct overtones of witchcraft, since, in another passage, Kroeber (1925 a) states: "Doctors and brave men are alike. The latter say: 'I do not wish to live long.' The doctor says: 'I shall not live a long time. I wish to die. That is why I kill people.' etc." The fact that Kroeber's text does not differentiate between doctor and witch lends substance to my informants' hints that the singers of semishamanistic song cycles may become not only healers but, possibly, also witches.

The total impression created by Kroeber's account is that he was not fully aware of the real scope and pervasiveness of the Mohave belief that supernatural powers may deteriorate and turn against their owners, causing them to embark, both psychologically and behaviorally, upon a course that leads to inevitable disaster, just as, in a Mohave myth (Kroeber, 1948) the deer inevitably go to meet Mountain Lion, who is both their maker and their doom. Kroeber did perceive, however, that the acquisition of certain powers, as exemplified by the power to sing semishamanistic songs, sets off a psychological drift toward shamanism. He also reported correctly that all doctors can bewitch and then crave death. On the other hand, he failed to perceive the unity of these two processes, because he did not see that becoming a witch is simply a further evolution of some "real" (=strong) healing shamans, whose initial defenses against their aggressive impulses, as represented by their healing activities, begin to decompensate, and, therefore, ultimately permit the eruption, first of overt, though magical, aggression and then of the self-punitive wish to be killed.

In summary, the singer of semishamanistic song cycles, so called, drifts first into therapy, then into witchcraft, and then into vicarious suicide, through a process which the Mohave themselves define as a gradual corruption of power, and which, from the psychological point of view, represents, first, a piling up and expansion of defenses, and then a final decompensation of these defenses. The pathogenic process itself is, from the cultural point of view, activated primarily by the subject's overt actualization of his powers. The fact that the singing of certain other—nonshamanistic—songs does not actuate a similarly fatal drift into a shamanistic neurosis and self-destructiveness may simply mean that harmless songs are dreamed only by persons whose anxieties are more moderate than those of persons who dream the semishamanistic cycles. Such relatively stable persons may require less extreme defenses for the control of their internal conflicts and are therefore less likely to experience an ultimate decompensation of their psychic defenses and balance. Whether or not a given person unconsciously chooses to dream a semishamanistic or a nonshamanistic cycle, because of some hitherto undiscovered differences between the latent contents of these two types of songs, is a question that cannot be settled in this context, since a detailed search for possible systematic differences between these two types of songs is beyond the scope of the present study. We simply suggest that the problem of possible basic differences between these two types of song cycles is a challenging one, which deserves the attention of the psychologically sophisticated anthropologist.

It should be emphatically stressed that the unity of this cultural process, in the course of which a Mohave drifts from singing to healing and then to witchcraft, was established by means of unequivocal anthropological field data. Only the psychodynamics of this drift have been afterwards elucidated psychologically. Hence, here too, the psychological analysis of data simply substantiates, and lends an additional depth to, findings that have been first formulated in purely anthropological terms. This proves that, instead of seeking to supersede the anthropological approach to cultural data, the psychological approach simply supplements and gives a broader meaning to anthropological findings and formulations.

THE CORRUPTION OF SHAMANISTIC POWERS

The involuntary process whereby a healing shaman turns into a witch who, after a while, seeks to be killed by his victims' relatives, is described elsewhere (pt. 7, pp. 387–426). Various limited aspects of this process, which the Mohave call nyayu: hudhu: tc takavekàm (then his-power turns-against-him, or comes-back-on-him), are also mentioned in part 2, pages 54–56, 57–71, and 83–89.

PATHOLOGICAL SEQUELAE OF INHIBITED AGGRESSIVITY OR POWER

The Mohave belief that the actualization of certain powers, or else prolonged contact with power-laden objects, can have psychiatric sequelae is completed by the symmetrical belief that the nonactualization of aggressivity or power results in a damming up of magical energy, which causes the self-inhibiting person to become insane. A related form of illness, caused by the damming up of the sexual impulse is the atcoo: r hanyienk convulsive seizure, which the Mohave themselves seem to consider as an orgasm-equivalent, or at least as an orgasm-substitute. Due to the fact that in this illness it is the sexual urge which is dammed up, this condition will be discussed in the chapter devoted to disorders of the sexual impulse (pt. 2, pp. 72–76).

The two psychopathological conditions that properly belong under the present heading are caused by (a) inhibited jealousy (hi: wa itck), and (b) by the inhibition of shamanistic powers that, even in their therapeutic manifestations, are essentially defensive reaction formations against aggressive impulses. However, since the Mohave view hi: wa itck as a mood disturbance, it will be discussed in connection with certain other disturbances of mood which the Mohave also connect with the heart (pt. 3). Nonetheless, in order to conform to the outline given in the introductory section of this chapter, hi: wa itck, too, will be characterized here, at least in a few sentences.

HI:WA ITCK (HEARTBREAK)

Older men, who are deserted by young wives for other men, are prevented by social regulations from seeking to win them back or to fight with their rivals. Hence, they develop a transitory agitated depression, presumably caused by the inhibition of their jealous vengefulness. This illness is described in detail in part 3, pages 91–106.

PSYCHOSES RESULTING FROM THE INHIBITION OF MAGICAL POWERS

The Mohave define shamanistic and other magical power as an impersonal, self-actuating, and ethically neutral energy, which can manifest itself in two radically different ways:

(a) Controlled by its owner, power can be directed at a given object with either good or evil intent. Indeed, strictly speaking, a shaman does not obtain the power to cure a given illness; he simply acquires an ethically neutral power over a given illness, so that he can both cause and cure it.[37]

(b) Acting on its own, power is inherently dangerous. Its harmful effects on the unauthorized dabbler ("apprentice sorcerer") with the supernatural manifest themselves almost immediately, while in the case of a legitimate shaman and of the owner of lucky charms

---

[37] A radiologist is, likewise, free to decide whether he will cause or cure certain neoplastic growths in experimental animals.

(pt. 4, pp. 202–212), the deleterious effects of contact with magical powers only become evident in the long run.[38]

However, the owner of shamanistic powers faces not only one type of risk; he is actually caught in a "double bind" (Devereux, 1939 d; Bateson et al., 1956). If he becomes a practicing shaman, his power may eventually "go wrong," and cause him to become a witch. This, in turn, involves him in an ever expanding series of vicious circles, sometimes culminating in the urge to commit vicarious suicide (Kroeber, 1925 a; Devereux, 1937 c). If, on the other hand, he refuses to utilize his powers, and does not become a practicing shaman, the damming up of his unexpended powers will cause him to become insane.

The fact that the shaman finds himself in a "double bind" may explain why the Mohave believe that some unborn children, who receive shamanistic powers while still in the maternal womb, simply refuse to be born. Such a fetus assumes a transversal position in the womb, killing both himself and his mother during parturition (Devereux, 1948 e). Given this attitude toward shamanistic powers, it is not surprising that some individuals, who have received shamanistic powers in dream, prefer to run the risk of becoming insane, by refusing to use their shamanistic powers, rather than expose themselves to the manifold tangible inconveniences and risks which confront every shaman.[39]

The motives of those who reject their shamanistic powers can be divided into two categories: sociocultural and intrapsychic.

Social and cultural motives.—The nuclearity of the shaman in Yuma—and Mohave—society and culture was given explicit recognition by Róheim (1932), who defined the Yuma shaman as the "group ideal." In fact, in contemporary Mohave society the shaman is, if possible, even more of a social cynosure (La Barre, 1946) than he was in aboriginal times, when the eminence of chiefs and tribal heroes rivaled his own. In addition, in a dream culture (Kroeber, 1925 a), such as that of the Mohave, shamanistic beliefs necessarily occupy a nuclear position within the framework of culture as a whole. Finally, the shaman's social and cultural significance is also highlighted by his indispensability as an anthropological informant.

These facts have tended to obscure both the genuine drawbacks and risks of being a shaman, and the extreme ambivalence of the Mohave toward all shamans, be they good or bad.

---

[38] In the same way, an untrained person working with X-rays may sustain burns almost at once, while expert radiologists, who take adequate precautions, may escape harm for many years.

[39] The rejection of supernatural powers, and even of positions of great social eminence, is known to occur in a great many primitive, as well as advanced societies. Hence, even though the present discussion is limited to the Mohave, many of the findings above are also applicable to other ethnic groups.

Every shaman is viewed as a potential source of danger, since, as stated above, he can both cause and cure the illness over which he has control. In fact, every shaman's first supernatural act is to be-witch someone publicly, so as to advertise his newly acquired shama-nistic powers (Devereux, 1937 c). Hence, not even a shaman who has an untarnished reputation as a healer is safe from sudden accusations of witchcraft. Thus, according to Hama: Utce:, "Hivsu: Tupo: ma is a good shaman, who never bewitched anyone. Yet, even as he was singing himself hoarse, night after night, trying to cure a young man, his patient accused him of having bewitched him (Cases 1, 44). It nearly broke the old man's heart." Accusations of witchcraft are readily believed even by the friends of the accused. Some months before his death Hivsu: Tupo: ma, who, as we just saw, was believed to be exclusively a healer, confessed to me that he had bewitched cer-tain people (Devereux, 1948 i). When, after his death, I communi-cated this information to Tcatc and to Hama: Utce:, who were his friends quite as much as mine, they were amazed, but did not doubt my word. Their implicit reaction was: "It just goes to show that you cannot be sure of any shaman, no matter how good his repu-tation may be." One wrongly accused shaman even committed suicide (Case 106).

The touchiness and uncertain temper of the shaman further in-crease the risk which he represents for society. In fact, many a quick-tempered person is, ipso facto, believed to be a shaman. Thus, when Tcatc was asked to comment on the rumor that she had shama-nistic powers, she replied indignantly: "It is not true at all! I only have a temper." Due to the shaman's susceptibility and quick tem-per, one never knows just how far one can go with him; should he suddenly decide that someone has offended him, or that a layman dis-cusses shamanistic matters too freely, or that another shaman's views deviate too much from his own, he may decide to bewitch the offender (Devereux, 1957 b).

The tendency of bad shamans to bewitch especially their own rela-tives, and other strongly, but ambivalently, loved individuals, makes them especially dangerous to their closest associates.

The Mohave are also quite critical of the shaman as a person: "All shamans are crazy and cowards at heart," is a frequently expressed opinion. Likewise, ostentatious misbehavior in childhood and ado-lescence is thought to be caused by the budding of shamanistic powers, and shamans are believed to be especially prone to commit extremely perverted acts and even incest (Devereux, 1937 c; and pt. 6, pp. 282–285).

The potential explosiveness of the Mohave tribe's ambivalence toward shamans is also underscored by the fact that, for several decades, nearly all victims of murders were said to have been witches. In fact, it is often the witch himself who incites other to kill him (Kroeber, 1925 a; Devereux, 1937 c).

Thus, despite his functional tribal nuclearity, the shaman is socially and culturally so dystonic (Devereux, 1956 b), and therefore faces so many inconveniences and risks, that these factors alone almost suffice to explain why some individuals refuse to become practicing shamans.

We might add that the conduct of at least the "bad shamans" clearly reveals their awareness of the social risks which they run. They are extremely furtive and reticent in their behavior, allegedly because they do not wish to incite antagonism. Yet, like other neurotics, they do not realize at all that their cautious, self-protective reticence only serves to make them more suspect than ever. Thus, the refusal of certain bad shamans to act as my informants greatly angered several of my Mohave friends, who viewed their refusal as proof positive of the cowardice of all real witches. One may even suspect that the shaman Hikye: t finally agreed to serve as a—very unsatisfactory—informant (pt. 1, pp. 9–13) chiefly because he sought to prove to the Mohave that, not being a witch, he was not afraid to function as an informant.

Intrapsychic motives.—It is generally recognized that intrapsychic needs, rather than specific social pressures and directives, cause an individual to become a shaman.[40] However, the fact that such intrapsychic needs are temporarily and partly resolved by becoming a shaman does not necessarily imply that either these needs themselves, or the acquisition and possession of shamanistic powers must therefore be wholly ego-syntonic.[41]

Many aspects of Mohave shamanism indicate that the acquisition of shamanistic powers, i. e., the developing of a culturally sanctioned system of defenses against certain atypically violent, but otherwise standard, unconscious conflicts, is a far from smooth and pleasant process. The Mohave assert that power-giving experiences first occur in utero, and are then remembered, and dreamed all over again, in adolescence (Devereux, 1937 c). This belief clearly indicates that the Mohave themselves experience these adolescent power-giving dreams as a return of the repressed, i. e., as a reactivation of conflicts,

---

[40] The shaman's dominant conflicts, like those of other members of the tribe, lie primarily in the realm of the unconscious portion of his ethnic personality, but tend to be of such intensity that he must cope with them not only by developing the typical basic personality of his group, but also by evolving an additional, culturally provided, but optional, pattern of defense against his strong anxieties and impulses: Shamanism (Devereux, 1956 b).

[41] Thus, an Omaha Indian, whose vision instructed him to become a transvestite, must have had this particular vision because he had intense, albeit unconscious, conflicts over his sexual identity. Nonetheless, the socially acceptable solution which his vision suggested to him was so ego-dystonic that he preferred to commit suicide rather than comply with this supernatural directive (Lowie, 1924).

impulses, and anxieties going back to early childhood.   Now, it stands to reason that the return of the repressed is not, and, by definition, cannot be, a pleasant experience, since otherwise the reemerging material would not have had to be repressed in the first place.   Hence, while the budding Mohave shaman apparently does not undergo periods of almost unendurable psychic pain and confusion, such as are reported for Siberian shamans (Czaplicka, 1914; Eliade, 1951), he, too, appears to be sufficiently disturbed during this period of psychic gestation to manifest highly obnoxious behavior.   Thus, even practicing shamans concede that budding shamans exhibit objectionable behavior.   For example, when "John Smith" (pseudonym) had, as an 8-year-old boy, a temper tantrum in our presence, Hivsu: Tupo: ma said that he would eventually become a shaman (Case 64).   Interestingly enough, this boy did, eventually, become successively an alcoholic (Devereux, 1948 i), a self-destructively reckless person, who had several almost fatal accidents, and, for a short time, even an actual psychotic requiring hospitalization.   It seems permissible to suggest that had this young man been less fully acculturated, he would have been able to find relief by becoming a culturally nondeviant shaman. However, since his acculturation made the shamanistic defense uncongenial and inadequate for him, he was obliged to improvise a series of idiosyncratic symptomatic defenses all on his own, which not only made him both abnormal and deviant, but also repeatedly caused him to endanger his life (pt. 5, pp. 222–243).   If this inference is correct, it means that, despite many tangible social and psychological drawbacks, being a shaman is, temporarily at least, a less risky and painful intrapsychic defense against one's conflicts, than are improvised, idiosyncratic defenses, which make the conflict-ridden individual both a symptom-ridden neurotic or psychotic and a social deviant, whose very deviancy automatically involves him in a whole new series of difficulties of a type that he could have avoided had he been sufficiently unacculturated to become a shaman.   This hypothesis helps one to understand why some ardent exponents of one type of irrational ideology often become vehement converts to another, equally irrational ideology.   Specifically, it explains why certain conflict-ridden individuals, who first sought refuge from their inner turmoil in violent Naziism, became, after the collapse of the Nazi system, convinced henchmen of Communism; the inference being that they had to do so in order to escape the necessity of having to improvise atypical defenses of their own, which would have caused them to become socially deviant psychotics.

It is hardly necessary to stress that only an intense intrapsychic turmoil could cause a child or adolescent to engage ostentatiously in obscene, perverted, or aggressive behavior, which reflects the attempt of the ego to express, and yet come to terms with, painful and disturbing psychic material, which erupts, or, rather, reerupts, at an unmanageably rapid rate. Otherwise expressed, the repressed material returns at a greater rate than the adolescent's ego—already overburdened with the task of managing his suddenly intensified sexual tensions—can handle, without being overwhelmed by it.[42] The fact that society ultimately rewards the shaman for his fantasies further aggravates the situation from the psychological point of view, since it further increases the rate at which repressed infantile material is permitted to reenter consciousness. The Mohave Indian's semihumorous tolerance for the misconduct of the future shaman, rationalized as: "It is his nature, he cannot help it," also has the same effect.

While the adolescent's ego may, conceivably, be able to cope with gradually reemerging conflictual material by means of improvised idiosyncratic defenses, the fact that society itself encourages the massive eruption of the repressed obliges the adolescent to utilize also, and even primarily, certain socially prepatterned defenses against, and means for, the distorted and partial expression of these ego-dystonic urges. As a result, he incorporates into his psychic structure the culturally determined "type solution" of the shamanistic pattern, whose ultimate expression is the self-definition: "I am a shaman."

Even though this symptomatic compromise or type solution is culturally prepatterned, individual phrasings thereof occur both among the Mohave and among other tribes. In fact, the Mohave shaman is so notoriously touchy about the validity of his particular phrasing of shamanistic powers, that, if the views of another shaman differ from his own, he will seek to bewitch the heretic. This "narcissism of small differences" clearly indicates that having shamanistic powers is an important restitutive mechanism, enabling the shaman to cling at least to the outer fringes of sanity and conformity by means of a culturally patterned "specialty" (Linton, 1936). The effectiveness of this culturally provided defense is, in turn, largely determined by its close articulation with the most characteristic type conflicts and tensions of Mohave society (Devereux, 1957 b).

It is extremely important to realize that even though the shamanistic solution is, for the time being at least, relatively effective, it is not a genuine "cure with insight," but simply a partial restitutional

---

[42] This specification is of great importance, since inhibited people are prone to imagine that giving free rein to fantasy and impulse is necessarily a pleasant and cathartic experience, affording considerable relief. By contrast, one of the most important technical objectives of the psychoanalyst is to regulate the rate at which repressed material reenters the field of consciousness, since too massive and sudden a return of the repressed is likely to overwhelm and totally disrupt the neurotic's weak ego.

process leading to a mere "social remission without insight." [43]   Actually the disturbed adolescent's attempt to stabilize his psychic situation by becoming a shaman is only partly and temporarily successful. Indeed, this socially sanctioned compromise solution does not protect the psyche permanently, the way a true sublimation does (Jokl, 1950; Devereux, 1957 a), against further crises and anxieties, to which the psyche again reacts by developing further compromise solutions. Thus, soon after the wife of Ahma Huma: re, a shaman specializing in the treatment of hiwey lak, died in childbirth while he stood by, unable to help either her or the baby, which could be seen moving in the dead woman's womb, the bereaved shaman "acquired in dream" the power to treat also obstetrical conditions (Devereux, 1948 e). In other instances the aggressive impulses eventually break through the socially supported reaction formation represented by the urge to cure, and cause the former healer to become a witch.   This, in turn, will involve him in a whole new series of subjective and social vicious circles, actuated by the internal interplay between aggression and feelings of guilt.   For a time his feelings of guilt over his magical aggression may find expression in the killing of witches; it being a characteristic feature of Mohave shamanism that some witch-killing heroes are themselves believed to be witches.   Thus, when a young visitor, belonging to a family of alleged witches (pt. 5, pp. 245–247) left, Tcatc said that he, too, was a witch who, should the occasion present itself, would, no doubt, also function as a witch killer.   In other words, witches, or potential witches, first seek to cope with their guilt feelings by means of projection, i. e., by killing other witches.   Later on, even this indirect or vicarious means of self-punishment ceases to be effective, and the witch eventually feels compelled to incite others to kill him.

This need to pile symptom upon symptom, e. g., by acquiring additional powers, as did Ahma Huma: re, or by becoming a witch, proves conclusively that being a shaman is a neurotic defense and not a true sublimation.   The effectiveness of a neurotic defense differs from that of a sublimation in three ways:

(1) Sublimation is nonspecific; it controls a large variety of conflicts related to a given impulse.   By contrast, a symptomatic defense is relatively specific and effectively controls only a few types of conflicts.   Hence, when new difficulties arise, they have to be dealt with either by means of new symptomatic defenses, or else the new conflict is artificially made to mean the same thing as the old one, in order to deal with it by means of the same symptomatic defense that, as a

---

[43] Ackerknecht's (1943) view that becoming a shaman represents a recovery without insight is, psychiatrically, a contradiction in terms (Devereux, 1956 b).

result of this unwarranted expansion of its applicability, turns at this point into a neurotic characterological defense.[44]

(2) Sublimations tend to provide permanent solutions, while symptoms gradually lose their effectiveness and become stale, so that, even if no new conflicts arise—which is unlikely, since symptoms themselves always create additional difficulties—they must eventually be supplemented by new, or more incapacitating, symptoms.[45]

(3) Defenses consume psychic energy; sublimations do not.

Given these inherent inadequacies of even socially sanctioned defenses, which are also in many ways quite ego-dystonic, since, as Lowie (1929) put it, "man is not a total abstainer from reason although he indulges with fanatical moderation," at least some potential shamans reject this defense altogether. However, if such a person is then unable to evolve a sublimation, or cannot find less ego-dystonic defenses against his conflicts, he will inevitably decompensate and become psychotic. Indeed, no matter how irrational it may be to believe oneself endowed with shamanistic powers, this symptomatic defense often does hold in check possibly even more irrational unconscious fantasies. Hence, when a potential shaman refuses to become a practicing one, his impulses, denied a socially sanctioned outlet, ultimately erupt in a wholly idiosyncratic form, and with a much greater irrationality and intensity than if they had not been first suppressed and/or repressed (Freud, 1925 a, 1925 b). Thus, modern psychiatry supports the Mohave Indian view that the person who received shamanistic powers, but refuses to become a practicing shaman, will become psychotic.

The preceding considerations will enable us to obtain a genuine understanding, both anthropological and psychological, of the case of Apen Ismalyk, who was believed to have become insane as a result of his unwillingness to become a practicing shaman.

CASE 4:

Apen Ismalyk (Beaver's ear), gens Melyikha, is a widowed and childless fullblood Mohave male born in 1889. He is related to a notoriously troublesome family (pt. 5, pp. 245–247).

Data.—Apen Ismalyk is one of the few Mohave psychotics for whom detailed medical records were available. The following sources of information were available:

(a) Colorado River Indian Agency Individual History Card (Form 5–153, Allotment No. 148T) (Card No. 180 B).

(b) Indian Field Service Field Matron's report (1931).

---

[44] While this theory of the transformation of symptomatic into characterological defenses is relatively novel, it is wholly compatible with the classical psychoanalytic theory of symptoms.

[45] Thus, an agoraphobic may first refuse to leave his home town, then his street, then his apartment, then his room and then perhaps even his bed, thereby creating increasingly severe socioeconomic difficulties for himself.

(c) Colorado River Indian Agency Hospital Record (1934–35).

(d) State Hospital Clinical Summary (1935).

(e) Information from my interpreter Hama: Utce:, whose husband, Sumurámurá (=soft or crumbly) of the Mah gens, is related to Apen Ismalyk (1936).

(f) Interview with Apen Ismalyk (at his house, which is located on the Arizona side of the Colorado River, opposite Needles, Calif., with Sumurámurá acting as interpreter). (1938.)

(g) Information from the shaman Ahma Huma:re, who is Apen Ismalyk's "own uncle" (=real uncle) (1938).

(h) Information from Tcatc, who is related to Apen Ismalyk (1938).

(i) Information from Pulyi:k.

Family history (Data a, e, g, i):

(1) Grandfather on father's side: Atcoo:r Hote:vá, a great chief, kwanámi:hye (brave), shaman and witch killer. Americans usually called him Arateva or Yarateva, while McNichols (1944) refers to him as Irataba. Like Apen Ismalyk, this grandfather also had a psychotic episode, allegedly for the same reason.

(2) Maternal grandfather: According to data (a) Hotcawaka, or Hatcawaka.

(3) Father: Ahma Thukam, gens Melyikha, a fullblood Mohave (individual history card 180), born 1869, died September 7, 1910.

(4) Mother: Melyikha, also of the Melyikha gens (!), a fullblood Mohave woman, born 1876, died April 9, 1910. (This identity of the spouses' gentes means, by Mohave standards, an "incestuous" marriage.)

(5) Younger sibling: Amasalya, a fullblood Mohave male born 1891.

(6) Younger sibling: A fullblood Mohave male born 1901.

(7) Half sibling: Ayulk Itcerk (leather feces) (data i).

(8) Other relatives: Apen Ismalyk is related to a certain family of the Mah gens, in which there were some cases of incest, and several members of which were shamans, witches, and witch killers (pt. 5, (pp. 245–247).

(9) Wife: Kat, gens Kat, was blind at least as far back as 1931, and died in 1933 or 1934, "of sickness."

(10) Children: None.

Socioeconomic status in 1931 (Data b):

Industrial situation of family: Good. Means of livelihood: Store-yard. Number in family to support: 2. Number of wage earners or workers: 1. Sources of income: Santa Fe Railroad. Kind of water supply: City. Distance of water supply from house: 200 feet. Danger of pollution of water supply: None. Are there facilities for obtaining cow's milk? Yes.

Medical status in 1931 (Data b):

Tuberculosis: No. Trachoma: No. Malnutrition: No. Sore eyes: No. Other diseases: No. Usual treatment: Shaman. Distance from medical doctor: ¾ mile. Distance from Field Matron: ¾ mile. Character of roads: City. Remarks: The wife is totally blind, but does very well. She carries the water about 200 feet.

Hygienic and sanitary conditions in 1931 (Data b):

Kind of house: Usual [i. e., adobe hut]. Number living in house: 2. Number of beds: 1. Sanitary conditions in house: Pretty good. Ventilation: Good.

Number of windows: 4. Number of doors: 2. Sanitary condition of premises: Good. Human waste, how disposed of? Toilet. Garbage and rubbish, how disposed of? Burned or buried. Prevalence of insects and vermin: Usual (i. e., considerable). Are there barns or stables: No. Are the animals well cared for: None. Insanitary practices observed: Pretty clean. General impression: "Unprogressive, inoffensive Indians" (sic!).

Colorado River Agency Hospital record (Data c):

Patient was in this hospital from July 7, 1934, to January 14, 1935. "Patient is constantly delirious and delusional. He is harmless but disturbs the other patients." On December 5, 1934, M. A. I. Nettle, M. D., recommended that the patient be transferred to a State Hospital for the Insane.

STATE HOSPITAL CLINICAL SUMMARY (Data d):

(Apen Ismalyk.)

The above-named patient was committed to this hospital January 14, 1935, and was discharged April 20, 1935, in care of his people from the Fort Mohave Reservation as recovered.

General information:

Apen Ismalyk resides on the Fort Mohave Reservation. He was born in Arizona and is about 48 (46) years old. He has lived in that vicinity all his life, sometimes on the California side of the river and sometimes in Arizona. His wife died about a year ago, when (whereupon) he went to live with his niece on the Fort Mohave Reservation. Patient has had no previous attacks; this attack was first noticed about 6 months ago. He was sick and was sent to the Hospital at Parker, Ariz., where he has been for some time. The Indians did not know that there was anything wrong with his mind, but learned a few days ago that he was being sent to Phoenix, and came to Phoenix to see that he was being taken care of properly. They did not want him sent here, but thought they could cure him with their tribal ceremonies and medicines.

Mental examination: 2-5-35.

Behavior.—Since admission this patient has been very well behaved, causing no trouble whatsoever on the ward, except on one occasion when he became noisy at night and refused to quiet down until he was put in restraint. At all other times this patient has been very quiet and cooperative. At present he resides on Ward J where he causes no trouble whatever. The mental examination of this patient was very unsatisfactory since we have no Mohave Indians among our patients to act as interpreter. This patient speaks English too poorly to give us a coherent story. However, I have been unable to elicit any hallucinations or delusions, and considering the information obtained that patient was suffering from typhoid fever at the Parker Hospital, it is my opinion that he was suffering with Psychosis with Other Somatic Disease, Typhoid Fever.

I would suggest that this patient be put to work on the farm or similar operations and be observed for another month or two before releasing him to his relatives in Needles.

Diagnosis: Manic-depressive psychosis, manic type.

Physical examination: 2-13-35:

This patient is a well-developed and nourished Indian male. *Head*—there is a marked flattening of the head posterially (probably due to cradling; Devereux, 1948 c), otherwise it is negative. *Eyes*—pupils are equal but react sluggishly to light; bilateral pterygli is present; nose and ears negative. *Mouth*—teeth in fair condition, but considerably worn. *Neck* is negative. *Chest* is of a hypersthenic type and clear throughout. *Heart* is negative. *Abdomen* obese. No findings of interest. *Extremities*—there is diffused discoloration of the left lower leg with several scars present, the result of previous ulcers. On the left thigh are multiple scars where pinch graphs have been taken.

Neurological examination:

Essentially negative in all respects.

Recommendation: 4–11–35:

To be discharged.

Discharged: April 1935.

(Name)

————————M. D.

Information from interpreter Hama: Utce: (Data *e*) :

Apen Ismalyk is a shaman. He sings and talks at funerals and it gives me the creeps. I thought at first that it did not mean anything, but found out that in reality he speaks of very old things, which the old-time Indians would have understood. Then he starts talking of God and of Christ, and prays. I like to listen to him, but I am scared all the same. Once he had a big bow and an arrow and I was afraid that he might shoot. Once I even took him to Yuma. He was here in the hospital, but the children were afraid of him, so they put him in the Yuma jail, for questioning before a Court of Commitment. He went out of his head, and the sheriff wanted to send him to the State Hospital for the Insane. When he is excited he mutters abruptly in English, "Go West, and go West, and to the East, with a pick and shovel, over 2,000, over 2,000,000 (repeats the numbers)." He talks to no one except my husband. My father-in-law thinks that, at some time or other, Apen Ismalyk had killed a white man— maybe a prospector—and worries over it. One day, when he was in the hospital, the practical nurse brought him a pair of pajamas to put on, and he flung them back at her. Then the practical nurse asked my husband, Sumurámurà, to help her get Apen Ismalyk into his pajamas. My husband took him to the lavatory and made him put them on. Quite often Apen Ismalyk just stares. Often he just lies on the ground with his legs crossed, his arms under his head, and says the things I told you about just now. He clenches his right fist in front of his belly and briskly strikes out sideways [demonstration]. Once he "preached" in front of the Harvey House at Needles. Another time he was lying with his head to the North and his face turned to the East, and said, "There is gold right there—someone gets it—I'll get it." Then my husband asked: "Who told you about it?" but Apen Ismalyk would not answer his question. He now lives at (near) Needles. He was released from the State Hospital after 3 months. Not until he went crazy did people know he was a shaman, but now that he practices, he is better. He cures colds, pneumonia, and the flu. He began practicing about a year ago, when he was released from the asylum. [In reply to a non-leading question, Hama: Utce: added that Apen Ismalyk also used to say, "I am dead."]

Interview with Apen Ismalyk (interpreter, Sumurámurà (Data *f*)):

I used to live just where the old schoolhouse is now, and was raised around there. Then, in 1901, I went away to school, to Fort Mohave. I was about 14 years old at that time. I stayed in school for 7 years, and then left because of illness. My heart was bad. Next, I worked off and on for the Santa Fe Railroad shops. After that, I quit for good at the Santa Fe, and when they started to build a levee—probably in 1911—I worked there as a laborer and as a teamster. I drove a team. After that was over, I stayed at Parker for a while and then went on to Yuma. Then I left Yuma and went to Blythe and worked there as a teamster. After that I returned to Needles to work once more at the Sante Fe shops, in the roundhouse. There was high water at that time and they were trying to stop the water from eating the banks away. I worked there for a while and then, around 1928, I quit because I hurt my left leg on the inside, just above the ankle. Look—you can still see a white scar, with a black area around it. They sent me to Los Angeles, to the Santa Fe Hospital, and I remained there for 1 month. Then I came home of my own accord, and stayed at Needles, on the California side of the Colorado River, until my leg began to ache once more. Then I went to Parker to get treatment, and got well. Another reason why I left Needles was that my heart was giving me trouble. It got so bad that people could hardly hear me when I spoke. (Note the culturally determined absence of any direct reference to his wife's death.)

Then they thought that I had gone insane and Dr. Nettle, together with M. L., and with Hama: Utce: and her husband, took me to Yuma for a lunacy hearing. I was first taken to jail and then to the State Hospital. The hospital was a nice place. I was there for 90 days. When I got well, O: oct, the wife of Modha: r Hoto: tcâ (penis pounds) (Devereux, 1954 b) came for me and took me home. That was in 1935.

[The following data were obtained in reply to direct questions.]

I was married once, but I lost my wife about 10 years ago or more. We had no children. I was married to her, roughly speaking, from 1916 until 1926 (actually longer).

I had venereal disease (hiku: pk) once and was circumcised (or incised?) by Dr. C. at Needles. I do not know from whom I got that disease, because I had been chasing around.

I am a bit of a shaman, but I have cured no one as yet. I do not know how to bewitch people.

[Why did they think that you were insane?] I do not know. [I heard that everyone was afraid of you. What were you saying or doing at the Parker Hospital?] I can recall nothing. [What kind of treatment did you get at the State Hospital?] They gave me a thorough examination and I was kept in bed. [Did you get any shots?] No. But I did get electric treatments, with wires attached to my elbows—it made me twitch. [What was your leg like when it hurt so much?] It itched and I scratched it a lot. I think the Santa Fe should pay for the wound on my leg. I think all the time about getting a compensation. (He may, conceivably, have thought of this when, in his delirium, he spoke of large sums of money.)

The Government gave me 10 head of cattle in 1931—I do not know why they did that. [Interpreter suggested that it may have been Relief cattle.]

[Where did you get the United States Indian Police badge, the one you showed me before the interpreter arrived?] I bought it myself. I never worked for the Government. [Apen Ismalyk looked rather sheepish when making this admission.]

[Does your leg still hurt?] No. [Is it just as good now as your other leg?] It still feels hot around the place where I got hurt.

[Do you dream great (power) dreams?] No. [Do you have ordinary dreams?] Yes. I dream that I go to swim, and then I get a cold afterwards. [Interpreter remarked that he, too, has such dreams and that all Mohave have them.] Sometimes I also dream of wading in water (due to sensations in his scarred leg?) It has the same effect on me. [Do you have falling dreams?] Yes.

The back muscles, behind my right armpit, twitch and feel as hot as my hurt leg. Sometimes, when that warm feeling comes, it goes right into my heart, but it does not make me short of breath. It stops at my heart and then it goes cold again (cf. pt 1, pp. 9–17). The first time it happened, it was like the bite of an ant. That was in 1934. When it started hurting I plunged into the river, because I did not know what else to do. It hurt for a whole week. Now I tend my cattle even when it hurts. This first attack came in June 1934. I do not know how it happened to come.

[What do shamans think about this?] They do not know. [Have you ever been treated for it by a shaman?] Yes, by (Hispan Himith) Tcilyetcilye. [What did he call it?] I do not know. He did not tell me. But the pain stopped after 2 days of doctoring. [Didn't they tell you that you too should be a shaman?] Yes. They were bound to think of that. [What can you cure?] [No reply.]

[Do you have any siblings?] Madhily Nyunye: (bread road) a younger uterine brother (actually his first cousin), and Ayulk Itcerk (= leather feces) (actually a half-brother). [Which one is the older one?] I do not know. They were born at Fort Mohave, and I am not certain of their relative ages. [Were you well treated as a child?] Yes. [What is your first memory?] They used to have shinney-games on the levee—the river, at that time, was further away. [What is your second memory?] The time when the Indians used to go in flocks to select land for allotment (1910).

[At what age did you have your first sex-experience?] I forget. I only recall going to school. [Do you still "chase around?"] No.

[Would you talk to one of my psychiatrist friends, who is going to visit Parker and Needles?] Yes. [How can I write to you, to let you know when he is coming?] There is no way to write to me, but I am always here, or else at the house of the neighbors.

[Do you get a pension?] No. [How do you earn a living?] I don't. I live off my relatives, but as soon as I get some payment from the cattle, I will live off that—as I do sometimes. I have about 600 head of cattle at Fort Mohave, but people steal them. [Interpreter remarked in whispers that Apen Ismalyk could not possibly own 600 head of cattle. "He must think that other people's cattle also belong to him."]

Information from Ahma Huma: re (Data *g*):

Apen Ismalyk is my own nephew. He is a very well-built man, who used to work at Needles, Calif., in the Santa Fe Railroad roundhouse. I visit him whenever he is (I am?) in Needles. Even before he became insane (yamomk) I noticed that he was not feeling well. Then I heard that he was yamomk. When he talks, he seems to know almost everything. I think it is due to the fact that he has knowledge of more things than he speaks about, but people say that he is yamomk.

[Half the time I could not understand Apen Ismalyk, even when he started pouring out a stream of words in English.] I know just what you mean! I heard Apen Ismalyk sing all the songs that were formerly sung and are still being sung by the Indians, and even heard him sing white people's songs.

People think that his insanity has two causes:

　　(*a*) He has dream power, but never used it; he is, therefore, so full of it that his mind is not open to other things. It seems to make him forget other things and causes him to speak only his mind, which is full of these unused powers. (Autism.)

　　(*b*) Some people also think that someone may have done something with him, by means of witchcraft.

Information from Tcatc (Data h):

Since Apen Ismalyk lives at Needles, I do not know very much about him, I only heard of him. He is about 30 years old. (Correct age: 49.) People say that he is a shaman, but he has never used his power. Hence, when he is full of his power, he goes crazy. He sometimes sings songs that are used in his (power) dreams, but he sings them only when he is alone (i.e., when he thinks he is alone). Today, even though he is insane, he has already cured some diseases.

I was at someone's funeral and he got there while they were singing some songs. First he gave a talk in English, and, naturally, I did not understand what he said. Then he began to talk in Mohave, but I did not understand that either. He also sang some songs, but people did not know what he sang. He did this all night long.

When he went insane, they brought him first to this (Parker) hospital, and then they took him to the State Hospital. Then I heard that Madhily Nyunye:, his nephew (actually first cousin, according to Pulyi: k), made a trip to the State Hospital and told the doctors that the Indians never want one of their people to be taken away from his home and family, to die some place else. He explained that the Indians always kept their seriously ill people home with them, partly so that they would know just how they died, and partly also because they want to take care of the remains according to Indian rites and customs. So, somehow or other, I finally heard that Apen Ismalyk was returned to Needles.

His grandfather Atcoo: r Hote: vå also had a spell of insanity before he began to cure; power seems hereditary in that family. Apen Ismalyk is also related to that family of the Mah gens in which there were cases of incest, shamanism and witchcraft, as well as of witch killing (pt. 5, pp. 245–247). One member of that family, Yellak Hi: ha, also called "Lakiha:", once doctored me when I had the black measles. He was the one who attempted to have sexual relations with his mother (Devereux, 1939a).

[Did you know that Hama: Utce:'s father-in-law thought that Apen Ismalyk may have killed a white prospector?] No, I didn't. It surprises me.

When people have power, but refuse to become shamans, they go crazy like Apen Ismalyk. After they begin to cure, it helps them some. His grandfather Atcoor Hote: vå also was that way for a while.

Information from Pulyi: k (Data i):

This informant was used solely for the purpose of clarifying some details, including Mohave names and their spelling. He defined the real kinship between Apen Ismalyk, Madhily Nyunye:, and Ayulk Itcerk, and gave the correct spelling of these and several other names. He explained that M. L.—a very progressive Mohave—was also present at Apen Ismalyk's lunacy hearing. However, he was unable to say whether Apen Ismalyk had been actually circumcised, or simply incised, to relieve phymosis. He agreed that Apen Ismalyk became insane (yamomk) due to his refusal to become a practicing shaman.

Comment

Diagnosis.—The official diagnosis of "manic-depressive psychosis, manic phase, complicated by typhoid fever delirium" seems insufficiently supported by the available evidence. The diagnosis of "transitory confusional state, probably triggered off by typhoid delirium" is suggested.

Mohave diagnosis.—The Mohave felt certain that Apen Ismalyk's psychosis was caused by his refusal to become a practicing shaman. The patient himself calmly admitted that people were "bound to think of that" when he lost his mind. He conceded that he had shamanistic powers, but avoided stating positively whether or not he had begun to practice.

When last seen, Apen Ismalyk gave the impression of a tense person in partial remission and relatively well rehabilitated socially. His total bearing left no doubt whatsoever that a recurrence of his transitory psychosis remained a definite possibility, even though episodes of this type tend to be rarer once middle age has been reached. Any suggestion that, in becoming a shaman, he had been genuinely cured—be it "without insight"—must be rejected out of hand, since Apen Ismalyk was quite obviously an ambulatory psychotic in a labile state of temporary remission.

Reference should also be made to the illness of Amat Válåka: (Case 34), which, though diagnosed as ahwe: hahnok, has certain aspects that suggest that a turning of powers against their owner also played a role in its etiology.

The single most important aspect of this case is that it demonstrates, as is shown by Ahma Huma: re's remarks, that Hikye: t was voicing a fairly generally accepted theory when he asserted that one cause of insanity is "lyelyedhu: tc hi: wa hakwi: lyk," which can be translated as "comprehension or knowledge exceed the heart." In modern psychology, this would mean that the emotions and the ego functions are swamped by autistic fantasy material erupting from the unconscious. Hikye: t's own theories of the etiology of psychiatric disorders are, in fact, a clear-cut example of his ego's inability to organize his fantasies into a logical system (pt. 1, pp. 9–17).

DISORDERS OF THE SEXUAL IMPULSE

The Mohave appear to differentiate, at least implicitly, between manifest sexual *misbehavior* and a derangement of the sexual *impulse* itself. The former is, for all practical purposes, defined as "endogenous," voluntary and controllable, while the latter is not, and is therefore considered to be symptomatic of insanity. Sexual misbehavior, which is theoretically controllable, is condemned and sometimes even punished, in terms of ethical considerations. Disorders of the sexual impulse—caused by some more or less impersonal "natural" illness or by witchcraft—are, by contrast, defined as "insanity," which must be dealt with therapeutically rather than punitively. The distinction is made especially clear by the radically different ways in which society reacts to the kamalo: y, who is not only promiscuous but also bad (ala: yk) (Devereux, 1948 f), and to the kindly nymphomaniac, who has the ya tcahaetk neurosis. The kamalo: y is despised and often even punitively raped. The woman suffering from ya tcahaetk is pitied, and her good human qualities are freely recognized.

Another useful contrast to be drawn is that between the shaman, whose sexual misconduct is due to the "acting up" of his own magical powers, and the misconduct of the bewitched woman, into whom an evil shaman injects his own powers. The misconduct of the shaman is rationalized by saying: "It is his nature, he cannot help it"; hence, no one tries to therapeutize him. The misconduct of the bewitched woman is, by contrast, defined as ego-alien and exogenous; she is held to be psychiatrically ill and attempts are made to therapeutize her.

Of course, the intellectual belief of the Mohave that the shaman is not, strictly speaking, "yamomk" is a cultural tenet rather than a psychiatric finding, and is therefore not a valid "certificate of sanity." In fact, the Mohave themselves seem to sense that the shaman is not really sane, since, when a new sexual outrage perpetrated by a shaman becomes known, people tend to exclaim: "All shamans are crazy." While, from the cultural point of view, the term "crazy" (yamomk) is used here in a strictly pejorative and nondiagnostic sense,[46] from the objective point of view this venting of feelings more nearly approximates psychiatric realities than does the official cultural tenet that the practicing shaman is not, strictly speaking, "yamomk," even though some of his actions resemble those of a psychotic.

In brief, it is a cultural bias, and not psychiatric insight, that leads the Mohave to differentiate between "yamomk" and "not yamomk" on the basis of whether the misbehavior is due to "illness" or else to ego-alien magical powers on the one hand, or to the subject's own unruly powers and/or basic makeup on the other hand. This "etiological" theory is of interest solely as a cultural fact, but has no psychiatric validity, except insofar as it seems to suggest that the Mohave have a dim insight into the difference between a (shamanistic) *character neurosis* and a (yamomk) *symptom neurosis*.

This point will not be elaborated further in the present context, since the entire problem of the Mohave Indian's differentiation between "yamomk" and "not yamomk" is analyzed in detail in part 1, pp. 24–35. Furthermore, since the present monograph is devoted exclusively to the study of Mohave psychiatric ideas, no consideration will be given to the perversions, which the Mohave do not consider "yamomk," and which, moreover, have been fully described in a series of previously published essays (see appendix to this section, p. 89).

ATCOO: R HANYIENK

The investigation of convulsive seizures was begun by describing to Tcatc the "fits" of a certain American man, who may or may not have been a true epileptic. Tcatc diagnosed his condition as atcoo: r hanyienk, and, in reply to a question, stated that no Mohave known to

---

[46] In the same way, an American may exclaim: "You must be out of your mind," without following up this pseudodiagnosis with the recommendation that his interlocutor consult a good psychiatrist.

her was currently (1938) suffering from this condition. Interpreter
E. S. agreed and added derisively: "Nowadays they just get drunk."

Etiology.—According to Tcatc:

Atcoo: r hanyienk means "hawks copulate."[47] I do not know how it starts.
Hawks have nothing to do with it. (By contrast, in discussing priapism—see
section on Sudhu: rk, pp. 76–77—Hivsu: Tupo: ma expressed the culturally more
plausible opinion that this illness is caused partly by the atcoo: r hawks and
partly by an excessive sexual urge and by masturbation.)

Symptomatology.—According to Tcatc:

When a person has this illness, it comes on him in spells. His mind somehow
turns (changes). He thinks that he sees pretty girls in the nude and then,
though fully awake, he ejaculates. He just falls down, foams at the mouth,
and even urinates. Then it just passes off again. (In between attacks) such
people are sane and all right. Only during their spells are they strange. A
woman, too, can be that way; she may think that she is "going through intercourse" and that she is reaching the climax. She thinks she sees men in the
nude, and that the men are "using her" sexually. [Have you ever heard of the
globus hystericus?] I never heard of it.[48] I am quite ashamed to talk of this
illness.

According to Hivsu: Tupo: ma:

Such persons dream of having intercourse every night and have nightly
pollutions. No, strictly speaking, they only have an orgasm, without pollution[49] (Ferenczi, 1926). This causes the penis to be constantly erect and also
causes a retention of urine. In addition, such people have awful fits. During
these attacks they feel as though they were copulating. A man who has such
an attack draws in his breath, producing the (aspirated) sound "ah . . . ah."
He clutches the ground and falls down just anywhere. He may even fall into
the fire. He might also fall into water and might even drown.[50] During the fit
he acts as though he were engaging in intercourse. He wants coitus so badly
that he gets sick from it. We call this illness atcoo: r hanyienk. It is, strictly
speaking, not real insanity (yamomk). Subsequently two informants mentioned
priapism as a symptom of sudhu: rk (pt. 2, pp. 76–77).

CASE 5 (Informant: Hivsu: Tupo: ma):

A man named Ahay Kuu: p had such fits.

CASE 6 (Informants: Hivsu: Tupo: ma and Tcatc):

Tcávákong, of the O: otc gens, acquired in 1900, at the age of 35, the power
to treat dysentery. He was a nonalcoholic epileptic. During one of his atcoo: r
hanyienk seizures he fell into the fire, burning his hand quite badly. He did
not seem to have any feeling (sensitivity) when he burned himself. Thereafter
he concealed his burned hand in a tobacco bag attached to a spoon which hung

---

[47] Hawks, like owls, are closely connected with death and ghosts.
[48] But cf. part 5, pp. 216–218.
[49] Significantly, Hivsu: Tupo :ma also said that very young boys who masturbate, or
have intercourse, have an orgasm, but do not ejaculate. However, the occurrence of or-
gasms without ejaculation was specifically denied by a sexually experienced boy (pt. 6,
pp. 260–286).
[50] Hysterics are careful not to harm themselves during their "fits."

from a cord tied around his neck. He was so poor that he sang and danced at the Harvey House, in Needles, for the tourists. In 1905, having declared that he had started the epidemic that was at that time killing many children, he was killed by a bereaved father, who had lost a son and daughter.[51] (Full details are given in Case 103.)

Comment

Tentative diagnosis: Epilepsy. (Less probably hystero-epilepsy.)

CASE 7 (Informants: Tcatc and E. S.) :

Isalyà Ukå (to curve) of the Melyikha gens, is said to have died at the age of 18 "70 years ago" (1868).[52] One day we were at school. The boys were seated on one side of the classroom and the girls on the other side. That morning the teacher asked us to sing. This boy was singing perfectly normally with the other boys, when suddenly he got up and made a choked, panting noise, which sounded like "ak'." We girls knew that he had fits and some of us had even seen him have a seizure. So all the girls said in Mohave: "It is getting him again!" Then all the girls, including myself, ran out of the room, and therefore I did not see the rest of the fit. We waited outside and could hear him make that noise. He was swaying and rolling around. [Here Tcatc mimicks the seizure.] We did not return to school that day. No one treated this boy, and eventually he died during a seizure.

Comment

Tentative diagnosis: Epilepsy.

CASE 8 (Informants: Tcatc and E. S.) :

Kumadhi:, a girl of about 18, died long ago during one of her numerous seizures. At the old Indian Agency, near the superintendent's residence, there was a big hole in the ground. She must have been near that hole when she had her last spell. She fell into the hole and broke her neck.

I (Tcatc) never saw her during one of her seizures.

Comment

Tentative diagnosis: Epilepsy (?).

CASE 9 (Informant: Hivsu: Tupo:ma [?]) :

A certain man was so addicted to masturbation that he eventually developed fits. During one of these fits he fell into a fire and burned himself rather severely. Later on, during another attack, he fell into an irrigation ditch and drowned.

Comment

Tentative diagnosis: Hystero-epilepsy.

The Mohave feel that a masturbating adult is quite atypical, in that he behaves in an infantile manner (Devereux, 1950 c).

CASE 10 (Informant: Pulyi:k) :

A girl named O:otc had seizures. She fell into the fire, and later on she also fell into water and drowned.

---

[51] A man, crippled by premature cremation, also danced at Harvey House (McNichols, 1944).

[53] This is probably a gross exaggeration, since he went to school with Tcatc, who was presumably not more than 75 years old in 1938.

Comment

Tentative diagnosis: Epilepsy.

CASE 11 (Informant: Pulyi: k) :

A man, of the Halypotà gens, is known to have fits.

Comment

Tentative diagnosis: Hystero-epilepsy? Epilepsy?

CONFIRMATORY CASE MATERIAL

In 1933 the late M. A. I. Nettle, M. D., reservation physician, stated that, between 1911 and 1933, she had known at least two Mohave epileptics, both of whom died status epilepticus. Unfortunately, I failed to ascertain which of the persons whom the Mohave knew to be suffering from seizures were those whom Dr. Nettle had definitely diagnosed as epileptics. Hrdlička (1908) mentions an epileptic girl child from Fort Mohave.

According to the Mohave, even whites may suffer from atcoo: r hanyienk.

CASE 12 (Informant E. S.) :

A certain American post-office employee at Parker also had convulsive seizures of the atcoo: r hanyienk type. One morning Huskiv Itcerk (dove feces) happened to go uptown and saw this man come out of the post office. Then, suddenly, he saw him fall down on the sidewalk and "act crazy." Some women, who happened to be nearby, came to see what was the matter with him. They were looking at him, when the man suddenly broke wind (epileptic defecation?), whereupon the women just turned around and went away. After a while the man got up and was all right once more. In telling this story Huskiv Itcerk commented that, when an accident happens, the women are always there; they stand around and want to see more of it.

Comment

E. S. volunteered the above case history immediately after he translated Tcatc's account of two Mohave cases of atcoo: r hanyienk. Its significance lies in the fact that the Mohave diagnosed the illness of a white person as atcoo: r hanyienk, which proves that the illnesses of whites are held to be identical with those of the Mohave. A detailed discussion of this finding, with confirmatory material, will be found in part 8, pp. 485–504.

The case of this white epileptic was apparently not widely known, since, when it was mentioned to Pulyi: k, he said that he hadn't heard the story before.

General comment

When speaking English, the Mohave generally designate seizures of all types by the term "fit." Atcoo: r hanyienk is believed to be due to an incapacity to discharge sexual tension even by means of masturbation or coitus that culminates in ejaculation. This view implies that the Mohave have some insight into the fact that a physiological orgasm need not necessarily also entail a psychic orgasm, even if the ejaculation is pleasurable. It will be seen in connection with the Mohave etiological theory of another derangement of the sexual drive (pt. 2, pp. 76–77) that they define this pathological process as a kind of damming up of the libido sexualis, whose final breakthrough occurs in the form of a convulsive seizure. This view is in harmony with modern psychoanalytic insight. One fact which may have enabled the Mohave to reach this conclusion is that, during the "tonic phase" of a seizure, there is a concave arching of the back, known as "arcus hystericus"—though it occurs also in true epilepsy—which duplicates the posture of the male during orgasm.[53] The idea of a damming up, followed by a flooding, may have been modeled upon the image of the periodic floods of the Colorado River, which played an important role in Mohave economy (Kroeber, 1925 a) and may have served the Mohave "psychiatrist" as a "thought model" for his theory of convulsive seizures (Devereux, 1958 b).

The likelihood of this interpretation being correct is increased by the fact that, in connection with another disorder of the sexual drive, the Mohave specifically mentioned the occurrence of masturbation, which is notoriously unable to produce an adequate psychic orgasm.

SUDHU : RK

This term is said to mean something like "to sneak after girls."

Etiology.—There is considerable confusion regarding the etiology of this disorder. The shaman Hilyera Anyay, when asked whether he knew of any case of priapism, made a somewhat obscure statement, whose interpretation depends entirely on the significance one wishes to assign to the term "hahnok." This word, when used in conjunction with a person, being, or entity believed to be capable of causing illness, means literally "due to," "caused by," or "derived from." Thus, ahwe: hahnok means "disease derived from contact with an alien" (ahwe:). However, Hilyera Anyay used in his account the expression "hiku: pk hahnok," although hiku: pk is already the name of a group of diseases (venereal diseases). In fact, this is the only recorded instance in which the term "hahnok" was used in connection with an actual disease, rather than in connection with a pathogenic agent. A reliable interpreter translated Hilyera Anyay's statement as follows: "When such a person was (sic!) hiku: pk hahnok, in some cases his penis stood up and never went down. I have heard of such cases:" This statement does not make it clear whether Hilyera Anyay viewed priapism as an actual epiphenomenon or symptom of syphilis, or as a symptom of an independent disease entity called "hiku: pk hahnok," presumably related to syphilis, or meant to suggest that priapism occurs in oversexed persons only if they also have

---

[53] Lordosis also occurs in female white rats, when their excitement reaches a peak during intercourse.

syphilis. While this question cannot be settled with absolute certainty, Hilyera Anyay's theory may have been based upon reports of priapism in syphilitics, who sometimes develop this condition as a result of syphilitic lesions of the nervous system.

By contrast, Hivsu: Tupo: ma emphasized the psychogenic component of priapism and related it to the atcoo: r hanyienk syndrome:

> Atcoo: r hanyienk is caused, on the one hand, by the atcoo: r hawk, and, on the other hand, by an excessive sexual drive and by masturbation. Priapism is due to excessive masturbation, which causes the penis to be in a constant state of erection. Sometimes, however, men also have painful and prolonged erections from other causes.

Priapism does not appear to be a widely known symptom. Thus, when asked about this ailment, Tcatc, as well as interpreter E. S. (who, later on, translated Hilyera Anyay's statement), burst out laughing and said they never had heard of such a thing.

Symptomatology.—According to Tcatc:

> (Forcible) seduction, called sakuve: râ (rape) should not be confused with sudhu: rk. A man suffering from sudhu: rk acts as follows: Suppose three or four families live together (i. e., in a small settlement). If a man just felt that way (i. e., had an attack), he went into the house of some girl, and cohabited with her. Sometimes the girl mistook him for her husband in the dark, but if she found out who the man was, she just kicked him off.[54]

Therapy.—According to Hivsu: Tupo: ma, shamans were usually able to treat such persons effectively. No shaman living in 1932–33 practiced this type of therapy.

No case histories could be obtained.

Comment

Sudhu: rk seems to be a variety of the atcoo: r hanyienk illness, and appears to affect only men.

YA TCAHAETK

Preliminary considerations.—Ya tcahaetk appears to be a comprehensive term applied to a variety of neurotic disturbances believed to be caused by an excessive sexual urge, which no amount of physical gratification can discharge entirely. Although the Mohave did not specifically state that the term "ya tcahaetk" included both the kamalo: y tâminyk neurosis of women, and the sudhu: rk neurosis of men, their ideas regarding the etiology and symptomatology of these

---

[54] A Mohave father cohabited with his sleeping daughter, who mistook him for her husband (Devereux, 1939 a). In many primitive societies (Barton, 1938; Devereux, MS., 1933–34; Hurley, 1936; Mead, 1928) men are known to rape sleeping women, who mistakenly believe them to be their husbands or lovers. It is superfluous, I think, to comment on the unconscious "cooperation" of the victims of such "mistaken identity rapes," especially if they are incestuous.

latter disorders are practically identical with those mentioned in connection with the ya tcahaetk syndrome.

Etiology.—This disease is caused by too much masturbation. Conversely, excessive masturbation is also a symptom and result of this disease. "These are the worst kinds of persons. They cannot get married, because no one wants them.[55] They cannot appease their sexual desires. Their excessive masturbation causes them to have 'fits.' " (Informant: Tcatc.)

Symptomatology.—Since such people are unable to discharge their sexual tensions, they create quite a problem for society. "If a woman or a girl is out by herself (i. e., alone), they take her without giving it any thought, and cohabit with her. They are crazy, even though they know what they are doing. I heard of such a person. I was afraid (of him). I do not remember his name. He was ya tcahaetk." (Informant: Tcatc. However, she later on supplied a series of case histories pertaining to this illness.)

CASE 13 (Informants: Tcatc, E. S., and Hivsu: Tupo: ma):

Nyoltc "Hukthar" (hukthar meaning primarily "coyote"; secondarily "crazy"), i. e. "crazy" Nyoltc, whose English name was not recalled, was the daughter of Ahwe: Ha: m (enemy traveling). At the time I (Tcatc) knew her, she was living near Ehrenberg, at a place called Hao: r (fine gravel), i. e., at Blythe, Calif. However, I did not know her very well and did not witness her "death" (meaning probably her cremation). At the time of her death, which occurred around 1913, she was about 25 or 30 years of age.

According to Hivsu: Tupo: ma:, Nyoltc Hukthar was, in her childhood, involved in a sexual experience with an oldish man. Once he masturbated her and she ended up by urinating on his hand, from sheer mischievousness. (This incident was not known to Tcatc.)   (See Case 79.)

Tcatc: I heard that this woman, though sane in every way, was extremely nervous and unable to keep still already in her childhood.[56] When one spoke to her, she could not keep her head still, but kept on looking around.[57] These symptoms of nervousness (hukthar hit'i: k) persisted throughout her life, and were among the reasons which caused people to nickname her "hukthar" ("coyote," i. e., "crazy"). The other reason was that she had been married many times, "chasing around with one husband after another." (Since her case history was given in response to a question concerning nymphomania, it may be assumed that her numerous marriages were attributed to her nymphomania.)

She died of illness at a young age. It happened during an epidemic caused by a shaman who was a relative of hers, and whose name I do not recall. Thus, her death was due partly to witchcraft and partly to suma: tc itcem, meaning "dream, or power, does not have" (lack of power obtained in dream). (Further data on this woman will be found in Case 79.)

---

[55] The case histories show that they do marry, but are soon divorced.

[56] The Mohave attribute nervousness to premature sexual experiences (Devereux, 1950 a).

[57] A desirable and eligible young woman always gives her undivided attention to anyone speaking to her.

Comment

Tentative diagnosis: Nymphomania and neurotic tensions in a hysterical character.

CASE 14 (Informant: Tcatc):

Nyortc Hatlyukwe: tc (or Hatlyukwa) of the Nyoltc gens, lived at Parker, Ariz., and died around the turn of the century, at the approximate age of fifty. She had been married successively to a large number of men, and must have had at least one child, since her name was changed to Nyortc, in accordance with the custom which requires that a female member of the Nyoltc gens should be so designated after the death of her child. I was told that Nyortc must have had bad luck, because all of her husbands died after living with her for a short time only. I knew her only in her old age, when she was single. I was told that even in her old age Nyortc still "copulated around," and that she was ya tcahaetk, i. e., a nymphomaniac. She died of some disease, the nature of which is not known to me. I suspect, however, that it must have been hiku: pk (syphilis).

Even her nickname indicates her sexual proclivities, since Hatlyukwe: tc means "looked for" or "sought after." Yet, at the same time, she was basically a very good woman. She was kind and she was very good to everyone . . . much like the woman you told us about.[58] That is why no one called her a kamalo: y, who is both dissolute and mean (ala: yk) (Devereux, 1948 f). Yet, she went with anyone for the asking. Of course, she did not actually solicit men; that wasn't necessary, since everyone knew she could be had, and therefore men came to her spontaneously. Such a woman is called ya tcahae: tk. [How did she get that way?] There is no real explanation for that. It may be something like this: You may not be known for doing something, such as getting angry, and yet, one day, without knowing it, you might become very angry. It was that way with Nyortc. She just did these things without knowing it; although sometimes she did know it. There wasn't any particular thing which made her do these things.

Comment

Tentative diagnosis: Nymphomania.

Tcatc's interpretative remarks suggest an attempt to explain Nyortc's behavior in terms of unconscious mechanisms, and, more specifically, in terms of an overwhelming of the ego by ego-dystonic or ego-alien id-forces. Indeed, it is quite obvious that the expression "without knowing it" cannot refer, in this case, either to a fuguelike state, or to an amnesia. There are also other indications that the Mohave sometimes relate abnormal behavior to "knowledge exceeding the heart" (i. e., exceeding the capacity to handle that knowledge) (Case 4). In such a statement the word "knowledge" must obviously refer to some internal urge, wish or fantasy, rather than to intellectual information.

CASE 15 (Informants: Tcatc and E. S.):

"Nyortc Huhual, of the Nyoltc gens, is (1938) a very old woman—she is even older than I am. (I. e., probably over 80 years old.) She had many sex partners and gave birth to four sons, one of whom, Huau Husek' (fly whip), gens Hualy, is still alive. He is married to a Kamia woman and lives near San

---

[58] Iris Storm, heroine of Michael Arlen's novel "The Green Hat."

Diego. (This may be a misstatement. Cf. Devereux, 1948 f.) Nyortc Huhual is related to M. L.'s wife. This M. L. is the one who was present at Apen Ismalyk's lunacy hearing (Case 4). She is also related to Uta: c, whose wife died insane (Case 38). Uta: c's father was her mother's brother, and his mother was her father's sister, two men having married each other's sister. Nyortc Huhual had been married to many men, all of whom died shortly after marrying her. In addition, she is said to have had affairs with the witch Kwathany Hi: wa, with Itha: v Kámuhan (alias Porkupork; cf. Devereux, 1950 a), and with a number of other people. I first knew her when she was 12 years old. At that time she lived near M. S.'s dwelling, at a place called Ah'a kapitan (Captain's cottonwood). She is like other men and women who have the ya tcahaetk illness: She is a good housewife and is good to everyone, but is known to copulate for the asking. Recently (1938), while going home from a party, she was waylaid by two allegedly drunken men, who pulled a sack over her head and robbed her. One of them even raped her.[59] (Cf. Case 128.)

"Although no one really knows who these men were, rumor has it that the one who raped her was one of her own nephews." At this point, someone present exclaimed in the typically Mohave bantering manner: "Lucky girl—at her age!" Tcatc replied quite seriously: "If she had not been copulating so much all her life, she would have died (of this rape?) long ago" (Devereux, 1939 a).

At this point I reminded Tcatc that, according to Hivsu: Tupo: ma and others, this selfsame alleged rapist is said to have cohabited also with his own sister, Mah (Devereux, 1939 a). Tcatc replied that she, too, had heard of that incident. Then the interpreter E. S. said: "This N. family are devils—and close relatives of mine, as well as of Hama: Utce: (Testicles charcoal)." Tcatc then closed the discussion with the remark: "They act just like white people do" (i. e., in an objectionable manner).[60]

Comment

Tentative diagnosis: Nymphomania.

CASE 16 (Informants: Tcatc and E. S.):

Hwet Isa: lye (Red hand),[61] of the Nyoltc gens, died around 1900 at the age of 60 or 65. He was married quite a number of times. Although he was a good man, who provided well for all of his successive wives, none of them lived with him for long. They just went away and left him, because he wanted to copulate all the time. Eventually he died from hiku: pk (venereal disease). That is all I know of him. I did not see him often.

Comment

Tentative diagnosis: Compulsive promiscuousness and sexual hyperactivity. Venereal disease.

This case closely resembles the following one. In both instances the man is said to have been a good provider, but sexually so demanding that every one of his wives deserted him. The assertion, also made in other contexts (Devereux, 1950 a), that wives may desert sexually hyperactive husbands is somewhat

---

[59] This is the only Mohave robbery and not partly traditional rape known to me (Devereux, 1939 a).

[60] For a discussion of this family, cf. part 5, pages 245–247.

[61] The Mohave stated that, for some unknown reason, the word "red" is in the Yuma, and not in the Mohave, language. In Mohave "red" is called "ahwat."

perplexing, since the Mohave themselves say that women are sexually more provocative (Nettle, MS., n. d.) and also more promiscuous than men (Devereux, 1950 a). There are, however, indications that the Mohave woman values her marriage less than does the man and therefore breaks it up more easily (Devereux, 1951 f). Also, precisely because Mohave women are more promiscuous than men, it is likely that they tire of sexual relations with one partner more rapidly than do the men. Yet, even so, one is forced to suspect that the men in question were simply hyperactive, but not satisfactory, sex partners, whose "goodness" in other respects may have been an unconscious attempt to make up for their inadequacy as sex partners.

CASE 17 (Informants: Tcatc and E. S.):

Sukuetc (Hamsukuetc?) (English name not recalled), of the Nyoltc gens, died around 1925, at the age of 40 or 45.[62] Except in one respect, he was like any other man. He was a very good man, but his successive wives would not live with him because he cohabited with them too often. After he had been married 10 or 15 times, he contracted severe gonorrhea (actually also syphilis). At that time the late M. A. I. Nettle, M. D., was our (reservation) physician, and she treated him. I recall hearing that his penis was just rotten and that one of his testicles had fallen off. His one remaining testicle, which was just about to fall off anyway, had to be removed surgically.[63] This is how this man died.[64]

Comment

Tentative diagnosis: Compulsive promiscuousness, and sexual hyperactivity. Venereal disease.

For additional comments, see below.

KAMALO : Y TÁMINYK

Preliminary considerations.—According to Ahma Huma : re, the term kamalo : y denotes a promiscuous and psychopathic woman (Devereux, 1948 f), while the term táminyk means "too much" or "excess." A woman suffering from kamalo : y táminyk is, however, not necessarily also an obnoxious and aggressive person. Informants knew of women, who, though extremely promiscuous, were, at the same time, amiable, kindly, and industrious, and, therefore, very different from the ethically obnoxious kamalo : y. Tcatc readily stated that my description of such women as "a bad lot, but a good sort," could

---

[62] He was the uncle of C. M., who was living around Parker at that time, and who is the stepfather of the juvenile delinquent discussed in Case 77.

[63] This case may have led to the belief (Devereux, 1948 g) that castration is fatal to the human male.

[64] At this point I realized that Tcatc had been working with me for several hours in a row, without any break in the form of the kind of banter which this lively octogenarian seemed to enjoy a great deal. I therefore said: "Don't I always ask nice and clean questions?" Tcatc's eyes began to sparkle and she replied with a smile: "Maybe others would not tell you such things. Maybe I am crazy to tell you." I replied quite seriously: "No, you are not crazy. You are simply my friend and that is why you tell me these things . . . to help me with my work." The purpose of these remarks was to humor Tcatc, who liked to pretend that she was reluctant to discuss sexual matters. The incident is cited as an example of field methods adapted to the specific temperament of a tribe, and to a typical member of the tribe.

very well be applied to one of her acquaintances, whose neurosis she diagnosed as kamalo:y tâminyk. Ahma Huma:re and Hivsu: Tupo:ma also mentioned this type of woman quite spontaneously.

Etiology.—The shaman Ahma Huma:re volunteered the information that this disease was similar to ya tcahaetk which, as stated above, is caused by an excessive sexual urge, which no amount of masturbation and coitus can satiate.

Symptomatology.—According to Ahma Huma:re, "People who do not think of their homes, and do not care for anything except running around and sex, are said to be yamomk (insane). The kamalo:y tâminyk illness is very similar to ya tcahaetk. Regardless of whether a person suffering from kamalo:y tâminyk gets married or stays single, he will be ya tcahaetk." According to Hivsu:Tupo:ma, "Such a woman is constantly in a state of sexual excitement bordering on orgasm. This condition, which is complicated by the retention of urine,[65] is due to coital dreams. Such patients have dream-orgasms without dream-pollutions." [66] Tcatc also described this illness in similar, though less specific terms: "People try to keep away from such a person. I personally know of no one who has kamalo:y tâminyk, but I have heard of such people. Nowadays one no longer meets such persons. Nowadays groups of people of both sexes go on drinking bouts and cohabit promiscuously, hardly knowing what they are doing. Thus, we no longer see extremes of sexual desire. When I was young, people behaved better. They had respect for each other, but now drinking has come in and things have changed. Nowadays I myself joke with men about this and that,[67] but when I was young I was afraid of sexual relations and also afraid to marry."

Summary.—The Mohave rate kamalo:y tâminyk as a psychosis. According to Ahma Huma:re, such people are yamomk (insane). "It is a true insanity, like hi:wa itck" (pt. 3, pp. 91–106). Tcatc also stated that such extremes of sexual desire were a form of yamomk.

Therapy.—According to Hivsu:Tupo:ma, shamans are sometimes asked to treat persons suffering from kamalo:y tâminyk, and their cures are said to be effective.

Tentative diagnosis.—Nymphomania; compulsive promiscuousness due to orgastic frigidity.

The informants clearly specified that such a woman is unable to discharge her sexual tensions either through coitus or through mastur-

---

[65] Mohave women sometimes void their urine either during orgasm, or immediately afterward (Devereux, 1950 a). This also occurs in Micronesia, etc. (Devereux, 1958 a).

[66] According to Ferenczi (1926), it is possible to have dream-orgasm without pollution, and vice versa.

[67] This is an indirect reference to her bantering conversations with me cited above (footnote 64).

bation. This indicates orgastic frigidity, which is almost always an outstanding and typical characteristic of nymphomaniacs, who can experience extremely intense excitement without being able to achieve an orgasm. Hence, they are driven to cohabit with many men, being constantly on the lookout for a male who can give them an orgasm, but never finding because their failure to reach a climax is psychologically determined.

Tcatc's spontaneous remark, that she was afraid of intercourse in her youth, and that the women of the older generation were better behaved, suggests an appreciable traditional (cultural) inhibition of the young Mohave woman's orgastic potentialities. Her comment, that this disease does not occur in the drinking and sexually dissolute younger generation has two—not necessarily mutually exclusive— implications: it suggests, first of all, that there occurred a breakdown of traditional internal inhibitions, not only to the point where orgasm can be readily achieved, but to the point where it can be achieved with anyone, including even the most casual partners. It may also imply that, as a result of drinking to excess, inhibitions which would operate in a state of sobriety are temporarily suspended, permitting orgasm to take place. This inference agrees with the well-known psychiatric epigram: "The superego is soluble in alcohol." (See Appendix, pp. 505–548.)

Kamalo: y táminyk, also reported from the Diegueño by Toffelmier and Luomala (1936), appears to be a variety of ya tcahaetk, but, unlike that disease, seems to occur only in women.

INSANITY RESULTING FROM MAGICAL COURTSHIP

Preliminary comment.—The shaman Hivsu: Tupo: ma called this condition nepu: k, an expression that my linguistic informant, Pulyi: k, failed to recognize. This may possibly indicate that "nepu: k" is simply a typical Mohave compression of several words forming a technical term, the way hiwey lak is sometimes abbreviated to weylak.[68] Pulyi: k agreed, however, that love magic exists, but specified that it did not include helticáthom (see further below, for a contrary statement).

---

[68] Similar compressions or abbreviations are used also in designating some individual who has a complicated name, made up of several words. In such cases he is commonly referred to either by one of the words only, or else by a two- or three-syllable word, made up of the last syllable(s) of one word and the first syllable(s) of the next word. Thus, the name of the mythical personage Hukthar Havi: yo was recorded by Kroeber (1948) as "Tharavlyo." Another type of compression occurs in songs, which often consist not of complete sentences, but only of "key words." In addition, in order to fit the text to the rhythm of the melody, already mutilated words may be further split up, by attaching their first syllable(s) to the preceding word and their last syllable(s) to the next word, to such an extent that no one may be able to unscramble the carefully recorded song of a singer. This was shown when a linguistic informant failed to unscramble the alyha: (transvestite=coward) initiation song dictated to the writer by Nyahwe: ra with the help of Hivsu: Tupo :ma (Devereux, 1937 b).

Hivsu: Tupo : ma's statement.—Shamans, especially those who specialize in the cure of so-called venereal diseases (hiku: pk and hiwey lak) are able to fascinate the objects of their sexual desires, regardless of whether these persons are heterosexual or homosexual (Devereux, 1937 b) love objects.[69] The shaman uses this power solely for the purpose of winning someone's affection and never for the purpose of keeping his wife, even when he knows that some other shaman, who seeks to seduce his wife, uses this form of love magic. If another shaman pursues his wife, he just keeps his peace, the way other men do. In fact, the shaman does not even use his status or power to become a domestic tyrant. The older shaman, especially, is sometimes inclined to use his powers, which he received from Avikwame, to win the love of a girl or of a woman. He can send out his power to steal a woman's love. Even though she might be a good woman, who has had no affairs, he can spoil her disposition and make her dislike everyone except himself. She might do for him things which she might never have done otherwise. Through his power he seems transformed in her eyes; he seems more handsome to her than he really is. Whenever she sees him, she is unable to turn her eyes from him, and wishes to be with him. No matter where she is, or who sees her actions, she turns her head toward him, and watches him almost against her will. Eventually he visits her and tells her that he heard of her strange behavior. She will then make all sorts of excuses and will never admit that he affects her in any way. Nonetheless, she will dream of him, and have fainting spells in the morning (Case 49). The shaman will continue to visit her in person until, in the end, she runs away with him. Then he will take his power back again and she will once more be the good woman she used to be. It is, however, not always safe to try this magic, because some shamans, who do not have full control over their power, might, later on, be unable to break the spell by taking back their power. If this happens, the woman goes insane, because his power just remains in her heart. [At this point interpreter Hama: Utce: interrupted Hivsu: Tupo: ma's account and related Case 18. Hivsu: Tupo: ma then resumed his story.] The relatives of the woman will, of course, seek to cure her, especially if she hasn't, as yet, gone to live with the shaman who bewitched her. They will ask a qualified shaman to cure her, by extracting the spellbinder's power and throwing it away. They might ask, e. g., (Hispan Himith) Tcilyetcilye (a shaman living in Needles, Calif., who claims to be able to cure this ailment) to treat her. The spellbinder will not seek to oppose the cure by magical means; i. e., the woman will not become a kind of battleground between the witch and the therapist. Furthermore, should the woman recover, the witch will not seek to fascinate her a second time. Also, regardless of whether the treatment is successful or not, once treatment is begun the woman can no longe hope to become the wife of the witch, because he would refuse to marry her.

If the shamanistic treatment is unsuccessful, the woman's relatives may call upon the spellbinder, and urge him to release the woman from his spell. The witch may, or may not, comply with this request. If he refuses to release her from the spell, or to cure here, her family will have her treated by still another shaman. A shaman usually practices love magic only on his own behalf, although he may use his powers also on behalf of a friend, either free of charge, or else for an honorarium, which usually consists of either a horse or a certain quantity of beads.

---

[69] Shamans do not have special sexual privileges. Apart from curing diseases related to sex, their only special duty in connection with sexual life is the distribution of sexually eligible prisoners to marriageable members of the tribe.

On the whole, the fascination resulting from such witchcraft is apparently halfway between the transitory fascination exerted by young shamans who wish to show off their newly acquired powers (Devereux, 1937 c), and the form of witchcraft that leads to neurotic sexual excesses. (See pt. 2, pp. 87–89.)

At the same time, this condition also appears to be related to courtship through an intermediary. According to information obtained by Hama: Utce: from Pulyi:k, and communicated to me in a recent letter (June 27, 1957)—

The word you ask about has two meanings:

1. Where one of two pals or chums will see someone he thinks would be a good mate for the other and will talk for that someone and do everything in his power to get the two together, this is called heltcáthom, meaning: Trying to bring the two together.

2. Hi:wa heltcáthom: Where a medicine man uses his power to turn one's heart to him and makes him or her fall in love with him. It really isn't love, but they are in their [sic!] power and are crazy enough about them to do anything from (sic!) them, even to dying for them. (Cf. pt. 7, pp. 383–386.)

In the first instance, two are brought together by an intermediary. In the second case the heart (hi:wa) is apparently the intermediary, i. e., the shaman's power, as it impinges upon the woman's heart. The person under the shaman's love spell is, literally, in the state known as "sexual thralldom," and the witchcraft element is emphasized by the thrall's willingness to die—presumably by witchcraft—so as to belong forever to the witch.[70]

CASE 18 (Informant Hama: Utce:):

My cousin married a man who was, at that time, officially a Christian. This man was generally believed to be a shaman, though he himself never admitted it. Eventually my cousin became ill and was brought to the reservation hospital. However, the doctor was unable to cure her. She was just plain goofy. Maybe she had reached menopause.[71] Then we took her to a shaman, who managed to help her. My cousin had such a temper, that her husband often remarked that he would never again marry a member of the Kunyii:th gens, which has the reputation of being very quick tempered. When I heard him talk that way, I said, "I, for one, will never marry you,"[72] but people who heard me, promptly

---

[70] It may be significant that Hama: Utce:, whose English is excellent, and who usually distinguishes carefully between singular and plural, began item 2, above, by speaking of a medicine man and then consistently used the third person plural pronoun (they, them) when referring to the medicine man (singular). This may conceivably indicate that she views the shaman's person and the shaman's power as plural, especially in a context where this power is a courtship intermediary. This suggestion is, of course, definitely speculative.

[71] Most old-fashioned Mohave deny the occurrence of menopausal emotional disturbances (Devereux, 1950 g). This informant was, however, quite acculturated.

[72] Interpreter made this remark because the Mohave believe that divorced and widowed persons tend to marry repeatedly into the same family or gens. At the same time her remark also voiced her claim to membership in the Kunyii:th gens, which is not a valid one, since, on her father's side, she is (partly ?) of white ancestry.

warned me not to talk that way: "He is a shaman. He might bewitch you, so that you will fall in love with him."

Comment

Tentative diagnosis.—M. A. I. Nettle, M. D., stated that this woman was either a hypochondriac, or else had a toxic psychosis caused by some kind of gall-bladder condition. She was never properly diagnosed, because she left the hospital before all diagnostic tests were completed.

It is not easy to decide why the interpreter felt impelled to interrupt the informant at a certain point of his narrative. The most plausible explanation is that she told this story in order to show that she, herself, had once incurred the risk of being subjected to love magic. This explanation is, of course, based upon the assumption that the conscious climax of the story is the threat that she, too, may be betwitched by a shaman. It is, however, also possible to suggest that the real, though unconscious, climax of the story is the cousin's illness. If that is so, then Hama: Utce: 's story, especially when viewed against the background of that portion of Hivsu: Tupo: ma's statement which immediately preceded her interruption, seems to hint at the existence of a latent belief that a woman's constant association with her shamanistic husband may affect her adversely, exactly the way close association with aliens may cause a Mohave to contract the ahwe: hahnok or ahwe: nyevedhi: ailments (pt. 4, pp. 128–150). This, partly speculative, inference is indirectly supported by two facts: On the one hand, the man in question, though reputed to be a shaman, never admitted publicly that he possessed shamanistic powers and did not use these alleged powers openly, although, according to Mohave belief, such self-restraint would predispose him to attacks of insanity and to complex psychosomatic illnesses (pt. 2, pp. 57–71). On the other hand, the Mohave believe that witches are especially prone to start their career of evildoing by first bewitching members of their own families, since, except for a fee (Devereux, 1948 h), shamans usually bewitch only those whom they both love and hate (Devereux, 1937 c).

The illness just described was, as we saw, thought to be a result of magical courtship, which seems to create a state of mind sometimes designated by the technical term "sexual thralldom," or, more colloquially, by the expression "being madly and helplessly in love." The fact that the case history suggests an altogether different kind of diagnosis even in terms of Mohave thought— i. e., the possibility that a shaman's wife may be adversely affected by his power—simply shows the difficulties and confusions that may arise in the study of unsystematic "primitive science." Be that as it may, the fact that the Mohave consider excessive emotional involvements a form of madness, fully accords with their reaction to the stories of Tristan and Isolde and of Romeo and Juliet. The audience seemed disgusted by these extreme manifestations of love, and Hama: Utce: remarked: "If a Mohave were running around in the bushes acting that way, someone might knock him on the head." Indeed, the Mohave are more inclined to be genuinely and lastingly fond of many people, than to "go overboard" for a single person, be he lover, husband, relative, or friend. This relatively homogeneous diffusion of the libido over a number of persons appears to be a general characteristic of many primitive groups (Devereux, 1939 a, 1942 d).

The warning issued to Hama: Utce: that, as a result of her challenging remarks, she could become the object of an irresistible magical courtship, may be partly related to the Mohave belief, that if a girl wantonly speaks ill of a man, "she is as good as his." (Devereux, 1950 a).

It is noteworthy that female shamans do not seem to resort to love magic, unless they also happen to be lesbians, who do not find it easy to secure sex partners (Devereux, 1937 b). (Cf., however, Case 49.)

This illness appears to be related also to sexual insanity due to witchcraft (see below) and to general insanity due to witchcraft (pt. 4, pp. 195–202).

INSANITY CAUSED BY INCEST

Although the Mohave did not mention a specific disease entity caused by incest, which automatically means also "incest with a witch" (Devereux, 1939 a), they reported a case of insanity caused by incest, whose symptoms resembled those found in various ghost diseases.

CASE 19 (Informant: Hivsu: Tupo: ma):

The shaman Uto: h (whom others call Tcamadhuly Vaha:) of the Nyoltc gens, his wife O: otc, their two married daughters (both named Nyoltc), and their two sons-in-law lived in the same house. One night, for no known reason, Uto: h cohabited with his younger daughter. Maybe he was crazy. What the rest of the family, including the daughter's children, were doing at that time is not known. The girl was half asleep and—like some other primitive women (see section on Sudhu: rk, pt. 2 p. 77)—thought the man approaching her was her husband. She therefore did not wake up completely, but let the man perform intercourse. When she finally realized that the man was her father, she sat up in bed and cried until dawn. This happened about 40 years ago (1892?). At that time Uto: h was about 40 years old and his daughter about 20. He was not punished, but was ostracized and held to be worse than a dog. This experience did not affect Uto: h's mind, but his daughter became practically psychotic. She thought that someone had bewitched her. She sat and spat about her, with an odd expression in her eyes. She died 2 years later. Her mother and older sister also began to behave queerly. In the end, they too became mentally deranged and died within a few years. At present only a son of the older daughter is still alive. His name is Nakue Mahay and he lives in Yuma. The rest of the family is extinct, as so often happens when there is incest in the family. I think this must have been a weak-minded family.

Comment

Mohave diagnosis: The symptoms cited are also found in various ghost diseases: stupor, spitting (indicative of the infantile delusion of having swallowed an evil and impregnating substance), etc. The self-diagnosis "witchcraft" may have been determined by the belief that only witches are incestuous. The insanity and death of the other female members of the family would also support this diagnosis, since witches preferably bewitch their own kin.

Tentative diagnosis: Psychogenic depression caused by trauma.

SEXUAL INSANITY RESULTING FROM WITCHCRAFT

Preliminary comment.—The madness which results from witchcraft differs from that induced by love magic. The latter is caused by a shaman's attempt to attract the love of a woman by magical means; the former is the result of a seemingly wanton magical aggression. Love magic seeks to divert a woman's love from her current sweetheart or husband to her shamanistic suitor, without causing her to misbehave sexually, except for a routine changing of her bed partner—a trifling matter in Mohave society. By contrast, a certain type of witchcraft can induce completely chaotic sexual misbehavior, which may even include sexual acts with animals (Devereux, 1948 g), but does not seem to produce any sexual advantage for the witch himself. One is reminded here of a similar act of wanton mischief, mentioned in Graeco-Roman myths. Hippolytus, the bastard son of Theseus and Antiope, was indifferent to love and exclusively devoted to the cult of chaste Artemis. This so offended Aphrodite that she caused Theseus' wife—the previously virtuous Phaedra—to fall incestuously in love with her stepson Hippolytus. When the horrified youth rejected her advances, she tore her clothes, screamed that she was being raped, and hanged herself. Misled by Phaedra's calumnies, Theseus then cursed his innocent son, which caused Hippolytus to die in a horrible, and supernaturally caused, accident.[73]

Tcatc's statement: There is something else that shamans will do. People sometimes see in their dreams a shaman who is bewitching (matadha : uk) them. You know, the way you see your sweetheart in your dreams. Sometimes they even bring some kind of animal into the woman's dreams. They also make the dreamer lie (though not necessarily cohabit) with a woman in his dream, or else they make him dream of using a dog or some other animal sexually.[74] Then they wake up. Ever after the dreamer always talks and thinks about that. In the end people who have such dreams are so much affected by them that they want to copulate with anyone—even with animals. [I heard from a Yuma woman, that a Yuma girl cohabited with a jackass. Is the condition you just described identical with the bestiality of young shamans who cohabit with donkeys and even with hens?] No. The zoophilia of shamans is not a form of insanity. They do such things simply because they are shamans (kwathidhe:) or braves (kwanàmi : hye). The man who was here a moment ago and brought us some ice—Madhi : ly of the Mah gens [75]—is a shaman. I was wondering whether, if he heard me talk about shamans, he would "land on my bottom" (i. e., hit me). He is also a brave. Should an epidemic come on the tribe, and should he find out who had caused it, he would just go and kill the witch.

No actual case history was known to this informant, and a subsequent informant, Pulyi : k, even said that he knew nothing of insanity caused by witchcraft.

There is also no information on whether female shamans, too, practice this type of witchcraft.

---

[73] Apollodorus: *Epitome;* Diodorus Siculus; Hyginus: *Fabulae;* Ovid: *Heroides;* Pausanias; Seneca: *Hippolytus;* etc.
[74] There are occasional instances of zoophilia (Devereux, 1948 g).
[75] This man belonged to a probably psychopathic family (pt. 5, pp. 245–247).

This disorder is also related to the derangements described in part 2, pages 83–87, and part 4, pages 195–202.

APPENDIX: THE PERVERSIONS

The present monograph does not include accounts of various Mohave perversions, since they were already described by me in a series of previously published articles. Mohave perversions include: masturbation (1950 c), mutual masturbation (1950 c), fellatio but not cunnilingus (1947 a, 1950 a), anal intercourse (1950 a, 1951 e), limited exhibitionism (1950 a), limited voyeurism (1950 a), group cohabitation (1948 i, 1950 a), punitive mass rape (1948 f), incest (1939 a), male and female transvestitism and homosexuality (1937 b), bestiality (1948 g), and extreme obscenity of speech and gesture (1951 c). One may also cite under this heading a type of female promiscuousness that differs from the nymphomania of otherwise kindly women, and is practiced by the so-called kamalo:y— who are not only promiscuous but also otherwise objectionable and aggressive (1948 f).

Several forms of perversion appear to be absent in Mohave society. They are: cunnilingus, sadism, masochism, fetichism, homosexual paedophilia, gerontophilia, true exhibitionism and voyeurism, frottage, the collection of sexual trophies (e. g., snipping hair, etc.), and certain other, more complicated, forms of perversion reported in psychiatric literature.

PART 3. MOOD DISTURBANCES

THE "HEART" NEUROSES

Three types of partly psychosomatic neuroses known to the Mohave are designated by terms containing the word "heart" (hi:wa), presumably because the Mohave think of the heart not only as an organ, but also as the seat of emotions. It may be suggested, in passing, that the widespread, though not universal, tendency to think of the heart as connected with the emotions may be due to the fact that certain persons react to emotional stress with precordial anxiety, tachycardia, and other disturbances of the cardiovascular system, just as other people react to emotional stress, e. g., with disturbances of the gastrointestinal tract.[76] The occurrence of the latter reaction pattern of the autonomous nervous system to emotional stress among the Mohave is probably responsible for the fact that a series of psychosomatic illnesses are grouped together under the general heading of hiwey lak (anus pain) (pt. 4, pp. 150–175).

A further attribute of the heart is conscience. Thus, the dictates of a man's better self (ego-ideal, rather than super-ego) are denoted by the term hi:wantc kinyai:m (heart does) or hi:wantc hidhu:m, or hi:wantc haniym, all of which can be freely translated as "the heart does" or "the heart says" or "the dictates of the heart"—i. e., man's better nature. Since, unlike the Chinese (Devereux, 1944 a) etc., the Mohave believe human nature to be good, rather than inherently corrupt, if one but listens to one's heart, one is impelled to do good deeds. Thus Case 101 shows that when a bewitched person became ill, the victim's family immediately asked the witch to perform a cure, because they hoped that the witch would yield to his hi:wantc kinyai:m, i. e., that he would follow the dictates of his heart or conscience.

There appear to be three main types of "heart neuroses"—i. e., three types of emotional stress to which people react, at least in principle, with their hearts. Of course, in reality the cases cited did

---

[76] It may even be possible to classify various ethnic groups in terms of the particular autonomous nervous system function(s) by means of which they react to emotional stress. Thus, the Sedang Moi of Indochina (Devereux, MS., 1933–34) seem to react to stress chiefly with the gastrointestinal tract, which may explain why they believe the liver to be the seat of emotions. The Greek seem to have reacted to emotional stress in several ways; witness their theory of temperaments: Sanguine (cardiovascular), phlegmatic (= mucus, respiratory tract, and mucous membrane reactions), melancholic (=black bile, gastrointestinal tract), and choleric (=yellow bile, gastrointestinal tract).

not always involve primarily cardiovascular reactions to emotional stress. The fact that they were nonetheless diagnosed as disorders of the hi: wa (heart) simply shows that, in Mohave psychiatry, the term "hi: wa" has lost its specific and literal cardiovascular connotation and acquired the broader meaning of one type of psychosomatic reaction to emotional stress. In the same way our own term "hysteria" (from: hystera=uterus) has also lost its original anatomical connotation, so that this technical term is now simply a holdover from an obsolete theory of hysteria.[77]

Strictly speaking, there are only three genuine hi: wa disorders:

(A) Hi: wa itck, or else hi: wa itce itc hi: m=heartbreak. (Hi: wa suh itck=he has heartbreak.)

(B) Hi: wa mava: rkh.

(C) Hi: wa hisa: kh= (roughly) heart rot.

At the same time, the emotional component of psychiatric illness is so routinely correlated with the "heart" that:

(A) Laymen tend to apply the nontechnical term "Hi: walyk yamomk hi: m" to almost any mild emotional or neurotic disturbance. This term, first mentioned by Tcatc, who—significantly—was not a shaman, was originally translated as "in-his-heart a-little-crazy," and was retranslated by the linguistic informant Pulyi: k as "in-his-heart will-be-crazy (or is-crazy)."

(B) Incidental references to the patient's hi: wa (heart), or to "cardiac" symptoms, occur even in shamanistic—i. e., supposedly "technical"— descriptions of a variety of psychiatric conditions, which definitely do not rate as disorders belonging to the "hi: wa" group.

HI: WA ITCK (HI: WA ITCE ITC HIM)

The type of subjective experiences about to be described is recognized as abnormal by the Mohave themselves, who apply to it the term "hi: wa itck." This term may be freely translated as "heartbreak" and is applied to certain psychotic, or possibly neurotic, episodes, which occur chiefly when an elderly Mohave man is deserted by his young wife. It rarely follows the desertion of a Mohave husband by a wife belonging to his own age group.

The social background.—Mohave marriages are extremely unstable, and, like all other interpersonal relations in that tribe, are characterized by only moderate object-cathexis (Devereux 1939 a, 1942 d). Marriage implies little more than common residence and continued sexual relations, which, in theory, should be limited to married couples. Divorce means simply that one of the spouses moves out

---

[77] It is interesting to recall in this context that when Freud first spoke of hysteria in men, a disingenuous critic ridiculed his views by resorting to the footless etymological argument that men could not have hysteria, since they had no uterus. Cf. also Usener's (1896) theory, that the most ancient Gods are those whose names have become true personal names and no longer have a known meaning.

(Nettle, MS., n. d.). The actual process of moving out is sometimes accompanied by much hubbub (Kroeber, 1925 b). Custom demands, however, that, once the divorce is completed, both partners accept it casually. As a rule, the Mohave comply with this cultural injunction. As stated elsewhere (Devereux, 1950 f), the socialization of the Mohave child occurs early in life, so that, thereafter, his libido and aggressions are distributed relatively homogeneously over the tribe as a whole. Hence, no single individual is invested with an unusually large and distinctive amount of object cathexis. An example to the contrary is afforded by the alleged marital fidelity of twins. This was attributed elsewhere (Devereux, 1941) to the fact that the preferential treatment meted out to twins, and a number of other characteristic events of their early lives, delay their socialization, and condition them to the formation of intense attachments. Another atypical example is that of persons who commit incest. I have tried to show (Devereux, 1939 a) that the Mohave interpret incest as a manifestation of an individual's unwillingness or inability to become detached from his proximate family, and to partake, through emotional socialization, in the complex give-and-take pattern of tribal relations.

A corollary of this attitude is the Mohave evaluation of "romantic love." The tale of Tristan and Isolde, and of Romeo and Juliet, which I related to them, caused a great deal of consternation. As for Tcatc, she once smilingly remarked: "You sigh every time you mention your sweetheart." The behavior of the lovelorn is considered undignified and unworthy of an adult, as soon as the breach is final. Before divorce occurs, the husband (or wife) may exhibit intense jealousy and even rage (Case 24). He may even compel his wife to submit to an examination of her private parts, for evidences of intercourse, and may even threaten to shoot her. In brief, he may go to great lengths in his attempts to preserve the status quo, without being unduly hampered by possible adverse reactions on the part of the group (Davis, 1936).

However, once the bond is broken, the finality of the new situation must be, and mostly is, accepted with equanimity. It is very seldom indeed that, acting in cold blood, a man paints his face black, like a warrior on the warpath, and, arms in hand, attempts to take revenge on the man who abducted his wife. As a rule, this procedure is only resorted to half jocularly, and one man, married to a passive male homosexual who deserted him, actually attempted to do this just to give the tribe something to laugh about (Devereux, 1937 b). This does not mean, of course, that even a deserted husband, who is supposed to display more equanimity than a deserted wife, shows no grief reaction whatsoever. In fact, in at least one case the deserted husband killed his ex-wife's new husband. These, however, are exceptions and are viewed by the Mohave themselves not as psychotic behavior, but as deplorable breaches of decorum.

The only serious clashes that may and do occur between divorced people pertain to claims of paternity, which are not easily validated, because certain Mohave theories postulate the possibility of changing the embryo's affiliation through subsequent intercourse with the pregnant woman (Devereux, 1937 d, 1949 c). Yet, because of the cultural stress laid on tribal continuity (Kroeber, 1925 a), paternity claims sometimes lead to severe clashes, involving, in one instance at least, actual murder (Case 131). Since this type of clash fits the general Mohave pattern, the participants, regardless of how wrought up they may be, are not held to be insane.

In brief, the Mohave ridicule romantic love in its more extreme manifestations, and demand that the deserted lover or spouse accept the situation as soon as the breach seems final. At the same time, their disapproval is tempered by a genuine compassion for those who are severely traumatized by the loss of a love object. The resultant of these two basic attitudes is a complex and delicately balanced ambivalence, which finds a formal expression in a well-known Mohave tale belonging to the class of the so-called Orpheus myths. Since the Halyec Matcoo: tâ legend was published elsewhere (Devereux, 1948 h), it will suffice to summarize here its most relevant features.

"Halyec Matcoo: tâ".—When a certain village was almost wiped out by an epidemic, the one surviving adult man found a baby girl clinging to her dead mother. He reared her and decided to marry her. Actuated by pride in his lovely bride, he prepared to give a great wedding feast. This party was attended also by a young married man, Halyec Matcoo: tâ, who fell in love with the bride-to-be, and abducted her, whereupon the jeering guests broke the old man's property and dispersed. The jilted man became depressed, and dispatched two evil shamans in pursuit of the fugitives, instructing them to bewitch the girl. They found her grinding corn for her husband, and killed her by magic. Her death "ended the old man's hi: wa itck." Distressed by the death of his young wife, the successful suitor now became afflicted with hi: wa itck. After many complicated adventures, involving his death by drowning while too fascinated by a vision of his dead wife to pay any attention to navigation hazards, and involving his resurrection as well, he bungled his chance to recover his dead wife, by being overly eager to seize her as yet half-formed reincarnated body. He then returned to his first wife, ill in body and sorely depressed. When his first wife and their son broke a taboo, whose observance would have led to his recovery, he turned into a bull-snake, amidst thunder in the hut.

Pathogenesis:

Hilyera Anyay's statement.—A man and a woman who are married and seem to be getting along well with each other, may sometimes leave each other for other spouses. On hearing of this new marriage, the deserted spouse may become afflicted with hi: wa itck, because of his great love for the departed spouse. Eventually they get over such attacks by themselves and are all right once more. Had they not loved each other so much when they married, and even when they separated, no hi: wa itck would have occurred. Hi: wa itck occurs in young people as well as in the old. [However, on being pressed, informant could recall no instance involving young couples.] When it occurs in a young person, it usually involves a young (?) person who is married to an older one. Hi: wa itck does not occur in good marriages, which last until one of the partners is dead. (But cf. below.) (Q) Hi: wa itck also occurs in women, but I have heard mainly of men who had it. [Interpreter commented: "When deserted, women fight, while men do crazy things."] [78] Women fight when they are deserted, but men do all sorts of funny things. Some cut off their hair, because they say that they are going to die, while others even kill horses (i. e., as at funerals, incestuous marriages, or after losing an eye). Still others say that they are going to die. I faintly recall one case . . . but not well enough to describe it, though I saw it happen. (Q) People do not kill themselves because of hi: wa itck.

Ahma Huma: re's statement.—I must laugh when I tell you about hi: wa itck. In days of old the parents of a girl often advised her to marry an older man, because he would think more of his home and of the things he could do for his wife, than he thought of himself (Devereux, 1951 f). Some such marriages were a success. In a few cases, however, the young bride did not find her old husband to her liking, and eventually deserted him for a man nearer her own age. On being informed of his former wife's new marriage, the old man would then have hi: wa itck. It would seem as though he did not know what to do. He would move from place to place. He would not know where he was going, nor what he wanted to do. When women get hi: wa itck they walk around and do not stay home. Some of them fight their rivals. Such things happen only when one of the spouses loves deeply and the other does not. The loving spouse loves more than he (or she) can help it.

Hivsu: Tupo: ma's statement.—The Mohave were not supposed to get upset about such things as desertions. A man might fight with his wife while she was staying with him, but, once the wife left, the man was supposed to forget about her. Sometimes, however, a man would go out and take revenge, either personally, or else by bribing an evil shaman to bewitch the faithless wife or her new husband. Occasionally a man went to fight his rival, just as a lark. One man even did that when his transvestite male "wife" left him (Devereux, 1937 b). Women were not obliged to show a similar self-control and therefore did not develop hi: wa itck. A woman could go and fight with her lucky rival (and/or, according to Tcatc, also with the rival's relatives). When a woman set out to fight her rival, many people went along, to enjoy the fun. A male transvestite also did that; he could do it because he could act like a woman. (A female transvestite also tried to threaten her (male) rival, Case 105.) (Devereux, 1937 b.)

Tcatc's statement.—Some people alternate between excitement and depression. This is caused by too much worrying. It goes to such an extreme that they are almost out of their minds. When people are very deeply in love, even though they be far apart, they see each other, because of their great love. You should know that, since you are so much in love. Among the Mohave there are cases of men loving their women so much that it causes their death . . . their heart breaks. Such cases do not occur among the unmarried, but among the married only. People marry those whom they love very much, and if the woman then starts going with someone else, it breaks the man's heart. They keep on living with her until she deserts them, because they cannot help loving her, even

---

[78] Characteristically enough, the only women I know who falsely) claimed to have had an attack of hi : wa itck, was O: otc, whom public opinion defined as a kamalo : y, i.e., as a "phallic" and dissolute person (Devereux, 1948 f).

though she hurts them. Recently a few white men even went so far as to commit suicide.[79] Hi : wa itck is generally limited to cases in which an older man marries a younger girl. The bride's father or mother may have advised her to marry an old man, because older people are more likely to be faithful to their wives. They also know more about planting (by which, be it understood, the bride's parents would profit), and they had mature notions about marriage. They were less likely to desert their wives (Devereux, 1951 f). Such a marriage was not always successful, however. If it broke up, the old man got hi : wa itck. His relatives would then advise him to forget about his faithless wife, and to think of some other girl. They would tell him that thinking of the deserting wife would make him feel just that much worse. They did not doctor such cases.

These reactions represent the views of four Mohave competent to evaluate the content of their culture. Although the data converge remarkably in almost every respect, they clearly reflect also the variety of viewpoints and emphases that a given cultural complex may be used to illustrate, depending on the personalities and subjective experiences of the informants. Three of these four informants had had subjective experiences that, to the psychiatrist, are symptomatic of mental disorder, although to the Mohave themselves these shamans were relatively normal persons, as far as shamans can be considered normal. The fourth informant, Tcatc, had such a temper that she was often suspected of shamanistic proclivities, although she denied having had shamanistic or other unusual subjective experiences. Yet, all four informants clearly dissociated themselves from the psychological state of individuals experiencing hi : wa itck, and regarded it unanimously as a mental disorder (yamomk). Their attitude, which is one of mingled contempt and pity, is symptomatic of the reactions of the tribe as a whole, including individuals, like the interpreter, who were normal in every sense, Mohave, Western, and clinical. In brief, we are confronted here with a condition that the Mohave, as well as ourselves, recognize as abnormal, and that involves a certain amount of social and personal strain.

Hi: wa itck and suicide.—The Mohave distinguish sharply between hi : wa itck, which they consider a mental disorder, and suicide, with or without murder, due to disappointment in love, which they do not consider a form of insanity. Love suicides are recruited from the ranks of men only, and appear to be limited to marriages in which both spouses belong to the same age-group. Furthermore, suicides do not seem to occur *after* the breach has become final, and the woman has settled down with another man. Rather do they occur when there is a danger of desertion, or actual acts of infidelity (pt. 7, passim).

By contrast, mainly widows attempt to throw themselves on the funeral pyre of their deceased husbands (Devereux, 1942 a). This is often a mere gesture, so that, even though the widow is sometimes

---

[79] Tcatc's wording did not equate such suicides with hi : wa itck.

severely burned, no instance of actual death could be recorded. As regards men, one widower (Case 110) attempted funeral suicide, and one father (Case 111) tried to throw himself on the pyre of his son, whom his constant nagging had driven to suicide.

CASE MATERIAL

CASE 20 (Informants Tcatc and E. S.) :

Kaly Yahway (or Ahwaly) (war club, colloquially called "tomahawk" in English) of the Mo: the gens, was born "about 115 years ago (1823?) and died as an old man." The events about to be described occurred when he was roughly 45 years of age. He was originally married to a young girl who left him eventually, whereupon he became angry and began to say that he was constantly thinking of killing. He talked about that until he became insane (yamomk) with hi: wa itck. During his psychotic episode he painted his face black (as did a lesbian (Devereux, 1937 b)), like a warrior going on the warpath, and actually seemed to believe that he was going to war. People began to notice that he was acting "queer" and suspected that he had become a shaman. They were apparently mistaken in this, since he never cured anyone. I do not recall whether he ever made a recovery, but I am sure his insanity did not cause his death—he died of an ordinary illness.[80]

CASE 21 (Informants: Tcatc and E. S.) :

Amo: Nomak (mountain-goat lost) was a member of the Nyoltc gens, who died many years ago at an advanced age. He was already old when the episode about to be described took place. He had been married to a girl named Mo: the of that same gens, who was much younger than he was. One day she just "got up and left him, because she got tired of him." [At this point informant and interpreter began to speculate on whether she left him because she wanted a man with a larger penis, or whether she merely wanter a "stronger" (i. e. more potent) husband. No decision was reached.] He showed no untoward reaction, until news reached him that the girl had settled down with another man. He thereupon became "insane" (yamomk) from hi: wa itck. He cut off his long braids of hair, the way mourners do, and painted his face black. [Here interpreter remarked: "His cutting his hair off makes me laugh."] He went into the winterhouse (ava: hatcor), sat down, laid out his bow and arrows, and declared that he would kill anyone who tried to come in. This frightened people so much that no one dared to enter the house, and that is why no attempt was made to doctor him. [Here interpreter and informant laughed out loud.] He stayed in his house for 2 days. Then he made a spontaneous recovery. He even picked up the braids he had previously cut off, and tied them back to his remaining locks. [Interpreter and informant laughed. Interpreter said, "It seems funny now," but informant replied: "At that time it was not funny at all."]

CASE 22 (Informants: Tcatc and E. S.) :

Katcidhomp, of the O: otc gens, died half a century ago (1888) at Needles, Calif., at the approximate age of 50. He was about 30 years old when the following events took place at Parker, Ariz. He was married to a women his own age, Hualy, of the Hualy gens. They seem to have had two children, both of

---

[80] Tcatc then remarked teasingly that I, too, had hi :wa itck, because (by Mohave standards) I, too, was deeply in love at that time. (See below.)

whom had died. They had lived together for a long time. Then Hualy got tired of him and deserted him. Three days later she married another man named Hamthuly Kudhap (i.e., a kind of lizard, which lives on the mesa, split open). When he heard that she had married again, he became afflicted with hi: wa itck; he lost his appetite and neither ate nor slept for 3 days. During these 3 days he ran around constantly.

Starting from his house, he ran to a lake known in English as Twelve Mile Slough, and in Mohave as Nyakro: muhuer (iron railed, or fenced). Thence he would proceed to the Colorado River, and eventually return to his own house. He ran this circuit for 3 days, stopping once in a while at the houses of his relatives, but even though they tried to press food on him, he would not eat.[81] He was never doctored for this mental disorder, but made a spontaneous recovery. [Here I commented: "You women are the very devil!" Informant replied: "Your own girl must be hukthar." (This word means properly coyote, and, by extension, "crazy," but not, insane.)]

CASE 23:

Tii: ly Koráu: lyva of the Tii: ly gens died at the age of 50, a long time ago. She was married to a man younger than herself, and had two boys and a girl by him. She nagged her husband so much that, in the end, he resented it and left her. She was about 40 years old at that time. She showed no unusual reactions until she learned that her former husband had married again. Then she picked up a stick and went to her former husband's new residence, which sheltered not only this man but also his new wife, and some of his relatives, and "just beat up everybody in that damn place." Finally they caught her, held her down, took away her stick, and brought her back to her own home. She then shut herself up in her own house and cried all night. Finally she made a spontaneous recovery and married someone else 2 years later. The events just described occurred at Kave: ly, a place south of Parker. None of the immediate relatives of this woman are now alive. (This is the only accepted case of hi: wa itck in a female that came to my attention. O: otc's self-diagnosis was rejected by all (Devereux, 1948 f).)

Dubious cases.—I first heard the term "hi: wa itck" in 1938, although in 1936 I recorded numerous cases of suicide, many of them due to amorous disappointments but none of them following a final break. These suicide cases also include suicide-and-murder cases. The term "hi: wa itck" was not applied to them in 1936, nor, on specific inquiry, in 1938. This indicates that hi: wa itck is, to the Mohave mind, a clear-cut clinical entity, regardless of how it may appear to the modern clinical psychiatrist, who cannot fail to recognize deep affinities between hi: wa itck and cases of suicide caused by the loss of a love object.

INFORMAL THERAPY OF HI: WA ITCK

Although hi: wa itck represents a striking deviation from the norm, persons afflicted with this ailment were not treated by shamans,

---

[81] The Mohave usually fasted during ritual running and travel (McNichols, 1944). Cf. the use of ritual as symptom also in the haircutting episode (Case 21).

possibly because such attacks were of a relatively brief duration. On the other hand, relatives as well as friends sometimes attempted to talk things over with the depressed or agitated man, and provided what might be called "supportive therapy." Such conversations followed no set pattern. "People just said whatever seemed appropriate." We may assume, therefore, that these interviews probably revealed many of the subtler and more private shadings of Mohave attitudes toward life and love.

If this assumption is a correct one, a verbatim report of such a conversation would be very valuable to the student of ethnopsychiatry, since it would provide a direct glimpse of Mohave sentiment in action. It is quite obvious, however, that, even if the anthropologist knew of a case of hi: wa itck, he could not be present during such a conversation without profoundly affecting its course and content. On the other hand, attempts to obtain accounts of such conversations proved fruitless, because my informants kept on insisting that "people just said whatever was appropriate."

These circumstances oblige me to lay aside the anonymity of the scientist and to report verbatim three conversations that took place between my old friend Tcatc and myself at a time when, by Mohave standards, I myself was suffering from hi:wa itck. The example of Freud (1953) justifies self-revelation in the interest of science, especially since, from the scientific point of view, Tcatc's remarks, rather than mine, are the important ones. Moreover, whatever merit my study of the Mohave may possess is solely due to the fact that I did not view the Mohave as trait lists to be unscrambled, but as friends, who shared their lives with me, because I shared mine with them.

The following conversation took place at a time when I was in love with a girl who did not reciprocate my feelings. The conversation with Tcatc was taken down verbatim, in the course of the conversation itself, with my old friend Hama: Utce: acting as interpreter.

Tcatc: "You sigh every time you mention your sweetheart. If you go on like this, you might end up by killing yourself."

G. D.: (Misogynistic remark.)

Tcatc: "You are crazy to think that. Among the Mohave, the women blame the men for going crazy (with hi: wa itck) and feel that all men should be wiped off the face of the earth.[82] You must feel better now that you have said it."

G. D.: (Derogatory remark about the girl's behavior.)

---

[82] The assertion that Mohave women wish all men to be killed is utterly false. On the other hand, the fact that Tcatc made this sweeping statement, in order to make her point, is typically Mohave.

Tcatc: "Maybe I should not say this, but you are very much in love with her and she is not in love with you. Maybe that is why she turned you down in this manner."

G. D.: (Restatement of my preceding remark.)

Tcatc: "The best thing to do is to forget about her and think about another girl. All this makes you feel bad, and things don't seem right at the present time. If a Mohave feels that way, we say that he has hi: wa itck. When a Mohave has that disease, his friends could only advise him to forget about his girl and to think of another girl. I think that this girl has been lying to you all along. The best thing, therefore, is just to stop thinking about her, right now. You'll only feel worse if you keep on thinking about her."

G. D.: "I know you are right—but it is just like telling a sick man to get well. It does not help."

Tcatc: "You should put all your mind and all your heart into the work you are doing with us."

G. D.: "I do just that when I am working with you. But what am I to do when I am not working with you—in the evenings?"

Tcatc: "Surely you have at least the courage to forget her!"

G. D.: "I know I am fortunate to be with friends such as you during these sad weeks."

Tcatc: (Nodding and smiling) "That is what friends are for—to know each other."

G. D.: "You are a very good and wise old woman, and I like you very much."

Tcatc: "I have known you for a long time, and all the time I have known you, you have been very good and I like to see you happy about such things. In my time I have advised many a young Mohave to choose a happy marriage rather than seek to be despised for being in love with a worthless woman. If this girl is that way, then there is nothing you can do to change her. Look at me! I have not been married once only. When my husband left me for another woman, I still loved him, but I could not help it. Time will heal your heart too. You will be happy, and you will be my happy friend once more. If you keep on feeling this way, you might even get sick from too much work, though I hope you won't."

The next day—probably because of Tcatc's support—I felt considerably better about the whole matter, and teasingly told Tcatc that she must be a shaman, because she had cured me of my hi:wa itck. Tcatc replied, "This girl is to be pitied, rather than thought about. In my own grief, I never thought afterward about such things. They just happen—and that is all there is to it. It would have been useless for me to feel bad about it, because I never knew anyone who died of heartbreak." (Note the distinction between hi: wa itck and suicide!)

After a few more days the beneficial effects of the initial conversation wore off and I felt rather unhappy once more. I asked Hama: Utce: to mention this to Tcatc and to ask her whether she felt that a woman could be in love with two men at the same time, since the girl seemed to seesaw between another man and me.

Tcatc: "No, that is not possible, and yet, this is a strange situation: She could marry the other man and she might even think that she belongs to him, but part of her will always be with you."

G. D.: (Association with a shallow person will spoil her.)

Tcatc: "It won't spoil her. I myself never forgot my first husband." (On another occasion Tcatc stated that she refused to believe in a repetition of earthly life in the land of the dead (Devereux, 1937 a), because she did not wish to experience once more the pain of losing her first husband.)

G. D.: "Should I stop seeing her?"

Tcatc: "This girl is a kwathidh: (shaman) and so are you. That is why your souls are together. If you were to make up your mind not to see her again, and married someone else, you two would bewitch each other and the weaker one of the two would die, because you two would be thinking of each other all the time. It is a form of madness, called ahwe: nyevedhi: (pt. 4, pp. 128–150). I think she bewitched you and is still trying to get you, even though she is in love with the other man." (Ahwe: nyevedhi: was mentioned presumably because, unlike the girl, I was foreign born.)

G. D.: "Should I write her what you just told me?"

Tcatc: "Yes, why not?"

When, at a later date, I again teased Tcatc, saying that she was obviously a shaman, she replied: "You may think so, because of the things I tell you. At any rate, I like to think that I cured your hi:wa itck."

Comment

Hama: Utce: afterward assured me that Tcatc would have given precisely the same advice to any one of her young relatives who found himself in a similar predicament. "She often tells me that you are just like a favorite grandson to her" (Devereux, 1951 b). When I replied that I felt the same way about Tcatc, Hama: Utce: nodded and said: "She knows it." We may therefore assume that the conversation given above accurately reflects the Mohave attitude toward hi:wa itck. Hence, it is rather striking to note that, except for references to witchcraft, a conversation of this type could have taken place also in a purely Euro-American cultural setting, between a young man and a worldly, wise, and kindly woman of 80. Only such extraneous and culturally determined details as references to witchcraft, etc., tend to obscure the basic unity of human emotions revealed by this conversation.

This finding has a direct bearing upon the validity of culture-and-personality studies in general, since it causes one to wonder to what extent an undue emphasis on culturally determined modes of expression may distort our picture of human realities because of our tendency to stress—possibly superficial—differences, at the expense of basic similarities. This question cannot be answered in a decisive manner until many more conversations such as the one given above are recorded. In the last resort, and despite the real value of projective and other personality tests, the ultimate, most sensitive and most revealing, test of human nature is concrete interaction in the real situations of daily life, which is only partially duplicated by the transference-countertransference relationship obtaining in the psychoanalytic situation.

Be that as it may, I realize in retrospect that the above conversations—and all they imply in regard to the possibility of a nearly culture-free man-to-man communication between human beings belonging to different cultures—had a decisive influence on my subsequent diagnostic and, especially, therapeutic work with neurotic Plains Indians (Devereux, 1951 a, 1951 i, 1953 b).

INTERPRETATION

Regardless of the close and obvious affinity, which, from the viewpoint of psychiatry, may exist between hi: wa itck and suicide, a useful explanation must be made in terms of sociologically meaningful variables, which are defined analytically.

We must, first of all, distinguish between types of breaches in the marital or love relationship.

(a) *Marital vs. nonmarital love relationships.*—Hi: wa itck seems limited to married couples, while suicide, with or without murder, may occur also in premarital, extramarital, adulterous, and even incestuous love relationships.

(b) *Age discrepancies.*—In hi: wa itck, but not in suicide, one generally finds a great age difference between the spouses. This is rather significant, because the flightiness of young Mohave women often enables old Mohave women, and even inverts, to obtain desirable husbands from among the ranks of young men, who crave a stable home (Devereux, 1951 f). In such marriages the senior partner craves love, and gives security and comfort to the junior partner, often closing both eyes to the casual infidelities of the latter. It is, hence, very significant that it is almost invariably the senior spouse who becomes subject to attacks of hi: wa itck. The average Mohave

can always find some form of security by calling upon the hospitality
of his relatives, which is never denied to him. Finding love is a
more difficult undertaking.

On the other hand we note that love suicide, with or without
murder, generally occurs when both partners are of the same age,
regardless of whether the relationship is marital, nonmarital, adulterous, or even incestuous. In these instances we find no barter gratifying one partner's need for security and the other partner's need for
love. It is, furthermore, significant that in all cases of love suicide
the person committing suicide is the male. It can be stated with a
fair measure of confidence that this fact is connected with the
proverbial flightiness of Mohave women, which is admitted even by
the female members of the tribe. The situation can be further
clarified by discussing the means of action available to the individual
wishing to restore the status quo ante.

(c) *Infidelity* sometimes leads to suicide or else to violence, but
never to hi: wa itck. At this stage the husband may compel his
wife to submit to an examination of her private parts, threaten her
with violence, or induce a group of his friends to abduct and rape
her, by way of "teaching her a lesson" (Devereux, 1948 f). Conversely, the woman may fight with her husband and his paramour,
nag him, and otherwise manifest her displeasure. In this specific
situation the husband is given relatively more elbow room, although
on a permissive basis only. Yet, Mohave public opinion condemns
excessive jealousy in either spouse, especially if it is not elicited by
valid reasons.

(d) *Simple desertion* consists of leaving the family domicile, or
else, in love affairs, in the denial of previously enjoyed sexual privileges. In cases of simple desertion the woman is given a greater
latitude in her attempts to regain the affection of the departed husband than deserted husbands enjoy. Attempts to restore the status
quo are not hampered by public opinion, unless they involve extreme
manifestations of emotionality in the man (Case 24). Simple desertion, sometimes followed by casual affairs, but not by a new marriage,
leads to suicide (and, occasionally, also to suicide after murder) but,
apparently, never to hi: wa itck.

(e) *Desertion and remarriage.*—Only suicide Case 125 falls into
this group, which includes all instances of hi: wa itck. In these cases
the breach was considered final, although there are instances in which
a woman oscillates back and forth between two men, or a man lives
alternatingly with two women. Such cases are, however, exceptional,
and do not seem to involve great emotional investments. Desertion
followed by remarriage was supposed to inhibit any attempt on the
part of men to reestablish the status quo, although women (and in-

verts) were at least permitted to fight with their successful rivals. In brief, the man was expected to respect the new situation, and to accept it, while the woman was allowed the privilege of "taking it out" on her successful rival. This inhibition may explain why hi: wa itck occurs only, or chiefly, in men, and is limited to cases of complete desertion followed by the establishment of a new relationship.

(*f*) *Funeral suicide* results from a situation which is irreversible (pt. 7, pp. 431–459). Once more the culture pattern demands that the male should accept it completely, while the female is permitted one last emotional outburst, in the form of attempted funeral suicide, which, if successful, enables her to go through subsequent metamorphoses at the side of her husband, thus restoring the status quo even beyond the grave. It should be added that a wife who dies long after her husband's demise cannot catch up with him, due to the lack of synchronization between their successive metamorphoses, which occur in a strict sequence (Devereux, 1937 a).

Summing up, male suicide is an equivalent not of hi: wa itck, but of the more aggressive attempts of women to restore the status quo. Female funeral suicide, on the other hand, is, within limits, the equivalent of hi: wa itck in the male, who is usually the senior spouse, and is a response to a situation, which, in theory and very often in practice as well, is irreversible. It may be added that the general failure of attempted funeral suicides, often followed by the remarriage of the widow, causes the Mohave to laugh and shrug their shoulders at these would-be suicides. Considering the flightiness of Mohave women, we may say that they reconcile themselves more easily to objective, man-made reality (desertion), than to the irrevocable dictates of fate (final breach or death). Culture supports them in this attitude, by permitting them a certain leeway of aggression.[83]

(*g*) *Absence of formal therapy for hi: wa itck.*—Although the Mohave had rites for the cure of most types of insanity, they lacked a formal therapy for hi: wa itck. This absence suggests that Mohave culture was not prepared to deal with very strong "object cathexes," of a highly individualized kind, and that such cathexes were felt to disturb the public order. A similar practical passivity existed also with regard to incest and suicide. At the same time, the fatal outcome of suicides somewhat mitigated the contemptuousness of public opinion, which was, however, manifested toward the would-be suicide who failed in his design.

Ambivalence was also less pronounced in cases involving death by murder-and-suicide, perhaps because of the Mohave fear of ghosts,

---

[83] A similar outlet is the frantic destruction of excess property not belonging to the deceased, which is thrown on the funeral pyre (Devereaux, 1942 a; cf. pt. 7, pp. 431–459).

and also because of the obvious similarity between these situations and the murder-suicide pattern of witchcraft (Devereux, 1937 c). Hi: wa itck, on the other hand, lacked this tragic aspect and was therefore considered a mental disorder. Public reaction was ambivalent and, in retrospect at least, emphasized the comical aspects of the situation.

(h) *Hi: wa itck and social integration.*—It should once more be stressed that hi: wa itck apparently afflicts chiefly persons who realize that, because of their age, they cannot expect to obtain a substitute love object as attractive as the spouse who may eventually desert them; such persons are, therefore, likely to invest a great deal of affection in their marital relationship. The special pattern of behavior obtaining between an old husband and his young wife should also be stressed in this context. If the wife was immature, the husband acted in loco parentis. He sometimes carried her around on his back and even took over some of the more strenuous feminine household chores, which the Mohave male scorns quite explicitly under normal conditions.[84] Last of all, the senior spouse was often exposed to jocular comments skirting the topic of incest (e. g., "Whom are you carrying around on your back? Is that your daughter?") (Devereux, 1951 f).

These factors tended to intensify and render more complex the marital relationship, and contributed to the isolation of the couple. Hence, if the junior spouse deserted, the senior spouse found himself isolated emotionally as well as socially, the act of desertion depriving him both of his love object and of concrete comforts. His abnormal behavior must therefore be interpreted also as a manifestation of the Mohave's sense of aimlessness (Kroeber, 1951) and as sensitiveness to isolation, rather than simply as a reflection of the difficulties involved in managing a simple affective frustration.

The lack of recent cases of hi: wa itck is balanced by an increase in love suicides. This trend reflects a profound social change; today, self-restraint in the male is no longer rewarded by an adequate increase in prestige; the difference between marriage and liaison has become insignificant; social relations in general are increasingly fluid and superficial. These factors are responsible for an increase in the sense of one's own uniqueness, as well as of that of the love object, and lead to a need for increasingly intense individualized object cathexes, which seem to serve as compensations for the increasing social and affective isolation of the average modern Mohave from his group.

One further psychological nexus may also be traced. Old malevolent shamans, who, through years of dream intercourse with the

---

[84] It should be noted, however, that braves of established reputation willingly worked for sick families (Stewart, 1947 c). Cf. in this context the nursing duties of the Knights of St. John of the Hospital (Devereaux and Weiner, 1950).

ghosts of their victims, have formed a strong object cathexis toward these ghostly beings, and have, therefore, withdrawn from social life, are so desirous of joining their victims in the land of the dead, that they proceed to bait the surviving relatives of these ghosts, until the aggrieved relatives kill them (Kroeber, 1925 a). Only this vicarious form of suicide enables witches to join forever the souls of those whom they have bewitched and to retain their empire over them (Devereux, 1937 c; cf. also pt. 7, pp. 387–426).

Summing up, hi: wa itck occurs only in individuals who, from the very beginning, are relatively handicapped in sexual competition and adventures, which constitute one of the chief safety valves of Mohave life. When their carefully built-up defense (i. e., their marriage to a young spouse) breaks down, they find themselves in a highly precarious position. Not only have they lost a, to them, exceptional and irreplaceable partner (Devereux, 1951 f), but they also find themselves without an emotional anchor, and without the security of social integration and marital companionship in their old age. In view of the fact that the Mohave have little use for highly personalized affective bonds, which, according to them, are silly, the formation of such bonds and the need for such marriages is already atypical and perhaps even pathological. The occurrence of such marriages is, thus, already an expression of a preexisting trend toward social isolation in a given individual. This is given explicit recognition by the Mohave, in their comments on marriages between mother-in-law and son-in-law, which occur when young men tire of the flightiness of young women and seek a stable home life. The Mohave say, "Women sometimes marry their former sons-in-law, but men are not crazy enough to marry their former daughters-in-law" (Devereux, 1951 f; but cf. Case 104, which has some aspects of such a union).

Marriage between mother-in-law and son-in-law is one of the minor patterns of Mohave culture, and appears to cater more to the infantile dependent needs of the young man than to the sexual and affective needs of the older woman. This may explain the discrepancy between the male-female ratio in hi: wa itck. The fact that social recognition is given to marriages between old women and young men may also be reflected in the (not conclusively established) Mohave habit of calling half siblings by kinship terms one generation apart.[85]

In brief, when seen against the background of Mohave culture as a whole, it is relatively easy to understand why Mohave psychiatric thought should consider hi: wa itck a distinct clinical entity. This social background also explains the attitude of normal persons toward

---

[85] This information was provided by the late Ruth Benedict in a private conversation, but could not be confirmed in the course of subsequent fieldwork.

this form of mental disorder. The most telling argument, however, in support of the thesis that the concept of hi : wa itck is almost wholly social in origin, is the fact that only people who satisfy a number of criteria are so diagnosed. When O : otc's husband was imprisoned for the slaying of the witch Anyay Ha : m (Case 104), O : otc professed to have hi : wa itck, presumably in order to rationalize her subsequent dissolute conduct (Devereux, 1948 f), but her claim was unanimously rejected by the tribe, since dissolute behavior is not held to be symptomatic of hi : wa itck. Thus, even though O : otc kept on saying that she had hi : wa itck, the tribe simply called her a kamalo : y (dissolute woman), and, instead of pitying her, severely condemned her conduct.

HI : WA MAVA : RKH

This illness was first mentioned in connection with the case history of a woman who had some psychiatric symptoms while hospitalized after an incomplete miscarriage followed by sepsis. No formal description of the syndrome itself was obtainable. When asked to describe this clinical entity the informants simply said that its symptoms are those mentioned in Case 24. They did not imply, however, that hi : wa mava : rkh is a necessary sequel of miscarriage [86] or that this illness cannot occur unless the patient first has an abortion or a miscarriage. One feels that Case 24 was diagnosed as "hi : wa mava : rkh" chiefly because of symptoms of depression. This suggests that, like other diagnostic labels in which the word "hi : wa" (heart) occurs, the term hi : wa mava : rkh is applied to certain illnesses characterized by disturbances of the mood, i. e., to an extreme affective reaction type. It must be clearly stated, however, that most of the preceding comments are simply inferences.

CASE 24 (Informant : O : otc, sister of the alleged kamalo : y) :

Introduction.—In 1938 I was informed by the reservation physician that O : otc, of that gens, a fullblood Mohave woman in her middle twenties, had had a confusional episode following an incomplete accidental (?) abortion complicated by sepsis. My Mohave friends said I could interview her without an interpreter and that I would probably be well received, since one of O : otc's numerous sisters was at that time married to Kamtoská Huanyeily (gens Vi : mak) and another sister to his brother N. S., both of whom were grandnephews of my old friend and informant Tcatc.

I found O : otc in her home, surrounded by her three children, and entertaining her amiable and intelligent brother-in-law Kamtoská Huanyeily. O : otc impressed me as a very intelligent, well-mannered, kindly, cooperative, and friendly person. She was somewhat thin and did not appear to be in good health. However, she seemed active enough and her movements were free and graceful.

---

[86] Miscarriages (huk'auvåk), as well as abortions (amayk kavo : råm = on-top step) frequently cause severe feelings of guilt and an appreciable depression (Devereux, 1948 d, 1955 a).

Though I had been told beforehand that one of her hands had been amputated, she concealed her crippled arm so unobtrusively that not until she herself mentioned her amputation did I notice it. Originally I had hoped to obtain only a brief account of her psychiatric illness. O: otc spoke so freely, however, that it was easy to rearrange her statements into an autobiography. All statements preceded by (Q), or by a question in brackets, were made in reply to a direct question, none of which was resented. Remarks in parentheses are either explanatory comments or else data obtained later on from informants Pulyi: k and Hama : Utce :.

Autobiography of O: otc:

My name is O: otc and I belong to the O: otc gens. I am about 27 years old and my present age-grade is thinyeak, which means "woman who has borne children." I am a fullblood Mohave Indian.

I was born on the Colorado River Indian Reservation, near Parker, Ariz. My mother died 12 months after I was born. I was not nursed, but fed on "tea." (This statement may refer to the period after her mother's death.) After my mother's death I went to live with a childless couple at Needles, Calif., both of whom were related to me. Except for the time I spent in boarding schools, I lived with them until I was about 12 or 13 years old. Both of my foster parents have died since then. I did not grow up with my father C. M., and my relations with him are indifferent. I don't bother him and he does not bother me. We meet only once in a while. (Pulyi: k stated that O: otc did not live with her father because they had "fights"—i. e., did not agree.)

I have quite a few siblings and half-siblings on my father's side, the oldest of whom is my half sister A. She lives at Needles and is married to F. W. I am very fond of her and she does everything she can for me. Then there are two older full siblings: my older brother P. and my older sister F., who is the one I see most frequently. She is married to Kamtoská Huanyeily (who was present during this conversation). Then there are my two half sisters by my father's third wife: Es. and El. I get along all right with my sister El. She is married to N. S., who, like Kamtoská Huanyeily, is a grandnephew of your old friend Tcatc. Before marrying N. S. she bore a girl child to someone else— to some fellow at Los Angeles, a Cherokee Indian. Now she is married to N. S. and her daughter stays with her. [Knowing that her half sister Es. is reputed to be a kamalo: y, and is alleged to have helped her husband to kill a witch (Devereux, 1948 f, and Case 104), I made a point of inquiring how she got along with Es. The reply was somewhat curt.] I get along all right with Es. too. Last of all, there are the three children of my father's present wife: my half sisters R. and F. and my half brother C. All my siblings are alive.

(Q) When I was a child I never played with my siblings or half-siblings. They were raised by different people. The people who raised me had no children of their own and I was pretty much brought up among adults, all the time. However, I did play, now and then, with the children of various neighbors.

(Q) The first thing I remember about myself is that I went with my foster parents to look for mesquite nuts.

(Q) My second earliest memory is about a carnival at Needles. Or maybe it was a circus. The noise frightened me, so I began to cry and got spanked for crying. I was still pretty small at that time.

I went to the Fort Mohave boarding school. The only time I was really ill was when my hand was caught in a mangle and had to be amputated. I was only a small girl at that time. After I hurt my arm, my father wanted me to come to Parker. I came and stayed with him for 3 or 4 years and went to school at Parker. Then I went back once more to the Fort Mohave boarding school and lived there as I had done previously.

[Q, asked in connection with her remark that she was in the habit of spanking her children.] They spanked me when I was at school. [Why?] [Before informant could reply, Kamtoská Huanyeily remarked jokingly, "Maybe they spanked her for flirting." "O: otc would do no such thing," I replied with a grin.] I got spanked for speaking Mohave.[87] I also got spanked once for running away one night from school, with a Chemehuevi Indian girl, because I did not like school. (Q) I do not recall how old I was at that time. (Q) I must have been about 12 or 13 years old, but do not recall whether I was already a masahay (pubescent) or still a màràtciny (=humar hàtciny=prepubescent), because I never went through the puberty ceremony.[88] We managed to get away from school and walked all the way to Needles. (Q) I was not scared while walking at night through the desert. I went to the house of my foster parents, but remained with them only for about an hour, because the school authorities discovered our escape and followed our tracks to my foster parents' house. They found me there and took me back to school. That is when I got spanked.

Around 1925 I was sent to Phoenix, Ariz., for further schooling. I remained in Phoenix for 5 years. (Q) I was quite happy there. I did not mind being away from Parker—I was used to being away. I left school in 1929, when my time was up. I made out pretty well at school, except in arithmetic. I went to the ninth grade. [Here, Kamtoská Huanyeily remarked, "O: otc has got me beat! I only went to the seventh grade, and I only got P's (poor) in most subjects," and then left us temporarily to chop wood for O: otc.]

When I left school, I came to Parker for one or two months and stayed with my father. Then I went to Needles, where one of my relatives lay dying. I went there with my aunt, and stayed with her, rather than with the people who had raised me.

I forgot to tell you that I was a church member once—a Presbyterian. My father was a religious, church-going man, and that is how I came to be baptized at the age of 12 or 13. I stopped going to church about two years ago. (I. e., roughly at the time of her divorce.) (Q) I actually used to believe what they told us in church. I obeyed the church laws and the religious laws. (Q) No, I did not get married in church.

(Q) My first husband, who belongs to the Mu: th gens, used to go around with my brother P. and they were coming to the house all the time. My first husband had been married before and had just been divorced from his last wife. (Q) He did not help around the house, the way suitors do. I was supposed to go back to Phoenix for some additional schooling, but I did not feel like going back. (The Mohave frequently get married for such trifling reasons.) He kept on coming to the house and after a while I realized that he came because of me. His sister used to go around with me and the two of us would go swimming with him (Devereux, 1950 e). Then, one day, he asked me to move to his place and marry him. He was about my own age or maybe a couple of years older and he got me while I was still quite young. He was pretty good to me for a while and I liked him. In 1934 we moved to Parker because he was ill and M. A. I. Nettle, M. D., wanted him to be near the Agency hospital. He

---

[87] This was formerly standard practice in boarding schools that tried to detribalize Indian children.

[88] This remark illustrates the psychological importance of the puberty rite (Devereux, 1950 g).

had heart trouble and high blood pressure and had to stay at the hospital for quite a while. When he came out of the hospital he went to work. He had a job up at the Agency school and we never had to live off our relatives. I lived with him for about 8½ years, and never left him during all that time.

I have three children by my first husband, a boy Morl. who is nine years old, a boy Mort. who is six, and a daughter J. who is four. My first child was born a year after we were married. I was glad when he was born, and took good care of him. I like girls better though—they are more obedient. (On the whole, the Mohave say that girls are more trouble than boys.) (Q) I nursed my children for one year only. (Q) I nurse them until they start eating. Then I stop. [That is not the old Mohave way. Don't you like to nurse them?] I don't really care one way or the other. [At this point her little daughter J., who had listened to our conversation, said, "I am going to play cowboy with Morl." J. also used the word "killing," but I was unable to make her tell me whom she wanted to kill. She had been carrying her toy revolver all day long, playing at being a cowboy. Then she told me that she was going to "stick me up." I immediately raised my hands to the ceiling, whereupon she hid behind her mother's skirt and grinned at me. Previously she had been playing alone, listening to us and talking to herself. She sounded as though she were talking to someone, and kept on calling out the names of little boys and girls. Her mother explained to me that her daughter saw the boys play cowboy with their toy guns and had also seen Westerns in the Parker cinema.]

(Q) I spank my children quite often, though, except at school, they did not spank me when I was small. (Q) They did spank me that time, at the circus. [Hivsu: Tupo: ma once said that the older Mohave think that only crazy people spank their children. He said that the old people are angry when they see the younger people spank their children. I think the old Mohave are right about that.] I know the old people don't like it. It makes them angry. [Kamtoskȧ Huanyeily remarked that he agreed with the old Mohave on this point, and shared my opinion about the iniquity of child beating.] [I saw Hitcu:y Kutask(w)elvȧ strike his stepfather when he was about 8 years old.] My children never strike back at me. (Q) I ask them to do something and if they don't do it, I spank them.

My oldest boy is not very good at school. My second son is already doing pretty well at school, although it is only his first year there. My little daughter is still too young to go to school.[89]

(Q) I speak both English and Mohave with my children. (Q) I do not teach them Mohave customs and tell them no Coyote (hukthar) stories, (Q) because I have only heard them vaguely myself, and do not remember them well enough to tell them to my children. (Kroeber, 1948; Devereux, 1948 h).

(Q) I like all my children equally well. There is no difference in my love for them. All of my children are alive. (This may be false. See below.) (Q) I have no children by my second husband. I did get pregnant by him, but had a miscarriage.

I left my first husband because he was drinking too much. (Hama: Utce: confirmed that the husband was kindly, but drank too much.) Whenever he got drunk he was mean to me and hit me, and was also mean to our oldest boy and hit him too. I could not stand it. One day my husband was drinking again. I had gone to an old woman's funeral and, by the time I came home, he had gone out to drink some more. When he finally came home, he talked

---

[89] The direct transition from spanking to schooling is significant.

loudly and was cantankerous. Since I had told my sister previously that I might leave my husband and come to live with her, that same night, or else next morning, I just left the house with my children and went to live with my sister. My husband came after me, however, and stayed with me at my sister's house for about 1 or 2 weeks. Then we both went back to our own old place and lived there for a while. However, since he kept on drinking, I left him once more and returned to the house of my sister. He did not come after me again, and that is how we were divorced. That was in 1937.

After a while I went to Needles with my children and stayed with my aunt M. H. At that time I would take a drink or two; in fact, after leaving my husband, I drank quite a lot. I drank only with women, however, and did not run around with men. (Hama: Utce: said that she did run around with men and lost the twins she bore to Huymánye:, a Yuma Indian.)

Eventually I left the house of my aunt, and, taking my children with me, went to live in the house of my brother P.

One evening I was in town with some of my male relatives. They wanted to sing Indian songs and we went to a place where we knew that there would be some singing. My future (second) husband was also at that party and the people asked him to sing for them. He consented and sang for a while. That is how I met him. We liked each other right away and went around together for the rest of the evening. After that he used to come around to visit me at my brother's house. He would chop wood and help with the chores (as a single girl's suitors do). My brother liked him pretty well. The only thing he did not like about him was the fact that he could not seem to find work, and my relatives began to think that he was lazy. He kept on coming to the house for quite a while.

Last January my first husband also happened to be at Needles. Someone was giving a birthday party and a bunch of us, both men and women, were drinking and doing an old Mohave dance in honor of our host's birthday. My former husband did not like what I was doing and beat me up. (This is atypical behavior for a deserted husband (pt. 3, pp. 91–106).) Luckily for me, some people interfered and stopped him. After that I never even spoke to him again.

The next morning my present husband came to the house to get me, and I moved over to his place and married him.

(Q) My present husband belongs to the [hesitates] Nyoltc gens, I think. He is about 33 years old. He was married several times before, and has children of his own. He had two children by his first wife, Nyortc. He also had two children, one of whom died a long time ago, by his second wife, Mah. (Q) Yes, Mah belong to that "famous" N. family. [See pt. 5, pp. 245–247]. (Q) I don't remember who my present husband's third wife was. He was married several times.[90]

I am happy with my present husband. We will have been married a year next January. As you see, my children are with me and they get along very well with my present husband. He is a good man.

When I fell ill after my miscarriage, we moved to Parker and he came along, to be with me. At first he had a job with Mr. W., up at the Agency,

---

[90] According to Hama: Utce:, O: otc's second husband was first married to E. N., a Yuma Indian woman, then to Mah (of the "psychopathic" family), then to Po: tá (who had been involved in two suicides, Cases 119 and 120), and then to Nyortc by whom he had two children. The fact that these two lists are not entirely in accord—and that it is possible that neither list is complete and/or correctly arranged—simply shows the casualness of marriage and divorce in contemporary Mohave society.

at a time when they were building a shed for the trucks. Then he was laid off for a long time. After a while he got another job, driving a truck, in connection with some road work and stayed on that job until last month. Then my brother-in-law Kamtoskå Huanyeily, spoke to Mr. S., who thereupon came down here and asked my husband to work on the Parker Dam, which is just being built. He works at the head gate of the dam. We are getting along all right on what my husband earns. My sister F., Kamtoskå Huanyeily's wife, used to live in this house, and it is a nice place to live in.

(Q) I myself am not related to your old friend Tcatc, but my brother-in-law Kamtoskå Huanyeily is her grandnephew. I am also a little bit related to that troublesome N. family, of the Mah gens. They are a strange family. I know that Mah is a shaman, because she treated a woman who was staying here. That woman's name was Vi꞉mak; she is a relative of Kamtoskå Huanyeily. Mah could not cure her, however, and she died (Case 93). (Q) Kwathany Hi꞉wa, the shaman, is just a litle bit related to me. He is definitely not a close relative of mine. (Q) I would not be afraid to interpret for you (even though he is a witch), if you should want to work with him, but he is ill and is "drying up." He is going to die. (Pulyi꞉k said: "He is suffering from huyatc avi꞉rk (breath finished), because he spent all his power bewitching people.") (Q) It is possible that some-one may have bewitched him at last. I too had heard that Kwathany Hi꞉wa had bewitched a number of people.

(Q) My favorite amusement is going to the movies. I also like to dance (Mohave dances) and I like to listen to songs, especially to the bird songs. I myself can't sing Mohave Indian songs. I also like to do housework. (Q) I really do. (She also went horseback riding once, cf. below.)

(Q) Yes, I do dream. (Q) I don't recall what I dreamed last night. Most of my dreams are about someone dying.[91] (Q) My recurrent dreams are about death. I see my dead relatives in a coffin.[92] After such dreams I wake up crying. These are bad dreams—suma꞉tc itcem. I dream that I am with them and am talking to them. (Q) I do not dream of being given food by them, or of eating with them (i. e., she does not have a nyevedhi꞉ type of illness.) (Q) I do not dream about my dead foster parents: only about my other dead relatives. (Q) I am very fond of my relatives.

(Q) I have falling dreams. (Q) I also dream of falling into water or of swimming. (Q) I cannot recall whether I ever dreamed about climbing. (Q) I never dreamed of running on all fours. Once I dreamed that I was flying, but I do not recall the details of that dream.

(Q) I never had a real suffocation nightmare. I did dream however, of being late; I was running and not getting anywhere. I also dream of people chasing me. They are gypsies. (Q) I saw real gypsies at the carnival at Needles. (Q) Not at the carnival which I saw as a child, when I was spanked for being scared and for crying. I saw the gypsies only last winter, at Needles. I must have heard about gypsies at school, or else I may have read about them in storybooks. (Q) I guess the closest Mohave equivalents of the bogeyman would be wolves and coyotes; also ghosts (nyevedhi꞉).

Not so long ago I dreamed of hikwi꞉r snakes. There were quite a lot of them. I looked down on them and was afraid to get off the wagon. They looked like snakes. There was more to that dream, but this is all I can recall. (See pt. 4, pp. 117–128, regarding the forgetting of snake dreams.)

---

[91] This indicates unconscious death wishes, which elicit guilt feelings and depression.
[92] Even nowadays the Mohave do not use coffins. They practice cremation.

(Q) I also dream of ordinary snakes. I dreamed that I was walking some-where and saw some snakes on the road, or on the path. [Very long pause.] I did not get ill after dreaming of real snakes, or of the hikwi: r snake (i. e., she does not feel she has the hikwi: r illness).

I had a miscarriage last June—I don't know why. I never before had a miscarriage. I was working at that time in Needles, cooking for a bunch of cowboys. (Q) I never had venereal diseases and had never been ill in my life, except the time I lost my hand. I had gone horseback riding just before I had my miscarriage (huk'auvâk). It was the first time I ever rode horseback in all my life.[93] I liked it, though the next day I was rather stiff. [I thought that Mohave women do not ride horses.] They used to ride in the past, though they don't nowadays. I went riding because I wanted to try it. I wore a pair of pants belonging to my husband. He too came riding with me. (Q) I don't know whether I would rather be a man or a woman.

Shortly afterwards I had a miscarriage and felt very ill. I was living on the Arizona side of the Colorado River, just opposite Needles, and I must have been ill for about two weeks when I began to get worse and started to have headaches. One day, when some Mohave, who came from some place, were passing by my camp, I asked them to take me to Needles, to see the doctor. The next day my brother P. went to town, to see the doctor about me, and asked him whether he could do anything for me. The Parker Reservation social worker—a Plains Indian girl who is married to a white man—happened to be in Needles at that time, and when she saw my brother at the doctor's office, she asked him what was the matter. When my brother told her that I was ill, the social worker had a talk with the doctor, and then drove to my camp and asked me to come to the Parker Indian Agency Hospital with her. When I agreed, the social worker put me in her car and drove me straight to the reservation hospital at Parker. The hospital doctor then told me that I had had a mis-carriage.

(Q) Yes, I was quite upset while I was at the hospital. (Q) They treated me with pills. (Q) The pills did not make me sleepy. The first day in the hospital I did not feel very ill. However, the next morning I got up and went to the bathroom, and when I came out again I guess I must have fainted. The nurse gave me some kind of medicine to smell, and that brought me around. Then they put me in a private room. I do not recall very much about the rest of my stay at the hospital. I was asleep most of the time. I had no pains, and nothing was worrying me, but my head kept on bothering me all the time. [Did you have headaches, or were you drowsy?] I had headaches, I think. (Q) I did not cry or shout. I was in the hospital for about a month. That was in the month of June of this year.

(Q) I had had fainting spells also in the past. I used to have them in school, all the time. (Q) The first time I fainted was after I had been in school, at Phoenix, for about two years. I must have been about 17 or 18 years old at that time. (Q) I don't think it had anything to do with my menses. (Q) I can't say that anything worried me, so as to make me faint. It just happened for no reason that I know of. (Q) I never had laughing or crying fits. (Q) No Mohave shaman ever doctored me, that I know of. I never was ill enough for that. (Q) They may have doctored me when I was a very small child. If they did, I do not remember anything about it. (Q) I don't know what the Mohave name of my ailment is. (Q) I do not think that any of the Mohave diseases

---

[93] This coincidence suggests an unconscious wish to abort.

which you just mentioned describe my condition. (Q) I recognize your description of hot waves in the head, and the sensation that I am going to lose my balance when I get up abruptly. I used to have these feelings before fainting. (The description pertained to dizziness associated with postural cerebral anemia caused by low blood pressure.)

(Q) The miscarried child was fathered by my husband.

(Q) At present my health is not very good. There is nothing special, really, but I just don't feel well sometimes. Perhaps it is some aftermath of my illness. (Q) I had no further fainting spells since I left the hospital. (Q) I don't think that I was even temporarily out of my mind, or yamomk (insane), while at the hospital.

(Q) I know Apen Ismalyk (Case 4). He is insane (yamomk). (Q) I don't know anyone else whom I would consider insane.

An interview with the reservation physician, James L. Troupin, M. D., disclosed that O: otc, 27 years of·age, was admitted to the hospital on June 2, 1938, with the diagnosis of incomplete abortion and postabortal sepsis.

On the day of her admission the patient stated that she had missed a period, which was due a month ago. If she was pregnant, her embryo would have been about eight to ten weeks old. About ten days before admission she began to have a flow, accompanied by clots. She denied all instrumentation or other interference. At the time of her admission this flow was continuing, though in somewhat lesser amount. There were no symptoms other than a slight nausea.

Except for the amputation of the right forearm, and for a few moist rales in both lungs (upper respiratory infection), no physical abnormalities could be found.

During the first 2½ weeks of her hospitalization, she had temperatures up to 100 and 101. About the third day, her nausea became worse and all food by mouth was stopped. On the eighth day she was able to take some food, and from then on she improved steadily. Throughout her illness, she was treated with hot douches, surgical interference being thought inadvisable. She passed small clots from time to time, and stopped flowing after about 2 weeks in the hospital.

The only symptoms suggestive of psychiatric complications were the refusal to eat during the first week, and considerable moaning and groaning during the first 2 days. There was no pain severe enough to cause the upset she displayed.

She was discharged as recovered on June 26, 1938, and since her discharge from the hospital had been perfectly well.

Comment

Tentative diagnosis:

(a) *Physical:* Incomplete abortion with sepsis. Upper respiratory infection.

(b) *Psychiatric:* Headaches, fainting, nausea, over-reacting to minor pain, anorexia. The entire picture suggests a transitory, mild, reactive depression.

Two aspects of this case deserve to be discussed in some detail:

(1) The "miscarriage" may actually be an abortion procured "accidentally on purpose." It is hard to understand otherwise why O: otc felt impelled to go riding horseback for the first time in her life at that precise moment, especially since Mohave women do not ride nowadays. This type of behavior is in a class with that of some occidental pregnant women, who suddenly decide to play, e. g., tennis, and manage to take a severe fall on the tennis court. This interpretation implies that some, or all, of her psychiatric symptoms were manifestations of a depression, caused by unconscious guilt over her so-called miscarriage. Why

she should have felt impelled to bring about a miscarriage is, unfortunately, far from clear, nor is it easy to see why, if she did wish to abort, she did not resort to the standard Mohave method called amayk kavo: râm (on-back step=abortion) (Devereux, 1948 d) and improvised instead the abortifacient technique of riding horseback, which no primitive woman seems to use (Devereux, 1955 a). However, since O: otc has had a lot of schooling, she may have heard that riding horseback is sometimes resorted to by white women who wish to abort.

(2) O: otc's recurrent dreams of death and of talking with ghosts should have made her feel that she had either hiwey lak nyevedhi: or else nyevedhi: taha: nà while her dreams of hikwi: r snakes and of real snakes should have suggested to her that she had the hikwi: r illness. Such, however, was not the case. Likewise, when this case history was read to other informants, they too ignored these diagnostic clues and said she was suffering from hi: wa mava: rkh. This suggests that their diagnosis—rightly, we believe—was determined primarily by O: otc's reactive depression, rather than solely by the manifest content of her dreams.

It should be noted that the fact that O: otc had psychiatric symptoms during her illness was not common knowledge. Thus, Hama: Utce: was surprised to learn that she had exhibited abnormal behavior while in the hospital, but took this information into account when she too, though a layman, made the diagnosis of hi: wa mava: rkh. As for Pulyi: k, who was likewise not a shaman, he declared himself unable to offer a diagnosis.

HI: WA HISA: HK (HEART ROT)

This illness was never formally described as a syndrome. The informant simply narrated the case history of an old woman and then stated that she suffered from hi: wa hisa: hk. Tentatively speaking, this disease entity does not seem to be one of the major Mohave diagnostic categories. Nyortc's illness appears to have been defined as a "mental disorder" only because this old woman had peculiar dreams and visions—which may not even have been true hallucinations—and was depressed and anorexic as well.

CASE 25 (Informants: Tcatc and E. S.):

Nyortc, of the Nyoltc gens, who died around 1928 at the approximate age of 70, was the wife of J. P., who was already dead in 1938. (Tcatc momentarily confused her with Mu: th Nyemsutkha: v, who was diagnosed as a hysteric by the reservation physician, M. A. I. Nettle, M. D.)

Nyortc was not ill, i. e., she had no pains. She just had a tired feeling all the time. One day she told me one of her dreams. She dreamed that she had died. Also, when she went to the outhouse toilet and sat down on it, she used to see a vision of herself. During the 3 years of her illness she got thinner and thinner, because she had no appetite. They did not know what had caused this loss of appetite, but they noticed that she coughed quite a bit. This was caused by hi: wa hisa: hk. She was never "out of her mind"; she was sane all the time. To my knowledge she had never been to the hospital. No one thought that she had been bewitched."

Comment

Tentative diagnosis.—Death from old age, perhaps complicated by an upper respiratory infection and some neurotic anorexia. The one truly psychopathological feature of this case is the fact that Nyortc dreamed that she had died and even saw herself—presumably as a ghost—while sitting on the toilet.

HI: WA HIRA: UK

The Mohave woman, who still nurses her own child, is reluctant to wet-nurse a small orphaned relative, lest her own child, on being given a rival at the breast, develop an illness called hi: wa hira: uk, meaning heart angry, which appears to be very similar to tàvàknyi: k. What little is known of this ailment will be discussed in connection with tàvàknyi: k (pt. 7, pp. 340–348). Hi: wa hira: uk is of interest in this context chiefly by virtue of the fact that it is an infantile equivalent of adult hi: wa neuroses (pt. 3, pp. 90–115), which clearly suggests that extreme jealousy in adulthood is rooted in the infant's unwillingness to share the breast.

PART 4. DISORDERS CAUSED BY EXTERNAL BEINGS

EXOGENOUS DISORDERS

This part of the report is devoted to a discussion of psychiatric and psychosomatic illnesses that, according to the Mohave, are caused by the impact of ego-alien and external beings possessed of various supernatural powers, to wit:

(a) An insane deity appearing in dream
(b) Supernatural snakes
(c) Aliens and alien ghosts
(d) Mohave ghosts who cause psychosomatic illness
(e) Mohave ghosts who cause depressions
(f) Funeral paraphernalia and rituals
(g) Witches
(h) Magic substances and narcotics

An Appendix briefly discusses alcohol, drug addiction, and trance states (the latter being related to "power") that, if one tries to think along Mohave lines, appear to be related to exogenous psychic disorders, as the Mohave conceive of them.

INSANITY DUE TO DREAMING OF AN INSANE DEITY

According to Kroeber (1948) "People who dream of Mastamho after he became a bald eagle know nothing and are crazy (yamomk) like him" (cf. pt. 2, pp. 50–54).

While Kroeber's data impress one as reliable, it is likely that this belief is not a key concept of Mohave psychiatric thought. Indeed— in reply to a direct question, illustrated by an account of the Indochinese Sedang Moi (Devereux, MS., 1933–34) belief that a person who dies insane turns into the "ghost of insanity," which seeks to make others insane—the Mohave denied that they had similar beliefs. Furthermore, since Kroeber recorded the actual text that describes Mastamho's insanity—which means that his (apparently sane) informant had (theoretically at least) dreamed this portion of the myth without going insane—this raises questions concerning the rigorousness of Mohave belief in this assertion. What Kroeber's informant probably meant was that anyone who dreams of Mastamho *only* as a fish eagle, and perhaps not necessarily in connection with this myth, may become insane. This view would be compatible with modern psychoanalytic insight. Indeed, the onset of a psychosis is often

116

marked by dreams that herald the overt psychotic break in rather clear-cut terms.[93]

Once we take into account these reservations regarding the real meaning of Kroeber's data, it is quite certain that the belief that he mentions is not incompatible, e.g., with the belief that the ghosts of the dead may, in dream, induce in the living a sickness complicated by a severe depression, which, according to the Mohave, indicates a psychic compliance of the living with the wishes of the dead, who desire to be joined by a beloved spouse, or relative, in the land of the dead. (This illness will be discussed in part 4, pp. 150–186.)

In brief, it is felt that dreams about Mastamho in his psychotic fish eagle (or osprey) avatar—though not necessarily dreams in which knowledge of the relevant portion of the Creation myth is acquired—may actually precede a psychotic break, since it is known that motifs derived from folk tales are often utilized both by occidental (Freud, 1925 c) and by Plains Indian (Devereux, 1951 a) dreamers. Otherwise expressed, certain Mohave Indians may dream of the insane Mastamho because—albeit unconsciously—they sense that they are about to have a psychotic break. In this respect the psychiatric interpretation of such a dream differs from the Mohave interpretation thereof only in that the Mohave consider it etiological, whereas modern psychiatry considers it as the first warning symptom of an impending psychotic break.

HIKWI:R HAHNOK

The disease caused (hahnok) by supernatural snakes (hikwi:r) was somewhat arbitrarily fitted into the class of mental diseases by the Mohave on the grounds that the dreams causing or heralding it are of a rather peculiar kind, and also because the physical illness sometimes involved delirium. The material obtained is rather instructive in several respects, but especially because:

(1) Hivsu:Tupo:ma's account seems to differ in every respect from the other three accounts of this illness, but becomes fully compatible with the latter if one assumes that the snake symbolizes the male organ.

(2) Ahma Huma:re's account contains several acculturation items fitted into a traditional pattern, thus illustrating the "gallant rear guard action" of Mohave culture that Kroeber (personal communica-

---

[93] This is also true of Indians. When I analyzed a Plains Indian woman, who had had three previous transitory psychotic episodes, she once reported a dream, in which there was much about doorknobs, locked doors, and hospital rooms. Having been at that time only a beginner—hers being my first psychoanalytic case—I analyzed only the latent content of the dream, expressed by means of symbols, but failed to take adequate notice of the fact that this dream's manifest content clearly indicated that she expected to be locked up in the near future. This experience taught me to emphasize (Devereux, 1951 a) the importance of analyzing also the manifest content of dreams, especially in the case of primitives.

tion, 1954) noted in the course of his most recent field trip to the Mohave.

(3) The same account implicitly relates supernatural snakes to white people, thus connecting the snake illness with the ahwe: nyevedhi: (foreign ghost) illness. This implicit nexus is indirectly suggested also by Tcatc's remark that the snakes appearing in pathogenic dreams wear the kind of funeral feathers that cause the insanity which affects misbehaving funeral ritualists (pt. 4, pp. 186–195), who are also shamans specializing in the cure of ahwe: nyevedhi: (foreign illness). This fact further increases the plausibility of the suggestion (cf. pt. 4, pp. 128–186) that aliens are more or less thought of as dangerous ghosts.

(4) Two of the three case histories are autobiographical, and include dreams.

(5) The same two case histories are those of a married couple, and suggest that the wife's "pathogenic dream" may have been influenced by her knowledge of her husband's pathogenic dream, parts of which provided material ("day residue") for her own dream.

(6) One of these two case histories underscores the dual function of snakes, which both cause and cure the snake illness. This dovetails with the Mohave belief that shamans can both send (cause) and cure certain ailments. In fact, in one of our cases the appearance of two hikwi: r as dream healers coincided with a real improvement in the patient's condition, but also served as a basis for the diagnosis of her ailment as the snake disease. (Cf. also Case 94 for healing in dream.)

Although three of the four accounts converge extensively on the manifest level, and the fourth also appears to be in harmony with the other three, provided that one accepts the symbolic equation snake= phallus, it seems expedient to reproduce the four accounts separately, in the order in which they were obtained, so as to illustrate the range—as well as the coherence—of Mohave psychiatric theories.

However, in order to obtain a real understanding of Mohave ideas concerning the hikwi: r hahnok illness, it is first necessary to describe briefly Mohave beliefs concerning snakes in general. As will be seen, snakes—be they real, imaginary, or mythical—play an important role in Mohave belief, custom, and fantasy.

(1) *Concrete snakes.*—If a Mohave is bitten by a rattlesnake he may not eat the first crops produced in the course of that year, lest he should "dry up" (huyatc avi: rk=breath finished) like an old witch who had spent his powers. If the penis touches any part of a rattlesnake's skin a permanent erectile impotency ensues. The penis becomes "paralyzed," and the paralysis will eventually spread also to the rest of the body (Devereux, 1950 a). If a pregnant woman or her husband kills a rattlesnake, she gives birth to a monster, whose head

resembles that of a snake. Such monsters are prone to bite the nipple, and their bite is believed to be poisonous (pt. 6, pp. 257–259).[94]

(*2*) *Snake dreams.*—If one dreams of being bitten by a rattlesnake, or of fire falling on one's finger, one will be bitten by a rattlesnake (Kroeber, 1902). A 12-year-old boy, attending fourth grade and getting B's and D's, dreamed, on the night of November 9–10, 1938, that he was bitten by a snake, and then woke up. He was unable to say what kind of a snake it was (Case 78; see also Case 77). It is noteworthy that dreams of real snakes usually involve being bitten, while the hikwi : r snakes appearing in dreams simply blow upon the dreamer, thus underscoring their supernatural shaman status, or else use guns and bayonets, thus resembling the "evil" white people. (For other snake dreams, see Case 24.)

(*3*) *Imaginary snakes.*—Snakes are feared so much that they are seen everywhere.

CASE 26 (Informant: Modhar Taa : p, gens O : otc) :

At a dance a boy went into the bushes to urinate and was badly frightened by what he mistook for the hissing of a snake. He immediately jumped to one side, in order to dodge the snake. After looking around more carefully he realized that what he mistook for the hissing of a snake was merely the sound of an old woman urinating. (Cf. Case 134.)

Comment

Freud's (1924 b) remarks about fausse reconnaissance are fully applicable to this misidentification, since in Mohave psychology urinary exploits, including the attempted exploits of women, are closely connected with phallic-exhibitionistic impulses and, therefore, also with snakes, which among the Mohave are phallic symbols.

Snakes also occur in alcoholic hallucinations. I reported elsewhere (Case 134) the case of an intoxicated man who, while walking home at night through the bushes, saw white snakes everywhere. Two maladjusted boys also had dreams of being bitten by snakes (Cases 77 and 78), and snake dreams are a characteristic feature of the hikwi : r hahnok disease.

(*4*) *Snake charms.*—See part 4, pp. 202–212.

(*5*) *Mythical snakes.*—A mythical snake plays an important role in the Creation myth of both the Mohave (Kroeber, 1925 a) and the Yuma (Harrington, 1908). It is a dangerous and destructive "shaman," who encircles the world and is eventually destroyed by certain supernatural beings, acting as witch killers. (For hikwi : r dreams, without hikwi : r illness, cf. Case 24.)

In addition to hikwi : r hahnok (disease from the hikwi : r snake)— the most commonly used term—the hikwi : r disease is known by other names as well, e. g.:

(*a*) Kumádhi: hikwi : r (thorn hikwi : r).

(*b*) Hitoly hiva : um hikwi : r. (Roughly translated as stomach pain, stands there, spreads.) (Or else hitoly hiva : um : hitoly havekwi :r.) (Cf. pt. 1, p. 11.)

Turning now to the four general accounts of this disease, it is proposed to present them in succession, each account being followed by a brief cultural comment.

---

[94] These monsters may be children suffering from hereditary syphilis.

Hivsu: Tupo:ma's statement (1933).—[95] The hikwi:r hahnok illness is caused by having intercourse under water. It only affects women. When, during swimming parties, couples cohabit in the water, they do it standing up. When intercourse is vaginal, the man may stand either in front or behind the woman; when it is anal, he stands behind her. Unless a woman does this too often, if her blood is good she will not contract this illness. I will now describe to you the symptoms of this illness: There are pains going from one side to the other in the abdominal region. The upper limit of the tender area is the navel and its lower limit the superior edge of the pubic bone. Unless a shaman is called in to treat the sick woman, death will occur in a matter of days. The shamans specializing in the cure of this disease are Harav He:ya (whisky mouth) of Needles, Calif., and Kwathany Hi:wa (lizard heart) of Parker, Ariz. [After translating this statement, the woman interpreter laughingly remarked, "I don't know why intercourse under water should cause disease. Why, it's only a good wash!" [96]]

This exchange of repartee put Hivsu: Tupo:ma in the mood for some typical Mohave banter. Turning toward one of his friends, he remarked sarcastically, "Of course, if you were to do that to a woman, the water would come out again, right away." (I. e., "you have so small an organ that it could not plug the vagina.") Put on his mettle, the man retorted, "Sure, it would come out again, but not via the vagina. It would come out via her mouth." (I. e., because his penis is so long that it would push the water high up.)[97] Hivsu: Tupo:ma had the last word, however, when he replied, "Indeed, there would be water coming out of her mouth! The water she drank!" (I. e., She would vomit, because cohabitation with so inadequate a man would nauseate her.)

This scurrilous conversation, so typical of Mohave banter, shows that the characteristically humoristic approach of the Mohave to all sexual matters not directly related to gestation (Devereux, 1951 c) may manifest itself even in the course of serious discussions about diseases that usually elicit considerable concern.

Comment

Hivsu: Tupo:ma's theory differs from that of others, in that he attributes this illness to the action of the male organ[98] whereas the other informants attributed it to the action of snakes. It also differs from the others in stressing the element of ribaldry, this being chiefly due to Hivsu: Tupo:ma's extroverted and Rabelaisian personality makeup. It is probable, however, that precisely this aspect of the informant's personality enabled him to translate the snake symbol into its real meaning and to offer, instead of the cultural and symbolic etiological theory of this illness, a nonsymbolic theory thereof (Devereux, 1957 a). His account tallies with that of others in stressing that this illness is contracted in, or under, water. The nefarious influence of cold water, especially on female organs, is standard Mohave belief (Devereux, 1949 d).

Hikye:t's statement: See part 1, page 11.

Ahma Huma:re's statement (1938).—The Indians believe that the hikwi:r is someone like a human being in the night (i.e., the nocturnal father, viewed as a sexual ogre). You, of course, might not believe this.

---

[95] Although this shaman did not specialize in the treatment of hikwi:r hahnok, he could give reliable information even about diseases not coming within the scope of his own therapeutic activities. The following account is therefore probably authoritative.

[96] This acculturated woman may have been familiar with douches.

[97] A related exaggeration is reported by the Berndts (1951) from Arnheim Land.

[98] Under certain conditions a harmful effect is ascribed to the penis (Devereux, 1948 b).

CASE 27 (Informants: Ahma Huma: re and Hama: Utce:):

A bunch of snakes lived along the banks of the Colorado River, near Needles. There was a white man who used to go there, looking for the skins of these snakes. A Mohave man told this white that he shouldn't take the (sloughed-off?) skins of these snakes, because he would be sure to contract some sickness. Despite this warning the white man came and took one of these skins. Not long afterwards he was taken ill. The Mohave man, who had warned him not to take the snake skins, thereupon visited him and told him that he was dying because of what he did. He said that he had warned him that some day those snakes would come to him in his dream and take away his soul. [Which of his four souls?] I know of only one soul.[99]

Finally, they took this man to Los Angeles and he died there.

In the dreams of persons suffering from this disease, these snakes are something like a hayiko (white person). They even use guns and bayonets! When a person dreams that this snake did something to him with a gun—that he stabbed or shot him with it, etc.—he awakens from his dream with a severe headache and has no appetite. Sometimes such a patient also hemorrhages from the mouth and becomes insane (delirium?). He will do a lot of talking about anything and everything. He will die from this disease. He also has a tendency to run away. [Was that the disease old Mrs. Uta: c (Case 38) had?] I don't know what her illness was. The (principal?) place where these snakes live is known as Amat kupa: ma (earth to-go-out, or earth to-exit), which is near Prescott, Ariz. This snake is also called hikwi: r nyamat (snake earth). These snakes are ipa: (persons), and whites are also persons.

Comment

We already stressed that this particular account contains references to objects of foreign origin (guns, bayonets) which are integrated with a basically Mohave belief, and that it compares white people to supernatural snakes. (The Mohave routinely refer to whites as beavers (apen), which are semiaquatic.) In addition, it shows that even a white man, who is culturally alien and therefore skeptical of Mohave beliefs, may contract this illness. Similar harm also befell a Mohave who disregarded this tribal belief (Case 30). The "stabbing" and "shooting" of the guns owned by these snakes can, I think, be at least tentatively thought of as symbolic of the nefarious thrusts of the penis mentioned in Hivsu: Tupo: ma's account. It is also noteworthy that whereas the skin of real snakes causes only impotency, that of the hikwi: r causes a more serious illness.

Tcatc's statement (1938)[1].—There is a lake where people used to get mud for their shampoo (Kroeber, 1925 a). I don't know exactly what there is about that lake, but after Hamuly Huk' yè: rà did something to it, they began to call it Hanyeo Masthidhe:. Before that it was known as Hanyeo Kwaahwat (Lake Red). They believe that if anyone now bathes in that lake, or takes mud out of it, he will have headaches and may even hemorrhage from the mouth, because the lake was bewitched by putting some hikwi: r into it. This is a snake "all by itself" (i. e., unique). [Interpreter E. S. remarked that he had never seen one.] It is not a rattlesnake. It is the kind of snake mentioned in the English version of the Halyeku: p song cycle, which you read to me out of Kroeber's book (1925 a). I saw one of these snakes myself.

---

[99] This is manifestly inaccurate (Devereux, 1937 a).
[1] Though Tcatc was a laywoman, she was extraordinarily well informed. Her account dovetails with the others perfectly and adds new and significant data to them.

It looks like the rattlesnake. There isn't much difference in color or appearance (pattern on the back of the snake) between the two, but the hikwi:r is larger. It is twice as big as a rattlesnake—it is about 4 or 5 feet long. I don't know just what causes the terribleness of these snakes. People who dream of this snake say that at night it is a person (ipa:). When one is going to get sick from this snake, one dreams that the snake appears in the form of a person, and tells the dreamer its name, which is a personal name, like that of human beings. Then the dreamer believes that the snake is a person. The patient suffering from this illness hardly ever knows how to tell what he dreams about this snake, nor can he tell all that this snake does (partial repression), because he has such a severe (tension?) headache. Nowadays the lake is no longer bad.[2] Nonetheless, because of all this business, hardly anyone ever goes down there nowadays. However, they are doing quite a bit of farming near that lake. It seems that the drainage system goes into the lake, and therefore the lake doesn't look any more the way it used to look. [P. H. told me that there was also a two-headed hikwi:r.] That is right, and there is only one of those. It has two heads; one at each end of its body. The Indians call this snake hi:dho havi:k (face two). It is at a place called Amat Ku:kiyet (earth cut-off). This snake is in a cave called Kuyanyåva: (cave-house), to the north of Fort Mohave. There is a group of hikwi:r there, who have only one head. The one with two heads is the only one of its kind; he is the chief (ipa: taha:nå) of these snakes. These hikwi:r are actually referred to as ipa: (persons). They use some kind of feathers.[3] They wear these feathers in the dreams of the people who see them, and they look like people. Atco:rå Hatè:vå knew more about these matters than I do and so does Kwathany Hi:wa. It would be hard to get Kwathany Hi:wa to talk to you about these things. He is a coward at heart and is afraid that one might do something (bewitch?) to him.

Comment

Tcatc's account brings into the dream imagery, characteristic of this ailment, the feathers that play so important a role in the psychosis of the funeral ritualist, who is also a healer of the foreign sickness. Thus, her narrative completes and clarifies Ahma Huma:re's concrete allusions to whites, who, are believed to be highly phallic and, thus, symbolize the nocturnal sexual father (Devereux, 1950 a). In addition, she introduces the theme of the bewitched lake, which is only tangentially mentioned in Ahma Huma:re's narrative, and which plays a significant role in Case 30. She also mentions the two-headed chief of the snakes. Psychoanalysis and mythological material alike suggest that two-headed beings are a condensation of two separate—or, at least, separable—beings (see Case 29, for a dream about two cooperating snakes). In this instance, the two heads are connected by means of a snake body—an imagery whose psychoanalytic meaning is fairly clear, especially in terms of "bridge-symbolism" (Ferenczi, 1926). Perhaps the most important point raised by Tcatc refers, however, to the fact that people who dream of the hikwi:r cannot recall the hikwi:r's personal name that was communicated to them in dream, nor even give a full account of the snake's

---

[2] Perhaps because Hamuly Huk'ye:rå died recently, allegedly bewitched by Kwathany Hi:wa. In reality his half brother, Hivsu: Tupo:ma, admitted to me that, motivated by sibling rivalry, he, personally, had disposed of him, through witchcraft (Devereux, 1948 i).

[3] Compare the psychosis allegedly caused by contact with the feathers of funeral regalia, part 4, pp. 186–195. Cf. also the Mayan feathered serpent.

activities in the dream. Instead, they have a (tension?) headache. This is clearly a description of the repression of the dream on awakening, which is made necessary by its painful or embarrassing (latent?) content. (Cf. Hivsu: Tupo : ma's account.) The inability of the dreamer to communicate the name of the hikwi : r is strongly reminiscent of the Mohave belief that a bewitched person knows the name of his magical foe, but cannot tell it to the therapist, either because the shaman "sealed the victim's lips" or else because the victim is actually willing to become the witch's beloved prey and a member of his faithful retinue of ghosts (pt. 7, pp. 383–386). Since the Mohave explicitly state that the mutual attraction between witch and victim is usually a sexual one, and is implemented in dream (Devereux, 1937 c), the dreamer's inability to recall the name of the hikwi : r must be related to the dreamer's repression of the snake's actions in the dream. While these remarks are admittedly speculative, they are not too fanciful to deserve consideration, at least as working hypotheses. The fact that the snake assumes in dream the form of a person has a twofold significance. We already saw (pt. 2, pp. 42–46) that, according to the Mohave, the only animal people dream of is the bull, and that the bull is a shaman in disguise. By contrast, in this instance it is a supernatural snake which is "disguised"—or would it be more correct to say "unmasked"?— as a person. The specification that the snake is recognized as a person only when it tells its name is also significant. Tcatc specifically said that this snake first appears in dream in a disguise, i.e., in the form of a snake; only as the "dream work" progresses (and as the mounting excitement overcomes the "dream censor") is the real identity of the snake revealed. Indeed, it is hardly necessary to argue the reasonableness of the assumption that only a person whom one does not wish to recognize needs to be smuggled into the dream in a disguised form. Were it otherwise, there would be no need for a disguise. Taking into account that, on awakening, amnesia partially blankets both the actions and the identity of the snake, and considering the nature of the attraction that, according to the Mohave, exists between witch and victim, the suggestion that such dreams may be oedipal ones does not seem farfetched. Indeed, in terms of what is known of dream symbolism, the "king" of snakes can only be the father's phallus, while the two-headed snake almost certainly symbolizes the primal scene.

One minor, but interesting, point to be stressed is that the hikwi :r snakes appear in dream disguised as persons. This belief may be related to the Mohave Indians' (erroneous) conviction that the only animal they dream about is the bull, and that the dream bull is but a shaman in disguise (pt. 2. pp. 42–46). This belief is complemented by the thesis that the hikwi :r, who have all the characteristics of supernatural shamans, appear in dreams in a human guise.

Hilyera Anyay's statement (1938).—This statement is of special significance, in that it was made by a person who claims to have the hikwi :r hahnok ailment.

[What makes people go insane?] A person may be sane to start with, but when he is (in a state of, or afflicted by) suma: tc itcem (dreams evil) (Wallace, 1947) sickness comes to him and he goes insane. When he is insane, they sometimes say that he is hikwi :r hahnok (snake contamination). Such people have bad dreams. When these dreams stop, they seem to get better. But if they keep on dreaming, having such dreams time and again, they naturally get worse. At that point it is no longer a plain (or 'straight') sickness like pains, or hemorrhages, as it was in the first stages. Yet it sometimes happens that when people grow old hikwi : r hahnok does not (any longer?) have an effect on them. On the other hand, if these bad dreams keep on coming, people get worse before they get old. They must be (have) suma: tc itcem (dreams evil). What I told you just now is a matter of general knowledge regarding the good and the bad aspects of hikwi:r hahnok. What I explained to you up to now is one kind of sickness. I am describing to you the various (mental) illnesses one by one.

Comment

Hilyera Anyay's statement is significant chiefly because it stresses that hikwi:r hahnok tends not to affect older people as severely as it affects younger ones. If hikwi:r hahnok should really turn out to be a mental disorder—and Hilyera Anyay listed it first among mental derangements—the specification above could fit both hysteria and manic-depressive psychosis. The informant's emphasis on the psychiatric aspects of the illness is interesting, in view of the fact that both he and his wife (Cases 28, 29) seemed unusually pleasant, neither of whom complained of overt psychiatric symptoms, though their hikwi:r dreams were obviously neurotic ones.

CASE 28 (Informant: The patient):

Dreamer.—Hilyera Anyay, a very old and nearly blind shaman, was most cooperative, unusually intelligent, and a very clear thinker as well. The events reported were stated to be recent ones.

"I was standing by the lake (Red Lake) and in my heart I knew that these hikwi:r things (snakes) were living somewhere along the bank. In my dream I knew that I had to get to the other side of the lake, so I went into the water and started to wade across. When I was halfway across, I suddenly felt warm around the legs. I knew that this warmth was the breath of one of these snakes."

Associations.—"Now, in my old age, I feel (have sensations in) my legs and have rheumatism. That is why I had this dream, which was the sign of the coming of rheumatism. Hence, I got sick after having this dream. When I get up and try to walk after sitting for a long while, my legs feel heavy and I have such sharp pains in my knees that it sometimes causes me to fall down. In my younger days I used to run races and ran long distances. Now, in my old age, the thing I have to think about, and must forget, are these pains."

Comment

Mythical as well as real snakes are pathogenic agents. The lake in question (Red Lake) is believed by some to have once been "good"; women used to go there to get mud for shampooing their hair. However, a malevolent shaman, Hamuly Huk'yè:rà did "something" to that lake, and now it is "bad." The breath of shamans and witches, both human and supernatural, is an important magical substance, used in therapy as well as in witchcraft. Heat is an important therapeutic agent among the Mohave. Mohave men literally sit on their upturned soles (Kroeber, 1925 a; Devereux, 1948 a, 1949 b), which is probably an uncomfortable position for an old man to assume. The Mohave are noted for their great ability to run incredibly long distances (Kroeber, 1925 a).

Tentative diagnosis.—Onset of rheumatism, eliciting an anxiety dream.

Interpretation.—This dream is stated to have heralded or caused the onset of rheumatism, which put an end to the dreamer's former agility and speed. The warm breath of the snakes on the dreamer's legs appears to be a denial of the illness, since old people suffering from rheumatism often have poor circulation, so that their legs feel cold rather than warm. One tentative interpretation of the warm feeling around the legs while wading may be that children—and sometimes even adults—urinate into the water in which they wade or swim, which causes a sensation of heat on the legs.[4] If this interpretation is correct, it ties up with Hivsu: Tupo:ma's statement that the hikwi:r illness is caused by coitus under water—both coitus and urination being phallic feats. Speaking in the most tentative manner, entering water often symbolizes a return to the womb and/or dying. It may be noted in this connection that the land of the dead is under the Colorado River (Devereux, 1937 a). Crossing water often symbolizes death and rebirth; the idea of rebirth being present in Mohave society, especially in connection with twins (Devereux, 1941). Another belief in the return to the womb is discussed in part 4, pp. 150–175. (See also Devereux, 1948 b.) The presence of snakes (=phalli) in the water may conceivably be related to the Mohave belief in an interaction between the phallus and the fetus within the maternal body (Devereux, 1948 b, 1949 c). It should be stressed, however, that the preceding interpretations are highly tentative. They are cited here not so much in order to offer a psychoanalytic interpretation of the dream, as in order to stress the importance of understanding the cultural meaning of personages or events occurring in a dream, before offering a psychoanalytic interpretation. Even if the preceding interpretation should prove incorrect, it is quite certain that a more correct interpretation of this dream would be impossible without taking into account the cultural significance of the elements occurring in this dream. On the other hand, it is extremely likely that one purpose of this dream was to bring the—possibly still only preconsciously perceived—onset of the illness in line with cultural beliefs regarding its etiology, and, as regards the warm breath of the snakes, to deny the illness, since heat is a recognized therapeutic agent in Mohave culture, while cold water (=wading through water) is deemed to be harmful. (Devereux, 1949 d, 1950 g). This interpretation suggests that in this dream the snakes perform a typically shamanistic double role: they cause illness, and yet blow warm breath on the legs of the dreamer. This is in line with the Mohave belief that shamans can both cause and cure a given illness (Devereux, 1937 c).

CASE 29 (Informant: The patient):

Dreamer.—The aged wife of the shaman Hilyera Anyay reported the following recent dream:

"I shall tell you first about my illness. My abdomen was swelling up and I could not breathe. Then, one night, I dreamed that I was standing by an adobe structure or house. A woman, whom I did not recognize, was sitting by my side. This woman told me that two people wished to treat me, and I said 'All right.' I lay down outdoors, near the south side of the house, when I noticed two snakes near the southwest corner of the house. As I lay down, I closed my eyes and wondered how it would feel to have two snakes doctor me. (Polyandrous fantasy?) The snakes came out of their hole, crawled on my abdomen and chest, and blew their breath upon me, the way shamans do when they doctor a sick person. Then, almost as soon as they had come, they went back to their hole again. When the snakes were gone I got up and stood there, looking at the hole into which they had disappeared. Then I woke up."

Associations.—"Shortly after I had this dream I began to notice that the swelling of my abdomen was decreasing. It went down so much that I could once more

---

[4] This interpretation was suggested by Martin H. Stein, M.D. (personal communication, 1957).

take long (=deep) breaths. I felt much better. But when the swelling went down, I had no appetite any longer, and by the time I was well again, I was quite thin. Now I am gaining weight once more. When I woke up, I told my dream to my husband. I did not know whether or not this was a good dream. The night (which is a 'person' who 'sends' dreams) seems to tell us what is going to happen . . . or is not going to happen. The name of my disease is hikwi:r hahnok (snake-caused). [How do you know it is not hiwey lak nyevedhi:=anus pain ghostly?][5] The two diseases are much alike. Both start the same way, but when the illness gets worse, the ghost (nyevedhi:) element comes into the picture."

Comment

Tentative diagnosis.—The fact that the swelling of the abdomen and the shortness of breath rapidly improved after a crucial night suggested to Martin H. Stein, M. D., and Ellis Devereux, M. D., the possibility that this old woman had been suffering from right heart failure, causing an accumulation of fluid in the body, which was alleviated in a single night by a (temporary) cardiac recovery.

Cultural comment.—In this dream, snakes function as healing shamans, treating an illness caused by snakes. This double function of snakes tallies with the belief that he who can cure a certain illness can also cause it (Devereux, 1937 c). The snake as a therapist is not a specifically Mohave cultural phenomenon. Snakes played a significant role in the ancient Greek Aesculapian cult, and its cult emblem, the caduceus, survives as a medical symbol to this day. The fact that these dream snakes spontaneously offer to treat the dreamer is, however, atypical, since real shamans wait to be consulted by prospective patients or their families; they are not ambulance chasers. On the other hand, the snakes cured the dreamer by standard Mohave means, e.g., they blew on the patient, though, unlike real shamans, they sang no songs. It is also significant that even though such snakes may appear in pathogenic dreams disguised as human scalper-funeral-ritualist-foreign-disease-healers, in this curing dream they appear in their real shape. The fact that two snakes treated the patient simultaneously is also atypical, since two shamans never treat a patient at one and the same time. Possibly the appearance of two snakes may be a dream expression of belief in the existence of a two-headed chief of the hikwi:r, the meaning of which is indicated above. With regard to the hole into which the snakes disappear, it is well known that snakes do not dig holes for themselves, but preempt holes dug by small burrowing animals, such as rats. The Mohave believe that the soul of a very young child, whose chin has not yet been tattooed, does not go to the land of the dead that lies under the Colorado River[6] but into a rat hole, and sometimes returns to the womb of its mother, causing pseudocyesis (false pregnancy), which is one of the forms of the hiwey lak nyevedhi: illness (pt. 4, pp. 150–175).

Interpretation.—Aristotle knew that one may perceive in dream the onset of an illness long before one becomes conscious of it in a waking state.

---

[5] The purposes of this question were: (1) To test the dreamer's conviction of the correctness of her diagnosis (pt. 1, pp. 24–35). (2) To clarify whether the manifest content of the *dream* preceding illness or the *symptoms* of the illness form the basis of Mohave diagnoses. Indeed, the swelling of an older woman's abdomen is often believed to be caused by a ghost pregnancy (pt. 4 pp. 150–175).

[6] It should be noted in this connection that even though the hikwi:r snakes are said to live in water, they were never mentioned to me in connection with the Colorado River.

In this case, however, it is the impending improvement that is heralded by a dream, perhaps because the heart temporarily resumed its normal functioning. The crawling of the snakes on the belly and chest may be related to the existing shortness of breath [7] and their departure may have been dreamed of at the precise moment when the functioning of the heart improved. The choice of snakes as dream figures is hard to interpret with any degree of confidence. In general, psychoanalysts find that the dream personage pressing down on the dreamer in the nightmare is a parental figure (Jones, 1931), and curing by blowing was interpreted by Róheim (1932) as a symbol of cohabitation. However, in this instance at least, the primary determinant of the appearance of snakes in the dream may be the fact that, the husband having had snake dreams causing hikwi:r hahnok, the wife felt unconsciously motivated to adopt a similar dream symbolism.[8] However, since reality factors (illness, and also the dream of the husband) seem to account for much of the dream's content and symbolism, and since the dream was not obtained in a psychoanalytic situation and the personal associations to the dream are relatively meager, it would be hazardous to interpret fully the unconscious content of this dream and the interplay of psychic forces in the dream work that caused Mrs. Hilyera Anyay to have this particular dream.[9]

CASE 30 (Informants: Tcatc and E. S.) :

Hu: kyev Anyay (=to bring together light), whose English name is forgotten, belonged to the Mu: th gens, and was married to Nyortc Kupu: yhà. This couple had no children.[10] Nyortc Kupu: yhà was a very nice (pretty?) girl, and had lovely hair. Hence, she frequently sent her husband to get mud for a shampoo from Red Lake, which is some four-fifths of a mile from Parker, near Ben Butler's farm. This lake had been bewitched by the shaman Hamuly Huk' yè: rà, simply because he was a shaman, and shamans do just anything to be odd. He did it just because people kept going to that lake. Hu: kyev Anyay had heard of the spell cast on the lake, but he kept going there all the same to get mud, because he did not believe in the spell. This happened around 1910, about the time the land allotments were made. As a result of his doing this, he became quite ill. He didn't do anything strange. He did not even talk or move the way Le: va (Case 35) did, who was also bewitched by the same shaman. He merely had an abdominal hemorrhage and, when he died, his stomach was puffed up with blood. He was treated by Hukuwalyevalye (=Kuwaly) who had hiku: pk suma: tc (venereal disease dream power), and was famous for having been the husband of more than one male transvestite (Devereux, 1937 b).[11] [Why did they get a hiku: pk shaman to doctor a patient

---

[7] Suffocation is characteristic of the true nightmare (Jones, 1931) and is specifically referred to in the German term Alp*druck*.

[8] Parallel dreams of closely associated persons, in which the dream of A. serves as a "day residue" for the dream of B., are known to occur. The most extreme forms of such a psychic interdependence are "folie à deux" and the "deputy lunatic" (Devereux, 1956 a).

[9] The interpretation of dreams to which there are few associations, especially if the dreamer's personality is not well known, is a highly speculative undertaking and may lead to off-the-cuff interpretations bordering on a psychoanalytic parlor game. Such over-interpretations have no standing in responsible psychoanalytic research.

[10] The designation of the wife as Nyortc, instead of Nyoltc, shows that she had given birth—presumably in a previous marriage—to at least one child, who died (Kroeber, 1925 a).

[11] If a transvestite happens to be a shaman, he or she is always a very powerful one indeed. However, a shaman married to a transvestite is not, ipso facto, an exceptionally powerful shaman.

who had hikwi:r hahnok?] I don't know why they chose him, rather than some other shaman. He specialized in venereal diseases. If you had been here at that time, and had had gonorrhea, he would have doctored you too. (A typical bit of Mohave banter.) Despite the treatment, this man died within a week after contracting this illness. His wife (Case 61) eventually remarried and had a child by her next husband. No close relative of this man survives; he was the last of his family. The same thing happens in many cases of witchcraft (and incest)—the family just dies out (Devereux, 1939 a).

Comment

Tentative diagnosis.—The clinical picture might suggest stomach ulcer with hemorrhage, though, since stomach ulcer is rare among primitives, it is more probable that the man had both tuberculosis and venereal disease. Psychiatric symptoms were denied, though his deliberate defiance of the dangers of a bewitched lake suggests that he had some self-destructive impulses, and that, once the disease became manifest, he may have had anxieties. This, however, is simply a probability, and not an established fact.

The diagnosis of hikwi:r was obviously made because of this man's repeated contacts with a lake which contained hikwi:r and was, moreover, under an evil spell. These facts impelled the Mohave to diagnose this case as "hikwi:r hahnok," complicated by witchcraft, even though obvious psychiatric symptoms could not be observed. The combination of hikwi:r hahnok with witchcraft would, in terms of Mohave medical theories, make this a "not straight" (multiple) type of illness.

THE AHWE: PSYCHOSES

Roughly speaking, the ahwe: disorders fall into three main groups: ahwe: hahnok (or mahnok or hahnotc) = foreign (enemy) contamination, ahwe: nyevedhi: = foreign (enemy) ghost, and ahwe: ma: n (pt. 2, pp. 43–45). The boundary between the first two conditions is not always sharply drawn. Ahwe: hahnok may only be a simpler, or earlier, or more benign form of ahwe: nyevedhi:, exactly as hiwey lak appears to be a less complex form of hiwey lak nyevedhi:, or as the nyevedhi: element may complicate the hikwi:r ailment. In fact, ahwe: hahnok may even be simply a "straight" disease, and ahwe: nyevedhi: a "not-straight" (multiple) disease, involving also either other disorders or ghosts, or else witchcraft. The third type, i. e., ahwe: ma:n, was discussed elsewhere (pt. 2, pp. 43–45).

The Mohave themselves spontaneously relate the ahwe: group to the scalper's psychosis (pt. 2, pp. 43–45) that Pulyi:k specifically designated as a form of ahwe:; a juxtaposition that, in the light of Mohave etiological theories, seems perfectly reasonable. At the other end of the scale, ahwe: nyevedhi: is said to be related to hiwey lak nyevedhi:, apparently because the dreams occurring in these two illnesses are extremely similar and involve dream interaction with ghosts. At first glance, the fact that dreams about the ghost of a deceased spouse or relative, i.e., of a person who is usually a Mohave, are capable of causing the ahwe: (alien) illness seems utterly paradoxical, at least on the (logical) conscious level. It is, however, perfectly reasonable, if one assumes that ghosts and aliens are affectively (unconsciously) experienced as the same kind of beings . . . an inference supported by the fact that the scalper, who is also a funeral ritualist, may, in his former capacity, contract the scalper's psychosis (said to be a type of ahwe: nyevedhi:), and, in his latter capacity, the psychosis caused by misconduct during memorial rites (pt. 4, pp. 186–195) ; in addition, he is also usually a ghost doctor (Fathauer, 1951).

Before presenting Mohave accounts of the ahwe: psychoses, it therefore seems desirable to outline briefly the Mohave's attitude toward, and fear of, aliens, since the "xenophobia of fear" is a major theme in Mohave culture.

Mohave xenophobia is determined by several considerations:

The Mohave refrain from all close contact with other tribes, and even more from intimate connections with alien races. Mexican blood is, however, relatively safe; Pulyi:k felt it was not too strong. As regards halfbreeds, Hama: Utce:, a halfbreed, reports that, in her childhood, people refused to eat from the same dish with her, though, needless to say, she was given as much food as anyone else. (However, she did play with other children and was made to carry around the baby of one of her relatives (Devereux, 1948 c).) Food received from aliens and nonaboriginal food also cause the alien sickness. K. M. Stewart (1947 c) specifies that, when female captives were distributed, only older men put in a claim for them, because they did not expect to live long anyhow. This suggests that the malignant influence of aliens requires some time to take effect. In addition, the Mohave believe that alien males are phallic, sexually potent (Devereux, 1950 a), and genetically prepotent. They believe this is true even of Mexicans. Thus, in connection with the belief that if a pregnant woman changes sex partners her new partner will modify the biological and social identity of the baby,[12] it is held, on the one hand, that it is hard for a Mohave to change the racial identity of a halfbreed fetus, and, on the other hand, that a single sexual act with an alien may suffice to change the racial identity of a full-blood Mohave fetus (Devereux, 1937 d, 1949 c). The extreme sexual effectiveness of the alien male is also reflected by his "dangerously" large male organ and hyperpotency (Devereux, 1950 a).[13] Last, but not least, the killing and/or scalping of enemies—or even a mere

---

[12] This belief is highly convenient in a society where marriages are very brittle, and children much desired and loved, since it enables the pregnant woman's new spouse to claim her previously conceived baby as his own.

[13] Since the partial breakdown of Mohave culture, men sometimes visit alien prostitutes in order to lend "spice" to the sexual act, whereas formerly only impoverished women had relations with whites capable of paying them for their services (Devereux, 1948 f).

participation in a raid—exposes the Mohave to the dangers of the ahwe: illness.

On an altogether different level, the Mohave stressed that all of Kroeber's informants died shortly after working with him,[14] apparently because, by imparting to him tribal secrets, or knowledge obtained in dream, they exposed themselves to the ahwe: illness, (and, perhaps, also to witchcraft).

Summing up, the three most intensive forms of physiological interactions—eating, cohabitation, and killing—and the most significant form of psychological interaction—discussing the knowledge one acquired in dream [15]—expose the Mohave to the dangers of foreign contamination. Less intensive contacts are, by contrast, not especially dangerous.

The second, and more general, factor is the streak of insularity in Mohave personality, which, paradoxically, is complemented by a tendency to explore distant countries,—e. g., for "name traveling" (McNichols, 1944)—secure in the knowledge that no one would dare attack even a single Mohave traveler, lest the dreaded Mohave clubbers should, later on, retaliate. Like many other Mohave paradoxes, this, too, becomes less paradoxical on closer scrutiny. Thus, Dr. A. M. Halpern (1938) informed me that men sometimes deliberately strayed into enemy territory, because they wished to be killed (pt. 7, pp. 426–431). Getting oneself killed by enemies is, needless to say, a way of expiating warlike aggression, guilt feelings of this type being quite common in many warrior societies. In another sense, the fear of aliens—and the deliberate incurring of risks by coming into contact with aliens—is but another facet of the type of reaction to conquest which, in other tribes, led to waves of suicide in early reservation days.

A third factor, related especially to impregnation by alien males, is tribal concern over the transmission of gentile affiliation. Among the Mohave, gentile affiliation is transmitted by the male, though the gentile name is used exclusively by females (Kroeber, 1925 a). Thus, both a man's sisters and his daughters may be called, e.g., O:otc, while he himself will have a strictly personal made-up name, although this name sometimes (though not often) is an allusion to his gentile emblem, which may, or may not, have been formerly a totem. Now, whereas the Mohave accept certain gentes of the related Yuman tribes as equivalent to their own, so that, e.g., a Yuma father of the Hipa:

---

[14] Needless to say, this was due to the fact that, like all anthropologists investigating a rapidly decaying culture, Kroeber worked chiefly with older persons.

[15] Compare in this context the fact that shamans are reluctant to speak of their own power dreams, medical theories, and therapeutic practices in the presence of another shaman, because they fear that the latter—offended by views partly differing from his own—may bewitch them (Devereux, 1957 b).

gens may transmit membership in the Mohave Hipa: gens to his children,[16] it is not known whether a Yuma father of the Wahas gens will transmit to his child membership in the Mohave Vaha:th gens, because of the similarity of names, or whether he will transmit to it membership in Syuly gens, because of the identity of the emblem (or "totemic reference"). As regards non-Yuman men, be they Indians or racially alien persons, they cannot transmit to their children membership in a non-Mohave gens, even if, in the father's tribe, gentile affiliation is transmitted in the male line. Originally this rule did not admit of exceptions; in more recent times it became more flexible, however. Thus, the daughter of an Italian father and Mohave mother, whose family name on the Agency register is that of her Italian father, is, by courtesy, sometimes called Mah, and was even considered sufficiently Mohave to have her nervous breakdown attributed to the foreign illness (Case 31), perhaps because she was raised entirely among the Mohave. She was certainly not believed to have the foreign illness because she was a halfbreed, since halfbreeds are apparently not believed to be—if one may use so daring a metaphor—"allergic to themselves." Also, as specific descriptions of the foreign sickness show, halfbreeds are considered racially alien, and therefore capable of causing fullblood Mohave Indians to contract the foreign illness. By contrast, even a decade or two earlier, the Mohave were less accommodating in this respect. Thus, when Hama: Utce:, who was of mixed blood, more or less considered herself to be—through her mother—a member of the Kunyii:th gens,[17] her claim does not appear to have been challenged by anyone, but neither was it ever formally accepted. In brief, the child of an alien father usually has no gens, and, if a female, does not wear a gentile name. Such persons either have a "funny name" [18] or else are known by the "English"

---

[16] Gifford (1918) published a tabulation of gentile equivalences among the Yuman tribes, which, while probably correct, has certain puzzling features, in that identically named gentes mostly do not have the same "totemic references" in all Yuman tribes. This may indicate nothing more than an obsolescence of the totemic *function* of the referents . . . but may also indicate that these referents were not true totems even in early times. In fact, they may simply be relatively recently adopted emblems, this being suggested also by the fact that some gentes have several unrelated referents in one and the same tribe. Thus, the Mohave Nyoltc gens has five referents: Sun, fire, deer, eagle, and humahnana beetle. While "sun" and "fire" may be interrelated, the relationship between these two and the other three is probably nil, and furthermore, the last three likewise do not seem to be related to each other. The problem is too complex to be discussed in this context. Suffice it to say that whereas it may be possible to establish, even at this late date, a gentile equivalence system in terms of the capacity of an alien (though Yuman) father to transmit his gentile affiliation to his half-Mohave child, it is almost certain that emblem equivalences are no longer susceptible of being established, and that the question of whether the Yumans ever had real totems will remain permanently in abeyance.

[17] The word "ipa:" means both person and lineage. The question "Kutc simu:ly ipa:?" (= what gens people) means actually: "To what gens do your people belong?"—but, because of the double meaning of ipa: (= person and also social group, lineage, family), it can also be translated as "You are a person of what gens?"

[18] This is far from unique. The Mohave revel in weird, self-chosen names, such as "Drygoods' anus" (Devereux, 1951 c).

name under which they appear on the Agency register. Now, even though almost the only function of the gentes is the transmission of gentile affiliation and the insuring of gentile exogamy, a disturbance of the gentile pattern is highly undesirable from the Mohave point of view, since a given ethnic group's "systems of classification" are among its most characteristic (Devereux, 1956 a) and most cherished cultural possessions.[19]

The pervasiveness and importance of xenophobia in Mohave society may best be ascertained by determining whether inherently unrelated material is forcibly coordinated with it, in a relationship of "artificial compendence" (Devereux, 1957 a). We have already stressed that not only aliens, but also the alien's foodstuffs, may cause the foreign illness. In this instance artificial compendence is relatively minimal, since the nexus is brought into being by means of a simple expansion of the concept "alien" to include not only the foreigner, but also all his works and possessions, by recourse to the pars pro toto principle. It is on this basis that alien food is held capable of causing the foreign illness.

The artificiality of the compendence is more pronounced in the case of magic-laden substances, or charms, which "do not really belong to the Mohave," but to alien tribes. Since the Mohave have no real "power over them," the Mohave possessors of these substances are ultimately harmed by these charms. However, in contradistinction to alien foods, these alien magical objects apparently do not cause the "foreign illness," but a disease which is sui generis, and which is caused primarily by contact with magic-laden substances and only secondarily by the fact that these substances belong to alien tribes (pt. 4, pp. 202–212).

We will postpone for the moment a closer scrutiny of the problem whether, in a roundabout way, "alien" and "magical" may mean the same thing, at least in the unconscious, and will examine instead the even more farfetched artificial compendence that the Mohave seem to establish between live foreigners and the ghosts of deceased Mohave Indians, both of whom may cause the "foreign ghost illness." Now, it stands to reason that the ability of the ghost of a Mohave Indian's own deceased parent, relative, or spouse to cause the foreign ghost illness is, to say the least, startling, especially since, officially at least, the Mohave believe that the ghost of a Mohave continues to be a Mohave also in the land of the dead.

At the same time it was possible to point out, in connection with the culturally atypical hoarding behavior that characterizes persons

---

[19] For example, the notion that "gender" is related to "sex" is so deeply ingrained in our culture that I once experienced considerable difficulties in persuading several behavioral scientists that the absence of gender in a given language does not imply that persons speaking that language minimize or ignore sex differences.

preparing for death (Kroeber, 1925 a), as well as in connection with the possessiveness of the recently dead (Devereux, 1942 a), and the acquisitiveness of twins, whom one set of Mohave beliefs defines as reincarnated ghosts (Devereux, 1941), that the Mohave do, in fact, ascribe to the dying and to the dead an acquisitive and selfish type of misconduct which they consider characteristic only of living aliens, and especially of whites. Hence, even though they formally deny that the ghost of a Mohave Indian turns into a kind of alien, their beliefs concerning the economic selfishness of supposedly Mohave ghosts and their conviction that the ghosts of one's own relatives may cause one to contract the foreign ghost illness, indicate that the formal belief concerning the nationality of Mohave ghosts is not echoed on a deeper attitudinal and affective level. (Cf. p. 139.) Without falling into the more extreme errors of the old-fashioned comparative method, it is not inappropriate to recall in this context that primitives often equate truly strange groups with the ghosts of their own ancestors. Thus, at least one Australian tribe argued that the newly arrived whites had to be the ghosts of their ancestors, since otherwise they would have been unable to find their way to that tribe's territory. In Melanesian "cargo" cults, whites also tend to be viewed at least as the emissaries of the tribe's ancestors.

If we now combine the culturally implicit, and psychologically more or less unconscious, tendency to equate aliens and Mohave ghosts with the fact that magic substances cause harm primarily because they do not truly belong to the Mohave, we must conclude, be it only tentatively, that—at least in psychological-attitudinal terms—the Mohave experience one and the same type of dread in connection with aliens, magical powers, and the ghosts of the deceased.[20] It is quite certain that such an identity of psychological reactions cannot take place in a cultural vacuum and cannot fail to have at least latent cultural consequences.

Thus, on the cultural level, the fear of magical substances and the dread of ghosts appears to be brought into a relationship of artificial compendence with the Mohave Indian's pervasive fear of all that is alien, partly because of the obnoxious acquisitiveness manifested by aliens, and partly because the alien's blood, soul, or "power" causes the Mohave to contract the alien sickness. In brief, on the cultural level, the Mohave Indian's xenophobia is the source of his dread of ghosts and magical powers.

By contrast, on the psychological level it is probable that the source of the Mohave Indian's conviction that aliens, as well as magical powers and substances, are dangerous, is, in the last resort, his fear

---

[20] It should be recalled that one and the same person functions as scalper, purifier of warriors, healer of the alien and the ghost sicknesses, and funeral orator.

of ghosts. The psychological transformation of the beloved relative's or spouse's ghost into a dangerous being is due partly to unconscious resentment over the beloved person's "desertion," and partly to the final eruption, triggered by the trauma of mourning, of the hitherto repressed aggressive component of man's unconscious ambivalence toward those whom he overtly loves. A further triggering factor is the feeling that neither ghosts nor aliens act as real, live Mohave should. We will return to this point in a moment.

Be that as it may, the Mohave themselves are quite conscious of their xenophobia, though, when accused of being terribly prejudiced, they at first strenuously denied it. However, in the end Hama: Utce: remarked: "The Mexicans are really closest to us; yet we would do more for an (American) Chinese or Japanese, than for a Mexican." Sometimes the Mohave neutralize their xenophobia by pretending that a likable alien is really a Mohave; a trait already mentioned by Garcés (1900). Thus, I, personally, was told time and again that I was not really a white but a Mohave, since I felt and acted the way a Mohave does.[21] Otherwise expressed, an alien who acts the way a Mohave should act, is, both emotionally and by courtesy, no longer a true alien. This, in turn, implies that a Mohave, such as Ha: wl, who is selfish like an alien, is felt to be "more like a white than like a Mohave." It is therefore reasonable to suggest that one reason why ghosts are implicitly viewed as sufficiently alien to be capable of causing the alien ghost illness is that their conduct is un-Mohave, which, in essence, means: not predictable in terms of Mohave "systems of classification" (Durkheim and Mauss, 1903) and of the expectations which are rooted in such a system of classification.[22]

It is of interest to note, at least in passing, that, even though the Mohave say that the Yuma are like the Mohave, and even though Hama: Utce: specified that the Mexicans were closer to the Mohave than any other racially alien group, I know of no instance where the expression "he is really a Mohave" was applied to anyone other than a white, and this despite the fact that the whites are the most foreign and most dangerous of aliens. Indeed, once in a while someone will even refer to ahwe: hahnok as apen hahnok (=beaver contamina-

---

[21] Since, to the Mohave, "white" means primarily "American," the fact that I had first come to them straight from France, also mitigated the odium of my being white, especially since those Mohave, who fought in World War I, admired French valor in general, and that of French officers in particular. "The officers were always the first to emerge from the trenches when the French attacked."

[22] From the psychological point of view it is important to note in this context that, for the small child, the behavior of adults—and especially that of parents—is essentially arbitrary and unpredictable (Devereux, 1955 b). It is therefore suggested, at least tentatively, that the relative unpredictability of ghosts and of foreigners is, psychologically, a major determinant of the tendency to equate ghosts, aliens, and also magical powers which, by definition, are unruly and unpredictable. In brief, the ghost becomes as unpredictable as the parent (= witch) sometimes seemed to the child. (Cf., however, pt. 5, pp. 254–255.)

tion) or apen nyevedhi: (=beaver ghost); the term "beaver" referring specifically to whites, who were formerly known as apen kutctha:ny (=beaver eaters), though nowadays they are called "hi:ko" by the older generation and—even when speaking Mohave—"Americans" or "whites" by the younger people.[23]

On the whole, Mohave xenophobia—which formerly led to the killing of halfbreed infants (Devereux, 1948 d)—appears to have been quite an effective barrier to miscegenation, since, as late as the 1920's, the reports of the Commissioner of Indian Affairs listed fewer halfbreeds among the Mohave and the other Yumans than among many other tribes.

The last point to be considered is the tendency of the Mohave to think of the alien disease as the most basic of all disorders. Hikye:t (pt. 1, pp. 9–17) more or less equated ahwe: nyevedhi: with ku: na: v nyevedhi:, and so did Pulyi: k. This latter term means, roughly speaking, "the foreordained ghost (disease)." [24] The implication of this name is that the disease in question was already foreseen and foreordained at the time the human world was first organized and that it was mentioned by Mastamho as the prototype of diseases. This was taken for granted by all informants, though it should be noted that Kroeber's (1948) version of the Mastamho myth does not discuss this illness in any way. This omission does not cast doubt either upon the accuracy of the text recorded by Kroeber, or upon the veracity of my informants, since everything that exists is automatically held to have been foreordained in the beginning. Furthermore, since the Mastamho myth does account for the origin of various nations, even before it accounts for agriculture, etc., it is clear that national differences are, in the opinion of the Mohave, among the most fundamental categories of the human order. This, in turn, necessarily implies that diseases due to contact with aliens must, ipso facto, be among the most basic of all disorders.

AHWE: HAHNOK

The first set of data to be presented pertains nominally only to the ahwe: hahnok entity, though it will be noted that it contains many references to ahwe: nyevedhi: as well. In fact, it seems evident that certain passages supposedly pertaining to ahwe: hahnok refer primarily to ahwe: nyevedhi:, which is believed to be a closely related, though more complex, disorder, whose nature is supposed to shed light upon the nature of the simpler ahwe: hahnok disorder, and vice versa,

---

[23] The word "hi:ko" also denotes Negroes, perhaps because—according to M. A. I. Nettle, M.D.—a Negro cavalry regiment, commanded by white officers, was once stationed in Mohave territory.

[24] Ku: na: v can be translated as: foreordained, prophesied, a prophecy, telling (in an impressive manner), to inform, something told.

of course.[25]   Both diseases closely resemble also moua: v hahnok (pt. 4, pp. 184–186).

Hivsu: Tupo:ma's statement (1933).—People who come into close or prolonged contact with foreigners go crazy. The stronger blood of the stranger "hits" (in some unexplained way) the weaker blood of the Mohave, causing him to become ill and to go crazy. Of course, a Mohave Indian's blood may also affect an alien adversely.[26] Formerly, there were shamans who could cure this illness, because they had ahwe: suma: tc (=foreign dreams, i. e., dreams pertaining to the treatment of the foreign sickness). Now there are none. (The Mohave insisted that Hivsu: Tupo: ma himself, as well as Ahma Huma: re, had the requisite powers, although both denied this not only to me, but also to the Mohave themselves.) It is possible, of course, that someone may have the appropriate dreams sometime in the future, and if that happens, there will again be a shaman who can cure this sickness." Some of Hivsu: Tupo:ma's subsequent remarks indicated that the term "blood"—at least as used in this context—may also carry a peripheral connotation of "power." Thus, once in a while he would say that the stranger's power hit the blood of the Mohave, although most of the time he said that this was done by the alien's blood.[27] Somewhat along the same lines, Tcatc stated that it was the soul of the alien that hit the soul of the Mohave. This was also the opinion of Hilyera Anyay.

Tcatc's statement (1938).—[What is the cause of insanity in general?] Insanity is, in general, caused by intermarriage with different tribes. This is called ahwe: (short for ahwe: hahnok). The soul (matkwisa:) and the blood of aliens are stronger than ours. They hit the blood and soul of the Mohave, who then contract this disease. [Which of the four souls is involved? (Devereux, 1937 a)] You, who saw your sweetheart in dream, should know that. It is the matkwisa: suma: tc mitcemvetc. (The soul wherewith one has bad dreams.) Even if your children are not real aliens, but merely halfbreeds, you will see this (stronger) soul among your children. (Weeks later, when summing up her remarks about mental disorders, Tcatc once more stated:) I have now finished telling you about all the crazy people I have known. Now that there are all these intermarriages with different tribes and with one's own relatives [28] there ought to be a lot of crazy people, but, oddly enough, there are not. [Why not?] There are no fullblood Mohave anymore.[29] Maybe— I am not sure of it—but it may possibly be that that is why they do not go

---

[25] In the same sense, any discussion of the psychodynamics of severe obsessive-compulsive states invariably contains references to the dynamics of paranoid schizophrenia, since a severe obsessive-compulsive may, if his analysis is not conducted with extreme skill, become a full-blown paranoid schizophrenic. While we certainly do not suggest that ahwe: hahnok and ahwe: nyevedhi: are effective and scientific nosological entities, in the modern sense, the Mohave feel that they are genuine clinical categories, and that ahwe: hahnok can develop into ahwe: nyevedhi:. If one accepts this Mohave view, the constant references to ahwe: nyevedhi: in discussions supposedly limited to ahwe: hahnok, and vice versa, are both logical and necessary. This view is in accordance with the principle that one may draw perfectly "logical" (though inherently false) conclusions from a set of coherent, but false, premises. An example of this is Plato's logically airtight, but factually fallacious, defense of slavery.

[26] This was not mentioned by any other informant and may be a personal opinion.

[27] Compare the belief that the witch killer becomes psychotic because he sees the blood of his victim in his dreams (pt. 2, pp. 45–46).

[28] The juxtaposition of tribal exogamy and incest further supports the inference that the "superpotent" alien symbolizes the sexual, "evil" paternal ogre (Devereux, 1950 a).

[29] This gross overstatement is made by many fullblood Mohave Indians.

crazy from the effects of all these foreign contacts. The "delinquent" boy Nepe: he (Case 76) is an example of this.

Ahma Huma: re's statement (1938).—A person who gets the ahwe: hahnok disease is suma: tc itcem (has evil dreams). A long time ago the original food of the Indians sometimes caused them to become ill. Le: va (Case 35) had this illness. It is called itcuma: tc.[30] They (sometimes?) dreamed that they were eating too much of some of this aboriginal food. But now that we have these foreign foods, they see in their dreams some other person—not a Mohave—who is preparing this food (for them) and dream that they eat too much of some of this food. When they have such dreams, they have no appetite. They vomit quite a bit and sometimes also have fever. The halfbreeds whom they marry may also cause them to have this sickness. The Mohave are said to have a weaker blood and weaker souls than other races. They may also dream of cohabiting with members of other tribes, or even with whites, and this causes them to contract the ahwe: hahnok disease. Ahwe: means the same thing as ahwe: hahnok.

[What is the apen hahnok disease?] There was a person who ate apen (beaver). The beaver is not what we would call the original food of the Mohave. Yet, even in the olden days, when people were hungry and meat was scarce, some people killed beavers and ate them. Some of them got sick from doing that. I do not know what dreams such people had. People who had this sickness suffered from a swelling of the body. I do not know in what way they would be crazy, but they did say that such people became crazy. By the way, whites are called apen kutctha :ny, which means beaver eater. Sometimes we also call the whites simply apen. It means beaver. [Is the term hi :ko still used to refer to whites?] No. Nowadays we refer to them mostly by the term "American."

Hilyera Anyay's statement (1938).—[What do you know about the ahwe: nyevedhi: ailment?] Ahwe: hahnotc (another form of the word hahnok) is a sickness that is contracted by coming in contact with other tribes and with persons of mixed blood. A Mohave is weaker in soul and blood than are other races. This sickness is accompanied by bad dreams. As time goes by, and the patient continues to have these bad dreams, he seems to be afraid of everyone and runs away. [Was this the trouble with Uta: c's father-in-law?] Yes. Such a person runs away from people not just once, but many times, because he is scared of people. Then people run after him and bring him back. Sometimes, in wintertime, when such a person runs away at night he may freeze to death.[31] At other times he falls into the river or into a lake and drowns. [Was this what happened to Tcȧvȧkong?] Yes.[32] [You explained all this very clearly. Thank you for helping me get this straight. A few of my other informants got me somewhat confused about this disease.] Even after a person reaches this stage of the disease, he will be all right again if his bad dreams cease. I am trying to tell you that when people suffer from this sickness they either get worse, or else they get well. Now ask me some more questions, so that I can explain everything to you just right. [Thank you. What sort of dreams do such people have?] Let me give you some examples: Should a Mohave marry a member of another tribe, he may see in his dreams the body of his spouse, or see humthi: ly (the discharge of the nose) on his own

---

[30] According to Pulyi : k the complete term is itcema : v hahnok, and is either actually the same as ahwe : hahnok, or very much like it.

[31] This may also happen to guilt-ridden intoxicated persons. Not long after Hivsu : Tupo :ma confessed to me that he had practiced witchcraft, he got drunk, fell asleep outdoors in wintertime, contracted pneumonia and died (Devereux, 1948 1; and Case 139).

[32] For a different diagnosis of Tcȧvȧkong, see Case 6 and Case 103.

face.[33] He might also see that his hair appears very greasy and oily. He also dreams of other things. He may dream of having the body secretions of his spouse, i.e., her saliva, urine, feces, or nasal mucus, on his own body.[34] If these dreams cease, he may be all right again. On the other hand, he may even dream that his spouse urinates on his body.[35] When a man has such dreams, he loses his appetite, and cannot keep the food down in his stomach. This condition is called suka :t lyidhi :k (=nausea). When he eats, he thinks of these dreams, and of these various secretions on his body. That is what makes him vomit. He is nauseated. In the ahwe: sickness, the person sees in his dreams only a person of mixed blood, and the power of the mixed blood.[36] [Does the dreamer also see his own sperm in dreams?] No, he doesn't."

The ahwe: hahnok case material will be found on pages 142–144.

AHWE: NYEVEDHI:

The ahwe: nyevedhi: disease greatly resembles the ahwe: hahnok disease and may be a more or less aggravated "not straight" form thereof.

Hilyera Anyay's statement (1938).—I will now explain to you the difference between the foreign disease (ahwe: hahnok) and the foreign ghost disease (ahwe: nyevedhi).

In the latter illness, a patient has dreams in which he mingles (consorts) with his dead relatives. He eats, plays, and talks with them. [Does this mean that this illness resembles hiwey lak nyevedhi :?] Yes. When these dreams continue, the patient seems to lose all interest in the activities of earthly life, because his heart and his mind are always with his dead relatives.[37] When he awakens from some such bad dreams, he sometimes sits for a long time without eating or talking, and sometimes he cries, remembering his dead relatives. A patient who has such bad dreams is advised to take young arrowweed tops and to fumigate himself with them, or to steep arrowweed roots in water and bathe in this, or to do both.[38] If the patient is suma: tc ahot (has good, or power-giving dreams) his bad dreams will then cease, and he will be all right once more. In other instances the patient is advised to take some tasi: lyk weed, soak it in warm water until it lathers, and then bathe in this water without disrobing. Then he must go down to the water (i. e., river) and bathe there. When he is ready to come out, he leaves his clothes in the river and is careful not to emerge from the water at the same place where he had entered it.

---

[33] When kissing, the partner's saliva may cause venereal disease (Kroeber, 1948).

[34] Compare the witch killer's dreams about blood (pt. 2, pp. 45–46), and the belief that evil creatures were born of Sky rattlesnake's body foam (Kroeber, 1925 a).

[35] Feminae venerea voluptate commotae nonnumquam super virum mingunt (Devereux, 1950 a). Mulier etiam temulenta, cum iuvenes nequam crinem pubis incendissent, incendium emissa urina exstinxit (Devereux, 1948 i). Mohavia mulier cum per venerem varie excitatur, sphincteres quos habet nonnumquam patefieri sinit: vel e vagina murmures emittit (Devereux, 1950 a) vel inflationem ructusque dat (Devereux, 1951 e) vel super mentulam in anum immissam cacat (Devereux, 1951 e) vel, dum fellat, salivam semine intermixtam ab ore ebullit (Devereux, 1947 a).

[36] Presumably the informant mentions here only mixed blood because most racially exogamous marriages nowadays involve Mohave halfbreeds rather than fullblood aliens.

[37] Witches are similarly obsessed with dreams and thoughts about their dead victims, who are frequently close relatives (Devereux, 1937 c). By contrast, scalpers and witch killers have unpleasant dreams about their victims (pt. 2, pp. 43–46).

[38] Bathing and/or fumigation rites are, in one form or another, also part of childbirth, menstruation, and funeral observances (Devereux, 1942 a, 1949 d, 1950 g).

If all this is done and the bad dreams cease, the patient may be all right. After all this has been done and the patient has put on different clothing, he is able to think straight again. Then he seems to forget his dead relatives and his bad dreams and gets well. (This suggests that this treatment psychologically duplicates and reinforces the basic function of the funeral ritual, which seeks to sever the bonds between the dead and the mourners.)

A woman who lost her husband may also have such bad dreams. She may dream that she is still living with her husband, and is doing all the things which they did during his life on earth. This sickness of widows is much the same as the illness of persons who dream of the dead blood kin. This illness, too, is called ahwe: nyevedhi:. If the sick widow performs those actions which are also prescribed for the cure of the previously mentioned ailment, the results are the same. [What if one dreams of one's dead spouse during the first 4 days after the death of that spouse?] [39] It is all right to have such dreams during that period; one does not get sick from them. It is not a sign of sickness if one dreams of one's dead spouse during the 4 days which follow cremation. Once in a great while one may even dream of one's dead spouse at a later date. People say that one has such dreams when the dead spouse thinks of the surviving spouse. When the widowed spouse has such bad dreams about the dead spouse, it is a sign of the coming of sickness. In the case of a woman, there seems to be some hard substance, or some "muscles," in her vagina. Then, in her dreams, she has sexual intercourse with her dead husband. This particular condition is known as ahwe: tci:. (Note that dead husband=enemy, i.e., ahwe: !) This hard thing, is roughly speaking, like a real object inserted into the vagina (i.e., an imaginary foreign body). It is not just that a part of the vagina is getting hard. (Phantom phallus.) [40]

Comment

The preceding account strikingly illustrates the connection between aliens, the ghosts of relatives, and the ghosts of dead spouses.

The "internal phantom phallus" has also been mentioned by Euro-American psychoneurotics. It must be specified that the "experience" of an "internal phantom phallus" in a waking state is very different from dreams of having intercourse, and represents an almost schizophrenic impairment of the body image. [41]

The pathogenic dreams related by Hilyera Anyay appear to differ from those which cause hiwey lak nyevedhi: only in that the latter type may involve also dream-incest, dreams "causing" pseudo-pregnancy (pseudocyesis) and dreams about one's childhood. [42]

---

[39] During this period the dead soul, which is not yet a true ghost, revisits its old haunts.

[40] At this point Hilyera Anyay was asked about the globus hystericus. His answer is reported in part 5, pages 216–218.

[41] An experienced psychoanalyst stated that when a psychoneurotic woman was speaking of her dead father, she began to experience the sensation of having some object in her vagina. The analyst promptly told her to get up from the couch and sit in a chair, since he rightly feared that if the woman remained in the prone position—whose purpose it is to facilitate the (gradual) emergence of unconscious thoughts and feelings—there might occur an uncontrolled and massive "return of the repressed," which may lead to a sudden schizophrenic break. The woman spent the rest of that hour sitting in a chair.

[42] This last type of dream is, of necessity, related to dreams about the dead, since one would see in dream a house which was burned down (Kroeber, 1925 a) at the death of a member of the household.

A supplementary statement by Hilyera Anyay is cited further below.

Ahma Huma: re's statement (*1938*).—[What causes ahwe: nyevedhi: ?] Such people have bad dreams which resemble hiwey lak nyevedhi: dreams. [Then what is the difference between the two ailments?] As regards dreams, there is practically no difference between the two. A person may dream that he has some sort of relations with his (dead?) relatives, but these relations need not necessarily be sexual ones. If the patient does not tell every single one of his dreams, then, even though he is being treated, there is no cure for him. The patient must tell his dreams just the way he dreamed them (this specification is also a part of the "basic rule" of psychoanalytic therapy), so that the shaman may know what his sickness is. Of course, if the person is bewitched, then it is only natural for him not to tell all his dreams.[43] If a patient is bewitched, it is death if he does tell his dreams (because the witch may take revenge), and it is death if he does not tell his dreams (because he cannot be cured). If the patient does not tell such dreams, he dies instantly, unless a shaman, who is not the bewitcher, happens to be treating him that very minute. In that case there is a chance that the patient may recover.

[Can dead people bewitch the living? Is that why hiwey lak nyevedhi: and ahwe: nyevedhi are so similar?] No. The dead can't bewitch the living in the sense in which we apply this word to the acts of living witches. Of course, ghosts also appear in dreams, etc., but that is not quite the same as witchcraft.

Hikye: t's statement (*1938*).—This informant asserted that ahwe: hahnok (foreign disease) is not identical with ahwe: nyevedhi: (foreign ghost) (pt. 1, pp. 9–38).

G. T.'s statement (*1938*).—This ahwe: nyevedhi: is also known as nyávudho:-ka. That is all I know about it. (According to Kroeber (1925 a) nyávudho: ka is also the name of a song cycle.)

Hilyera Anyay's statement.—[Do you know what nyávudho: ka is?] There are several things by that name. [Interpreter, after conferring with Hilyera Anyay, suggested that it would be better to ask Ahma Huma: re about this term, since Hilyera Anyay thought that this term designated the entire group of ghost diseases.]

Hivsu: Tupo:ma's statement (*1933*).—Kunyoo:r, who can take people by the hand and make them visit the land of the dead (Fathauer, 1951) can also cure insanity caused by dreams about one's dead relatives.[44]

---

[43] A witch who is not yet ready to make himself known as a witch, i.e., who is not yet ready to be killed, "seals" the lips of his victim, or else appears in his victim's dreams disguised as another person, whose shape he deliberately borrows in order to escape detection (Devereux, 1937 c). This belief is extremely interesting, since psychoanalysis has shown that persons whom one does not wish to recognize appear in dream in the guise of other persons. This belief implies furthermore that the Mohave tend to interpret dreams symbolically, whereas most primitives interpret dreams either directly or else by opposites. Even Homer is quite primitive in this respect, since his epics contain only one dream, that of Penelope ("Odyssey," bk. XIX), which is interpreted symbolically . . . and this despite the fact that Homer was a keen observer of dreams—witness his comparing the flight of Hector from the pursuing Achilles ("Iliad," bk. XXII) to a dream in which one runs and runs and does not advance at all.

[44] Hivsu: Tupo: ma, who did not specialize in the treatment of this group of diseases, always felt free to list all living specialists known to him ; e. g., it was he who referred me to Ahma Huma: re, Harav He: ya, and Kunyoo: r. Ahma Huma: re, on the other hand, being a specialist, only mentioned a dead specialist, Hulo: k. The fear of being bewitched by his competitors probably played an important role in silencing the reliable and cooperative Ahma Huma: re.

Two points mentioned in the preceding statements deserve special notice:

Hikye:t, a somewhat weird and probably quite disturbed witch, whose opinions often seemed quite idiosyncratic,[45] denied that ahwe:nyevedhi: is fundamentally identical with ahwe: hahnok.

G. T., an intelligent layman, related the ahwe: nyevedhi: syndrome to the Nyávudho:ka song cycle. Kroeber (1925 a) calls this song cycle Nyava-dhoka, but only states that little is known about it, that it begins at Aha'av'ulypo (the primal house), and that the singer slaps his thigh. Hilyera Anyay was puzzled by G. T.'s statement, and Ahma Huma:re, to whom he referred me for further information, was, unfortunately, not available at that time for consultation. In the absence of other information about this song cycle, the problem of its relationship to ahwe: nyevedhi: cannot be resolved.

INCIDENCE

All informants agreed that whereas one would expect to see many cases of foreign sickness, one actually sees very few of them nowadays.

Tcatc's statement (1938).—[Do you think that there are more insane people nowadays than there were formerly?] In the past more people became insane, because they had more Mohave blood in them. They were fullblood Mohave and were therefore constantly exposed to insanity (through contacts with aliens). Nowadays there are a lot of halfbreed Mohave. No wonder, then, that there are so few insane. Yet, there should be more of them around because, in the olden days, they went insane if they married an alien.

THERAPY

Tcatc's discussion of the basic principles of all psychotherapy re-veals the importance she attached to ahwe: hahnok, which seemed to represent for her the very essence of all mental disorders.

Tcato's statement (1938): [Do shamans now living know how to cure insanity?] No. [Then what do the Mohave do when someone becomes in-sane?] In the old days there were ailments which we called straight sicknesses. In those days, when our only food was corn, pumpkins, melons, beans, hamo:se and hatev-i:ly, we got sick from these foods, but these ailments were called "straight (ordinary) illnesses." When we began to eat strange food, the sickness (which it caused) was no longer called a "straight" one. All shamans who doctored such ailments in the olden days seem to have gone by now. When

---

[45] The tendency to present personal views as cultural material may be quite common among the Mohave. Thus, Kroeber (1948) reports that when a woman named Māha (= Mah) told him a certain "Coyote" story in the presence of other people, the latter vehemently protested that she did not tell a traditional story, but simply a (private) dream. Kroeber failed to add, however, that many personal dreams may eventually become part of Mohave culture, provided that they fit the Mohave cultural pattern—which Mah's dream seemed to do—and provided also that the narrator's "dream inspiration" is accepted as genuine. In fact, even a budding shaman must first demonstrate his power publicly, if he wishes to persuade others that he is, indeed, a shaman who had the proper power-dreams. Even then he does not rate as an established shaman until he has a few cures to his credit (Devereux, 1937 c). The growth and renewal of Mohave "dream culture" is, thus, largely determined by a given dreamer's ability to persuade others that his addition to Mohave culture or mythology has genuine "dream authority" behind it. This, in turn, depends to a large extent on the congruence of the new material with the basic pattern of Mohave culture.

shamans treated such ("straight") ailments, there was only one who would
doctor such a sickness, because the patient had only one sickness (at a time).
Nowadays, however, when a person has ahwe: hahnok, he also has other sicknesses at the same time, so that a number of shamans have to be called in.
No shaman now living knows how to cure the ahwe: nyevedhi: illness. Nowadays, if someone contracts this illness—and some people do contract it—he goes
to the hospital. And, if nothing can be done for him, he dies.

GENERAL COMMENT

The principle that polar opposites are often interchangeable and
may symbolize each other is often of great importance both in primitive cultures and in the individual unconscious.[46] This principle explains why the Mohave Indians' deceased relatives and spouses, as
well as their enemies, can cause them to contract the foreign ghost
illness. This suggests that gentile exogamy, combined with tribal
endogamy, is a typical compromise solution between the oedipally
motivated urge to commit incest and the reaction formation against
this urge, which impels one to marry a complete outsider. It is this
reaction formation against incestuous wishes that provides the motivation, e.g., in the legend of King Cophetua who married a beggar
girl. The same defense against incestuous wishes is often also a major
motivating factor in disparate unions, as exemplified by hypergamy
or by miscegenation.

CASE MATERIAL

It is proposed to present, first, cases of ahwe: hahnok, and then
cases diagnosed as ahwe: nyevedhi:. It is noteworthy that whereas
the accounts of the former "clinical entity" are more elaborate than
are the accounts of ahwe: nyevedhi:, our case material contains more
examples of the ahwe: nyevedhi: illness than of the simpler ahwe:
hahnok ailment. Since one of the ahwe: hahnok cases was also observed and described by the reservation physician, it is this case which
will be presented first.

AHWE: HAHNOK CASES

CASE 31 (Informant: James L. Troupin, M. D., reservation physician (1938)):

M. D., 21 years old, is the daughter of an Italian father and a fullblood Mohave
mother of the Mah gens. (According to Pulyi: k this young woman is permitted
to claim membership in her mother's gens on a courtesy basis, but does not seem
to have a supplementary Indian name or nickname to differentiate her from all
the other women named Mah, so that she is commonly called—and referred to—by
her "English" name.)

---

[46] Among the Sedang Moi of Indochina, that which is big in the land of the living is
small in the spirit world, and vice versa. Hence, the share of the sacrificial animal
which is given to the spirits is always very small. Likewise, whereas both human beings
and the supernaturals associated with the Sedang tribe walk and stand in the normal
position, the Thundergods of the enemy Halang tribe are believed to stand on their
heads (Devereux, MS., 1933–34).

This patient was seen by me for the first time in January 1940. Information about her was obtained from her mother (through an interpreter), from her younger sister, and from members of the tribe who have known her since childhood. Much of the data received from the latter source is unreliable and colored by individual imagination.

The father was an Italian who was apparently normal, but who met a death of violence some years ago. He was shot by the watchman while attempting robbery. The mother is a mild-mannered Mohave woman who speaks fairly good English, but cannot understand all that is said to her, probably because of the speed of the speech. She seems to be above the average in intelligence (among her own) [sic!]. The patient is bedridden and is constantly attended by her sister L., age 19, the latter even accompanying her to the hospital for her brief stay.

The relatives say that Mah was quite normal as a child. She was willing to play with other children, and a history of moodiness and of self-centered and introspective characteristics was not obtained. At the age of 6 she went to the Indian boarding school at Fort Mohave, and returned there the following September for her second year, but, for some reason which was not clear, the mother took her home at Christmas and she never returned to school. Another informant said that formerly Mah played with other children at campfire meetings, etc., by running from them and squatting in the grass a short distance away, giggling, and covering her face.

Her life was uneventful for the next few years; that is, her relationships with the remainder of the tribe were practically nil, but stories are told of periods of excitement, during which it was necessary to chain or tie her to the bed. There was apparently some movement on foot to commit the patient, for there are stories of the mother standing by with a gun and threatening to shoot the first one to lay a hand on her. About 5 years ago, the patient took to her bed, and has been there ever since.

Attempts to elicit a history of delusions, hallucinations, or illusions have met an absolute blank, not because the family is trying to hide anything, for indeed they are most cooperative, but because they have seen so much of the patient, for so many years, that they do not remember. As one looks at the patient, however, one sees a continual movement of the lips as though she were talking to some invisible person. She also makes sharp movements with her head, as though she suddenly saw something to one side or the other.

The patient seems to recognize her surroundings, and is alert enough to respond to visual and auditory stimuli. There are many grimaces of lips and eyebrows, but no actual speech. The sister claims that the patient is capable of asking for food and water, though she is incontinent and has been so for years. There is contracture of both knees in a flexed position, but motion is relatively free with arms. At one time, the patient was surprised in the so-called "fetal position," under a blanket. When she learns to know someone, she is perfectly willing to smile and shake hands.

The mother was very anxious to know the prognosis, and she is almost desperate for a new treatment for Mah, as she has tried everything suggested to her, and at one time was trying to scrape together 10 dollars for a blood test, which some doctor wanted to do. A diagnosis of schizophrenia, hebephrenic type, was made, and a poor prognosis given. The mother was advised to put the patient in an institution, so that the sister may have a more healthy and normal life, but the mother would like to keep her at home.

Comment

Mohave diagnosis.—Ahwe: hahnok. This diagnosis is culturally most interesting, since this woman is a halfbreed. The fact that such a diagnosis was made may be due to her having been granted a kind of courtesy membership in her mother's gens, making her a real Mohave.

Tentative diagnosis.—Schizophrenia, hebephrenic type. Less probably: recurrent transitory confusional state, resembling a so-called "three-day battlefield schizophrenia." This patient is the only Mohave who, during her psychotic episode, is actually known to have assumed the typically schizophrenic fetal position.

AHWE: NYEVEDHI: CASES

CASE 32 (Informant: E. S., son of patient) :

I am going to tell you what my mother, Vi: mak Kuko: thå (=to hit a barrier), of the Vi: mak gens, told me about the time when she, herself, was temporarily insane. It happened before I was born. She was at that time already married to my father, who was the son of a Cocopa Indian, of the Nyoltc gens,[47] and of a Mohave woman. My mother never told me about the dreams she had had at that time, but she said that while she was insane her father and her mother [48] came to her. First they called her, and then they ran away. At least that is what she thought was happening. My mother then ran away, thinking that she was running after her parents. My mother thought that this hallucination made her get up (from her sick bed) and run away. Naturally, people immediately ran after her. They must have been the ones she mistook for big balls that seemed to be chasing her. My father, too, must have been chasing her, because she used to see a red ball among the big balls that were chasing her. The other balls were all black. The shaman who treated her—I forgot his name—told her that this red ball was a halfbreed. That means that it represented my father, who was half Cocopa.[49] That is all my mother told me about the time she was insane.

Comment

Mohave diagnosis (*inferred from symptoms*).—Ahwe: nyevedhi: (Pulyi: k was not sure this woman had an ahwe: disease.)

Tentative diagnosis.—Anxiety state with hallucinations, suggesting a transitory confusional state. It is unlikely that Vi: mak was delirious at that time, since her son did not mention any organic illness.

CASE 33 (Informant: Ahma Huma: re) :

Nyortc, of the Nyoltc gens, a Mohave woman of about 70, lived at Needles, Calif. Since she was not married at that time, she lived with her daughter, Mrs. C. F., and got along well with her daughter and her son-in-law. She died in the middle 1930's. One day this old woman ran away from her daughter's house, went down to the riverbank, fell into the mud, and remained there for

---

[47] The Mohave recognize the Cocopa gentes as being the equivalents of their own. However, Gifford (1918) does not list a Nyoltc gens among the Cocopa, and neither does Kelly (1942).

[48] One must not assume that Vi: mak's parents were already dead at that time.

[49] This is puzzling. Most Mohave informants say that red is associated with women, and black with men. Only Pulyi: k said that black paint was used only by shamans and by the kwanàmi: hye braves). One explanation may be that only the husband's mother was Mohave. This is, however, not a satisfactory cultural explanation of the fact that a red ball symbolized the husband.

2 days. The first day of her absence her relatives called for help upon the now-deceased shaman Loho: hà (whose gens was probably Tü: ly and who had no English name). He was the only shaman who, at that time, knew how to treat this ailment. He was asked to call the lost woman back. In accordance with his sumac: tc (power) he sang some songs, and called her, and, after 2 days, she did come back. Then he treated her for a few days, and she made a full recovery.

Comment

Mohave diagnosis.—Ahwe: nyevedhi :.

Tentative diagnosis.—Fugue, caused by delirium or, less probably, by senility.

In this instance the shaman does not appear to have used the trance technique for locating a person lost in enemy territory, nor could he deal with this problem as one does with soul loss, since in this case the patient herself was lost. One infers that he treated her in absentia for ahwe: nyevedhi:, and that this therapy at a distance (McNichols, 1944) was thought to have been sufficiently effective to bring about a partial recovery, enabling the woman to return home on her own and to undergo the rest of the treatment under normal circumstances. Be that as it may, this is the only instance known to me in which a shaman undertook such a task.

CASE 34 (Informants: Tcatc and E. S.) :

Amat Válàka (earth open) of the Mah gens, died around 1888, at the age of 80 or 90. His case history, though reported in reply to an inquiry about flexibilitas cerea, suggests senile dementia, or perhaps paralysis caused by a stroke. This is the only person Tcatc ever saw in that particular condition.

In the beginning, his illness took the form of a lot of coughing. He did not have his full appetite and sometimes ran a high fever. (The Mohave seldom mention fever in any context.) He did not become insane at any time during his illness. He was sane right up to his death and did no insane talking whatsoever. In fact, he did not talk at all, and, in the later stages of his illness, he could not move at all. If they spread his hands palms upward, he could not put them back into a normal position. If they turned his head sidewise, he could not right it. People were very much puzzled by his condition, since he himself had been a shaman who could cure precisely this type of disease. Some people even thought that his power had turned back on him and had produced these symptoms.[50] An alternate, or possibly supplementary, theory was that he had been bewitched by the shaman Tcàvàkong, who was one of his relatives, and who had already bewitched several of his own relatives, as witches usually do. In fact, Tcàvàkong himself freely admitted that he had bewitched Amat Válàka. Eventually Tcàvàkong was killed by his own first cousin, Aoo: rà.[51] (For a different version of this murder, cf. Case 6 and Case 103.)

Comment

Mohave diagnosis.—Ahwe: nyevedhi: hahnok (sic!) and suma: tc itcem (dream bad).

---

[50] It should be recalled that a shaman is said to be able to cure because he can kill, and vice versa.

[51] The data given above indicate that various members of this shaman's family practiced shamanism, witchcraft, and witch killing. It is therefore interesting to note that, in accordance with Mohave expectations, this family was also guilty of "incest," in that Aoo: rà's daughter's son married the daughter of Aoo: rà's brother Altonio. This marriage, which Tcatc had forgotten, was described in detail by the shaman Hivsu: Tupo: ma (Devereux, 1939 a) (Case 89).

Tentative diagnosis.—Senile dementia and/or stroke causing paralysis. This case is a typical illustration of the "complications" theory of ahwe: nyevedhi:, which is defined as an illness that is "not straight." The present case involves, in addition to the ahwe: element, references to witchcraft—which is a typical complicating factor in various diseases—and also to the "activity psychosis" (pt. 2, pp. 45–56).

CASE 35 (Informants: Tcatc and E. S.) :

Le:va (no English name) belonged to the Kumadhi: gens, and, at the time of his death, which occurred around 1914, was about 40 or 50 years of age. (Q) I do not recall how long before the onset of his illness his parents had died, but I do know that they were already deceased when he became ill. Le:va's younger maternal half brother, Madhuly Hi: dho (sugar eye), was a shaman specializing in the cure of the food disease (itcema:v). Madhuly Hi:dho's daughter, Nyo:rtc, known as Nyo:rtc Tce:vs, was the mother of the shaman Hivsu: Tupo: ma, and, by another man, also the mother of the witch Hamuly Huk' yè: rà (who was eventually bewitched and killed by Hivsu: Tupo: ma (Devereux, 1948 i)). Le: va was also related to S.S.'s family. He was a heavy-set man, resembling C.S. in build. He was a good man, and much respected by his tribe.

Le:va lived where he had been born and raised: near a lake called Hanyom Masthidhe: và (Lake dangerous, lake to be dreaded). Some shamans occasionally have the urge to bewitch someone, for no special reason whatsoever. They do it simply because they know that they have the power to do such things. They tend to bewitch their closest relatives, because they claim to have the power to take the souls of their victims to a certain place, and to keep them there, so that they can visit them [Devereux, 1937 c]. That is what happened in Le:va's case. His great-nephew Hamuly Huk' yè: rà bewitched him. He used this lake, and, in some way, through his power, he did something to the lake with Le: va, in Le: va's own dreams. (I.e., he guided Le: va's dreams.) As a result of these dreams Le: va became ill. He was unable to get around and, on his deathbed, he did quite a bit of talking. [E. S. guessed that he was delirious.] He said just anything; sometimes he would even call out the names of all his dead relatives. (This, being taboo, is, by definition, "typically insane behavior.") He would try to get up and pick up anything within reach and would then throw these objects around. He remained in that condition for more than a year. All he did in his delirium was talk about his dead relatives. Sometimes he would also talk about his good planting and harvesting, and at other times he would tell precisely who had bewitched him. He also spoke of that lake. I specifically recall that, just before his illness reached its final stage, he sometimes called for his dead father and mother. We believe that his spirit eventually went to the place where his father and his mother were, namely, to the land of the dead called Cálya: yt (Devereux, 1937 a). When he began to speak of his parents, the Mohave knew that he was nearing his death. I knew Le:va's parents, having become acquainted with them when they lived at Needles.

In the end Le:va's physical condition deteriorated quite rapidly. He did not have his full appetite and ate very little, yet he would eat something anyway, just because he did not know that he was eating something. In the final stages of his disease, this formerly heavy-set man was nothing but skin and bones. His brother Madhuly Hi: dho tried to treat him, but could not effect a cure. At the very end, just before his death, he ceased to talk for about half an hour. Then he died.

Comment

Mohave diagnosis.—Ahwe: nyevedhi: complicated by witchcraft.

Tentative diagnosis.—Possibly delirium, but more probably involutional melancholia. The presence of a serious organic illness is probable.

The Mohave diagnosis is not easy to justify in cultural terms. It may have been determined by the fact that Le:va cured itcema:v, which Ahma Huma:re related to the ahwe: group of illnesses. The fact that Le:va was bewitched and also called out the names of his dead parents and relatives would suggest to the Mohave that he dreamed of them. This would place his condition in the ahwe: nyevedhi: class. On the other hand the fact that his bewitchment had something to do with the bewitching of a lake into which hikwi:r snakes had been placed by the same witch (pt. 4, pp. 117–128) could have led to the diagnosis of hikwi:r. Finally, the fact that he, who had been able to cure the itcema:v (food) illness, which is related to the ahwe: illnesses, eventually displayed a, possibly neurotic, aversion to food (anorexia nervosa) suggested to the Mohave that, in addition to everything else, his illness was also complicated by what we have called "activity psychoses" (pt. 2, pp. 46–56). Given these multiple diagnostic possibilities, the fact that his illness was called ahwe: nyevedhi:, rather than hikwi:r or something else, reveals the importance which the Mohave assign to the dangers of all contact with aliens.

The tentative diagnosis just offered is, admittedly, speculative, and was determined by the fact that depression, preoccupation with one's dead parents, ideas of being bewitched, and anorexia, occurring at the age of 40 or 50, suggest involutional melancholia. The patient's boasting of his skill as a farmer is, however, not typical of involutional melancholia, which is characterized by feelings of worthlessness. The boast may therefore represent a defense against feelings of worthlessness, which are necessary for the development of paranoid ideas (belief in being bewitched).[52] His boast may also have been specifically related to his marked anorexia, because he stressed his skill in producing food precisely at a time when his intake of food was minimal.

CASE 36 (Informants Tcatc and E. S.):

Matkwisa: Namak (Soul leaves) of the Nyoltc gens, a resident of La Paz, was married to Va:hath, and was father of two boys and two girls. He died at the approximate age of 50, around 1890, when I (Tcatc) was about 20 years old.

This man had ahwe: nyevedhi:. He had a bad dream, which may have been a recurrent one. He dreamed that he was visiting his father and his mother, who had died, and toward the end of the dream he even ate food prepared by his dead relatives. After he woke up, he hardly ever ate anything, because the food he ate in his dream had decreased his appetite. In the end he was nearly starved, because he had no appetite for real food. Every time he ate anything, he would vomit it out again. He had a kind of stomach trouble which they call suma:tc nyevedhi: (dream ghost). This term refers in this context exclusively to the man's gastric troubles. In the later stages of his disease he also had severe headaches.

---

[52] Anne Parsons' (1956) recent attempt to differentiate formally between delusional persecutory ideas and the fear of being bewitched is overintellectualized psychodynamics, and also reflects a trend in certain sociological circles to justify at all cost the essential "rightness" of society (or of culture) even if it happens to be one which destroys the human being psychologically.

During daytime he sometimes talked of his dead relatives.[53] It seemed just as though he did not know the things that were going on in real life. They call this matkwisa: hidha: uk—"The dead souls have taken his soul" (soul loss). That is why he did not know anything. (According to Pulyi: k, this condition is also called ahwe: hidha: uk meaning "enemy took-it," which once more suggests a tendency to equate ghosts with enemies.) When Matkwisa: Namak reached this stage, his wife looked for a shaman who could cure him. The two walked from La Paz to Hipaly Kuvlyeo (Tongue white), where I (Tcatc) used to live in my youth. During the trip the wife went off looking for something, and left the patient under a cottonwood tree, telling him to stay there until she came back. This much we know for certain. Now for the rest. When his wife left him, the sick man must have gotten up and gone on the road alone. He must have kept on walking until, somehow or other, he began to walk toward the river. We do not know how far he went. We think that he may have crawled under a mesquite tree, and died there. No one found his remains at that time. However, 10 years later the Mohave ex-policeman, Kohovan Kura :u, found a skeleton in that place. Everyone thought it was the skeleton of this man. The skeleton was neither cremated nor buried, but left where it had been found. The bones were scattered all over the place and the skull was the only part of the body which suggested that these bones were those of this man. On second thought I think that they did bury the skull, but I am not sure of this. [How did they dispose of the dead man's property?] After searching in vain for a week, this man's relatives foregathered at a place called Ah'a Dhoku :pit (cottonwood owl) and held a mourning ceremony, in the course of which all of this man's property, including his dwelling, was burned.

This is a simple case of psychosis (yamomk), since the man was not a shaman, and was not thought to have been bewitched.

Comment

Mohave diagnosis.—Ahwe: nyevedhi :, complicated by suma: tc nyevedhi : (dream of ghost) and by matkwisa: hidha :uk or ahwe: hidha :uk, i.e., soul loss or theft. It was also specified that he was yamomk (insane).

Tentative diagnosis.—Involutional melancholia.

It may be simply a striking coincidence that the self-chosen name of a person suffering, inter alia, from soul loss should have been "Soul leaves." On the other hand, the choice of this name may, conceivably, have been determined by his long-suppressed dim awareness that he was losing his mind . . . a far from rare occurrence in psychoses which have a slow and insidious onset.

CASE 37 (Informants: Tcatc and E. S.) :

Cii :p (straight erection, a baby name which was never discarded) of the Mah gens, was the son—others say, the nephew—of Mr. and Mrs. Uta :c (Case 38). He died at the approximate age of 24, many years before the death of his mother. One day, on his way home from school, Cii :p stopped by a fallen cottonwood tree and began to cry. People who saw him asked him why he cried, but he replied that he did not know. After this incident he became ill and had severe headaches. As a result of these headaches he died in a short(?) time. I myself did not witness these events. I only heard about them. Some people

---

[53] This is a violation of a very important Mohave taboo, and therefore almost a critical symptom of psychosis in a tribe where such a taboo obtains.

claimed that Cii :p had been a victim of witchcraft, but there is plenty of room for doubt on that score.

Comment

Mohave diagnosis.—Ahwe: nyevedhi: (?) perhaps complicated by witchcraft.

Tentative diagnosis.—The crying incident followed by headaches suggests simply the onset of some physical illness. On the other hand, the fact that Cii :p had this crying spell while coming home from school, but did not die until he was about 24 years old, suggests that the crying spell and the death were not connected.

The fact that this man's baby name was Cii: p (= straight erection) suggests that he had frequent "tension erections" in babyhood. If this supposition is correct, it is possible that his mother may have felt inadequate as a mother, which would then explain why, when she, too, had a transitory psychotic episode, cried a lot, had headaches, and believed herself bewitched.

CASE 38 (Informants Tcatc and E. S.) :

Mrs. Uta : c, 85 years old, of Parker, Ariz., had, according to some informants, married into a family allegedly addicted to shamanism, witchcraft, witch killing, and even incest (pt. 5, pp. 245–247).

Mrs. Uta :c was bewitched by Hikye :t. She had been living a normal life and no one knew why Hikye :t should have wanted to bewitch her. She was all right until about a year before her death, which occurred in the late 1930's. Around that time she became ill and had severe headaches, but felt better after a few days. While she was going through this crisis, she had spells, during which she cried out the names of her dead grandparents, saying that they were dead and that people should cry (mourn for them). When the spells ended, she became normal once more, but kept on having slight headaches.

Approximately 6 months before her death she was taken to Needles, to attend the funeral of one of her relatives named Coo: tâ. While at Needles, she again had one of her spells. She got up in the middle of the night and complained that her chest was hurting her. Then, all of a sudden, she lost her mind. She began to talk—about anything at all—and kept on raving for about half an hour. I myself (Tcatc) did not see this, I only heard about it. Eventually she quieted down and went back to sleep. In the morning her husband visited the shaman Masahay Tcammahay (an untranslatable name, which has something to do with a girl bird) of the Mu :ha gens, who, at the husband's request, consented to treat her.—I (E.S.) was present when Mrs. Uta :c was taken to Masahay Tcammahay's house, where she had breakfast with her niece (sister of another Mah, who is alleged to be an incestuous witch (Devereux, 1939 a)). Toward 10 :00 or 10 :30 a.m. she had another attack, during which she did not lose her mind, but merely complained of pains in her chest. The shaman immediately began to treat her, whereupon she felt better almost at once, and had no further attack until about 4 :00 p.m. Then she once more complained of pains in her chest, and was treated again by the same shaman. She then slept well all night. I left the house in the morning, so that I myself did not witness the rest of the incident.

Two or three days later she was brought back to her home at Parker by C. N., who is said to be (at least potentially) a shaman-killing brave. During the last two weeks of her life she was completely out of her mind. At times she rose from her bed as though she were well, and then suddenly tore off her clothes, so that her two nieces, both called Mah, had to hold her down. Sometimes they even had to restrain her by wrapping her into a blanket. During these attacks she would talk about her dead relatives, but especially about her parents, describing their deaths, and urging people to mourn with her. At one time she also said something about her dead son (?) Cii:p (Case 37) and grabbed her husband, Uta:c of the Mah gens, asserting that he was her son.

I (Tcatc) did not visit her during her last illness, although she was my contemporary, having been born just one night before I myself was born. During her last illness they had put her in the hospital, but, when death seemed imminent, they took her home again, since the Mohave like to die at home.

Mrs. Uta:c herself claimed that she had been bewitched by Hikye:t. As a result, her husband called on Hikye:t, asking him to treat her, in the hope that his better nature (hi: wantc kinyai:m=heart says) would induce him to cure her, if he were asked to do so. Hikye:t accepted the assignment and treated her for two nights, but finally gave up the case as hopeless. Uta:c then asked Kapel Tcukye:va to treat his wife. He, too, failed to cure her, however. At present, all of Mrs. Uta:c's relatives have a personal grudge against Hikye:t.

In conclusion, Tcatc remarked teasingly: "Maybe you too will be like that, but I hope not." This remark referred to the fact that I was at that time believed to be hi: wa itck (heartbroken), due to disappointment in love. This jocular remark may suggest a slight nexus between ahwe: nyevedhi: and the relatively mild and somewhat humorously viewed ailment called hi: wa itck (pt. 3, pp. 91–106).

Comment

Mohave diagnosis.—Ahwe: nyevedhi: (?) complicated by witchcraft.

Tentative diagnosis.—Senile dementia. (Highly uncertain.) The similarity between Cii:p's and Mrs. Uta:c's symptoms is quite striking. Also noteworthy is her insistence that others help her mourn her dead relatives,[54] and her mistaking her husband for her dead son.

CASE 39 (Informant not recorded, perhaps Pulyi:k.):

Tcatc (not to be confused with the informant of that name) suffered from ahwe: nyevedhi:. (No other data were obtainable.)

THE HIWEY LAK GROUP

An important group of psychiatric or, more specifically, psychosomatic conditions is known by the name of "hiwey lak" (anus pain). Many Mohave informants tend to view hiwey lak primarily as a kind of venereal disease, even though every Mohave who had the characteristic symptoms of gonorrhea or spyhilis was diagnosed as having hiku:pk.

Broadly speaking, there are two types of hiwey lak diseases:

(1) Hiwey lak proper, which rates as a "straight disease"

(2) Hiwey lak nyevedhi: (anus pain ghostly), which is a "not straight" disease and is closely related to ahwe: nyevedhi: (pt. 4, pp. 128–150).

---

[54] Compare the insistence of transvestites, who profess to have given birth to a stillborn baby, that their "husbands" should also mourn for this "fecal baby" (Devereux, 1937 b).

Hiwey lak is certainly an ancient diagnostic category, since Kroeber (1925 a) mentions an apparently unrecorded song cycle called Wellaka, which is used in the cure of diarrhea.[55] "Wellaka" is certainly a contraction of hiwey lak, since I, myself, first recorded the name of this illness as "weylak."

Generally speaking, all forms of hiwey lak seem to involve a variety of nutritional disturbances, from actual diarrhea to seemingly neurotic anorexia. The significance of the fact that pseudocyesis, too, is assigned to this group will be discussed at the proper point and will be shown to form no exception to the statement that hiwey lak is chiefly related to nutritional disorders. One may even venture to suggest that just as the hi: wa group of illnesses (pt. 3, pp. 90–115) seems to lump together cardiovascular emotional reaction patterns, so the hiwey lak group seems to be made up of gastrointestinal emotional reaction patterns.

THE DATA AND THEIR CONTEXT.—The connection in which one seeks information about a certain topic radically affects the range, scope, and patterned orientation of the data which one obtains. Hence, one's information on a given subject is bound to be incomplete unless that topic is studied in relation to every major cultural matrix to which it belongs (Devereux, 1957 a). Data on hiwey lak were obtained in four contexts, two of which were spontaneously mentioned by the informants themselves:

(1) *Venereal disease.*—The term "hiwey lak" was first mentioned by Hivsu: Tupo:ma, in response to questions about venereal diseases. When asked to describe this illness, he explained that he was not an expert on hiwey lak and advised me to consult two recognized specialists, Harav He:ya and Ahma Huma:re. He added that Harav He:ya was actually qualified to treat all sex-linked disorders, since he could treat not only hiwey lak, but also hiku:pk (gonorrhea, granuloma inguinale, and syphilis). In fact, even though Ahma Huma:re treated only hiwey lak, but not hiku:pk, Hivsu: Tupo:ma was of the opinion that it was more or less natural for a shaman to treat both of these groups of diseases.[56] This view was shared even by Ahma Huma:re, who definitely considered hiwey lak as a "venereal disease without eruptions," though he, himself, did not treat hiku:pk, and, naturally, it was shared also by Harav He:ya, who treated both hiwey lak and hiku:pk. He specifically mentioned the transmission of hiwey lak by saliva, which, according to the Mastamho myth

---

[55] Diarrhea is far more common among the Mohave than is constipation. As I recall, my Mohave informants mentioned constipation only in connection with the faked "pregnancies" of transvestites (Devereux, 1937 b) and with tuberculosis (Case 44).

[56] It might be noted in passing that, in referring me to these experts, Hivsu: Tupo:ma simply transposed to the fieldwork situation the standard shamanistic procedure of referring patients whom one is not qualified to treat to the proper specialist.

(Kroeber, 1948) is the way in which venereal disease (i.e., chiefly hiku: pk) was to be transmitted in times to come. Ahma Huma: re, on the other hand, seemed to view hiwey lak as a broadly sexual rather than as a specifically venereal disease, and therefore spontaneously referred to the connection between hiwey lak and obstetrics, which was his second specialty (Devereux, 1948 e) and which appears to be also the second cultural context or matrix of the hiwey lak group of diseases.

(2) *Obstetrics.*—Ahma Huma: re fully agreed with the definition of hiwey lak as a sexual disease but, due to his subjectively determined interest in obstetrics,[57] emphasized chiefly its connection with this latter specialty. In fact, just as Harav He: ya, who also treated hiku: pk, stressed the connection between the power to cure hiwey lak and the power to cure hiku: pk, Ahma Huma: re asserted that shamans who treated hiwey lak specialized in obstetrics also, even though, at that time, he appears to have been the only Mohave shaman who had this dual competence. This fact illustrates the great flexibility of even major Mohave systems of belief. It should be stressed, however, that in postulating a necessary nexus between the two specialties, Ahma Huma: re did not introduce any radically new point of view into Mohave medical theory, since the connection between hiwey lak—one of whose symptoms may be ghost pregnancy (i.e., pseudocyesis)—and obstetrical difficulties is, in a way, "natural," so that both logically (culturally) and subjectively (psychologically) Ahma Huma :re was on solid ground.

(3) *Psychosomatics.*—During the 1938 field trip devoted to the study of Mohave psychiatric theories, Ahma Huma :re was once more asked to discuss hiwey lak, but this time with special reference to ghost pregnancy (pseudocyesis), viewed as a psychosomatic condition. While discussing this hiwey lak symptom in this particular context, Ahma Huma: re spontaneously provided data which led to additional questions concerning the purely psychiatric aspects of this group of ailments.

(4) *Psychiatry.*—While discussing hiwey lak from the psychosomatic and psychiatric point of view, 6 years after discussing this illness as a sex-linked disease, Ahma Huma: re demonstrated that he had been aware all along of the psychiatric aspects of that disease and had simply failed to elaborate this aspect of the problem at a time when he was expected to discuss its sex-linked (venereal) aspects. It should be stressed that, though very cooperative, Ahma Huma :re was by no means suggestible. It is quite certain that in discussing

---

[57] As stated elsewhere (Devereux, 1948 e) Ahma Huma :re obtained obstetrical powers in dream, shortly after his wife and unborn child died.

the psychiatric aspects of hiwey lak, he did not, in an overcompliant manner, improvise a psychiatric approach to this group of illnesses, but simply provided additional information that he had neglected to give at a time when he was asked to discuss hiwey lak as a sexual illness. In brief, the psychiatrically oriented leading questions, asked in 1938, did not put words into his mouth but simply served to focus his attention on the psychosomatic and psychiatric aspects of this illness.[58] Had Ahma Huma:re been simply suggestible, he would not, in 1932–33, have spontaneously related hiwey lak to obstetrics, nor would he, in 1938, have discussed this illness psychosomatically (i.e., with reference to the role of ghosts in an organic illness) in such a manner as to make a supplementary inquiry into its purely psychiatric aspects mandatory.

What is to be retained here is that the data obtained when hiwey lak was being discussed as an (organic) venereal disease are not, in an absolute sense, more authentic or more important than the data obtained when this illness was discussed in, e. g., a psychiatric context. The fact is that hiwey lak has at least four cultural matrices: venereal, obstetrical (Cases 45 and 46), psychosomatic (ghost), and psychiatric. Any investigation of this disease that fails to take into account all four of these matrices is bound to yield only fragmentary data.

In brief, the following accounts do not simply provide further data belonging to one and the same matrix or cultural frame of reference, but reveal the functional nexus between hiwey lak and its four distinct cultural matrices and, implicitly, also the functional connection between these four matrices themselves. Thus, the additional data not only increase our knowledge of the factual aspects of the hiwey lak complex, but, above all, expand our insight into the nature of Mohave cultural matrices and help us to understand the manner in which these matrices are not simply juxtaposed, but also integrated into a whole, both on the abstract level (Devereux, 1951 a) of the cultural pattern and on the concrete level of actual belief and practice. In addition—especially in the passage in which Ahma Huma:re establishes a connection between hiwey lak and obstetrics—we also gain insight into the manner in which personal interests and biases can exploit a latent and implicit, but a priori logical, connection between two existing patterns so as to conjoin them in a manner which is in harmony with the basic orientation of that culture as a whole. Indeed, in postulating a necessary nexus between the practice of obstetrics and the treatment of hiwey lak, Ahma Huma:re did not breach the latent cultural pattern underlying Mohave medical theories,

---

[58] In the same sense, a good internist, when asked to discuss peptic ulcer, will stress primarily its organic apects, but will, when asked about its etiology and prognosis, describe also its psychiatric aspects.

but simply developed and institutionalized an already present, but previously only latent, nexus. In brief, he did not revolutionize Mohave medical theories but expanded and elaborated them in a manner which, both substantively and procedurally, fitted the basic orientation of Mohave culture and medicine.

THE DATA

Hivsu: Tupo: ma's statement (1932).—Some women contract a sexual illness called hiwey lak (anus pain) which is caused by a ghost pregnancy. A woman who was never pregnant and never lost a child cannot dream of being pregnant with a ghost child and therefore cannot have pseudocyesis. This illness is contagious and is transmitted through intercourse. The man's sperm carries it to the woman and the woman's discharge during the orgasm transmits it to the male.[59] You should ask Harav He:ya and Ahma Huma:re for information about this illness. They are specialists in its treatment and know more about it than I do.

Comment

It is extremely interesting that, just as in the case of hikw:r (pt. 4, pp. 117–128), Hivsu: Tupo:ma gave a relatively nonsupernaturalistic, down-to-earth account of the manner in which hiwey lak is transmitted, whereas the two experts, Harav He:ya and Ahma Huma:re, gave highly supernaturalistic explanations. Yet, even this nonspecialist's theory of the transmission of this disorder by means of the genital secretion of living persons is ultimately rooted in the mythical theory of the transmission of venereal disorders by means of saliva. It is simply restated in more realistic terms, modeled upon the now-known means whereby true venereal disorders are transmitted. This observation tends to strengthen the thesis presented elsewhere (Devereux, 1958 b) that real science comes into being when culturally and supernaturalistically "tainted" or "obfuscated" knowledge is stripped of its cultural connotations, thus making possible a subsequent elaboration of the factual core of what was previously nothing more than "temple science."

It is also tentatively suggested that the mythical theory that venereal diseases are transmitted by means of saliva, i. e., while kissing (Kroeber, 1948), may not date back in its entirety to aboriginal times, since the practice of kissing does not seem to be an ancient one. If that is so, then the nefarious effects attributed to kissing (saliva) may, in part, reflect a resistance to acculturation which is rooted in the belief that the aliens, and all their works, are harmful to the Mohave (pt. 4, pp. 128–150) and in the attitude that occidental techniques of lovemaking are obnoxious (Devereux, 1948 f, 1950 a). If this view is correct, then it is necessary to predicate a connection between the foreign illness (pt. 4, pp. 128–150) and at least the type of hiwey lak caused by ghosts, since, as Fathauer (1951) has shown, there are also many other indications that the Mohave equate ghosts with aliens (pt. 4, pp. 128–150). On the other hand, due consideration must also be given to the probably ancient Mohave belief that the body fluids of a slain monster produced harmful small creatures (see further below), and that dreams of contact with the various secretions of a spouse (pt. 4, pp. 128–150) or of a slain foe or witch occur in

---

[59] This etiological theory, presumably inspired by the "transmission through the saliva" theory mentioned in the Mastamho myth (Kroeber, 1948), may explain why hiwey lak is thought to be a veneral disease.

certain serious illnesses (pt. 2, pp. 43–46). We may therefore suppose that the mythical explanation of the transmission of venereal diseases by means of saliva—rather than by means of other secretions—simply combined into a unified scheme the Mohave's ancient dread of secretions and their explicit (Devereux, 1950 a) anti-acculturational (Devereux and Loeb, 1943 a) rejection of occidental patterns of lovemaking. An additional reason why precisely saliva was chosen as the chief vehicle of sexual contamination may be the fact that the supposedly "venereal" hiwey lak disease group is, at least in theory, a gastrointestinal ailment that is caused, in part, by eating the food of ghosts, is characterized by anorexia, diarrhea, and the like, and is specifically called "anus pain." In fact, it is almost necessary that the Mastamho myth should mention saliva as the principal means whereby sexual diseases are transmitted, if not only hiku: pk, but also hiwey lak, were to be defined as predominantly sexual ailments.

Harav He:ya's statement (1933).—Harav He: ya of Needles, a nearly blind old specialist in the treatment of hiwey lak and hiku: pk (venereal diseases), was an exceptionally willing informant, who gave a detailed account of hiwey lak and sincerely tried to help me record his curing songs. Unfortunately, despite the admonitions of his wife and nephew, he was at first altogether unable to sing slowly and clearly enough to enable me to record his songs accurately. In fact, most of the time he mumbled so badly that even my two expert assistants, Hivsu: Tupo :ma and Hama: Utce:, could not understand all the words of his songs well enough to repeat them for me in their entirety. Furthermore, when they asked him to repeat a word, Harav He:ya simply began to sing the song once more from the start.[60] By contrast, his meticulous prose account of hiwey lak could be recorded in its entirety.

In the following account the noncapitalized pronouns "he" and "they" refer to shamans or to the laity, as the case may be, while the capitalized pronouns "He" and "They" refer to the "Ancient Ones," from whom Harav He:ya derived his shamanistic powers. Unfortunately, the exact identity of these "Ancient Ones" is one of the unsolved problems of Mohave ethnology. All we know is that shamans whose power comes from the "Ancient Ones" are said to be more powerful than those whose power comes from the gods and that they use the right, rather than the left, hand in treating their patients. The most likely hypothesis concerning the identity of these "Ancient Ones" is that they are the culture hero Mastamho (cf. Ahma Huma: re's account) and his contemporaries.

In ancient times They divided the crowd and Them. Some were to the right and some to the left. The shamans on the left were given the power to cure hiwey lak, and They were telling them what will cause them (the people) to be sick. In this house (Matavilye's?), They are telling them how they are going to become sick and then taught them the method by which this illness may be cured. They also described the symptoms of this illness. Even in their own homes (i.e., even where they are not exposed to contamination by aliens(?)) their dreams may be such that they will get sick. In everyday life, wherever they go, they will perhaps become ill; and, when they are ailing, they will think of the shaman to whom the power is given to cure. Then, while they were still gathered together, the power to cure was distributed. There was to be sickness also in the coming generations. The boy is like

---

[60] This indicates that a Mohave song forms a Gestalt exactly as an occidental melody does and can therefore only be remembered as a Gestalt.

Heaven and the girl is like Earth.[61] If they see all the things which He tells, and grasp its meaning and have it in their hearts, it will be in their power to cure hiwey lak and also other ailments of that type.[62] In later times this sickness will be very common. At present, however, it is less common, because I am curing it. Hiwey lak is sometimes accompanied also by some other sickness, which makes the cure very difficult. In such cases I do my part and, then, if the patient is still sick, I send him to another shaman who will cure the remaining sickness. When a man receives the power to cure, he calls himself by a name. He folds his arms behind his back and declares to heaven and to all (cardinal) directions that he has the power to cure certain sicknesses and gives himself the name Maikwitcedhom. (Cf. Mastamho calling himself Pahotcate; Kroeber, 1948.)

Now I will tell you also about the different disorders which resemble, or result from, this disease.

When a man and a women live together, the woman may have a child (who dies?). Sometimes, immediately afterwards, her (menstrual) blood may seem to turn back instead of flowing out, and may cause a sickness called idhotk. I can do some good also in connection with this ailment. Such a woman may (then?) have one or two more children, but, later in life it (idhotk) will come again. It will seem as though the spirit of her dead child had entered her womb again. Yet, even though some people claim that it is a dead child (that is troubling her), in reality it is only that something is wrong with her blood.[63] When this condition occurs, I call it hiwey lak nyevedhi: (anus pain ghost) and cure it. Even the woman herself may think that the child's spirit returned to her womb. She may dream that she is pregnant, or in labor and nearing the moment of delivery, or else she may dream that the child, a little tot about one or two years old, is running beside her, or that a slightly older child is playing at a distance and is approaching her, calling her "mother." Then, when people call on me to help, I see it all. I call this hiwey lak nyevedhi: and cure it. I myself have had hiwey lak during my life.[64]

In such cases the spirit of the child enters its mother in order to kill her. She won't even eat her favorite dishes. Her lack of appetite may even go so far that the very smell of food will nauseate her, so that she will throw up something that has a greenish, or yellowish, or white color.[65] If that happens, it becomes evident that the child tries to go into her and kill her.[66] This too I will cure. Each dream makes the woman a little more ill and every one of her illnesses will be a little worse than the previous one.

---

[61] This appears to be an allusion to that portion of the Creation myth which describes Matavilye's parents as Sky Male and Earth Female (Bourke, 1889).

[62] This is, presumably, an allusion not only to the Mohave method of grouping certain illnesses together, but perhaps also to the combining of various specialties, such as hiwey lak and hiku:pk in Harav He:ya's own case, or of hiwey lak and obstetrics in Ahma Huma:re's case.

[63] A childless woman, or one who had no child that died, cannot, in theory, dream of a ghost pregnancy.

[64] In many primitive societies the healer is a former patient. It is psychologically of the utmost importance that Harav He:ya mentions his own illness after describing essentially feminine symptoms. This is clearcut evidence of a (neurotic) partial feminine identification, perhaps related to the belief that transvestite shamans are more powerful than heterosexual ones (Devereux, 1937 b).

[65] Sucklings jealous of an unborn sibling are said to have stools of this color (Devereux, 1947 a).

[66] Certain bewitched or shamanistic fetuses also try to kill their mothers (Devereux, 1948 e).

The patient may also dream of the old home in which all members of his (or her) family were formerly living. In dream the patient sees once more the old house, as it was when he (she) was happy there. In other cases, however, the home of the patient's youth appears all battered and abandoned in his (her) dreams. He (she) will also see the path which he (she) used to take when he (she) went to the fields or for wood. A young man may dream of how he picked up an ax or some other implement which he once used and will see the roads which he used to travel. The patient will dream of his youth and of the (puberty?) ceremonies he participated in, in order to gain endurance (Devereux, 1949 a).

Some women are generous and some hold a high position in the tribe. The patient may dream about the objects which (such?) women use in their everyday life, e.g., he may dream about their metates, etc.[67] All such dreams cause disease. In dream, one may find it difficult to grind the corn on the metate or else one may dream that one is tired and that one's legs and hands ache. Then, as one's endurance decreases, one wonders why this happens. These fatigue dreams then cause one to have the same kind of pains also when one is awake. This too is a form of hiwey lak. Yet, if the patient has a great deal of resistance, he may not become ill in spite of the pains that rack him.

If one dreams of cohabiting with persons whom one likes, in dream one may even like their way of spitting, and may therefore allow them to slobber into one's mouth (while one is kissing them) in dream,[68] and one will do whatever the loved one wants.

When I speak of such dreams to patients, they may recall certain of their forgotten dreams. I mention every type of dream that may cause this sickness, so that the patient may recognize (recall?) his dreams. A patient may also have incestuous dreams about the dead.

It is really not right for me to tell you all I know, because another shaman may be offended by my way of doing things, or else he may so greatly resent the order in which I am telling things that he will send out his bewitching power and bewitch me. If that happens, I may carry on for two or three more years and then die bewitched (Devereux, 1957 b). Professor Kroeber's interpreter, Jack Jones, who interpreted everything, and especially the Creation myth, died from this.[69]

Cure: I use my right hand, because my power comes from the Ancient Ones. I may, however, also use my left hand, as do those whose power comes from Avikwame. [At this point the interpreter remarked: "The same power may have been given also to Ahma Huma :re:, but Harav He :ya goes deeper. There are fundamental differences between their respective methods."] [I was told there were certain food taboos.] Some shamans (e.g., Ahma Huma : re) forbid certain foods, but I don't, even though some foods may pull down the resistance of the patient. I give them whatever food is handy, and should it harm them, I will cure them of that illness too. As to their relatives and myself—we can eat what we want. [Is intercourse taboo?] My treatment does not involve sexual taboos. With my right hand I gently press the abdomen, and the region just below the solar plexus. It is only a sort of massage, because

---

[67] Homosexually inclined boys are attracted to female regalia and to female occupations (Devereux, 1937 b).

[68] Compare in this context the ahwe : syndrome (pt. 4, pp. 128–150). Cf. also the mythical theory that saliva transmits veneral diseases (Kroeber, 1948).

[69] These remarks were indirect allusions to the fact that this interview took place in the presence, and with the help, of the shaman Hivsu : Tupo :ma.

the patient is too weak for me to hurt him. Then the stomach gas goes out either way (eructation or flatus).[70] I blow on the solar plexus first and then immediately press my hand on the same spot, to keep my breath on it. I may also blow on the patient, starting from the upper part of his chest and progressing toward his abdomen, to remove the pains. If the pains are strong, I will also boil the bark of the white mesquite tree, or make a willow bark tea and give it to the patient to drink.

Summing up, at first the child's body consists only of menstrual blood which is kneaded into human shape by the father's sperm. If the pregnant woman then cohabits with some other man or men, the semen which she receives molds the child to the likeness of the new partner(s).[71] The ghost of the dead child sometimes returns to its mother's womb and, without help from human semen, makes a body for itself out of the menstrual blood which accumulates between (two or more) menstrual periods. This disease kills the mother. We believe that the ghost child kills its mother and takes her soul to the land of the ghosts.

Curing songs: The final version of the following songs approximates rather closely the actual text of Harav He :ya's songs, which varied considerably as he repeated them. Harav He :ya's singing was interspersed with copious throat clearings, stage whispers, explanations given in a kind of recitative which could barely be told apart from the songs themselves, and even with extra syllables, allegedly caused by "shortness" (sic) of breath, (e.g., oh-eyam, instead of eyam). The entire performance of this toothless, stubborn, but willing old man, who lost his bearings and had to start all over again whenever he was asked to sing more slowly, caused the interpreter to exclaim, "If we hadn't had Hivsu: Tupo:ma along, who had heard these songs before, I couldn't have grasped a single word for it." In fact, even Harav He : ya's alert old wife and his highly cooperative nephew, who had heard him sing these songs many times, were unable to catch certain words well enough to repeat them for me.

There are four songs altogether. The first one had to be recorded three times and the second and third twice. The fourth was recorded only once because, by that time, Harav He :ya had finally learned to sing more slowly. The differences between the various recordings suggest that the actual text of the songs is flexible. This supposition is wholly compatible with the fact that, unlike the ritual formulas of obsessive-compulsive ethnic groups, the effectiveness of Mohave songs does not depend on their letter-perfect reproduction, but on the singer's possession of the necessary powers. In fact, several informants stated that when a certain illness is not treated by anyone for a number of years, because no one had received suitable powers in dream, the text of the traditional songs may be lost forever, so that the next person to receive the necessary powers will simply recite the (condensed?) prose text of the relevant myth, instead of making up new songs.[72] The variability of Mohave ritual texts is, both from the anthropological and from the psychological point of view, too complex a problem to be discussed in this context (Devereux, 1957 b).

---

[70] Jones' (1951) analysis of Hindu pneuma-theories is illuminating in this context (see also part 1, pp. 9–17).

[71] Note the nexus between this theory of modifiable paternity (Devereux, 1949 c) and theories of ghostly pseudocyesis.

[72] It may be assumed, however, that even such narratives will approximate the singing style and will consist primarily of a series of key words.

To illustrate the flexibility of Harav He:ya's texts, as well as the difficulties met with when trying to record them, all versions are reproduced as recorded. The numbers in parentheses indicate how often a given word was repeated.

First song:

    (*a*) *Final version:* miyo:a (4) look at / amay (4) sky / miyo:a (4) look at / amay vadho miyo heavens face-toward you'll see / . . . (This song, repeated several times, refers to dreams about the homestead of one's youth.)

    (*b*) *First recording:* vangiyu (9) meaningless? / eyo angiyu (8) ? / eyo . . . (11) ? / eyo haymauay ohemay hamanay ? / .

    (*c*) *Second recording:* vidhaue to take / eyam? / amaye heavens / vidhaue to take / .

Second song:

    (*a*) *Final version:* miyo:a (12) will see / vangi:yo (12) meaningless? / hemat body, kwisau soul or shadow / idhau take / miyo: will see/. (This song refers to the ghost or shadow which comes and assumes a shape.)

    (*b*) *First recording:* e-matkwisa: soul or shadow / idhau take / hiyuk to see / vangi:yu meaningless?/. (The interpreters first thought that "hiyuk" may be an onomatopoea for hiccoughing or sneezing. In fact, one of them suspected that what I had recorded as hiyuk was an actual hiccough: However, Pulyi:k later on translated it as "to see.")

Third song:

    (*a*) *Final version:* eyam meaningless? / ama:ye heavens / vedho:a will be / midha:ua will take/. (This song refers to pseudocyesis and to the ghost of the dead child.)

    (*b*) *First recording:* hongoyi meaningless / manyau monoyi where you were / myoyima (2) all gone / nyoyima hohima moved on / eyam hamauayh ? heavens / midho: a is there / manyaui gone invisible / monoyi where you were / .

Fourth song:

    Final (and only) version: manga: ui (12) all gone / eyam meaningless? / ama:uay heavens / amat earth / kwisa: soul or shadow / idhauem taken / havi:yum meaningless / anyaue vanished /. (This song refers to the destruction of the old homestead, when "all is over," i. e., when, after the death of a person, the building in which he lived is burned down.)

Epilogue.—The interview with Harav He: ya had an aftermath, which casts an interesting sidelight upon the psychological effects of listening to a shaman who is discussing his powers:

Interpreter: "After listening to Harav He:ya, I dreamed of dying and became ill."

Anthropologist: "I will doctor you for it and you will never dream of it again."

Hivsu: Tupo:ma: "I, for one, do not want helpers around me when I discuss such things with you, because, should the assistants become ill later on, they will blame their illness on me.

Comment

(1) It is quite striking that, after specifically denying that the baby actually returns to the mother's womb, Harav He:ya promptly proceeded to interpret most of this illness precisely in terms of this supposedly untenable theory. This seeming self-contradiction illustrates, in the anthropological frame of reference,

the degree of latitude permitted to the individual shaman in evolving his personal medico-etiological theories. However, from the psychoanalytic point of view, the two, seemingly incompatible, theories actually say the same thing.[73] Indeed the menstrual blood from which babies are formed is simply equated with a ghostly fetus, because many psychic and somatic effects of a pathological retention of the menses and of a natural pregnancy are, according to the Mohave, almost identical (Cases 45 and 46).

(2) The narrative contains two passages which reveal a certain confusion about sexual self-identification. The first of these passages opens with a description of ghost pregnancy and motherhood, immediately followed by the, logically extraneous but psychologically relevant, remark that the singer—a man— formerly had hiwey lak. The second passage states that male hiwey lak patients may dream of female regalia and possessions, at which point we noted that such dreams and interests are said to be highly characteristic of future transvestites. What is especially relevant in this context is that male transvestites who have "husbands" not only fake menstruation and pregnancy, but even deliberately constipate themselves so as to be able to "give birth" to a fecal "child" (Devereux, 1937 b). This practice may be the (implicit) link which connects ghostly pregnancy (pseudocyesis) with a disease whose very name (hiwey lak = anus pain) indicates that it is believed to affect primarily the digestive tract. Thus, the entire concept of hiwey lak nyevedhi: appears to be a culturally structured and implemented fantasy about the oral-anal origin of babies, such as children evolve during the anal stage of psychosexual development (Devereux, 1951 e). Indeed, both normal children and adult schizophrenics sometimes fantasy that babies are conceived orally and are born through the anus or navel. Mohave male transvestites actually implement this fantasy, by drinking a constipating decoction and by "giving birth" to a hard fecal mass, which they choose to call a "stillbirth," while in hiwey lak nyevedhi: the retention of the menses and the ghost pregnancy resulting from it are said to cause major gastrointestinal disturbances.[74]

Ahma Huma:re's first statement (1932).—The disease called hiwey lak may come from dreaming about intercourse with a person of the opposite sex, or about drinking stagnant water or else water found in the hills. The person one dreams about is not responsible for these dreams or for the subsequent illness.

Symptoms: The chief symptoms of this disease are stomach troubles because (sic!) hiwey lak is a venereal disease without skin eruptions. Once a person has such dreams, even his favorite dishes will not seem to taste good. There will also be frequent headaches, and vision will be disturbed and hazy (migraine?). When the patient looks at a distant object, the thing he looks at seems deformed. There is, furthermore, a general nervousness of the eyes; one cannot look at things for any length of time, because one's vision becomes hazy and flashy (scintillating scotoma?). Unless a shaman is asked to cure the sick person, death may be considered a certainty.

Origin of power: I do not say that my power comes from Matavilye, because I believe that Matavilye lived and died without telling about, or giving, the power to cure this illness. In this respect, our religion differs from the religion

---

[73] Cf. the basic identity of two, supposedly incompatible, etiological theories of the hikwi:r illness (pt. 4, pp. 117–128).

[74] The fact that the same illness may be caused also by dreaming of the homestead of one's youth, which was destroyed when a relative, who lived in that house, died, is psychologically also related to this retentive process and is a defense against the sense of psychic and material loss which death, followed by the destruction of property previously available to the survivor, entails (Devereux, 1942 a).

of the whites, who claim that God gave every power. Mastamho, who came after Matavilye to teach, was the one who did it; he had the power to teach in dreams. My personal experience of this power is as follows: I see things only at night. As a child of seven or eight, I saw Mastamho in my dreams, and he, who came to me in my dreams, told me about hiwey lak, gave me the power to cure this sickness, and described its symptoms to me. He came only at night [75] and taught me from sunset to sunrise. He said to me, "It is fine from sunrise to sunset. Therefore, let your right arm be like the day (the day too, being a dream-bringing "person") and your left arm like the night—for with the left arm you will be able to cure. The power will be in your left arm when you touch people who claim to have this sickness. And if the illness they have is really *this* one, the touch of your left arm will cure them." Thus, if the patient is not cured by the time I am through with the fourth song of the curing rite, he does not have this disease. (Traditionally, right=paternal, life=maternal kin.)

Hiwey lak nyevedhi: is a form of the hiwey lak sickness. It is caused by dreams of intercourse with the dead and is cured the same way as ordinary hiwey lak.

Cure: When they bring me a patient who claims to have hiwey lak, I ask him to tell me his dreams, so that I may be sure that he does have hiwey lak and not some other disease. If I discover that he does not have this illness, I will advise him and tell him which shaman he should consult. I must also take into account that a patient's bad dreams may be balanced by his good dreams. I can cure not only Mohave Indians, but also whites who have this disease.[76]

I forbid the patient to eat any kind of watermelon or pumpkin, other than the grayish-white variety of pumpkin. The rest of his food will be prepared as usual. I prescribe a diet only in very serious cases. No other taboo of any kind need be observed. The patient, his relatives and the shaman are neither painted nor dressed in any special way. The ghost who appeared in the patient's dreams is not contacted and has no connection with the cure. The patient is treated at some convenient place, i. e., generally at the house of the shaman, if the latter is married and has a home of his own. If he is single, or has no home of his own, the patient may be treated wherever it is convenient to everyone concerned.

Audience: An audience, as numerous as possible, is useful. The audience just sits around and says, "Yes, yes," whenever I sing. I press the patient's abdomen with my left hand, blow on it, and sing my four songs.

Songs: Before presenting Ahma Huma:re's songs, as sung in 1932, it is desirable to quote first his 1938 description of the manner in which he acquired them:

"I know the traditional songs while some other shamans don't. However, the fact that they do not know these songs does not affect their healing powers in any way. What matters are not the songs themselves but the power to cure, which one receives in dream. When I was a child, some of my old relatives were still alive. They, too, used to treat hiwey lak [77] and would sing the songs which I now use. I did not pay much attention to them or to their songs, at that time. Yet, once in a while, these songs would come to me and

---

[75] The night itself is also a "person" (ipa :) who brings dreams.

[76] Despite this statement, both Ahma Huma : re and Hivsu : Tupo : ma refused to treat me both for a genuine indigestion and a recent "typical hiwey lak" dream. (See dream B, pp. 170–171).

[77] Shamanistic powers supposedly run in certain families.

I would sing them.[78] Whenever I sang these songs in the presence of these old people, they said that I too would eventually treat hiwey lak, and their prediction seems to have come true. [I commented that his spontaneous remarks dovetailed perfectly with the conclusions I had previously reached regarding the manner in which "learning" took place in a dream.] What various shamans tell about their suma:tc (dream power) is not always the same thing. But the questions you now ask about insanity refer to something whose causes we can describe as we hear and see them.[79]

(1932) "My songs are in archaic Mohave and relate certain events in a 'preaching' (schematic and telegraphic) style. The Yuma, Cocopa, Yavapai and Maricopa, and even some Walapai may understand my songs but the Havasupai and the Diegueño cannot understand them. Unless the case is a very severe one, it can be cured in one night—the treatment takes place at night. As a rule, the illness is cured before the sun sets next day. In severe cases I (first) tell (in prose) about the songs which I am going to sing, because the sick person must be helped before the fourth song is finished. If he is not cured by that time, he does not have hiwey lak."

First song:

> Hamayvi tcami:ye, tcami:ye—(heavens, under control, under control.)
>> (Pulyi:k translated it as: heavens, put-down-lower-and-lower.)
> Hamayvi tcami:ye, tcami:ye
> Mayvi tcami:ye, tcami:ye
> Mayvi tcami:ye, tcami:ye
> Mayvi tcami:ye, tcami:ye, tcami:ye
> Mayvi tcami:ye, tcami:ye, tcami:ye
> Hamayvi tcami:ye, tcami:ye
> Mayvi tcami:ye, tcami:ye
> Etc.[80]

Second song:

> Hamayvi kono:(h)yi: ko(h)ono:yi (as we are on earth, they are in
>> heaven.) (Pulyi:k said it meant: heaven, right down here—patted down
>> with the hand on the patient.)
> Mayvi kono:(h)yi ko(h)ono:yi
> Hamayvi kono:(h)yi ko(h)ono:yi ko(h)ono:yi
> Mayvi kono:(h)yi ko(h)ono:yi ko(h)ono:yi

---

[78] This is a clear-cut description of the quasi-involuntary and preconscious manner in which ritual knowledge is acquired and explains why these songs are afterward also "relearned" in dream. This process resembles that which Pötzl (1917) tested by means of his now famous experiments: He briefly flashed a picture on a screen and instructed his subjects to describe what they had seen. The morning after, he recorded his subjects' dreams. It was found that those details which the subjects had not consciously seen and recalled, appeared as elements in the dreams they had during the following night. This may be due to the fact that uncompleted tasks are remembered better than completed ones (Zeigarnik, 1927).

[79] This concluding remark clearly differentiates between dream knowledge and empirical data (Devereux, 1957 b).

[80] This song goes on for a long time and there is no strict rule as to where and when the meaningless syllable "ha" should be inserted before "mayvi." There is, likewise, no rule as to whether one should repeat the word tcami:ye twice or three times in a given phrase. These things vary according to the melody. In fact, the song changes a little every time it is sung. Whenever tcami:ye is repeated three times, the melody becomes a little less monotonous, but this is not an absolute rule. In brief, the song changes whenever the singer wishes to change it. For this reason, only the basic lines of the following songs will be recorded. These lines may be repeated as often as the singer wishes and may recur at any time during the singing of this song.

Third song:

Meya me-eya me-eya (An exact translation could not be obtained from
Ahma Huma:re. He said it refers to "their" (whose?) physical makeup.
Pulyi:k said it referred to a contest or argument with the illness.)

Hameya me-eya me-eya (Sometimes me-eya is sung thrice.)

Fourth song:

Hono:me yono:me yono:me (This still refers to "their" makeup. Pulyi:k
stated it meant: He goes after the illness saying in effect: "Do you
hear me?")

No:me yono:me yono:me (Sometimes yono:me is sung thrice.)

As a general rule, every line is repeated at least once. Every time the second
word is repeated thrice, the melody loses its shuffling monotony and becomes
quite pleasing. The song is sung moderato, mezzopiano, and, at the end,
morendo (fading away). The phrasing is rather abrupt, and the rhythm is
dotted.

Translation: "Your interpreter (Hama: Utce:) cannot really translate this
for you. All the words have, of course, a real meaning in everyday language
but in this song they mean more than that." (I.e., they are catch phrases or
slogans.) The interpreter also agreed with this statement. "I am not giving
you a real running translation of these songs. I will translate to you what
Ahma Huma:re says his songs mean." These remarks reveal that the Mohave
themselves realize that in shamanistic songs each word is surrounded by a halo
of implied meanings derived from mythology. Thus, in a sense, the shamanistic "poet" seeks to transcend the limited meaning of words, and to compress
the story of, e.g., the "Creation" in the two words "heaven and earth," in order
to convey to the patient and to the audience certain general ideas which seem
to transcend the everyday "core meaning" of Mohave words. A discussion of
the complex problem of "translating" Mohave ritual songs will be found elsewhere
(Devereux, 1957 b). For the moment, it suffices to stress that a ritual song can
be translated on three different levels:

(1) One can translate the "core meaning" of the words, as was done some 15
years later by the excellent linguistic informant Pulyi:k.

(2) One can translate the "halo meaning" of the words, as was done by Hama:
Utce:, in consultation with Ahma Huma:re.

(3) One can explain the meaning of the songs as a whole, as Ahma Huma:re
did.

The meaning of the songs: In the first song I tell about the whole of heavens;
how beautiful and full of life it is. I also say the same thing about the earth. I
say that people were meant to be healthy and full of life and that, as I sing, this
sickness, which is foreign to (does not fit in with) all this life, will leave and
disappear. In the second song I say, 'You will have to tell your dreams and by
the time I am through with my singing, you will be healthy.' The third song is
really just a 'different pronunciation' (sic) of the first song and is supposed to
convey the same meaning. The fourth song is also the same; it conveys the
idea that it is in my power to cure."

Left hand: I use my left hand because my power comes from the supernaturals on the mountain Avi:kwame:.

Cases: At this point Ahma Huma:re briefly referred to three patients whom
he had treated recently (Cases 40, 41, 42).

Ahma Huma:re's second statement (1933).—Sometimes the ghost of a dead
child returns into the mother's womb, causing hiwey lak nyevedhi:. Its body
is just a clot of menstrual blood. This condition is treated by shamans like
myself, who specialize in obstetrics. This disease is due to the fact that the

dead child tries to kill its mother so as to take her soul with it to the land of the dead."

Ahma Huma:re's third statement (*1938*).—Lay people call ghost pregnancy hiwey lak, but we who have power (shamans) call it nyevedhi: utu:y (or utu:ly). The disease is caused by dreams of intercourse with dead relatives, which precede dreams about the return of dead babies. Such dreams of intercourse with the dead cause the woman to have a ghost baby in her womb. This condition, too, is called nyevedhi: utu:y (or utu:ly). [Is the man with whom the woman cohabits in dream the father of the ghost baby?] Yes, he is. [Do ghosts have semen?] They do. [Can it be seen?] No. [Does the woman who dreams of intercourse have a dream "pollution"?] [81] Yes. [Does this happen only to women whose baby died?]. Yes. In order to have such dreams one has to have both a dead baby and a dead husband. [If the woman did not have a baby who died, this cannot happen?] No. [Do such people act queer?] Yes. [What do they do?] Yavoo:k means that they talk without knowing what they are talking about. They do a lot of talking. [Do they speak Mohave or an unknown language (glossolalia)?] They speak Mohave, but sometimes they also hear other languages and then they speak that way too. It is, naturally, always a language that they have heard, like Yavapai or Yuma. They do not act peculiar in other ways—they only speak—it is only a sort of queerness. [Do they speak fast?] Yes. [Do they throw themselves about so that you can't hold them?] Yes. [Do they have fugues?] Yes, some of them do, but not all. [Is there also retardation—like this (mimic)?] Yes. [Are they sometimes excited and at other times retarded?] Yes, they alternate. When I treat them, I have to blow in their ear and if my power is able to cure this type of sickness, it will cure it. All three types of hiwey lak make people act that way and I can cure all three types. [I describe a manic female patient whom I saw in a mental hospital.] Yes, that is how they act. [What are the physical symptoms?] They seem to run a temperature. Their body is very shaky and they have stomach troubles. I can cure all three conditions. [Have you had patients of all three kinds?] Yes. [Can you tell me this afternoon about your patients, one by one?] Certainly. [Did you ever treat a nyevedhi: utu:y (or utu:ly) case?] I never had such a case on the reservation. I know about it from my dreams. [Whence comes this term?] I heard it in my dream. Utu:y (utu:ly) is a well known name for sickness. [Interpreter remarked: "Even I know it."] I have heard of such cases, but I have never doctored one personally. I just heard of them but know of no special case. I personally never had a case where real insanity (yamomk) was one of the symptoms of this disease, nor have I heard of such a case. [When ghosts dream of living people, do they get sick too?] Nobody knows about that.

Ahma Huma:re's fourth statement (*1938*).—[Why do you, and others as well, hint that hiwey lak is a kind of insanity?]- In their younger days people live with their own parents. Then, because of death in the family, they sometimes move from one place to another. For example, they may lose their own parents and then have to move to another place (because the death house is burned down (cf. Kroeber, 1925 a)). In such cases they may get hiwey lak nyevedhi:, because they have suma:tc itcem (bad dreams). In their dreams they see these dead relatives and may also see their old home which was destroyed. In other instances they dream that they are doing the things they did when

---

[81] The Mohave believe that women also ejaculate. Their "sperm" seems to be the vaginal moisture (Devereux, 1950 a).

their parents or dead relatives were still alive. Sometimes they have dreams in which the dead relatives prepare foods, such as pumpkins and melons, which are supposed to be the original food of the Mohave. When they awaken from such dreams, their appetite is lost, their bowels are loose, and they urinate to excess. In their dreams they see before them the body of a dead relative; they see the matkwisa: (soul) arise from that body and then step aside, turn around and speak to them. Then the dreamers talk to the ghost and answer. At that point the person who has such dreams goes insane. The spirit that arises from the body and steps away from it is said to be itc tu:atck (the end, the termination).

A sick person also has another kind of dream. He sees that his dead relatives have come back. They tell him that they have come for him. They say 'The place you are living on now (i.e., the earth) is bad.' The clothing which the dreamer destroyed at the funeral of his dead relatives is supposed to be in the land of the ghosts. The land of the ghosts is called Câlya:yt (Devereux, 1937 a) or Nyevedhi: nyámat (ghost earth). That place also contains the nyevedhi: nyeva:tce (ghost dwellings) and Ahatc kupi:lyk. When he discovers that his dead relatives have come for him, the dreamer may decide to go back with them to the land of the dead. I mean, of course, that his soul, matkwisa: sumatc mitcemvetc (soul of evil dreams) may do so. When one reaches that stage (has such dreams), that too is a cause of insanity. When the dreamer tells of having such a dream, people know that he has hiwey lak nyevedhi:. This is so well known that even ordinary (lay) people know (can make) this diagnosis. [In English we call this autistic regression. You are quite right, it sometimes does involve insanity. By the way, I heard of two other things that cause this disease: The return of the dead child into the womb, and dream intercourse with ghosts.] As regards the return of dead children into the womb, ordinary people may, perhaps, call it hiwey lak nyevedhi:, but we, who have power (shamans), call it nyevedhi: utu:y or utu:ly. We also apply that name to dreams of intercourse with ghosts, because they precede dreams about the return of the dead baby and do, in fact, cause ghost pregnancy. But when one merely dreams of intercourse with ghosts, the resulting sickness is called hiwey lak nyevedhi:. [What if one dreams of intercourse with sexually tabooed living relatives?] That only causes straight hiwey lak (Case 42) and not hiwey lak nyevedhi:. [Can women conceive babies that way?] No. they can't.

[I am getting a little confused—there seem to be so many kinds of ghost illnesses.] There is, first of all, nyevedhi: taha:na (ghost real) [see pt. 4, pp. 175-184]. A person who has this ailment sees his dead relatives in dream; they prepare food for him and he eats this food. He also dreams of engaging in various activities with his dead relatives, much as he did when they were still alive. Hiwey lak and hiwey lak nyevedhi: are just about the same illness. Their symptoms are the same.

There was a man here at Parker, by the name of Hulo:k, who also had the power to cure this illness. He is dead now and there is no longer anyone who can treat such cases. [Then what do you do with people who have this illness?] They just die. There is only one man left who might know something about it, but I am not sure of it. That is Kapel Tcukye:va. [I asked people to tell him I wanted to talk to him, but he doesn't seem to want to talk to me. Why doesn't he?] He must be afraid of these things. Persons who are called real shamans, because they have bewitched people, are very touchy about telling anyone their dreams and power. This applies also to Hikye:t[82] and to Kwathany Hi:wa (lizard heart) as well as to Kapel Tcukye:va. No matter how much money you offer them, they don't want to say anything about their powers.[83]

Acatc's statement (1938).—Hiwey lak seems to be connected with menstrual troubles and with the pseudocyesis which such troubles cause. Menstrual blood is bad blood, which is expelled from the body. Some women bleed little, however, because they are sick; such women are eventually killed by this disease. Some of them do not get with child even from men who already fathered other children. Something is wrong with their blood and with their stomach, and is likely to kill them. They dream of having children and then their blood forms some sort of "child" inside of them. That is one cause of hiwey lak.

Hiwey lak dreams.—With the exception of dreams of incest with living relatives (Case 42), all hiwey lak dreams supposedly concern the dead, either directly or indirectly. An important exception to the rule that such dreams cause illness is the belief that during the four nights following death the soul of the deceased—which is not quite a ghost as yet—revisits its old haunts, and may even have intercourse with the surviving spouse, without harm to the latter. The belief that witches may have erotic dreams about their victims—whose souls they temporarily prevent from going to the land of the dead, i.e., from becoming real ghosts (Devereux, 1937 c)—without becoming ill is, in a sense, simply a more complex expression of the basic belief that only relations with fully fledged ghosts, already residing in the land of the dead, can cause disease.

The chaotic variety of dreams cited in the preceding accounts actually falls into a very few, closely interrelated categories:

(1) Dreams restoring the status quo ante.—These include dreams of the house of one's youth, of the rites one underwent at puberty, of the actions one performed and the roads one traveled while one's relatives were still alive; dreams of female (i.e., maternal) regalia and possessions, which recall the future transvestites' preoccupation with female regalia; activity dreams which cause one to feel tired first in dream and then also on awakening, etc. This latter type of dream suggests a nexus between hiwey lak and the activity psychoses (pt. 2, pp. 46–56).

(2) Dreams accepting the loss.—Dreams of the old home, which appears battered and abandoned in dream, as it now is also in reality.

(3) Social interaction with ghosts.—One is visited by, or else visits, the ghosts of one's relatives, who seek to persuade one to join them in the land of the dead. Sometimes the ghost rises from the corpse and engages the dreamer in conversation. At other times one engages in various routine activities with the ghosts of one's relatives.

(4) Food.—The ghosts prepare aboriginal food for the dreamer, who then partakes of it and thereafter has no appetite for human food. One may dream

---

[82] This shaman did, eventually, consent to an interview. However, his extremely confused statements and his air of embarrassed vigilance indicated that Ahma Huma:re was right in saying that he would be afraid to speak of his powers (pt. 1, pp. 9–11).

[83] The implications of this remark are: (1) Ahma Huma:re talked to me not simply for pay, but chiefly from friendship, and (2) unlike the shamans just mentioned, he was not a witch who is afraid of revealing the nature of his powers.

of drinking unusual types of water, such as stagnant water or water found in the hills (which may symbolize the water drunk by the dead).[84]   The various cannibalistic dreams reported in connection with nyevedhi: taha:na (pt. 4, pp. 175–184) suggest that eating the food of the dead symbolizes eating the dead themselves.   This meaning of ghost food is so close to consciousness that one woman actually saw that the fish she ate had the head of her dead mother (Case 47).   The feeding of the dreamer by the ghosts of his relatives, which causes him to lose his appetite for earthly food, is clearly part and parcel of the ghosts' attempt to lure their children, etc., to the land of the dead, by providing them with imaginary (infantile?) oral gratifications.

(5) *Coitus with the dead* also appears to be a means of luring the living to the land of the dead.   It is also to be noted that witches begin to long for death *after* cohabiting in dream with the souls of their dead victims, who often happen to be their close relatives.   The dead sex partner acts either like a succubus or like an incubus, regardless of his or her real sex.[85]

(6) *Incest with the dead* appears to be the principal form of coitus with the dead and the one whose effects are most likely to be fatal.   It is interesting to note that Harav He:ya took pains to stress that in such dream intercourse one allows the saliva of one's ghostly sex partner to dribble into one's mouth; this combines the sexual and oral devices by means of which the dead lure the living to the land of ghosts.

(7) *Pregnancy, childbirth, and motherhood* dreams occur chiefly in women who lost both their baby and their husband.   The dead baby reenters the mother's womb in order to kill her and take her to the land of the dead.   Since unborn shamans, who do not wish to be born, also seek to kill their mothers during childbirth, it may conceivably be relevant in this context that evil shamans are said to be prone to commit incest (Devereux, 1937 c and 1939 a).

(8) *Incest with a living person* occurring in dream causes hiwey lak, but not hiwey lak nyevedhi: (Case 42).

On the whole, the dead are believed to resort to a variety of means to lure their living relatives to the land of the dead.   These means range from persuasion to oral and incestuous sexual gatifications, or else involve dreams related to mourning.   Apparently the manner in which the deceased person died does not affect the quality or intensity of his wish or ability to lure the survivors to the land of ghosts. Thus, it was specifically ascertained that the ghosts of women who died in childbirth are no more eager than other ghosts to induce the living to follow them to the land of the dead.   A partial exception to this rule may be the ability of bewitched persons to make their killer long for death (Devereux, 1937 c).

The two physiological means of luring the survivors to the land of the dead, and of arousing in them a desire to die—i.e., by incestuous coitus and by feeding them aboriginal food (= milk)—reflect a remarkable insight into the oral components of the Oedipus complex,

---

[84] Thus, twins in heaven drink rain water (Devereux, 1941).

[85] This point was made when I mentioned to the Mohave the Navaho belief (Bailey, 1950) that in coitus inversus the man may become pregnant, a notion which made the Mohave laugh out loud.

against which the Mohave struggle all their lives and which causes them, e.g., to taboo, as suggestive of incest, the oral titillation of the mammae during foreplay (Devereux, 1947 a and 1950 a).

It should be noted, however, that at least one of my own two dreams which the Mohave diagnosed as hiwey lak dreams did not fit any of these patterns. This suggests a tendency to diagnose as hiwey lak dreams certain anxiety dreams in which the "ego is split." Thus, Kohovan Kura:u, who had a "dream within a dream," was convinced that this was an unlucky and probably pathogenic dream, although he did not specifically mention the possibility that it may be a hiwey lak dream. By contrast, a dream in which he saw the white town of Parker almost deserted, was interpreted by him simply as a prophetic dream, heralding the great economic depression of 1929–1934—perhaps because he knew that the white man does not destroy his house when one of its inhabitants dies.

MISCELLANEOUS SUPPLEMENTARY DATA
From Various Informants

Predisposition.—Women who menstruate little or irregularly are especially likely to develop ghost pregnancies. Apparently even irregular or scanty menses, occurring naturally during puberty, or else during the menopause, are sometimes considered pathological, since of the two women who misdiagnosed their pregnancies as hiwey lak nyevedhi:, one was still in her middle teens (Case 46), while the other was old enough to have reached the menopause (Case 45). It should be noted that in both instances the shamans consulted were quite proud of having made the correct (naturalistic) diagnosis, and of having "debunked" the patient's supernaturalistic self-diagnosis (McNichols, 1944).

Witchcraft.—Unlike the other veneral disease, hiku:pk, hiwey lak can also be caused by witchcraft. It is desirable to recall in this context that another type of murderous attack upon the mother by a living and real fetus can likewise be caused by witchcraft (Devereux, 1948 e). On the other hand, it should also be specified that at least one reliable informant asserted that a witch cannot send the ghost of a dead child back into its mother's womb and is also unable to shift a real fetus from one woman's womb to that of another. Yet, even this informant believed that witches can cause simple hiwey lak and, perhaps, also those forms of hiwey lak nyevedhi: which do not involve a ghost pregnancy.

Dreams.—Sometimes a dream about a (dead?) baby causes itc hira:v, a disorder seemingly related to hiwey lak.

Symptoms.—Ahwe: tci is a sort of hard object in the vagina, which is caused by dreaming of coitus with a dead husband (pt. 4, pp. 138–141). This condition, which may or may not be related to hiwey lak, is not generally known to laymen, since Pulyi:k professed to know nothing about this symptom and had never even heard the term ahwe: tci. (Note that dead husband=ahive:= enemy!)

Diagnosis.—The initial diagnosis of hiwey lak is sometimes far from easy, so that a hiwey lak patient may first be treated for another illness, which he does not have (Case 44).

Treatment.—Supposedly, usually successful.

Treatment despite bad prognosis.—In hiwey lak nyevedhi: dreams one actually goes to the land of the dead. This means that one part of the soul

(Devereux, 1937 a) actually takes such a trip. If the fourth soul, which is the real self, does so, the case is hopeless. Yet, even in such instances, people may ask a shaman to do whatever he can for the patient.

Obscure points.—A number of interesting points could not be clarified. They are:

(1) Asked whether stillborn babies or (usually halfbreed) babies who were killed by burying them alive (Devereux 1948 d) could return to cause ghost pregnancies, Hama: Utce: and Pulyi: k replied: "We do not know—we are not shamans."

(2) Given the fact that ghost pregnancies are called "anus pain ghostly," several informants were asked whether the ghost of the dead child entered its mother's body via the anus or was eventually expelled via the anus.[86] This question was also motivated by the Mohave belief that young girls who eat mesquite sap become barren (Devereux, 1948 b), and by the practice of "married" Mohave transvestites first to constipate themselves with a decoction of mesquite and then to deliver a "fecal child" (Devereux, 1937 b). Informants were unable to answer this question.

(3) The Mohave differentiate between "complete" and "incomplete" beings (Kroeber, 1925 a, Devereux, MS., 1935). Hence, informants were asked whether only "incomplete" (e.g., untattooed) dead babies returned to the womb. Unfortunately, no one was able to answer this question.

(4) Several informants spoke of the role of the various secretions in the hiwey lak group of diseases. A shaman's story, published by Kroeber (1925 a), states that Halypota, the primordial spider, grew from the "himata hakamalya" of the killed gigantic Sky Rattlesnake. Kroeber translated this Mohave expression as "body form," whereas my informants translated it as "body foam." This latter translation is both logically and mythologically more plausible than Kroeber's.[87] Indeed, quite apart from the fact that all over the world mythologies mention dangerous creatures born of the secretions (blood, etc.) of a slain monster, the rest of Kroeber's own account makes it almost mandatory to assume that "body foam" is meant, since all the other disagreeable and dangerous creatures born from the corpse of Sky Rattlesnake were formed out of the various sticky fluids of its body: its blood, sweat, and the "glue of its joints," i.e., precisely from the type of secretions which certain sick Mohave see in their dreams not only when they have hiwey lak nyevedhi: but also when suffering from certain other neuropsychiatric conditions (pts. 2, pp. 42–46 and 4, pp. 128–150).

Erroneous diagnoses of hiwey lak.—The number of cases (45, 46) in which the patient was erroneously believed to have hiwey lak is greater than is the number of all other recorded cases of false diagnosis. This suggests that hiwey lak is a "fashionable disease," not only among Mohave laymen, but even among shamans, perhaps because its symptoms are sufficiently numerous and vague to fit a great variety of illnesses. In addition, hiwey lak is also, in a sense, the prototype of "not straight" illnesses, since it is believed to occur quite often in conjunction with other diseases (e.g., nyevedhi:). As a result, it appears to

---

[86] Compare Harav He :ya's comment on "gas" and Hikye :t's remarks on internal smoke (pt. 1, pp. 9–17).

[87] Although the Mohave are quite preoccupied with the concept of "taking a certain shape," Kroeber (1925 a, p. 775) himself appears to have been puzzled by the highly abstract idea of something being made out of the "body form" of a dead creature, since he himself placed these words in quotes.

play in Mohave diagnostics the role of a "catchall" or "wastebasket" diagnosis, which can be made to fit a variety of obscure ailments.[88]

CASE MATERIAL

DREAMS

When making a general study of Mohave dreams, I deliberately told several of my own dreams to my Mohave friends, in the expectation—which turned out to be correct—that if I shared my dreams with them, this would encourage them to tell me theirs. Two of my dreams were diagnosed as symptomatic of hiwey lak. Since neither of these dreams resembles the dreams mentioned by the various informants as being pathognomonic of hiwey lak, one is forced to conclude that a certain type of anxiety dream tends to be considered symptomatic of hiwey lak, no matter what its actual content may be, especially perhaps if it is dreamed after listening to accounts of hiwey lak. This point is of sufficient importance to justify the publication of these—now respectively 37- and 28-year-old—personal dreams.[89]

Dream A:

Dreamer.—The anthropologist. I had this dream when my 14½-year-old younger brother died under rather tragic circumstances in 1924. I dreamed that he came back and this made me so happy that I ran around on all fours. (1924.)

Associations.—Even nowadays (1936), when I am very sad, I sometimes dream of my dead younger brother. I was only 16 when he died.

Hivsu: Tupo:ma's interpretation (1936).—

(a) Your brother longed for you and came back to see you.

(a) The shock of seeing him made you run on all fours in dream.

(c) The reason you dream of him when you are unhappy is that he thinks of you. He never forgot you.

Dream B:

Dreamer.—The anthropologist. Exutus ipse puellam quam amo exutam bracchio teneo. Then I, or my double, chase myself. Still carrying this burden, I take off and fly away, while my pursuer remains on the ground. (1933.)

Associations.—I met this person just before my first Mohave field trip and thought a great deal about this meeting.

Tcatc's interpretation (1936).—This is a dream of good luck.

Hivsu: Tupo:ma's interpretation (1936).—I am sure Tcatc was afraid to tell you the truth, because she is very fond of you. So am I, but I think you should know the truth.

(a) Your attire means that you will become poor. (Hivsu: Tupo:ma knew that I was quite "broke" in 1936.)

(b) Your flying off means that you will meet someone else and have better luck.

---

[88] In fairness to the Mohave diagnostician, it should be stated that such fashionable "catchall" diagnoses also occur in occidental psychiatry. Thus, at the turn of the century the favorite "when in doubt" diagnosis was hysteria, whereas today the diagnosis of schizophrenia is often applied so indiscriminately that many thoughtful psychiatrists are beginning to bend over backward to avoid making this diagnosis whenever it is at all possible to do so . . . . partly perhaps to forestall the possibility that the patient so diagnosed would be subjected to so-called shock therapy, or to a lobotomy.

[89] Additional reasons that favor the publication of such personally revealing material will be found in part 3, pp. 97–101.

(c) The one who chases you is also yourself. It is your "shadow soul." You are also the one who carries this burden. It is fortunate that you dreamed of both of your selves. Had you dreamed only of one, it would have meant death. This is a hiwey lak dream.

At this point I asked Hivsu: Tupo :ma to treat me, but he refused to do so on the grounds that he was not qualified to treat a white . . . but failed to add that he was not a hiwey lak specialist either.

Dream C:

Dreamer.—Tcatc (N), a middle-aged woman. I dreamed on two separate occasions that some women tried to have intercourse with me. Once I dreamed about one woman and another time about another woman. Both of these women were either close friends or else relatives of mine. I knew even in dream that they were women, though they acted like men and tried to pull up my skirt. Both managed to throw me down and then tried to get on top of me. Fortunately I managed to fight them off in both instances, so that neither of them actually succeeded in having intercourse with me.

Associations.—Had these dreams culminated in intercourse, I would have become very ill. [Do you desire women also in a waking state?] Definitely not.

Cultural comment.—In principle, incestuous dreams are supposed to cause hiwey lak. In this instance the dreamer did not specify that she might have contracted hiwey lak, had these female relatives succeeded in having intercourse with her. This omission may be fortuitous, since this is the first dream I obtained, early in my first field trip.

Tentative interpretation.—The dream reveals unconscious, homosexually incestuous wishes. The fact that the women "acted like men" is a tentative denial of the fact that women have no penes. (Small children often fantasy that the powerful mother has a phallus.) The dreamer strenuously resists her attackers, partly because her homosexual wishes are not ego-syntonic but perhaps also because, had she allowed them to go ahead, she would have discovered in the end that women do not, after all, have a phallus. These aggressively masculine female relatives may symbolize the dreamer's mother, such as the small girl sometimes fantasies her mother to be. The aggressivity of the women is presumably related to the child's "sadistic theory of intercourse" (i.e., "father does dreadful things to mother.") Narcissistic elements are also present.

ACTUAL HIWEY LAK CASES

The most interesting aspect of the recorded cases of genuine hiwey lak is the fact that two of the patients were brother and sister and that incestuous elements, combined with witchcraft and murder, played a great role in the etiology of their illnesses. It is equally interesting that none of the other recorded hiwey lak cases involved obvious psychiatric symptoms. This fact further confirms the impression that the Mohave view this illness as psychosomatic rather than as strictly psychiatric.

CASE 40 (Informants: Ahma Huma : re and Hama : Utce:) :

A young man was once brought to my house for treatment. He was all swollen up. His whole body was swollen from the dreams which he had had.

I cured him in one night, so that the next day he was able to walk home. (Allergy?)

CASE 41 (Informants: Ahma Huma: re and Hama: Utce:):

I recently cured an old woman who had hiwey lak.

CASE 42 (Informants: Ahma Huma: re and E. S.):

Huau Husek' (fly whip) of the Mu:th gens, 35 years old, dreamed that he had intercourse with his (living) sister, Mu:th Nyemsutkha:v (= a certain feather for the hair). I treated him and his dreams ceased in 4 days.

Comment

Tentative diagnosis.—Anxiety state caused by incestuous dreams.

The first point to be noted is Ahma Huma:re's specification that the dreams ceased in 4 days. No mention is made of a physical illness. This leads one to suppose that the patient called the shaman as soon as his anxiety dreams began, thereby indicating that, for a man of 35, he was unusually old fashioned. His conservativeness also expressed itself in the fact that he was the last Mohave to kill a witch, who, after seducing Huau Husek's wife, proceeded to threaten both him and his wife with witchcraft (Devereux, 1948 f, and Case 104).

An equally important feature of this case is the fact that, in violation of the Mohave custom of not meddling with the domestic affairs of others, Mu:th Nyemsutkha:v went out of her way to inform her brother of his wife's infidelities. This suggests an unusually intense and unconsciously incestuous relationship between brother and sister, who should not discuss sexual matters with each other. This inference is, in turn, strongly supported by the fact that, soon after Mu:th Nyemsutkha:v brought him this news, her brother had incestuous dreams about her. It is also to be noted (Case 43) that, soon after the murder of the witch, Mu:th Nyemsutkha:v herself contracted hiwey lak.

CASE 43 (Informant: Ahma Huma: re and E. S.):

Soon after her brother Huau Husek' and his wife murdered the witch Anyay Ha:m (Case 104), Mu:th Nyemsutkha:v, a woman in her 30's, became hysterical and quite ill. Although the informant himself stressed that this illness began shortly after the witch's murder, he denied that there was any nexus between the two events. No further details could be obtained, since the woman was still too ill at that time to be interviewed.

Comment

It is known also from other sources that Mu:th Nyemsutkha:v was indirectly responsible for the murder of the witch and for the imprisonment of her brother who killed him, since she took it upon herself to tell her brother that his wife had an affair with the witch. It is also known that, soon after she made this disclosure, Huau Husek' had incestuous dreams about her. This frightened him sufficiently to induce him to consult a shaman, who diagnosed his case as hiwey lak (Case 42). It is, therefore, probable that Mu:th Nyemsutkha:v, too, had an incestuous fixation on her brother and that her illness represented partly a guilt reaction to the tragedy caused by her talebearing and partly an identification with her brother's hiwey lak illness.

CASE 44 (Informants: Hivsu: Tupo: ma, Ahma Huma: re, and Hama: Utce:) :

(Hivsu: Tupo: ma) : Sudhu: râ of the Mah gens is the son of Atci: Akw(o)-ath, who is very old fashioned and antiwhite. Sudhu :râ impregnated his second cousin Tcatc (N), whereupon his mother made him marry the girl (Case 90). This incestuous marriage worried the girl so much that she died of tuberculosis. Then Sudhu :râ, too, fell ill. He was taken to the Agency hospital with pulmonary tuberculosis, but he got worse and worse and the doctor gave him up. He was then taken home and I was asked to treat him for an old horse kick. I work with you during the day and at night I treat him.

(Hama: Utce:) : Poor old Hivsu: Tupo :ma is singing himself hoarse every night to cure Sudhu :râ, who keeps on saying that it is Hivsu: Tupo :ma who had bewitched him. For a while some of Sudhu: râ's relatives were even talking about beating up Hivsu: Tupo :ma, but they finally gave up the idea, because they are afraid of the American law.[90] It just about broke the old man's heart to have his kinsman Sudhu: râ accuse him of having bewitched him, when he was actually trying to cure him.[91]

(Ahma Huma :re) : Since, despite the treatment he had received so far, Sudhu: râ kept on getting worse, I was asked (on January 5, 1933) to take over the treatment and I agreed to do so, Sudhu: râ is getting worse and is also badly constipated.[92] It is because of this "stomach" trouble that I was consulted. He believes that two sisters, Mah (W) and Mah (E), who belong to a family of witches, bewitched him, causing him to die conscious and in great pain.[93] Perhaps some of his relatives made him think that. He suffered so much that he begged his relatives to shoot him. I decided that he was suffering from hiwey lak and hiwey lak nyevedhi:, and that his illness was caused by the ghost of his deceased wife, who was also his second cousin (Case 90). I treated him exactly the way I told you I treat this illness. I had also treated a certain old woman in exactly the same way. I am supposed to have improved his condition somewhat, thus proving that he had hiwey lak and hiwey lak nyevedhi:.

(Hama: Utce:) : Ahma Huma : re is quite proud of his success, which greatly increased his reputation as a shaman. However, in the end, Sudhu :râ died of tuberculosis. There used to be quite a lot of people in that family, but whenever incest occurs people seem to die off. That family practically died out on both sides (i.e., on the right (husband) and on the left (wife) side.)

Comment

Diagnosis: Tuberculosis.   Anxiety reaction with paranoid components.

The belief that Sudhu: râ's fatal illness was due partly to his having contracted an incestuous union, and partly to the ghost of his wife—who was also his second cousin—fits both the standard Mohave theory of hiwey lak and beliefs concerning the fatal consequences of incest (pt. 7, pp. 356–371). Hence,

---

[90] The fact that Hivsu: Tupo :ma, though already in his fifties, was still a huge and powerful man, as well as the fact that he, too, was a member of the Mah gens, may also have had something to do with the decision not to beat him up after all.

[91] When Hivsu: Tupo :ma confessed to me that he had bewitched his half brother and his neice, he denied that he had bewitched Sudhu :râ (Devereux, 1948 1).

[92] Constipation is rare among the Mohave and therefore causes concern. It is a relatively common symptom in the terminal stages of tuberculosis. The possibility of a symbolic unconscious nexus between constipation and incest cannot be disregarded (Devereux, 1939 a).

[93] If tuberculosis spreads to certain parts of the nervous system, the pain is sometimes very severe. Whether that happened in this case is not known.

Ahma Huma:re's view that Sudhu: rà's illness was caused by his wife's ghost and not simply by his incestuous marriage was somewhat unusual, as was the fact that the Mohave readily accepted this somewhat surprising etiological and diagnostic explanation. What may explain both Ahma Huma: re's diagnosis and its ready acceptance by the tribe, is the fact that it appears to be patterned upon certain theories accounting for the death of a type of twins. The Mohave hold that twins, one of which is a boy and the other a girl, were spouses in heaven (or else, according to another theory, in the land of the dead) and, while still young, sometimes quarrel on earth, the way spouses do. When that happens, the offended "spouse" may decide to die and will soon be followed by the surviving twin (pt. 7, pp. 348–356). Since Sudhu: rà married his second cousin, who belonged to his own gens, and since this woman had died, Ahma Huma: re apparently felt impelled to equate Sudhu: rà's illness with the fatal illness of the surviving twin-spouse, which, in a way is—in twins—a pediatric equivalent of the ghost diseases of adults, except that, in the case of twins, "marriage" precedes the sibling relationship, while in the case of incestuous marriages the blood relationship precedes the union. Moreover, when viewed in this context, Ahma Huma: re's diagnosis implicitly takes into account also the harmful effects of incestuous marriages. The considerations which induced Ahma Huma: re to make this diagnosis were, thus, probably also responsible for the tribe's willingness to concur with it. As for the view that Sudhu: rà's illness was aggravated by worry and remorse, it is fully compatible with modern medical knowledge.

Ahma Huma:re's avoidance of any reference to Hivsu: Tupo:ma's efforts to cure Sudhu:rà was partly due to rivalry between shamans (Devereux, 1957 b) but partly also to the fact that the woman Melyikha: had, shortly before, oscillated back and forth between the two men to such an extent that during this period she could not even get credit at the local stores, because no one knew which of the two men was her current husband and would assume responsibility for the debts she contracted on a given day. When, at long last, she finally settled down with Ahma Huma:re, Hivsu: Tupo:ma accepted her decision without resentment, as a good Mohave should. Thus, since there was no hostility between the erstwhile rivals, my friendship with Hivsu: Tupo:ma did not impair my friendly relations with Ahma Huma:re. However, the somewhat grotesque aspects of their former rivalry led to a certain amount of embarrassment between the two men, who avoided each other, presumably because they realized that they had made themselves quite ridiculous in this particular situation.

The statement that the patient had been "discharged" from the hospital as an incurable tuberculotic also calls for comment. It simply means that the dying man was removed from the hospital at his own request and that of his family, partly in order to make a final attempt to cure him by shamanistic means, and partly because the Mohave wish to die in their own homes. It most definitely does not mean that the hospital authorities callously discharged the patient because he was incurable, nor even that they did not do everything possible to discourage his removal from the hospital. In fact, such discharges at the point of death, against medical advice, are a frequent cause of friction between the Mohave and the hospital authorities.

This case history shows that the test of the correctness of a diagnosis is the effectiveness of the treatment and therefore leads us directly to the presentation of those cases in which the patient's condition was erroneously diagnosed as hiwey lak.

CASE 45 (Informant: M. A. I. Nettle, M.D., reservation physician) :

When I came to Parker 20 years ago (1912?) as reservation physician, N., who at that time was only 4 feet tall, already had a child. A little while ago (1932?) she thought she had reached the menopause and, on noticing the symptoms of pregnancy, went to consult the shaman, Kwathany Hi:wa, who specializes inter alia in the cure of ghost pregnancies. She has a baby right now and her previous child is seven years old. There are also several other women on the reservation who menstruate regularly at the age of 45 (Nettle, MS., n.d.).

Comment

Tentative diagnosis.—Psychological crisis due to a presumably unwanted pregnancy.

The preceding case illustrates the implicit nexus between hiwey lak nyevedhi: and menopausal disturbances, which, in this case, caused N. to mistake the symptoms of a late (and perhaps unwanted) pregnancy for hiwey lak. Compare this case, which was known also to my Mohave informants, with that of G. A. (Case 46), who mistook an early (and certainly unwanted) illegitimate pregnancy for hiwey lak nyevedhi:. Both cases also demonstrate the tendency of Mohave patients to make an initial diagnosis of their condition and then to consult a shaman who specializes in the cure of the disorder which supposedly affects them.

CASE 46 (Informants: Ahma Huma:re and E. S.) :

G.A., 17 years of age, single and without gentile affiliation—since her father was not a Mohave—became ill and was taken to the hospital where "they couldn't do anything for her." They didn't know that she was pregnant. She was then taken to my (Ahma Huma:re's) place and I told them that she was pregnant. People didn't believe me, however. Since women are not well when they are pregnant (being an obstetrician) I treated her all the same and she eventually felt better. Subsequent developments proved that she was pregnant and, in due time, she gave birth to a child, which is still alive. The father of this child is unknown, since G.A. is a kamalo:y (lewd woman) (Devereux, 1948 f).

Comment

Tentative diagnosis.—Unwanted pregnancy causing physical psychic malaise.

This case illustrates the nexus between hiwey lak nyevedhi: and obstetrical conditions. It is significant that the therapist was Ahma Huma:re, who appears to have been the first to formulate this nexus explicitly. His skillful diagnosis of G.A.'s real condition appears to have received considerable publicity, since years later Pulyi:k, a layman, woh was simply asked to give G.A.'s Momave name, spontaneously referred to the fact that she did not have pseudocyesis, but was simply pregnant.

NYEVEDHI: TAHA:NA

(GHOST GENUINE)

An attempt to understand the nyevedhi: taha:na (ghost genuine) illness brings one face to face with one of the fundamental ambiguities of Mohave culture.

On the one hand, the Mohave do everything within their power to terminate, once and for all, any connection between the living and the dead. The funeral ritual provides the mourners with every opportunity to abreact massively their grief, thus abridging the period of mourning. In addition, the property and dwelling of the dead are destroyed and his name is not mentioned again.

On the other hand, they dream of ghosts, insultingly mention the name or relationship of a dead person to his surviving relatives (Kroeber, 1925 a), and even hire a ghost doctor (nyevedhi: suma:tc, ghost dreamer) to take them as visitors to the land of the dead. Such visits are risky indeed, since, should the client become separated from his shamanistic mentor, and should the latter fail to find him before morning, both will be stuck in the land of ghosts. Furthermore, the visitor's dead relatives make considerable efforts to pull him away from his mentor and to induce him to remain in the land of ghosts (Fathauer, 1951). Even a shaman sent to the land of the dead to recover a patient's soul may be kept there by his own dead relatives (Kroeber, 1925 a).

It is quite certain that whereas these two formal patterns are, logically speaking, mutually incompatible, psychologically (attitudinally) they complement each other, exactly as the two mutually contradictory sets of Mohave beliefs concerning twins form a psychological whole, in that they reflect the two aspects of ambivalence toward twins (Devereux, 1941).

One of the most interesting aspects of Mohave attitudes toward the dead is that they impute to them their own mourning reactions (Devereux, 1956 a) and reluctance to break old bonds and habits. Thus, the data on hiwey lak nyevedhi: (pt. 4, pp. 150–175) are quite ambiguous in one respect, in that it is hard to decide whether, when a living person interacts with his dead relatives in a dream, this represents a visit of the living person's soul to the land of the dead, or a visit of the ghost to the land of the living (pt. 4, pp. 150–175). In addition, even though persons on the point of death are supposed to do everything within their power to break all relations with the living and with earthly things, and may even already be spoken of as ghosts, there are indications that this cultural demand is not complied with altogether wholeheartedly. Thus, since at the death of a person everything pertaining to him, including even his pictures, are supposed to be destroyed, my old friend Tcatc would not allow me to photograph her. Yet, shortly after she died, I was amazed to receive from a young Mohave friend two photographs of Tcatc. In his accompanying letter this young man stated that, sensing that she did not have much longer to live, Tcatc dressed up in her best clothes, put on her seldom-used aboriginal ornaments, and asked him to photograph her for me, so that I would never forget her (Devereux, 1951 b).   In brief, despite her orthodoxy and her previous refusals to leave so much as a photograph of herself behind her, when Tcatc felt that she would soon die, she made sure that I at least—whom she often called her favorite grandchild—would never forget her.   (Pl. 9, *b*, *c*.)

The data concerning nyevedhi: taha:na, about to be presented, combine information published by Fathauer (1951) with data obtained when my informants described the powers of (Hispan Himith) Tcilyetcilye, Kuskinave: and Kunyoo:r, who could not only recover souls that had strayed or had been taken to the land of the dead (matkwisa: namak=soul leaves, matkwisa: hidha:uk=soul to take), but could also help their clients visit their relatives in the beyond.

Kunyoo:r could also cure mental illness caused by dreaming of one's (bewitched?) dead relatives.[94]

The most important aspect of such planned soul travels is that the visitor deliberately exposes himself to the fatal blandishments of these ghosts, who seek to take him to, and keep him in, the land of the dead, even if they themselves, being twins, are in heaven, or, being victims of witchcraft, are in the evil shaman's "place."   Yet, at the same time, the Mohave greatly dread dreams in which their dead relatives visit them or in which, without being escorted by a shaman, they visit their dead relatives.

On the whole, there are only five situations in which the living can have contact with the dead, without contracting the ghost disease.

(1) Association with live twins is not harmful, even though twins are reincarnated ghosts, who must be treated very politely.

(2) If one observes the relevant taboos, one can safely participate in all funeral observances.

(3) A mourner, and especially the spouse of a deceased person, may be visited by the soul of the deceased during the first 4 nights following death, and the spouse may even cohabit with that soul in dream, without being harmed by this act.   From the point of view of Mohave belief, the innocuousness of "contact" with the dead during these four nights seems to be due to the fact that the newly deceased is not, as yet, a fully fledged ghost already inhabiting the land of the dead, but simply a detached soul revisiting its former haunts and repeating the major activities of its life on earth (Devereux, 1937 a).

(4) Witches temporarily delay the transformation of the souls of their victims into fully developed ghosts, by segregating them "in a place of their own."   Until they themselves die or, preferably, are killed, they dream of their victims, enjoy their company, and engage in sexual relations with them.   Although such contacts do not cause witches to contract the ghost disease, presumably because their

---

[94] No one was able to answer the question whether one dreamed only of dead relatives who had died of witchcraft.

victims are not, as yet, true ghosts, they enjoy these contacts so much that they begin to long for the constant company of their ghostly captives and therefore induce others to kill them (Devereux, 1937 c and pt. 7, pp. 387–426). A further reason why the witch eventually seeks to be killed, is that another witch may kidnap his ghostly retainers and permanently deprive him of their company (Devereux, 1937 c).

(5) Ghost doctors may go to the land of the dead and bring back the soul of a patient who strayed there, without contracting the ghost disease, although they do run the risk of being kept there by their dead relatives, which may be another way of contracting ghost disease.

All other contacts with ghosts are believed to expose the living to the dread ghost illness.

Before describing this illness, it is important to discuss why it is called "nyevedhi: taha:na" (ghost real), rather than simply, e.g., "nyevedhi: hahnok" (ghost contamination).

As already mentioned, a patient's illness may either be "straight" or "not straight." In the former case the patient has one disease only. In the latter case there is added to his basic illness a second pathological condition, which, in most cases, is related either to witchcraft or to ghosts. Thus, ahwe: hahnok (foreign contamination) (pt. 4, pp. 128–150) and hiwey lak (anus pain) (pt. 4, pp. 150–175) are "straight" diseases, while ahwe: nyevedhi: and hiwey lak nyevedhi: are "diseases that are not straight" because ghosts play a major role in their etiology and symptomatology. In fact, the ghost disease appears to occur mostly in conjunction with other illnesses, so that, when it occurs by itself, it seems necessary to stress that the disease is the genuine (unadulterated) ghost disease, nyevedhi: taha:na.

This supposition is so important for an understanding of the relationship between the ghost illness and certain other disorders, that it must be examined in some detail.

When asked to describe the nyevedhi: taha:na illness, Ahma Huma:re declared that he had already done so when he described the hiwey lak nyevedhi: illness, i.e., that form of hiwey lak in which the patient dreams of intimate contact with ghosts, and especially of eating food prepared by ghosts or of committing incest with ghosts. Fathauer (1951), in turn, stresses that "the 'enemy dreamer' cured people who became insane as a result of dreaming of their dead relatives," i.e., he treated patients who had not only the "straight" ahwe: hahnok disease, but also the "not straight" ahwe: nyevedhi: illness.

Since one and the same person usually had the power to function as a scalper, as a healer of the foreign disease, as a funeral orator, as a healer of the illness (insanity) of those who violated funeral taboos, and as a ghost doctor as well, Fathauer concluded that these various powers were either inherently interrelated, so that one and the same individual necessarily exercised all of these functions and held the various statuses pertaining to them cumulatively, or else that the foreign disease itself was closely related to the ghost illness.[95]

It is proposed to show that the accumulation of these various powers by a single shaman is, as Fathauer's first hypothesis indicates, due to the inherent relationship obtaining between these various powers, and that such a patterned co-occurrence of interrelated powers in one and the same shaman is actually an important characteristic of Mohave shamanism. This, in turn, implies that Fathauer's second hypothesis is simply a corollary of his first hypothesis.

The basic point is the fact that shamans who treat hiwey lak usually have the power to treat also either the other "venereal" disease called hiku:pk (e. g., Harav He:ya) or else those real obstetrical complications (e. g., Ahma Huma:re) that more or less resemble the difficulties experienced by women whose hiwey lak takes the form of a ghost pregnancy (pseudocyesis) (pt. 4, pp. 150–175). Otherwise stated, it is in the nature of Mohave medical practice to combine related specialties.[96]

Thus, the real problem is not whether scalpers specialize also in the treatment of the foreign illness, of the ghost illness, and of illness (insanity) caused by a violation of funeral taboos, but why these various specialties form a pattern, and how they are interrelated.

In this connection, Fathauer (1951) suggests that there is a natural affinity between aliens and ghosts, since both these pathogenic agents are, in a sense, not real Mohaves. It was shown elsewhere (pt. 4, pp. 128–150) that, even though the Mohave are convinced that the ghost of a dead Mohave remains a Mohave even in the land of ghosts, there is a definite psychological tendency to equate, affectively at least, aliens and the ghosts of one's relatives, not only in connection with illness, but also otherwise.[97]

The fact that these various powers are interrelated does not necessarily mean that all scalpers acquire all of these powers. Even less does it mean that these various powers are necessarily acquired simultaneously. Thus, even though Hivsu: Tupo:ma was a practicing

---

[95] Fathauer's third supposition, that, due to the breakdown of their culture, the modern Mohave tend to confuse these various functions is, as will be seen, unconvincing.

[96] The fact that the hiwey lak specialist may specialize either in the treatment of hiku : pk, or else in the treatment of obstetrical complications has its parallel in occidental medicine, in that a syphilologist may, in addition, specialize also in the treatment of the other venereal diseases (granuloma inguinale, gonorrhea), or else in dermatology.

[97] Thus, alien males, who are supposedly oversexed and endowed with huge phalli, are actually projections of the small child's grossly fantastic image of the father, whose "mysterious" (sexual) activities during the night make him in the child's eyes a nocturnal ogre on the prowl (Devereux, 1950 a).

shaman and funeral orator, who could cure illness caused by a violation of funeral taboos, and could also have functioned as a scalper
had his contemporaries been able to engage in independent warfare,
he does not appear to have had the power to treat either the alien or
the ghost sickness. He might, of course, have acquired these powers
later on, had some subjective experience focused his interest on these
illnesses, exactly as the death of his wife and unborn child during
labor caused Ahma Huma:re, a hiwey lak specialist, to acquire also
obstetrical powers, though relatively late in life (Devereux, 1948 e).

Thus, in a sense, it is natural for the ahwe: specialist to treat also
the nyevedhi: taha:na illness, since, as Fathauer rightly suggests, the
two are fundamentally interrelated, by means of the affective equation
alien=ghost. In addition, the dreams of ahwe: *nyevedhi:* patients
greatly resemble the dreams of hiwey lak *nyevedhi:* patients, not because the "straight" forms of ahwe: hahnok and hiwey lak are the
same illness, but because both "nyevedhi:" types are "diseases that
are not straight," in that the ghost factor is superimposed on the basic
ahwe:, respectively hiwey lak, "straight illness." This, in turn, explains why, even though the ahwe hahnok and ahwe: nyevedhi:
specialist can treat also the nyevedhi: taha:na illness, the hiwey lak
specialist, who also treats (part of?) hiwey lak nyevedhi:, is not,
ipso facto, also a nyevedhi: taha:na specialist.

What remains to be explained is precisely why the hiwey lak
specialist can also treat hiwey lak nyevedhi:, without being, at the
same time, also a nyevedhi: taha:na specialist. We can perhaps
visualize this situation better if we cite a parallel instance from occidental medicine. Thus, even though tertiary syphilis (tabes dorsalis,
general paresis, etc.) is, strictly speaking, a neurological disease, most
syphilologists are also quite expert in diagnosing and treating this
late (neurological) manifestation of syphilis. The Mohave parallel
of this is the ability of hiwey lak specialists to treat also the nyevedhi:
factor (i.e., the additional ghost sickness) in hiwey lak nyevedhi:,
because the two occur together so often. In fact, this combination
of illnesses is so common that, as stated above, when asked to describe
the nyevedhi: taha:na illness, Ahma Huma:re declared that he had
already done so when he described the hiwey lak nyevedhi: illness.
At the same time, there are some indications that when the treatment
of hiwey lak by means of the specific hiwey lak songs is not altogether
successful, the patient is sometimes referred for supplementary treatment to a different kind of specialist who, one supposes, is likely to
be a ghost illness specialist, or else a healer of bewitched persons. This
latter possibility is suggested by the belief that hiwey lak may also

be caused by witchcraft, which ties in with Fathauer's finding that the nyevedhi: taha:na illness is sometimes due to witchcraft.[98]

The next point to be discussed is the fact that instances in which the ghost illness occurs in combination with other illnesses, such as ahwe: hahnok or hiwey lak, are more common than unadulterated cases of nyevedhi: taha:na. This is presumably due to the tendency of all psychologically "primitive" persons to "somatize;" i. e., a depression such as nyevedhi: taha:na is very likely to trigger off also physical symptoms, or at least hypochondrial complaints, while physical illness, in turn, often elicits in psychologically primitive persons considerable anxiety and a depression.[99]

The last point to be considered concerns the classical symptoms of the ghost illness, and the extent to which our case history fits the characteristic symptomatology of this psychosis, which does not seem to include any organic pathology.

According to Fathauer (1951):

People afflicted with the ghost sickness were afraid of darkness, experienced nightmares, were unable to sleep at night, and cried for long periods of time. The shaman could also produce these symptoms by witchcraft, causing the victim to see whirlwinds in which ghosts traveled, and to have bad dreams, which produced the sickness. (It is necessary to stress in this connection that when a Mohave notices that one of the small whirlwinds, which occasionally arise in the desert, heads toward him, he immediately dodges it, lest it carry his soul to the land of the dead, causing him to die.)

Fathauer's description suggests that the ghost illness is a psychogenic depression of considerable severity, uncomplicated by organic symptoms. The case history given below (Case 47) confirms this impression. The only part of Fathauer's description which calls for clarification is his statement that the patient has "nightmares." In psychiatry the term "nightmare" is applied almost exclusively to suffocation dreams, and especially to those in which an unbearably heavy mass seems to press down upon the dreamer's chest (Jones, 1931).[1] Since our data make no mention of suffocation dreams, we must presume that Fathauer used the term "nightmare" in the colloquial sense of "severe anxiety dream." This being said, Fathauer's characterization of the ghost illness perfectly fits Case 47, which is a typical example of the nyevedhi: taha:na. In her dream, the patient cannibalizes her dead mother, who first appears disguised as a fish, presumably because, even in a dream, the patient could not have

---

[98] Lack of space makes it impossible to show that the witch operates in many ways as though he were a ghost.

[99] There are certain indications that each type of physical illness has distinctive emotional-psychiatric sequelae, or at least a distinctive psychic climate (Menninger and Devereux, 1948).

[1] Compare the German term "Alpdruck" (pressure of a spirit called Alp) and the Hungarian term "lidércnyomás" (pressure of a spirit called lidérc).

forced herself to eat the undisguised body of her mother. Such a hallucinatory disguising of the identity of a member of one's family, whom one wishes to cannibalize, also occurs among Canadian Indians afflicted with windigo, who often hallucinate that their wives and children are fat beavers. (Landes, 1938.) [2] Only after the cannibalistic act has already taken place is the true identity of the "fish" revealed.

Thus, this Mohave woman's depression dream has every hallmark of authenticity and could not possibly have been either invented or appreciably distorted in telling it. The dream in question expresses and fuses the following elements: The oral incorporation of the dead mother, the infantile fantasy that the seemingly omnipotent mother is not only female, but, at the same time, also male (fish), or that she symoblizes maleness per se (Fenichel, 1954) and, finally, the infantile notion that the sexual act is an essentially oral process.[3]

In summary, the dream in question is so classical a depression dream that any psychoanalyst whose patient has such a dream would envisage the imminence of an acute psychotic depression.

CASE 47 (Informant: E.S.):

The following case history was volunteered by E.S., in order to illustrate Ahma Huma:re's account of the ghost illness, which he had just interpreted. E.S. first told his story in Mohave to Ahma Huma:re, and, when the latter agreed that this was indeed a case of nyevedhi: taha:na, he repeated it for me in English.

Tcatc—not your informant Tcatc, but another woman of that gens—was, around 1930, about 30 years old. She had been to boarding school and had just(?) returned to the reservation. She was at that time single and childless. She is still living (1938).

Her illness began as follows: She began to dream that she saw a fish being prepared for a meal. When the fish was cooked, she sat down, meaning to eat it. However, after taking two or three bites, she looked at the head of the fish and saw that it was her mother, who had been dead for quite some time. After she woke up, she was unable to eat . . . she simply could not keep the food down in her stomach. She also cried now and then, without knowing why she cried. Her "Indian relation" maternal grandfather [4] Kuskinave: (or Kwiskwinay)—the one who had homosexual relations when he was in prison (Devereux, 1937 b)—fortunately knew how to treat such cases. He made her tell him her dream and then performed the usual cure for nyevedhi: taha:na, singing all the proper songs. This treatment enabled her to recover her health."

---

[2] It is interesting to note that in "The Gold Rush," the starving bully first hallucinates that Charlie Chaplin is a chicken and then tries to slaughter him for the pot.

[3] These elements are richly represented in Mohave culture where male transvestites drink a constipating infusion so as to be able to "give birth" to a fecal "child" (Devereux, 1937 b). Compare also the belief that the first (female) witch, Bullfrog, bewitched her father, the god Matavilye, by swallowing his feces, because he incestuously stimulated her by touching her genitalia (Bourke, 1889).

[4] I.e., her classificatory grandfather on the maternal side.

Comment

Mohave diagnosis.—Nyevedhi: taha :na.

Tentative diagnosis.—Transitory manic-depressive psychosis, depressive phase,

The pathogenic dream in question fully substantiates Abraham's (1927) well-known interpretation of the psychogenesis of manic-depressive psychosis. The fact that in this particular "genuine ghost disease" dream the patient was not, as in hiwey lak nyevedhi:, simply offered food by a dead relative, but was actually induced to eat her mother's body, strongly supports Freud's (1925 d) view that the mourning reaction is an attempt to incorporate the lost love object. The choice of a fish to represent the dead mother may be partly determined by the fact that the land of ghosts lies to the south and under the Colorado River (Devereux, 1937 a) from which the Mohave obtain their fish. A further reason why a fish is made to represent the dead ("phallic") mother is, presumably, the fact that the fish is not only a common masculine symbol but, among the Mohave at least, also a female symbol.[5]

The suggested diagnosis, manic depressive psychosis, depressive phase, is based both on this patient's symptoms and on the fact that the first symptoms of this psychosis usually appear in persons 30 years old or less.

To clarify further the cannibalistic element in this patient's dream, it was deemed desirable to append to this case history summaries of three cannibalistically tinged dreams of nondepressed Mohave individuals who, by Mohave clinical standards, did not have the ghost disease. These dreams show, on the one hand that, despite his horror of cannibalism (Devereux, 1948 d and 1951 b), even the "normal" Mohave has impulses of that kind and, on the other hand, that this depressed patient's dream exceeds in explicitness and in the intensity of affect the more allusive, and less anxiety-tinged, cannibalistic dreams of nondepressed "normal" Mohave Indians.

The occurrence of dream cannibalism is far from exceptional among the Mohave.

Dream D:

The night of November 16–17, 1938, Hama: Utce: dreamed that she was rinsing meat in the *bathtub* and that there were lots of dead mice mixed up with the meat. She felt disgusted and nauseated, and was sick the next day. She told this dream in the presence of E. S., who, as he himself pointed out next day, promptly responded to Hama: Utce:'s dream with a cannibalistic dream of his own.

Dream E:

The very next night (November 17–18, 1938) E. S. had two dreams. The first dream concerned his father's cremation; it included the sudden appearance of the father, who told E. S. that he had to leave, because some people (ghosts?) were waiting for him. The father then went off. At this point, E. S. woke up, but soon fell asleep again and then had a second dream, which, oddly enough, he reported to me first.[6] In this dream he thought he saw a whole steer boiling

---

[5] Thus, a Mohave greatly offended his host's wife when he kept on saying: "Phew, you women smell like fish" (Devereux, 1951 c). Note also that in this case the therapist was someone who had had homosexual relations (Devereux, 1937 b).

[6] The reporting of dreams in reverse order often means that the second dream is a more disguised and therefore less embarrassing version of the first dream.

in a bathtub (cremation?) but when he went nearer, to examine it, he realized that it was really a man. Because this man had (long) hair and whiskers, E. S. thought the man was Jesus. This man then talked in a language which E. S. did not understand. After narrating this (second) dream first, E. S. proceeded to tell me a dream which he had had several days earlier and which concerned his deceased parents. Only then did he tell me the first dream of the previous night, which had something to do with his father's cremation. In other words, E. S. was unable to report first the key dream, which revealed that the core of this entire dream series was the cannibalization of his dead father's corpse. Instead, he had to work himself up to the telling of the key dream by degrees. Such evasive maneuvers are quite common, not only in the psychotherapy of members of the occidental culture area, but also in that of "primitives" (Devereux, 1951 a).

The various ghost diseases known to the Mohave (pt. 4, passim) are, in a genuine sense, also soul loss diseases, which, among many North American tribes (Hultkrantz, 1953), are believed to cause insanity. Among the Mohave, the concept of soul loss appears to be applied chiefly to depressions and to anorexias, whose relationship to true depressions was convincingly demonstrated by Gerö (1953). In fact, one is tempted to say that the "ethnic psychosis" (Devereux, 1956 b) of the Mohave appears to be depression (including anorexia and suicide), which perfectly dovetails with their cyclothymic disposition (Kroeber, 1925 a, Devereux, 1939 b). This finding proves once more that so-called "culture and personality studies" which fail to take into account the characteristic ethnic neuroses and psychoses obtaining in a given group are incomplete both psychologically and anthropologically.

MOUA:V HAHNOK

The moua:v hahnok (relatives, disease from, or relatives, contamination by) illness was not mentioned by the informants at the time when psychiatric disorders were investigated, which explains why relatively little is known about it. It was mentioned by Tcatc, when she listed the disorders Anyay Ha:m (light passing; also called Amat Hu:dhap—earth rent or torn and I-lyi, the latter being a distortion of his English name) of th Hipa: gens was qualified to cure.[7]

Tcatc's statement (1938).—Anyay Ha:m could cure hisa:hk (=body sores), hikwi:r (pt. 4, pp. 117–128), hu:the:rv (colds and pneumonia), and moua:v hahnok (relatives, contamination by). [What is this last disease?] Sometimes a man who lost his brother (which is a severe emotional blow (cf. pt. 7, pp. 459–484)), dreams that the soul of the deceased returns to earth and goes around the way he used to do when he was still alive. Then, when the surviving brother wakes up, he grieves so constantly over his brother's death that he may not even be able to eat, from lack of appetite. (For other data on Anyay Ha:m, see Cases 42, 43, and 104).

---

[7] This witch is mentioned in Cases 42, 43, and 104.

Hama: Utce:'s statement (1958).—"Some people dream of the dead. R. H.'s mother, an old lady, even now mentions that she dreams of the dead, who put out their hands, seeking to shake hands with her." [8]

Comment

Moua :v hahnok is apparently a mourning reaction, since such depressions are often characterized by a lack of appetite (pt. 4, passim). It is probably significant that the witch Anyay Ha :m specialized in the cure of this ailment, since he openly confessed that he had bewitched his own son, R. E. L., as well as the 48-year-old Arapa :k Thume: (a kind of feathers for the hair), of the Mu :th gens, and Arapa :k Thume's 30-year-old wife Kat, of the Kat gens, who were the parents of his son's uncle-in-law Huau Husek' (Cases 42, 43 and 104).

It must be presumed that Anyay Ha :m specialized in the cure of excessive mourning reactions chiefly because—being a witch—he, himself, developed an abnormally intense longing for his victims, dreaming of them, boasting of his evil deeds, threatening Huau Husek' and his wife O :otc by telling them that he would bewitch them as he had bewitched Huau Husek's parents and, adding insult to injury, by having an affair with O :otc. In other words, this man cured an illness whose chief symptom—longing for a dead relative—was exactly the same as the principal symptom of the suicidal depression of witches: dreams about one's relatives whom one bewitched, eliciting longing and depression.

Since many tribes, in various culture areas, believe that in order to be able to cure certain illnesses the shaman himself must have had that illness, the similarity between Anyay Ha :m's suicidal depression and the moua :v hahnok illness which he was qualified to cure is, both anthropologically and psychoanalytically, quite understandable and therefore requires no further comment.[9] At any rate Anyay Ha :m's provocative behavior, which included confessions, threats, and adultery, so exasperated Huau Husek' that, assisted by his wife O :otc, he eventually killed Anyay Ha :m (Devereux, 1948 f and Case 104).

The moua :v hahnok disease appears to differ from the ahwe: and the hiwey lak groups of disorders, chiefly in that the deceased relative who appears in dream does not make a specific effort to lure the survivor to the land of the dead, either by cohabiting with him, or by feeding him, or by urging him to leave the earth and go to the land of the dead. He simply appears in dream and behaves exactly as he did

---

[8] Hama : Utce : did not imply that this old woman had moua :v hahnotk. She simply cited this case as an example of contact with the dead, which frightens the living. (Cf. also "John Smith's" dream of D. S. (Case 64).)

[9] Compare the fact that Ahma Huma :re acquired the power to treat obstetrical complications after he lost his wife and unborn child, due to some obstetrical complication (Devereux, 1948 e).

while he was still alive; it is his mere "presence" which once more elicits a strong mourning reaction in the survivor. However, since in moua :v hahnok dreams the deceased behaves much less seductively than in those dreams which cause the ahwe: and hiwey lak groups of disorders, it is permissible to assume that the moua :v hahnok psychic illness is less severe than the two related groups of depressions. Moreover, the fact that it was only mentioned once, and then only in passing, suggests that it is a less common (or "fashionable") disorder than either the ahwe: or the hiwey lak depressions.

The fact that, despite the stringent cultural rule against thinking of the deceased after he is cremated, the Mohave do develop delayed mourning reactions amounting to real depressions suggests, at the lowest estimate, that those who experience such delayed mourning reactions did not manage to abreact most of their grief in the course of the funeral itself. On the other hand it also seems legitimate to infer that even psychologically quite sound ready-made defense mechanisms—such as culturally encouraged extreme grief reactions during funerals—do not always suffice to allay completely man's anxieties, nor to decrease to a satisfactory extent the impact of some genuine misfortune or loss. In other words, it seems evident that culturally provided ready-made defenses become maximally effective only after being also "customized" and adapted to the specific needs of each individual.[10] The process of "customization" is, in fact, easily observable in the case of shamans, who strenuously insist that their particular version of some myth or ritual is the only correct one, and therefore bewitch other shamans whose beliefs or curing rites differ from theirs (Devereux, 1957 b).

The last point to be made is that the existence of a depression called "contamination by one's dead relatives," whose chief dream symptom closely resembles the principal dream symptom of the depression that is due to aliens and enemies (ahwe:) (pt. 4, pp. 128–150) further supports the inference that the unconscious tends to equate one's nearest kin with one's hated foes, or at least with inherently dangerous strangers.

PSYCHOPATHOLOGY RELATED TO FUNERAL OBSERVANCES

Death is a crisis that necessitates considerable readjustment, both psychological and practical, on the part of the survivors. Affective bonds are broken, ingrained behavior patterns and expectations are destroyed, benefits as well as obligations are discontinued, the network of social and interpersonal relations must be rearranged, the

---

[10] The easiest way to visualize this process is to think of a ready-made suit which the department store tailor then "customizes" for the person purchasing it.

social position of the survivor is changed, expenses are incurred, and material objects belonging to the dead, which were formerly available for use, are withdrawn from circulation. In fact, funeral customs may deeply affect a society's chances for accumulating the surplus goods which form the basis for socio-economic progress. Thus, the destruction of the dead person's house and property among the Cocopa represented such a drain on their economy as to make the accumulation of surplus impossible (Kelly, 1949). The same is true of the Mohave, who not only destroy the defunct individual's property, but even cast goods, expressly purchased for that purpose, upon the funeral pyre of the deceased (Devereux, 1942 a, McNichols, 1944).

Needless to say, the necessity of responding to the crisis represented by death with extensive behavioral and attitudinal changes arouses both anxiety and resentment. Thus, while the Mohave do not go so far as the Hopi, who slap the face of the corpse, accusing the deceased of having died solely in order to grieve the survivors (Kennard, 1937), they, too, are inclined to interpret death as a voluntary, if inevitable, act. For example, in a Mohave myth (Kroeber, 1948) some deer (consciously?) head for a fatal meeting with their maker, the mountain lion, who is also their destroyer.

The Mohave tendency to see suicide even in certain types of death from natural causes (pt. 7), and the ease wherewith the wish to die is said to be mobilized in witches (Devereux, 1937 c) and in persons suffering from certain ghost ailments (pt. 4, pp. 128–186), also show that, in one way or the other, the living define death as a desertion. Hence, like many other groups, the Mohave, too, turn a previously beloved relative into a dangerous ghost and taboo his name (Kroeber, 1925 a). The fact that funeral and memorial rites are defined as acts of piety toward the honored dead does not imply that they are truly loved and defined as beneficial or at least harmless, since the dangerousness of certain supernaturals is often denied either by renaming the "Erinyes" (furies) the "Eumenides" (gracious ones) or, like small children, by splitting their image into a good and a bad part, as seems to have been done when the words "deus" and "diabolus" were evolved from the common root "dev."

Even the love that the deceased is supposed to harbor for the living may harm the latter. Thus, the ghost of a spouse or relative may long so much for the survivors that it will visit the latter in dream, so as to lure them to the land of the dead, either by offerings of food, or else by means of dream intercourse (p. 4, pp. 128–184). Similar seductive maneuvers on the part of his victims are held to motivate, at least in part, the witch who seeks to be killed by the surviving relatives of his victims (Kroeber, 1925 a, Devereux, 1937 c). In other words, the mourner's own separation anxieties and mourning depression are, so to speak, ascribed to, and projected upon, the dead, so that, by means of a typical paranoid maneuver, the mourner seems to say: "I no longer feel bound to you and only seek to forget you; it is you who long for me and try to lure me to the land of the dead." [11]

The obligation to destroy the property of the dead person, which was previously available to the living for their use, and the casting of specially purchased additional property upon the funeral pyre in a frenzy of destruction—which represents spiteful giving—also reflect the degree of resentment experienced by the survivor (Devereux, 1942 a and pt. 7, pp. 431–459).

In other words, after being a source of love and support, the deceased turns into a source of danger and into a being who is parasitical on the living. The Mohave even attribute at least to some ghosts a tendency to violate certain basic Mohave ethical patterns and attitudes. Thus, according to one set of belief, twins are acquisitive ghosts, who return to earth solely in order to obtain a second set of funeral goods (Devereux, 1941), and whose graspingness is a clear-cut violation of the Mohave code of unselfishness and non-acquisitiveness. (Devereux, 1939 b.) This point is of considerable importance, since interestedness and grasping avariciousness are among the principal sins of the Mohave value system and are, furthermore, supposedly highly characteristic of the hated white conquerors. Thus, even though the ghost of a Mohave is expressly stated to remain a Mohave,[12] at least some of the behavior attributed to ghosts, is, in principle, radically un-Mohave. In fact, it is just the kind of behavior that they ascribe to the despised whites.

It is, likewise the ghost rather than the living who, in defiance of Mohave custom, seeks to breach the barrier between the living and the dead, by haunting the living and trying to lure them to the land of ghosts—sometimes by seducing them into incestuous dream-intercourse, which, in itself, is a gross violation of Mohave sexual ethics.

In brief, the Mohave seem to attribute to the dead the actualization of certain wishes—such as the desire to accumulate surplus property, to engage in incest,[13] and to breach the barrier between the living and the dead—that are severely inhibited by Mohave custom. Tentatively speaking, this may mean that, more or less unconsciously, the Mohave define not only their traditional foes, but also the dead, as persons who openly "act out" that which the average Mohave must inhibit and control in himself. The fact that many primitives be-

---

[11] Homer's "Odyssey" (book XI) describes Achilles' emotional state in the underworld in terms which unmistakably characterize a mourning depression (Devereux, 1956 a).

[12] This was ascertained by means of direct questions (pt. 4, pp. 128–150).

[13] It was suggested elsewhere (Devereux, 1939 a) that there may be a psychological nexus between avariciousness and incest.

lieve the world of the dead to be an "upside down" symmetrical rep-
lica of the world of the living, where, e.g., big is small and vice versa,
also fits the tentative assumption that ghosts are sometimes unconsciously viewed as representatives of man's socially tabooed and
psychologically repressed urges.

This hypothesis gains additional support from the fact that some
basic behavior patterns are violated not only by the dead, but even
by those who are preparing for death.   Thus, Kroeber (1925 a) reports that old women sometimes hoard property, in order to have it
cast on their funeral pyres.   He mentions, however, that an old
woman could be persuaded to sell him some of this property.   She
rationalized her act by saying that she would invest the money in
food, which would pass into her body, and thus, in a way, would still
be burned with her.   Equally striking is the fact that when Tcatc,
who had repeatedly refused to violate Mohave custom by allowing
herself to be photographed, thought she would die in the near future,
she dressed up in her best finery, and had herself photographed by a
young Mohave, whom she then instructed to send me this photograph,
so that I would not forget her (Devereux, 1951 b).   This was a
definite violation of the Mohave rule that the dead should be forgotten as soon as possible, and that no memento of them should be
kept.[14]   It is even conceivable that modifications of behavior were
permitted to elderly people because of an unconscious feeling that
they must be allowed to prepare themselves for the socially abnormal
behavior befitting ghosts.   Thus, Tcatc stated that, owing to her advanced age, she felt free to speak up in all-male councils and to
usurp also certain other male privileges.[15]   This hypothesis is appreciably strengthened by the fact that not only a ghost, but even a hopelessly ill person on the verge of death may, according to Pulyi:k,
be referred to by the Mohave as "nyevedhi:" (ghost).[16]

Given this psychological situation, which is largely determined by
the internal readjustments necessitated by death in the ingroup, and
also by the socio-economic deprivations resulting from the death itself,
as well as from the destruction of property and from other funeral
expenses, it is probably unnecessary to argue that one purpose of
funeral rites is to control or replace an unstructured psychic upheaval
by an anxiety-binding ritual (Freud, 1924 a).   How easily psychological mourning may turn into a genuine psychotic depression may

---

[14] The discarding of mementoes calls for a real effort in every society. Thus, when
Hama : Utce :'s beloved father-in-law died, her husband toyed, throughout the wake, with
the fine bead belt she had recently made for the deceased (Case 107).

[15] The widespread lifting of sex-linked taboos in the case of post-menopausal women may,
perhaps, have a similar basis.

[16] It is interesting to note in this context that the Crow call objectionable people "ghost-
like" (Lowie, 1935).

be inferred from the fact that Nyakyusa mourners feign insanity during the funeral, in order to avoid becoming insane afterward (Wilson, 1954).[17] We may call this a "lightning-rod defense."

The Mohave themselves seem to contrast, at least implicitly, intensely emotional funeral rites followed by a forgetting of the dead, with emotional control during funeral rites and the remembering of the dead. Thus, the Mohave Creation myth which I obtained specifically contrasts the piety of Yuman mourners at Matavilye's funeral with the callousness wherewith other groups, and especially the whites, deserted the scene. It is significant that, after mentioning this point, several Mohave informants spontaneously referred to the fact that whites freely and callously mention the names of their dead relatives. Another proof that the Mohave correlate the intensity of mourning with the compellingness of the taboo on the name of the dead is the fact that, when lists of Mohave names were collected, Hama: Utce:, half apologetically and half humorously, turned to the other informant, Modhar Taa:p (penis cover, foreskin, also condom) and said: "So far, I mentioned several of your dead relatives. Soon it will be your turn to mention mine." Since one obviously mourns for one's own relatives more intensely than for other persons, the taboo on mentioning one's own dead relatives is an especially strong one. In fact, among the Mohave, as well as in some other tribes, uttering the names of one's dead relatives is a frequently mentioned symptom of psychosis. This symptomatic act may therefore be thought of as the socially standardized "signal symptoms," whereby mentally deranged persons notify the community of their claim to be considered insane.

Speaking more generally, it is both psychologically and anthropologically plausible that the extreme emotionality of primitive mourners during the wake and the funeral permits a massive abreaction of grief (and unconscious hostility) and therefore facilitates a subsequent emotional detachment from the dead.[18] (pt. 7, pp. 431–459).

In the case of ordinary persons, who will be missed only by members of their primary group, the funeral ritual apparently suffices to permit the mourner to abreact his grief and to detach himself from the deceased. However, in the case of leading personages (ipa taha:na), who are presumably missed by the tribe as a whole, a further opportunity for ritual grieving is afforded by the Mohave

---

[17] A psychological analogue may be the following custom: Should a Dayak dream that his house burns down, he promptly builds a model house and sets fire to it. In this manner the dream is permitted to come true, without causing material loss.

[18] There was a striking contrast between the violent keening and grief of Sedang Moi mourners accompanying a dead child to its grave, and the casual and almost lighthearted chatter of the same persons during their return from the graveyard (Devereux, MS., 1933–34).

"memorial rite," in which representatives of the entire tribe participate (Kroeber, 1925 a, K. M. Stewart, 1947 b).

Mohave memorial rites, often called in English "talking to the
feathers" (i.e., to the feathered staves), consist essentially of a highly
stylized mock battle, enacted by a line of male runners, flanked on each
side by a girl runner and by a horseman. In addition, there is also
a great deal of funeral oratory or singing, by funeral orators who, by
definition (Fathauer, 1951, 1954) are also scalpers (pt. 2, pp. 43–45)
and therefore qualified to cure the alien sicknesses (pt. 4, pp. 128–150).
The feathered staves used in this rite are apparently laden with a
certain impersonal power. Hence, they may be used only by qualified individuals, who must fast and refrain from intercourse during
the ritual and must be purified afterward. Apparently these staves
are not ordinary personal property, since, when a funeral orator
dies, they are not burned with the rest of his property, but, like certain feathers which only shamans may own, are buried in the mud.
(See further below.)

There appear to be three types of "insanity" which are related to
funeral and/or memorial rites.

(a) The derangements of funeral orators and other memorial ritualists who
violate taboos obtaining during the ritual period.

(b) The neuroses of nonritualist mourners who violate certain taboos.

(c) Hiyam ahwat (mouth red), which afflicts lay persons who presume to
handle feathered staves (and, apparently, also certain types of feathers which
only shamans may own).

DERANGEMENTS OF TABOO-VIOLATING FUNERAL RITUALISTS

In the course of a lengthy account of his powers and activities as
a funeral orator, Hivsu: Tupo:ma (with Hama: Utce: acting as interpreter) gave the following incidental information:

(a) [Could you sing for me the songs, or recite for me the orations which are
used by memorial service orators?] No, I cannot do so, because every time I sing
these songs I must undergo a purification and I would be starved by the end of
that period.[19] Also, I would have to bathe in the river and it is too cold to do so
in winter. When we bathe, we are not even allowed to warm ourselves near a
fire, lest we should begin to shake and become insane. You would not want your
old friend to submit to such an ordeal, would you?

(b) People (who participate in the ritual?) must refrain from intercourse
for 4 days after each cry, regardless of whether or not it is followed by a
memorial feather ritual. If they don't, they go crazy, or else become ill.

CASE 48 (Informant: Hivsu: Tupo: ma):

My friend C. S. did not believe in this prohibition. One day both of us participated in a funeral (memorial rite) at Needles; we were among the runners.

---

[19] Hivsu: Tupo:ma was a notoriously heavy eater, always ready to joke about his
voraciousness.

Our respective girl friends sat at the end of the row (of mourners and spectators) and watched us run. Both of us ran all night, and at seven o'clock in the
morning we had to jump into the river. That wasn't bad, because it was
summer. When we came out of the water, we met our girls and paired off. I did
nothing with my girl friend that I should not have done, but C. S. had intercourse with his girl friend and told me about it afterwards. I warned him of
the consequences, but he just laughed it off. This C. S., who was also a funeral
orator, became paralyzed a few years ago, and could hardly talk. Finally a
shaman, who has died since then, doctored him and improved his condition
somewhat. However, he still mumbles before he begins to talk (stroke?) and
therefore can no longer function as a funeral orator. When his illness began, he
dreamed of having intercourse with that girl friend of his. The funeral took
place about 10 years ago (1922?), and C. S. became ill 2 or 3 years later. At
present (1932) he is about 45 or 50 years old.

Comment

C.S.'s condition, and his subsequent improvement, suggest a mild stroke. The
fact that, at the onset of his illness, he specifically dreamed of intercourse with
the girl with whom he violated a major funeral taboo, suggests that, despite his
professed skepticism, he felt guilty for having violated an important taboo. The
onset of his illness, which he seems to have interpreted as a penalty for his misconduct, presumably reawakened in him the memory of his misbehavior so that,
in accordance with the Mohave cultural tenet that the cause of illness becomes
manifest in dream, he began to dream of the very act which allegedly caused
him to become paralyzed.

NEUROSIS OF TABOO-VIOLATING MOURNERS

Hivsu: Tupo:ma's statement.—Mourners who violate funeral taboos may become afflicted with psychiatric disorders.

(a) Funeral ceremonies usually take place on the fifth day after death.[20]
On the fifth day the house of the dead is burned down and his property is
cremated or spoiled, because anyone keeping the possessions of the dead will be
driven crazy by these objects.

It seems plausible to suggest that this etiological theory is based upon
two assumptions: (1) That the preservation of the dead persons' property deleteriously prolongs mourning and postpones the severance of
the dead from the living; and (2) that the dead themselves drive insane
the living who refuse to part with these objects. Here, as in many
other instances, the psychological explanation and the socio-cultural
explanation of a given phenomenon or belief are not mutually exclusive, but rather complement each other.[21]

(b) People are not supposed to sleep or doze off during the memorial rite.
Now and then, however, a girl who had intercourse during this period falls

---

[20] This delay is presumably determined partly by the Mohave tendency to do things by
fours, and partly by the belief that, for 4 days, the ghost lingers on earth and revisits its
former haunts before departing for the land of the dead. These 4 days may, without undue
imaginativeness, be interpreted as a "mourning period" on the part of the ghost, forming
a counterpart to the mourning period of the living. Compare, above, the demonstration
that mourning reactions are also ascribed to the dead.

[21] It is probable that much anthropological hostility toward the psychological explanation of cultural phenomena is due to a failure of psychologists to demonstrate that the
two types of interpretations supplement and complement each other.

asleep, but when the orator sings about Pahotcatc she wakes up with a jerk, in a real terror. Then she has a fit and makes various noises, which awaken other people who may also be napping. I (Hivsu: Tupo:ma), who sing of Pahotcatc, will immediately cure her, by talking (ritually) to her. During such a ritual certain other persons, who also happen to be unwell, will likewise be awakened and become noisy.

It is obvious that the preceding statement does not imply that the orator punishes such dissolute girls by supernatural means. It does, however, suggest that young Mohave women are prone to become emotionally disturbed in public, and especially during public ritual activities. This is also suggested by the fact that young shamans first display their powers by mildly bewitching a girl at a gathering. The tendency to have a fit in public is clearly a hysterical trait and causes one to question the validity of the traditional supposition that the Roman morbus comitialis (illness occurring at a gathering) was always true epilepsy and not hystero-epilepsy.[22]

HIYAM AHWAT

Informants: Tcatc and E. S.:
Only those who have obtained the appropriate powers in dreams may use and handle the funeral feathered staves, and take care of them. If anyone else picks up these feathers, it is a usurpation of shamanistic-oratorical powers. Hence, the contact with these feathers will drive the usurper insane. He will hemorrhage from the mouth and will have bad dreams. Also, when he uses these feathers, or feathered staves, he has severe headaches. In his dream he sees this hemorrhage and then he goes crazy.[23] He may even go down on his knees and plow the ground with his head. It is very much like having a spell (convulsive seizure). They just go insane.

Comment

It is tentatively suggested that we may be dealing here with tuberculosis complicated by a reactive neurosis.

From the cultural point of view, the Mohave etiological theory of this disorder is rooted in the "apprentice sorcerer" motif. Hiyam ahwat differs from the misfortunes that befall unauthorized meddlers with shamanism in that, in the present instance, the illness is not caused by retributive witchcraft exercised by some irate shaman protecting shamanistic prerogatives, but is directly due to the impersonal power which resides in the feathered staves. In fact, certain feathers—such as those of two or three species of hawks, one of which is called su:kwily (chicken hawk?), those of a turkey, those of a white, cranelike

---

[22] In Haiti, at folklore shows held in the Théatre de la Verdure, professional performers sometimes uncontrollably go into a trance. Dr. Louis Mars told me that a Haitian troupe, performing in Paris, was greatly embarrassed when one of the performers went into a spontaneous trance, right on the stage.

[23] Compare the belief that scalpers and witch killers dream of blood (pt. 2, pp. 43–46), and that in another mental disorder the dreamer sees himself covered with his wife's secretions (pt. 4, pp. 128–150).

bird called thu :dhilyk and those of the uro :ta (pelican?)—must be purified by shamans before laymen may own them or use them in the manufacture of war bonnets. As for eagle feathers and the feathers of the atcoo :r hawk, neither of which is used in the manufacture of war bonnets, they may only be owned by shamans and may not be used for war bonnets. In fact, when the shaman dies, these feathers are not even cremated with the rest of his possessions, but are buried in the mud. It was not ascertained whether the feathers of the saksak—who is either the fish eagle or else the white osprey (Kroeber, 1948)—may also be owned only by shamans. This is a regrettable gap in our knowledge, since anyone who dreams of Mastamho, after he turned into a saksak, is said to become insane (Krober, 1948 and pt. 4, pp. 116–117).

I also failed to investigate who may bury the deceased shaman's eagle and atcoo :r hawk feathers, without incurring supernatural risks. It seems reasonable to suggest that this was done by some other shaman, who is presumably a funeral orator. On the other hand, it is not altogether impossible that even a lay mourner may bury these feathers and that the general purification of the mourners may also effectively protect such a lay person from the dangers which he incurred by burying a shamanistic relative's stock of feathers.

The chief point to be stressed in this context is that these feathers—and apparently also the feathered staves—are not burned but buried. This is at variance with accepted Mohave funeral practices, since the Mohave only bury stillborn children (Devereux, 1948 e) and living, but unwanted, halfbreeds, and puppies (Devereux, 1948 d). The one known violation of this rule occurred when a Mohave woman vengefully caused her dead child, whose father refused to recognize it, to be buried in the Parker cemetery (Devereux, 1950 f). The practice of burying feathers remains, therefore, unexplained and deserves further investigation. The only lead to a possible explanation is provided by the fact that these feathers seem rather unique in that, in spite of their being, like charms, laden with autonomous power, unlike charms they do not necessarily turn against their legitimate owners in the end (pt. 4, pp. 202–212). Even this statement must be partly qualified, since there were some vague indications that funeral orators, too, may become insane, independently of the fact that, in their role of scalpers, they are exposed to the scalper's insanity (pt. 2, pp. 43–45). Another question to be clarified by future fieldwork is whether these staves, which clearly resemble the feathered staves that tribal officers carry into battle (K. M. Stewart, 1947 c; Fathauer, 1954), are actually identical with the latter. The answer will probably be in the affirmative, since the memorial rite is, itself, a kind of mock battle, commemorating important tribal officials.

A further comment concerns the fact that the illness is called hiyam *ahwat*—mouth *red*. This may or may not be related to the fact that the "spirit language" spoken by the funeral orator is called *ahwat* cukwarekwi kusumany (Fathauer, 1954).

The preceding discussion suggests that much remains to be known about the basic meaning of death and of funeral practices in Mohave society. The latter have, so far, been investigated chiefly from the viewpoint of the ritual itself. However, such a study is less likely to yield deep insights in the case of an essentially unritualistic society, such as that of the Mohave, than in the case of a highly ritualistic tribe, such as the Hopi.

In summary, three types of mental derangements seem to be related to various funeral observances. In some cases the derangement is due to sexual activity at inappropriate times, such activity being, in many groups, deemed to be incompatible with mourning. In other cases the neurosis is caused by preserving items belonging to the dead, which should have been placed on the funeral pyre. In still other instances the disorder results from unauthorized contact with ritual objects used in the memorial rites. Thus, the common denominator of this group of ailments is the fact that all of them are caused by violations of funeral taboos. This fact, taken by itself, suffices to lend plausibility to the basic hypothesis that unauthorized contact with objects pertaining to funeral rites, and/or a failure to forgo economic advantages or sexual gratifications during the mourning period, counteract the beneficial effects of the mourning ritual upon the mourners' psyche. Deprived of the social support that compliance with mourning taboos appears to provide, the mourner's chaotic grief reaction may get out of hand, transforming objectively justifiable sadness into a psychotic depression, characterized by guilt feelings (Cases 38, 47), panic and other forms of psychic self-aggression. Otherwise stated, funeral rites must be viewed as socially provided and culturally standardized defenses or "type solutions," which society places at the disposal of individuals struggling with certain statistically frequent "type conflicts" (Devereux, 1956 b).

INSANITY CAUSED BY WITCHCRAFT

There are many indications that the Mohave expect victims of witchcraft to display abnormal behavior. In fact, it is conceivable that the abnormal behavior of a given patient may, in itself, be the reason why his illness is attributed to the effects of witchcraft. Although this inference is, admittedly, not supported by direct statements, it is significant that many of the illnesses mentioned in this work were diagnosed as being due to witchcraft at the time the patient began to behave abnormally. The fact that, in several instances, this abnormal behavior was not due to a neurosis or psychosis, but to fever delirium, seemed irrelevant to the Mohave themselves, and is, therefore, irrelevant also from the anthropological point of view.

A detailed discussion of witchcraft and of witches is beyond the scope of this section, which is limited to the discussion of the abnormal behavior of patients believed to be victims of witchcraft. Of course, it is not suggested that the Mohave believe in the existence of a specific psychiatric syndrome caused by witchcraft. On the contrary, it is almost certain that, had these cases been recorded in the course of the 1938 field trip, which was devoted to the study of Mohave ethnopsychiatry, the informants would have spontaneously discussed these cases from the "psychiatric" point of view and would have attached a traditional diagnostic label to each of them. However, since they were recorded in the course of an earlier field trip, devoted partly to the collection of data pertaining to witchcraft, the cases were cited as examples of sorcery and—as a glance at the material will indicate—emphasized the role of the witch, rather than the role of the victim.

In view of these considerations, each case will be followed by a suggested Mohave diagnosis, as well as by a tentative psychiatric diagnosis. The suggested Mohave diagnoses are in every case so plausible, that only the strictest adherence to scientific accuracy caused, e.g., Case 49, on magical courtship, to be assigned to the present part, instead of to part 2, pages 83–87, to which it obviously belongs.

CASE 49 (Informants: Hivsu: Tupo: ma and Hama: Utce:, 1935):

The patient in question, Pi :it Hi :dho Kwa-ahwat (Pi :it eyes red), also known as Kwakuy Tadhuk (Old-woman?),[24] was the 30-year-old fullblood son of a woman also said to be a member of the O :otc gens, and therefore named O :otc. He was the classificatory "younger brother" (isutck) (Gifford, 1922) of Kumádhi: Atat, who bewitched him, causing him to have fits, because she loved him passionately, without being loved in return. A proper presentation of his case requires a detailed discussion of Kumádhi: Atat's personality.

Kumádhi: Atat, of the Kumádhi: (horn or ocatilla cactus) gens [25] was, in 1932, about 35–40 years old. This fullblood Mohave woman was relatively well behaved. "She is not a habitual drinker and does not run around with men." According to Hama: Utce:, "She is sociable; she talks, laughs and jokes.[26] She is also smart, well educated and speaks good English (few middle-aged Mohave women spoke good English in 1932.) I, personally, like her." According to Hivsu: Tupo :ma, however, "In the old days she would have been dead (killed) long ago. They say that she is a shaman, even though she does not cure anyone.

---

[24] Men's names are often a slur on women, and vice versa (Devereux, 1951 c).

[25] "And she sure is a thorn in some people's side," Hama: Utce: said.

[26] This remark presumably was meant to suggest that she differed from other witches, who tend to be stealthy and unsociable (pt. 2, pp. 57–71).

They think she is simply a killer. In that respect she is an exception, since few shamans are exclusively killers. Yet, if she wished to do so, she could use her power to cure witchcraft, since she knows how to bewitch people. Of course, some shamans can only bewitch, but cannot cure witchcraft, because they do not have enough power for that. I think, however, that she could cure witchcraft, if she chose to do so" (perhaps because women shamans are, by definition, "stronger" than male shamans).

(Be that as it may, Kumâdhi: Atat was hated and despised by many Mohave.) "Several people would like to kill her, because she is killing people all the time. She is alive only because of the new law" (which prohibits the killing of witches).[27] At any rate, after she killed her husband, her two children, and the man she was in love with,[28] people made it so unpleasant for her at Needles, Calif., that she decided to move to Parker with her sister and brother-in-law.

Kumâdhi: Atat was first accused of witchcraft sometime between 1931 and 1938, when her husband, Tcakwar Ala :y(e), a 25-year-old fullblood Mohave of the Kat gens, and their two children, Pi :it,[29] a boy of 4, and Kat, a girl of about 3, died within a relatively short time. First she bewitched her husband, because she knew that he was having an affair with another woman and was planning to leave her. Then, the same year, she also bewitched her children who, before they died, accused their mother of witchcraft, saying: "Our mother bewitched us." [This seems strange to me.] Hama: Utce: retorted a little impatiently: "It is not strange at all—she just wanted to have them with her in the Hereafter." [30]

Her next victim was Pi :it Hi :dho Kwa-ahwat, with whom she was in love. He did not return her love, partly because he was satisfactorily married to a young woman named Tcatc, of the Tcatc gens, and partly because he was so closely related to Kumâdhi: Atat that the latter had to call him isutck (younger brother). This meant that she could not have married him without first performing the already obsolete horse-killing rite, which dissolves the relationship between bride and groom (Devereux, 1939 a; and pt. 7, pp. 356–371).

She had two reasons for killing the man she loved: She had had a quarrel with the young man's mother, and, in addition, she was angry with him because he did not wish to leave his wife and marry her. Yet, even though she was angry with him, she also loved him—she did not hate him.[31]

When she started to bewitch him, the man began to dream of her all the time. He saw her in his dreams and her dream image was so real to him that the next day he would have a convulsive fit. Hence, even though he had a good

---

[27] Many Mohave hold this law responsible for the prevalence of witches, which is believed to threaten the tribe with extinction.

[28] This is one of the very rare cases in which the Mohave described another Mohave as "being in love," since intense and exclusive sexual attachments are altogether exceptional in this tribe. Her "being in love" may have been due to her relatively high degree of acculturation, in accordance with La Rochefoucauld's maxim, that few people would be in love, had they not read about being in love.

[29] A very common name among the younger Mohave, and said to have no meaning. The Mohave rejected my suggestion that it may be a Mohave form of "Pete," which is a very popular English name in that tribe.

[30] A witch segregates the souls of his or her dead victims in a certain place, and delays their subsequent reincarnations until he or she, too, dies (Devereux, 1937 c)

[31] The Mohave believe that the witch usually both loves and hates his victim. Compare also the firm belief of the Mohave that if one openly professes to hate a person of the opposite sex, one actually loves that person very much (Devereux 1950 a).

job at Needles, Calif., he left town and moved to Parker, Ariz., in order to escape her influence.[32]

As a result of his fight, his condition improved for a while, although, in some obscure way, he always knew in advance when Kumádhi: Atat would visit Parker, and he would have a fit. Thus, the day before his death he happened to be at my house, visiting my cousin's ailing son, when, all of a sudden, he stood up, exclaimed: "She is coming!" and had a fit. He kept on frothing at the mouth even while they were taking him back to his house. The next day he got up again, and began to walk about restlessly. He paced the floor and said over and over again: "She is coming! She is getting closer!" Then he had another fit. A little later on, about 20 minutes before his death, he said: "She is here. She is on the last lap of her trip. She is already at the Colorado River" (i.e., some 5 miles from his house). Then, around 5:00 p.m., he died and, sure enough, 20 minutes later Kumádhi: Atat did arrive.

[Why did she kill her husband and children by witchcraft, when she knew that she would not be killed anyhow?] It is true that nowadays she is not likely to be killed and would therefore be unable to retain her hold over her family, the way witches retain their hold over the ghosts of their victims. On the other hand, as long as she is alive she would still have the satisfaction of feeling that they belonged to her, and would dream of them at night. In addition, by killing her husband before he deserted her, and by delaying his subsequent reincarnations until she, too, died (Devereux, 1937 c), she made sure that he would belong to her also in the other world, though not the way a victim belongs to his bewitcher, but the way a husband belongs to his wife. That would not have been the case if he had already deserted her for another woman.[33]

As for Pi: it Hi: dh Kwa-ahwat she will lose her grip on him if, as seems certain, she does not die a violent death (Devereux 1937 c). However, in the meantime he does belong to her, since she put him in a certain place, with her other victims. Until she dies, she can dream about him and have intercourse with him in dream. That may explain why, unlike other women, she remained a widow and did not have affairs with men.

At any rate, she never confessed that she had killed her family, as well as the man she loved. There would have been no sense in her doing so. Since nowadays she cannot hope to be killed, a public acknowledgment of her deed would only have made things unpleasant for her.

Comment

Suggested Mohave diagnosis.—Epilepsy, due to magical courtship (pt. 2, pp. 83–87).

Tentative diagnosis.—Epilepsy, culminating in death while in status epilepticus. The triggering mechanism of the seizures appears to have been the patient's culturally determined belief that he was a victim of witchcraft.

Special considerations.—According to one informant, Pi: it Hi: dho Kwa-ahwat's mother was that O: otc, of the O: otc gens, who was responsible for Hipily Tcukup's suicide (Case 126). Since Pi: it Hi: dho Kwa-ahwat too was of the O: otc gens, his mother appears to have been guilty of gens incest. Hence

---

[32] Cf. Hivsu: Tupo :ma's flight from Parker to Needles, while in his late teens, to escape the obnoxious, but nonmagical, advances of an older, syphilitic woman (Devereux, 1950 a).

[33] The notion that the members of a family stay together in the course of their various reincarnations in the Hereafter only if they die at approximately the same time, is responsible for the funeral suicide of wives (Devereux, 1942 a).

she must have experienced great anguish (caused by a resurgence of all her old guilt feelings) when Kumádhi: Atat, a close relative of her son, expressed the desire to marry him. This, in turn, may explain why she quarreled with Kumádhi: Atat. As regards Pi: it Hi: dho Kwa-ahwat, his absolute refusal to cohabit with a woman who "threw herself at him" is extremely atypical for a Mohave, and may indicate that his puzzling chastity was also partly motivated by shame over his mother's intra-gens "incest." At the same time, it should be stressed that even though Mohave women do most of the (extramarital) courting (Nettle, MS., n.d.), they tend to dislike women who pursue men too insistently. The suspicion that Kumádhi: Atat was a witch, and therefore likely to bewitch primarily members of her own family, may also have deterred Pi: it Hi: dho Kwa-ahwat from marrying her. The final deterrent may have been the Mohave belief that families guilty of incest soon become extinct.[34]

Several years later, when these events were once more discussed with another informant, it was again stressed that Kumádhi: Atat would not join her victims if, instead of being killed outright, she was bewitched by another shaman. "In that case, all her victims would belong to the shaman who bewitched her, and he will separate her from them. That is why shamans are so afraid of being bewitched by another shaman, because, in that case, they lose their ghostly followers."

It is perhaps significant that, in the end, Kumádhi: Atat, who, as we saw, was relatively well educated, developed syphilis of the central nervous system (Case 75), a condition long known to be far rarer in American Indians (Kraepelin, 1904) than in whites.[35] Bold as the hypothesis may be, we cannot entirely disregard the possibility that her tertiary syphilis was, in some obscure way, related to her relatively high educational level,[36] and, possibly, also to her neurosis.

CASE 50 (Informants: Hivsu: Tupo: ma and Hama: Utce:) :

Kanvotce, of the Nyoltc gens, was a fullblood Mohave girl in her late teens. At that time (1890?) I (Hivsu: Tupo: ma) was just about 15 years old, and Kwathany Hi:wa (lizard-species heart, also called Himey Kuvalákas), a fullblood Mohave of the Nyoltc gens, then approximately 20 years of age, were attending the Parker (Reservation?) School. Kanvotce was Kwathany Hi:wa's girl. He bewitched her by the very slow method (Devereux, 1937 c), so that she had fits once in a while. I used to say in school that Kwathany Hi: wa had done this, whereupon he would say: "This kid is a shaman!" I, however, would reply: "No, I am not. I just know. You had better cure her!" When he left school he married her and, for a while at least, she was well. However, when she deserted him for Kumet Ahmat, of the Nyoltc gens, a 35-year-old fullblood Mohave, and moved with him to Needles, Calif., she soon began to have fits once more. I was at that time in Needles,[37] and realized that Kwathany Hi:wa was

---

[34] Note in this context that, according to the Mohave, only witches tend to commit incest (Devereux, 1939 a). Since witches also tend to bewitch chiefly those whom they love, and members of their own families, this may explain why families in which incest occurred are believed to become rapidly extinct.

[35] The causes of this difference are not fully understood, and an examination of the various attempts to explain it is beyond the scope of this work.

[36] The late William A. White, M.D., for many years superintendent of St. Elizabeth's Hospital, Washington, D.C., once informed me that the only paretic Indian he himself had seen was an Apache miner, who had lived most of his life like a white (personal communication, 1935).

[37] Hivsu: Tupo :ma had fled the attentions of a syphilitic older woman, going from Parker, Ariz., to Needles, Calif. (Devereux, 1950 a).

once more at work. Later on this girl returned to Parker and died of her seizures. Neither she nor her second husband was related to Kwathany Hi:wa.

In order to understand the preceding case history, it is necessary to give additional data about Kwathany Hi: wa, who was so definitely thought of as "the" leading witch among the Mohave, that one informant even alleged that he was the "only witch in the Parker Valley." In discussing him, Hama: Utce: spontaneously asked Hivsu: Tupo:ma whether Kwathany Hi:wa was responsible also for the big 1918 influenza epidemic. Hivsu: Tupo:ma explained that no one had been blamed for that particular epidemic, but that subsequent epidemics were said to have been caused by Kwathany Hi:wa and also by a certain Anyay Ha:m, also called I-lyi:, who was later on murdered by a married couple (Case 104) whom he had threatened with witchcraft (Devereux, 1948 f). One reason that Kwathany Hi:wa was blamed for such epidemics is that he happens to specialize, inter alia, in the treatment of colds, aching joints, rheumatisms, and witchcraft.

He is said to have started to practice witchcraft at the age of 20. In addition, by the time he was 25, he was also a recognized healer, although this did not cause him to desist from the practice of witchcraft, thus antagonizing many people, including Hama: Utce:, who specifically accused him of having "bewitched all my family."

He bewitches people because he likes them. However, he also bewitched Wàlàpa: e Nahakwe (Walapai's knife), of the Vi:mak gens, a fullblood Mohave, approximately 55 or 60 years of age. This man was a powerful shaman, who specialized in the treatment of bewitched persons. Wàlàpa: e Nahakwe doubted Kwathany Hi:wa's powers, but the latter was the stronger of the two and bewitched his antagonist about 9 years ago (perhaps in the 1920's) just to show him. On another occasion Tcatc said: "Once Kwathany Hi:wa told me that he had exiled this shaman's ghost beyond the sacred mountain Avi-kwame, to the west, and that he would keep him there until he, too, died, at which time the soul of the other shaman would (automatically) be released and go to the land of the dead. I was so afraid of Kwathany Hi:wa that I never repeated his confession to anyone. People would like to kill him, but they are afraid of the law."

When Hivsu: Tupo:ma was asked whether it would be possible to talk to Kwathany Hi:wa, he replied: "He would tell you nothing. He is afraid to talk. Even his own relatives accuse him of witchcraft, because he killed some of them. Were it not for the Indian Agent, he would have been killed long ago. Whenever a dying relative of his accuses him of having bewitched him, Kwathany Hi:wa breaks down and cries, and denies having done it. His married niece, Po:tà, of the Po:tà gens, who died recently, also kept saying that he had bewitched her."

Po:tà was not the only one who was obsessed by the idea that Kwathany Hi:wa might bewitch her. The same notion literally haunted Hama: Utce: for quite a while. Thus, when he repeatedly passed Hama: Utce:'s house, where we were working, Hama: Utce: was genuinely scared, and said: "He bewitches us, because he likes us. He is very superstitious. He is a killer and a coward at heart. We say that all shamans are cowards at heart, though I would not say so in front of Hivsu: Tupo:ma, who is, himself, a shaman."

Hama: Utce's fears appear to have had a personal, though culturally sanctioned, basis.[38] "When my cousin's former husband told me that he would

---

[38] The relevance of the following passage is depedent upon the accuracy of my recall that the person who had married Hama: Utce:'s cousin was, in fact, Kwathany Hi:wa. Unfortunately, the relevant page of the original field notes was lost, and the typed notes contain no name.

never again marry a woman of the Kunyii:th gens, because they are so quick-tempered, I replied: "I, for one, would never marry you." When this remark of mine became known, people warned me, saying: "He is a shaman, even though he denies it, and may make you fall in love with him." The reference is apparently to magical courtship (pt. 12, pp. 83–87) since only curers of venereal diseases (hiwey lak and hiku:pk) are especially lucky with women.

It is true, of course, that one informant denied that it was possible to obtain a wife by witchcraft. However, the case of Kanvotce does not contradict even this, possibly subjective, opinion, since, even before Kwathany Hi:wa began to bewitch her, Kanvotce was considered "his girl." On the other hand, the inference that genuine magical courtship was at work in this instance is supported by Pulyi:k's assertion that the victim of this form of witchcraft sees the witch in dream, in the very act of bewitching her and making her ill. The exceptions to this rule are cases which do not involve love magis, so that the personal identity of the witch need not necessarily be disclosed to the victim in dream. In such instances the witch may appear in his victim's dream, e. g., in the guise of a less powerful shaman, whose soul the witch "borrowed" so as to disguise his identity. "Suppose Kwathany Hi:wa took Anyay Ha:m's soul, in order to deceive a victim. (Hispan Himith) Tcilyetcilye, who is as powerful as Kwathany Hi:wa (and who also happens to be a "ghost doctor," cf. Fathauer, 1951), would see the truth (when called in to treat the victim?), and would tell it, if he is not afraid of Kwathany Hi:wa." At this point Hama: Utce: interrupted Hivsu: Tupo:ma and said that she, too, had heard of such "goings-on."

In other instances—which may include ordinary witchcraft, as well as magical courtship—the witch may appear in his victim's dreams in his true shape, but may forestall a cure by "sealing the lips of the victim" (he:ya averk, or he:ya tcahana:p).

Even so, conclusive evidence of witchcraft may come to light after a shaman's victim dies. Thus, according to Tcatc, "Two years ago (1936), the corpse of Jenny Honadick rose up on the cremation pyre, because she had been bewitched by Kwathany Hi:wa. She died of a hemorrhage at the mouth."

Comment

Suggested Mohave diagnosis: Magical courtship (pt. 2, pp. 83–87).
Tentative diagnosis: Hysteria, followed by death from other causes.

CASE 51 (Informants: Hivsu: Tupo: ma and Hama: Utce:):

Hi:wa Maa:ma, whose vital statistics are no longer remembered, lived at Fort Mohave. He had the power to cause, as well as to cure, a type of convulsive seizure (fit) believed to result from excessive masturbation (pt. 2, pp. 72–76). He bewitched several women between the ages of 35 and 40, as well as some men and children, causing them to have convulsive seizures. My informants specified that Hi:wa Maa:ma "gave his victims these fits," without first having to compel them, by means of witchcraft, to engage in masturbation.

"Eventually he was killed. We do not know who did it, nor how it happened. They just sent word that he had been killed."

Comment

Suggested Bohave diagnosis.—Atcoo:r hânyienk (pt. pp. 72–76) induced by witchcraft.

Tentative diagnosis.—Hysterical attacks in a woman approaching menopause (cf. the specification "between the ages of 35 and 40").

The true nature of this derangement can best be grasped by reading the preceding pages in connection with the data presented in part 2, pages 83–87 and 87–89, which also deal with disorders of behavior directly related to the effects of witchcraft.

PSYCHOSES OF THE OWNERS OF MAGICAL SUBSTANCES AND NARCOTICS

The Mohave attribute supernatural or magical powers to several substances, which interpreters usually designate by the term "drugs," although, strictly speaking, they are charms endowed with personality and power. However, since the Mohave believe that the principal sources of success in human life are dreams, charms play a relatively marginal role in their life and custom, despite the fact that they have been more or less coordinated with dream and ghost patterns. The impression that this coordination or compendence is an artificial one is strengthened by the fact that, according to the Mohave themselves, these magic substances do not "belong" (nyuu :yk) to the Mohave, who have "no power over them," but to the Yuman Walapai and Yavapai Indians, and to the Shoshonean Chemehuevi Indians. Indeed, we find that the charm tcapany is probably identical with the Walapai "drug" tcipa'n, that greasewood is part of the pharmacopoeia of the Walapai (Kroeber, 1935) and of the northeastern Yavapai (Gifford, 1936), and that minerals (turquoise) are used as amulets by the Walapai (Kroeber, 1935), the north-eastern Yavapai (Gifford, 1936) and the south-eastern Yavapai (Gifford, 1932). Since these charms are believed to be "persons," and since the Mohave affirm that all intimate contact with aliens is dangerous to them, it is not surprising that these drugs should be both coveted and feared. As a matter of fact, the final evil influence of these charms is spoken of as "hahnok" (influence of, or infection from), and is specifically compared with the so-called "foreign disease" ahwe: hahnok (foreigner's contamination) (pt. 4, pp. 128–150). Furthermore, in view of the connection between these charms, which, like shamanistic powers, eventually turn against their owners, and such typically Mohave culture elements as dreams of ghosts and of curative powers, it is to be expected that charms would usually be owned by shamans rather than by laymen.

MAGIC SUBSTANCES

(a) *Tcapany* is the root of a certain weed, which grows in the vicinity of the Steffens ranch.[39] "It smells like mint, and, when it seeds, it

---

[39] The Walapai describe "tcipa'n" as a short plant with leaves about 6 inches in length, and with a short, gray root, which grows around springs. It is powdered, chewed, or pounded (Kroeber, 1935).

looks a little like alfalfa." "The parched and ground tcapany seeds are merely ordinary articles of Mohave diet, since the magical power of tcapany is in its root." "We fear this plant because we have no power over it. Power over this plant was given to the Chemehuevi, Yavapai, and Walapai Indians." "The Mohave have a little power over this plant, however. They use it to cure rheumatisms and pains in the joints, since the tcapany weed has the power to cause these ailments." This belief resembles the theory that witches can cause only those diseases which they can also cure (Devereux, 1937 c).

The tcapany root should be handled and owned only by shamans, since it has "dreadful effects" upon ordinary young men who presume to handle it. In the same way, those who, without being shamans, presume to sing shamanistic songs will be seriously harmed by the power of these usurped songs (Devereux, 1937 c). This is, of course, the well-known "apprentice sorcerer" motif.

A bit of tcapany root, a little more than an inch in length, is believed to bring good luck to its owner, especially luck in gambling and in love. Furthermore, should he walk or ride about at night, the root will not only protect him against snakes, causing them to refrain from biting him, but will even cause the snakes to warn him of their presence on the road. (Cf. snake charm, below.)

On obtaining the root, one must refrain from intercourse and from salt and meat for 4 days. Should a man violate this rule, his joints will swell, his tongue will become paralyzed, knots will appear on his skin and his blood will be "corrupted." This last sanction reminds one of the belief that the "stronger blood" of aliens "hits" the "weaker blood" of the Mohave who come in contact with them (pt. 4, pp. 128–150).

CASE 52 (Informant not recorded; probably Tcatc):

A certain old man, who was still alive in 1933, used tcapany in the following manner: He chewed a bit of root, spat its juice on three fingers, and then traced stripes across his calves and lower thighs. The charm brought him luck for a while, but, in the end, it "turned against him," and paralyzed his tongue. He did not regain his powers of speech until he was treated by a competent shaman.

Tentative diagnosis: Stroke (?).

All informants agreed that the owner of this charm must remain continent while actually handling it. Other informants even alleged that tcapany frequently became jealous of its owner's wife or mistress, and therefore haunted and even destroyed him. It is significant to recall in this context that witches too, are haunted by the ghosts of their beloved victims (pt. 7, pp. 387–426) and mourners by the ghosts of their dead relatives (pt. 4, pp. 128–186), who attempt to lure them to the land of the dead, e.g., by having intercourse with them in dream.

(*b*) *Talyaveh* (or *talavey*) *tcukac* is the root of a plant which, like tcapany, belongs not to the Mohave but to the Chemehuevi, the Walapai, and the Yavapai. It is used like tcapany, and, like that substance, is believed to bring its owner good luck, especially luck in gambling. Should a person whom the charm dislikes approach it, his entire body will be covered with a rash of red pimples. The irrational dislikes of this charm remind one somewhat of the irrational dislike which infant twins sometimes conceive for certain persons (Devereux, 1941).

(*c*) *Amatàta:vos* was described by Hivsu: Tupo:ma as a powdered, blue and yellow striped rock (devil's diamond?), and by Tcatc, who said that quantities of amatàta:vos are to be found on the other side of Wickenburg, on the road to Phoenix, Ariz., as a "crumbly, fuzzy thing on rocks." The Mohave have no "power" over this charm, which belongs to the Chemehuevi, the Yavapai, and the Walapai Indians. A person who acquires this charm must remain continent for 4 days and must not partake of salt or meat for the same length of time. This substance is carried in a little bag, which is worn either in the breechcloth, or else under the clothing, against the skin. When the owner of this charm goes to a dance or to a gathering, the power of this charm will attract the women whom he happens to like. "If he is near her, she will be attracted to him and turn toward him, and he will win her favor." However, since this charm does not belong to the Mohave, its power will affect the owner the way the power of tcapany does. In fact, the power of this charm is so great that "it can cripple not merely its owner, but also his close relatives, who will dream of it and may even die from its effects." One is reminded here of the belief that evil shamans bewitch mostly their own relatives (Devereux, 1937 c).

(*d*) *Hunyavre itcerk* (bug excrement) is said by some to be a mineral substance; a powdered, glistening, and sparkling black-and-white rock. Others, however, said that it is found on greasewood (*Sarcobatus vermiculatus*) branches.[40] The Mohave have no power over it, since it belongs to the Chemehuevi, the Walapai, and the Yavapai. It is acquired and kept for the same reasons as other charms. The person who acquires this potent substance must remain continent for 4 days and must also refrain from salt and meat for the same length of time. It brings luck for a certain length of time, but, when it becomes malevolent, "it causes terrible headaches; one aches all over." (The Mohave seldom mention headache as a symptom.) In the end, it kills its owner. Should one attempt to chew this substance

---

[40] The magical use of greasewood by the southeastern Yavapai is mentioned by Gifford (1932).

it causes the tongue to become stiff. (Paralysis? Astringent effect?) In some instances, people who own this charm also partake of datura. It was possible to record only a Yuma Indian instance in which the owner of this charm also drank datura.

CASE 53 (Informant: Hama: Utce:):

I knew a Yuma Indian who owned this charm and also drank datura. I was even present at his funeral, because it took place the very day (1933) on which I arrived at Fort Yuma in order to attend the cremation of my aunt, who had married a Yuma Indian. This man was an exceptional shinney player and also excelled in all other sports. He used to own some of this ground white-and-black stone charm, in order to win favor with the girls. When he died, his older brother, contrary to custom, decided to keep the corpse until next morning. When the other brothers protested, he offered to remain with the corpse all night, and told the others to go home. The younger brothers were so indignant, however, that they threatened to kill him: "You will be the next one to die," they said. When, despite their protests, their oldest brother refused to yield, they went home, but one of them became so indignant that he got drunk, came back to where his oldest brother kept his vigil and stabbed him. The wounded man was eventually discovered in a ditch and was transported to the hospital. Informant implied that this family tragedy was caused by the charm which the dead man had owned, since the behavior of the oldest brother was unusual and highly irregular.

(e) *Katc humu:kwa*, called in English "the stone," is a lodestone. In discussing this substance I propose to deviate from the system of presentation adopted for the description of other charms and will reproduce instead Tcatc's account. This narrative, which shifts from case history to theory, and back to case history again, was related in the tense, clipped, preaching style of Mohave orators (Kroeber, 1925 a), which conveys more convincingly than could any formal statement the awe which this substance inspired in an old, very level-headed and rather skeptical, though old-fashioned, Mohave.

"The lodestone is a 'drug' which brings luck, but also drives people crazy. They call it katc humu :kwa, which means 'the stone.' They get it for luck. It is usually a shaman who gets it—not just anyone. They think that they are lucky in love then—that they can get any woman. They also think that it makes them lucky in gambling. They carry it all the time. When you carry something like that, you cannot copulate, nor eat salt or meat."

CASE 54 (Informant not recorded; probably Tcatc):

About 10 years ago (1928?) Hulymânyo:va, of the Nyoltc gens, who was at that time quite young—maybe only 20—and was living at Blythe with his wife Po:ta, got himself a lodestone. When he became sick, people claimed that his illness was caused by that lodestone. They brought him to the hospital here, at Parker. Dr. Nettle was our doctor there. You could hear him—he went out of his head! They wanted to take him to Needles, but old Atci: Akw(o)ath, whose wife was related to Hulymânyo:va, said that they could not take him away, although (because?) they thought that he was dying.[a] He was out of his head and fought everyone who came near him. This lodestone drives you crazy and also deforms you. When he got a little better they took him out, although he still complained of pain in his hip. He got over it eventually, but his whole hip sticks out now and his knees are drawn up. He is deformed. He must have had a way with the ladies, for when his wife Po :tà left him because of his deformity, he married Mu :th, a nice young girl just out of Riverside Indian School, and had a baby by her. When Mu :th also left him, he married another young girl, Nyortc, who had had a baby of uncertain paternity, which had died. When Hulymånyo :va and Nyortc also separated, he went back to Mu :th—perhaps because they had had a baby. These lodestones are insanely jealous. Had Hulymånyo :va observed the taboos, and had he not married, he would have been all right.

Tentative diagnosis: Delirium, due perhaps to an inflammatory disease of the joints.

CASE 55 (Informant not recorded; probably Tcatc):

Hulymånyo :va's first wife, Po :tà is also believed to have a lodestone. Maybe that is why men kill themselves over her. (Po :tà caused two men to commit suicide. (See Cases 119 and 120.) Maybe she got it while she was working at Fort Mohave. That must have been 20 years ago. She is crippled and has funny noises in her ears (tinnitus?). She is just about deaf with them. Yet, men still love her. She lives at present with Kutenyam Lyivec, a 40-year-old Yuma Indian. Her first husband, Hulymånyo :va, is now about 31 or 32 years old (1938).

Tentative diagnosis: Disease of the joints, due perhaps to *venereal disease.*

CASE 56 (Informant not recorded; probably Tcatc):

We are not sure of it, but we also suspect some other people owning lodestones. One of them is Ma :le, a Chemehuevi woman about 40 years of age. She is married to Aha Ksuu :k (or Mat-ha Månye:) of the Mah gens, whom A. W. allegedly raped in his youth (Devereux, 1950 a).

CASE 57 (Informant: Tcatc):

I myself used to see lodestones when I was cooking for railroad workmen, over there at the Boundary Cone. One sees these things in dream. These stones are like living people. You find them together, like villages. When you dream of them, it seems as though all those little lodestones were coming to visit you. They are real persons (ipa:). You find men and women among them. They have souls. They have little children too. When one gets sick, one sees all the little lodestone kids that are coming to visit one. They are people, and have children, and increase and decrease in numbers, just like people. They do not die. How could they die when they are like ghosts (nyevedhi:)?

Tentative diagnosis: Hallucinations (?) during organic illness.

The attitude toward charms is, perhaps, best revealed by the fact that Tcatc, after speaking of insanity induced by witchcraft, and its cure, spontaneously switched to a discussion of charms. Hence, it seems best to describe the attitude toward charms in Tcatc's own words:

There are altogether five such substances: tcapany, talyaveh tcukac, amatåta :vos, hunyavre itcerk, and katc humu :kwa. They are all people, and what

---

[a] Dying patients are usually taken home from the hospital, so that they can die in familiar surroundings.

I said of lodestones is true of all of them. If you get sick from these charms, you dream of young boys and girls coming around you. You mâhnok (from) them, as with alien tribes.[42] It is like the influence through which you contract ahwe: hahnok (disease from contact with foreigners). It is not matadhauk (witchcraft), although you do go out of your head because you get very sick.

There is no one alive now who knows how to cure witchcraft. It is not enough to be a witch in order to be able to cure witchcraft. You have to have special powers. The charm-sickness can be doctored, however, by Kwathany Hi:wa (Case 50). But the ahwe: nyevedi: (foreign ghost) disease—which you contracted because you are so much in love with that girl who does not love you—no one knows how to cure *that ailment*. (Cf. pt. 4, pp. 91–106. Note also the equating of hi:wa itck with ahwe: nyevedhi:—perhaps because I was felt to be a "Mohave.")

CASE 58 (Informant: Tcatc):

Nyaipatcem, of the Mu:th gens, was a shaman who lived 40 years ago. He was as much feared in his time as Kwanthany Hi:wa or (Hispan Himith) Tcilyetcilye is feared nowadays. Yet, even he died from one of those charms. He got sick from that and was doctored by a Mohave-Apache (Yavapai?) shaman, who is a relative of your interpreter's half sister, the one who is a twin. In fact, he was that twin's grandfather. This (Yavapai) shaman, Tceyakâm Uva: thâ, also doctored me when I got sick from a pain in my leg and was partially paralyzed. This man treated Nyaipatcem and he got well. Two or three years later, however, he kept on going out of his mind, and in the end he could no longer speak. He was in a kind of daze. He never acted as though he knew or understood what was going on. He just sat there. He stayed that way for about 2 weeks, and then he died. This second attack came over him all of a sudden. He lived on the east side of the river, directly east of Riverside Mountains.

"The shaman who had treated him had moved to the Mohave Reservation because he had married a Mohave woman named Hualy, who had no English name. They had three boys, two of whom died young. Only the third, Ahma Sokam (quail-soul), lived. He, like his Yavapai father, was of the Tcatc gens. The Yavapai also have the Syuly gens, but no other gens.[43] He was the father of your informant's half sister, who was one of a pair of twins.

Tentative diagnosis: Stroke?

Rattlesnake teeth and lizard tails are worn by some women in their hair, because they are supposed to bring them luck. These "lucky pieces" are not thought to harm their owners, which is of some interest, since contact with any part of a rattlesnake is usually avoided, especially by men, who fear an impairment of their potency (Devereux, 1950 a). The use of rattlesnake teeth and lizard tails by women as "lucky pieces" may be due to feminine penis envy and to the spiteful desire to render men impotent (Deutsch, 1944–55). Some male gamblers also had rattlesnake charms, which eventually crippled them (Kroeber, 1948), but did not cause the hikwi:r illness.

Transvestites, like magic substances, are said to bring luck to their spouses (Devereux, 1937 b.)

---

[42] Mâhnok, from hahnok, means, roughly speaking, a supernatural infection or influence.
[43] This is apparently incorrect (Gifford, 1932, 1936).

NARCOTICS

Datura (ismaly katuh), which plays an important role in the ritual of the Diegueño Indians (Toffelmier and Luomala, 1936), is not thought of as a genuine charm, although, according to Kroeber (1925 a), persons who drink datura are believed to dream for 4 days and to acquire thereby luck in gambling. As a rule, the few Mohave who use datura do so principally for the purpose of obtaining a narcotic dream experience (Drucker, 1941). According to my informants, the entire plant, according to Kroeber (1925 a), only the western foliage of datura—the eastern leaves being thought of as poisonous (a tenet which was not known to my informant Pulyi:k)—and, according to Drucker (1941), only the root is pounded, soaked in water, and wrung out.[44] The liquid is left standing until the undesirable particles suspended therein settle on the bottom of the container. The remaining liquid is then decanted and drunk. My informants described the effects of datura as follows: "If a person drinks datura, he will walk around, and may even fall into shallow water and sleep for 4 days." At present, the few Mohave who partake occasionally of datura no longer soak it, but merely chew a piece of the root. According to Spier (1936) the Mohave, like the other Lower Colorado Yumans and like the Maricopa, take datura individually to forecast the future, and, unlike the Maricopa, also indulge in drinking datura in groups. My informants simply specified that the Mohave take datura in order to divine a boy's future as it relates to his warlike or other activities.

Pulyi:k's statement.—If a boy's close relatives wished to find out what he would become in adult life, they pounded the root of datura, and made him drink it. Then, if the intoxicated boy was to become a warrior, his actions would betray him: He would hit and try to kill people and would find carefully hidden weapons. If he was to become a shaman, he would blow (saliva?) and press (people?) with his left hand."

This test, while formally different from the test to which children suspected of transvestite inclinations were subjected (Devereux, 1937 b), has in common with the latter custom the fact that it is a test of the youth's real inclinations, powers, and potentialities. The fact that in a state of intoxication he could find hidden weapons is somewhat reminiscent of the trance seance in the course of which persons who were lost in enemy territory, as well as thieves, were located (pt. 7, pp. 426–431). (Cf. also Kroeber, 1957.)

Although the intoxicating, sedative, and hypnotic effects of datura were generally known, the Mohave did not take datura as a sedative, and did not administer it to insomniac infants, whose fretfulness was treated by means of sympathetic magic (pt. 6, pp. 257–260). There is,

---

[44] My informants stated that only the root is used in divining a boy's future as a warrior, shaman, etc.

however, a somewhat puzzling reference in Bourke (1889) to the drugging of Matavilye's daughter—whom Bourke calls Catheña—because she prevented her sons from marrying. Bourke's informant apparently did not name this drug; he simply compared it to "kloky-fum" (=chloroform). However, since the Mohave knew no other intoxicating drug, Bourke's informant was probably referring to datura.

Likewise, even though the Mohave knew that large doses of datura could kill a person, murder by poisoning was not mentioned by any informant, and only one person—an unjustly accused shaman (Case 106)—appears to have drunk datura in order to kill himself.

CASE 59 (Informant not recorded; probably E. S.) :

At X Indian school a bunch of Indian school girls of various tribes drank some datura. When the teacher found them, she did not know what was the matter with them, and the girls were unable to tell her what they had done, since, by that time, they were "goofy" and foamed at the mouth. The teacher called a doctor, but even he did not know what was the matter with them. The girls recovered, however.

Tentative diagnosis: Datura poisoning.

The nexus between datura, witchcraft, and suicide is shown by the fact that a shaman, unjustly accused of witchcraft, drank datura and drowned himself in the Colorado River (Devereux, 1937 c; and Case 106).

The relationship between datura, dreams, witchcraft, charms, and transitory toxic states (Case 59) suggests that charms are the psychological equivalents of datura, and vice versa. It is also probable that, in many respects, magic substances, drugs, and alcohol (Appendix, pp. 505–548) satisfy a constellation of interrelated psychological needs, most of which are rooted in the oral-sadistic stage, and are intimately interwoven with death wishes and with the conscious denial of these wishes (Lewin, 1946).

INTERPRETATION

The integration of charms with Mohave culture.—Although the general problem of the cultural integration of borrowed traits is beyond the scope of this discussion, it may be said that, usually, borrowed traits either fill a major, but previously unsatisfied, need, or else serve to expand a conspicuously significant cultural preoccupation. In the former case a vigorous new trait modifies the existing cultural equilibrium, whereas in the latter instance it reinforces it.

Charms, being allegedly alien objects, and hence dangerous ones, were—a trifle artificially—coordinated with the rest of Mohave culture, without ever acquiring the significance of, e.g., Plains Indian medicine bundles, and without ever being able to challenge the primacy of dream experience as a source of power and of luck. To be specific, charms

were coordinated with the dream-power-witchcraft-ghost complex of
Mohave culture, thus preserving and even reinforcing the overall
equilibrium of that culture.

The nexus between the power-complex and charms is revealed in
many ways:

(*a*) Despite the danger that a magic substance may eventually turn
against its owner, few Mohave hesitated to acquire a charm. In the
same way, only a few persons shrank from accepting shamanistic
powers, despite the risk that these powers too might eventually "go
wrong" and cause their owners to become witches (pt. 7, pp. 387–425).

(*b*) When charms turn against their owners, they destroy them,
and sometimes even kill off their families as well. In the same way,
when a shaman's powers turn evil, he bewitches mainly his relatives
and those whom he loves. The ghosts of his beloved victims then
haunt him, and attempt to lure him to the land of the dead, until the
witch deliberately induces his victims' surviving relatives to kill him
(Kroeber, 1925 a) (pt. 7, pp. 387–425).

(*c*) Another point of similarity between shamanistic powers and
charms is the fact that both are dangerous to laymen who attempt to
usurp them. This obvious apprentice sorcerer motif, together with
the "insane jealousy" of these charms, probably justifies an oedipal
interpretation of these magic substances and powers. This interpretation is also supported by the belief that charms bring luck in
gambling, which is believed to be an orally determined trait (Bergler,
1943; Devereux, 1950 d); and in promiscuous amorous pursuits,
which, according to psychoanalytic theory, are determined partly by
a vain pursuit of a parental imago, and partly by unconscious homosexual tendencies (Fenichel, 1945). The unconscious confusion between the maternal and paternal imago is probably determined by
oral fantasies, since, according to Mohave belief, unborn children are
"nursed" by their mother's husbands or lovers (Devereux, 1937 d;
1949 c). Summing up, among the Mohave, belief in magical substances appears to be due to a deviation, at the phallic-oedipal stage,
from "normal" (i.e., occidental) psychosexual development.

The unconscious significance of charms is a matter of conjecture,
although, from the viewpoint of psychoanalytic theory, they obviously fall into the general category of magical substances, whose
infantile prototypes are such body products as the excreta, milk,
semen, saliva, and sweat. The first of these is mentioned in Mohave
mythology (Bourke, 1889) as the means whereby the first act of
witchcraft was perpetrated. Saliva and sweat, which I have elsewhere linked with milk and semen (Devereux, 1947 a), also play a
significant role in witchcraft, as well as in shamanistic therapy. In
brief, there can be no doubt that magical substances, like shamanistic

powers, are intimately linked with infantile fantasies of omnipotence. This inference is particularly convincing if one recalls that shamans are, by definition, persons who remember their intra-uterine existence (Devereux, 1937 c). As regards the excreta, they play a significant role also in the myth which accounts for the origins of agriculture and the end of large-scale infanticide (Devereux, 1948 d). Last, but not least, female secretions occur in the pathogenic dreams of certain neurotics (pt. 4, pp. 150–175).

Yet, it is almost impossible to determine precisely which body product is the ultimate prototype of magic substances in Mohave psychology. The most obvious source of this difficulty seems to be the fact that, due to Mohave child-training techniques, the oral and anal stages of development tend to overlap with the phallic and oedipal stages, which probably accounts for the paradoxical belief that the first orally absorbed nourishment of children is not milk, but semen (Devereux, 1937 d, 1947 a, 1948 b). It is, hence, impossible to do more than underline the significance of oral elements in such practices as the chewing of charms, the drinking of decoctions, and the pulverization of rocks, and in the belief that some of these dangerous substances paralyze the tongue—just as contact with rattlesnakes paralyzes the penis (Devereux, 1950 a)—causing loss of speech.   In this latter context it is important to recall that the mother of a child born mute is believed to have performed fellatio during pregnancy (pt. 6, pp. 248–251). The most telling argument in favor of an oral interpretation of these beliefs is, however, the fact that charms and shamanistic powers are closely connected with fantasies of omnipotence, which, as is well known, belong primarily to the oral stage.   The fact that semen is so systematically equated with milk is probably due to the relatively complete fusion of the "partial drives" with genitality in Mohave society, which, in turn, is made possible by the fact that the various stages of psychosexual development tend to overlap to an unusual extent in Mohave maturation (Devereux, 1947 a, 1951 e, 1950 c, 1950 b).

The fact that "good" charms and powers tend to turn "bad" in the long run seems to be due to the successive emergence into the field of consciousness of the two poles of an ambivalent attitude, which probably mirrors the process whereby "good objects," such as the mother or her milk, turn into "bad objects," such as the denying and frustrating mother (Devereux, 1947 a) and feces. It is not improbable that this process is ultimately responsible for the basic characteristics of all sacred objects, which, as Durkheim has shown, are invariably thought of as both sacred and dangerous.

Although the above interpretations are, admittedly, tentative ones, it is at least reasonably certain that charms are adult representatives of infantile magical objects. The conjectural nature of our interpretation is due partly to the relative paucity of ethnological material, and partly to the fact that the entire psychoanalytic problem of "good" and "bad" objects is still in a somewhat chaotic state.[45] A fuller and more dogmatic interpretation of insufficient ethnological material, in terms of a still incomplete theory, is, hence, undesirable, since it would violate the most elementary rules of scientific discretion.

Though admittedly tentative, the interpretations given above are likely to be correct, especially as regards oedipal factors. Indeed, the fact that the mythical, counter-oedipally possessive, *"Catheña"* (Bourke, 1889) had to be intoxicated—perhaps with datura—before her sons could marry, suggests a definite link between *drugs* and *oedipality* and therefore also between oedipality and *charms*.

ALCOHOL

The Mohave had no alcohol in aboriginal times. It is therefore understantable why, even though some people are nowadays known to drink too much, the Mohave continue to consider drunkenness not as an aboriginal neurosis (yamomk) but as an alien form of misconduct or badness (ala: yk). Since this work seeks to present primarily Mohave theories concerning psychiatric illness, the Mohave view, that alcoholism is *not* a neurosis, made it necessary to relegate a discussion of Mohave drinking to a special Appendix (pp. 505–548). Needless to say, from the strictly psychiatric point of view, alcoholism, of course, is a genuine neurosis.

---

[45] We suggested elsewhere (Devereux, 1953 a) that good objects turn into bad ones as a result of their being ejected.

PART 5. OCCIDENTAL DISEASE CATEGORIES

NEUROSES, PSYCHOSES, AND NEUROLOGICAL DEFECTS

The present chapter contains the psychiatric information which was obtained in response to questions regarding the occurrence of classical psychiatric syndromes among the Mohave. The form of the questions explains why, in answering them, the Mohave simply provided descriptions or explanations, but used no Mohave diagnostic labels.

Although it would have been easy, in some instances, to correlate these data with Mohave clinical entities, it was felt that such a procedure would inextricably mix what the Mohave themselves specifically said about certain Mohave disease entities and what, for the best of reasons perhaps, I decided to correlate with those entities. Hence the two sets of data were kept apart. Nothing is lost thereby, since the reader himself will readily correlate psychopathy with disorders of the instinct of aggression, manic depressive psychosis either with disturbances of the mood or else with nyevedhi: taha:na, etc.

ANXIETY AND ANXIETY STATES

Anxiety is one of the key concepts of psychiatry. It is either consciously present in neuroses and psychoses, or else it is effectively barred from the field of consciousness by such defense mechanisms as isolation, albeit at great cost in terms of incapacitating symptoms and disorders. In some instances anxiety is detached from its original cause or source and is attached to some less anxiety-arousing item, by means of the defense mechanism of displacement. When the subjective awareness of anxiety is suppressed, e.g., by means of isolation, it can usually be elicited by means of deep psychotherapy. In such instances the patient must be brought to experience anxiety subjectively, before the anxiety itself can be dealt with therapeutically. The chief objective of many symptoms is the reduction of anxiety.

In addition to anxiety as a symptom of various neuroses and psychoses, there are also two neuroses, called "anxiety state" and "anxiety hysteria," in which the subjective experience and symptom of anxiety plays a dominant role. In other instances anxiety is elicited by situations of stress or else by definite "phobic situations, or objects." In still other instances anxiety attacks occur in a seemingly random manner, so that the pattern only becomes manifest in the course of deep psychotherapy. Anxiety is an excruciatingly painful experience, which has great motivating force.

The Mohave themselves mention anxiety in connection with a variety of mental disorders, as well as in connection with "pathogenic dreams." The clue to the Mohave Indians' preoccupation with the general problem of anxiety was obtained accidentally, in connection with questions pertaining to obsessive-compulsive states, and led to the discovery of a fairly perceptive Mohave conception of anxiety.

Anxiety was well understood by the informants, who spontaneously differentiated between "intelligible anxiety" over the major problems of life (which, depending on the nature of one's dreams, may culminate either in a socially valuable sublimation, or else in neurosis or even in a psychotic decompensation), and more or less free-floating "neurotic anxiety," whose object is unknown to the neurotic and/or puzzling to the observer.

In accordance with the policy of using, whenever possible, Mohave categories of classification, I have, for the sake of brevity, labeled these two types of anxiety: "intelligible anxiety" and "neurotic anxiety." It should be emphasized, however, that the use of these terms is a strictly heuristic one, and does not imply that anxiety over the major problems of life, at a time when the responsibilities of adulthood begin to supersede the easy-going irresponsibility of youth,[46] is necessarily free from neurotic components, regardless of how valid and intelligible such an "Angst der Kreatur" may seem to the objective observer. In brief, we have used the terms "intelligible" and "neurotic" anxiety solely because they seem to fit the ideas of our Mohave informants. Hence, anyone is free to designate what we have called "intelligible" anxiety by another label which, in his estimate, is more appropriate either in terms of psychoanalytic theory, or in terms of Mohave ideas about the nature of anxiety.

INTELLIGIBLE ANXIETY

Tcatc's statement.—[What is your opinion about the inability to "let up," and to relax and enjoy things?] Among the Mohave, boys and girls under the age of 18 or 20 have less knowledge of the bigger things in life (than the adults have). Therefore, they have less worry on their minds, and are able to enter into recreational activities and sports wholeheartedly (Devereux, 1950 e). As they grow older, they are able to think maturely. This causes (hahnok) some weight on their minds, and brings worries in its train. Among the Mohave of long ago, the mature ideas (preoccupations) of young people were the following: How to grow their crops, how to develop physically and mentally,[47]

---

[46] Compare Gladwin and Sarason (1953) for another primitive instance of such an anxiety.

[47] Even the non-shamanistic fetus in the womb is believed to think of ways and means of developing and of being born (Devereux, 1948 b).

how to care for one another, what to do in times of sickness, and how to do good within the tribe. Of course, these ideas bring worry to the young people, so that they think a great deal about them. And so their good times became more mature (i.e., they outgrew their "good times"), and (after a while) it seemed to them that they (i.e., the past and the present) were not good times at all. The solution of these mature ideas (problems) sometimes came to them in dreams (Devereux, 1956 c.). This (i.e., the general problem of living) may be the cause of worry. They may still have good times, but it just does not seem like good times to them. A pi-ipa: taha:na (i.e., "person real"=usually a tribal officer), who is interested in the welfare of Indians (Devereux, 1951 b) would sometimes be thinking of the advice he could give to the people. (Then) he does not seem to be happy in the so-called good times. At times he would sit and think out loud.[48] When you are young, you have fewer worries. When you grow older, you have more mature ideas and, therefore, that which you do for fun may not seem to be fun at all. But, for a short time, it will seem to be fun. [What about people who are always looking for a general meaning in everything that happens? Or who can never "cut their losses," but have to throw good money after bad?] [Interpreter stated that he was unable to explain this in Mohave: "It is too complicated for us and for the Mohave language."] [How about compulsive thinking?] The Mohave, when they are intelligent and have a full knowledge of something, keep thinking about it, until it becomes a constant preoccupation with them. This condition is called lyelyedhu: tck hi: wa hakwi:lyk (comprehension or knowledge, heart, to exceed). Let me give you an example of this: Chiefs are thinking day and night of the welfare of the tribe.[49] [That is not the kind of thing I meant. I was wondering whether you knew people who constantly worry about something silly, like a Dickens character about King Charles' head, or the loss of a handkerchief, or the shape of the minister's nose, and suchlike.] I don't think I understand this. There are some people who at times sit in silence and think intently."

Other informants also mentioned the chiefs, and their constant preoccupation with matters affecting tribal welfare, as "examples" of "compulsive rumination" and "obsessive thinking."

Hilyera Anyay's statement (1938).—[Do you know of obsessive acts or thoughts?] Some people who think of doing something (i.e., are making realistic plans), think about it all the time. Eventually they get so that they talk to themselves wherever they are. They call such persons ipa: matum ku:na:và (person, to himself, talk, or prophesy, or institute, or ordain). Sometimes such a person, if he happens to be (have) suma:tc itcem (dreams bad) may go insane. On the other hand, if such a person has suma:tc ahot (dreams good=power dreams), he can become an ipa: taha:na (person real=tribal official). Such pi-ipa: taha:na advise people about the right way of living, and tell them what things are not right.

It is quite obvious that Tcatc's statement, and especially that of Hilyera Anyay, clearly indicate that we are dealing here with an intelligible "Realangst," or "Angst der Kreatur," i.e., with the anguish of man confronted with the great problems and responsibili-

---

[48] Informants, who are trying to figure out an answer, sometimes also resort to a sort of soft monologue, as though they were "testing" their utterances (Devereux, 1949 b, 1949 e).

[49] If one may judge by Lévi-Strauss' (1944) description of the duties of Nambikuara chiefs, the primitive leader carries a heavy psychological load indeed. (Cf. also Devereux, 1951 b.)

ties of life, rather than with neurotic ruminations. Yet, Hilyera Anyay's remark, that such intense thinking or planning may lead either to a neurosis, or else may become a source of success and supernatural powers, depending on one's dreams, firmly assigns the entire process to the unconscious, without suggesting, however, that it is primarily an obsessive-compulsive mechanism. Good dreams are, in this context, indications of a successful sublimation, which harnesses the energy behind anxiety to constructive goals, while bad dreams suggest a failure of sublimation.

NEUROTIC ANXIETY

Hilyera Anyay's statement (1938).—I have known such people, but I cannot tell (recall) their names. Such a person is sane in every way, but there seems to be fear in his heart, a fear of something that he himself does not know. Such people are not very sociable. They keep to themselves and do not seem to know what their worries are. Sometimes they just sit and brood—seemingly over nothing at all.

Tcatc's statement (1938).—People who worry, but don't know what they are worrying about, are hi:wa :ly yamomk him (in their hearts, a little crazy). Such people are not really insane. One can get along with them, but they just worry and worry.

CASE 60 (Informant: Tcatc.):

Ave: Pu:y's daughter G. A. is also that way. They say that she is tcitcekwa :r mâtum (talkative, is-not). (Some Mohave allege that this woman is a kamalo :y, i.e., a psychopathically promiscuous and obnoxious person. Cf. Devereux, 1948 f; and Case 46).

THE HYSTERIAS

There appears to be no general term applied by the Mohave to the various forms of hysteria.

(*1*) *Hysterical laughter, screaming and crying.*—Tcatc stated that such cases do occur. First she specified that such behavior occurred principally in old women, but promptly contradicted herself when describing the behavior of Nyortc Kupu :yà (Case 61), whose attacks began when she was about 20, and tapered off as she got older.[50] "[How do they deal with such crises?] We don't do anything to such a person, except tell her that there is nothing to laugh about. After a while such a person gets terribly tired, lies down and sleeps."[51]

(*2*) *Hysterical anesthesias.*—These occur, according to Tcatc, among old people, and are symptomatic of illness. She was unable, however, to cite a concrete case. It seems extremely probable that she had misunderstood the question and described not true hysterical

---

[50] A decrease in the frequency of hysterical attacks, as the subject grows older, is often characteristic of this neurosis.
[51] Sleep following the crisis occurs both in hysteria and in convulsive seizures.

anesthesias, but disturbances of the sensorium of organic origin, observed in old people.

(*3*) *Echolalia and echopraxia.*—A description of the latah syndrome of the Malay (Yap, 1952) and of the imu syndrome of the Ainu (Uchimura, Akimoto, and Ishibashi, 1938) was given to informants, who were then asked whether such behavior occurred among the Mohave. Hilyera Anyay stated that he had never heard of such seizures and then proceeded to describe a kind of fugue state, which may be hysterical.

(*4*) *Hysterical fugue states.*—Hilyera Anyay said that certain people sometimes just sit still and seem to be almost in a kind of trance. "They do not seem to hear what is being said, nor to see what is being done. At times such a person may get up and move around, and he may talk in such a way that no one understands him (Glossolalia?)[52] They may even grab people by the hair[53] and get into a fight. I have heard of such things happening, but do not know anyone who had this condition."

(*5*) *Globus hystericus and hysterical seizures.*—"[After Hilyera Anyay mentioned the "phantom foreign body" in the vagina of widows suffering from ahwe: nyevedhi: (pt. 4, pp. 128–150), he was asked about the globus hystericus.] It is something that comes upward and chokes them. Then they have a fit (convulsion). They are also unable to urinate.[54] This illness, too, can be treated. [How is that done?] They take young arrow-weed tops, or some greasewood (*Sarcobatus vermiculatus*) branches and warm them by holding them near a fire. Then they put the warm twigs on this hard spot. They also heat water and make the patient drink it. If they are (have) suma:tc ahot (have good dreams, or dream-power), they get well, and their urination becomes normal again."

(*6*) *Charms.*—The presumably hysterical reactions of the owners of charms and magical substances are described in part 4, pages 202–212.

Hysteria is an extremely common neurosis in primitive society. It is therefore quite probable that a number of cases cited in this

---

[52] Glossolalia—the "speaking in tongues"—is known to occur in primitive society (May 1956).

[53] The Mohave club-wielding warriors would grab the foe by the hair and smash his face with an upward stroke of their "potato-masher" clubs.

[54] This specification is of extraordinary interest, since it reveals real clinical acumen. Indeed, unlike epileptics, hysterics usually do not void their urine during their seizures. In fact, this is an important diagnostic criterion in differentiating between epilepsy and hysteria. In addition, the retention of urine during such attacks characterizes especially "retentive" hysterics, who often have what is sometimes called a "spinal cord bladder." Such hysterics may retain their urine for incredibly long periods of time, and must be frequently catheterized. Our Mohave data clearly suggest that the hysterics in question are of the "retentive" type, since, on the one hand, the globus hystericus is "stuck" in the throat and "chokes" them, and, on the other hand, the widow, who remains fixated on her defunct spouse, seeks to retain his phantom phallus in her vagina by means of a muscular spasm.

monograph, which the Mohave diagnosed otherwise, were actually hysterical attacks.

CASE 61 (Informant: Tcatc and E. S.) :

Nyortc Kupu :yhá (to die) was a very nice girl, with beautiful hair. She is said to have been a good singer. (The good singer is very popular in Mohave society.) First she married Hu :kyev Anyay [Case 30], but had no child by him. After his death she contracted another marriage and had a child by her second husband. She died around 1928, at the approximate age of 60. I used to play with her when we were both young. She was roughly 20 years old when her fits began, and became less frequent as she got older. For example, a man once told a funny story . . . I don't recall the story, but it was a very funny one, and we all laughed about it. However, Nyortc Kupu :yhá just kept on laughing and seemed unable to stop. The rest of us tried to stop her, but she just kept on laughing. Finally we just watched her and let her laugh, until she sat down and fell asleep. This happened to her a number of times. She would laugh at anything. This is the only such laughing fit I recall.

Comment

Tentative diagnosis.—Hysteria.

This diagnosis is supported by the cogent observation that the frequency of attacks decreased as she became older, and that her fits of laughing ended with her falling asleep.

CASE 62 (Informant E. S.) :

When I was a student at Sherman Institute, we were rehearsing a play. There were a lot of us, both boys and girls, on the stage. Suddenly one of the boys made a remark about a mouse. He said that one of the directors of the play looked like a mouse,[55] whereupon a Pueblo Indian girl of 17 began to laugh hysterically and could not stop laughing, even when people slapped her and told her to stop it. In fact, she didn't even seem to hear what was said to her. She just laughed and cried, and then laughed and cried some more. Finally they took her to the hospital and put her to sleep. After that she was all right again.

Comment

Tentative diagnosis.—Hysteria.

This story was first told to me in English, and then translated into Mohave for Tcatc's benefit. She was then asked what, if anything, the Mohave did in such cases. Her answer is recorded on page 216. Stimulated by this account, Tcatc then proceeded to describe the case of Nyortc Kupu :yhá (Case 61).

PHOBIC STATES

Classical phobias are characterized by the occurrence of anxiety bordering on panic in the presence of certain situations or objects which the phobic, for idiosyncratic reasons, defines as dangerous. Common phobias pertain to cats, high places, stairs, bridges, enclosed spaces, open spaces, etc., and some of them are known to occur in

---

[55] Victorian ladies were notoriously prone to become hysterical when they saw a mouse, because they were afraid that it might dive under their skirts and run up their legs.

certain Indian tribes (Devereux, 1951 a). True phobias appear to be absent in Mohave society.

Isolated, pseudo-phobic symptoms are, however, known to occur in various mental disorders of the Mohave. Thus, numerous case histories specifically mention a strong aversion to food which, in some instances, borders on anorexia nervosa. Persons and objects habitually dreaded by the Mohave are, likewise, known to appear in pathogenic dreams. These items include: Ghosts, witches, aliens, snakes, blood, secretions, etc. Although all of these items are dreaded, it is of the utmost importance that not one of them is a formally tabooed person or object. This suggests that the lack of genuine phobias in Mohave society cannot be due to the great flexibility of their ritual and taboo system. This is not surprising, since taboos are psychologically more closely related to obsessive and compulsive phenomena (Freud, 1924 a) than to phobias, and, even though severe phobics sometimes also have obsessions and compulsions, the psychological mechanism that actuates obsessive compulsive symptoms is distinct from the one that actuates phobias.

We must therefore content ourselves with pointing out the absence of true phobias, at least among Mohave adults. Whether or not typical childhood phobias occur in Mohave children was not investigated.

THE PROBLEM OF OBSESSIVE-COMPULSIVE STATES

Perhaps the most striking result of the investigation of mental disorders among the Mohave Indians was a negative finding. The most persistent inquiries, fully explained, and illustrated with concrete examples, failed to disclose the occurrence of genuine obsessive-compulsive states. Furthermore, it soon became obvious that, for the first and only time, every single informant failed to grasp the meaning of these questions. Their answers consisted either of a description of the unceasing and vigilant concern of the chief for his tribe, or else of remarks about the "constant worrying" of adults over the major problems of life (pt. 5, pp. 212–216). Since the Mohave did not hesitate to describe any other mental disorder, and since, furthermore, they specifically stated that the symptomatology of many disorders includes a constant preoccupation with, e.g., certain dreams, it is quite evident that the obsessive-compulsive symptoms that I described did not resemble anything known to them. Their answers to my questions are given in part 5, pages 213–216.

These negative findings shed a great deal of light both on the basic orientation of Mohave culture and on the structure of the Mohave basic personality. Were Mohave culture a highly ritualistic one, it would be possible to claim that formal rituals replace individual compulsive rituals (Freud, 1924 a), and represent a standardized defense against the types of anxiety and conflict that, in our society, produce obsessive-compulsive neuroses. However, since Mohave culture constantly under-emphasizes ritualism (Kroeber, 1925 a), it is evident that this explanation fails to account for the striking absence of this well-known Occidental syndrome. Since the inference, that the Mohave are "racially" incapable of developing an obsessive-compulsive defense system is, obviously, an inadmissible one, one is forced to conclude that Mohave culture does not produce the type of anal character structure which, in our own society, may evolve into an obsessive-compulsive neurosis. This conclusion can be substantiated not merely by reference to the fact that toilet-training in Mohave society is both a lenient and a belated one—so belated, in fact, that it overlaps with the early stages of the oedipal period (Wallace, 1948; Devereux, 1951 e)—but also by pointing out that the psychological manifestations of anal retentiveness are consistently penalized by the Mohave, who value generosity almost above any other virtue (Devereux, 1939 b, 1951 e). If this conclusion is correct, then the argument that a genuinely permissive upbringing cannot prevent neurosis seems to stand in need of revision.[56]

The Mohave Indian's total inability to understand the meaning of compulsive acts is exemplified by Hilyera Anyay's remarks.

Hilyera Anyway's statement (1938).—[Do you know people who have some small compulsion, like jingling coins in their pocket, or getting up at night, time and again to check the door, or something else?] People who jingle coins might be called name:hlåk (=willing to do it). As for getting up at night—I just can't seem to understand what you are driving at. There seems to be no term to denote such things. The nearest thing to it might be hi:wantc kunyume: him (=heart changed, doubting). They know that certain things are thus and so, but if they have a feeling that if they do not *see* that things are actually that way—well, this might be called in Mohave hi:wa hak hu:dhauk (=heart??). That is as near as I can come to explaining it to you.

Tcatc's statement (1938).—Some people just do things without knowing it. When a person is that way, they say that he is nyåmmåna:k (habit?). I can't give you an example of such behavior,. because none occurs to me just now.

The Mohave Indians do not seem to be unique in not producing obsessive-compulsive neurotics, since anthropological and ethnopsychiatric sources contain almost no references to this type of neurosis

---

[56] One often hears the statement that the children of early psychoanalytic enthusiasts, who were brought up in a very permissive atmosphere, eventually developed neuroses. This line of reasoning disregards certain crucially important social aspects of the problem. The permissively educated child is constantly rebuked by his contemporaries, teachers, and other associates outside the home. He has a "neurosis of sanity," i. e., he is a "freak" among "well-adjusted" neurotics (Devereux, 1951 a). It is, furthermore, quite obvious that a child growing up in a permissive home is psychologically unprepared to adjust himself to what Jones (1951) calls our "anal culture."

among primitives. One of the rare exceptions is an Attawapiskat Cree of northern Ontario (Honigmann, 1954) who had a handwashing compulsion. As for the Dobuan mentioned by Fortune (1932), whose constant urge to work was exploited by the other members of the tribe, one cannot be certain whether he was a genuine obsessive-compulsive or something else.

The problem of the Yurok (Kroeber, 1925 a; Erikson, 1943) is more complex. Members of this tribe have a basically anal character structure, and devote all their thoughts and actions to the acquisition of money. While their unbridled pursuit of wealth, implemented by many rules and avoidances, is certainly pathological from the psychiatric point of view, we are dealing in their case not simply with an aggregate of individual obsessive-compulsives, but with an inherently sick society, which produces an obsessive-compulsive ethnic character, whose symptoms are provided by Yurok culture itself. Thus, there seem to be three varieties of obsessive-compulsive personalities: The culturally deviant obsessive-compulsive neurotics exhibiting, like the aforementioned Attawapiskat Cree, some concrete and circumscribed non-cultural symptom, such as a handwashing compulsion; the culturally deviant, though sometimes socially somewhat useful, obsessive-compulsive character, who may become an overmeticulous "red tape artist," and, finally, the Yurok representative of a basically obsessive-compulsive ethnic character (basic personality), who, even though he is fully adjusted to society, represents a "group ideal" (Róheim, 1932), and has no idiosyncratic "private symptoms," is nonetheless emotionally sick, because he is generally tense and has fundamentally a high level of anxiety. Ackerknecht's attempt (1943) to dub this latter type of personality "autonormal," though "heteropathological," is an evasion of both psychiatric and cultural realities, and fails to prove that such personalities are not very neurotic (Devereux, 1956 b).

HYPOCHONDRIASIS

Severe and chronic hypochondriasis is often a prodromal stage of acute psychosis. Although serious hypochondriasis seems absent among the Mohave, minor "imaginary illnesses" are known to occur. Thus, a very young girl (Case 46) as well as a middle-aged woman (Case 45) mistook their pregnancies for hiwey lak, while two other women (Cases 24 and 63) greatly exaggerated the severity of their pains and the seriousness of their condition.

The following case was, unfortunately, recorded in such a manner that it does not disclose the sex of the patient. It may, perhaps, be identical with Case 18.

CASE 63 (Informant, M. A. I. Nettle, M.D.) :

One of my Mohave patients may have been a hypochondriac. Unfortunately this patient ran away from the hospital before the diagnostic workup was completed. It is therefore possible that the patient was not a hypochondriac, but had either a pellagra psychosis, or else a toxic psychosis due to an infection of the gall bladder.

It seems worth mentioning that hypochondria is far from rare in primitive societies and may account for the success of many shamanistic cures. The victims of hypochondria are quite often magnificent specimens of health. Thus, I once noticed in a psychiatric hospital a Kiowa Indian, who stood well over 6 feet 2 inches, looked like the archetype of a Plains Indian brave and seemed in splendid health. In reply to my inquiry, his physician told me that he was a chronic hypochondriac.

THE GROUP OF SCHIZOPHRENIAS

A careful analysis of my data indicates (except for Case 31?) a near absence of genuine (chronic) schizophrenia. There occur, however, certain transitory reactive confusional episodes, which resemble schizophrenia but differ from the latter in being of brief duration.

All leading questions regarding schizophrenic symptoms, including even the question, "Did you ever hear of someone who believed himself to be someone else?", were answered in the negative by Tcatc, Hilyera Anyay, and all other informants.

If one accepts the (oversimplified) theory that early oral frustrations play a decisive role in the etiology of schizophrenia, then the prolonged "demand breast-feeding" of Mohave children would, in itself, suffice to explain the absence of schizophrenias. Since, however, schizophrenia also appears to be absent among the orally frustrated Marquesans (Kardiner and Linton, 1939), it is probably preferable to attribute the absence of schizophrenia among the Mohave to the basic structure of primitive culture, which, by its very nature, seems to play a role in preventing the occurrence of genuine (chronic) forms of schizophrenia (Devereux, 1939 d), at least until a primitive society is subjected to massive and oppressive acculturation, as in South Africa. It is true, of course, that the Mohave have become appreciably acculturated in most external ways. However—and this point was agreed upon in a personal conversation with A. L. Kroeber (1954)—the "dream core" of Mohave culture is still relatively intact, so that the essence of that culture continues to be the basic orientational framework of almost all Mohave Indians.

There is, admittedly, the case of a young man of mixed ancestry (Case 64), who was diagnosed by psychiatrists as a catatonic schizophrenic. However, on the basis of an intimate acquaintance with the facts of the matter, I cannot persuade myself that they warrant our regarding his symptoms and general condition as suggestive of a genuine schizophrenia. While it is admittedly extremely hazardous to make a psychiatric diagnosis at a distance, it is my conviction that he simply developed a deceptively schizophrenia-like transitory confusional state, of a type known to occur in primitive society.

On a more general level—and speaking from years of experience with Indians hospitalized in neuropsychiatric wards—I am firmly convinced that, due to cultural differences, also reflected in differences in ethnic character, far too many Indians are wrongly diagnosed as schizophrenics. The following examples will illustrate this point.

(1) One Plains Indian case, so misdiagnosed, was published in great detail (Devereux, 1951 a, and 1951 i).

(2) Another Plains Indian, also misdiagnosed as a schizophrenic, became violent only after being subjected to shock "therapy," but made a prompt recovery when, at my insistence, he was given a brief supportive psychotherapy.

(3) An educated Plains Indian woman, presented at a staff conference, was diagnosed by all nonanalysts, except one, as a schizophrenic, and by all analysts as a hysterical psychosis. A subsequent psychoanalytic study of this woman supported the latter diagnosis (Devereux, 1953 b).

(4) An experienced psychiatrist, who had done a great deal of work with psychotic Indians, told me of a Navaho, who had been locked up in a cell for years, because he was diagnosed as a homicidal paranoid schizophrenic. Yet, when this physician released him from his cell and gave him ground privileges, the patient made a prompt recovery and was able to return to the Reservation (Devereux, 1942 c).

Cases like this could be multiplied indefinitely and force one to express serious concern over the current tendency to diagnose both Indians and other "primitives" (Laubscher, 1937, etc.) far too readily as schizophrenics, on the basis of entirely inadequate data, and also because of a lack of real understanding of cultural and characterological differences. Such misdiagnoses are especially deplorable in view of the fact that, given the financial, and often also linguistic, impossibility of giving "natives" intensive psychotherapy, many of them are unnecessarily subjected to shock "therapy" and perhaps even to lobotomy, both of which appreciably reduce the colorfulness, multidimensionality, and general level of functioning of the patient, and, in most cases, simply make him more "manageable."

CASE 64:

Preliminary note.—For various reasons it was necessary to disguise the identity of the Mohave Indian whom I propose to call "John Smith."

One way of disguising data likely to betray the subject's identity is to distort them, or to replace real occurrences with similar but invented incidents. These means of disguising facts are psychologically unsatisfactory, because every omission, distortion, or substitution affecting the data automatically distorts also the psychological climate of the case history and disrupts the subtle internal logic of the events.

It was therefore decided not to alter the data, but to refer to facts likely to betray the subject's identity in abstract, rather than in concrete terms. For example, a certain older man is simply referred to as a "father figure," which makes it unnecessary to define the precise relationship between John and this older man. Likewise, it was found possible to discuss points of similarity, complementarity, and difference between this father figure's fatal accident and John's own accident proneness, without describing the actual nature of these two sets of accidents. However, in some instances it was deemed necessary to clarify the seemingly paradoxical psychological characterization of some occurrence by citing, usually in a footnote, some comparable incident. Thus, the seemingly puzzling statement that John's unions were sociologically exogamous, but psychologically (affectively) endogamous, was clarified by citing other primitive examples of such complex modes of mate selection.

This mode of disguising the facts has two drawbacks:

(1) The necessity of characterizing certain critical incidents in abstract, rather than in descriptive, terms, forces one to refer to certain simple matters in a complicated technical jargon (e.g., "father figure" replacing a simple kinship term). Much time was spent on editing and reediting this case history, so as to reduce the scientific jargon to an absolute minimum.

(2) The fact that certain details could only be characterized in abstract terms, may arouse the suspicion that, in some instances, I "overstated the case," so as to strengthen the plausibility of my conclusions. I wish to stress that exactly the opposite policy was adopted. Whenever some detail could not be described in straightforward terms, its abstract characterization invariably understates the case. Thus, if it was not possible to say explicitly that two objects were "identical," they were simply described as "similar," etc. Under no condition was a mere "similarity" transformed into an "identity," etc. In brief, had it been possible to describe the relevant facts in straightforward words, the inferences I drew from them would have seemed far more convincing than they appear to be now.

LIFE HISTORY:

For obvious reasons John's life history can only be described in somewhat general terms.

Social life history:

Parents.—John's pregnant mother was deserted by his father, who took no interest in his son, either then or subsequently.

Birth.—Socially speaking, John's birth created appreciable difficulties for John's mother, since neither his father, nor his father's family, contributed to John's support.

Siblings.—For all practical purposes John was an only child.

Psychosexual development.—(See special section devoted to that topic, below.)

Education.—John received only the type of education available to the average Mohave Indian, but, since his family was rather progressive, he successfully integrated his education with the rest of his personality. (See section on Self-definition, below.)

Economic status and work patterns.—During the first eight or ten years of John's life the family was relatively poor. The adults had to earn a living outside the home, so that John was usually alone during the day and had to perform a number of household tasks usually performed by adults. The economic status of the family began to improve when John was about ten years old. However, by then, John had learned to work hard and to show initiative and was therefore able to earn his own pocket money. By the time John was in his late teens, the family was quite prosperous by Mohave standards, John's own industriousness contributing appreciably to its prosperity. Since many Mohave are quite industrious (Kroeber, 1925 a), John's work history differs from that of other Mohave Indians only in that he began to perform useful and responsible work somewhat earlier than other Mohave children.

Unions.—Many Mohave Indians contract several unions before they find a spouse with whom they can settle down permanently. It is therefore significant that at least one of John's earliest unions came to an end through no fault of his own. His most recent and apparently permanent union is characterized by a great deal of mutual tenderness and devotion between the spouses.

Fatherhood.—John's father deserted him before he was born so that the role of the father had to be filled by a certain father figure who, fortunately for John, was a singularly kindly and affectionate person. These facts explain why John eventually turned into a highly responsible and affectionate father, keenly conscious of the duties and pleasures of fatherhood, even in connection with the offspring of a dissolved union.

Social relations.—Despite his childhood temper tantrums (see below), John was most of the time a very nice child, well liked by his playmates, schoolmates, teachers, and by the adult members of the tribe. He grew up into a fine adolescent and man and is today a respected and well-liked member of the tribe, noted for his industriousness, generosity, intelligence, and kindness.

The capacity to love is an important aspect of emotional maturity. John's devotion to his current wife and his lifelong ability to form lasting friendships prove that, in some respects at least, he was always relatively mature. On the other hand, his pattern of mate selection, his lasting attachment to his mother, and his extreme reaction to the death of a father figure suggest that he had to struggle with oedipal fixations even during his early manhood.

Mode of life.—John spent most of his life on the reservation, engaged in pursuits similar to those of other Mohave Indians. His mode of life differs from that of other Mohave Indians chiefly in that, being more prosperous than most, he was able to engage in certain self-destructive and expensive pursuits (see below).

Medical history:

Birth.—Apparently uneventful.

Childhood ailments.—The usual childhood diseases.

Other diseases.—Ordinary minor ailments. One relatively serious illness shortly before his psychotic episode. Recurrent accidents of considerable severity, one of which left him slightly disabled for a few years.

Psychiatric history:

Childhood.—Severe temper tantrums and anxiety dreams (see below).

Adulthood.—Prolonged mourning depression of nonpsychotic intensity, followed by self-destructive "acting out." Psychotic episode followed by complete recovery and by the termination of accident proneness (see below).

SELF-DEFINITION AND EGO-IDENTITY:

(I) *Ethnic identity.*—John's "ethnic" origins, like those of many younger Mohave Indians, are somewhat complex. However, unlike the mixed breeds of earlier years, who were sometimes disposed of at birth (Devereux, 1948 d) or were at least rejected because contact with them was believed to cause illness (pt. 4, pp. 128–150, etc.), John was not discriminated against in any way.

(II) *Sociocultural identity.*—Due to the absence of discrimination, John grew up to think of himself—quite rightly—as a genuine Mohave Indian.

Moreover, precisely because he experienced no discrimination, his Mohaveness was not a defiant or self-vindicating, but a matter-of-fact and generally accepted, self-definition. Thus, John's sociocultural self-definition as a Mohave contrasts with that of some of the older members of his family, who are somewhat insistently Mohave, precisely because, when they were young, it was still hard for a Mohave of mixed ancestry to be accepted by the tribe.

(III) *Body image.*—Once, while talking and kidding with a boy his own age and with a friendly and well-educated older adult, John spontaneously made a series of drawings (pl. 1), which shed a great deal of light upon his "body image" and self-definition at the age of 11 or 12. These drawings, as well as some scribblings which accompanied them, are of some importance, and will therefore be discussed in some detail.

(A) *6×9 ruled sheet (pl. 1, a):*

The center of the sheet is occupied by a head in three-fourths profile, facing left, 3½×4½ inches in size, which makes it the largest head of the series. The drawing is that of a somewhat microcephalic but large-chinned boy, with a curiously distorted tip-tilted nose and a huge chin. The hair is stubbly, i.e., apparently clipped short, which, in Mohave culture, suggests mourning. This inference is confirmed by the four huge tears rolling down the boy's left cheek. The grossly exaggerated Adam's apple has three probable meanings:

(a) *Swallowing.*—This is a plausible inference in the case of a design that shows a person who is apparently mourning, since eating and swallowing fantasies are highly characteristic of mourning depressions in general (Freud, 1925 d), and of Mohave depressions in particular. (Pt. 4, pp. 128–186.) This interpretation also agrees with John's dreams of starving, thirsting, and experiencing oral deprivation in general.

(b) *Choking.*—Suffocation and the feeling of strangling are common in vehement grief and crying. Suffocation plays a conspicuous role in John's dreams.

(c) *Masculinity.*—A developed Adam's apple is characteristic of adult males.

The top of the piece of paper in question is occupied by John's elaborate signature, which, for obvious reasons, cannot be reproduced. It has the following characteristics:

(a) The careful shading of all loops.

(b) The running together of the (English) given name and surname. (As in "Johnsmith.")

(c) The tallest letter is the initial of the given name (1 inch), the next tallest are such "tall" letters as "b" or "f" (¾ inch), and the third tallest letter is the initial of his surname (½ inch) (minimization of surname?). The rest of the letters are only a shade less tall (⅜ inch) than the initial of the surname.

(d) There is some exaggeration of the horizontal elements.

(e) The "signature" ends in a small backward and upward loop, which cuts—with some justification—through one of the last letters of John's surname.

The bottom of the page is occupied by the very awkwardly scrawled given name of one of John's male playmates. This scrawl is so overloaded with very awkward curlicues that it is barely legible, and, if one uses John's own elaborate signature or the drawing as points of reference, it is written "upside down." (180° rotation of paper, clockwise.)

The back of the sheet was written as follows:

(a) *First line.*—The awkwardly written given name of the playmate, and then the very carefully written full name of the playmate, with all loops shaded, much as in John's own elaborate signature on the reverse side of the paper. In this line the words are arranged as follows:

(Playmate's given name) ⎫
(Playmate's given name)   ⎬
(Playmate's surname) ⎭

(b) *Second line.*—The fairly well-written given name and the grossly misspelled last name of the playmate, in a relatively neat writing. The last half of the playmate's given name is partly obliterated by means of the superimposed cipher "0."

(c) *Third line.*—The scribbled given name of the playmate, with the initial written twice, as in "PPeter."

These three lines are parallel with the 9-inch side of the 6 × 9 sheet, and the writing is very large. (Tall letters, 2 inches; short letters, nearly 1 inch.)

It will be noted that, while using this sheet, John had rotated the paper at least twice, after using it in the normal position. While using the paper's front surface, he rotated it clockwise 180° before writing the playmate's given name. Before writing on the reverse side, there was a 45° counterclockwise rotation of the paper.[57]

The fact that the playmate's name was written more often than John's own name is probably significant, and may represent a kind of self-depreciation. By contrast, the repeated misspelling of the playmate's name and its partial obliteration by means of the cipher "0" probably reflect hostile impulses.

(B) *8½ × 11 unruled sheet (pl. 1, b):*

This sheet of paper contains drawings of two heads, an extremely elaborate capital "A" somewhat similar in design to an "Athletic Letter," five of John's normally written signatures, of which only one is really neat, a surprisingly neat quasi-"mirror signature" (i.e., nhoj htims) without capital letters, another legible signature with a crooked arrow pointing at the "sandwich nose" design, the given name of the playmate with a crooked arrow pointing at the "jugeared" design, the genuine signature of another male playmate, a genuine signature of the educated adult, two complete and quite clumsy attempts of John to imitate the adult's signature, plus two attempts at imitating only the first two letters of that signature, and finally, the true "mirror-writing" hand-"printed" surname of the educated adult, written, at John's request, by the adult in question.

(a) *Portrait of playmate.*—In this drawing the playmate has old-fashioned feminine bangs covering the forehead, small "piggy" eyes, a huge, "potato" nose, and a long, thin mouth, with part of the lower lip covered by three huge rabbit-like upper incisors.[58] The entire face, up to the zygomatic arches, is covered by what seems to be a stubbly beard, drawn in a manner which corresponds to the way in which John drew the stubbly hair of his "weeping" self-portrait. The playmate's portrait also includes huge jug ears, practically no chin, a rather scrawny neck covered with stubbles, and a portion of the shoulders, approximately down to the clavicles, clothed in what appears to be a checkered shirt. The facial expression is that of a grinning moron, and probably implies a depreciation of the playmate.

(b) *Self-portrait.*—The head is drawn in full profile and faces left. It is topped by a hat somewhat resembling a "beanie," with uptilted front and rear peaks. The hair is normal. The eyes are wide open and have a pleased but startled expression. The collar is that of a plain white shirt. (Identification with the adult?) The nose, shaped exactly like a frankfurter, juts horizontally

---

[57] For a discussion of Mohave clockwise and counterclockwise circuits, see Kroeber (1948).

[58] The phallic shape of these three incisors is quite conspicuous.

forward and is caught between two objects shaped like long buns. The entire arrangement looks like a so-called "hot-dog bun." The three layers of the "hot dog bun" are tied together with a thin string, whose two loops and loose ends are so arranged that the knot represents two testes and a penis pointing upward. Some fluid drips from the tip of the phallic nose. The tongue protrudes from between the open lips and curves upward, apparently seeking to reach the "hot-dog bun." It is almost impossible to escape the conclusion that this design represents the well-known symbolic equation: nose=phallus (Devereux, 1949 a) and also coitus, the latter being represented by the sausage inserted between the two halves of a bun.[59] The oral element is also markedly conspicuous and may perhaps be related to the Mohave belief that the fetus in utero feeds on semen (Devereux, 1948 b, 1949 c). This inference is somewhat strengthened by the puzzled but pleased expression of the face, and also by the fact that the face is neither entirely boyish nor entirely girlish. The design probably reflects some of John's difficulties in identifying himself wholeheartedly either with his "masculine" mother or with his gentle "father figure."

On the reverse side is a fierce-looking, toothy white (?) (pl. 1, c), with a phallic nose.

Taken as a whole, these drawings and scribblings reflect a rather high degree of anxiety, an oscillation between self-depreciation and the depreciation of the playmate, and a high degree of rather infantile phallic pride which, however, is combined with, and threatened by, markedly feminine incorporative urges. As for the element of grotesque humor, it probably represents a typically Mohave defense (Devereux, 1950 a) against the mourning, crying, and general depression so clearly present in the first self-portrait.

If one examined these drawings without reference to certain Mohave cultural items, such as the belief that fetuses feed on semen, etc., one would probably be tempted to detect in them some of the germs of John's subsequent "catatonic" episode. However, when these drawings are viewed in their cultural context, it seems more likely that John's subsequent decompensation was a "hysterical psychosis" or "transitory confusional state," rather than a catatonia. This conclusion is further supported by the observation that the skill or quality of the handwriting and of the various drawings is highly variable, which suggests that many of John's resources and potentialities were at that time severely inhibited by anxiety, in a typically oedipal-hysterical manner.

NORMAL AND NEUROTIC IDENTIFICATIONS WITH THE PARENT FIGURES:

(I) *Identification with the father figure:*

(1) *General aspects.*—Since John's father had deserted him, he chose to identify himself with an available father figure, a masculine, but also extremely kindly person, to whom John was greatly devoted. Since the mother also had a very high opinion of this man, John knew that he could win her approval by behaving like this father figure. As a result, John too became an extremely kind, warm-hearted, good-natured, tolerant and industrious person, endowed with a genuine sense of humor.

Unfortunately, John's need to identify with a father figure also had certain compulsive aspects, which, later on, forced him to seek to duplicate also this admired father figure's accidental death,[60] for which he gratuitously blamed himself.

---

[59] Some neurotic children are known to visualize coitus as a sausage between the two halves of a bun (Bird, 1958).

[60] It is, moreover, not altogether unlikely that John's marked preference for violently temperamental girl friends (see further below) was also due in part to his identification with this father figure, who was known to have admired John's mother's strong—and occasionally explosive—personality.

(2) *Self-destructive identification with the father figure.*—When John was a young man, he had to be absent from the reservation for highly creditable reasons. His absence obliged the admired father figure to perform, at some distance from the home, a certain economically productive but hazardous task usually performed by young men, whose quick reflexes enable them to retain control of the situation, and which, had John been living on the reservation, he, and not the middle-aged father figure, would have performed. In the course of this activity the father figure sustained fatal injuries, and died before anyone found out that he had had an accident.

This death severely depressed John, probably because he held his absence from the reservation responsible for the father figure's death. As a result, he began to manifest a markedly chaotic and self-destructive loss of self-control.[61] John's chaotic behavior lasted a few months and did not cease until a friend, belonging to the father figure's generation, provided some emotional support and temporarily functioned as a psychological substitute for the deceased. Unfortunately, this did not suffice to eradicate John's excessive mourning reaction. It only suppressed the first chaotic manifestations of John's self-destructiveness, but did not prevent the subsequent appearance of a far less chaotic, but also considerably more self-destructive, form of "acting out," which repeatedly endangered John's life.

Since the nature of these mishaps cannot be stated without revealing John's identity, the discussion will be limited to a characterization of some of the basic similarities, differences, and complementarities between the father figure's fatal accident and John's own recurrent mishaps.

(*a*) The two activities were not aboriginal Mohave pursuits.

(*b*) The father figure's accident fitted his moderate degree of acculturation, while John's accidents corresponded with his relatively high degree of acculturation.

(*c*) In both types of activities events had to be controlled through the rapidity of one's reflexes.

(*d*) The father figure was unable to control the situation because, due to his age, his reflexes were relatively slow. John was unable to control the situation because he usually engaged in this risky activity at a time when his reflexes were slowed down.[62]

(*e*) Both activities necessarily took place at a distance from human habitations. In this context it should be specified that John was most distressed by the fact that the father figure died without receiving help from anyone, because his accident was not discovered until he was dead.

(*f*) Both activities resemble each other not only in objective and descriptive ways, but also in terms of their symbolic significance. In other words, a person who has difficulties controlling some of his basic and violent impulses, could dream either of the type of accident in which the father figure lost his life, or of the type of accident in which John was repeatedly injured.

It may be objected that these similarities might be fortuitous. The best way of disproving this objection is to examine the differences between the two types of accidents and to demonstrate that John's accidents were a "playful" re-enactment of the father figure's accident. These "complementary differences" are the following:

---

[61] Comparable self-destructive losses of self-control following the death of a beloved kinsman are cited in part 7, passim, and especially pages 387–484.

[62] A comparable form of self-destructiveness would be the compulsion to perform strenuous or dangerous tasks preferably when one is feverish or exhausted.

(*a*) The father figure's accident involved a necessary and economically productive activity, while John's accidents occurred in the course of a gratuitous and economically unproductive activity.

(*b*) The father figure's activity was a nontraditional but nowadays commonplace type of performance among the Mohave. By contrast, the activity whereby John repeatedly endangered his own life is without parallel among the Mohave. It is almost as unusual as though he had decided to become a professional big game hunter or bullfighter.

(*c*) The element of risk in the father figure's activity was inherent and unavoidable; in John's activity it was gratuitous and superimposed on the basic activity.

The costliness, unproductiveness, riskiness, and social uniqueness of John's activity thus contrasts with the economic productiveness and routine nature of the activity in which the father figure lost his life. It is this set of "complementary differences" that suggests that whereas the father figure's activity was a normally motivated one, John's activity reflected a neurotic and uncontrollable need to reenact the father figure's death. This finding is completely compatible with, and almost predictable on the basis of, the manifest tendency of Mohave suicides to "cluster," i.e., for one dramatic death or suicide to serve as a model for a second death or suicide (part 7, passim).

(3) *John's accidents seen in relation to his mother.*—John's self-destructive activities were quite expensive, so that he could not have engaged in them had his mother been unwilling to subsidize these activities on several occasions. Since the mother knew that these activities were extremely dangerous, the most obvious, and superficial, "off-the-cuff" psychoanalytic interpretation of her behavior would be that her seeming generosity was actually hostile giving (Devereux, 1956 a), which masked a great deal of unconscious hostility toward her son. It is proposed to show that this off-the-cuff interpretation is not valid, because it disregards basic Mohave ethics, as well as certain traumatic events in the mother's own life.

(*a*) Mohave culture strongly emphasizes the value of generosity, especially toward one's children and toward members of the kin group. This ethical value does not seem to admit any exception to the rule:

Several kindly Mohave, including John's mother, allowed themselves to be exploited by shiftless and selfish relatives because they did not wish to be ungenerous.

Although, due to their lack of mature judgment, children sometimes ask for things they should not have, Mohave parents seldom if ever refuse to give their children whatever they desire. Thus, Hivsu: Tupo:ma clearly implied that even though candy is bad for children suffering from tàvàknyi:k if the ailing child asks for candy, it will be given what it asks for (pt. 7, pp. 340–348).

(*b*) Mohave Indians often react to rejection on the part of their relatives, and especially of their parents, by developing suicidal impulses (pt. 7, pp. 459–484). Moreover, the Mohave believe that three pediatric illnesses, which they define as suicides (pt. 7, pp. 331–356), are caused by the frustration of the child. In brief, had John's mother refused to subsidize her son's self-destructive activities, her refusal would probably have caused John to commit suicide by even more effective and direct means.

(*c*) Subjective psychological reasons made it impossible for John's mother to refuse to subsidize the particular activity her son chose to engage in. In fact, it would have been impossible for her to do so even if Mohave culture did not insist on absolute generosity and even if young Mohave men were not notoriously prone to react to rejection by suicide. Indeed, the refusal of certain members of the mother's kin to help two members of her own immediate family to purchase certain objects that were practically identical with those that John desired led, in one case, to an actual catastrophe, and, in the other case, to a depression that could easily have culminated in a catastrophe.   Hence, though the mother might possibly have refused to help John purchase some other potentially harmful item, she could not bring herself to refuse to obtain for him the object he did, in fact, desire.

In brief, both cultural and psychological factors made it impossible for the mother to refuse to subsidize John's self-destructive activities.

Of course, logically speaking, this does not necessarily mean that, in addition to cultural and general psychological reasons, her compliance with her son's unreasonable demands was not determined also by unconscious hostilities. This, however, is beside the point. What matters here is that the cultural and psychological explanations just offered are based on demonstrable facts, whereas the mother's hypothetical "hostile giving" is not. Moreover, the cultural and psychological explanations just cited represent legitimate psychoanalytic constructions, whereas the explanation that the mother's compliance represents "hostile giving" is simply "pseudo-psychoanalysis by rote," which is as illegitimate in the analysis of anthropological data as in the clinical and therapeutic practice of psychoanalysis.

(II) *Identification with the mother:*

John's relationship with his mother was, if possible, even more complex than his relationship with the father figure, because the mother was the dominant— and almost masculine—member of the household. This meant that, in seeking to achieve masculinity through identification, John was, paradoxically enough, obliged to incorporate into his personality makeup also some of his mother's character traits. At the same time, since the mother was also a truly feminine, though strong-willed and temperamental, person, she was, in some ways, a more than usually possessive mother. Last but not least, as the most significant woman in John's early life, she inevitably aroused in him the oedipal impulses that are an integral part of the psychosexual development of any normal boy. Thus, throughout his life, John was obliged to effect numerous and complex compromises between his identification with his mother's masculine traits, his dependence on her as a mother, and his normal oedipal strivings. This complex situation must be discussed under several headings :

(*A*) Maternal possessiveness
(*B*) Identification with, and imitation of, the mother :
  (1) Positive identification (character traits)
  (2) Identification with the "enemy" (temper tantrums)
  (3) Dreams.
(*C*) Oedipal strivings, as reflected in John's pattern of mate selection.

(*A*) *Maternal possessiveness.*—There are some indications that John's mother was somewhat more possessive than other Mohave women. This is suggested by the fact that—despite John's industriousness and his ability to earn money while still in his early teens—she managed to make him dependent on herself by providing him with certain luxuries, including even the means which enabled him to reenact, in a highly self-destructive manner, the much admired father figure's accidental death. (See above.) It is also quite noteworthy that the mother, who genuinely respected education, made no attempts to encourage her intelligent son to obtain more education than was available on the Reservation, perhaps because she was unable to allow her son to leave her and to become psychologically independent of her. In addition, being herself an admirer of the Mohave way of life, it is likely that she preferred to have her son become a good Mohave, rather than a detribalized, characterologically deteriorated Mohave, obliged to make his way in the white man's world, i.e., in a competitive and materialistic system that is completely uncongenial to the real Mohave.

(B) *Identification with, and imitation of, the mother:*

(1) *Positive identification (character traits).*—John identified himself with his mother by incorporating into his personality makeup some of his mother's most characteristic traits:

(a) He became a goal-directed and practical person, capable of considerable initiative even before reaching puberty and combined this practicality with honesty, reliability, warmth, outgoingness, real generosity, and efficient helpfulness.

(b) Although his formal education was limited to that which was available on the Reservation and in the nearby small town, because of his mother's respect for education he integrated his schooling with the rest of his personality more effectively than most Mohave Indians of his generation. Thus, to take an example almost at random, whereas even those young Mohave, who speak English better than Mohave, handle the English language as though it were a perfectly learned foreign tongue, and the Mohave language as though it were their half-forgotten mother tongue, John, who also spoke good Mohave, spoke English like a native American, and spoke Mohave as though it were the second language of a bilingual person.[63]

(c) Though not as temperamental as his mother, he resembled her a great deal in his reluctance to receive thanks or rewards for his helpfulness. He therefore often did extremely kind things in a somewhat gruff manner, as if to ward off the beneficiary's thanks or tokens of appreciation.

(d) During a certain period of his childhood all adults in the home had to work for a living, so that John was obliged to perform a number of household chores ordinarily performed only by women.[64] Although John resented these onerous tasks and viewed them as part and parcel of the adults' desertion (see section on temper tantrums), he was able to perform them without thereby impairing his masculinity, since most of the housework was actually done by the mother who, functionally at least, was the "masculine" member of the household. This may explain why, despite his obvious masculinity, John later on developed a genuine liking for at least one type of housework.

(2) *Identification with the "enemy" (temper tantrums).*—Between the approximate ages of five and nine or six and ten John had marked temper tantrums, in the course of which he was highly aggressive and destructive. Although some older member of the tribe viewed his tantrums as manifestations of budding shamanistic powers, John's destructiveness was so great that even some of those who believed that he would become a shaman and who were strongly opposed to American ways of punishing children (Devereux, 1950 h) felt that his bouts of destructiveness called for energetic countermeasures. Hence, even though the tolerant father figure sometimes interceded on his behalf with the mother and showed a great deal of good-humored patience, John was sometimes given corporal punishment by his affectionate but quick-tempered mother. John's temper tantrums had at least five significant aspects:

(a) *Getting attention.*—John's tantrums occurred almost entirely during the

---

[63] This type of bilingualism is psychologically quite complex, and was quite common before World War I in the ethnically mixed Austro-Hungarian Empire. The primary tongue is the one in which affective, strongly charged words—such as "mother," "country," "love," "hate," etc.—seem most "real" and most "evocative."

[64] Only three types of Mohave men perform housework: Tribal heroes who, like the Knights Hospitaler, took care of ailing families (K. M. Stewart, 1947 c), middle-aged men married to very young girls (Devereux, 1951 f), and male transvestites (Devereux, 1937 b).

years when, due to an economic crisis, all adult members of the household had to work away from the home. Hence, John not only had to amuse himself all day long, but also had to perform a variety of household chores, which were relatively onerous for a small boy (see above). He therefore craved attention and—since the adults were usually quite tired when they got home after a hard day's work—he soon discovered that he could get a sufficiently massive dose of attention only by making himself obnoxious.

(b) *Retaliation.*—Since John felt "deserted" by the adults, he was quite hostile to them (see dreams) and manifested his anger by means of temper tantrums.

(c) *Expiation of guilt.*—John was extremely angry with the adult members of the household, and therefore harbored strong death wishes toward them. At the same time—as is shown by the terrible things that happened to him in his dreams—he also felt extremely guilty for harboring such wishes, so that, in order to alleviate his feelings of guilt, he had to force his mother and other adults to punish him. However, since Mohave parents only punish children for extreme forms of misbehavior, the only way he could force adults to punish him was to develop extremely destructive temper tantrums, which, needless to say, only made him feel even more guilty. This interpretation of the facts is not only plausible in terms of our data regarding John's temper tantrums, but is also fully compatible with what is known of the dynamics of temper tantrums in general (Devereux, 1956 a).

(d) *Need for external controls.*—The average child learns to control its impulses (temper) by identifying with the adults or with older children who provide certain external controls. Unfortunately, during this crucial period, the older members of the household were absent most of the time, so that John's ego received relatively little external support in its struggle against ego-dystonic impulses. He therefore had to explode periodically, so as to force the adults to provide, in a single massive dose, the amount of external control which, had the older members of the household been present in the home all day long, he would have received in a series of small doses, throughout the day. This "call for help with the control of impulses" is a well-established function of temper tantrums (Devereux, 1956 a).

(e) *Identification with the "enemy"* (Anna Freud, 1946).—Repeated references were made to the fact that John's mother is a fine, generous, warm-hearted but also extremely quick-tempered person, whose sudden explosions frightened John a great deal. In fact, as one of his dreams (see below) indicates, John at times visualized her almost as a kind of ogress, capable of tearing down the house with her bare hands. One way in which a young or psychologically relatively simple individual can protect himself against an ogreish aggressor is to identify with the "enemy," so as to acquire the aggressor's irresistible strength and seeming invulnerability.[65] Otherwise expressed, the threatened individual seeks to turn the tables on the aggressor: He borrows the enemies means, the more effectively to resist his ends. This protective device can also be observed on the social level, where it manifests itself in the form of antagonistic acculturation (Devereux, 1943 a). In brief, in developing temper tantrums John appears to have identified with his mother's sudden outbursts which, to judge by his dreams, must have paralyzed him with fright.

The inferences stated above regarding the dynamics of John's temper tantrums are strongly supported by the following considerations:

[65] Identification with the enemy and the uncontrollable compulsion to imitate his words and actions (echolalia, echopraxia) are highly characteristic of such ethnic neuroses as *latah* (Malay), *imu* (Ainu), and *myriachit* (some Siberian tribes).

(*a*) Even during the years in which he had temper tantrums, John was most of the time an extremely nice boy, liked both by adults and by children and doing rather well in school. This finding suggests that his tantrums represented an admittedly neurotic attempt to come to terms with a difficult situation and to control his impulses. Otherwise stated, John's tantrums appear to have been simple hysterical manifestations, rather than symptoms of a severe disorganization of his personality.

(*b*) The temper tantrums disappeared completely as soon as it became possible for the adults to spend more time at home, and for John—who was by then about 10 years old—to move around more freely by himself, visiting and playing more often with other children.

(*c*) Although, as John well knew, his temper tantrums led many Mohave Indians to expect that he would become a shaman, and would therefore behave even worse during his adolescence, he actually became an extremely nice adolescent, friendly, alert, generous, and responsible in every way, and did not develop into a shaman.[66]

(*d*) Although his internal conflicts were not abolished, he eventually developed sufficient internal controls to "dream out" his conflicts, hostile impulses, and wishes for punishment, instead of having to "act them out" through continued misbehavior.

This last finding leads directly to a closer scrutiny of John's dreams, which were recorded approximately when he reached puberty.

(3) *Dreams.*—The following dreams were dreamed and recorded by John during his early teens and are reproduced verbatim:

(*a*) I dreamed that I lived in a tent near a ditch and there was a girl lived near us that (who) goes to school and there were many children besides her. We were playing on the ditch bank and a storm came and we were laying (lying) together in the ditch and it started to rain and the water came down the ditch and it carry us both and we (were) saw a fall and were just about to go of (off) when they caught us and I woke up and I nearly fell out of bed.

(*b*) My mother and I were home and (the father figure) was gone and left us alone and my mother was crying and she went and tore down the house and left me in the house and she went away, locked me in the house and I stayed in the house two weeks and I was hungry and thirsty and I was choking and I woke up and I couldn't breathe for a long time. Then when I went to sleep I dream I was sleeping in the house and I kept on talking to myself and my mother was trying to wake me up ant (and) it was morning.

(*c*) (The night of November 9–10, 1938) I was home alone and a man told me a lady died. I (it) was a lady named D. S. and we went to the cry house and all of a sudden her hand started to move and she uncovered herself and she had a cement all over her head and to (two) holes for her eyes and mouth. Another boy and I started to go and it (she) started after us and every time I went slower and slower and she caught me and she was choking me and I couldn't breath and I wcke up and I couldn't get my breath back till a long time.

The principal scientific significance of these dreams is that they appear to be the only immediately recorded dream experiences of a non-Occidental who, later on, had a psychotic episode. With the wisdom of hindsight, it is possible to say that the high level of anxiety that is made manifest through these dreams—and also through certain of his drawings (see above)—foreshadows

---

[66] A further reason why John did not become a shaman was that he was too acculturated to do so. This, however, is not highly relevant in the present context.

John's subsequent temporary psychic decompensation. On the other hand the dreams in question seem quite incompatible with the diagnosis "schizophrenia, catatonic type" made by at least one psychiatrist when John suffered a temporary breakdown. They are, however, fully compatible with the diagnosis: "transitory confusional state," i.e., with a type of psychotic episode which is commonly found among "primitives."

The latent content of John's three nightmares is fairly obvious:

(a) The first dream differs somewhat from the other two in being a typical pubertal anxiety dream, reflecting the adolescent's dread of his increasingly intense sexual impulses, which—once they are aroused through "playing" with a girl—become stormy and uncontrollable to the point where both he and his girl friend are carried away by a torrent. The real climax of the dream is the fact that, on waking up, he nearly fell out of bed (= detumescence).

(b) The mother is seen as a potentially destructive ogress.

(c) The dreamer identifies himself with a threatening mother figure (temper tantrums), and betrays this identification by means of a slip of the pen; he writes: "*I* was a lady named D. S." instead of "*It* was a lady named D. S."

(d) He wishes his mother were dead, since D. S., a mother surrogate, appears in dream as being dead.

(e) John's death wishes are partly neutralized by his fear of desertion, although in dream he is deserted by a kindly father figure (= "good mother") rather than by the ("bad, violent") mother, who, however, also deserts him in the end. The experience of being deserted is characterized in dream chiefly in terms of oral deprivation: hunger, thirst, and lack of air.

(f) The fantasied gratification of the death wishes is immediately followed by punishment: The dead mother surrogate turns into a kind of masked ghostly monster and this ghost chases John and his young friend.

(g) At the same time, the dreamer knows that the "monstrous" mother is also a loving mother, since it is she who awakens him from the dream in which she herself behaved like an ogress gone beserk.

(h) The presence of suffocation (or at least of drowning) in all three dreams clearly indicates that the dreams in question are nightmares, whose oedipal nature was conclusively demonstrated by Jones (1931). This finding leads directly to the next topic.

(C) *The mother as oedipal love object.*—A detailed discussion of this aspect of John's relationship with his mother will be found in the section on mate choice, in which the interplay between John's identification with his mother in her "masculine" role and his oedipal attachment to her in her feminine role is analyzed in some detail.

PSYCHOSEXUAL DEVELOPMENT:

Outwardly John's psychosexual development was relatively uneventful and conformed to what is known about the development of sexuality in Mohave society (Devereux 1950 a, 1951 d). He functioned like a normal Mohave male and showed no tendency to become dissolute, or to become involved in scandals, though, like many other Mohave boys, he had performed coitus before he was 10 years old.

However, on a less obvious and deeper level, John's development into a man and his behavior as a man were largely determined by the atypicality of his oedipus complex. Unlike most Mohave children, he was brought up in a home whose dominant adult member was his strong and temperamental mother. The fact that he was nonetheless able to achieve genuine functional masculinity was largely due to his effective identification with a beloved father figure who, despite his real gentleness, was a completely masculine person. On the other hand the fact that, in his childhood, the dominant figure was his temperamental mother, deeply affected his choice of girl friends, as well as his choice of spouses. The relationship of his choice of partners to his somewhat atypical oedipus complex can be discussed under five headings.

(1) *Pseudo-exogamous tendencies in the choice of partners:*

It is a psychological truism that human beings sometimes protect themselves against some ego-dystonic impulse by seeking refuge in its polar opposite. For example, a man sometimes masks his oedipal cravings by developing a marked preference for women as different from his mother as possible. This trend was markedly present in John. Thus, already in elementary school he showed a preference for non-Mohave girls, in a ratio of two or three to one. Subsequently he developed a marked taste for non-Mohave partners, was known to have admired the Japanese-American girls who had been sent to a nearby War Relocation Camp, and contracted only tribally exogamous unions.

John's *ostentatiously nonoedipal* preference for non-Mohave girls appears to have masked markedly oedipal inclinations. He professed to have liked non-Mohave partners because they were aggressively violent in their responsiveness, whereas Mohave girls, although they admittedly do most of the courting (Nettle, MS; n.d.), are trained to be quite passive during the consummation (Devereux, 1950 a). This taste for aggressively violent—i.e., necessarily non–Mohave—partners must be presumed to have strongly oedipal roots, because their violence appears to represent a sexualized version of the mother's explosive temper, which played so important a role in the etiology of John's childhood temper tantrums. Otherwise expressed, John's preference for aggressively violent girl friends suggests that, like many other neurotics, he too dealt with his fear of his mother's explosive temper first by identifying with her and developing childhood tantrums of his own, and later on by "erotizing" his fear of physical aggression and developing a marked preference for violent partners. This inference is strengthened rather than weakened by the finding that he contracted his most durable union with a rather gentle girl, because in that union he managed to gratify his oedipal cravings through more devious means, which will be discussed in the next section.

(2) *Cultural evaluation of John's quasi-permanent mate choices:*

Conformism:

(a) John's real unions carefully conformed to the rule against marrying a member of one's extended family and gens.

(b) John's unions also conformed to the minor Mohave practice of marrying an affinal relative of some member of one's own family.

Rebellion:

(a) John complied so excessively with the letter of the aforementioned mandates that, in so doing, he violated the rule against tribal exogamy, thus exposing himself "self-destructively" to the ahwe: illness (pt. 4, pp. 128–150).

(b) "Accidentally on purpose," he contracted unions which were impeccably and even excessively "exogamous" in terms of the Mohave kinship system, but were completely "endogamous" from the psychological point of view.

The last comment calls for a brief clarification. A union is socially exogamous but psychologically oedipal and endogamous if, for various reasons, the original relationship between the future spouses is emotionally of the familial type. Common examples of such unions are mother-in-law marriages among the Mohave (Devereux, 1951 f), stepdaughter marriages (Kroeber, 1940), and the inheriting of one's widowed stepmother(s), which is quite common in many African tribes. The legitimacy of the view that such socially exogamous marriages are psychologically endogamous ones is strongly supported by the fact that at least one African tribe found it necessary to help the son of the deceased and the dead man's widow(s) whom he inherits, to discard their existing inhibitions and to shift from the asexual "stepson-stepmother" relationship to the "husband-wife" relationship. Customs providing this type of encouragement would not have been invented, had they been unnecessary.

John's pattern of mate selection, which achieved forbidden endogamous ends by means of an overcompliance with the rules of exogamy, represents a well-known neurotic maneuver, which, by means of a "mock overcompliance" with a given rule, reduces that rule ad absurdum, by violating the spirit of the law through too literal a compliance with the letter of the law. Such a neurotic maneuver gratifies forbidden unconscious striving in the very act of "bribing the superego" through an outward compliance with its dictates.

(3) *Psychological evaluation of John's mate choices:*

As stated above, John's mate choices gratified his endogamous oedipal cravings, by means of an overcompliance with rules whose purpose it is to frustrate such cravings, by enforcing exogamy. He did so by imitating his mother's mate choices in several respects.

(a) He chose mates belonging to the precise groups into which his mother had also married, though normally young men tend to imitate the mate choices of father figures.[67] This imitation of the mother's example was presumably due to the fact that in John's own home the mother was the "masculine" parent.

(b) In each instance John had to go rather far out of his way to imitate the example of his mother by contracting extremely exogamous unions which duplicated in every respect the mother's own exogamous unions.[68]

(4) *John's mate choices and his relationship to mother:*

Normally, when a man marries, the bonds between himself and his mother become attenuated. John's marriages were, however, so contrived that, even though they seemed to deintensify his maternal ties, they actually reinforced the bond between himself and his mother. In his last and seemingly permanent union his basic relationship with his mother was actually reinforced by superimposing upon it a further kinship bond.[69]

(5) *John's mate choices and his relationship to father figures:*

While both of John's unions reinforced his relationship with his mother, they also brought him a great deal closer to two father figures. It is possible, and even probable, that this intensification of the bonds between John and certain father figures was not an accidental byproduct of his mate-selection pattern, but one of the many unconscious determinants of John's distinctive mate-selection

---

[67] Compare the well-known song: "I Want a Girl, Just Like the Girl who Married Dear Old Dad."

[68] A fictitious example will help clarify this statement: A son whose mother married first a judge and then a pianist would have to go far afield to marry first a lady lawyer and then a female violinist.

[69] An illustrative parallel is an occurrence from the Sedang Moi village of Tea Ha. When Mbra :o's wife, the mother of his sons, died, he married one of his dead wife's younger sisters, while one of his adult sons married another of his dead mother's younger sisters. This made the son also his father's brother-in-law, while his aunt also became his wife. Thus, the son's marriage doubled preexisting kinship ties both between himself and his father and between himself and his aunt. At the same time they also deintensified the son's ties with his father who now became, in one context at least, his brother-in-law, rather than his father.

pattern.[70] This inference becomes a near certainty once it is realized that John began to seek closer ties with various father figures only after the death of the father figure who had played so decisive a role during the psychologically critical years of his life.

As can be seen, John was extraordinarily successful in achieving a great variety of neurotic-oedipal objectives through a rigorous and even excessive compliance with certain social regulations that seek to frustrate oedipal strivings and to loosen the bonds between a man and his mother, and was able to do so more than once. Moreover, in his last, and most durable, union, he managed to gratify these forbidden strivings even more successfully than in his earlier one. These findings suggest that we are dealing with a genuine psychological pattern and not with mere "coincidences." The subtlety of the maneuvers whereby John achieved forbidden ends through an overcompliance with the rules that forbid these very ends will not startle the psychiatrist, who is accustomed to the subtle and devious ways in which symptomatic behavior effects compromises between forbidden unconscious strivings and the rigid rules of the superego.

PSYCHOTIC EPISODE:

John's delicately poised and extremely complex symptomatic compromises were eventually disrupted by certain external occurrences. These events threatened one of his most vulnerable spots, which, until then, had not been subjected to any kind of trauma.

Predisposing situational factors.—Although John's last union appears to be a permanent one, and is characterized by a great deal of mutual devotion and tenderness, the young spouses experienced a series of severe disappointments related to one of the basic aspects of their union. These events greatly distressed John, who, for no good reason, felt that he was personally responsible for them. Unfortunately it is not possible to state the nature of these disappointments, without revealing John's identity. Suffice it to say that these disappointments were extremely threatening to John's self-definition as a Mohave man, and were, moreover, inextricably intertwined with a variety of oedipal problems and also with the more threatening aspects of his identification with his mother and with the most important father figure in his life. It is also possible that he viewed this series of disappointments as a punishment for a quite minimal derelection that he committed in another, slightly similar context.

Precipitating factors.—While John was still convalescing from a rather serious physical illness, he carelessly and quite unnecessarily overexerted himself and had a brief relapse. While he was convalescing from his relapse, he and his wife once more had to endure a major disappointment, which caused John's wife to become desperately ill at a time when John—himself still a convalescent—was obliged to work extremely hard. Being devoted to his wife, John hardly slept at all for several days; he worked hard all day and nursed his sick wife all night long. As a result of worry, overexertion, and insufficient sleep, John, who was at that time still convalescing from his own recent illness, lost his appetite, and became quite cranky. In brief, by the time John's wife was beyond danger, John was utterly exhausted physically and depleted psychologically. Nonetheless, due to the exigencies of the season, he continued to work extremely hard, though he was occasionally almost in a daze and, by his own admission, did not even know at times where he was. Finally several members of the kin group, who noticed his condition, pressured him into taking some rest. Unfortunately, by this time the prolonged physical and emotional strain

---

[70] A comparable example is marriage with the employer's daughter.

to which John had been subjected made it impossible for him to rest. He suffered from severe insomnia and became more and more disturbed and confused. A very observant Mohave described his state at that time as follows: "He seemed to withdraw from people and did not talk, drink, or eat anything for several days in a row. Even after he began to eat and to drink once more, he was still quite confused and refused to speak to anyone."

John's condition so distressed the members of his immediate family that, despite the objections of their more conservative relatives, who—suspecting an ahwe: illness (pt. 4, pp. 128–150)—wished to consult a shaman, they decided to have John hospitalized.

Admission.—After considerable efforts, John was admitted to a reputable public psychiatric hospital, which, like nearly all public psychiatric institutions, was both overcrowded and understaffed. Since John's mutism prevented him from giving the admitting official the necessary information, he was placed for several weeks in a ward for deteriorated schizophrenics.

The milieu.—The Mohave who visited John in the hospital were horrified by the atmosphere of this "back ward," though this ward was infinitely better than what one sees in many public institutions. As for John, he was so depressed by his environment, that when he began to talk once more, he asked one of his visiting Mohave relatives: "What have I done to be put in such a place?"

Psychotherapy.—Since John did not respond to the ward psychiatrist's initial attempts to obtain a case history from him and since many Western hospitals appear to operate on the assumption that it is impossible to communicate with Indian psychotics, including even those who, like John, speak English fluently, he was given no formal psychotherapy. This decision appears to have been both injudicious and overly pessimistic. Indeed, when a kindly hospital employee—who held an advanced degree in one of the auxiliary medical professions, but was not a qualified psychotherapist—took an interest in him and encouraged him, day after day, to ventilate his problems and anxieties, John proved to be quite accessible, although he continued to remain aloof from the ward psychiatrist. It is extremely probable that John's recovery was largely due to the effort of this interested and kindly employee.

Other "therapy."—Like most not immediately accessible psychiatric patients, John was subjected to a type of "therapeutic" intervention that is routinely used in all but the very best—and most expensive—psychiatric hospitals.[71] Fortunately for John, he does not appear to have been given a so-called "full course" of this type of "treatment," since he emerged from it without any flattening and discoloration of his personality.

Visitors.—While in this hospital, John was periodically visited by certain members of his family and it is to the credit of the hospital that these visits were facilitated and encouraged by the staff in every way.[72] A Mohave who visited him during this period reported that John could not accept the reality of the disappointment which had precipitated his breakdown; i.e., in psychiatric terms, John dealt with this trauma by denial, "not remembering" it.

Remission.—After a relatively short period of hospitalization John began to improve quite rapidly, and, according to an observant Mohave visitor, "seemed to be himself most of the time," although he was still somewhat confused at times and occasionally still attempted to deal with the precipitating trauma by means of denial. However, a few weeks later he ceased to be confused, accepted the reality of the traumatic occurrence, and recovered sufficiently to

---

[71] For a critical evaluation of this type of treatment see the section on Diagnosis, below.

[72] Indian patients, especially if they do not speak English, rapidly deteriorate in mental hospitals, due to the impossibility of forming real relationships with the staff and with the other patients (Case 65).

be returned to the reservation on a so-called "trial visit," which was eventually changed into a formal discharge from the hospital as "recovered."

Convalescence.—During the first weeks following his return to the reservation John still tired rather easily, but gave the impression of being fairly happy and no longer psychotic in any respect. At the same time, those who knew him best felt that he still was not quite "his own self."

Recovery.—John's complete recovery, as distinct from a mere remission, appears to have been brought about by two, objectively very distinct, but psychologically closely interrelated, events:

(*1*) An extremely fortunate development in John's marriage strengthened the very foundations of his union, put an end to the series of disappointments which had precipitated John's psychosis and demonstrated in a conclusive manner that he need not have blamed himself for the earlier disappointments.

(*2*) John had one last—and this time near-fatal—accident, which differed from his previous mishaps in one, descriptively minor but psychologically highly significant, detail that mercilessly highlighted the unconscious purposiveness of his accident proneness. It occurred at a time when his reflexes were *not* slowed down. This accident restricted John's behavior pattern in two ways:

(*a*) The shock of this near-fatal accident had a sobering effect on John, who suddenly realized that his next accident could very well be fatal and would prevent him from enjoying the recent and long hoped-for improvement of his marital situation.

(*b*) The near fatal outcome of his last accident apparently made John feel that he had, at long last, atoned for the father figure's death and was therefore no longer obliged to follow him into the beyond.[73] This, in turn, enabled him to transform his infantile-oedipal commitments into mature ones, thereby achieving a genuine psychological adulthood.

Degree and permanence of the recovery.—Today, several years after his discharge from the hospital and his last accident, John is, in the very best sense, once more his own self. He is no longer accident prone and shows no residual psychic stigmata of any kind. He is the poised, effective, industrious, responsible, and warmhearted head of a happy family and a useful and respected member of the tribe, leading a calm and relatively uneventful life. These findings suggest that he made a complete and permanent recovery, and oblige us to reevaluate the diagnosis that had been made during his hospitalization.

DIAGNOSTIC PROBLEMS:

Symptoms.—The hospital's diagnostician noted withdrawal and mutism, resistiveness, catatonic posturing, bizarre behavior, and hallucinations. It is likely that the degree of John's withdrawal and negativism was overestimated by the diagnostician, who was probably unfamiliar with the Mohave Indian's aloof distrust of whites. It is also possible that some of John's so-called "catatonic posturings" were simply traditional Mohave kinesic patterns, which probably included the distinctive and traditional Mohave sitting position (Kroeber, 1925 a), certain typical Mohave gestures (Devereux, 1949 b, 1951 c), etc. The absence of any reference to "delusions" is, if possible, even more significant, since the beliefs of Indian patients are very often listed by diagnosticians as "delusions" (Devereux, 1951 a). Hence, the absence of any reference to delusions strongly suggests that communication between John and his diagnostician was quite minimal.

---

[73] Despite the marked tendency of Mohave suicides to occur in "clusters," no Mohave ever tried to commit suicide twice.

Even more disturbing is the fact that, with the sole exception of delusions, the list of symptoms includes every single symptom characteristic of catatonia. Otherwise stated, the clinical description of John's "catatonia" is simply too perfect to be convincing, since it is a well-known psychiatric fact that the "classical textbook case" is the exception, rather than the rule, except in the case of the so-called "ethnic psychoses" which are strongly prepatterned by the cultural matrix in which they occur (Devereux, 1956 b). Since true catatonia is not an "ethnic psychosis" of the Mohave, it is hard to see how John—who is psychologically a genuine Mohave—could have developed a textbook case of catatonia. On the other hand the list of John's symptoms is perfectly compatible with a textbook case of "transitory confusional state (hysterical psychosis)" which is a genuine ethnic psychosis not only among the Mohave (pt. 2, pp. 50–54), but also among most other primitives.

Psychiatrist's diagnosis.—Acute schizophrenic state (catatonic type).

Mohave diagnosis.—Uncertain. Some relatives suspected an ahwe: illness.

Suggested correct diagnosis.—Transitory confusional state (hysterical psychosis) dynamically related to the hysterias. This diagnosis is based on the following considerations:

(1) *Pattern of life history.*—The nature of John's childhood tantrums, the character of his anxiety dreams (nightmares), the marked preponderance of oedipally motivated "acting out" over preoedipally motivated "acting out," adequate sexual-emotional functioning, the presence of genuine and lasting friendships, the formation of at least one meaningful, tender, and durable union, adequate functioning as a father, and the nature of the traumata that precipitated the psychotic break.

(2) *Personality structure.*—An outgoing and friendly disposition, the absence of shyness, withdrawal or compensatory pseudomanic hypersociability, the capacity to love, noncompulsive industriousness, a nonobsessive sense of responsibility, the absence of ruminative tendencies, the capacity for realistic initiative, and the absence of excessive preoccupation with dreams and dreamlike autistic experiences. The latter trait is especially significant, since, had John been autistically inclined, both the shamanistic tenets of his culture and the knowledge that, because of his tantrums, many Mohave expected him to become eventually a shaman, would have facilitated the emergence of autism, had such proclivities been present. What neurotic traits John did have were largely hysterical in character.

(3) *The sudden onset and short duration of the psychosis.*—Although modern psychiatry no longer subscribes to Kraepelin's (1919) thesis that chronic mental illness is practically synonymous with "dementia praecox" (schizophrenia), on the whole a psychosis of short duration, with a sudden onset, and with highly dramatic symptoms is not—or should not be—diagnosed as a schizophrenia, unless a scrutiny of the patient's premorbid life history and personality makeup discloses the presence of markedly schizoid traits. Since such traits cannot be found in John's premorbid personality and life history, the short duration of his psychosis militates against the diagnosis "schizophrenia." Otherwise expressed, the present writer agrees with many dynamic psychiatrists in questioning a recent tendency to label certain forms of hysteria and manic-depressive psychosis as schizophrenias of the hysterical (or manic-depressive) type.

(4) *Degree of recovery.*—During his psychotic episode John was subjected to a type of "treatment" which, in the opinion of many competent dynamic psychiatrists, does not resolve the patient's internal conflicts, but simply suppresses their outward, symptomatic manifestation, by bringing about a radical im-

poverishment and flattening of the patient's personality. Otherwise stated, whenever the disappearance of a schizophrenic patient's symptoms is actually due to this type of intervention, the patient's post-treatment personality is invariably impoverished, colorless, nuanceless, and relatively sluggish, both in the sphere of the emotions and of imagination.[74] Hence, had the disappearance of John's symptoms been due to the type of treatment he received, his postmorbid personality would have been little more than a flattened and discolored version of his premorbid personality. Since this did not happen, one is obliged to conclude that John had—fortunately for him—not received enough such treatments to cure his alleged "schizophrenia" in the only way in which such treatments "cure" the schizophrenic: by impoverishing his personality, in order to flatten out and to deactivate his symptoms. His recovery was therefore presumably due to something else than the treatment he had received, i.e., presumably to the fact that, during this emotional crisis, he was able to abreact and to ventilate the conflicts of a lifetime and the anxieties aroused by the precipitating trauma in one massive act of catharsis—an inference which is strongly supported by the fact that John's last remaining symptoms disappeared shortly after his near-fatal accident. If this interpretation of John's recovery is correct, it almost automatically excludes the diagnosis of schizophrenia, and strengthens the proposed diagnosis of "hysterical psychosis," since such a massive temporary decompensation and catharsis sometimes suffices to alleviate the symptoms of a hysterical type of disorder, but not those of a genuine schizophrenia, and especially not to the point where one is entitled to speak of a genuine recovery, as distinct from a mere remission.

In view of the preceding considerations, the diagnosis of an "acute schizophrenic state (catatonic type)" seems untenable. On the other hand, these considerations are fully compatible with the diagnosis of a transitory confusional state (hysterical psychosis), of a type which is known to be extremely common in tribal societies.

CONCLUSIONS:

The present case illustrates the etiological significance of culturally atypical traumata and techniques of education, whose impact, because of their atypicality, cannot be counteracted by culturally provided readymade defenses (Devereux, 1956 b). The patient's mother is a very progressive Mohave, whose personality is, in some respects, different from that of the run-of-the-mill Mohave. Her cultural atypicality was further underscored by the fact that the principal father figure was an almost ideal Mohave personality. This combination made John's education confusing in the extreme. Hence, even though older people expected John to become a shaman, the atypicality of his conflicts—like those of other young Mohave Indians—made this type solution wholly unattractive for him (Devereux, 1956 a, 1957 b), quite apart from the fact that, due to his acculturation, he did not sincerely believe in shamanism, so that he could not even have been effectively treated by a shaman. By contrast, despite his acculturation, John was psychologically still sufficiently a Mohave—rather than a white man "gone native"—to develop the typically archaic psychiatric condition: "transitory confusional state" followed by a complete remission, instead of developing a true chronic schizophrenia, such as a similarly traumatized member of our own culture might have developed.

---

[74] At a time when the now obsolete metrazol convulsion treatment was still in use, some dynamic psychiatrists spoke of patients subjected to a full course of metrazol convulsions as "the zombies."

Appendix 1.   A Havasupai Case
CASE 65:

X STATE HOSPITAL, CLINIC SUMMARY:

Havasupai Indian.
Diagnosis.—Dementia praecox, hebephrenic type.
The above-named patient was admitted to this hospital on April 20, 1929, and is (years later) still an inmate in this institution.
Personal and family history.—This young Indian boy, who is a ward of the Government, is totally inaccessible. He sits around the ward and laughs, smiles, and grins in a silly fashion. He also has some mannerisms.
Mental examination.—When spoken to, he will answer with a silly grin; otherwise, it is impossible to get him to answer any questions whatsoever. Considering the history that he gave on his admittance paper, and his general appearance and actions since being in this institution, it is felt that this is undoubtedly a case of dementia praecox—hebephrenic type.
Neurological examination.—The neurological symptoms are negative, with the exception that his pupils are inclined to be dilated, ovoid, and rather irregular. This dilated and ovoid condition of the pupils is found very frequently in the dementia praecox conditions, and especially in this type.
Physical examination.—Physically, he is in excellent condition and does not show somatic pathology of any kind.

Comment

On being told that this young patient had been unable to speak to anyone for approximately 9 years, because no one in that Hospital could speak the Havasupai language, I asked him in the related Mohave tongue one or two questions. Although the patient did not reply, his face lit up with so happy a smile that the physician felt impelled to remark that, as far as he knew, this was the first time this patient had ever shown any sign of an appropriate reaction. The tragedy implicit in this case is too obvious to stand in need of discussion.

Appendix 2.   Two Yuma Cases
CASE 66:

A.B., a Yuma Indian, had to be hospitalized in X State Hospital.
Diagnosis: Unknown.

CASE 67:

A. H. M., a Yuma Indian woman, had to be hospitalized in Y State Hospital.
Diagnosis: Unknown.

Comment

The need for hospitalization suggests in both cases the likelihood of a pseudo-schizophrenialike condition—probably a transitory confusional state, aggravated and made chronic by hospitalization away from the tribe.

MANIC-DEPRESSIVE PSYCHOSIS

According to Tcatc "Some people alternate between excitement and depression. This is brought about by too much worrying. This worrying goes to the point where they are almost out of their minds."

The shaman Hilyera Anyay also heard of cases in which manic attacks alternated with depressions:

They seem to be taken up by some thought and seem very sad and quiet. At other times they are so excited that they even get into quarrels and fights. [Is there a flight of ideas?] No—they just pick arguments with people, but do not pour out words. This disorder is closely related to hi:wa itck (pt. 3, pp. 71–106).

The meagerness of data concerning manic-depressive psychosis is doubly significant. On the one hand it shows that mood swings must be excessive indeed before the characterologically cyclothymic Mohave consider them in any way abnormal. On the other hand the "manic-depressive psychosis" of one of the rare Mohave who was sufficiently disturbed to require hospitalization, was believed to have been caused by his unwillingness to admit that he possessed shamanistic powers, and to use these powers (pt. 2, pp. 57–71). The Mohave Indians' casual acceptance, and even institutionalization, of extreme mood swings may, thus, explain why acute manic-depressive psychosis is so rare in this tribe, especially in its manic phase. On the other hand, it explains also why depressions, with or without anorexia, seem to be the characteristic "ethnic psychosis" (Devereux, 1956 b) of the Mohave Indians.

ARTIFICIALLY INDUCED STATES OF DISSOCIATION: ALCOHOLISM, DRUG ADDICTION, AND TRANCE

Habitual drunkenness and occasional bouts of intoxication are known to occur in Mohave society. Since Mohave alcoholism is fully described in a special Appendix (pp. 505–548) it is not discussed in the present section.

Drug addictions are unknown, and no extreme addictive craving for tobacco, such as is known to occur among the paleo-Siberian tribes (Bogoras, 1904; Sverdrup, 1938), was reported from the Mohave. Peyotism is also absent.

Nonritual "intoxication" by voluntary temporary self-suffocation, causing anoxemia, which occurs among the Groenland Eskimo (Peter Freuchen, personal communication), is also absent, though suicide by suffocation (Case 123) does occur, as does the inducing of trance by such means (pt. 7, pp. 426–431).

Temporary trance states, many of whose symptoms are somewhat similar to those of intoxication, are rare, and occur only in a ritual context; for example, in divining the whereabouts of a person lost in enemy territory. Since the Mohave do not consider such a (suffocation) trance state to be a mental disorder, it is discussed in this monograph in a different context (pt. 7, pp. 426–431). It should be stressed, however (Devereux, 1956 b), that the fact that a given form of abnormal behavior is socially sanctioned and exploited does not mean in the least that it is not psychopathological in the strictest sense of that term.

PSYCHOPATHY

Few nosological concepts are as controversial as psychopathy, sociopathy or constitutional psychopathic inferiority, perhaps because social circumstances and consequences play so great a role in the evaluation and diagnosis of persons who give the clinician the initial impression that he is dealing with a "psychopath."

In most cases, the psychopath has no obvious symptom beyond that of being chronically "in trouble" with society. Speaking in a general way, nothing in particular and everything in general is wrong with him. Sometimes he gives the impression that he is unable to control his impulses, an observation which underlies the diagnostic label "impulse-ridden psychopath." The correctness of this designation has been challenged elsewhere (Devereux, 1951 g) and an attempt was made to show that the "impulse-ridden psychopath" is, in reality, a "defense-ridden psychopath." The provocativeness of the psychopath, while pronounced, is, likewise not uniquely characteristic of him, since it can be shown (Devereux, 1940 a) that "social negativism" is a fundamental characteristic of all symptoms. The general instability of the psychopath is striking indeed, but can be easily misdiagnosed if one disregards the social situation. Thus, a certain Negro was first diagnosed as a psychopath, on the grounds that he had held some 15 jobs between 1929 and 1939. This justification of the diagnosis "psychopathy" became untenable, however, once it was pointed out that 1929–39 were depression years, when Negroes were the last to be hired and the first to be fired. Hence, the fact that this Negro patient managed to find and hold 15 jobs during that period suggested not psychopathy but extreme energy and ingeniousness.

Hence, I urged elsewhere the view (Devereux, 1953 b) that the psychopath's one truly unique characteristic may be his ability to manipulate *for his own selfish ends* the cultural loyalties of others, without his having any cultural loyalties of his own.

On the whole, psychopathy appears to be a relatively rare disorder among primitives. A systematic search of the anthropological and ethnopsychiatric literature, over a period of 28 years, for case material on mental derangements among primitives, yielded only a negligible number of possible cases of psychopathy. By contrast, the psychopath is a relatively conspicuous predator in occidental society. It is therefore tentatively suggested that psychopathy may be one of the typical "ethnic neuroses" (Devereux, 1956 b) of our civilization, or, perhaps, of higher cultures in general.

Be that as it may, there appears to be one Mohave family of the Mah gens, many of whose members could, loosely speaking, be classified as psychopathic. They have a record of brazen incest, witchcraft, and troublemaking, and are generally suspected and disliked by the rest of the tribe. Their objectionable activities often have a marked quality of wanton provocativeness, of a seemingly inexplicable "impulsiveness" and instability, etc., that might induce Occidental psychiatrists to diagnose them as psychopaths. Since the proper diagnosis of the various members of this family cannot be adequately settled in this work, we simply propose to list the incidents in which members of this family appear to have been involved over a period of several generations:

Incest:

Mah (Devereux, 1939 a)
Yellak Hi :ha (=grebe spittle) and Atceyer Hita :pk'à (=bird brought-over, or bird put-in) (ibid.)

Incest and robbery:

See Case 15.

Maladjustment in childhood:

See Case 77.

The responsibility for diagnosing, or not diagnosing, this family as psychopathic is, thus, left to the reader. By ordinary clinical criteria they may be diagnosed as psychopaths and Mohave society does view them as chronic troublemakers. On the other hand, they do not fully satisfy our criterion that the psychopath is a person who, having no cultural loyalties of his own, predatorily exploits the cultural loyalties of others for his own selfish ends, because several members of this family appear to have been *bona fide* shamans, which is proof of a certain degree of social and psychological conformity, and/or potential witch killers, which is indicative of a certain degree of (possibly misguided) cultural loyalty and sense of responsibility toward the tribe.

The fact that we are dealing here not with a single individual, but with a whole lineage, also suggests a certain degree of conformity, at least on the primary group level, since no really convincing case has ever been made for the assertion that "psychopathic inferiority" is truly constitutional, or hereditary.

In brief, the diagnosis of this lineage is left open. It is simply noted that various members of this lineage were reputedly engaged in a series of antisocial acts and that the lineage as a whole is therefore more or less in disrepute. The real psychiatric meaning of this finding is a moot question both on the clinical level, because of a lack of really adequate data, and on the theoretical level, because of the basic inadequacies of current concepts of psychopathy. The one thing we can be sure of is that neither the concept of delinquency (pt. 6, pp. 260–285) nor the concept of "patterns of misconduct" (Linton, 1936) is broad enough to cover all the misdeeds ascribed to members of this lineage, especially if we consider that one of these men, Yellak Hi:ha (commonly called Lakiha) was, despite his bad reputation, called in by Tcatc to treat her when she had the measles, while the incestuous Mah was, in 1938, considered to be an effective healing shaman as well as a witch, as was Mah's brother C. N., "because the power to be a shaman runs in this family." [75]

TICS

A tic, according to Tcatc, is called ave:tc kådhonk, which means "mouse dig-in" or "bury-in." This condition was treated by shamans who had sumatc ave:tc kådhonk power. The last shaman, who died long before 1938 and who knew how to treat this disease, was Tcåvåkye: (to bring a boat ashore) of the Tcatc gens. He was a first cousin of the blind half-Cocopa man Hi:dho (eyes).

Three case histories were obtained. Although all three were diagnosed as ave:tc kadhonk, it is certain that only the first (Case 68) was a genuine tic. The other two seem to be involuntary or idiosyncratic movements of the eyelids.

CASE 68 (Informants: Tcatc and E. S.):

Tånyo: (to do it repeatedly) of the O:otc gens, a married man approximately 40 years of age, had a tic since childhood. It consisted of occasional spastic movements of the face.

Comment

Tentative diagnosis.—Facial tic.

The other two cases which Tcatc and E. S. diagnosed as ave:tc kådhonk cannot, by any stretch of the imagination, be considered as genuine cases of tic. They are therefore not presented in the form of numbered case histories, but as part of the main text, and as examples of "lay" (i.e., non-shamanistic) misdiagnoses pertaining to a very minor defect:

(1) "W. W., of the Mah gens, has no Mohave name. He is the cousin of your friend Sumurâmurâ. For some 4 or 5 years past he has tended to close his eyes involuntarily. [Is he under strain at such times?] I don't think so . . . he does not seem to be having any difficulties."

(2) "Matha:tc Nutuhu:lyk (wind blow) of the Matha:tc gens, used to close her eyes spasmodically whenever she coughed."

Both of these pseudotics are, obviously, simple reflex actions.

---

[75] Apen Ismalyk (Case 4), who refused to become a shaman, and therefore became psychotic, was also related to this lineage. In fact, this relationship was cited in support of the supposition that he had obtained shamanistic powers in dream.

CHOREA

Since it is notoriously difficult to describe a choreiform seizure in words, I simply imitated a person known to me, who had Huntington's chorea, and then asked my informants whether they knew anyone having such symptoms.

Tcatc said that this type of disorder was unknown among the Mohave, but Hilyera Anyay declared that such cases do exist.

I have seen some people act that way, but I cannot recall their names. These people have died, and I don't think about the dead.[76]

CASE 69:

A Yuma informant, Barney Jackson, then visiting Parker, Ariz., stated that a Yuma Indian was known to be suffering from this disease.

SPEECH AND HEARING DISORDERS

It is not in the least surprising that a tribe that admires orators and skillful conversationalists (Devereux, 1949 e) should equate deaf-mutism with yamomk, i.e., with psychosis. This viewpoint was expressed with great clarity by the shaman Ahma Huma:re (1938):

Suppose there is a person who is mute, or a person who goes insane from (hahnok) sickness. There is one, and only one, name given to this. When we describe insane acts, we use the term "yamomk." That is all.

Even when discussing the general problem of the etiology of mental disorders Ahma Huma:re systematically equated psychosis with muteness:

Insanity, the way I have been told about it, is known (revealed) in two ways. One way is that a person does not talk, but uses signs instead. Such a person is called "crazy." Then there is an insanity caused by (hahnok) sickness. Should the Mohave intermarry with their relatives, there will, in some cases, be mutes among their offspring. These mutes are understood by their parents and by such of their relatives as may be living with them, but they are the only ones who can interpret the signs which such persons make. The Mohave believe that a person who is that way (i.e., mute) is merely fulfilling a kind of prophecy given to the Indians: (It was instituted at the time of Creation that) persons who marry their relatives will sometimes have mute offsprings. The Indians call these mute persons "yamomk" (insane). (Pt. 5, pp. 251–253.)

Speech disturbances may be due to a variety of causes:

Supernatural causes:

The Mohave believe that no one is able to climb "Superstition Mountain" (Avikwame). According to Hivsu: Tupo:ma—

They say that some whites, who tried to climb this mountain, lost their way and died, despite the fact that a search had been organized to find them. In

---

[76] It is taboo to mention the names of the dead (Kroeber, 1925 a).

fact, it is dangerous even to dream of climbing Avikwame. Should one dream that one has climbed to the top of this mountain, one also dreams that, on reaching its top, one suddenly goes up into the air and disappears. This dream will cause the dreamer to become deaf and dumb.

Incest:

See page 48.

Perverted act of pregnant woman:

Another cause of congenital muteness is oral cohabitation (Devereux, 1947 a) with a pregnant woman. This act is believed to damage the child's "throat-cap" causing it to be born mute. It seems probable that this belief reflects unconscious aggressive wishes directed at the unborn child (Devereux, 1949 c).

CASE 70 (Informants: Hivsu: Tupo:ma and Hama: Utce:) :

A group of men found a notoriously alcoholic pregnant woman in a state of intoxication and cohabited with her serially. In due time this woman bore an almost mute daughter.

Comment

The sexual abuse of intoxicated women is quite common in Mohave society (Devereux 1948 i, 1950 a). Since this woman was sufficiently intoxicated to be nearly unconscious, she could not have performed fellatio. Moreover, even though the birth of an almost mute daughter is the whole point of the narrative, the story itself does not specify that fellatio had, in fact, taken place. If it did not take place, one is forced to assume that the Mohave attributed the daughter's defect to the abuse to which her mother had been subjected and/or that the fetus was damaged by being (forcibly "overfed," since the more developed fetuses are believed to feed on sperm injected into the womb (Devereux, 1948 b).

CASE 71 (Informant: Hivsu: Tupo:ma) :

On February 9, 1933, Hivsu: Tupo:ma introduced me to an allegedy feeble-minded and almost mute girl, whose condition was said to be due to the fact that her mother, while pregnant with her, had performed fellatio. However, she did not impress me as being feebleminded, nor did she seem to have any of the more obvious stigmata of hereditary syphilis. This girl was also mentioned to me by the late M. A. I. Nettle, M.D., as one of the few mute Mohave Indians.

Comment

It is possible that this case is identical with Case 70.

CASE 72 (Informant: Hilyera Anyay) :

Hu:piny (called Opinynya by the Americans), who lives at Needles, is dumb. He is single and has no children, but did have sexual relations with women, as is shown by the fact that, on a certain occasion, he had contracted a venereal disease (hiku:pk). [Was this man dumb because his pregnant mother had performed fellatio?] Of course; that is what we believe. [Does anyone actually know that she had performed this act during her pregnancy?] No—but her son's muteness proves that she had done so.

Comment

Although Kroeber (1948) rightly stressed that Mohave myths seldom if ever describe sequences of events in terms of the logical sequence: "because . . . . therefore," the present case history vividly demonstrates that, in "medicine" at least, the Mohave shaman not only thinks in terms of cause and effect, but is intellectually bold enough to infer the cause from the symptom in terms of a clear-cut etiological frame of reference. The fact that Mohave theories regarding the causes of congenital dumbness happen to be incorrect must not be permitted to obscure the fact that the Mohave shaman was capable of evolving a type of reasoning—etiological reconstruction—which is an empirically validated and practically indispensable mode of reasoning also in modern, scientific medicine.

Since incest, as well as attempts to harm unborn children, are severely condemned by the Mohave, muteness, which sometimes also results from the violation of other pregnancy taboos (Devereux, 1948 b), causes considerable concern to the Mohave.

Hilyera Anyay's statement (1938).—Some women bear children who do not cry even at birth. Such a child never cries. When given commands, the child can carry them out, but when you ask it anything, the child only uses its hands, making signs. I myself have seen such children. They grow up to be men and women, but they never talk. However, their children need not be dumb. It is not inherited. Now I am going to tell you about such a person (Case 72).

Stammering:

Stammering is called tcakwar itu :r.

CASE 73 (Informant: Pulyi :k) :

Tuhum Hiwey (=drygoods' anus) stammers.

Temporary aphasia due to overexcitement:

Tcatc's statement (1938).—[Do you know of anyone who temporarily lost his speech, due to overexcitement?] If people are asked bad (obscene) questions of a kind they are not accustomed to answer, they will hardly be able to find the right words.[77] [The question was repeated, with further explanations.] I know what you mean. I heard of such a case.

CASE 74 (Informants: Tcatc and E. S.) :

Hispan Tcáliyak (vagina open), of the Nyoltc gens, must have been about 50 or 60 years old in 1875 or thereabouts. He had a house at Parker, just west of where the church now stands. One night his house burned down and when people came running and asked him what had happened, he was so excited he couldn't say anything at all.

Partial mutism due to neurosis:

The importance that the Mohave attach to speech disturbances as neurotic symptoms may be inferred from the fact that mutism and/or abnormal speech are mentioned in connection with a great variety of cases. The informants whom I questioned about a certain boy who,

---

[77] This reply was due to a misunderstanding of the question, but was also part of Tcatc's coy pretense of being shocked by sexual questions which, in reality, she enjoyed a great deal and answered in great detail.

as a result of a humiliation, became severely withdrawn and spoke so little that he was almost mute at times, invariably mentioned his speech disturbance *first* (Case 77).

Deaf-mutes:

According to the late M. A. I. Nettle, M.D., in 1932-33 there lived on the Colorado River Reservation one almost deaf-mute Mohave Indian and several completely deaf-mute Chemehuevi Indians. My own informants did not describe any Mohave Indian as a deaf-mute, though it is probable that at least one of the mutes mentioned in this section was the person whom Dr. Nettle described as an almost deaf-mute Mohave Indian.

Comment

The importance that the Mohave attach to speech disturbances can be partially understood in terms of their admiration for orators and clever conversationalists. On the other hand it is possible to suggest, at least tentatively, that the Mohave tendency to emphasize the pathognomonic import of speech disorders in "insanity," may also be partly determined by their xenophobia, since the stranger is, by definition, someone with whom one cannot communicate verbally. While this comment is admittedly speculative, it should be noted that even in our society people who seek to mimic "insane behavior" usually babble rather than gesticulate, and that grotesque imitations of foreign languages and of foreign accents are often used to poke fun at "those crazy foreigners." [78] The popularity of dialect jokes may also be due to the tendency to equate foreign speech with grotesque "craziness."

In conclusion, it is worth mentioning that the only other physical defect the Mohave use as a symbol of psychic derangement is, according to Kroeber (1925 a), blindness, which is understandable since sight is man's main means for testing reality.

FEEBLEMINDEDNESS

The Mohave readily understood descriptions of feeblemindedness, but denied its occurrence among members of that tribe. Thus, when asked whether a certain girl named E. (native name not recorded)— who, according to various employees of the Indian Agency, was a mentally defective person—was, indeed, feebleminded, all informants said that there was nothing the matter with her intelligence. In fact, even when describing the behavior of mutes (pt. 5, pp. 248-251) or

---

[78] Such grotesque and derisive imitations also occur in primitive society. When the headman of Kon Pley visited the Sedang Moi village of Tea Ha in Indochina, his "odd" pronunciation was imitated for days afterwards and never failed to elicit derisive laughter (Devereux, MS., 1933-34).

when discussing snake-headed monstrous births (see below) they never referred to mental defect—an omission that is comparable to their marked unawarenes of the psychological and intellectual deterioration of the aged (pt. 5, pp. 254–255). Last, but not least, not once did a Mohave refer in my presence to another Mohave as "stupid." [79] Conversely, the Mohave hardly ever say that someone is especially intelligent (Case 49). This is not necessarily a primitive trait, since e.g., the Sedang Moi of Indochina (Devereux, 1947 b; MS., 1933–34) are greatly interested in the presence, development, and deterioration of intelligence. [80]

In brief, stupidity (dull normal intelligence) was never mentioned at all, and feeblemindedness, when taken cognizance of, was simply considered a form of "craziness" (yamomk), *but only if a marked abnormality of behavior was present.*

The tendency not to take cognizance of simple stupidity, nor even of actual mental defect, goes hand in hand with the tendency to impute an adult intelligence to shamanistic fetuses (pt. 7, pp. 331–339), to newborn twins (pt. 7, pp. 348–356) and possibly even to sucklings (pt. 7, pp. 340–348) who, if they become ill because they are weaned too suddenly, can be cured by reasoning with them, though the person who reasons with them must be a shaman who has the necessary supernatural powers. Likewise, intelligence is not held to be impaired in the psychoses of shamans, whose confused and ineffectual behavior is believed to be due to the fact that their "comprehension" or "knowledge" (=autistic-supernaturalistic fantasy) exceeds their "heart" (pt. 1, pp. 9–38). Finally, in discussing the development of children, the Mohave stress ethical maturation, rather than an expansion of intelligence or performance.

In psychiatric parlance one would say that the Mohave do not believe in genuine mental defect and view all intellectual limitations as "pseudodebility"; as an inhibition of an inherently normal intelligence. [81] Needless to say, this statement does not imply that the Mohave actually discovered the existence of pseudofeeblemindedness, in the scientific sense of that term. Rather do they believe that every

---

[79] After translating Case 19, Hama: Utce: added that "this must have been a weak-minded family." It seems probable that she simply meant to say that this was a mentally unstable family. However, even if she meant to say that they were stupid—which they were not—this does not mean that the Mohave tribe is preoccupied with problems of stupidity, since Hama: Utce: is, even by American standards, an unusually well educated person, and therefore more likely to think of people as either intelligent (cf. her comments on Kumádhi: Atat, Case 49) or stupid.

[80] Thus, in discussing children, they will say: "So-and-so already has (or else, does not have as yet) intelligence; he can (or else, cannot as yet) do such-and-such work." In discussing adults, they nearly always say whether or not they have intelligence. An old man, who was mentally still very alert and an exceptionally good informant, often complained that he was now less intelligent than formerly (Devereux, MS., 1933–34).

[81] "Pseudodebility" is a technical term, suggesting pseudofeeblemindedness resulting from the neurotic inhibition of an inherently normal intellect.

human being, including the even small child, has a normal intelligence. Whether or not this normal endowment does, or does not, manifest itself in normal performance depends to a large extent on whether the individual has the proper power-giving dreams (Devereux, 1956 c), exactly in the sense in which a woman's dreams enable her to become a mother or a man's dreams enable him to be a good hunter, etc.

This being said, the Mohave describe a type of monstrous neonate who is clearly grossly feebleminded. If the husband of a pregnant woman, or the pregnant woman herself, kills a snake, the woman will give birth to a snakeheaded monster, whose bite is said to be poisonous and who is therefore not nursed at the breast. Such an infant is kept alive by feeding it in one of two ways:

(1) Its jaws are pried open with two sticks, or
(2) Its jaws are kept open by inserting in its mouth a corncob or a piece of wood.

The milk is then squirted into its mouth, without allowing its lips to touch the nipple, lest it should bite and "poison" its mother.

Other informants said that such babies are fed only gruel or mush, by means of a small stick.

This mode of feeding is sometimes successful, since, in 1933, there died an old Yuma woman, who had been a snakeheaded monster and who had been fed in this way when she was a baby.

The real cause of such monstrous births is far from certain. The most plausible guess would be that such infants are either congenital syphilitics or the victims of maternal rubella (German measles). In still other cases such cranial and facial defects may be due to birth injuries.

The most important point to be noted is that, in discussing such monsters, the Mohave did not describe them as feebleminded, and neither did the Yuma. This is probably due to the fact that the majority of such babies die in early infancy, as do most defective children born into a primitive tribe,[82] so that their mental defect has no chance to manifest itself.[83] However, at least one such Yuma girl did live to a ripe old age.

Since feeblemindness of this type is not correlated by the Mohave themselves with yamomk (craziness), neither a detailed discussion of this defect nor the presentation of one, very dubious, case is called for in this section, especially since these data have already been cited in part 5, pp. 248–251.

---

[82] The vitality of feebleminded children is usually much lower than that of normal children.
[83] It is possible that some twins, who supposedly die voluntarily, are actually defective babies, injured during delivery, or else are congenitally abnormal (cf. Case 85).

SENILITY

The Mohave seem to have no conception of mental decline in old age, though they are ready enough to complain of the deterioration of their physical powers with advancing age. The idea of a functional decline in old age is so alien to them that, according to reliable informants, it is generally believed that formerly men remained potent and women sexually active until death (Devereux, 1950 a). This lack of a conception of senile decline is not wholly due to the fact that formerly the Mohave did not live long enough to become senile, since, as late as the 1950's, I knew of no Mohave who showed signs of senility, though there may have been some formerly (Cases 33, 34, 35, and 38).

It is not even possible to suggest that in primitive society only persons who are not likely to become senile ever reach old age, since among the Indochinese Sedang Moi even my intellectually still very alert old informant, Mbra:o, complained that, with advancing age, he lost his "mana" (called pån) as well as his "ear" (=intelligence and judgment). In support of this statement he cited the fact that he now occasionally beat his good wife, whereas previously he had never chastised her. Thus, both the apparent absence of prolonged senile deterioration and the absence of the *idea* of senility among the Mohave can only be recorded, but remains unexplained, unless we assume that many of the psychoses in elderly persons (e.g., Case 34) cited elsewhere in this work, were instances of (terminal) senile psychosis. Even if this view is accepted, the absence of the *conception* of psychic senility remains unexplained.

Be that as it may, the only undesirable psychological change the Mohave associate with aging is the tendency of singers of "semi-shamanistic" song cycles (Kroeber, 1925 a) to become shamans, and the proneness of aging shamans to turn into witches. These undesirable trends are, however, limited to certain small classes of individuals; according to the Mohave most people become more responsible and serious minded as they become older, and therefore become socially more useful than ever before. In brief, the *social image* of the stupid, crazy, or "evil" old person is an exception in Mohave society; the predominant social image of the aged is that of a socially useful and responsible old person. Tentatively speaking, the lack of a cultural *concept* of senile deterioration, insanity, or evilness may, perhaps, be due to the fact that, on the whole, Mohave parents treat their children kindly and display a great deal of reasonableness and patience toward their early efforts to grow up (Devereux, 1950 f) and even to experiment sexually (Devereux, 1951 d), so that the *image* of a stupid, tyrannical, unreasonable (Devereux, 1955 b), and envious "older generation" (=witch) is only rarely evolved in childhood.[84]   (See also pt. 4, p. 134 fn., and pt. 7, pp. 356–371).

The above data—combined perhaps with Mohave beliefs concerning the deleterious effects of hyperactivity (pt. 2, pp. 46–56)—represent the sum total of what is known concerning Mohave conceptions of the psychopathological aspects of aging.

SYPHILIS OF THE NERVOUS SYSTEM

Parenchymatous neurosyphilis as well as tabes dorsalis is extremely rare among the Mohave—perhaps because they usually have extremely marked primary and secondary lesions. The Mohave themselves are not aware that syphilis can produce neurological lesions, or psychiatric symptoms, and did not recognize descriptions of paretic megalomania and euphoria, syphilitic paralysis or tabes dorsalis. Although they mentioned that certain persons suffering from various forms of mental derangement had had venereal disease (hiku: pk), they did not estab- lish a nexus between syphilis and subsequent psychiatric symptoms.

The only possible hint that "venereal diseases"—which, in this con- text, are defined in the Mohave sense, and include all forms of hiwey lak as well as hiku: pk and alyha:—may produce mental disorders was contained in the following statement:

People will say that one's blood isn't good and causes stomach trouble. One feels a hard lump in one's side or under the ribs. One loses one's appetite and with every new bad dream one's health declines further. One's bowels and urine are also affected and one may not even be able to vomit anymore. The lump will go up to the mouth, but will not be vomited out. One might also go crazy.

Various details of the preceding statement indicate that the descrip- tion refers to an ailment of the hiwey lak group, which some Mohave consider to be venereal diseases (pt. 4, pp. 150–175). Hence, while a Mohave may state that a "venereal disease," in the Mohave sense of that term, may cause "insanity," this remark must not be interpreted to mean that the Mohave are cognizant of the psychiatric sequelae of syphilis.

The one mention of paresis by a Mohave occurred in a letter written to me by a highly educated member of that tribe, who was fully aware of the causes of paresis.

CASE 75 (Information from a personal letter written by Hama: Utce:) :

(Kumàdhi: Atat, the middle-aged woman referred to in this letter, was said to have been a witch, greatly dreaded by many Mohave Indians; see also Case 49).

---

[84] If this assumption is correct, the presence of the *concept* of senile deterioration among the Sedang Moi may be due to the exploitation, and occasional ill treatment, of children, and to the, at least partial, inhibition of their urge for sexual experimentation after the age of 7 to 10 or thereabouts.

By the way, we had a case last month that would have interested you. It was a woman (Kumádhi: Atat) that went crazy (syphilis). Over a year ago I brought her down from the town of N. and we were going to take her to Ph. State Hospital but her sister wouldn't agree to it, so we took her back to N. About a week later she was in the city jail in N. and they committed her to Ph. State Hospital. It seems she died a few weeks later and none of the folks were notified. A year later some Indians going through the town of S. stopped off and asked about her and found that she had been dead over a year, and did that cause talk! The Indians were almost ready to go on the warpath. Your friend X [85] and some (northern Mohave) Indians went over to S. and after a lot of talking they found out that she hadn't been buried. The body had been released to L. Hospital and that is where they found her, over a year after she had been dead. They got her home, cremated her and everything was all right after that. By the way, she was supposed to be a medicine woman. A much feared one at that. (Case 49.)

---

[85] A Mohave for whom neither my Mohave friends nor I had any respect or liking. In discussing him, we therefore always called him *"your* friend."

PART 6. PSYCHIATRIC DISORDERS OF CHILDHOOD

CHILD PSYCHIATRY

GENERAL INTRODUCTION

The Mohave differentiate between presumably "organic" (i.e., genetic or constitutional) defects, caused by certain inappropriate acts of the parents, and "functional" psychiatric disorders affecting children.

The former category includes mental defect, conditions which may be due to defects of the nervous system, "snake-headed monsters," and speech defects, each of which is discussed separately in the following pages. (See also pt. 5, pp. 248–253.)

The latter category includes the relatively transitory "acting out" period of budding shamans and nonshamanistic "problem children." These disorders are discussed on pages 260–285.

The susceptibility of children to traumata and their tendency to become depressed is an axiom of Mohave psychiatry. Future shamans seek to kill themselves while being born (pt. 7, pp. 331–339), infants who have to be weaned because their mothers are pregnant again make themselves sick (pt. 7, pp. 340–347), sucklings whose mothers also nurse a young orphaned relative contract the hi:wa hira:uk illness (pt. 3, p. 115), young twins may decide to return to heaven (pt. 7, pp. 348–356), and so forth. Yet, interestingly enough, actual child suicide cases are completely unknown, presumably because the Mohave child is loved and feels fairly secure.[86]

"ORGANIC" CONDITIONS

According to the Mohave, all congenital or constitutional defects of children are due to certain actions of the parents, such as "incestuous" marriage, fellatio performed by a pregnant woman, the killing of a snake during pregnancy, etc. (Devereux, 1948 b). Despite the fact that the condition of defective children is living proof of the misconduct of the parents, the Mohave do not destroy such children; instead, they make considerable efforts to keep them alive, even though, e.g., the breast feeding of snakeheaded (heredosyphilitic?) monsters

---

[86] This good treatment is not wholly due to the belief that ill-treated children can make themselves die. The Sedang Moi (Devereux, MS., 1933–34) have the same belief, which does not prevent them from being quite harsh with their children. Hence, the suicide of the young is sufficiently common among the Sedang to have led to the inclusion into Sedang law of the provision that an adult oppressor whose acts drive a helpless young person to suicide can be fined.

must be avoided, because their bite is believed to be poisonous. The Yuma kept one such woman alive until she died of old age in January 1933. This reluctance to abandon defective children to their fate can be properly understood only if one contrasts it with the now obsolete practice of killing halfbreed babies and sometimes even full-blood Mohave infants whose fathers refuse to recognize them (Devereux, 1948 d).

The most plausible explanation of this discrepancy is the Mohave feeling that children are the means of insuring the continuity of the tribe, rather than that they are the "personal property" of their parents. Thus, a child that refuses to be born is asked by the obstetrical shaman to remember that the tribe needs children; i.e., it is asked to give up its personal reluctance to be born and to think of itself as a link in the tribe's continuity (pt. 7, pp. 331–339). Likewise, when a suckling makes itself sick because it resents its mother's new pregnancy, the pediatric shaman asks it not to be jealous of the unborn, and to allow another Mohave to come into being (pt. 7, pp. 340–348). In brief, both adults and children are expected to think of the child first and foremost as a link in tribal continuity. By contrast, children whose fathers refuse to recognize them belong to no gens and therefore do not qualify as individuals capable of insuring social and tribal continuity. Hence, such children can be destroyed without a biological loss to the tribe. The idea that they should not be killed because they too are human beings was a distinct innovation, introduced by a kindly old man (Devereux, 1948 d). This reform, which reflected a breakdown of Mohave insularity, found ready acceptance, perhaps for the same reasons that induced the Pawnee not to resist the man who suddenly decided to rescue a captive about to be sacrificed to the Morning Star and to declare that such sacrifices were not to be performed in the future (Linton, 1922). It must be presumed that, in both instances, the killings, though culturally sanctioned, had been essentially ego-dystonic all along, so that, when conquest weakened the effectiveness of cultural imperatives, the people were only too glad to abandon a custom that was never wholly congenial to them.[87]

---

[87] The Sedang Moi of Indochina explicitly state that certain rules, established by their violent and unreasonable gods, are ethically objectionable, and are complied with only because of fear (Devereux, 1940 c). Hence, some of them were not at all displeased when the French forbade them to engage in ritual slave raids. As for their ritual cannibalism, it began to decline even before the French conquest. At first, they still sacrificed captives, but merely pretended to eat their livers. As Mbra :o put it: "I never really ate any part of the sacrificed slave's liver. I only touched my lips with it." On another occasion a man was simply tied to the sacrificial pole and was symbolically pricked with a knife, without even piercing his skin; actually, they killed a pig tied to the same sacrificial pole. By 1933, they only sacrificed buffaloes tied to the customary sacrificial pole, to which they also attached a small basket filled with wax figurines representing slaves (Devereux, MS., 1933–34). These observations bear witness to the fact that not only man's destructive impulses, but also his "better nature" may be at odds with cultural pressures (Devereux, 1939 c).

By contrast, the fullblood defective, whose paternity was not in dispute, was, at least in principle, viewed as a bona fide link in tribal continuity, i.e., as a recognized member of the ingroup, who could not be killed without violating a major value of Mohave culture. Hence, no matter how humiliating his existence may have been for his parents, and no matter how difficult it may have been to raise him, he was cared for to the best of his parents' ability, presumably, and in part at least, because his parents felt that they had to make up for the harm they have done to their child.[88]

In brief, defective children are not consciously rejected by their parents, because Mohave society defines them as representatives of the tribe's future quite as much as normal children.

The present chapter need not include a discussion of such organic conditions as speech defect (pt. 5, pp. 248–251) or feeblemindedness (pt. 5, pp. 251–253) since these ailments have already been dealt with in earlier chapters. The same is true of various "psychosomatic illnesses" in infants, which have important psychic components (pt. 3, p. 115; pt. 7, pp. 329–356). The only "organic" defect to be discussed in this section concerns the deleterious aftereffects of a certain type of "sedation" administered to fretful children suffering from insomnia.

If a child—usually because of illness—fussed too much, it was put to sleep by dipping a twig of arrow weed into black paint mixed with the charred and powdered eyes of a certain small bird that goes to sleep at sunset, and by painting its eyelids, just above the lashes, with this paste. This method of putting a child to sleep was said to be infallible, but, when used to excess (?) could cause a lifelong somnolence.

N. C.s statement (1932).—When my son was a baby, he used to sleep all day long and cry all night. At last, in order to get some peace, I used this method to make him sleep. This treatment had such lasting effects that, even though he is now already 27 years old, he still wants to sleep all the time and is quite lazy. The fact that N.C. blamed only herself for her son's sleepiness and laziness is typically Mohave (Devereux, 1948 c).

The fact that the Mohave use only sympathetic magic to cause fretful children to sleep, and do not resort to the administration of datura, which they believe to be a sedative and hypnotic, is fully compatible with the nonpharmacological orientation of Mohave medicine.

A variety of other defects of children, which the Mohave themselves consider to be unrelated to "craziness" (yamomk), and which probably come within the scope of neurology rather than of psychiatry, were discussed in another publication (Devereux 1948 b) and therefore need not be discussed in the present work.

---

[88] The parents of Occidental defectives often "love" them passionately and make great sacrifices for them, in order to alleviate their own guilt feelings over their children's condition, for which they (often erroneously), blame themselves (Devereux, 1956 a).

DEVIANT CHILDREN

"FUNCTIONAL" DISTURBANCES

Data concerning deviant children were obtained chiefly in the course of investigations of Mohave sexuality, psychopathology, and suicide. Thus, in contrast with earlier articles on child rearing (Devereux, 1947 a, 1948 c, 1950 f, 1950 h), which present primarily formal data on child-rearing techniques and the routine life of children, the present chapter consists mostly of case material. This may create the erroneous impression that a *large* number of Mohave children are either deviant or delinquent.

Indeed, even though child-rearing techniques resist acculturation rather tenaciously, it is, nonetheless, self-evident that the inconspicuous lives of most well-adjusted children are more likely to be forgotten than the escapades of a few young scamps. Hence, case material pertaining to "good" or well-adjusted children, who lived many years ago, would be almost impossible to obtain, even if the Mohave taboo on the names of the dead had not already erased their memory.[89]

On the whole, if one uses as one's diagnostic base line the Mohave notion that children are entitled to sexual information, as well as to freedom of sexual experimentation (Devereux, 1951 d), the average Mohave child may be described as pleasant, outgoing, and trusting, and also as well behaved by aboriginal Mohave ethical standards; furthermore, the Mohave child usually grows up into a kind, trustworthy, and generous adult. Even the instability of Mohave marriages, which is responsible for the fact that many children grow up in a variety of households, does not seem to undermine the emotional security of most such "displaced" children, because the Mohave give all children a great deal of love and acceptance, even though they do not look after them very consistently.

Two facts illustrate the Mohave Indian's ready acceptance of the child:

(1) It is believed that, if a pregnant woman changes husbands, her sexual relations with the new spouse modify the biosocial identity of the unborn and transform the fetus into the biological and social

---

[89] These remarks are not to be thought of as lending indirect support to Wallace's (1948) view that Mohave children were sexually less active than my previously published data (Devereux, 1951 d) indicate. When, in the course of a later field trip to the Mohave, I confronted my informants with the discrepancy between Wallace's data and my own, my informants unanimously declared that Wallace's principal informant—well known to all of them, as well as to me—was a somewhat rigid person, as well as an atypical Mohave, known, e.g., to be quite selfish, exploitive, and ungenerous. Psychoanalytically speaking, such "anal characters" are often quite "moralistic," which would account for his puritanical account of the behavior of Mohave children. In addition, several informants, so challenged, supported the statements they made during my earlier field trips by citing autobiographical data, going back to their own childhood. Thus, e.g., Hitcu:y Kutask(w)elv described in some detail his first sex experience, which took place at the age of 7 or 8.

child of the mother's new husband (Devereux, 1949 c). This facilitates such a child's acceptance by its mother's new husband.

(2) Many Mohave children are genuinely devoted to their stepfathers (Devereux, 1950 f).

On the other hand, the Mohave child is not trained to be devoted
only to its nearest kin and to expect no real love from others. The
libido of the Mohave child is diffused early in life over a substantial
segment of the tribe, so that, later in life, the adult Mohave will be
truly fond of many persons, but seldom if ever deeply in love with,
or tied hand and foot to, one person. In brief, the Mohave's "primary affect hunger" (Levy, 1937) is gratified throughout life by a
large number of persons, which may account for the great emotional
security of the average child. Indeed, Levy (1937), Spitz (1945,
1946), Spitz and Wolf (1946), Brody (1956), and most other analysts believe the need for love to be a fundamental and primary
need, and hold that a frustration of this need is responsible for much
negativism, depression, and other anomalies of behavior in children
deprived of love. On a broader level, "affect hunger" may be simply
an aspect of the even more fundamental (and probably biological)
"need for response" stressed by Linton (1945), that involves ultimately
both favorable and unfavorable responses, i.e., a controlled exchange
of stimuli between the individual and the organic, and even the in-
organic, environment. Thus, students of animal ecology found that
two goldfish in a bowl containing a certain noxious solution will
survive, while *one* goldfish in a bowl half that size, containing the
same noxious solution, will die (Allee and Bowen, 1932).

On a broader level, it was suggested (Devereux, 1951 e) that the
infant's capacity to perceive, and to over-react to, minimal
tokens of love is one of the infant's chief homeostatic survival mechanisms. Its capacity to sense slights, and to exaggerate their importance and intensity is, in terms of the present hypothesis, an accidental
byproduct of, and epiphenomenal to, its more basic capacity to perceive and to "amplify" such tokens of love as it may receive, e.g.,
in the form of biologically seemingly "meaningless" caresses, body
contact (Montagu, 1953), etc.[90]

In brief, the fact that the Mohave child is seldom alone and par-
ticipates actively both in juvenile and adult group life provides it
with a degree of security that, despite many material deprivations,
usually suffices to keep the child emotionally on an even keel.

The Mohave child's emotional position may, thus, be characterized
as follows:

The Mohave are intensely fond of children. The child receives
much love but, in keeping with the somewhat noncompulsive character

---

[90] Compare in this context the goldfish example cited above.

of the Mohave, little systematic "looking after." This love is given quite indiscriminately by parents, kinsmen, and fellow-Mohave, so that any child is a welcome visitor wherever its fancy takes it. Similarly, partly because of the type of socialization prevalent in Mohave society, and partly also because of the extreme mobility and variable composition of Mohave households, the child's affections, as well as its hostilities, are spread quite early over much of the tribe. Thus, whatever capacity for love the child possesses is not monopolized by a few persons—such as members of his immediate family—but is evenly distributed over a large area of the social body (Devereux, 1939 a, 1942 d, 1950 f).

Under these conditions it is almost certain that, at any given moment, the child will receive love at least from some people, although these givers of affection may not always be the same. This means that, time and again, great demands are made upon the child's ability to shift its emotional attachments from one person to another. Thus, even though the child seldom, if ever, lacks food and/or love, there is often no real constancy and continuity in the composition of its "emotional environment." In brief, even though a stepmother or stepfather, a grandparent, a kinsman or even some benevolent but unrelated adult Mohave, may nurture the orphaned or neglected child as generously as its own parents would, this constant shifting about, together with the Mohave insistence on the importance of gens affiliations, may, in some instances, cause the child to feel—quite erroneously—that it lacks both love and care.

The preceding statements apply primarily to the fullblood Mohave child, mostly regardless of whether it was born in or out of wedlock.

The fate of halfbreeds (Case 76), or of children resulting from the marriages or casual matings of a Mohave woman with members of other tribes is, on the other hand, very different. The same is true of children who, though conceived as fullblood Mohave Indians, are considered aliens because of the Mohave belief that the racial, tribal and even gens affiliation of the fullblood fetus can be changed if the pregnant woman has intercourse with a person other than the original impregnator (Devereux, 1949 c). Hence, unless the intruding male is a Mohave, who is willing to claim his wife's child as his own, or else is a lesbian who proudly proclaims her "paternity" (Devereux, 1937 b), the "halfbreed" infant was sometimes killed (Devereux, 1948 d). Such infanticides were motivated not so much by crude racial prejudice as by the Mohave Indian's genuine fear that prolonged association with a "halfbreed" would cause him to contract the allegedly often fatal "foreign disease" (pt. 4, pp. 128–150). Hence if such children were permitted to survive, their fate was a rather unenviable one; they were rejected by their maternal kin, and shunned by the rest of the tribe. This meant in practice that, in some instances, they were *less* frequently shunted from household to household than were some orphaned fullblood Mohave children, because fewer people were willing to care for such "carriers of the foreign illness." Thus, "affect hunger" often became a major factor in shaping such children's lives and ideologies.[91]

It is on this screen, to which Mohave generosity and improvidence contribute further elements, that the following case histories should be projected.

The preceding observations are of great importance also for a deeper understanding of Mohave society and culture. Indeed, it should be borne in mind that child behavior is a significant and revealing part of the tribal culture pattern. Hence, any attempt to define certain modes of behavior as "normal" or as "abnormal," independently of the characteristic themes, interests, and value-systems of Mohave culture, would automatically result in a gross distortion and misevaluation of the life and role of children in Mohave society. It should be added, however, that this specification does not imply cultural relativism in psychiatric diagnosis and should be considered simply as a corollary of the general theory of actual differences between normal and abnormal (Devereux, 1956 b).

An important point to be stressed is that the Mohave tend to consider as neurotic only those children who are, *at the same time*, also delinquent by tribal standards. This finding obliges us to discuss, at least briefly, the real meaning of delinquency.

"Social negativism" is necessarily present in all symptom formation (Devereux, 1940 a, 1954 a), so that all neurotics are also more or less deviants. Hence "delinquency" is, of necessity, a highly elastic term, whose primary meaning is a strictly sociocultural one. We therefore cannot consider any Mohave child as "delinquent," unless it was specifically called a delinquent either by *older* persons (Cases 76 and 77), who are less contaminated by American views than are the younger members of the tribe, or else by a playmate (Case 78). Thus, sexual activities, unless carried to certain extremes, are not defined by the Mohave as tokens of maladjustment or of neurosis. However, when the sexual activity of a Mohave child exceeds certain limits, the Mohave themselves are the first to define such misconduct as maladjusted and neurotic. It must be explicitly stated that, *in terms of Mohave standards*, the sexual behavior of the three boys discussed in this section was neither deviant nor delinquent. This is proved by the fact that, by his own account, no *adult* Mohave ridiculed Hamteya:u for having contracted gonorrhea at the age of 10 (Case 77), because, by Mohave

---

[91] Ideologies can be shown to result from childhood situations (Schilder, 1936).

standards, his sexual activities were neither extreme, nor incompatible with his age.   The fact that he was slightly maladjusted and neurotic, *even before* this sexual act, obliges the psychiatrist to suspect that his sexual activity was also neurotically motivated.   This does *not* mean, however, that we are entitled to consider him, *at that time* and *for that reason*, also as a *delinquent*, in the sociological sense of that term.

By contrast, if a child's sexual activities violate the usual Mohave norm for such actions, the child may, in certain instances, be considered delinquent.   However, even in such cases a detailed examination of the Mohave attitude toward juvenile sex activity is necessary, before a valid psychiatric evaluation of the sexually hyperactive Mohave child becomes possible.

If the sexual excesses and the obstreperousness of a child happen to fit the behavior pattern which the Mohave expect the budding shaman to manifest, the child will be called "wild," "crazy" or "obnoxious"—i.e., it will be considered delinquent.   Yet, at the same time, the tribe recognizes that it is dealing not with a "simple delinquent," but, specifically, with a future shaman.   In such instances the Mohave show a great deal of—slightly exasperated—tolerance and, on the whole, seek to avoid open clashes with the "bad" child.   This tolerance is not motivated by a fear of magical retaliation, since, according to the Mohave, such misconduct *precedes* the actualization of the budding shaman's powers.   Rather is this tolerance motivated by the belief that the misconduct is a supernaturally and temperamentally determined characteristic of the budding shaman, and cannot therefore be controlled, either by an act of will on the part of the child, or by familial and/or social pressures.   "It is his nature, he cannot help it."   Thus, even though the behavior of Nyoltc Hukthar (Case 79) was deemed delinquent and scandalous enough to earn her the lifelong nickname of "crazy Nyoltc" (hukthar=coyote=crazy), no real pressure seems to have been put on her to make her behave, presumably because her conduct conformed to, and did not exceed, the "pattern of misconduct" (Linton, 1936) expected from budding shamans.   By contrast, a great deal of pressure was put on Nepe:he (Case 76), whose petty thefts violated the basic Mohave value of honesty [92] and did not fit the "social image" of the "pattern of misconduct" which budding shamans are expected to exhibit.   Similarly today, when there seem to be more than a few true juvenile delinquents among the Mohave, the tribe is more disturbed by the gross violence and altogether "un-Mohave" crimes against property than by the sexual acts of these acculturated Mohave juvenile delinquents.   It is also quite probable that, in earlier

---

[92] A theft by a Mohave was an almost unheard-of occurrence.

times, many of these modern juvenile delinquents would, sooner or later, have become shamans.

The public attitude toward a turbulent child was neatly expressed by Hivsu: Tupo:ma, when he witnessed the destructiveness of a certain boy. Instead of expressing moral indignation, Hivsu: Tupo:ma simply said: "This boy behaves badly, because he is going to be a medicine man; he already shows the destructive tendencies typical of future shamans." Nevertheless, the unusual actions of a child believed to be a future shaman give rise to a great deal of gossip, whose *Leitmotiv* is not "How awful!", but rather: "Have you heard the latest trick of so-and-so?" Otherwise stated, disapproval is, in such cases, always tempered by amused curiosity.

Now, it is of special interest that, insofar as I am able to determine on the basis of extensive data collected in the course of a half a dozen fieldtrips spread out over two decades, all turbulent and sexually hyperactive children whose behavior fitted the "pattern of misconduct" expected from future shamans did, in fact, become shamans and/or witches—or, if they could not, or refused to, become shamans, eventually developed a psychosis (pt. 2, 57–71, and Case 64)—but did not become simple (nonshamanistic) delinquents.

It is possible that this is due, at least in part, to the social evaluation of, and reaction to, the supposed "significance" of their misconduct, which may have encouraged them to define themselves as shamans. On the other hand, the fact that, unlike Nepe:he (Case 76), they did not steal, or violate in some other manner the type of patterned misconduct expected from budding shamans, and finally "settled down" into the shamanistic pattern, strongly supports the thesis (Devereux, 1956 b) that the conflicts of the future shaman are rooted in the unconscious segment of his "ethnic personality" and differ from those of other individuals only in their intensity. This, in turn, explains why socially expected and provided symptoms appear to enable them to cope—at least for a while—with their internal conflicts and ego-dystonic impulses, without having to supplement them with truly idiosyncratic symptoms of their own devising. Thus, like the rest of the Mohave, they are able to use sex as their chief generalized safety valve—albeit in a more symptomatic and excessive form than ordinary persons—and, unlike, e. g., Nepe:he (Case 76), do not have to resort also to symptomatic theft. Likewise, they find magical aggressions (witchcraft)—and sometimes also the socially sanctioned killing of other witches—a sufficient outlet for their aggressivity and do not also have to abuse physically, e.g., a helpless small sibling, the way Hamteya:u did (Case 77).

The same is also true, mutatis mutandis, of Mohave transvestites, whose basic difficulty is an "ethnic neurosis," as this term was defined elsewhere (Devereux, 1956 b), and not a true, idiosyncratic neurosis. The tolerance accorded the Mohave transvestite resembles that accorded the budding shaman. Like the latter, the budding transvestite exhibits a socially defined and expected "pattern of misconduct." Also, as in the case of budding shaman, no real pressure is put on the budding transvestite, although when certain young girls begin to show lesbian tendencies, there are occasional half-hearted and not very hopeful attempts to discourage them from becoming inverts. When these efforts fail, they are subjected to a ritual, which is half "test" of their true proclivities and half "transition rite" and which authorizes them to assume the clothing and to engage in the occupations and sexual activities characteristic of their self-chosen sex (Devereux, 1937 b). Here too, the high predictability [93] of the future and actual transvestite's behavior in terms of a socially formulated "pattern of misconduct" suggests—as indicated elsewhere (Devereux, 1956 b)— that we are dealing simply with unusually strongly developed instances of a type of conflict which is, at least statistically, highly prevalent in a given culture, i. e., with an "ethnic neurosis," whose symptoms are provided by society itself, in the form of a preestablished "pattern of misconduct."

The preceding considerations explain, at least in part, the difficulties experienced by psychiatrists who seek to interpret the essentially socio-cultural problem of delinquency in psychiatric terms. These difficulties are made especially obvious by the purely heuristic attempt to deal with this problem by means of the relatively new diagnostic category, "sociopathy," which is, logically, "neither fish, nor flesh, nor good red herring," and which, strictly speaking, leaps from psychic determinism to social repercussions, without ever facing squarely the crucial intermediate problem of symptom formation.[94] The same is also partly true of the more authentically psychiatric concept "psychopathy" (pt. 5, pp. 245–247). The notorious reluctance of many judges, lawyers, and law enforcement officers to accept psychiatric testimony in criminal cases may well be due, in part at least, to a dim awareness of the inadequacies of present-day psychiatric attempts to bridge the gap between the *social* concept of delinquency and the *psychiatric* concept of neurotic aggressivity and predatoriness. (Cf. also U.S. Senate 1955, for recent data.)

---

[93] It was shown elsewhere that the alleged unpredictability of neurotics, etc., is not real, but simply a consequence of misguided attempts to predict their behavior by means of a frame of reference which is not the proper one for the understanding, control, and prediction of their behavior (Devereux, 1951 h, 1952 a, 1952 b).

[94] But compare some of my papers, which seek to grapple with this triple problem (Devereux, 1939 c, 1940 a, 1942 b, 1944 a, 1951 g, 1954 a, 1955 a; Devereux and Moos, 1942; Devereux and Loeb, 1943 a, 1943 b).

CASE MATERIAL

The case material about to be presented was obtained from three types of sources:

(1) The principal of the reservation school named three boys who, from the point of view of the school, were "problem children."

(2) All three boys were discussed with reliable adult Mohave informants, who considered Nepe:he (Case 76) and Hamteya:u (Case 77) as neurotic delinquents, but did not think that Case 78—the only one of the three who hoped to become a shaman—was truly neurotic or deviant, though one of his playmates did consider him a delinquent or, at least, a problem child.

(3) All three boys were interviewed personally—two of them being seen more than once—with one of their friends and age mates, Hitcu:y Kutask(w)-elvâ, acting as interpreter and social mediator on all occasions except one, when this role was performed by a friendly and tactful adult, E. S.

It was found in every case that, even though these children spoke fluent English, they answered some questions in English less freely than questions put to them in Mohave by the intermediary. However, one cannot exclude a priori the possibility that they were somewhat timid and therefore "slow on the uptake," so that the fact that a question was first put to them in English and was then repeated in Mohave, gave them more time to grasp its full meaning, and to formulate a satisfactory answer. This, however, is not the whole story, since it is easy to observe that questions which, when asked in English were either not answered at all or else were answered in the negative, but, when asked in Mohave, were answered quite readily and in the affirmative, usually pertained to activities which are known to be condemned by whites, though not by the Mohave. It is quite probable that the child *experienced* such acts in the Mohave way and even in the Mohave language, which means in practice that he experienced these acts without an occidental sense of guilt. However, questions regarding such acts, when asked in English, inevitably evoked for the child also a halo of disapproving occidental ways of visualizing these acts or experiences, which were simply not part of the actual experiences. This meant in essence that there was a real affective discrepancy between the *act* experienced in the *Mohave* manner and the *questions* pertaining thereto, which—being asked in *English*—seemed to demand that the child should think of his act in occidental terms of sin and guilt. Given this incompatibilty between the (Mohave) act itself and the (English=puritanical) questions pertaining to the act, the child was affectively truthful in giving a negative answer to such an *English* question and an affirmative answer to the same question asked in *Mohave*. In the same sense, a young and chaste bride, very much in love with her husband, would answer the question: "Did you make love with your husband?" affirmatively, but might answer a crudely formulated question of the same kind in the negative,— and would be right in so doing, since what she did, in fact, experience was a genuine act of love and not a "dirty" gratification of "base" impulses. This interpretation of the facts is greatly strengthened by my personal observation that similar obstacles to communication are quite common also in psychoanalytic work, and especially when one tries to confront the patient with the fact that his *way* of reporting and interpreting certain of his activities is incompatible with the known *objective* aspects of the reported experience.

A very young girl, who had been sexually involved with one of the aforementioned boys (Case 77), was seen, but could not be interviewed, because she was simply speechless with shyness. Although it would have probably been possible to induce her to talk eventually, by making her realize that the interviewer was discreet and friendly, information obtained from the boy who had been involved with her, and from other sources, made it seem unlikely that the expenditure of so much time during a relatively brief field trip would have been justified by the results.

General background material, especially on cultural attitudes, case material on turbulent budding shamans (Devereux, 1937 c), which provide a basis for the evaluation of the three case histories presented in this chapter, and a few minor data on the three boys in question, were obtained over a period of years from various reliable informants.

The most important fact to be borne in mind while reading the following case material is that only two of these children were considered delinquent by the adult Mohave themselves and that neither of these two was thought to be a budding shaman, in the sense in which my young interpreter was believed to be a future medicine man, whose turbulence was attributed to the gradual unfolding of his magical powers. The fact that, in the end, this boy did not become a shaman but developed, at least for a while, certain other behavior problems may be due to the fact that he and his family were so exceptionally acculturated that this obsolescent, culturally provided, "type solution" was no longer available to him, because it was incompatible with his degree of acculturation and sophistication.

Before presenting the actual case material it is also desirable to justify briefly the frankness wherewith sexual questions were tackled. Such a direct approach may well have frightened and confused an occidental boy, who is expected and accustomed to gratify the occidental adult's culturally determined need to deny the existence of infantile sexuality, by pretending that he has no sexual impulses. By contrast, the Mohave take infantile sexuality for granted and freely discuss sex with, or in the presence of, children. Of course, these boys, like other Mohave children, knew from experience that the white group's attitudes differed in this respect from those of the Mohave. However, by approaching this topic in the calmly casual Mohave manner—as exemplified for instance by the interpreter's own, spontaneous interventions—it was possible not only to obtain significant, and indeed indispensable, data, but also to promote a better rapport than would have been possible had the interviewer conformed to the occidental pattern, by failing to take overt cognizance of his prepubescent subjects' socially recognized masculinity. A general justification of the technique of tackling frontally that which is *not* tabooed and repressed in the patient's society, even if it is tabooed and repressed in the therapist's society, was presented elsewhere (Devereux, 1951 a, 1953 b). This justification is applicable in every respect also to fieldwork techniques, as exemplified by the following case material, which was investigated with careful attention to what are not potentially explosive topics in *Mohave* culture and in *Mohave* personality dynamics.

CASE 76 (Informants: Nepe: he and E. S., and, on some details, Tcatc.)

Nepe:he (no meaning), of the Melyikha: gens, was about 10 or 11 years old in 1938. By modern standards he was considered to be primarily a Mohave, being the son of a Mohave father, Mepuk Sulyi :tc (knee pierce) of the Melyikha: gens, who is the brother of C. M. Sr.[95] the stepfather of Hamteya :u (Case 77).

Mepuk Sulyi :tc married, at the approximate age of 24 or 25, H. F., a full-blood Chemehuevi Indian woman approximately 20 years old, who did not re-

---

[95] These men are Tcatc's "nephews," since her grandfather and the grandfather of these men were brothers.

main faithful to him very long. For example, she had affairs with two of her husband's brothers, C. and K. M. Despite these affairs, her four children were presumed to have been fathered by her husband. The oldest one, Melyikha (L. M.), married a Walapai Indian, and had a son, who, since his mother's death, lives with his part-Chemehuevi maternal grandmother K. F. H. F.'s second child, Tcekuvar Mânye: (good laugh) was, in 1938, about 17 years of age and single. Her third child was stillborn. Her last child was Nepe:he.

Nepe:he's mother died when he was about 4 years old, so that he, and also his older brother Tcekuvar Mânye:, had to be raised by their grandmother, K. F., who sent them for their education to the Agency elementary school. In the summer Nepe:he never stays long in any one place, but lives in a variety of homes. Sometimes he stayed for a while with his father, who was married at that time to Syuly (H. N.). This household also contains Syuly's three children by a previous husband, Sukat of the Nyoltc gens, son of Amily Nyunye: (a certain kind of edible field-rat's road.)

At other times, Nepe: he lives in the household of this paternal aunt Melyikha (I. B.), the wife of Hayu: ny Himitc (cricket's cry) of the Tcatc gens. The same household also contains Melyikha:'s daughter Tcatc (P.) her daughter's husband, Hanavtci :p Humatc (a-little-bird food—so called because he is very thin), of the O :otc gens, and their 2-year-old son Me :ta (no meaning).

K. F.'s house may be thought of as Nepe: he's principal residence. This old woman's mother was a Mohave woman named O :otc. Her father was mostly Chemehuevi, with, apparently, some admixture of white blood. K. F. is quite fluent in the Mohave language and also speaks some English. She is described by all as a very kind person. Her household also shelters several other children, most of whom are Chemehuevi.

In reply to a direct inquiry, informant E. S. said that Nepe: he does not feel discriminated against because of his mixed blood: "No one ever made fun of him because of that." When I suggested that Nepe: he may perhaps be reacting against, and trying to forget, the fact that he is part Chemehuevi, (a group whom the Mohave consider inferior) E. S. stated that K. F. herself suspected something of that kind, since she occasionally remarked that Nepe:he does not seem to like the Chemehuevi. In this context it may be interesting to note that, during the school year, when Nepe:he can play with *Mohave* children *at school*, he lives with his grandmother and her Chemehuevi foster children, whereas during his vacations he tends to move around among his Mohave relatives.

Nepe :he's delinquency appears to have two main facets:

(1) He does not remain in one household, but moves around a great deal. "Maybe he will get worse as he gets older."

(2) A more usual fact, according to the Mohave themselves, is his tendency to steal. He does not steal systematically from any particular person, but pilfers small things whenever he can conveniently do so. For example, once, while staying with his paternal uncle K. M., the uncle caught him trying to break into the B. home, which is located near the plumbing plant. The owner of that home, Mr. B., is said to be a Cherokee Indian, married to a Chemehuevi woman. When the uncle asked Nepe:he precisely what he had intended to steal, the boy refused to answer. He was not given corporal punishment, and was merely told not to do such things. This happened roughly in 1937, when the boy was about 10 or 11 years old. Since he began to misbehave in so atypical a manner at so early an age, the Mohave assume that he will get worse as he grows older.

Yet, Nepe:he is not held to be wholly bad, witness E. S.'s remark that, when one meets Nepe:he, he gives the impression of being a nice boy, because he never fails to inquire after one's relatives.

At the time of this inquiry (winter 1938–39) Nepe:he was staying with his grandmother.

Interview with Nepe:he (November 25, 1938; interpreter E. S.).—It is expedient to reproduce the interview verbatim. It should be noted that, even though Nepe:he spoke very good English, he more than once refused to answer English questions, but readily answered the same questions when they were repeated by E. S. in Mohave. Nepe:he is known to understand Mohave and also speaks Chemehuevi quite fluently.

Q. In what grade are you at school?

A. I am in the fourth grade.

Q. What kind of grades do you get?

A. In art, I get B's; the rest of my grades are C's and D's.

Q. How do you get along in school?

A. Quite well. Sometimes, however, I get mad and fight.

Q. With whom do you fight?

A. With C. T. He, too, is in the fourth grade.

Q. Who is your teacher?

A. Mr. X. I don't go to the Valley school, but to the uptown school.

Q. Why?

A. Because I live up north, which is nearer to the uptown school.

Q. Is C. T. a Mohave?

A. Yes.

Q. What are you?

A. I am half Mohave and half Chemehuevi.

Q. Who is taking care of you?

A. K. F.

Q. What tribe does she belong to?

A. She is a Chemehuevi.

Q. What relation of yours is she?

A. She is my grandmother.

Q. How does she act toward you?

A. She is good to me and I like her.

Q. How do you get along with your father?

A. He does not take care of me.

Q. Does your father's sister take care of you?

A. Yes—I go down to her place sometimes.

Q. Why do you move around so much?

A. Sometimes I just get tired of staying in one place.

Q. Do you like your father?

A. [Pause.] Ahem. Yes. [Nods.]

Q. Do you really like him—or do you just like him a little?

A. [Long pause. No reply.]

INTERPRETER. I guess he does not know his father very well.

Q. Do you like your paternal aunt?

A. [Pause. Suddenly Nepe:he burst out crying and cried for nearly 10 minutes, during which period both E. S. and I comforted him.]

Q. Do you get enough to eat?

A. Yes.

Q. Is there anything you want?

A. I don't know what I want.

Q. Do you have any friends among the children?

A. M. McC. He was the one I was playing with when you picked me up, to talk to me.

INTERPRETER. One day I was with Huskiv Itcerk at a funeral which was held at C. N.'s place. Nepe:he too was there, and I was talking to him. It was a very hot summer day and Nepe:he had walked barefoot quite a ways on the hot ground. So, after we talked to him, Huskiv Itcerk said he would ask the Reservation social worker to give Nepe:he a pair of shoes. Huskiv Itcerk told me, later on, that he did ask for a pair of shoes, but did not get them. People know Nepe:he. They know all about his condition and feel sorry for him, but that is all they can do.

Q. Nepe:he, what would you like most?

A. I want clothes most.

Q. What kind of clothes?

A. A shirt and pants. Denim pants, and a shirt to go with it.

Q. Do you have a blanket?

A. No, I don't.

Q. I will buy you a pair of pants and a shirt and a blanket.

A. [Nods and seems pleased, but not very hopeful.]

Q. Whom do you like among the children?

A. Sometimes I go to C. W.'s place and play with him. I do not like Hamteya:u (Case 77) nor E. St. I like (Case 78) and Hitcu:y Kutask(w) elvà and F. S. and F. S.'s brother B. S. That is all.

Q. What are these children? I mean, to which tribe do they belong?

A. They are Mohave.

Q. Do you also play with Chemehuevi kids?

A. I also play with some Chemehuevi children—with the boys who are around K. F.'s place. I also play with by brother Tcekuvar Mànye:, and with H. McK., Wi. and We. F. and also with P. H. All these kids live at K. F.'s place, except for We. F., who lives with L. F.

Q. Do you think Mohave and Chemehuevi children are alike?

A. [Hesitates.]

INTERPRETER. Judging by my contact with the Chemehuevi kids with whom I went to school, I would say that there was no difference. The Chemehuevi children seem all right.

Q. If someone asked you what you were, would you say you were a Mohave or a Chemehuevi?

A. I'd say both.

Q. How about if you could choose?

A. Both are all right.

Q. Do you smoke? [I offer a cigarette.][96]

A. I do not smoke.

Q. Do you play with girls?

A. No.

INTERPRETER. Do you play with M. P.?

A. Yes.

Q. Do you play with Syuly's children?

A. No.

Q. Do you play with O:otc's (Case 24) daughter?

A. No.

Q. Why don't you play with any girls at all?

---

[96] The Mohave allow even small children to smoke.

A. I like to play football and girls don't play it.

[At this point Nepe:he asked E. S. to tell me that P. H.'s situation is similar to his own. His mother too is dead, and his father too went away, so that now K. F. also has to take care of him.]

Q. How does K. F. manage to take care of so many children?

INTERPRETER. The general idea is this: These children are close relatives of hers and have nowhere to go. So K. F. feels that they might as well all starve together. Besides, B. F. is working—that is how they manage to live. And the Reservation social worker, Mrs. W., gives them food. The first of this month they gave K. F. $13.00 in cash and also some food. Tcekuvar Mànye: also contributes some food, since he is much older than Nepe:he and is therefore able to work for his clothing.

NEPE:HE. I washed L.F.'s car this morning and earned a quarter. [He takes the quarter from his pocket and proudly displays it.]

Q. What are you going to do with the dollar I promised to give you for talking to me?

A. I am going to get tennis shoes with that.

Q. Can you get sneakers for a dollar? I said I'd buy you shoes and other things.

A. Yes, they are much cheaper than other kinds of shoes. [Pause.] I cough and my stomach hurts; it is like cramps—as if someone were poking it.

Q. Does anyone tease you?

A. E. St. does, and also Hamteya:u. (Case 77).

Q. E. St. is quite tough, isn't he?

INTERPRETER. He is.

Q. Do you know about E. St.'s sexual escapades?

A. No.

Q. Did you have breakfast today?

A. Yes—we had potatoes. [After a pause.] And mush, bacon and biscuits. [This did not sound convincing.]

Q. What do you want to do when you grow up?

A. I don't know.

Q. Do you want to go to school and learn something?

A. I don't know.

Q. Do you feel lonesome?

A. Sometimes.

Q. What makes you feel that way?

A. I don't know—I just feel that way sometimes.

Q. Are you going to get married when you grow up?

A. I don't know.

Q. Haven't you already picked out the girl you wish to marry? [97]

A. No.

Q. Do you want to have children?

A. I don't know.

Q. Do you ever dream?

A. Sometimes.

Q. Do you remember your dreams?

A. No.

Q. Did you dream anything last night?

A. No.

---

[97] Some very young boys, like Hitcu:y Kutask(w)elvá, already had plans of marrying certain girls when they grew up.

Q. Do you ever have failing dreams?

A. No. [Pause.]   When they took out my tonsils, I did dream that I went up into the sky like a steamshovel and then came down fast.

Q. Umquamne somnias te cum puellis cubare?

A. No.

Q. Vidistine umquam quemquam concumbentem?

A. No.

Q. Num ipse umquam concubuisti?

A. No.

Q. Concumbuntne cum puellis tuae aetatis pueri?

A. No.

Q. Manune te ipsum stupras?

A. No.

Q. Do other boys?

A. Yes.

Q. Then how does it happen that you don't?

A. I don't know.

Q. Truly? Never?

A. I tell you the truth—I never did it in my life.

Q. Habesne ejaculationes seminis nocturnas?

A. No.

Q. Did you do any bedwetting?

A. No.

Q. How old are you?

A. Eleven years old.

Q. What is the story behind this alleged attempt to steal something from the B. home?

A. J. H., M. H.'s brother, wanted to get his bathing suit, because we were going to swim in that basin down there. J. H. untied a string and got into Mr. B.'s tent. Then he went in and got his bathing suit, and I went to my uncle K. M.'s house to get my own,—and then we went swimming.

Q. Why was J. H.'s swimming suit in the B.'s tent?

A. They just visited there and left it there on one occasion.

Q. Did you ever take anything that did not belong to you?

A. Yes [Pause.] There were some piñon nuts belonging to my grandmother and I stole them. I took a pocketful.[98]

Q. Were you punished for it?

A. No one found out about it, so I was not punished.

Q. Anything else?

A. Once I took a watchfob from a Mohave at Needles. It was lying on the table and I took it. Someone told my grandmother that a watchfob was missing and my grandmother showed them the one I had. They recognized it as the missing one, and my grandmother spanked me.

Q. When was that?

A. A long time ago.

Q. What else do you get spanked for?

A. For running away, and for going uptown, and for stealing.

Q. What is the trouble you have with your paternal aunt?

A. Nothing.

Q. Then why did you cry?

---

[98] This is not theft by Mohave standards, since children are free to "swipe" food (Devereux, 1950 h).

A. [No reply.]

Q. Is she mean to you?

A. No—she got me clothes a long time ago. I sometimes stay with her when my grandmother goes to Needles. When she does that, she tells me to stay with my aunt. I also stayed with my father once. That was when they had the rodeo. I also stayed with him the time I went to get some horses. My uncle, K. M., wanted to plow, so I got the horses for him.[99]

Q. How do you get along with your father's present wife, Syuly?

A. She is all right.

Q. Does your father ever spank you?

A. No.

Q. Do you ever go up to your father's house to play?

A. No.

Q. Do you really feel unable to remember any dreams?

A. I can't remember any.

Q. Are you a shaman?

A. No.

Q. Will you be a shaman when you grow up?

A. I don't know.[1]

Q. Do you ever get so angry that you want to kill someone?

A. No. [Grins.]

Q. Vidistine umquam canes coeuntes?

A. Yes.

Q. Iuvatne te spectare?

A. No. [Expression of disgust.]

Q. Riguitne umquam mentula tibi?

A. No.

[After a few other questions of this type which Nepe:he did not answer, he again repeated his denial.]

INTERPRETER. [Spontaneously repeats the same question *in Mohave.*]

A. Yes, now and then.

Q. Num umquam experrecto tibi mane riguit mentula?

A. No. [Pause.] Case 78 semper rigidam habet mentulam. I saw it once. Masturbatur quoque iste, sed ego non facio.

Q. Venitne tibi in mentem aliquid cum riget mentula tua?

A. No.

INTERPRETER. Vidi aliquando Nepe:he cum mentula rigida. Eramus in conventu; mingere parabat; cum illo loquebar, et paulo post "Euge!" inquit. Cum adspicerem, mentulam eius rigidam factam vidi. Ex eo quaesivi num puellis egeret, at ille negavit.

After the conclusion of the interview, Nepe:he was given the promised dollar. Then all three of us drove to town, where I bought him the promised shirt, trousers, sneakers, and blanket. Not until then did Nepe:he actually seem to believe that I would keep my promise.

Comment

Tentative diagnosis.—Maladjustment, *of a distinctly nonshamanistic type,* in a neglected and half-orphaned child caught in a double culture conflict (Indian vs. American; Mohave vs. Chemehuevi) and torn between two racial allegiances

---

[99] The lending of draft animals is quite common within the family.

[1] This question was deliberately superogatory, because stealing is not characteristic of budding shamans.

(Mohave vs. Chemehuevi). This boy's four outstandingly atypical symptoms are:

(1) Theft—which is almost unheard of among the Mohave and which is invariably a symptom of emotional deprivation.

(2) Spontaneous and voluntary—i.e., neurotic—oscillation between several homes, the mobility cycle being apparently synchronized with the differential availability of *Mohave* playmates during the schoolyear, as against the vacation period.

(3) A degree of sexual inhibition which is atypical for the average Mohave boy approaching puberty.

(4) A tendency to overreact to material deprivation of a type that many full-blood Mohave children also experience without a comparable sense of frustration. This overreaction to *material* deprivation must be viewed as a displaced manifestation of his sense of *emotional* deprivation.

CASE 77 (Informants: Hamteya:u of the Mah gens and Hitcu:y Kutask-(w)elvà):

Preliminary comment.—The two interviews with Hamteya:u were highly productive, which is noteworthy, since both the school principal and the Mohave described him as negativistic and uncooperative, and the Mohave emphasized especially that he hardly spoke at all. (Neurotic mutism.)[2] The productiveness of the interviews was largely due to the great skill of my teenage interpreter. At the same time, the length of the interviews, the large number of persons mentioned in them, and the constant shifting from topic to topic made it inexpedient to reproduce the material in the order in which it was obtained, or in the form of a dialogue. Instead, the material was reorganized and is presented in the form of a systematic narrative, with occasional passages in dialogue form.

Family background:

Father.—E. Sr., of the Mah gens, is a member of a notoriously troublesome family (pt. 5, pp. 245–247). He deserted his wife, Hamteya:u's mother, named Nyoltc, when Hamteya:u was (allegedly) 3 years old, because there was some question regarding the paternity of Nyoltc's last child, M., who, in 1938, was roughly 2 years old. Since, despite doubts regarding his paternity, M's English surname is the same as that of E. Sr., Hamteya:u was presumably 10, rather than 3 years old when his father left his mother. "I see my father occasionally and I like him. He stays with Uta:c." (See below.)

Mother.—Nyoltc of the Nyoltc gens, married C. M. after being deserted by E. Sr. "I like my mother best."

Stepfather.—C. M. "He is a good man and I like him, even though he is only my stepfather." [3]

Siblings:

(1) Mah (W.) is a middle-aged woman. (Hamteya:u mistakenly said her name was Nyoltc, which is not the name and gens of his sister, but of his mother. As in Case 78, the mistake is socially due to the absence of the father; it is symptomatically a perseveration and dynamically a manifestation of the oedipal tendency to equate an older sister with the mother.) Mah never married and has a bad reputation, partly because of sexual misconduct (Devereux, 1939 a) and partly because she is believed to be a witch. She lives in the

---

[2] Compare pt. 5, pp. 248–251 for a discussion of the Mohave tendency to consider any speech disturbance as a major symptom of "craziness" (yamomk).

[3] Mohave boys especially are often devoted to their stepfathers (Devereux, 1948 i, 1950 f).

house of P. G., where the second sibling, E. Jr., and the recently widowed Uta:c (Case 38) also reside. "I like her, because she does not get mad at me."

(2) E. Jr., an adult man, lives in the home of P. G., but was also said to live "at Parker." His exact residence was not ascertained. Tcatc believed E. Jr. to be a potential shaman, witch and witch killer (pt. 5, pp. 245–247). He and one of his brothers (or else a cousin with the same English surname) are said to have robbed and raped an elderly female kinswoman named Nyortc Huhual (Case 15).

(3) C. is a man approximately 20 years old. For some reason his English surname was said not to be the same as that of his other siblings. [Did he have a different father?] "I don't know.[4] He and I sleep in the same bed. He gets mad at me when I pester him to play with me and he does not feel like it." [Does he hit you when he gets mad at you?] "No, he doesn't."

(4) Mah (L.)

(5) Mah (G.) is about 13 years old. When Hamteya:u was asked whether he had "fits" he said he didn't, but added that his sister Mah (G.) fainted in the hot season. In 1938 she was at school in Phoenix, having been sent there for "financial reasons" which Hamteya:u could not explain clearly enough to make them intelligible.

(6) HAMTEYA:U, whose name was chosen by his mother, is 12 years old and is in the fourth grade.

(7) M., approximately 2 years old, has the same English surname as E. Sr., though his real paternity appears to be in dispute. His birth caused E. Sr. to desert his wife Nyoltc.

The home.—C. M., Nyoltc, C., Mah (L), Mah (G) when not at boarding school, Hamteya:u, and M. all live in a two-room home. One room is the "bedroom" and the other is a combination of dining room and kitchen. "M., the baby, sleeps with his (uterine) sister Mah (L.). I sleep with my brother C. We have enough to eat."

Language.—At home the family spoke Mohave.

Sibling rivalry.—"I hit my baby brother M. and make him cry. Then my mother hits me and I hit her back. I do not like the baby. He cries too much. I do carry him around, however." One is led to assume that Hamteya:u's resentment toward this baby is not simply sibling rivalry, but is largely motivated by the fact that the infant's birth and uncertain paternity caused the breakup of the parental home. The obligation to carry around (Devereux, 1948 c) this "intruder" may also explain Hamteya:u's dislike of his uterine sibling. It should be noted that he, in turn, pesters C. to play with him (cf. above).

School.—"I go to the reservation school. I am in the fourth grade of the Valley School and my grades are C and lower than C. Sometimes my teacher gets mad at me, but he does not beat me. I do not speak in class (see below) and do not like anyone at school. I do not like white people. Sometimes Mr. D. whips us until we cry. I like my teacher, but the kids sometimes laugh at me. Thus, Case 78 laughs at me, and the white children laugh at me too. Yet, Case 78 is a friend of mine. He thinks everything is funny. He kids you if you fall down, or are defeated in a football game." This matter appeared to agitate Hamteya:u a great deal, since his—almost breathlessly insistent—final remarks were as follows: "Please tell Case 78 not to laugh at me anymore. When he laughs at me the teacher does not say anything to him. Do please ask my teacher to stop Case 78 when he laughs at me. I think I shall make

---

[4] C. may have been conceived during a temporary separation between Nyoltc and her husband. The matter was not investigated.

good grades this time. Say nothing about this to my family. I want football 'gear' (helmet) from the Variety store, and they do not want to get it for me. They scold me whenever I ask for it. That is why I am mad at my mother and refuse to try for good grades in school. Perhaps you can speak to my mother about that. If they get me the football helmet I will speak up in class. Really I will. It costs 98 cents." [5]

Playmates.—"As a rule I play alone. At school I only play with boys, never with girls." It was noted above that, despite his pleas, his older (uterine?) brother refuses to play with him.

Dreams.—"I often have anxiety dreams and wake up frightened, but I do not recall what it is I dreamed. I think I dream of something that bites—maybe of snakes.[6] (Q) I have falling dreams but no suffocation nightmares. (Q) Non habeo somnos humidos. [Hitcu:y Kutask(w)elvå sua sponte dixit se somnos habere humidos.] I had no dream last night (November 7–8, 1938). I went to the show with the 25 cents you had paid me."

Nonheterosexual experiences.—"Nullus umquam puer mentulam meam tractare conatus est. Ego interdum solus onanizo; emissio seminis non fit, sed fit titillatio, quae me iuvat. Adultos numquam vidi coeuntes.[7] E. S., puer XIII annorum, mihi monstravit quomodo coeatur, copulans me praesente cum puella XIII fere annorum (E. W.). Numquam antea fututationem videram; non timebam (Devereux, 1950 a) sed me pudebat. Hoc evenit eadem aestate qua cum R. concubui; septem fere dies antequam ego feci."

First sex experience.—"Concubui aestate anni MCMXXXVII (de facto MCMXXXVI) cum R., puella Mohavia XI (de facto IX) annorum. Ulcera illius accepi. Non nisi semel id fecimus: factum est domi eius; ista stuprum poposcit. Puellam futuens semen emisi.[8] Haec est una quacum concubui, atque semel tantum factum est. Nunc non facio—timeo ne iurger, atque me pudet."

Attitude toward the partner.—R. aliis quoque pueris familiariter utitur, at ego, qui illam non diligo, neque furore neque invidia affligor. Concumbit cum quibus iuvenibus Mexicanis qui prope habitant. [In this context Hitcu:y Kutask(w)elvå commented that "girls are looser than men; most girls run around, while only a few boys are loose. Aliquae puellae adhuc ludum litterarum frequentantes cum viris adultis concumbunt."] [9]

Hospitalization.—"Ulcera habui postquam cum R. coii, at non in mentula mea.[10] I did not get shots at the hospital, but they made some tests. The treatment did not hurt. The Mohave said I had hiku:pk. In nosocomio me futuisse non dixi quia me pudebat."

Publicity and humiliation.—"I did not tell the truth to my parents either. I was afraid of what they might do to me." [At this point, Hitcu:y Kutask-(w)elvå said with some bitterness: "Some people don't care what they do to children."] Dixerunt quidam—utriusque generis adulti—matri meae me futuisse, sed illa (primo) non credidit. She thought maybe I just had some kind of sore, but not hiku:pk."

---

[5] At this point the interview was concluded; Hamteya:u was given the dollar he had been promised. Also he was taken uptown, to the Variety store, where a football helmet, which he craved, was purchased for him. In the course of the interview itself there was a brief interruption, during which we went to the Trading Post to purchase candy for Hamteya:u and my young interpreter.

[6] His playmate, Case 78, also had snake dreams.

[7] Given the setup at home, this is obviously untrue (Devereux, 1951 d).

[8] Cum onanizat, semen emittere non videtur, ut vide supra.

[9] Hitcu:y Kutask(w)elvå voiced a standard Mohave opinion, which, according to the late M. A. I. Nettle, M. D. (MS., n. d.), accurately describes the conditions prevailing at that time.

[10] But compare the hospital record, below.

"While I was still in the hospital, R.'s mother wanted to fight my mother, because she did not want anyone to say things about her daughter; however, in the end, they did not fight after all.[11] After I got out of the hospital, my mother beat me. She asked me why I did it, and told me not to do it again." [12] [At this point I commented that the older Mohave do not approve of child beating, whereupon my young interpreter said: "My mother (who is well educated and admits that the Mohave acquired the habit of beating their children through being beaten by their teachers in school) even used to throw stones, bricks, and knives at me, but she doesn't do it any more. Nowadays she just whips me. Even my stepfather whips me occasionally nowadays, but most of the time he intercedes with my mother on my behalf."] [13]

"At that time I was in the town school and not in the Valley school, where I am now. I was not punished by the teachers for what I had done." (Extraordinary as it may seem, no white appears to have suspected that Hamteya :u and R. had had sexual relations, even though all the Mohave knew it, and even though both children were hospitalized at almost the same time with gonorrhea.)

Public ridicule and neurotic response.—"I used to be known as a clown before all this happened.[14] But, when I got out of the hospital, people made fun of me. Then I stopped talking and became contrary (negativistic) and uncooperative. I know a little Indian girl named E.; she is like me, but she talks even less than I do. She just stands around and no one plays with her.[15] Children, not adults, laughed at me; chiefly Case 78, E. S., A. B., and a girl of 14 I. T. All these are school children like I am, but only Case 78 attends the Valley School like I do."

As was shown above, Hamteya: u spontaneously attributed his neurosis and bad grades to ridicule and to tensions in the family. He felt certain that, if the ridicule ceased, both his behavior and his grades would improve.

Plans.—"When I grow up I will work at any kind of job I can get." [Are you a budding shaman?] "No."

Sex-identification.—This topic was approached indirectly, by asking first my interpreter whether he would rather be a boy or a girl. The interpreter said he preferred to be a boy, and Hamteya :u agreed with him. "It is much easier to be a man. You can work; you can make a house. Women must get married to make a living. Of course, some women can work in an office and rent a room. Most women know how to cook, while only a few men can also cook. [Do males envy the procreative functions of females?] Well—some people want babies badly, but cannot have them, and so they adopt some."

Hamteya:u's medical record:

This 10-year-old boy was admitted to the hospital with gonorrheal urethritis (9 days after R. was admitted to the hospital with vaginal and urethral gonorrhea; no connection seems to have been suspected). He was placed in an isolation ward.

---

[11] Mohave parents are inclined to fight the parents of children who harmed their own offspring (Devereux, 1950 h).

[12] This beating was presumably due to anger over the humiliating publicity.

[13] The stepfather was an extraordinarily sweet-tempered person, even for a Mohave (pl. 10, *b*) (Devereux, 1950 f).

[14] Excessive clowning in a child is a well-known neurotic attention-getting device, which often conceals much underlying sadness and loneliness.

[15] The case of this girl was not investigated. The above data do not enable one to decide whether she was simply abnormally shy or else mentally retarded. Later information suggests that she was not feebleminded (Case 71).

Presenting symptoms.—Inability to urinate for 2 days.—Discharge of pus from urethra. It hurts him to urinate and he experiences a burning sensation. The prepuce is inflamed; it is reddened and slightly edematous. Otherwise the patient is in good health and appears well nourished.

Laboratory findings.—A smear was taken and the presence of intracellular micrococci, presumably gonococci (diplococci), was demonstrated.

Etiology.—The patient denied any form of exposure to infection.

Other findings.—After 28 days of hospitalization the patient was briefly under observation for cerebrospinal fever. The findings were negative.

Treatment consisted of local applications of argyrol, etc., for about a month. During the treatment period the meatus was stuck together several times. Thirty-two days after admission there had been no discharge for 3 days past and no inflammation. Patient was discharged.

R.'s medical record:

This 9-year-old girl was hospitalized (9 days before Hamteya:u) with an acute gonococcic urethritis and vaginitis.

Presenting symptoms.—The patient complained of pain when urinating. She also had pains when sitting down. There was a vaginal discharge; the vagina was markedly excoriated, and the labia maiora were swollen. The entire genitals were covered with a pustular exudate and the labia maiora were excoriated with breaks in the mucosa. The genitalia were swollen, and tender to the touch of the cotton swab. The eyes were apparently not infected. The condition was of several days' duration. Otherwise the patient seemed healthy and well nourished.

Laboratory findings.—Smears were taken.

Etiology.—The patient reports that other members of her family have also had discharges.[16] She denies immoral contacts (sic!).

Discharge against medical advice.—Three days after the patient's hospitalization there arrived at the hospital a delegation of the family, led by W. S., a fairly well acculturated man. The delegation charged that the patient was being neglected and asserted that the child's pads had not been changed for 2 days; all of these charges were proved untrue.[17] Since, despite this demonstration, the family demanded that the patient be discharged, the child was permitted to leave the hospital against medical advice.

Comment

Tentative diagnosis.—Neurotic negativism in a badly ridiculed boy who overreacted to ridicule because he was an insecure, depressive, "attention seeking" clown even before this traumatic teasing.

The fact that he was not ridiculed by adults, but only by other schoolchildren—whose attitudes were presumably actively influenced by the occidental morality of their teachers—reveals certain basic aspects of the Mohave Indians' attitude toward juvenile sexual activities.

From the Mohave point of view Hamteya:u was delinquent only in that he abused his small sibling and was a truant and an exceptionally bad student. From the point of view of the adult Mohave, his sexual activity was one suitable

---

[16] Gonorrhea was common among the Mohave.

[17] For years after the death of their much-beloved reservation physician, M. A. I. Nettle, M.D., who was "our doctor" for some 22 years, the Mohave refused to place real trust in their subsequent Agency physicians, and often complained of being neglected, though at least in the case of one first-rate doctor, James L. Troupin, M.D., I myself was able to ascertain that the charges were totally unfounded.

for his age, and his having contracted gonorrhea a commonplace misfortune. The mother's punitive reaction presumably did not reflect *moral* condemnation, but simply represented a personal reaction of anger over a difficult and "messy" situation, which could have easily led to administrative difficulties with the Agency.

It is especially significant for a proper evaluation of Hamteya :u's delinquency, which was so labeled by the Mohave themselves, that no one considered him to be a budding shaman or witch, even though he belonged to a family in which shamans and witches are said to be quite numerous.[18] This means that his misconduct diverged so extensively from the "pattern of misconduct" usually exhibited by budding shamans that not even his membership in a notoriously shamanistic family could persuade the Mohave that he was simply a typically "difficult" future shaman, rather than a genuine neurotic delinquent. It should also be noted that, quite unlike Case 78, Hamteya :u himself did not plan or wish to become a shaman, presumably because he sensed that becoming a shaman would not solve his highly idiosyncratic problems. Thus, Hamteya :u should be viewed psychiatrically, culturally, and in terms of his self-appraisal as well, strictly as a neurotic delinquent.

CASE 78 (Informants: The subject and Hitcu :y Kutask (w) elvå) :

I am 12 years old. I am in the fourth grade and get D's and B's in school. My mother's name is Mah. My stepfather is T. D. The three of us live together. My father is dead. [To what gens did your father belong—I mean what is your gens?] I don't know. [Q] I have no siblings. My mother and stepfather treat me well.

[Q] I play with several Mohave kids; I play with Hamteya :u (Case 77) D. S., L. S., a Yuma boy named G., and with the interpreter. I also play with two American boys: O. J. Sk. and P. Sm. [Do you play with Mexican kids too?] Yes—with D. M. and M. M. and with R. P. [Why don't you play with girls as well?] I do not like it.

[Do you get beaten at home?] No, I am neither beaten nor punished. [Are you in good health?] I had measles a long time ago. I stayed home; they did not take me to the hospital. [Q] They feed me well at home. [Q] No one is mean to me, and I am not mad at anyone. [Q] I speak mostly Mohave at home, but I am not told Mohave stories and no one teaches me Mohave customs at home.

[Q] I have dreams and remember them. [Q] I have never been drunk in my life. [Q] I smoke cigarettes and any other tobacco I can get hold of.

[Q] Ego numquam coii. [Hitcu :y Kutask(w)elvå, qui est amicus Case 78, hoc dicto non confisus sodalem sua sponte interrogavit, nonnullarum mentionem faciens tenerae aetatis puellarum. Case 78 se coitum expertum esse negabat, sed furtim cachinnabat ita ut manifeste dicto suo contradiceret.]

[Q] Habeo somnos humidos—de grandibus puellis plus XIV annorum.[19] [Q] Ego non onanizo. [Cum interpres iterum sua sponte Case 78 rogaret, plane dubitans de eo quod dixerat.] Sane, inquit, aliquando onanizo. Ut verum tibi dicam, coii cum puella XIII annorum cui nomen est Mah. (Same gens as his mother.) Come to think of it, I must belong to the Mah gens—at least I think I do.[20] Saepe cum Mah coivi. [Q] Per vim cum illa concumbere coepi. W. H. et ego illam rapuimus: clamitabat puella sed non destitimus, etiam

---

[18] The Mohave believe that shamanistic powers run in certain families (Devereux, 1937 c).

[19] A girl of 14 rates and functions as a woman in Mohave society (Devereux, 1951 d).

[20] This is unlikely, since his mother is of that gens. His error may be due *symptomatically* to perseveration, *dynamically* to oedipal impulses, which become intensified during puberty and *socially* from the lack of a father (cf. Case 77).

cum alii supervenissent adulescentes.²¹ Placet mihi coitus, sed emissio seminis mihi non fit.

[Q] Last night (November 9–10, 1938) I dreamed that a snake bit me. Then I woke up. I don't know what kind of a snake it was. The night before that (November 8–9, 1938) I dreamed about a lot of stuff. [Q] I have no recurrent dreams. [Q] Yes, I want to become a shaman later on. [Do you dream about the gods, like shamans?] No. [How long ago did this business with Mah happen?] Last summer. [Do you have a girl now?] No.

[Num umquam vidisti futuentes?] Vidi F. St. futuentem, sed non vidi Hamteya:u (Case 77) neque umquam adultos vidi hoc facientes. [Q] We live in a one-room house—all three of us sleep there. We also have another house for cooking. [Q] All three of us sleep in one bed. [Sed tu negas te umquam adultos futuentes vidisse?] I do.²²

[Q] When I am grown up, I want to work at anything I can get.

[Whom do you want to marry?] I don't know. I'll marry anyone who wants to marry me.²³

[Why are you a truant?] I just get lazy spells and stay home. [Don't your parents tell you to go to school?] No—well, they do tell me to go, but I just refuse to go and I do not get punished, either at home or at school, for not going to school. Sometimes I do not go to school because I do not have lunch.

[Q] Yesterday I got punished in school for drawing, I had to stay in during recess.²⁴

[Do you ride horseback?] Yes. I even have a horse.²⁵

[Q] I fight with E. St.; he is bigger and stronger than I and he makes me cry. Of course, anyone can make Hamteya:u (Case 77) cry. [Quis te docuit quomodo coeas?] Nemo. [Quomodo masturberis?] Nemo: solus didici. [Iam emittis semen?] Non facio—facio.²⁶ Multa emissa est materia, et mentula dolebat mingenti. Colei quoque tumuerunt, sed in nosocomium non me contuli. Aliquid puris evenit. [Factumne est hoc postquam cum Mah concubuisti?] Antea fuit. [Adhucne venit pus illud?] Interdum solum.²⁷

[Do you have enuresis?] No, not now. I had it long ago, when I was still small.

[Vidistine umquam animalia coeuntia?]²⁸ Vidi—heri vidi canes hos facientes. Iubet spectare; mentula mihi fit rigida, at non onanizo.

[Q] Puellam masturbantem numquam vidi." ²⁹

[Question addressed to Hitcu:y Kutask(w)elvâ: Vidistin umquam puellam hoc facientem?] Non vidi—ut verum dicam, vidi F. W. hoc facientem. Id facere solebat, mihique spectare libebat: mentulam mihi reddidit rigidam."

[Question addressed to Case 78: Why do you tease Hamteya:u?] I don't know why.

---

²¹ Non fit raro inter Mohavios, adultos quoque, ut coeant caterva facta (Devereux, 1948 f), et inopinata irruptione facta desistere nolint (Devereux, 1939 a).

²² This denial is a Mohave convention; it does not reflect actual facts (Devereux, 1951 d).

²³ This is a typical Mohave attitude (Devereux, 1951 f).

²⁴ This boy likes to draw and made several drawings during our conversation (pl. 2).

²⁵ Case 78 presumably refers here to the finest horse on the reservation, which his stepfather had meant to use as a stud horse. However, this horse was stolen from him, allegedly by a white man, and by the time he recovered it the fine stallion had been gelded by the thief.

²⁶ A typical Mohave answer to a sudden embarrassing question.

²⁷ This may have been a simple urethritis of unknown origin.

²⁸ A common amusement of Mohave children (Devereux, 1948 g).

²⁹ Interdum, puella nervis infirmis laborans publice se ipsam defricat (Devereux, 1950 c).

Comment

Tentative diagnosis.—From the Mohave point of view, Case 78 is neurotic only in that he is aggressive and cruel to Hamteya:u. In fact, he was interviewed partly in response to Hamteya:u's plea (Case 77) that I should ask Case 78 to stop tormenting him. This aggressivity, which fits the rest of the type of behavior that one expects, by definition, to observe in a boy who wishes to become a shaman (Devereux, 1937 c), is also reflected in the drawings that he decided to make for me. All of these drawings (pl. 2) represent rough-looking men with threatening guns or teeth.[30] It should be noted, however, that, in 1938, Case 78 was not considered (as yet?) to be a budding shaman, though of the three boys interviewed only he expressed the desire to become a shaman.

Apart from his aggressive behavior toward Hamteya:u, Case 78 makes a favorable impression and is, on the whole, simply a typical, exuberant and uninhibited Mohave youngster. The occasional truancy impressed only the white school principal as a sign of maladjustment, but was ignored by the boy's own family, as well as by various informants, who unanimously denied that he was neurotic. His extreme exuberance is, however, clearly narcissistic and exhibitionistic, as is shown, e.g., by the ornate manner in which he wrote his initials and also his full name (not reproduced in this work).

His aggressivity toward Hamteya:u appears to be triggered in part by the desire to make Hamteya:u cry, the way E. S. makes him cry. This is a typically infantile way of mastering an injury, by "handing it on" to someone weaker than oneself. It should be noted that, unlike Hamteya:u's aggressive ill-treatment of his baby brother (Case 77), Case 78's aggressivity is not directed at a helpless infant, but at a playmate his own size, and is not as obviously an expression of neurosis as Hamteya:u's aggression is. Otherwise stated, Hamteya:u's victim is actually helpless, because he is a mere infant, while Hamteya:u can be victimized by Case 78 only because his neuroticism makes him a "sissy."

BORDERLINE PSYCHOSES OF YOUNG SHAMANS

It is proposed to present in this section an account of the abnormal behavior exhibited early in life by the female shaman Nyoltc Hukthar (Nyoltc coyote="crazy Nyoltc") who, according to the Mohave themselves, suffered all her life from a disorder of the sexual impulse called ya tcahaetk (Case 13), as well as from "nervousness" (hukthar hit'i:k) (Case 79).

The theoretical objective of this section is to demonstrate the validity of the general thesis (Kroeber, 1952; Linton, 1956; Devereux, 1956 b) that, even though the shaman is socially more or less "adjusted" (Ackerknecht, 1943) and performs socially valued functions, he or she is, nonetheless, psychiatrically a genuinely ill person, and is specifically recognized and diagnosed as such by other members of the tribe. Since this point of view is expressed also in other chapters of this work, the present discussion is limited to an account of this woman's behavior in her childhood and youth, followed by certain

---

[30] Biting is equated with shooting, e.g., in Ahma Huma:re's account of the hikwi:r illness (pt. 4, pp. 117–128).

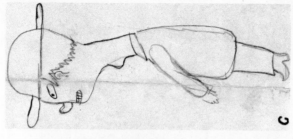

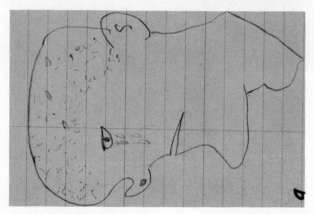

a, "John Smith's" self-portrait.   *b, c,* Drawings by "John Smith."   (× approximately 2/3.)

Drawings by Case 78.   (× approximately 1/2.)

general comments. The information about to be presented was obtained from Hivsu: Tupo:ma in 1933, in connection with an inquiry into shamanism. Hama: Utce: acted as interpreter. Additional data, pertaining specifically to Nyoltc Hukthar's neuroticism in adulthood, as well as her vital statistics, are given elsewhere in this work (Case 13) (pt. 2, pp. 77–81).

Girls who will become shamans behave even worse than boys. Of course, their power also surpasses that of male shamans.

Eiusmodi puella virgunculas suae vel inferioris aetatis proicit humi, quibus superincumbens corpus illarum corpori suo affricat. Interea sua vel amicarum pudenda continuo manu tractat, et per omne tempus seipsam defricat. Non sunt tuti ab illa vel pueri, quos huiusmodi puella supinos humi proicit et insuper subsidens mentulam pueri correptam contra volvam fricat suam—nonnumquam tam vehementer ut virga praeputiumque laedantur. Talis puella olim pueri virgam rigidam tam violenter tractavit ut urethram eius ruperit. Propinqui puellae illam hoc fecisse primo negabant, sed alia quae id viderat puella illam prodidit. The two families fought bitterly over this incident.[81] Postea, talis puella rogat pueros ut digitos immittant in volvam suam perscrutenturque eam— id quod maximo odio est Mohaviorum feminis normalibus, quae hoc sibi fieri non sinunt nisi in adulterii suspitione. (Devereux, 1950 a.)

CASE 79 (Informants: Hivsu: Tupo:ma and Hama: Utce:) :

Memini puellae cuiusdam, quae postea magna *shaman* facta est, quaeque omnia quae tibi narravi faciebat antequam XI annos nata esset. Eo tempore senex quidam illam ad flumen ducebat—natandi causa, ut dicebat. Senex iste licet fuerit, at mentula eius minime senilis erat; saepe coierunt. Quod istae tantum placebat ut senem domi suae viseret, quippe qui desiderio puellae satisfacere posse videretur. Audivisti Harav He:ya dicentem suo tempore viros usque ad mortem amore potentes fuisse. Tam famosa illorum societas facta est, ut senis denique uxor suspitionem ceperit, quae, quamquam valde irata, tamen quid ageretur certior fieri cupiebat antequam aliquid faceret.

Senex iste aliquando puellam ad flumen natatum deducebat. Nabant autem in lacu quodam qui plenus aquae manebat etiam post annuas inundationes. Anus illa quae ambos abeuntes viderat, in arbustis latitabat. Vidit senem, qui puellae in ripam deductae anum intra et extra lubrica quadam argilla lubricabat, qua argilla saepe salivae vice utuntur (Devereux, 1950 a).[32] Senex virgam in anum puellae immittere conabatur, et quandocumque paene immisisset, puella dolore affecta prorsus se iactitabat, ita ut mentula elaberetur. Tum anus irata baculo suscepto eos adgressa est. Senex statim puellam in aquam intrusit, iubens ut ad citeriorem lacus ripam naret; ipse ad iratam uxorem versus baculo vapulavit. Quae cum iram explevisset, "Non est," inquit, "operae pretium: iam illam habebis. Memet tu non vis: praestat ut te deseram." Deseruit eum, ipsaque hoc postea mihi narravit.

Postera aestate—eo tempore quo, exundante flumine Colorado, victum degimus arvaque serimus—vetus iste matrimonium unâ habitare cognovimus. Erat illis filius, sodalis meus, quocum ludum litterarum frequentabam. Certo die,

---

[81] Parents fight off children who are nasty to their own offspring and also fight with other adults about quarrels among children (Devereux, 1950 h).

[32] Sicut Patwinii (Kroeber, 1932), Mohavii saepe primum cum parvis puellis coitum per anum efficient (Devereux, 1951 e).

cum anus fabas quae *mesquite* vocantur colligeret, puella illius absentia fructa senem rursus visit.   Ego et senis filius e ludo domum ibamus constitueramusque melopepones in eorum domo obtinere.   Cum ad domum venerimus, mirum quiddam conspeximus: senex puellam consederat ad perticam quae est in media domo, cruribus dispessis, tunica sublevata; ipse sedebat ad pedes eius, digitos volvae inserere conans.   Quod cum vidissem, dixi ad sodalem: "Ecce pater tuus ad solitos reversus est dolos!   Appropinquemus clam et capiamus eos!"   Cum assentisset, procubuimus in ripa fluminis quae XX fere passus a domo aberat. Post aggeris molem abditi pronique iacentes super ripam oculos coniciebamus. Senex digitum pedetemptim immittere conabatur, sed quandocumque altius impelleret, puella spasmo convulsa digitum retrahi cogebat.   Saepe conatus quattuor denique digitos vaginae immisit, dum puella podicem versabat ut illum se defricare adiuvaret.[33]   Subito lympham aliquam de senis cubito stillantem vidimus; primus vidi ipse, et, "En," inquam, "stillat!"   Puella adeo excitata visa est ut in manum senis mingeret.[34]   Lympham istam liquorem qui dicitur Bartholinus fuisse Hivsu: Tupo:ma negavit; lotum fuisse asseruit, quia puella 'tam plena erat diaboli.'   Denique, cum iam ad ludum decurrere decreverimus, quia tintinnabulum sonaturum erat, vidimus puellam manum capiti senis imponentem, ut volvae caput appropinquaret lotoque suo umectaret.[35]

At that point we decided to make our presence known, and cleared our throats noisily.   At the first sound we made, the girl raced out of the house and ran away. Then we walked up to the house, and the old man asked us what we wanted. When we said: "We want melons," he said: "Go and pick some in the field!" So we went out again and picked some melons and returned to school where we discussed what we had seen in every detail, and with a great deal of disgust. This happened about 50 years ago (probably not later than 1882).

For 2 years I continued to keep an eye on the old man's doings.   I kept this up until I went off to Needles, wishing to escape the woman I told you about some time ago (Devereux, 1950 a).   When, 6 years later, I returned to Parker, this young girl had grown up into a handsome married woman, but was already then generally known as Nyoltc Hukthar (Crazy Nyoltc).

As for the son of that old man, he got a steady job at the Agency as an interpreter, with a salary of $10.00 a month, and married Nyoltc Hukthar's older sister.   Thus, there lived in the same house, the old man, his son, his daughter-in-law, and Nyoltc Hukthar with her husband.   The old fellow knew that I knew all about his scandalous behavior, and seemed rather pleased about it. He would say to me: "Don't you ever mention it aloud!   I get my meals here, and if they found out about it, they might throw me out."

I don't know whether the old man and Nyoltc Hukthar ever had any further sexual relations, but I do not think they did.   Ego tamen senem appellabam "Siup pip siup," id quod est sonus exsilientis loti.   Not only wasn't he ashamed of this name, but he even laughed at it and seemed to be pleased with it.[36] No one else ever called him by that name.

As for Nyoltc Hukthar, she turned out to be a great eye-doctor, later on.   (For further data about this woman, and about her death, see Case 13, pt. 2, pp. 77–81.)

---

[33] Mohavii mulierem in coitu podicem versare rem nimis salacem ac turpissimam esse existimant (Devereux, 1950 a).

[34] In compluribus Micronesiae partibus viri mulieres usque ad mingendum excitant; mictus quoque post-orgiasticus ex illa regione nuntiatus est (Gladwin and Sarason, 1953; Devereux, 1958 a).

[35] Omnes Mohavii cunnilingum fieri negant et facies virum volvam humidam tangentem caecum fore asseverant (Devereux, 1948 f, 1950 a).

[36] The Mohave deliberately select grotesque names even for themselves.

Comment

Tentative diagnosis.—Borderline psychotic behavior.

Psychiatrically, the most striking aspect of the preceding case history is the masculine role which this young girl assumed in her relations with younger girls. Conservatively speaking, it suggests a total absence of the latency period, and may conceivably even imply a direct transition from oedipal attitudes to a premature (psychological) puberty. In this context it should be noted that when a female chimpanzee in oestrus is caged with another female who is not in oestrus, the rutting female will play a male role in her sexual and social behavior toward the non-rutting female (Yerkes, 1939). As regards Nyoltc Hukthar's aggressive and destructive sex play with boys, it must be viewed as an expression of rivalry with, and hostility toward, the male, and of a wish to perform phallic-urethral "feats."

The conduct of the old man can, to a considerable extent, be interpreted not so much as a senile person's debauching of the young, as a response to the deliberate seductiveness of an abnormal girl child. Indeed, in many occidental cases that are legally defined as "contributing to the delinquency of a minor," the *actual* and *tenaciously active* seducer is the girl child, who is acting out her oedipal impulses with a near-psychotic intensity.

The preceding case history adequately supports the view that the budding shaman has, at the lowest estimate, a borderline psychosis, possibly of the "hysterical psychosis" type, characterized by certain homosexual tendencies. The same impression is created also by all general accounts of the misconduct of the budding male shaman (Devereux, 1937 c), cuius in maxime indignis artificiis hoc est, ut inter mulieres mutonem sibi quoque deesse fingat mingatque "sicut equa." These quasi-homosexual acts of budding shamans of both sexes may be responsible for the Mohave belief that female shamans are stronger than male ones, and transvestite shamans stronger than either male or female ones (Devereux, 1937 b). The detailed case history of a lesbian shaman, who earned her living as a prostitute (Case 105), also fits this interpretation of the data. The proneness of future shamans to engage in zoophilia—often in a form that involves extraordinary and wholly un-Mohave brutality toward the misused animal (Devereux, 1948 g)—the tendency of witches to engage in incest (Devereux, 1939 a) and, finally, the notorious suicidal impulses of older witches (Kroeber, 1925 a), fully prove the thesis that—always in his youth, sometimes also in adulthood, and quite frequently in his old age—the Mohave shaman of either sex is to be diagnosed either as a borderline case, or else as an outright psychotic, and is, in fact, so diagnosed by the Mohave themselves. The same is true of so many other tribes as well, that Ackerknecht's (1943) attempt to give the shaman a clean bill of psychological health is both culturally and psychiatrically fallacious.

PART 7. SUICIDE

GENERAL INTRODUCTION

It is a basic Mohave tenet that all possible events in life, as well as all beliefs, customs, and rituals constituting culture, were established during the period of creation, usually by means of a mythical precedent. It is therefore desirable that—as an introduction to the study of suicide in Mohave culture—we should first examine the Mohave myth concerning the origin of death, which is so lengthy that it can only be cited in an abridged form.

The mythical origin of death.—The precedent for all deaths, from any cause whatsoever, was set by Matavilye. He decided that man had to be mortal, lest the earth should become so crowded that people would have to void their excreta on each other.[37] He was in the primal house when he resolved to die, so as to set a precedent. He was ill at that time and felt the need to defecate. Rising from his bed, he headed toward the door and, according to the Yuma version (Harrington, 1908), on passing near his daughter, he deliberately touched her genitals.[38] According to the Yuma account, it was this act which exasperated his daughter, while according to the Mohave account she was offended because her father wished to void his stools. Be that as it may, the daughter, who was also the first witch, immediately dived into the ground,[39] emerged exactly under her father, and, by swallowing his excreta, bewitched him. Shortly thereafter Matavilye died, as he intended to die, thereby bringing death into being. When they cremated him, Coyote—leaping over Badger and Raccoon, the shortest persons present—grabbed his heart and ran away with it.[40] Later on, as a punishment, Coyote became a foolish (=insane) tramp of the desert (Kroeber, 1948).

If one examines this account with special reference to self-destruction, the following points help one to understand the place of suicide in Mohave culture:

(1) The first death, which is the cause and prototype of all deaths on earth, was due to an act of will: Matavilye decided to die. Other-

---

[37] This specification is psychologically closely related to the way Matavilye died (cf. below).

[38] Another example of this type of seductive contact occurs in the story of a runaway "Coyote" girl (Devereux, 1948 h), who also resented it.

[39] A typical action in Mohave myths (Kroeber, 1948).

[40] Earlier accounts of this prototypal death were published by Bourke (1889), Kroeber (1925 a, 1948), and Devereux (1948 f). All accounts are similar, at least in their broad outlines.

wise expressed, the prototypal death was a vicarious suicide. It is, therefore, not surprising that the Mohave should believe in the existence of at least three types of vicarious suicide (pt. 7, pp. 371–430).

(2) More specifically, Matavilye chose to become the willing victim of witchcraft (pt. 7, p. 373 fn.), and induced his daughter to bewitch him, by means of a provocatively seductive act which angered her and presumably also made her anxious, since it stimulated her oedipal impulses.[41] In brief, when she bewitched her father, Matavilye's daughter "loved him but was angry with him"; moreover, she bewitched her sexually most tabooed relative, who had aroused her incestuous impulses. This is precisely the state of mind which the Mohave ascribe to the witch (pt. 7, pp. 387–426).

(3) Coyote stole Matavilye's heart, exactly the way the Mohave witch, fearful of being betrayed by the owllike creature into which his cremated victim's heart becomes transformed, seeks to steal and to kill this creature before it calls out his name, for everyone to hear (pp. 390–392).

Needless to say, this abridged myth fragment contains also many other culturally well-established items, such as underground travel, the magical use of excretions, and several other cultural practices and beliefs.[42] What concerns us chiefly in the present context is, however, the fact that this myth fragment, even in its abridged form, illuminates the whole range of Mohave beliefs related to death from any cause whatsoever, including especially suicide. In fact, it is doubtful that any purely rational attempt to bring together so many threads and skeins of belief, practice, and ritual in a brief narrative could even approximate the many-faceted, dreamlike complexity of this myth, which emerged from some early Mohave's unconscious, and was elaborated by his preconscious. It is this obvious multivalence of their myths that presumably enables the Mohave to cling to the belief that everything in life duplicates some mythical event and makes it possible for him to "acquire in dream" the magical powers needed for coping with such new problems as gunshot wounds (Devereux, 1942 c).

---

[41] The anal offense and the genital offense are psychologically equivalent. Indeed, not only are children prone to develop theories of anal birth, but such beliefs are even institutionalized among the Mohave, where male transvestites pretend to give birth anally (Devereux, 1937 b). Compare also the seeds in Coyote's stools which made agriculture possible and infanticide obsolete (Devereux, 1948 d). All this is one more proof in support of the thesis (Devereux, 1953 c) that, *on the latent level,* all versions of a myth—including even deliberately bowdlerized ones—say the same thing.

[42] According to Freud, were one able to analyze one single dream completely, this would be tantamount to a complete analysis of the dreamer. It is tempting to suggest that the same may be true of any myth, if one could trace all its implications and ramifications. In fact, it is especially tempting to suggest this with regard to Mohave myths, in which condensation plays a tremendous and recognized role (Devereux, 1957 b). Be that as it may, the myth fragment just cited contains, in a condensed form, allusions to practically every form of death, suicide, and funeral practice.

Be that as it may, it is quite certain that the myth fragment concerning the origin of death is, in fact, all the Mohave believe it to be: A condensed precedent for all forms of death, including suicide, which explains practically every cultural—and, in part, also psychological—aspect of death and suicide and whose most striking feature is that, in the last resort, it views voluntary death (vicarious suicide) as more basic than death from natural causes.

Since it is extremely likely that the Mohave tendency to derive death from suicide will be utilized by the champions of the primary self-aggression (death instinct) theory as an argument in support of their views, the following observations are in order:

(1) The Mohave do not possess a better "phylogenetic memory" than anyone else. Their myths do not show how life and death did, in fact, start. They only show what the Mohave happen to believe about the origin of life and death.

(2) It is psychologically almost a certainty that the Mohave belief and the occidental theory, both of which derive natural death from suicidal impulses, are simply psychic defenses against the unpleasant realization that—due to perfectly natural causes—man would die even if he never once experienced self-destructive impulses. The attempt to make the inevitable appear as a product of our own will is, thus, a megalomanic defense against the realization of man's inevitable mortality.[43]

It seems desirable to inquire at this point into theories regarding the origins of death. According to the Freudian death instinct theory, the prototypal death is suicide, while according to many mythologies death is brought into being through murder or its equivalent. In fact, even though the Bible postulates that man is inherently mortal, the first death recorded in the Bible is that of Abel, slain by his brother Cain. As regards the Mohave, their mythology takes a somewhat ambiguous position regarding the origin of death: Mata-

---

[43] The pretense that events independent of our will are the consequences of our acts can be observed among psychotics, among a few *irresponsible* students of parapsychology and also in children. As regards psychotics, I myself saw a paranoid schizophrenic pretend that the leaves on a bush, which could be seen from his window, moved because he sang certain magical songs "long enough." Actually, this " feat" simply took place on a slightly windy day, when mild gusts of breeze alternated with total calm. As regards some *irresponsible* students of parapsychology (telekinesis), the Journal of the American Society for Psychical Research published a devastating critique of a certain individual's alleged abilities to dispel a type of clouds by an act of will. This man simply chose clouds of a type which always disintegrate in a short time (D. Parsons, 1957). As regards children, Romain Rolland, in his novel *Jean Christophe,* describes better than any clinician a boy's attempt to control the movement of clouds. If they refused to drift in the prescribed direction, he stamped his feet and "ordered" them—with most satisfactory results— to move in the direction in which they had been drifting all along. Even humor takes cognizance of such omnipotence fantasies ; witness the story of the dog owner who boasted of his dog's absolute obedience : "When I tell him : 'Are you coming or are you not?' he either comes or he doesn't." Needless to say, humor often illuminates deeply buried unconscious processes (Freud, 1938).

vilye's death is intentional, and therefore represents suicide, but is actually brought about through witchcraft, and therefore represents murder.

It is unnecessary to repeat in this context what was said elsewhere (Devereux, 1958 b) regarding the cultural thought models underlying the doctrine of the death instinct, which is unacceptable to many classical analysts (Fenichel, 1953). The point which concerns us here is the fact that many cultures explain the origin of death in terms of suicide and/or murder, rather than simply in terms of man's inherent mortality.

As far as I know, it has never been pointed out that there exists a radical difference between murder and suicide on the one hand and death from natural causes, such as old age, on the other hand. This difference consists in the fact that it is possible to die of illness or of old age without either imagining or accepting the fact of death, whereas, at least in the human being, both murder and suicide presuppose the idea of death and its acceptance. It is suggested that this fact suffices to explain why intellectual explanations of the origin of death—even when they are heavily tainted with fantasy, as in myths concerning the origin of death—tend to favor theories, hypotheses, and mythical occurrences which include the psychic representation of death and the acceptance of the idea of death, and therefore view either suicide or murder, or some intermediate model, such as the Mohave myth of the death of Matavilye, which blends murder and suicide into a unified whole, as the basic prototype of death.

Actually, of course, one meets both with killing (murder) and suicide also in the animal kingdom. Yet, the studies of Zuckerman (1932) indicate that even primates, such as baboons, seem unable to recognize the state of death. Likewise, no sound animal psychologist, no matter how sympathetic he may be to the idea that primates are capable of relatively complex acts of mentation, would, even for a moment, entertain the idea that the self-destructive and, indeed, practically suicidal male *Macacus rhesus* monkey described by Tinklepaugh (1928), "knew" what he was doing, in the sense of having an operationally definable idea of death and an operationally definable idea of suicide.

In brief, it is suggested that the real problem of interest to the psychoanalyst is not the truth or falseness of the death instinct theory—which is a pseudo-problem, in Carnap's sense—but the motivation which impels both a genius of the first magnitude, like Freud, and the primitive myth maker, to explain death in terms of a theory—or myth—in which the basic model of death is murder and/or suicide, and which therefore presupposes from the start the idea of death and the acceptance of that idea. The fact that death can be triggered off by psychic and/or psychosomatic processes does not justify a psychologizing of physiology any more than the influence of brain lesions or of drugs upon our psychic functioning authorizes us to physiologize psychology. A reminder of such basic facts is, perhaps, especially necessary in an age of interdisciplinary research and may seem less bigoted when it comes from a student working in an interdisciplinary field, than it would be if it came from a more narrowly specialized scholar.

THE THEORETICAL FRAMEWORK

METHODOLOGICAL ASPECTS OF MOHAVE SUICIDE

Delimitation of the subject matter.—The present portion of this work seeks to study the Mohave Indian's conception of suicide, regardless of the fact that certain occurrences and activities viewed by the Mohave as suicides are not suicides in the modern, scientific sense of that word. Hence, no distinction will be made between deaths actually due to suicide and deaths—or symbolic deaths—which are obviously due to other causes. It also seemed desirable to accept unquestioningly, and to operate primarily in terms of, the categories of suicide defined by the Mohave themselves. Thus, we will consistently differentiate between funeral suicides and suicides not committed during funerals, even though it is possible to show that many of the latter are also due to more or less disguised and delayed mourning reactions.

A systematic adherence to this policy is greatly facilitated by the fact that the Mohave are a relatively small tribe. Were the Mohave very numerous, one would no doubt meet with many cases that it would be hard to assign to one category of suicide only. Thus, in a very large tribe there would almost certainly be cases of twin braves straying into enemy territory, of shamans killing themselves because of the infidelity of their wives, etc. As is, every single real or alleged case of Mohave suicide could be unhesitatingly assigned to one suicide category only, and this despite the fact that several types of suicide appear to have highly similar basic motivations.

METHODOLOGICAL CONSIDERATIONS

The "cultural mass" of the idea of suicide in Mohave society.—The basic datum in any discussion of suicide in Mohave society is the enormous sociocultural "mass" (Devereux, 1940 b) of the *idea* of suicide. The magnitude of this "mass" can be ascertained (Devereux, 1957 a) by demonstrating that a number of occurrences which cannot be called suicides by any objective standard are forcibly brought within the scope of suicide, by establishing an "artificial compendence" between that occurrence and real suicide. This is true even if suicide is defined in the broadest possible psychoanalytic sense of the term, and is made to include also certain psychosomatic ailments, accident proneness and other unconsciously motivated self-destructive acts.

The Mohave apply the term suicide to the following occurrences:

(1) Certain stillbirths, with or without the simultaneous death of the mother, which are believed to be caused either by the spontaneous unwillingness of a future shaman to be born, or else by the fact that the bewitched nonshamanistic fetus was taught by a witch "the fatal trick" of killing both itself and its mother at birth (Devereux, 1948 e, and pt. 7, pp. 331–339).

(2) The death of a suckling who, because its mother is pregnant once more, has to be weaned suddenly and therefore allegedly makes itself sick from spite (Devereux, 1947 a, pt. 7, pp. 340–348).

(3) The death of one or both twins either at birth or at any time before they get married (Devereux, 1941, and pt. 7, pp. 348–356).

(4) The symbolic or social pseudo-suicide of a man who, on marrying a kins-woman, consents to his own partial social death by allowing a horse to be killed at his wedding. The death of the horse (=bridegroom) supposedly dissolves the bonds of kinship between the future spouses, and enables a "new boy" to marry the "former" kinswoman (Devereux, 1939 a, and pt. 7, pp. 356–370).

(5) A bewitched person may actually wish to become the victim of the be-loved witch and may therefore refuse to cooperate with his or her therapist (Devereux, 1937 c, and pt. 7, pp. 383–386).

(6) An aging witch may overtly (Kroeber, 1925 a; Devereux, 1937 c) or tacitly incite the relatives of his victims to kill him, so that he can join—and perma-nently retain his hold over—the beloved ghosts of his victims (Devereux, 1937 c and pt. 7, pp. 387–426).

(7) A warrior, weary of life, may deliberately stray alone into enemy terri-tory, in order to be killed (Halpern, 1938, and pt. 7, pp. 426–431).

(8) Funeral suicide (Devereux, 1942 a, and pt. 7, pp. 431–459).

(9) Real suicide (pt. 7, pp. 459–484).

Methodological difficulties.—No deviant act is more difficult to ap-praise anthropologically, and no psychic derangement is harder to explore psychodynamically than suicide, chiefly because this deed represents a negation of the basic drive—the instinct of self-preservation—so that complete empathy with the suicide is almost an impossibility for the normal person. Moreover, not only is it actually impossible to obtain information from the successful suicide, but it is also altogether questionable whether one can obtain broadly valid data from persons who consult a psychiatrist because they ex-perience suicidal impulses, or were prevented from attempting suicide, or made unsuccessful attempts to kill themselves, or were "acciden-tally" saved at the very last moment. In none of these instances can one be entirely certain that the motivation is rigorously identical with that of individuals who actually killed themselves. This problem was outlined elsewhere (Devereux, 1955 a) approximately as follows:

Statements obtained from persons who have *unsuccessfully* attempted suicide do yield some clues, but are open to criticism on the score that, as all psychiatrists know, a really determined person can kill himself even when restrained and under constant supervision. Hence, the range of phenomena, from threats of suicide—motivated by the desire to dramatize oneself or to blackmail someone, etc.—to seemingly bona fide suicidal attempts that were frustrated at the last possible moment through the seemingly "chance" intervention of some external agency, forms a continuum. This does not mean, however, that we must lapse into a complete interpretative nihilism. Indeed, even though many last-minute "chance" rescues may have been unconsciously "engineered" by the would-be suicide, one is nonetheless entitled to wonder precisely how many actually successful suicides were intended originally as simply exhibitionistic "attempted suicides," which just "happened" to succeed because of an accidental failure of the intended rescuer to appear at the right moment. Of course, at this point one may begin to suspect that the "chance" failure of the rescuer to turn up in time was also "engineered" by the would-be suicide, and that the suicide was therefore a genuine one, and so on, ad infinitum. Moreover, we must also take into account the possibility that in some instances a seemingly genuine and intentional suicidal act may not have been seen by the victim himself in that light. Thus, a minimally acculturated middle-aged Navaho Indian, who worked far from his reservation as a railroad track worker, contracted a severe upper respiratory infection and had to be hospitalized in a setting where no one spoke Navaho. When, after improving slightly, he was still not permitted to leave the hospital, he appears to have evolved the conviction that he had been—incomprehensibly and unjustly—imprisoned. Wishing to escape "imprisonment," he therefore jumped off the roof terrace of the four-story hospital. In this instance it is almost impossible to know whether this man really thought that he could escape alive in that manner, or whether he actually tried to kill himself. Due allowance being made for a great scientist's dictum, that nature is unconcerned over the greatness of the analytical difficulties wherewith its phenomena confront the mathematician, somewhere or other a line must be drawn between excessively obsessive methodological refinement-mongering, and naively sweeping generalization-mongering.

In practical terms, this means that we will make use of whatever data we possess in our attempt to understand Mohave suicides and Mohave beliefs concerning suicide, but will always bear in mind that both our data and our interpretations are necessarily segmental ones and possess only a limited validity. However, since the real focus of this work is the place of suicide in Mohave culture, our interpretations would be valid, at least in that cultural frame of reference, even if every seemingly fully intended Mohave suicide turned out to be an accidentally botched exhibitionistic suicidal attempt, and even if it were demonstrable that every rescued would-be suicide did retroactively falsify his real motivation, either in order to save face, or because he now totally repudiates his presuicidal motivation and can no longer understand it,[44] or because the actual physical and psychic trauma of the conscious or else disguised suicidal attempt radically restructured the would-be suicide's psychic economy, for example by gratifying his need for punishment and by alleviating his guilt feelings (Case 64).

Theoretical frames of reference.—Existing theories of suicide fall, by and large, into five categories:

Legal theory views the suicide as an antisocial being (felo de se), whose act deprives society of the services of one of its members. In our own society, the law has a double standard: The person who bungles his suicide is, in principle at least, defined as a malefactor, though in practice he is usually simply hospitalized. By contrast, the successful suicide is automatically held to have been "unsound of mind." In neither case is there any attempt to bring before the court those who drove a person to suicide. By contrast, the Sedang Moi of Indochina fine the oppressor who drove a relatively helpless individual, such as a young girl, to suicide (Devereux, MS., 1933–34). Since the Mohave have no legal theory of suicide, and since modern legal theory is based upon an obsolete conception of human psychology, no attempt will be made to interpret Mohave suicide legalistically.

Sociological theory is best represented by Durkheim's (1897) conception of anomie, which, with some additional refinements, is readily applicable to our Mohave data. According to Durkheim, people kill themselves only if their ties with society, and orientation in society, are impaired. In aboriginal times the Mohave killed themselves when their ties with society *as a whole* were weakened. Next, there came a stage where the defections of certain socially proximate *and* emotionally significant persons were experienced as a rejection by society as a whole. The nagging of a father (Cases 111, 116) or the flightiness and irresponsibility—though not necessarily also adultery—of a housewife (Case 118) could elicit in the ill-treated individual a sense of *social* rejection, since his expectations regarding these persons were rooted in the culture pattern. Otherwise expressed, the Mohave counted upon support from his father and on a correct performance of duties on the part of his wife, not primarily

---

[44] Loss of contact with some unusual act of one's own—the feeling "did I really do that?" or "I can't understand what made me do it"—is a psychological phenomenon whose detailed analysis has, so far as I know, never been undertaken and would be most rewarding.

because of the personalized bond between himself and his father or wife, or because of the distinctive personality makeup of these individuals, but chiefly because of certain basic specifications of Mohave culture regarding behavior to be expected from participants in such socially defined relationships. Only in relatively recent times do we begin to meet with suicides motivated by the fact that the individual is rejected by a beloved person, such as the girl he is courting (Case 121), who does not—or does not, as yet—have *culturally defined* duties toward the individual. This change parallels a gradual shift in the Mohave Indian's pattern of allegiance to his society. In aboriginal times his chief emotional anchor was the tribe as a whole; i. e., its collective presence and also the sense of its continuity in time, as represented by the Mohave Indian's intense awareness of his national identity (Kroeber, 1925 a). At present, however, Mohave society is moving from the Gemeinschaft toward the Gesellschaft pattern (Tönnies, 1887), so that the individual's chief emotional anchor is increasingly his subjective relationship with a limited number of people of his own choice, who are emotionally meaningful to him and who—like a girl one loves (Case 121)—may, *on a purely cultural basis*, have no explicit obligations toward him. Hence, functionally at least, the total effect of a total social rejection in aboriginal times can be elicited today by rejection on the part of an emotionally significant person who, socially speaking, has no formal obligations toward the individual. This analysis is, on the whole, applicable to all types of genuine suicide, and can even help one to interpret Mohave *beliefs* concerning imaginary suicides. The only further specification to be made is that "social rejection" may, either in reality or else in Mohave belief, be replaced by a prior rejection *of* society *by* the neurotic person—such as the witch (pt. 7, pp. 387–426)—or else by the failure of the child to mature to the point where it can successfully transfer its basic allegiances from its mother to all members of society and to society as a whole, defined here as a Durkheimian (Durkheim, 1912) "collective representation."

The Mohave themselves seem rather keenly aware of this shift in the affective structure of their society, and of its relationship to new types of suicidal motivation. This is clearly shown by Tcatc's statement—quoted elsewhere in this section—that "white people commit suicide all the time." Now, it is quite certain that Tcatc's remark is not an inductive statement based on a careful study of the few cases of white suicide known to the Mohave (Case 82). It simply reflects the Mohave feeling that suicide must be frequent indeed in a society that, in their opinion, is characterized by a "shocking" lack of mutual support and by a corresponding "ridiculous" proneness to fall violently in love. Once this is clearly understood, Tcatc's belief that the modern Mohave are more prone to commit suicide because of marital and amorous disappointments than was formerly the case, clearly reflects her implicit belief that the modern Mohave is emotionally more deeply involved with his girl friend or spouse than was the case in aboriginal times, and that this greater concentration of the modern Mohave's emotional allegiances took place at the expense of a broader, though less intense, affective commitment to, and emotional dependence upon, the kin group and the tribe as a whole.[45]

Statistical theory—as distinct from the statistical *documentation* of sociological or psychological theories—does not provide any real understanding of suicide, which is an occurrence best discussed, at least to start with, in idiographic, rather than in nomothetic, terms. Attempts to formulate a purely statistical theory of suicide are doomed to failure in advance, since such a theory simply seeks to turn a disorderly confusion into a regimented chaos, without diminishing in the least the inherent scientific worthlessness of the junk pile of facts *which have not yet been given a meaning* in terms of some sociological or psychological theory. For this reason, and also because our data are neither numerous enough nor perfectly reliable in regard to readily quantifiable factors, such as age, dates, etc., no attempt will be made to "decorate" this work with pseudo-statistics.

Psychoanalytic theory interprets suicide in two ways. The more recent trend is to view suicide as the ultimate implementation of a primary instinctual self-aggression, which can, in theory, exist even in the absence of any frustration whatsoever (Freud, 1922; Menninger, 1938). True or false as this theory may be—and there are reasons to assume it to be false (Fenichel, 1953)—it is simply not usable in anthropological discourse, since it places the ultimate motivation of suicide wholly outside the scope of culture. The anthropologist who accepts this theory could, at most, discuss only the sociopsychological factors responsible for the *disinhibition* of this alleged "instinct." By contrast, the earlier psychoanalytic theory of suicide (Freud, 1930 [46]), which postulates the sequence: libidinal needs—frustration—aggression directed at an external object—frustration or inhibition of this aggression—aggression directed toward oneself, does give a wide scope to anthropological interpretations of the real motivation of suicide. While this fact does not *necessarily* prove the falseness of the anthropologically unexploitable "primary death instinct" theory, the anthropologist can defend his preference for the earlier theory on satisfactory heuristic grounds. Moreover, true or false though it may be, the *primary* death instinct theory has no known use even in clinical psychoanalysis, since it stops a priori all attempts to interpret the patient's "basic" self-aggression (Devereux, 1953 a).

---

[45] For additional comments see "Suicide and Cultural Change" below (pp. 314–326).
[46] Originally published in 1905.

Ethical theory is exceptionally useful for the anthropological interpretation of Mohave data, since the place of suicide in the Mohave value system, as reflected by Mohave attitudes, is of crucial interest to the anthropologist. The Mohave seem to view suicide as a means to an end, rather than as a self-contained action. Specifically, in terms of Allport's scheme (1937), Mohave suicide seems to be due quite often to "pull" rather than to "push," in that some Mohave suicides seem to seek something better than what *is*, more than they seek to escape some present evil. This is especially conspicuous in the vicarious suicide of witches, who cause themselves to be killed because they wish to join their beloved victims in the land of the dead (pt. 7, pp. 387–426), in the suicide of twins who simply decided to return to heaven (pt. 7, pp. 348–356), and also in the symbolic suicide of a person marrying a kinswoman (pt. 7, pp. 356–371) who uses his symbolic death as a stepping stone to "incestuous" marital bliss. The situation is less unequivocal in other types of suicide, so that each reader will have to decide for himself to what extent, if any, other forms of suicides are motivated by pull rather than by push.

Anthropological vs. psychological interpretations.—The precise relationship between the psychological and the sociocultural interpretation and understanding of a given event is one of the most vexed problems of the interdisciplinary field of ethnopsychology and ethnopsychiatry. A basic discussion of this problem is not only beyond the scope of the present study, but also quite unnecessary, since we repeatedly urged that there exists a complementarity relationship between the *simultaneous* sociological and psychological understanding of a given event. Indeed, the more fully we understand *at a given moment* the psychological motivation of, e.g., a certain suicide, the less fully we understand, at the same moment, its sociocultural determinants (Devereux, 1945 a). This problem is further discussed in part 7, pages 371–431.

Broadly speaking, the anthropologist is entitled to view suicide as an institution, albeit as an aberrant one, which represents a "pattern of misconduct," in Linton's (1936) sense. The anthropologist's task is therefore practically completed once he has clarified the institutional basis of suicide in a given society and has described the sociocultural determinants and meanings of recorded suicidal acts. In fact, he may even be quite legitimately indifferent to whether an attempted suicide was actually successful or not, or else may be interested in its outcome for statistical purposes only. His main concern is the sociocultural position of suicide in a given group, and, in his capacity as an anthropologist, he is entitled to take into account only sociocultural motivation. Thus, as anthropologists, the focus of our interest must be the elaborateness of ideas pertaining to suicide in Mohave society, and the variety of occurrences that the Mohave believe to be suicides (cf. above).   In addition we may also take cognizance of the fact that Mohave suicidalness is part and parcel of the general rebelliousness that pervades Mohave life and culture. Above all, as anthropologists, we must operate as though we accepted unquestioningly the manifestly erroneous Mohave supposition that certain deaths at childbirth, weaning, etc., are actually suicides, if we are to grasp the *function* and *"mass"* of the *idea* of suicide in Mohave culture.   Otherwise stated, for an anthropological understanding of Mohave suicide certain deaths at childbirth, or the symbolic suicide of the young man marrying his cousin, are quite as important as an understanding of bona fide instances of actual suicide.

In fact, we must even urge the need for distinguishing between two aspects of socially marginal behavior. For example, the statement that most petty thieves are drawn from the poorer classes is, strictly speaking, a psychoecological, rather than a sociocultural one. A truly anthropological and sociological study of the role of poverty and deprivation in theft must analyze almost exclusively such basic institutional aspects of culture and society as the significance of property, the cultural meaning of wealth and of poverty, social attitudes toward acquisitiveness, sociolegal distinctions between the legitimate and the illegitimate transfer and acquisition of property, etc. In brief, the socioanthropological purist is entitled to treat the role of poverty in theft chiefly as a social factor, derived from the basic sociocultural pattern, and to differentiate it from its psychomotivational force. The distinction just made corresponds to the basic distinction between the pure science of "social pathology" and the applied or remedial science of "social work." Moreover, it is precisely our failure to differentiate between these two meanings of "poverty as a cause of theft" which seems to handicap us in understanding such phenomena as juvenile delinquency also in psychiatric terms. Indeed, the psychoecological and sociological motivation of the impoverished juvenile thief is so understandable that it tends to obscure his subjective, though usually unconscious, motivation. Hence, such a limited understanding of the poor boy's thieving can shed no light at all upon the thieving of the rich juvenile delinquent, who is obviously not driven to theft by poverty. If, however, we view poverty as one aspect of a broad institution, which includes attitudes toward property and deprivation and also toward the various ways in which property can be acquired, we automatically deepen also our psychiatric understanding of the rich juvenile delinquent, for example, by realizing that, due to an inner quirk, he derives neurotic gratification from the acquisition of property in a reprehensible manner (Devereux, 1940 a) and enjoys the thrill of taking senseless and gratuitous, but "romantic," risks.

The position just taken implies that the psychiatric or psychological understanding of any form of conduct presupposes primarily an understanding of basic social and cultural facts and institutions, rather than an infinitely more superficial understanding of the most obvious effects of such basic sociocultural facts as hunger, poverty, or deprivation. This thesis tallies with our previously expressed view that some of the major roots of psychological conflicts are to be found in the basic culture pattern, rather than in superficial social techniques for the implementation of these basic patterns (Devereux, 1951 a, 1956 b). In other words, the locus of the real interplay between sociology and psychology is not the more manifest and superficial level of the personality or of society, but the bedrock of ethnic character structure on the one hand and the bedrock of the culture pattern on the other hand. This implies that, certain views to the contrary (Kroeber, 1952) notwithstanding, one of the principal objectives of both the ethnopsychiatrist and the so-called "real" anthropologist, is precisely the understanding of the nature of culture as a phenomenon sui generis (Devereux, 1946 b).

In brief, the fundamental source of the individual Mohave suicide's motivation is the bedrock of his tribe's culture and of his basic personality. Only the specific paths and mechanisms by means of which this basic motivation is translated into an overt act of suicide are the primary concern of the psychologist functioning solely in that capacity. For this reason we will seek to study primarily the social *causation* of the suicide's psychic *motivation*.

ETHNOPSYCHIATRIC ASPECTS OF MOHAVE SUICIDE

Suicide and ethnic personality.—An attempt to understand suicide in terms of Mohave ethnic personality must take into account from the start an aspect of ethnic personality which is usually completely neglected: the difference between the ethnic group's conception of its own characteristic personality type, which we may call the group's self-image, and the characteristic personality type of the group as seen by outside observers. This latter can, in turn, be divided into, e. g., the Mohave personality type as seen by unsophisticated whites in daily contact with the Mohave and as seen by anthropologists (Kroeber, 1925 a; Devereux, 1939 b) and other professionals.

(1) *The self-image* of the Mohave is radically at variance with characterizations of the Mohave published by anthropologists. The Mohave view themselves as a sober, stoical, strong, and silent people, or at least affirm that the Mohave had this kind of character structure in aboriginal times. They view this personality type as ideal and judge both the average and the deviant contemporary Mohave in terms of the extent to which he conforms to, respectively deviates from, this

ideal type. At the same time the Mohave also sees himself as a warm and generous person, although he feels that he is unable to show this side of his personality to whites, who are cold, unethical and graspingly acquisitive.

Now, whereas the self-image of the Mohave as a warmly generous person fully dovetails with the findings of anthropologists (Kroeber 1925 a; Devereux, 1939 b), his self-image as a stoical and aloof person is at variance with the views of those who studied him. It is tentatively suggested that this part of the Mohave Indian's self-image has two sources:

(*a*) One source of this part of the Mohave's self-image is Wild West literature, to which he is much addicted. It includes not only trash, but sometimes also such works as Stanley Vestal's biography of Sitting Bull (1932), which was seen in a Mohave home only a few months after its publication. A further source of this self-image may be Hollywood Wild West films, the lay American's image of the stoical Indians being likewise almost entirely derived from his stereotype of the Plains Indian, though we know of course that, e.g., the Crow (Lowie, 1935) were much addicted to humorous horseplay.

(*b*) A second source of this part of the Mohave Indian's self-image may well be his familiarity with such emotionally rather stolid groups as the Chemehuevi Indians, even though they have relatively little respect for that tribe. Indeed, the Mohave is quite prone to characterize both himself and "the Indian in general" in almost identical terms, and to contrast this composite image with his stereotype of whites. Hence, the incorporation of observable Chemehuevi, etc., traits into the Mohave self-image is not at all surprising. Moreover, the evolving of such a composite self-image could even have been predicted on the basis of the suggestion (Devereux, 1951 a) that, as a result of acculturation, the formerly important minutiae of tribal differences tend to be obliterated by the increased functional importance of what I termed the "areal basic personality," which, too, may eventually be superseded—at least as regards its functional importance—by a more generalized "American Indian basic personality." Needless to say, should this latter type of personality pattern, or self-image, ever come into being, it will be largely made up of traits wherein all Indians *do* differ, and/or *seek* to differ, and/or are *forced* to differ, from whites. In other words, should this personality type ever come into being, it will inevitably be the product not of a creative synthesis of various Indian areal character types, but of what may be termed "antagonistic acculturation" (Devereux and Loeb, 1943 a). Perhaps the strongest argument supporting this prediction is the current evolving of an Afro-Asian block of nations, made up of culturally disparate and sometimes historically antagonistic groups, whose collective—and purely syncretistic—self-image is almost exclusively a product of their collective antagonism to whites.

In brief, the Mohave Indians' self-image appears to be derived, at least in part, from Wild West literature and films, and, perhaps, also from their contacts with more stolid Indian groups, such as the Chemehuevi. Be that as it may, the behavior of the suicide is appraised both in terms of this standard of stoical strength of character and of the standard of generosity. The suicide is defined as weak, overly emotional, and selfish, i.e., as a person who does not live up to an ideal standard of conduct.

(2) *Lay characterizations* of the Mohave, by whites living near the reservation, do not directly contribute to our understanding of Mohave suicide and may therefore be disposed of in a few words. Due partly to cultural and language barriers and due also to the quiet and stolid deportment of the Mohave when visiting the town of Parker, the local whites consider the Mohave, *as a group*, a rather stolid people. On the other hand the *individual* Mohave who is personally known to a white and *individual* Mohave Indians who participate in some spectacular and scandalous occurrence which becomes known to whites, are described as unstable and emotional. The whites' tendency to view the Mohave as primarily stolid people agrees with Róheim's (1932) finding that the whites of Yuma call the culturally and temperamentally kindred Yuma Indians "the Indian Sphinx." In the Mohave as well as in the Yuma case this layman's view of their temperament simply shows that Western whites are successfully deceived by the Indians' façade of stolidity, which is due partly to a deliberate attempt to have as little to do with whites as possible, and partly to the seeming inability of most Mohave to communicate *affectively* in English.[47]

(3) *Professional characterizations* of Mohave ethnic personality (Kroeber, 1925 a; Devereux, 1939 b), which are implicitly supported by all anthropological publications on the Mohave, consistently stress the warm and mercurial temperament of the Mohave, his adaptability, his proneness to extremes and also his determination, which sometimes verges on stubbornness. It is interesting to note, however, that even though Kroeber strongly underscored the tremendous preoccupation of the Mohave Indians with autistic processes, such as dreams and their cultural counterparts, he does not refer to this aspect of their personality in his characterization of their disposition—perhaps because this side of their makeup is hard to reconcile with their generally extroverted temperament. Yet, it would appear (Devereux, 1939 b) that these seemingly divergent trends are actually highly complementary. Indeed, the Mohave is too firmly rooted in reality to have

---

[47] Compare in this context the fact that a delinquent boy (Case 76), who spoke good English, tended to answer embarrassing English questions in the negative, but gave affirmative answers when these questions were repeated in Mohave.

to dread the more shadowy corners of his inner world; he seems to sense that he can plunge into the unconscious without having to fear that he may not be able to reemerge from it unscathed.[48] Moreover, the Mohave Indian's thirst for experience—which may be due to his sense of aimlessness (Kroeber, 1951)—would naturally push him to explore the deeper layers of the unconscious, be it his own or that of someone else, precisely in the way in which he feels impelled to travel alone to distant tribes, simply for the sake of the experience (pt. 7, pp. 426–341).

In terms of this conception of the Mohave personality, the Mohave suicide does not seem to be a person who negates the world and seeks to destroy it by destroying himself, who perceives the world. Hence, one is inclined to assume that the psychic mechanism underlying his suicidal act is a depression and not a quasi-catatonic world destruction fantasy, implemented by suicide. On the other hand the Mohave themselves seem to feel that suicide is committed primarily by very young children and by persons who show certain markedly regressive and infantile trends. It is therefore not altogether impossible that at least some suicides, or self-destructive acts, in Mohave society may be unconscious attempts to escape a true psychotic break (Case 64). If this—admittedly highly tentative—assumption is correct, many cases of Mohave suicide may be viewed as psychosis equivalents. The chief argument in favor of this tentative explanation is the "social" or "human" quasi-death of Mastamho, who, after completing his work as a culture hero or god, turns into a mindless fish eagle, whose condition closely resembles catatonia (pt. 2, pp. 50–54).

The limitations of our data and the inherent difficulties of really understanding suicide unfortunately make it inadvisable to elaborate further any of these explanatory hypotheses, whose tentativeness cannot be emphasized too strongly or often enough. Thus, the only facts we can be reasonably certain of are the following:

(1) Mohave autism complements Mohave reality-directedness.

(2) The Mohave preoccupation with autistic processes and their cultural equivalents is part and parcel of the Mohave Indian's thirst for intense experiences.

(3) Most types of suicides, so defined by the Mohave themselves, involve persons who supposedly retain memories of their intrauterine existence, i.e., they involve relatively autistic persons. This finding possibly suggests that suicide in Mohave society may be both a product of a depression and an escape from, or substitute for, a severe psychotic break.

---

[48] This fear is a very real one in most people. I was personally present when an apprentice psychotherapist flatly refused to "go down" with the psychotic he was interviewing into the more hidden layers of the patient's psyche, "because I am afraid I might not be able to come up again." The Mohave Indian's ability and readiness to empathize with the unconscious of others is discussed in part 8, pages 485–504.

Prenatal factors are held to play a role in the majority of types of suicide known to the Mohave. The groundwork for all stillbirths is laid already in the womb. The suicide of sucklings is motivated by their continued awareness of what is happening in the mother's womb. The suicide of twins, regardless of whether they are held to be heavenly beings or returned ghosts, is largely determined by their continued awareness of their previous existence. Shamans retain all their lives a memory of their intrauterine existence. Great—and suicidal—warriors are persons who already dreamed in utero of becoming braves. Moreover, the Mohave themselves see a connection between the suicidal wishes of shamans and the braves's statements that they will not live long (Kroeber, 1925 a).

By contrast, the prenatal element is far less explicit in the four remaining types of suicide. In the case of incestuous marriages, the nexus is quite tenuous. Formerly the Mohave did not kill a horse at such marriages, but alienated part of the bridegroom's land, and it is implicit in one of their myths (Kroeber, MS., n.d.) that it is the possession of land which turns "persons" (ipa:) into human beings. An additional fact to be considered is that even though such cousin marriages are not necessarily contracted by shamans, in principle only evil shamans—i.e., persons who remember their prenatal existence—are said to be prone to commit incest. It is also quite conceivable that contracting a marriage which, by Mohave standards, is incestuous, may represent the kind of "acting out" a nonpracticing potential shaman would engage in.[49] As regards bewitched persons who consent to become the victims of a witch, their only connection with prenatal life, if we can call it that, is their relationship to the witch. In funeral suicide the nexus with prenatal existence is, for all practical purposes nil, save only that the suicide seeks to be metamorphosed into (reborn as) a ghost at the same time as the mourned-for person. Real suicides appear to have no memories of prenatal life, the only exception being the shaman (Case 106) who killed himself because he had been unjustly accused of being a witch.

It cannot be sufficiently stressed that nothing said in this section should be interpreted as lending support to theories of intrauterine self-awareness or psychic life, though Menninger (1940), after citing my Mohave data on shamanistic intrauterine "experiences," did suggest that possibility.[50] Whatever the merits of that thesis may be, it suffices for the present purposes to note the cultural fact that the Mohave *fantasy* a great deal about intrauterine life and that many

---

[49] Compare the psychoses of persons who could be shamans but refuse to practice (Case 4). They too are subjectively evolved substitutes for being a shaman.

[50] There are many solid arguments against, and only very tenuous ones militating in favor of, the reality of an intrauterine psychic life.

profess to have memories of, and to be motivated by memories of, their prenatal existence. The fact that in five of the nine types of suicide the suicidal impulse is explicitly stated to be directly related to prenatal existence, while in the four remaining ones it is possible to suggest at least some indirect connections with prenatal existence, does, on the other hand, have a psychodynamic significance. It suggests that the Mohave may unconsciously view suicide as regression to prenatal bliss—an element pointedly stated especially in regard to twins who, according to one theory, die in order to return to their heavenly home (Devereux, 1941, and pt. 7, pp. 348–356). Needless to say, this Mohave theory of suicide is but one cultural phrasing of man's great reluctance, or even basic incapacity, to believe in his own death and permanent cessation (Devereux, 1942 b).

The motivation of suicide.—According to the Mohave, each type or category of suicide has a different type of motivation. For this reason it seems more expedient to discuss motivation in connection with the type of suicide that it is supposed to cause. Suffice it to say for the present that most motives imputed to "suicides" involve resentment, a dislike and depreciation of life, an urge to kill, and an element of self-punitiveness which, in the case of witches longing for their beloved victims, is—at least in cultural belief—masked by the cultural tenet that unless a witch is killed, he may lose his hold over his ghostly retinue of former victims (Devereux, 1937 c and pt. 7, pp. 387–426). By contrast, culture itself emphasizes the element of guilt in the voluntary "social suicide" of men marrying their cousins (pt. 7, pp. 356–371). A detailed discussion of specific motives will be found in the individual sections devoted to various types of suicide. On the other hand the general role of aggression will be described in the next paragraphs.

Aggression.—Frustrated as well as manifest aggression is so conspicuous in all forms of Mohave suicide, that it would be tautological to demonstrate its presence in every type of suicide known to the Mohave. The present section simply seeks to clarify the role of aggressivity in Mohave life as a whole.

The first point to be made is that our own culture, of which our sociological and psychological sciences are products, systematically minimizes and distorts the creative value of aggression. Some psychoanalysts, like K. A. Menninger (1938), almost seem to imply that only the most sublimated and disguised aggressivity has any social value whatsoever. While there is certainly nothing to be said either for blind, hateful, destructiveness or for the vicarious aggressiveness of the effete Roman spectator watching gory combats, a certain basic willingness to protect one's life—and way of life—seems indispensable for social and individual survival. In fact, even stoical courage is no real substitute for a healthy amount of assertiveness. The French nobility of 1789 mounted the steps of the guillotine without showing fear, but lacked the basic self-assertiveness to fight for its survival sword in hand—perhaps because it had lost faith in the legitimateness of the system that had created it and supported it. This phenomenon may, conceivably, be responsible also for the sudden and puzzling decline of Greece, and especially of Athens, after the Peloponnesian War, and for the revival of mysticism—i.e., for the whole complex phenomenon which Murray (1955) called "the loss of nerve" of Greek society and which he was unable to explain even to his own satisfaction.[51]

The Mohave were a strongly self-assertive group in aboriginal times, though they were neither habitual predators nor sportive fighters viewing war as a highly ritualized and exceptionally risky game. In this respect their aggressivity was normal and had genuine survival value (Stewart, 1947 c; Dobyns, 1957).

On the other hand the tribe also included certain hyperaggressive individuals, animated by hostility rather than by anger; by the simple urge to destroy rather than by the wish to assert themselves. All of their exceptionally aggressive witches and great braves (kwanámi:- hye) appear to have shown marked depressive features. Thus, according to Kroeber (1925 a), shamans said that they did not wish to live long, while braves declared that they would not live long. Moreover, the destructive potential of both these social types was ultimately derived from certain power-given dreams, which were supposedly first experienced in utero. Now, it is quite obvious that an aggressivity that is rooted in so schizoid a fantasy is, of necessity, an ambivalent and complex one. This may explain why the Mohave state one minute that shamans are like braves and then, in the next breath, contemptuously describe them as "cowards at heart." Such complex forms of sheer hateful destructiveness, rooted as they are in schizoid processes, cannot indefinitely be directed toward the outer world. In the long run they are bound to elicit guilt feeling—which healthy self-assertiveness does not do to the same extent—and to be deflected from the outer world to the self. This finding fully agrees with the observation that practically all types of suicide involve either persons who still have a *culturally predicated* awareness of prenatal existence, which simply means that they have—or are alleged to have—fantasies of intrauterine regression, pathognomonic of schizoid processes in the

---

[51] On the historical stage one pathognomonic characteristic of this "loss of nerve" is the tendency to let someone else do one's fighting: mercenaries, professional soldiers, hired allies, and bribed barbarians.

psyche. The "you will be sorry" attitude,[52] that is markedly character-istic of several types of Mohave suicide, also shows the extent to which the psychic attitude of the suicide approximates certain typically re-gressive and infantile patterns.

Thus, it suffices to stress that several types of suicide known to the Mohave are committed by genuinely or supposedly hyperhostile and schizoid (or autistically infantile) persons, who need almost no reasonable provocation to become suicidal. In this context the term "reasonable" denotes types of provocation or injury—such as neglect, nagging, unjust accusations of witchcraft, bereavement, etc.—which the Mohave themselves define as bona fide traumata. While the Mo-have do not approve of suicide even for "good" reasons, they consider a person who does kill himself as a result of such traumata as weak, but not as a violator of the code of Mohave ethics. By contrast, the child who refuses to be born and wishes to kill its mother during parturi-tion, the weaned child who begrudges another Mohave the chance of being born, the shaman who caps a career of destructiveness with vi-carious self-destruction, etc., do violate the basic Mohave code. The basic difference between suicides who are inherently suicidal, and those who become suicidal as a result of some truly traumatic occurrence thus seems to correspond to a difference between abnormally destruc-tive and hostile persons on the one hand, and more or less normally self-assertive and aggressive individuals on the other hand. In psy-chiatric terminology, the former group's psychic makeup includes a basic, inherent self-destructive element, while the latter group's suicidalness is reactive, i.e., due to situational factors. Needless to say, in making this statement—which seems to reflect the implicit ideas of the Mohave fairly well—we ignore the fact that it is the *adult* Mohave who *imputes* to the stillborn child, the weaned infant, and the very young twin a culturally objectionable hatefulness and meanness. Whether or not this imputation has a basis in reality will be answered in the negative by the classical psychoanalyst and in the affirmative by followers of Melanie Klein, who view the child's psyche as a kind of self-perpetuating nightmare. What does matter is that,

---

[52] The "you will be sorry" type of masochistic self-destructiveness is well known in psychiatry and psychoanalysis. A characteristic childish reaction is : "It serves my parents right if I freeze my hands playing with snow ! Why didn't they buy me mittens?" The deliberate attempt to make oneself appear "pitiable," in order to induce the supernatural beings to show compassion was, interestingly enough, extremely pronounced among certain very warlike Plains Indians. The youth setting out to obtain a vision dressed himself in rags and was ostentatiously rejected by his family, so as to appear pitiable. A Crow orator, inciting his tribe to make war upon the foe, spoke of the fierce and often victorious Crow nation as a pitiable people, imposed upon by a ruthless enemy, mourning the sad lot of Crows taken prisoners by the enemy and therefore deserving compassion (Lowie, 1935). Psychologically such self-pity is closely related to the "you'll be sorry" or "you must be sorry" attitude, which has markedly aggressive components (Devereux, 1951 a, Kubie and Israel, 1955).

in the last resort, the Mohave implicitly equate the pathological destructiveness and self-destructiveness of shamans and braves with
that of infants, and implicitly differentiate it from the reactive suicidalness of traumatized individuals. In so doing, they actually—
and legitimately—differentiate between healthy assertiveness and
pathological, hate-laden destructiveness.[53]

The psychic state of the prospective suicide must be sharply differentiated from his motivation, although, needless to say, one's motivation and the affect which accompanies the behavioral implementation
of one's motives are closely interrelated. The point to be stressed
here is that the affective state of the prospective suicide need not be
depression pure and simple, nor even depression combined with other
ego-dystonic or dysphoric affects. Indeed, it is reasonable to suppose
that "heroic" or ostentatious forms of suicide are characterized by
exaltation rather than by manifest depression.[54] The affective state
which the Mohave impute to most suicides is not a sudden surge of
violence. Few Mohave seem to become suddenly so enraged and desperate that they kill themselves. In almost every instance the suicide
was stated to be the culmination of a long process of psychic incubation, although the actual act may have occurred at a moment when
the individual suddenly felt that he had endured as much as he
might reasonably be expected to endure. Thus, the Mohave do not
feel that the suicide is necessarily insane, as does occidental juris-
prudence, which views suicide as the outcome of a temporary insanity
that, presumably, strikes its victim "out of the blue." Rather do
they view the suicide as a person lacking in psychic stamina and
resiliency. (Cf. the section on attitudes toward suicide, pt. 7, pp.
308–313.)

Needless to say, from the anthropological point of view it is
wholly beside the point whether or not the Mohave are right in viewing every form of suicide as the final product of a long process of
incubation. What matters is that they would so view it even if every
single case of suicide were demonstrably the product of a sudden
breakthrough of self-destructive impulses of psychotic intensity.
Indeed, the notion that all decisive steps in life are taken after a
long period of meditation is deeply embedded in Mohave culture.
Normal fetuses think of how to be born, while shamanistic fetuses
think of how not to be born (Devereux, 1948 b); forcibly weaned
infants constantly think of their future rivals, who currently
occupy the maternal womb (Devereux, 1947 a; and pt. 7, pp. 340–348);
twins appraise life carefully before deciding whether to live or to die

---

[53] It is interesting to note, at least in passing, that the chief champions of primary self-
destructiveness, or of the death instinct, do not even seem to be aware of the importance
of this distinction.

[54] Compare in this context descriptions of the behavior of self-appointed martyrs, including heretics, etc., at the stake.

(Devereux, 1941; and pt. 7, pp. 348–356); adolescents think a great deal about their power dreams (Devereux, 1957 b); the bereaved think of the dead despite the fact that they should forget them (pt. 4, pp. 128–186); witches long for their beloved victims before they incite someone to kill them (pt. 7, pp. 387–426), etc. This tendency to meditate and to brood is of considerable interest for an understanding in depth of the seemingly mercurial (Kroeber, 1925 a) Mohave personality, which, as suggested elsewhere (Devereux, 1939 b), manages to be also introverted precisely because it has one foot firmly planted in reality—and vice versa, of course.

Thus, no matter what the objective facts may be, the role which the Mohave assign to a long period of psychic incubation would inevitably lead them to postulate also that nearly all types of suicide and nearly all concrete cases of suicide result from a prolonged preoccupation with one's grievances or longings and with the notion of contriving one's own death. On the other hand, so great a cultural emphasis on mulling over all important decisions—which both contrasts with and forms the depth psychological counterpart of the Mohave Indian's proneness to engage in seemingly aimless activity (Kroeber, 1951)—could not exist without leaving its imprint upon the Mohave Indian's ethnic personality. Hence, it seems reasonable to conclude that the informants who, in nearly every case of real suicide, strenuously emphasized that the actual suicide was but the culmination of a constant preoccupation with grievances, longings, and the like, actually described at least one very genuine and important aspect of the psychic process that caused these individuals to kill themselves.

Generally speaking, the psychic state that ultimately leads to suicide is called by the Mohave *ivaly idhi:k*, which can best be translated as "brooding." It was first described in connection with berdaches, who— according to all informants with the exception of Pulyi: k—were prone first to brood and then to kill themselves if they were teased too much and were told too insistently that they did not really possess the genitalia of their adopted sex (Devereux, 1937 b). In some ways even the longing of the aging witch for his victims and other forms of preoccupation that culminate in real or alleged suicide contain a very genuine element of brooding, in that, in each and every one of these instances, the prospective "suicide" harbors feelings in which fear of loss, frustrated aggressivity, inhibited resentment, and feelings of guilt play an important role.

Summing up, according to the Mohave practically all real or imputed acts of self-destruction are preceded by a period of brooding, until a point is reached where even a relatively minor new annoyance, or one more habitual annoyance, suffices to trigger off the suicidal act. Yet, Kroeber (1925 a) asserted that the Mohave do not brood over grievances!

SOCIOCULTURAL CONSIDERATIONS

ABORIGINAL CONDITIONS

Expressions denoting suicide.—It is psychologically interesting that no language (so far as I know) has a special root-word denoting suicide.[55] This suggests that, both historically and psychologically, the concept of self-killing is derived from the concept of killing someone else—a rather telling argument against the reality of a genuine "primary self-aggression," first postulated by Freud (1922) and then carried to an extreme by K. A. Menninger (1938).

In Mohave, real suicide cannot be designated in less than two words, and vicarious suicide in less than three words. Hiweyk ma :tâpu'yem (=self kill) denotes nonvicarious suicide; vicarious suicide may be referred to by saying either hiweyk aa :rum tupu'ytcitc (self wants killed) or else hiweyk tâpu :yum hauytcum (self kill wants-it-done). From the metalinguistic point of view these two sets of expressions do not really differ from each other. Thus, although the expression denoting vicarious suicide consists of three words, while the one denoting active suicide consists of only two, both expressions are descriptive and declarative statements, rather than nouns in the sense in which the modern term "suicide" (which was originally also a descriptive statement) is now a genuine noun. This finding is quite compatible with the purely anthropological observation that the Mohave consider vicarious suicide quite as genuine a form of self-destruction as real suicide. However, while this observation is not without interest, it would be hazardous indeed to do more than mention it. All we can do is to note in passing that a comparative study of terms applied to killing, self-killing, and vicarious self-destruction in a variety of languages would be of considerable value to students of psychopathology, as well as to the student of the cultural history of suicide.

Attitudes toward suicide.—Generally speaking, the Mohave condemn suicide, and seek to prevent it by all means at their disposal. On the other hand, they do not disapprove to the same extent of all forms of suicide, the intensity of their disapproval being, to a large extent, determined by the actual or imputed causes of the suicidal act. Moreover, even though the Mohave disapprove wholeheartedly of suicide per se, they are quite capable of being lenient toward those individuals whose suicidal motivation seems more or less "adequate" and "reasonable" to them—i.e., toward those with whose despair they are able

---

[55] The English (and French) word "suicide" resulted from a combination of two roots: *sui* and *-cide*, which long usage alone causes the nonphilologist to apprehend as a single, self-contained word. In the German "Selbstmord" and in the Hungarian "öngyilkosság" the composite nature of the technical term is still quite clear; both of these terms conjoin, without any modification whatsoever, the words "self" and "murder." In the Mon Khmer Sedang language the idea of suicide can only be expressed in two words: to-kill self (kînde :e cih), etc.

to empathize. A further cause of the Mohave Indian's leniency
toward the individual suicide is his basically nonlegalistic and personalized approach to individual differences, including even individual
quirks.

The suicide of stillborn children is deplored, since it interferes
with the perpetuation of the tribe. The unborn child which is slow
to emerge from the womb is reminded of the mythical precedent
set by a deity, who, after refusing to be born, finally decided to emerge
from the womb, in order to set an example for future babies. The
reluctant unborn baby is therefore urged to set a similar example
for future generations, lest the tribe become extinct.

The suicide of forcibly weaned babies is viewed somewhat more
critically. The sick baby suffering from a weaning trauma is ad-
monished not to be jealous of its unborn sibling and not to begrudge
another Mohave the chance to be born.

The suicide of twins elicits a rather ambivalent reaction. On
the one hand, in accordance with the theory that twins are heavenly
visitors, the Mohave blame those who have offended the twins. On
the other hand, however, in accordance with the theory that twins are
acquisitive ghosts who return to earth for additional funeral gifts
and property, the Mohave blame twins for being overly sensitive
and demanding and admonish them to be more tolerant and patient.

The symbolic social suicide of a man who marries his cousin is criticized not so much because it is a form of suicide, but because such a
marriage disturbs the smooth functioning of the intratribal system
of kin and gens exogamy and also because it jeopardizes the survival
of the incestuous couple's entire extended kin.

The willing victims of witches, who refuse to cooperate with their
therapists, are blamed for their foolish compliance with the wishes
of murderous witches.

The vicarious suicide of witches is viewed as the inevitable consequence of their personality makeup and of their nefarious activities.
Hence, persons not related to a slain witch sometimes overtly express their satisfaction over the slaying of the witch (Case 101). In
fact, whenever the guilt of the witch is generally accepted, his own
relatives often refuse either to protect him or to avenge him. Thus,
the Mohave Indians' disapproval of such witches is not due primarily to their vicarious suicidal behavior; they are criticized for being
witches. On the other hand, when the slain shaman is not believed
to be a witch, he is sincerely pitied (Case 100) and his killers are
condemned. An unjustly accused shaman, who commits suicide is,
likewise, pitied rather than blamed (Case 106).

The suicidally motivated straying of senior warriors into enemy
territory is viewed as behavior compatible with the character struc-

ture of braves, who know that they are not meant to reach old age (Kroeber 1925 a). Here, as in many other contexts, the "official" Mohave reaction seems to be: "It is their nature; they can't help it." Yet there are indications that this superficial tolerance masks quite a lot of resentment, since the lost warrior's male relatives sometimes frustrate the attempts of a shaman to discover, with the help of a medium, his fate and whereabouts.

Funeral suicides elicit a rather complex reaction: while the attempt itself is, more or less, a minor custom, it is not one which has the unambivalent backing of Mohave society. The suicidal attempt of a widow (Case 109) was ridiculed, because her subsequent marriage allegedly proved her gesture to have been hollow exhibitionism. A father who threw himself on the pyre of his son, whom his nagging had driven to suicide (Case 111), was criticized more because of his cruelty toward his son than because of his suicidal gesture. Finally, males attempting to commit funeral suicide are criticized more than females, since funeral suicide is viewed as a typically feminine gesture.

Real suicides are condemned more consistently than other types of suicide. This disapproving attitude is present—at least in theory—even where explicit cognizance is taken of the fact that the suicide has been seriously wronged. This, however, simply means that the Mohave criticize not only the suicide, but also those who have wronged him. The suicidal person is considered "weak" or "crazy" and is said to lack the Mohave Indian's traditional strength of character and stoicism. It is worth recalling here that the mercurial Mohave tend to think of themselves as highly stable and almost stolidly stoical persons, even though they are simply skilled in presenting a stoical and stolid façade to whites, for whom they do not care, or whom they do not know. It should also be noted, however, that the term "crazy" is applied to suicides only when the informants contrast the supposed emotional liability and "weakness" of the younger generation with the imaginary glories of Mohave character in aboriginal times. A further discussion of this point appears in the section on "Suicide and Ethnic Personality" (pp. 298–301).

In addition to being called "weak and crazy," the person who commits suicide is also blamed for being stubborn, since he refuses to listen to well-meaning persons who try to comfort him and to dissuade him from killing himself. It should be noted that the stillborn babies, infants who die at weaning, and twins who voluntarily return to the land of the dead, despite all efforts to persuade them to choose life instead of death, are also blamed for not listening to their "better selves," for being stubborn, and for causing grief to their relatives and to the community.

Yet, even though the Mohave feels impelled to condemn those who are "weak, crazy or stubborn" enough to kill themselves, he is far from consistent in his attitude. A few days after Hama: Utce: expressed the traditional opinion that all suicides were weak and crazy, I went with her over the actual list of suicides which we had compiled and asked her to express an opinion about each of these concrete persons, instead of about the suicide as an abstract "social type." To my surprise, she said: "All of them were pretty good people. No one thought they would do such a thing. They were brave. People mourn for suicides, but, underneath it all, they are appalled that anyone should grieve his family and kin." While this statement definitely reflects the Mohave tendency to condemn the "sin," but to be lenient toward the "sinner," it is quite likely that Hama: Utce:'s sudden tolerance also had personal causes. Indeed, just at that point she had come to feel that she, herself, had reasons for toying with the idea of self-destruction (Case 115). Moreover, her explicit reference to the grief of the survivors was probably motivated by her conscious wish and hope that her death would shame and grieve her aunt, whose cantankerousness was responsible for her suicidal thoughts. The inference that Hama: Utce:'s sudden leniency had at least partly subjective causes is strongly supported by the fact that the other informant, Hivsu: Tupo:ma, continued to voice his disapproval of anyone who committed suicide: "People despise suicides, and a certain man who tried, but failed, to kill himself is often teased for his abortive suicidal attempt" (Case 117).[56]

On the whole, no great significance should be attached to the Mohave view that suicides are objectionable simply because they are weak enough to experience extreme psychic distress. This attitude is nearly always voiced only in the form of general statements about suicide. Thus, even though Hivsu: Tupo:ma never retracted or qualified his general condemnation of suicide, whenever a concrete case was discussed he, like every other Mohave, nearly always added a word of regret, made a more or less lame attempt to justify the suicide, or tried at least to arouse compassion for the person who killed himself.

Finally, there is a marked difference in the Mohave Indian's reaction to those who kill themselves because their feelings were hurt in some manner, and to those who kill themselves because they grieve over the death of a brother or relative. The latter are hardly ever described as "crazy" or "weak," perhaps because the idea of following the dead to the land of ghosts pervades many aspects of

---

[56] One of the most common oversights in anthropological fieldwork is the failure to take into account the *mood* of the informant who makes certain sweeping statements, especially in connection with attitudes and values. The above information was reproduced in great detail, in order to underline the importance of evaluating the informants' statements not only as regards their objective validity, but also in terms of personal motivation and bias.

Mohave culture (Devereux, 1937 a) and is specifically held responsible not only for the nyevedhi: group of psychiatric disturbances (pt. 4, pp. 128–186), but also for the suicide of the second of a pair of twins and for that of witches and of a dead brave's young admirer. At the same time no informant so much as hinted that a person who *actually* killed himself did so because he was haunted by the ghost of one of his dead relatives. In fact, haunting was never even alluded to in connection with actual suicides. On the other hand, haunting is so consistently mentioned in connection with various psychosomatic ailments and also in connection with certain forms of vicarious suicide, that psychosomatic death appears to represent for the Mohave a type of vicarious suicide.

In the preceding paragraphs we differentiated between the Mohave Indian's reactions to the *act* of the suicide and his reactions to the *person* who kills himself. The best way of justifying this distinction and of demonstrating the intensity of the Mohave Indian's condemnation of suicide is to examine his reaction to the suicide of aliens, and especially of white persons. The Mohave view of the white suicide is quite uncharitable and therefore clearly reflects the intensity of his basic condemnation of suicide, even if one makes allowances for the fact that, in Mohave opinion, nearly everything a white does is *necessarily* bad.

The chief difference between the Mohave Indian's evaluation of the suicide of a white person, and of that of a Mohave is that, in his opinion, the Mohave suicide regrettably failed to live up to both ideal and (supposedly) real Mohave standards, whereas the white who killed himself acted in a manner which is (supposedly) precisely what one can expect from members of a characterologically and ethically defective group, which consistently fails to live up even to the most basic standards of human (= Mohave) dignity.[57] The basic ethical code in terms of which Mohave and white conduct are judged is the same. However, whereas the Mohave is condemned for violating tribal standards, whites are blamed for conforming to their (unethical) national standards. In brief, whereas the Mohave suicide is viewed as a *maladjusted* member of an *ethical* society, the white suicide is held to be a *fully adjusted* member of an *unethical* society.

The following case histories, obtained from Mohave informants, but involving aliens, reveal the intensity of the Mohave Indian's condemnation of suicide.

Suicide of foreigners.—Since the Mohave disapprove of both suicide

---

[57] This manner of evaluating objectionable conduct is a basic characteristic of the Mohave ethical system. If a Mohave is stingy, he is said to violate basic human ethics and to be ethnically atypical. If a white is stingy, he is held to have conformed to Western "ethics," which violate all basic human (=Mohave) standards of decency, and is therefore felt to be typical of his group.

and aliens, they are naturally inclined to impute suicidal proclivities, as well as especially disgraceful kinds of suicide, to foreigners.

(*a*) *The suicide of both Mohave and non-Mohave but Indian homosexuals* was mentioned in a derisive manner. "Male homosexuals sometimes jumped into the fire if people teased them too much and called them 'modha :re' (penis)."

CASE 80 (Informants: Hivsu: Tupo :ma and Hama: Utce :) :

About 40 years ago (1890?) a Yuma male transvestite killed himself.

CASE 81 (Informants: Hivsu: Tupo :ma and Hama: Utce :) :

A Yavapai lesbian transvestite killed herself by hitting herself on the head with a ta :kyat hit'a :(w)à (ax small).

(*b*) *Whites* are so lacking in dignity that they commit suicide whenever they are disappointed in love. According to Tcatc and E. S., "White people who are in love and cannot get married kill themselves. The Mohave don't do such silly things." [58]

CASE 82 (Informants, Tcatc and E. S.) :

"When a white man objected to his son's wish to marry a certain girl, the two young people went to a deserted house, where the girl first shot the boy and then herself. They left a note—that is how people found out what happened. The Mohave who are in love don't do such things, though nowadays young Mohave men sometimes kill themselves from jealousy. I know of two recent cases of this kind. One of them was that of Amalyk Tumàdha :p (Case 113). [59] If you don't stop fretting over that sweetheart of yours, you too might kill yourself in the end."

Funeral and mourning rites.—Although the Mohave disapproved of suicide, they did not discriminate against the suicide's corpse, and they disposed of it exactly as though the death had been due to natural causes. Stillborn children were buried, while other "suicides" were cremated. If the "suicide" was old enough to have ceased sleeping in the cradle, the house in which he had lived was burned down; if he was still young enough to sleep in the cradle, the mother either threw the cradle into the Colorado River—thus signifying that she was willing to bear other children—or else burned it, hoping that this would render her permanently sterile (Devereux, 1948 c). In brief, the suicide was cremated and mourned like any other dead Mohave. The survivors cried, cut their hair short, performed the usual mourning rites and observed the customary mourning taboos. Moreover, even though certain observances at the marriage of cousins apparently represented a partial funeral rite (pt. 7, pp. 356–371), at the death of a person who had contracted such a marriage the regular funeral rite was probably performed in its entirety.

---

[58] This is manifestly false. Compare case material for modern examples.
[59] This is incorrect; the suicide in question was due to a delayed mourning reaction.

Eschatology of suicide.—The fate of a suicide's ghost was the same as that of other persons. The souls of ordinary stillborn children and of ordinary infants, who died before they were old enough to have their chins tattooed, went into a rathole (Devereux 1937 a), while the souls of twins returned to heaven or to the land of the dead (Devereux, 1941.) The soul of the willing victim of a witch first joined the witch's other victims in a special place; then, when the witch was killed, the victim's soul accompanied him to the land of the dead and— instead of joining his own deceased relatives—lived in the witch's camp (Devereux, 1937 c). All other suicides proceeded, like ordinary persons, to the land of the dead where, before being metamorphosed into something else, they relived their earthly life, including even their death by suicide (Devereux, 1937 a). The ghosts of suicides did not differ from other ghosts, were not believed to be especially dangerous and, with one exception, were not thought to make special efforts to induce others to commit suicide. The one—rather dubious—exception is the victim of witchcraft, whom the witch temporarily segregated in a "place of his own." This captive ghost, or dead soul, (voluntarily?) haunted the witch [60] by cohabiting with him in dream until, overcome by longing for his ghostly captives, the witch provoked someone into killing him (Devereux, 1937 c, and pt. 7, pp. 387–426).

The failure of the Mohave to discriminate against suicides and the absence of a special eschatology of suicide suggest that suicide may have been fairly common in aboriginal times. Had it been something exceptional, the Mohave, who have very elaborate and imaginative ideas about death and the fate of the soul, would certainly have evolved a special eschatology for those who died in so dramatic a manner.

SUICIDE AND CULTURAL CHANGE

Due to the lack of reliable early data on Mohave suicide, and also because of the Mohave taboo on the names of the dead, it is nearly impossible to form an opinion about the frequency of suicide in aboriginal times and to contrast it with the frequency of suicide during the last 75 or 100 years.

Mohave beliefs concerning changes.—It was possible to point out, in the section on the relationship between ethnic personality and suicide, that just as the Mohave tend to idealize the stoical strength of character which they impute to their forebears, so they idealize also conditions prevailing in aboriginal times. Hence, in view of their disapproval of suicide, it is almost unavoidable that they should feel convinced that it was rarer in aboriginal times than it is at present.

---

[60] Compare the haunting of people by their dead relatives, which causes them to contract ghost diseases (pt. 4, pp. 128–186) and note that the favorite victims of a witch are his own relatives.

Tcatc's statement (1938) : There are more suicides now than there were formerly. [Why?] Most suicides seem to be due to unsuccessful marriages.
[Were people more happily married formerly than they are now?] There were
just as many unhappy marriages then as there are now, but people did not
commit suicide so much. [Why not?] So-called (*sic!*) civilization must have
something to do with it. White people commit suicide all the time (cf. Case 82).
[Did you ever hear of children *actually* committing suicide?] No.

Comment.—Since Tcatc was a very conservative person who idealized the
good old days and felt convinced that the Mohave had deteriorated as a result of
their contact with occidental civilization and its representatives, her remarks
should be viewed solely as characteristic Mohave utterances, rather than as
factual statements. They shed light upon the Mohave attitude toward suicide
and acculturation, but contribute nothing reliable to our actual information
about historical trends in the incidence of suicide.

Inferences regarding suicide in aboriginal times.—Many facts
suggest that suicide was not uncommon even in aboriginal times.

(*1*) *Mythology:* Although there seem to be no mythical episodes
involving actual suicide, the idea of self-destruction is explicitly present in the Mohave myth concerning the origin of death: Matavilye decided to die in order to institute death and funeral rites by setting a
precedent. Some narrators even say that the coming into being of
death was willed not only by Matavilye himself, but also by his evil
daughter. The psychoanalytic meaning of this myth having been discussed elsewhere (Devereux, 1948 f), it suffices to note here that,
in Mohave belief, the first death was a voluntary vicarious suicide. Brief mention may also be made of the fact that, in a Mohave
tale, Coyote commits what is usually termed "partial suicide." He
commits autophagia after being wounded through his own "accidentally on purpose" injudicious behavior (Devereux, 1948 h).

(*2*) *The cultural mass of the idea of suicide:* The variety of deaths
and symbolic deaths which the Mohave traditionally define as "suicide" proves that the idea of suicide played a great role in Mohave
culture and thought. It is therefore permissible to assume that, even
though real suicides may have been less common formerly than they are
at present, vicarious suicides may have been more frequent than they
are now, since, due to American interference, witches are no longer
slain. Indeed, some Mohave opinions to the contrary notwithstanding,
the modern witch's knowledge that he would not be killed, no matter
what he did, may very well inhibit not only the provocative behavior
of at least some suicidal aging witches, but, possibly, also the urge
to commit witchcraft. Indeed, Hivsu: Tupo:ma—who, though generally believed to be a "good" shaman, had confessed to me that he
too had bewitched people (Devereux, 1948 i; and Case 92)—
sounded almost wistful when he said that in former times he would
never have reached old age; moreover, not long after making this
statement, he got drunk, accidentally on purpose, slept outdoors in

freezing weather, and contracted pneumonia, which proved to be fatal.

The second argument in support of the assumption that, in the case of the Mohave, effective laws against the killing of witches actually reduced the incidence of witchcraft by making it impossible for the unkilled witch to maintain forever his hold over his beloved victims (Devereux, 1937 c), has a Malay parallel. According to Linton (1956), when the Dutch forbade the killing of amok runners, who seek to die in glory (Anonymous, n. d.), and sentenced them instead to hard labor on the rock pile, the incidence of amok decreased very appreciably.

Probable changes in the incidence of real and alleged suicidal acts.— A further point to be considered in any scrutiny of historical changes in the incidence of both real and fictitious suicides is the fact that, in prereservation days, obstetrical mortality, the mortality of infants and twins, and the death rates of sick people were, of necessity, higher than at present. Hence, there were many more deaths of a type that the Mohave *defined* as "suicide." In support of this inference one can cite the Mohave belief that "due to recent changes in the weather" more twins are *born* nowadays than was formerly the case. This Mohave belief is certainly attributable to the simple fact that, thanks to the Indian Agency's medical resources, nowadays fewer twins *die*, either during birth or in early infancy, than was formerly the case (Devereux, 1941).

Thus, while it is possible that the number of actual suicides is nowadays on the increase, other forms of "suicide" (neonates, twins, witch's victims, etc.) were presumably more frequent in aboriginal times than at present.

There are indications that the frequency of real suicides may actually have increased in modern times, as a result of acculturation. This is suggested by the fact that an unduly large proportion of modern suicides appears to have been better educated than the average of the Mohave tribe. It should also be recalled that a wave of suicides appears to have swept over a great many Indian tribes when they were placed on reservations and were denied access to their traditional means for directing aggression against outsiders, instead of against themselves. This discouragement and sense of frustration had, of course, also a great many other roots (Devereux, 1942 c), at least some of which deserve mention, since they are intimately related to the entire problem of gratifications in relation to self-esteem.

The basic problem can best be visualized by contrasting a 19th century Mohave Indian, half naked but wearing the *best* clothes his tribe could make, and accustomed to run long distances *as rapidly as anyone else*, to the same Mohave Indian in 1932, fully dressed in *shabby* occidental clothes and driving a *ramshackle* model T Ford. Though he is now warmly clad and possessed of faster and less strenuous means of transportation than ever before, he was, in aboriginal times, as well, or better, off than most, while in reservation times he was shabbier and poorer than the whites living within his purview.   In such a situation the *absolute* advantages of warmer clothing and faster transportation are more than canceled by the narcissistic blow of being a pauper among *relatively* well-to-do persons, instead of being simply a respected member of a group whose whole economy is a relatively marginal one.

The situation of the Mohave differed, of course, from that of the Plains Indians who, as Wissler (Preface to Mead, 1932) rightly stressed, had been rather prosperous hunters before being confined to reservations.   The Mohave had never been rich to begin with, chiefly because, like the Cocopa, they destroyed everything belonging to the dead, thus making a gradual accumulation of capital impossible (Kelly, 1949).   In fact, contrary to what happened to the Plains Indians, American conquest actually enriched rather than impoverished the Mohave.   However, since—unlike the Plains Indians—the Mohave were contemptuous of wealth, this "absolute" enrichment was counteracted by their *relative* poverty, which contrasted with the "wealth" of the invading Americans.   Yet, despite their contempt for wealth, the Mohave, like other human beings, do not enjoy being inferior to others, and since there was nothing they could do about it, they developed a compensatory contempt for whites, specifically related to the white man's all-absorbing interest in property.   Needless to say, the very nature and intensity of this contempt makes it clear that it is both a reaction formation against their culturally controlled desire to acquire or keep wealth [61] and a denial of their envy of the "rich" white man.   In this context it is interesting to note that the Mohave continue to be quite generous with food they themselves produce and—by extension—also with store-bought food, but are somewhat less ready to give away other store goods,[62] while continuing to be extremely generous with money (and its equivalent—labor for pay), perhaps because it is less "real" to them than actual goods are.[63]

A second deleterious aspect of their acquisition of American goods, including especially labor-saving devices and also a few relatively valuable frame houses, requiring little upkeep, was the increasing unavailability of means for the utilization of leisure, which, in aboriginal times, consisted of feasts, warfare, and other meaningful group activities.

---

[61] Compare the marked regret of Hama : Utce's husband over having to burn a fine bead belt, which Hama : Utce : had made for her beloved father-in-law shortly before he died (Case 107).

[62] Yet, already several decades ago the Mohave used store-bought cloth, etc., as funeral gifts, to be thrown on the cremation pyre (Hall, 1903).

[63] As late as the 1930's all informants, and as late as 1950 informants who were also friends, showed marked embarrassment when being paid their daily wages.

The third, and perhaps most important, frustration experienced by the reservation Mohave was the depressing realization that the world in which they now lived, and which affected their welfare, stretched far beyond their horizon and was almost entirely beyond their control. This change in the size and center of gravity of the Mohave's human universe was as distressing for him as was for post-Copernican European man the realization that the earth was not the center of the universe, nor the Delphic Omphalos the navel of the world.[64] Closely related to this was their realization that the whites could produce and control absolutely things the tribe now needed, but could neither produce nor control. Being, therefore, no longer in full control of their own fate, they began to feel less responsible for it, and began to seek escapes where formerly they looked for commitments and responsibilities within their "universe," which they controlled as the leading military power and cultural model (Kroeber, 1920) of their cultural sub-area. In aboriginal times the world which the Mohave had, in William James' terminology, an "acquaintance with" and the world they had "knowledge about" were practically coextensive and congruous. With the advent of the white man, the Mohave's horizon expanded immeasurably. The world with which he was actually acquainted became a small dot, surrounded by a much larger area—the United States—which he had some "knowledge about," and this area was, in turn, surrounded by an immeasurably larger "outer world," of which he simply knew that it existed, and whose unknown dangers bewildered and frightened him.

This point is sufficiently important to justify additional comment. The first Mohave who reached this "outer world," by serving in France during World War I, adjusted to its strangeness by identifying the gallantry of the French infantryman with the traditional courage of Mohave braves, who also fought on foot. Similarly, the well educated Hama: Utce: spontaneously compared Mohave warriors to "Spartans" (pt. 7, pp. 426–431). Areas not visited by any Mohave continued, however, to be defined as dangerous and exotic. Thus, when the Mohave learned that I was planning to go to Indochina to study headhunters, they expressed a great deal of concern, and after I reached Indochina, Hivsu: Tupo:ma actually asked Hama: Utce: to write to me that he was "praying to his Holy (sic!) Pahotcatc" for my safety. Similarly, Hama: Utce:, who, like most Mohave, disliked unkempt hair a great deal, habitually described such hair as resembling that of "South Sea Islanders," who, never having been visited by

---

[64] A comparable phenomenon was observable among the mountain jungle tribes of Indochina in 1933, when the repercussions of the 1929 economic collapse of the Western World just began to undermine their economy. They were frightened and puzzled by the realization that, for some utterly incomprehensible reason, money and trade goods had suddenly become far more "expensive" than they had been; and that a given quantity of rice or rattan had to be sold for less than ever before (Devereux, MS., 1933–34).

a Mohave, necessarily represented something dangerous, or at least objectionable.

The idea that they, themselves, might represent the "dangerous" outer world to anyone would certainly have bewildered them, since they thought of themselves as being the kind of people everyone should be, and as living where everyone should live. This is clearly shown by the fact that, even though the Mohave shared all my joys, concerns, and griefs and frequently asked for news about my parents and sister, it never occurred to them that my family might be worried over my being with what they—being Europeans—believed to be "wild Indians." Similarly, it never struck them that I might be homesick for my home town, or for Paris where I had studied. They could understand and sympathize with my being lonely for the girl I was in love with (pt. 3, pp. 91–106), but the idea that anyone could be homesick while living among his Mohave friends simply did not occur to them.[65]

The preceding data indicate that, despite the expansion of their geographical horizons, and despite their awareness that their country is but a tiny dot on the map, the Mohave simply took cognizance of objective realities without modifying in the least their *emotional* conviction that the Mohave are the only real "home folk" and their country the only real "home base." Hence, despite their dislike of, and contempt for, whites, I never once heard a Mohave say either directly or indirectly: "What are the whites doing here? Why don't they go home?"—as though they took it for granted that everyone should gravitate to the Colorado River Reservation.[66]

Our next task is to discuss the Mohave Indian's psychocultural adaptation to the stresses of acculturation, with special reference to suicide.

Adaptation to culture change.—One of the primitives' traditional "escapes" from many acculturation difficulties is, of course, a nativistic-revivalistic cult epidemic. No such cult arose among the Mohave, nor did outside cults of this nature ever gain a foothold among them (Kroeber, 1925 a), for a number of reasons:

(1) Since the Mohave are not ritualistic or liturgically oriented (Devereux, 1957 b), a new cult would not have solved their problems.

(2) Many of these cults hold out the promise that the dead would return. Such a notion would have repelled the Mohave, who do their

---

[65] In fairness to my Mohave friends' perceptiveness, I feel obliged to add that I never did feel homesick while living among them, though I often enough feel homesick for the Mohave country when I am elsewhere.

[66] The Mohave felt somewhat differently when, during the last war, a Japanese relocation camp was established on the reservation. Though genuinely committed to helping the whites to win the war, they pitied the Japanese Americans who had been forcibly uprooted and had not come to Arizona of their own free will. As regards the landless Hopi, transplanted en masse to the Mohave Reservation, the Mohave were resentful partly because this invasion jeopardized their own right to the land and partly because they felt that the Hopi too had not *really* wanted to come. (U.S. Senate, 1955). Moreover, they intensely disliked the Hopi ethnic character and spoke scathingly of their callous cruelty to animals (Devereux, 1948 g).

best to forget the dead as soon as possible (Kroeber, 1925 a). Moreover, even though they are keenly aware of the lure of the dead (pt. 4, pp. 128–186 and passim), they are convinced that all contact with ghosts is a threat to the living. Finally, the idea of a return of remote ancestors is utterly incompatible with the basic Mohave belief that, after a number of metamorphoses, there is a complete cessation of existence (Devereux, 1937 a).

(3) A number of such cults promise at least the return of former prosperity, which, as stated above, the Mohave never did experience in aboriginal times, and do not profess to have experienced even in their retrospective idealization of all other features of days gone by.

(4) Many such cults have marked "cargo" features, promising new wealth to the faithful. Such a promise would have held no special appeal for the Mohave, who do not value property very highly. In this context it is permissible to suggest, at least tentatively, that such cults chiefly arise among, or are adopted by, tribes who were formerly relatively prosperous and are inclined to value property more than the Mohave do.

This avenue of escape having been denied to the Mohave, both by their geographical position and by the specific beliefs and value systems of their culture, they had to resort to more personalized escapes, which will be considered next.

Their horizon having expanded, while their place in it shrank, the Mohave began to look for compensatory escapes. It is quite possible that one such early escape may have been an increased preoccupation with the inner world, resulting in a further elaboration of their myths and nonmaterial culture in general and in an increase in the number of shamans. This statement is admittedly inferential, and possibly even speculative. Is is, however, precisely what one would expect to occur in a tribe oriented to the inner life and so essentially unritual-istic that a nativistic cult, such as the Ghost Dance religion, would have provided no solution for the psychological and cultural conflicts resulting from the forcible acculturation to which it had been subjected. Be that as it may, even a very few years ago Kroeber [67] could still comment on the "gallant rear guard action" of Mohave dream culture, in the face of overwhelming acculturation pressures. As for shamanism, it was still very much alive and generally accepted as recently as the early 1950's, witness the fact that a progressive mother was blamed for taking her son to a psychiatric hospital, instead of to a shaman (Case 64). Notice should also be taken of the recurrent assertions of some informants that, as little as 15 years ago, shamanism was on the increase (pt. 7, pp. 387–426).

[67] Personal communication, 1950.

Confronted with such a loss of scope in tribal life, and with a general increase in leisure accompanied by a simultaneous loss of normal outlets in daily living, the Mohave, like many other underprivileged people, increasingly looked for escape in a somewhat chaotic sexuality and, to a lesser extent, in drinking alcohol (Devereux, 1948 i), not only at formal feasts, which seem to have become less frequent, but also in ordinary life. This meant that, in the course of the last few decades, people spent more time than formerly within the relatively narrow circle of family and friends, while the rest of the time they had many, increasingly superficial and fugitive, contacts with "outsiders," which included even some non-Mohave, as well as the white people of Parker and Needles. This, in turn, meant that whereas in aboriginal times the Mohave had meaningful relations of medium intensity with a large number of persons,[68] after being subjected to acculturation he began to evolve a few intense emotional commitments, while reducing the affective content of his numerous fugitive relationships to an absolute minimum. In the sexual sphere this led, on the one hand, to an increasing tendency to "fall in love" with a particular woman, while on the other hand it led to many passing and hasty sexual contacts, almost wholly devoid of subjective elements and affective commitments. Though the average Mohave is still a warmhearted and sincerely outgoing person, the trend just described is definitely present, especially among the young. This point need not be labored further, since it was discussed systematically in the section on the relationship between ethnic character and suicide. The one point to be retained is that the Mohave themselves are keenly aware of the nexus between this trend and the supposed increase in the suicide rate. As an expert informant put it: "Nowadays people commit suicide when disappointed in love. In aboriginal times people did not, as a rule, fall so intensely in love; they had plenty of other interests in life."

Be that as it may, the Mohave believe that there have always been suicides, though they are convinced that suicides are more frequent today than they were formerly. The Mohave themselves attribute this trend to the breakdown of their culture; a view indirectly substantiated by the fact that an unexpectedly large proportion of suicidal persons had had some education. At the same time it is necessary to point out that, in view of the taboo on the name of the dead, old cases of suicide are more likely to be forgotten than relatively recent ones, which may create a mistaken impression regarding the aboriginal vs. modern frequency of suicides. It might also be mentioned, at least in passing, that no informant seems to have realized that far

---

[68] Thus, the Mohave applies the English term "relatives" both to the immediate and to the extended family.

more men than women commit "real" suicide, although one would have expected them to notice this fact, since the Mohave themselves stress that modern suicides are largely due to disappointments in love and firmly believe that women are far more flighty than men are, which would necessarily imply that they would be less likely than men to kill themselves because of disappointment in love (pt. 7, pp. 459–484).

Statistical trends, as seen by the Mohave, are as follows:

(1) *Prenatal suicides* were said to be decreasing in numbers. This statement is probably correct, since many Mohave women now have their babies in the reservation hospital.

(2) *Suicide at weaning:* No statistically significant statements were made. A decrease seems probable, due to better medical care.

(3) *Suicide of twins:* The number of twins is said to be increasing. This is correct, but only in the sense that many more twins survive today than in former times.

(4) *Symbolic suicides* markedly decreased in numbers because the ritual of killing of a horse at the marriage of cousins is now obsolete. However, cousin marriages, being less openly condemned than formerly, were said to be increasing in numbers, thus "causing whole families to become extinct."

(5) *The willing victims of witchcraft* were said by some to have become more numerous in recent times, because witches now ply their evil trade without fear of being killed. Others felt that such deaths had become less numerous, because it is no longer worthwhile for a witch to bewitch anyone, since he knows that he cannot always provoke others into killing him in the end.

(6) *The vicarious suicide of witches* is markedly on the decrease, since witch killing is now prohibited by law. The Mohave also implied that suicidal witches were usually older persons, who had had time to bewitch a number of persons. No informant stressed the preponderance of male over female suicidal witches, though they said that there were few female shamans in aboriginal times.

(7) *The vicarious suicide of braves* is wholly obsolete, though it should be noted that, during World War II, even men in their forties tried to volunteer for service. One such man even tried to join the Marines, in order to see "real fighting."

(8) *Funeral suicide* is now wholly obsolete.

(9) *Active suicide* is said to be increasingly frequent—a statement that is probably correct. No informant pointed out the preponderance of male suicides over female suicides.

Trends in means used for committing suicide.—In aboriginal times the suicide poisoned himself with datura, jumped into the river and—even though every Mohave is said to have been a swimmer (Devereux, 1950 e)—determinedly floated downstream until he drowned; or stuffed his mouth with earth and suffocated himself. The use of knives, guns, and hanging seems to be modern, and even if one makes allowances for the fact that an old woman would not have found it easy to get hold of a gun, it is altogether compatible with female conservativeness that the last person to suffocate herself by stuffing earth into her mouth was a woman (Case 123).

Actually, the means used for committing suicide are probably also closely related to such noncultural factors as the individual's determination to kill himself. Thus, nearly all suicidal attempts involving guns were successful, whereas no suicide who used a knife managed to kill himself. It is also extremely interesting that all suicides who used traditional means (geophagy, datura, drowning) were successful. The hanging—which was executed with extraordinary determination (Case 124)—may have been successful chiefly because it is, fundamentally, a modern variant of self-suffocation by geophagy. These facts are simply noted, without attempting to make too much of them, since the data are not numerous enough to permit one to draw from them irrefutable conclusions regarding the nexus between the means a Mohave uses to kill himself and the degree of his determination to die.

Cultural data which lend themselves to tabulation are presented in table 1.

TABLE 1.—*Summary of cultural suicide data*

Type of suicide	Mythical precedent (specific)	"Prenatal" connections	Age	Sex and sex ratio	Cause of death	
					Imputed	Probable
Prenatal:						
Shamans	Yes	Planned in womb to be stillborn	At birth	(?)	Intentional stillbirth	Obstetrical complications.
Bewitched	(?)	Persuaded in womb to be stillborn	do	(?)	Compliant stillbirth, due to witchcraft.	Do.
Forced weaning	(?)	In rapport with uterus which it still considers its place.	At weaning 0–4 years	(?)	Self-induced illness	Pediatric disease and malnutrition.
Twin(s)	Yes(?)	(1) Recall heavens all their lives. (2) Perhaps recall that they are ghosts revisiting the earth.	From birth to marriage.	(?)	Self-induced illness	Stillbirth, or illness, or malnutrition.
Incestuous marriage	(?)	No explicit nexus	At marriage	M	Slaying of horse, which symbolizes partial social death of bridegroom.	No real death.
Willing victim of witchcraft	Yes(?)	No explicit nexus	Any age	F>M(?)	Witchcraft and cooperation of the victim with the witch.	Illness, perhaps psychosomatic.
Witch	(?)	Recalls intrauterine existence	Middle-aged or old	M>F(?)	Provoked murder, or refusal to escape murderers.	Murder.
Warrior	(?)	May perhaps recall intrauterine existence.	Adult	M	Slaying by enemy, through deliberate self-exposure.	Slain by enemy.
Funeral	(?)	No explicit nexus	Adult	F>M	Attempted self-cremation	Attempted self-cremation.
Active	(?)	No explicit nexus, except for unjustly accused shaman.	Adult	M>F	Suicide	Suicide.

Type of suicide	Motivation		Alleged (A) and real (B) technique
	Imputed	Probable	
Prenatal:			
Shamans	Innate hatred of life and wish to kill mother	None	Refuses to be born (A). Lies transversally in womb (A, R).
Bewitched	Hatred of life (and wish to kill mother?) induced by witchcraft.	None	Do.
Forced weaning	Resentment over weaning. Resentment toward unborn sibling. Spite.	Weaning trauma. Sibling rivalry (contributory).	Makes self sick from spite (A). Illness (R).
Twin(s)	(1) Hypersensitivity. Dislike of the earth. Longing for dead twin (heavenly twins). (2) Purpose of mission to earth completed (twins as ghosts). (?)	None if stillborn. Possible sibling rivalry and general hypersensitiveness.	Dies intentionally in utero (A). Makes self sick (A and R?).
Incestuous marriage	Desire to marry a cousin, regardless of the risks involved.	Guilt over "incestuous" marriage	Kills self socially by having a horse killed (A, R).
Willing victim of witchcraft	Enthralled victim of witchcraft willing to die bewitched.	Masochistic impulses (contributory)	Refusal to tell name of witch to therapist (A, R). Illness (R).
Witch	Longing for beloved victims. Fear of their being kidnaped by another shaman. Desire to retain control over them, which requires that the witch be killed.	Guilt reinforced by cultural beliefs regarding advantages of being killed.	Provokes others to kill him, or refuses to flee killers (A, R).
Warrior	Tired of life.	Guilt over having killed enemies(?). Desire to cause a retaliatory raid(?).	Strays into enemy territory (A, R).
Funeral	Guilt feelings. Desire to go through various incarnations with the deceased.	Guilt feelings. Aggression toward the dead and identification with the dead. Delayed mourning. Hysterical self-dramatization.	Leaps on funeral pyre (A, R).
Active	Adultery of wife. Disappointment in love. Accusations of incest. Unjust accusations of witchcraft. Illness. Neglect by son. Longing for a dead brother. Insults. Nagging, etc.	Brooding resentment. Identification with a previous suicide. Delayed mourning. Masochistic revenge, etc.	Gun, knife, hanging, self-suffocation, datura poisoning, drowning (A, R).

TABLE 1.—*Summary of cultural suicide data*—Continued

Type of suicide	Success versus failure	Recent increase (I) or decrease (D) in frequency; its cause	Social action	Attitudes
Prenatal:				
Shamans	S>F	D; modern medicine	Call shaman	"It is their nature, they can't help it." Feel sorry nonetheless.
Bewitched	S	D; modern medicine	...do	Feel sorry, consider this an act against tribal survival.
Forced weaning	(?)	D; modern medicine	Call shaman	Worried. Child is told not to be jealous and to let another Mohave be born.
Twin(s)	S>F(?)	D; modern medicine	Call shaman	Worried. Ask twins to stay on earth, promise them preferential treatment. "It is their nature; they can't help it."
Incestuous marriage	S	D; obsolete custom	Try to prevent such marriages	Disapprove. Fear extinction of family. Demand that such a marriage be permanent.
Willing victim of witchcraft	S>F(?)	D; modern medicine	Call shaman	Worried and exasperated. Angry at witch; may retaliate.
Witch	S>F (formerly)	D; U. S. law prohibits witch killings.	If witch believed guilty, no interference with killers. If witch believed innocent, try to prevent killing or avenge it.	"It is their nature; they can't help it." "Crazy." Gloat. Regret it, if related to witch. Some ambivalence.
Warrior	S>F	D; tribal warfare obsolete	Seance to discover what happened. Retaliation against enemy.	Angry at enemy. Indirect indications of anger toward the brave. Desire to retaliate.
Funeral	F	D; obsolete custom	Always prevent it; this is known to prospective suicides.	"We feel sorry for them, but it is a crazy thing to do." "Showing off." "His conscience hurt him."
Active	S>F	I; acculturation, anomie	Seek to comfort the distressed person	"Coward," "Brave," "Crazy," "Pretty nice people," "Weak," "We are sad." Marked ambivalence.

SUICIDE AND KILLING

Suicide and killing are closely interwoven in Mohave culture. This is not surprising either psychoanalytically, or in terms of Mohave culture, which postulates that all deaths are patterned upon that of the God Matavilye, who decided to bring death into being by setting a precedent.

In some instances a killing precedes suicide; in other instances the dead cause the living to die, or to commit suicide.

Killing precedes suicide.—The future shaman kills his mother during birth, by assuming a transversal position in the womb and then, inevitably, dies himself. If a pair of twins, composed of a boy and a girl, quarrel, the offended twin dies, whereupon the offending twin also decides to leave the earth.[69]   At incestuous marriages the killing of a horse is the means whereby the groom's social identity is destroyed. Witches first kill their victims and then become suicidal. Senior warriors seek to be killed by an enemy tribe, some of whose members they themselves had slain in battle. One man attempted to commit funeral suicide, by leaping on the pyre of his son whom his nagging had driven to suicide and for whose death he was blamed as much as though he had killed him (Case 111). Several persons attempted to commit suicide after first threatening or trying to kill someone (Cases 113, 120, 126), while one woman first expressed death wishes toward her hated aunt and then said that she herself wished to die (Case 115). The suicide of suddenly weaned sucklings is, in a sense, only a partial exception to this rule, since the infant is supposed to hate the unborn rival, which presumably means that, being unable to harm the fetus, he kills himself. The only true exceptions are the willing victims of witchcraft, who are not supposed to have killed anyone before allowing themselves to die of witchcraft.

In brief, in all types of suicide except one, the Mohave explicitly or implicitly hold that suicide follows aggression, or even murder.

The dead as killers.—One of the basic tenets of Mohave eschatology is the belief that the dead seek to lure the living to the land of the dead, and that the living wish to join the beloved dead before the latter undergo further metamorphoses (Devereux, 1937 a). The shamanistic fetus wishes to die together with its mother. If a twin dies, its twin soon follows it to the land of the dead, or to heaven. Although the Mohave did not specify that the longing of the surviving infant for its deceased twin is directly due to attempts on the part of the dead infant to lure its surviving twin to the other world, it is extremely likely that such a belief exists, but was simply not recorded. When a man, who marries his cousin, commits "social

---

[69] In view of the fact that one can cause the death of a twin by offending it (Devereux, 1941), the death of the first twin may be considered as a killing.

suicide," the kin group cries, because such marriages often cause the complete extinction of the lineage. The voluntary victim of a witch realizes that his or her ghost will cohabit with the witch in dream, thus arousing in the witch a longing for his victim, which will cause him to incite *his victim's relatives* to kill him. The vicarious suicide of a warrior usually induces one of his young admirers to persuade the tribe to make a retaliatory raid. If he succeeds in mobilizing such an expedition, the dead brave's admirer will recklessly expose himself, in the hope of being slain, so as to be able to join his admired mentor in that part of the land of the ghosts which is reserved for braves (Fathauer, 1952). In funeral suicide the nexus between the death of a spouse or close relative and the attempted funeral suicide of the survivor is equally explicit. As regards actual suicides, several of them were directly due to the death (or suicide) of a beloved person, usually a brother (Case 113, etc.).

Summing up, the dead are, by definition, eager to lure the survivors to the land of the dead. The survivors succumb to this lure either by contracting a ghost disease (pt. 4, pp. 128–186), or else by killing themselves in one way or the other. In this respect the Mohave myth of the origin of death, various eschatological beliefs concerning the seductiveness of the dead, and the actual fact that genuine suicides often occur after the death (or suicide) of a loved person are perfect cultural expressions of the basic psychic mechanism of mourning (Freud, 1925 d), of which suicidalness is but the most extreme manifestation.

Significantly, the most insightful and unequivocal statement concerning the nexus between killing and suicide was obtained in response to a general question regarding the causes of suicide.

Hivsu:Tupo:ma's statement (1936).—It is hard to explain in a general way just why people kill themselves. Let me try to give you an imaginary example. You know that your interpreter is as devoted to her husband as he is to her. Suppose, now, that your interpreter suddenly became promiscuous. Well, her husband would not kill her . . . he would kill himself.

The point of Hivsu: Tupo: ma's fictitious example seems to be that only a man *accustomed* to the exemplary loyalty and devotion of his wife has an *understandable*, or *justifiable*, reason for killing himself. As the main informant on matters pertaining to suicide, Hivsu: Tupo: ma knew, of course, that some men killed themselves over women who had not been devoted wives to begin with, but felt that such suicides only proved the men in question to have been fools and weaklings. It is also noteworthy that every single suicide that was preceded by an attempted murder involved an unreasonable attachment to a woman who was "worthless" to begin with. In brief, actual killings seem to occur only where jealous anger is the chief motivating factor. Where the chief trauma is loss of love and trust, life seems meaningless and suicide, often without murder, the only possible means of escape.

The preceding considerations also have major methodological implications. It is quite evident that certain basic "psychological" reaction patterns, fantasies, etc., are institutionalized in certain cultures by means of standardized beliefs and practices, even though, in other cultures, these selfsame beliefs may either be wholly repressed, or else may be reflected in culture only in a highly disguised, distorted, or even inverted form. Precisely which basic psychological reaction will be overtly implemented in a given culture, and which will be repressed, depends on the nature of the culture under consideration.[70] A systematic study of a set of cultures in terms of the basic reaction patterns which each of them implements culturally, respectively refuses to take cognizance of, would be a difficult, but also highly rewarding, undertaking and might shed new light on the nature of differences between various cultures. A pendant to such a study would be an analysis of the manner in which one and the same idea or fantasy is implemented in a variety of cultures: in myth, religion, medicine, material culture, humor, or daily practice.[71] A study of the exact context in which each of a set of cultures implements a given basic fantasy would also increase one's insight into the nature of cultural differences.[72] These two fields of inquiry are, so far, more or less unexplored.

PSYCHOSOMATIC SUICIDE

GENERAL CONSIDERATIONS

Three types of death are, from the Mohave point of view, definable as psychosomatic suicide, i.e., as deaths caused by physical illness of psychological origin: Stillbirth due to a malposition of the child in utero (pt. 7, pp. 340–348), the death of the infant who, because of the mother's new pregnancy, must be weaned rather suddenly (pt. 7, pp. 340–348) and the death of one or both twins before they have contracted marriages (pt. 7, pp. 348–356).

The idea that psychic distress can cause—sometimes fatal—physical illness has a long history. The possibility that death may be caused

---

[70] This finding has important implications for therapeutic work with neurotics from other cultures. Thus, whereas it proved safe to interpret to a Plains Indian professional cowboy his castration anxieties fairly early in his treatment, his hidden passive dependent needs had to be passed over in a short-term treatment, because, in his culture, dependency must be severely repressed (Devereux, 1951 a).

[71] For a tentative examination of the fantasy of the "retractible or reversible penis," cf. Devereux, 1954 b and 1957 a. For a scrutiny of the fantasy of "people without an anus," cf. Devereux, 1954 c. This latter study could have been greatly expanded, had Norbeck's essay (1955) been published earlier.

[72] It was stressed years ago (Devereux, 1942 e) that cultures differ more in the manner in which their constituent "elements" are put together, than in terms of discrepancies between their culture element inventories. (Cf. also Devereux, 1951 a.)

by shock or by a "broken heart," etc., has always been taken for granted by clinicians, as well as by the man in the street, and has been exploited by many writers of fiction. Equally ancient appears to be the idea that witchcraft can cause the death of a person who believes himself to be bewitched. The actual mechanism of such "voodoo deaths" is still incompletely understood, and may, possibly, result from either one of two mechanisms. Cannon (1942) shows that death can occur from fear and rage, leading to shock due to the workings of the sympathicoadrenal system. Richter (1957) demonstrates that death can occur from hopelessness, which affects the parasympathetic system ("vagus death"). In the "fear-rage death," outlined by Cannon, death occurs during the systole; in the "hopelessness death," described by Richter, it occurs during the diastole.

What is to be retained in this context is simply the fact that external life stress can result either in psychological or in physical illness, or both (Hinkle and Wolf, 1957; Hinkle et al., 1957) and that psychic distress can produce severe, or even fatal, physical illness. Thus, the Mohave belief, that a traumatized person can make himself reactively ill and may actually die from such an illness, is supported by the most reliable findings of modern psychosomatic research. Moreover, the Mohave belief that children are especially prone to die as a result of psychic traumata perfectly dovetails with Spitz's (1945, 1946), and Spitz and Wolf's (1946) richly documented finding that emotionally starved children die even if they receive excellent physical care in hygienically impeccable orphanages or hospitals.

This finding is of some importance for an objective evaluation of Mohave psychiatric thought. Even though it is obvious (pt. 8, pp. 485–505) that a given primitive belief can be objectively "correct" without thereby being necessarily also a product of scientific induction, in this particular instance it seems legitimate to suggest at least tentatively that the Mohave concept of the "psychic suicide" of children has some of the formal characteristics of a scientific theory.[73] It is, on the other hand, very important to understand that even the objective correctness of the Mohave theories in question, which admittedly have some of the formal characteristics of scientific theory, does not mean that every pediatric case diagnosed by the Mohave as "suicide" is actually a death from psychic causes. This mistake is, however, not due to an inherent defect of their theory, but to an error in its application; i.e., it is a misdiagnosis. The most striking

---

[73] It should be noted that the Mohave are far from unique in believing that the "soul" of the child is especially easily traumatized, and that such traumata can cause death. This belief is also held by many other primitive tribes, including the Sedang of Indochina (Devereux, MS., 1933–34), though this latter group did not evolve a theory of such deaths that has the formal characteristics of a scientific theory.

example of such a misdiagnosis is the belief that the stillbirth of certain children is due to psychic causes.[74]

Summing up:

(1) Some deaths may be due to psychic causes.

(2) Small children deprived of psychologically significant gratifications actually become—or "make themselves"—ill and sometimes die of such illnesses.

(3) The Mohave theory that death from psychic causes, especially in children, is a form of psychic suicide is, generally speaking, correct. Moreover, it actually possesses some of the formal characteristics of a scientific theory. In other words, it is not only objectively correct, but also scientific in the conventional sense of that term.

(4) The correctness and scientificality of this Mohave theory does not prove that all Mohave diagnoses of psychic suicide are actually correct. In some instances—and especially in the case of stillbirths diagnosed as psychic suicide—we are clearly dealing with a misdiagnosis.

(5) The occurrence of such misdiagnoses demonstrates the greatness of the "cultural mass" of the Mohave Indians' preoccupations with the idea of suicide in general and with the idea of psychic suicide in particular, because they demonstrably force certain deaths *not* due to psychic causes into the procrustean bed of their belief that all deaths occurring under certain circumstances are *necessarily* psychic suicides (Devereux, 1957 a).

PRENATAL SUICIDE, OR SUICIDE DURING PARTURITION

According to well-established and quite elaborate Mohave beliefs, some children refuse to be born and therefore kill both themselves and their mothers by assuming a transversal position (breech presentation) in the womb.

The principal significance of this belief for an understanding of the role of suicide in Mohave culture is that these "suicides" are thought to be planned by such infants while still in the womb. Hence, the belief that such deaths are suicides gives added meaning and depth to the observation that a great many types of "suicides"—as defined by the Mohave—are committed by persons who have relatively explicit connections with, or memories of, their intrauterine life (pt. 7, pp. 302–303, and passim).

Like all major aspects and events of Mohave life, "intentional" death during childbirth, too, has a quite explicit mythical model.

The mythical precedent.—The account of Matavilye's birth describes what we may tentatively call either the first real birth, or else

---

[74] On the basis of my account of this Mohave belief, K. A. Menninger (1940) suggested that such deaths may actually be due to "prenatal instinctual conflicts." The least that can be said of this thesis is that it is unconvincing.

the precedent-setting birth.[75]   At the same time a knowledge of this
myth, which is acquired in dream (Devereux, 1957 b), is a necessary
part of each obstetrical shaman's power and therapeutic equipment.
The following version was obtained from Ahma Huma:re, who was
originally a hiwey lak and hiku:pk specialist, but, after helplessly
watching his wife die in childbirth, while the movements of his
unborn child were still visible, also obtained the power to be a real
obstetrician, and not only, inter alia, a specialist in the cure of
ghost pregnancies (pt. 4, pp. 150–175).

> In a land west from here (Parker, Ariz.), at Amata Vihamok, there were
> Motutc ipa: (Sky-person Male) and Mokukumat(à)[76] (Earth Female).
> Other supernaturals, also born from the union of sky and earth, such as
> Mastamho, who, according to most versions, is Matavilye's son (Kroeber, 1948);
> and Pahotcatc, who, according to Kroeber (1948), is either Mastamho or else
> Mastamho functioning in a special capacity,[77] were also present. Only
> Matavilye was still in the womb, acting like a fetus who wishes to die during
> birth. He tried breech presentation and all other presentations as well . . .
> except only the normal presentation although he knew the way out (from the
> womb.)[78] Finally he decided to be born head first, so as to set an example
> and a precedent for mankind. In the meantime Sky Male and Earth Female
> were under the earth.[79]

Bourke (1889) supplies the additional information that Matavilye's
birth was accompanied by earthquakes.

The only comment called for is that Matavilye, who eventually died
because he *chose* to die (pt. 7, pp. 286–290), appears to have entertained suicidal ideas already in the womb.   He gave up these suicidal
wishes temporarily, in order to set an example for mankind, but, toward the end of his career, his suicidal wishes apparently returned and
induced him to die, so as to bring death into being.

Shamanistic rites for the alleviation of obstetrical complications
include formal and explicit references to this myth.   (See below.)

Prenatal preparations for suicide and murder at birth.—In the following discussion no reference will be made to infants who have a
difficult birth because their parents violated certain pregnancy and
birth taboos (Devereux, 1948 b).   It is simply noted that obstetrical
difficulties caused by breaches of taboos are dealt with exactly the way
the birth difficulties of shamanistic or bewitched fetuses are.

---

[75] It will be remembered that Matavilye's death was, likewise, the first and precedent
setting death (part 7, pp. 286–290).

[76] If Bourke (1889) is right, it might repay the efforts of a linguist and expert on Indian
religions to investigate further this name.

[77] Compare such references to Zeus as "Nephelegeretes"=cloud gatherer; "Soter"=he
who saves; "Zeus katachthonios" (Aeschylus)=Zeus under the earth (Hades); etc.

[78] This specification implies that, like all fetuses (Devereux, 1948 b and 1948 e) Matavilye,
too, thought of ways of being born while still in the womb.

[79] A detailed discussion of the extraordinary statement that, during his delivery, Matavilye's parents were both inside the earth—which implies that the mother was in her own
womb—was given elsewhere (Devereux, 1948 e). Unfortunately even a brief summary of
that discussion would take us too far afield to warrant its inclusion in the present work.

After 6 lunar months of pregnancy have elapsed, the fetus has an immutable identity (Devereux, 1937 d, 1949 c) and an autonomous psychic life. At that time the normal child begins to dream of ways of being born, while the shamanistic fetus dreams of ways of *not* being born, and, due to his "devilishness," assumes a transversal position in the womb. He wishes to kill the first person he can get hold of, even though that person is, of necessity, his own mother—whom he does not hate, but loves—and even though he realizes that this trick will kill him too. He does not mind dying, since he does not wish to be born. Such an unborn shaman cannot hurt anyone except himself and his mother. "The murderous unborn does not *take* its mother to the land of the dead; both proceed there *together*."

It is to be noted that future shamans are supposed to dream of shamanistic powers already in the womb: One of the deities "repeats" for the future shaman the portion of the creation myth that pertains to his future speciality. This point is of some importance for the understanding of the association between shamanistic power and suicidalness. Since, in his therapeutic work, the shaman necessarily deals with matters related to life and death, it is permissible to infer—even though no specific statements to that effect were either asked for or volunteered—that, in the course of this intrauterine "repetition" of creation, all shamans would, of necessity, dream not only of the incident of Creation which pertains to their speciality, but also of Matavilye's precedent-setting intentional death (quasi-suicide), which, as we have seen, represented psychologically a resurgence of those suicidal impulses which this deity already manifested when he temporarily refused to be born. This myth may therefore explain the close relationship between birth, death, and suicidalness in Mohave belief.

In addition to suicide shamanistic fetuses, who spontaneously (?) decide not to be born, there are also fetuses who compliantly assume a transversal position because a witch "taught them this trick meaning death." The fact that these bewitched fetuses are said to assume this lethal position (instead of being thought to have been passively rotated in the womb by the magical powers of the witch) implies that, like the cooperative adult victims of witches (pt. 7, pp. 383–386) they are compliant because they are willing to die, in accordance with the wishes of the witch. The voluntary nature of their malposition is further underscored by the fact that, when appealed to by the obstetrical shaman, they—like shamanistic fetuses—are capable of resuming the normal (head first) position in the womb.

Mohave beliefs concerning voluntary suicide and murder at birth have certain interesting psychological implications.

(1) They clearly reflect the—culturally predicated—close connection between suicidalness and murderous impulses (pt. 7, pp. 327–329).

(2) They emphasize that, even though the weaned infant, who no longer spends most of its time in the carrying cradle (Devereux, 1947 a and 1948 c), ceases to consider the womb as "its place," at least some adult Mohave continue to remember the womb (pt. 7, pp. 302–303, passim) and may unconsciously long to return to it, as do the ghosts of certain dead infants, who, in reentering the womb, are also likely to kill their mothers (pt. 4, pp. 150–175). Were such ideas and wishes not present even in the adult Mohave unconscious, this tribe would not have evolved the notion that some infants refuse to be born and that certain dead infants return to the womb, nor would they have been able to accept (Devereux, 1948 h) such ideas through diffusion from another culture.

(3) Many unborn shamans, whom the obstetrical shaman persuaded to give up their murderous and suicidal impulses long enough to be born, eventually turn into murderous witches who, in the end, long to be killed, and incite others to kill them (pt. 7, pp. 387–426).

(4) The fetal shaman is in an exceptionally favorable position for insuring that he and his mother would never be separated. By killing her and by dying himself during birth, he never has to emerge from her womb and can therefore go through all future reincarnations with his mother, without ever being separated from her. Hence, unlike adult shamans, who must delay the entrance of their victim's ghosts into the land of the dead until they themselves are killed (pt. 7, pp. 383–426), the infant shamanistic murderer can automatically achieve this end by killing his mother at the same time as he, himself, commits suicide.[80]

Needless to say, the four beliefs just cited shed light only upon the psychology of the Mohave *adult*, who imputes certain impulses, actions, and ideas to the unborn child. They do not, and cannot possibly shed light upon the "psychodynamics" of the unborn child, for the very good reason that the fetus has no psyche in the ordinary sense of the word. Hence, K. A. Menninger's (1940) attempt to use these Mohave beliefs in order to demonstrate the existence of prenatal instinctual conflicts and to support the theory of the primary death instinct is untenable.[81]

Diagnostic problems.—The Mohave believe death at birth to be usually pathognomonic of fetal shamanistic, murderous, and suicidal impulses. Indeed, in their opinion the overwhelming majority of obstetrical deaths and stillbirths are caused by shamanistic fetuses, and most of the rest by the fact that the fetus had been bewitched.

---

[80] Fantasies about obstetrical deaths may be the infantile models of so called "suicide pacts."

[81] It might be added in passing that a great many of our supposedly "scientific" ideas about child psychology appear to be little more than projections of the adult mind. Differently expressed, they are adult fantasies, imputed to children. This criticism applies not only to the views of such psychoanalytic (?) extremists as Melanie Klein and her school, but also to much of our academic child psychology (Devereux, 1956 a).

This matter is of such importance, that, in 1936, Hivsu: Tupo:ma was asked to dictate his opinion in Mohave. Since Hivsu: Tupo:ma was not a first-rate linguistic informant, in 1950 the excellent linguistic informant Pulyi:k was first asked to read the texts dictated by Hivsu: Tupo:ma and was then asked to repeat them—if he agreed with the statements—in his own words. For the sake of completeness both versions are given.

(1) Transversal (buttocks first) presentation was held by Hivu: Tupo:ma and Pulyi:k to be indicative of the fact that the stillborn fetus was a shaman.

Hivsu: Tupo:ma's version: Kau:lym (how) yalynyidhu:tck (to think) cupa:um (they knew) hi-itckwa (they said) kwathidhe:y-nye (shaman he was)? (Why did they assume he was a shaman?) Hipa: râm (end, butt end) suyavak (coming first) hidhu:m (it was) cupa:um (they knew) hi-itc-(i)ntaha (they said already). (From the breech presentation they inferred and declared that it was a shaman.)

Pulyi:k's version: This informant only modified the preceding text by placing *cupa:um* before *yalynyidhu:tck,* and by replacing *suyavak* with *cuya:uk.*

(2) The fact that the fetus killed its mother during birth was held by Hivsu: Tupo:ma and Pulyi:k to prove that the fetus was a shaman.

Hivsu: Tupo:ma's version: Kwathidhey-pak (shaman) hidhu:m (he is) hinta:y-nye (mother his) tapuypak (he killed) hidhu:m (he is) cupa:um (they knew) hi-itc-(i)ntaha (they said already). (He is a shaman; he killed his mother; that is how they knew it and why they said it.)

Pulyi:k's version: Kwathidhe:yk (shaman) hidhu:m (he is) hamcuvya:(w)k (butt end first) hitpa:kâm (comes out) hidhu:m (he does) hi-inta:ye (his mother) tâpu:yâm (kill) ha(w)-intaha (he does). (He is a shaman; he comes out butt end first, he kills his mother.)

These statements leave nothing to be desired in the way of explicitness. One may add, however, that bewitched fetuses also behave in this manner, which causes one to wonder in precisely what way—if any—the Mohave differentiate, or profess to differentiate, between these two types of death at birth since, despite careful inquiries, Hivsu: Tupo:ma could only repeat the texts already quoted above. Likewise, no informant could explain why the death of Hualy Hore:e in childbirth (Case 83) was held to have been caused by her unborn child's shaministic nature, rather than by witchcraft, or by a breach of pregnancy taboos.[82] This inability to differentiate diagnostically between these three types of obstetrical complications is rather striking. Indeed, as this work shows, the Mohave are, if anything, rather overmeticulous diagnosticians, not adverse to splitting diagnostic hairs in terms of their own nosological scheme. Their inability to differentiate between these various obstetrical complications probably explains why all such difficulties are treated by the same method, and

---

[82] For a possible explanation, see Case 83.

why all obstetrical powers are acquired by dreaming of Matavilye's intentionally difficult birth. In brief, only the obstetrical shaman's hunch determines the alleged cause of a given obstetrical difficulty.

The one troubling point is the theoretical possibility that the Mohave failure to differentiate between the two most prevalent obstetrical difficulties may ultimately be due to a—perhaps obsolete and forgotten—belief that certain unborn infants become shamans only because they are "made into shamans" by the magical power of shamans already born and practicing their craft.[83] The one positive datum suggesting that such a belief may once have existed is the tenet that "shamanism runs in the family." This belief appears to be significant, not only because it seems to be the only Mohave reference to the inheritance of psychological traits, but also because witches mostly bewitch their own relatives.

The obstetrical crisis.—Sometimes a woman is unable to give birth because her child assumes a transversal position in the womb. The Mohave laymen are unable to deal with breech presentations, since they do not know how to rotate the child in the womb. All informants were emphatic in their insistence that both shamanistic and bewitched fetuses assume this lethal position voluntarily.

Statement of the obstetrical shaman Harav He:ya (1933).—The fetus is lying crosswise in the womb, even though it knows the proper way out. It is as though a person, who knows quite well the shortest highway to a certain place, deliberately took a devious side road. Such children do not care that, in killing their mothers, they also kill themselves. Both good and evil future shamans at first resist being born.

It is true, of course, that breech presentation may also occur if the pregnant woman ignored, e.g., the rule against lying in the doorway of the house (Devereux, 1948 b). Whether in such instances the baby is automatically *placed* transversally in the womb, or whether it *assumes* this position—perhaps because it resents its mother's careless action—could not be ascertained. Fortunately, this point is, practically speaking, relatively unimportant since, even though the Mohave have this belief and taboo, most breech presentations are automatically diagnosed as being due to the unborn child's typically shamanistic suicidalness and murderousness.

When such difficulties occur, the lay people present first try to help delivery along by various simple physical means, but, in the end, usually call in the shaman (Devereux, 1948 e). In at least one instance (Case 83) the shaman was called in so late that, by the time he arrived, the woman and her baby were both dead.

Obstetrical therapy.—A detailed discussion of Mohave obstetrics having been published elsewhere (Devereux, 1948 e), it suffices to outline, in the present context, the main features of shaman-

---

[83] For a suggestive hint, cf. Devereux, 1957 b.

istic rites for the alleviation of obstetrical difficulties caused by the self-destructive and murderous behavior of unborn shamans and bewitched fetuses.

The obstetrician Ahma Huma :re said that he first spoke to the woman from a distance, either in a language that can be understood, or else in a language that cannot be understood.[84] He then circles the woman clockwise, singing one song each from the South (right arm of the woman), the West (left arm), the North (left leg) and the East (right leg). At each of these stops he also talks to the unborn child, asking it to emerge the natural way, saying: "If you come out the natural way, your example will be followed by the Mohave still to be born and the tribe will increase. If, however, you do not come out, your bad example will also be followed by children yet unborn and then there will be no new generation to follow ours and perpetuate the tribe." Ahma Huma :re then confidently declared that, after he spoke to the child from all four directions, it would be born regardless of what the difficulty might have been.[85]

This last statement implies that even though the obstetrical difficulties may have been due to witchcraft—which is said to be very hard to treat—or to a violation of some pregnancy taboo (Devereux, 1948 b), these difficulties are, in the last resort, also referable to Matavilye's difficult birth, which was due solely to his reluctance to be born. Be that as it may, it was specifically asserted that bewitched fetuses respond to this treatment quite as satisfactorily as future shamans do.

It should be noted in passing that obstetrical shamans apparently do not knead the woman's abdomen and do not perform an internal examination. Thus, a medical account of Mohave obstetrics (Nettle, MS., n. d.; cf. Devereux, 1948 e) stated quite explicitly that the kneading of the abdomen is performed by nonshamanistic persons, before the obstetrical shaman is called in. Hrdlička (1908) also stated that, in case of severe distress, the woman is examined internally, but did not specify whether this is done by shamans or by lay midwives. The data obtained both from Ahma Huma :re, who was an obstetrical shaman, and from Hivsu: Tupo :ma, who appears to have described Harav He :ya's modus operandi (Devereux, 1948 e), suggest that no internal examinations are performed by shamans.[86]

The shaman's appeals to the unborn child's reason, sense of fairness and responsibility for the perpetuation of the tribe vividly underline two salient features of the Mohave world view: The notion that tribal continuity is the responsibility of everyone, and the view that even

---

[84] In my article on obstetrics (Devereux, 1948 e) I suggested that the "unknown tongue" was probably an archaic Mohave text. I would now add that the "understandable" tongue may refer to a recital of the prose version of the relevant myth, in more or less ordinary language. (For a justification of this view cf. Devereux, 1957 b.)

[85] Being an honest man, Ahma Huma :re added, somewhat regretfully, that "nowadays all the women call in the reservation physician. Hence, even though I have the power to help in cases of difficult birth, so far I have not yet been called upon to help, though people do consult me for other ailments which I can cure." This statement highlights the Mohave shaman's faith in his own untested powers.

[86] Female obstetrical shamans were not mentioned by any informant.

the unborn child is a sentient and reasonable being, capable of responding both to objective reasoning and to an emotional appeal to the Mohave value system.[87]

Responsibility.—In obstetrical deaths caused by future shamans, the blame clearly rests with the fetus. Indeed, even though it is a shaman's nature to act in this manner, it was, in principle, possible for the fetus to yield to the obstetrical shaman's appeals, urging it to be born. In not heeding these appeals he showed himself a bad Mohave, not interested in setting a good example for future generations.

As regards the obstetrical death of a bewitched infant, the person blamed is the witch, whose powers the fetus could not resist, nor the obstetrical therapist neutralize. The Mohave seem to feel that the power a witch uses for such purposes is very great indeed, since obstetrical difficulties caused by witchcraft are said to be the most difficult to alleviate.

It is especially important to note that the mother never seems to be blamed for such mishaps, although some women not only resort to mechanical means for abortion (Devereux, 1948 d, 1955 a), but may even ask a witch to kill the child in the womb by magical means. If the witch agrees to do so he "presses her sides" . . . the implication being that, in this manner, he sends his evil power into the woman, so as to destroy the child in the womb. This operation is called hi :toly matadha :uk masahaye (or thinyeak) (belly bewitch girl, or woman).[88] Unlike the bewitching of the fetus, such magical abortions are not believed to harm the woman herself.

In brief, since the Mohave deem it inconceivable that any woman would be "crazy enough to ask a shaman to bewitch her foetus in this manner, so as to be able to die with her unborn child," the mother who dies without being able to deliver her shamanistic or bewitched baby is never held responsible for the double misfortune.[89] The only women who are blamed for obstetrical deaths are those known to have violated the relevant pregnancy taboos (Devereux, 1948 b).

---

[87] Compare in this context the appeals made to suddenly weaned children suffering from tavåknyi :k (pt. 7, pp. 340–348), the belief that all children begin to think already in the womb (Devereux, 1948 b) and the thesis that, from the moment they are born, twins have the intelligence of adults (Devereux, 1941). For a discussion of Mohave patriotism, compare Kroeber 1925 a.

[88] This text having been obtained in 1932, at the very beginning of my first field season, it may conceivably be in "simplified" Mohave, since the words seem to lack suffixes.

[89] In this respect the Mohave seem more sensible than certain extreme exponents of "natural childbirth," who see in every obstetrical complication maternal anxieties, reluctances, and the like. While psychological factors certainly play a role in some cases, a wholesale "psychological" approach to obstetrics seems unreasonable, as a minimal familiarity with obstetrical difficulties in animals will prove. It is also half distressing and half amusing to note the persistence of the myth that "primitive women bear their children painlessly and easily," when every tribe appears to have elaborate rules and taboos for preventing obstetrical calamities, and means, both technical and ritual, for dealing with such difficulties when they do arise. The magic surrounding the term "natural" in "natural childbirth" does not make natural childbirth any more pleasant than the "natural" eruption of teeth is for the baby.

The "suicidal" neonate, whom the shaman finally persuades to live, is not discriminated against in any way, though his difficult birth will be remembered and people will knowingly refer to it when such a child begins to misbehave in a way characteristic of future shamans (Devereux, 1937 c). It is also possible that children, who overhear references to their difficult birth, may begin to think of themselves as potential shamans.

Even neonates whose mothers actually died in birth are not discriminated against, though it is not always easy to find a woman, with a living infant of her own, who is willing to nurse such an orphan. This, however, is not due to discrimination, but to the Mohave woman's reluctance to give her own child a rival at the breast (Devereux, 1947 a and pt. 3, p. 115, and pt. 7, pp. 340–348).

The chief reason why such children are not discriminated against is that the Mohave are fond of any fullblood Mohave child capable of insuring the perpetuation of the tribe (pt. 6, pp. 257–259). A subsidiary reason is that the shamanistic neonate's suicidal and murderous behavior is routinely explained in terms of characterological compulsions implicit in his being a potential shaman. The final reason is the simple fact that, even though the Mohave do not admire shamans as people and dread them as potential witches, they believe them to be necessary for the welfare and survival of the sick.

The following obstetrical death was cited as an example of the prenatal suicide of a future shaman, although the informants were unable to say why it was believed to be a suicide of this type, rather than the complaint suicide of a bewitched fetus or a death caused by the breach of a taboo. It is tentatively suggested that the diagnosis may have been determined by the fact that the mother was the daughter of a shaman, so that—in view of the belief that "shamanism runs in families"—the conclusion that the infant unwilling to be born was also a future shaman was practically inescapable.

CASE 83 (Informant not recorded; probably Haray He:ya):

Hualy Hore:e, a 30-year-old fullblood Mohave woman, the wife of Nyilas and the daughter of a shaman specializing in the cure of the ahwe: illnesses (pt. 4, pp. 128–150) had a protracted labor. She and her female attendants waited all day and all night for the baby to be born. It was "lying across" in the womb. "We could feel the head bulge." "We also knew it from the way it moved." In the end they called in the shaman Haray He:ya, who knew how to cure such cases. He arrived at about 10:00 a. m., but by that time both the woman and the unborn baby were dead. They were cremated together.

Comment

The remark concerning the "bulging head" can be linked with the fact that certain old women are believed to be able to diagnose impending twin births by abdominal palpation. As for the late arrival of the obstetrician, Mohave shamans habitually attribute their therapeutic failures to the fact that they were not consulted in time (McNichols, 1944).

SUICIDE AT WEANING (TÁVÁKNYI:K)

Under ordinary circumstances the Mohave child is nursed for 2 or 3 years, and great care is taken not to traumatize it by weaning it too suddenly or by means which might frighten or distress it. Moreover, the intensity of the weaning trauma is even further reduced by the fact that it occurs at a time when the mouth is no longer the chief erotogenous zone of the child who, at the age of 2 or 3 has already reached the anal stage of psychosexual development (Devereux, 1947 a; Devereux, 1951 e). Similarly, Mohave toilet training also occurs relatively late (Devereux, 1951 e, Wallace, 1948)—at least by occidental standards—i.e., at a time when anal erogeneity is largely superseded by phallic-genital interests. Thus, the control of oral, respectively of anal functions, requires less self-constriction and less renunciation on the part of the Mohave child than on that of the occidental child. This finding probably sheds a great deal of light on Mohave character structure and also on the character structure of other tribes in which weaning and toilet training occur at a point in time when the renouncing of oral, respectively anal, interests is appreciably facilitated by the fact that, as a result of normal psychosexual development, the pleasure to be renounced is no longer the child's principal source of gratification. This point is of some importance for the understanding of certain types of character structure, although a detailed discussion of this matter is beyond the scope of the present study.

Yet, despite the lateness and gentleness of the weaning process, the belief that certain weaned children develop the "suicidal" táváknyi:k disease shows that some Mohave at least empathize rather readily with the plight of the infant about to be weaned. It is probable that this insight into the weaning trauma is not exclusively due to the proverbial insatiability of the oral drive. Indeed, there are, even in Mohave society, certain infants who experience such intense oral frustrations and rivalries that they remain orally fixated for the rest of their lives.

Genuine oral frustrations and rivalries are experienced by three types of persons likely to reach adulthood: [90]

(1) Children who must be weaned suddenly, because of the mother's new pregnancy.

(2) Twins who have, from birth, a rival for the breast.

(3) Children whose mothers give them a rival for the breast, by suckling also a small orphaned relative (pt. 3, p. 115).[91]

It seems extremely probable that at least a few such persons later on become shamans specializing in the cure of the táváknyi:k disease.

---

[90] Snake-headed monstrous births, whose bite is so greatly dreaded that they are not nursed, seldom reach adulthood, and are therefore unlikely to contribute to the genesis of new beliefs and opinions (pt. 6, pp. 257–259).

[91] The only one to mention a white child's Mohave wet nurse is McNichols (1944), who does not tell us what had happened to the woman's own child.

This inference is supported by the fact that Hivsu: Tupo: ma, a noted tåvånyi:k specialist, was so voracious an eater that even he sometimes joked about his appetite. Moreover, even the name he had selected for himself alludes to food; Hivsu: Tupo:ma means "burnt raw," and refers to the parching of corn. It is true, of course, that Hivsu: Tupo:ma justified his choice of this name by saying that the totem of his gens, Tcatc, is corn (Spier, 1953), but this explanation does not account fully for his choice of a food-connected name, since Mohave men show no preference for personal names that have a totemic reference. It is, therefore, far more likely that, since the best concealment for unconscious impulses is notoriously a seemingly realistic "reason," he simply took advantage of the fact that his gens had an edible totem, to justify his choice of a name referring to food. Finally, it is known that Hivsu: Tupo:ma was quite jealous of his male half sibling, and eventually bewitched him, "because my mother preferred him to me" (Case 139) (Devereux, 1948 i).

It is highly characteristic of the Mohave that they impute radically different psychological reactions to children who have to be weaned because of the mother's new pregnancy, and to those who have to share the maternal breast with another child. Only forcibly weaned children are said to become "suicidal." Most children who must learn to share the breast with another suckling are believed to be able to tolerate and to accept the competitive situation in which they find themselves; hence, only a few develop the hi:wa hira:uk ailment (pt. 3, p. 115). One might almost say that whereas the forcible weaning of a newly pregnant woman's child is viewed and explained in infantile terms related to the nursing process, the sharing of the breast is brought within the scope of the mature and ideal pattern of generous sharing, which characterizes Mohave social interaction. Hence, the sharing of the breast will be discussed only in order to highlight the differences between the psychological reactions imputed to forcibly weaned children and those attributed to children who must learn to share early in life.

In regard to twins, the Mohave feel that they readily adapt themselves to the need of sharing the maternal breast, and nurse either at the left or at the right breast. On the other hand twins become resentful and also very jealous of each other if they are not treated exactly alike and are not favored above all *other* children. Moreover, twins, one of whom is a boy and the other a girl, sometimes quarrel with each other, the way spouses do. In all such instances the slighted or offended twin causes himself (or herself) to die, and is usually soon followed into death by the surviving twin. Finally, twins are said to be exceptionally prone to develop tåvåknyi:k if their mother becomes pregnant before she had time to wean them (pt. 7, pp. 348–356).

Thus, it seems quite certain that even though simple reality factors—such as the lack of practical alternatives—compel the Mohave to deny that twins are rivals for the maternal breast, they implicitly, albeit in a displaced form, recognize the existence of this rivalry, by insisting that twins are especially susceptible to slights, to unequal or non-preferential treatment, and also to a "marital discord" type of quarrel with the other twin.

Sometimes even a child who had no twin had to endure the trauma of being given a rival for the maternal breast, for example, when its mother had to nurse also a small orphaned relative. Although Wallace (1948) rightly stresses that this was the normal and accepted procedure, my informants—who were somewhat older than his—were quite emphatic in saying that the average Mohave woman was somewhat reluctant to wet-nurse another child, because she was afraid that her own child might react to the intruder's presence with hi:wa hira:uk (heart angry or mean, where the word hira:uk is derived from hwara:uk=anger) (pt. 3, p. 115). Hence, they sometimes subjected the orphan's grandmother to a galactopoietic treatment, whose efficacy in the case of A. W.'s mother was medically attested in 1933 by the late M. A. I. Nettle, M. D. (Devereux, 1947 a). Finally, there seems to be no case on record in which a pregnant, but still lactating, woman agreed to nurse an orphan, in addition to her own child.

The one puzzling feature of the practice of nursing an orphan simultaneously with one's own child is the tendency to give one's own child the right breast, and the foster child the left breast. The point to be considered here is that, in Mohave parlance, the left side is the maternal side,[92] while the right side is the paternal side. One explanation may be that the woman's own child is given the right breast because it belongs to its father's gens. This hypothesis is, however, not entirely satisfactory, since it could just as well be argued that the woman's right breast represents the kin of *her* father, to whose gens she, but not her child, belongs. The chief argument in support of this second interpretation is that the child necessarily receives milk from its mother—and, by extension, from its mother's gens—rather than from its father, who "nurses" the child only in the uterus (Devereux, 1937 d, 1949 c).[93] There certainly exists no absolutely convincing interpretation of this fact, which is cited only because of its rather puzzling features.

---

[92] Thus, according to McNichols (1944), when a Mohave refers to the death of his interlocutor's mother or maternal kin, he tactfully says that there is grief on the "left side."

[93] Compare in the context the fact that if a Sedang Moi marriage is matrilocal, the husband must make a gift to the girl's mother, to "buy her milk" (to be given by her daughter) for his potential children. If the marriage is patrilocal, the bride "buys the milk" of her new mother-in-law, so as to be able to nurse her future babies (Devereux, MS., 1933–34).

The hi:wa hira:uk illness of sucklings, who are given a rival for the breast, appears to resemble the tàvàknyi:k illness; its most interesting aspect is, however, its designation. It is called "anger" rather than "envy," perhaps because envy is particularly odious to the Mohave, who seldom if ever use this latter term, perhaps because they do not care to recognize its existence,[94] though it is clear enough that the motivating force behind such "anger" is jealous envy (pt. 3, p. 115). From the cultural point of view, the crucial difference between the suckling's reaction to a rival for the maternal breast and its reaction to a weaning necessitated by the mother's new pregnancy seems to lie in the fact that, in the former case, the conflict is rooted in a present and real situation, whereas in the latter instance it is actuated by "prenatal" factors which, according to the Mohave, seem to possess a greater motivating force—especially where self-aggression is involved (pt. 7, pp. 302–303, passim)—than do the events of post-natal life.

The only weaning trauma capable of arousing suicidal impulses in the suckling occurs when, due to a new pregnancy of the mother, the infant must be weaned rather *abruptly*, because the milk flow ceases. It would therefore be understandable if the Mohave explained the difficulties caused by such a sudden weaning in terms of the sudden cessation of the milk supply. Indeed, as soon as a lactating woman becomes pregnant, her milk rapidly deteriorates both quantitatively and qualitatively, causing her infant to be both psychologically frustrated and physiologically undernourished.

However, perhaps because the Mohave are conditioned to deny their oral enviousness, which is not quite respectable, while placing preoccupations with prenatal experiences on a cultural pedestal, they believe tàvàknyi:k to be caused primarily by the child's awareness of its mother's new pregnancy.

The differences between the Mohave and the scientific interpretations of the psychosomatic process which culminates in tàvàknyi:k are summarized in table 2.

TABLE 2.—*Differences between Mohave and scientific interpretations in tàvàknyi:k*

Physiological state of mother	Psychological state of suckling	Mohave explanation	Scientific explanation
Pregnant but lactating. Milk scanty and of poor quality. Milk flow decreases.	Hungry and frustrated. Hungry and angry.	Knows mother is pregnant. Feels hurt and sad. Misses the milk. Feels hurt when scolded for fretting. Angry at the unborn intruder.	Severely frustrated. Finds it difficult to drink less milk and to eat more mush and solid food, all of a sudden. Angry at mother.
Milk flow has ceased.	Hungry, angry, ill.	Spitefully seeks to kill itself through sickness, after first making everyone thoroughly miserable.	Self-aggression, complicated by psychosomatic factors: Malnutrition and "organic compliance" with self-aggression. Marasmus.

[94] All groups are markedly reluctant to call a socially penalized affect by its proper name. Thus, in our own society, the experiencing of mere "lust" is usually denied both to others and to oneself, by masking it with a variety of more ego-syntonic and culture-syntonic euphemisms.

It is of some interest in this context that, according to the Mohave, the pregnant woman ceases to have milk after the sixth lunar month of pregnancy has elapsed. This belief is presumably due to the belief that the 6-lunar-month-old fetus has an immutable sociobiological identity that is no longer susceptible of being modified by intercourse with a man who is not the original impregnator (Devereux, 1937 d, 1949 c); begins to feed orally, "chewing and swallowing" its food (semen) inside the womb [95] (Devereux, 1948 b); and also starts dreaming those dreams that pertain to the modalities of birth (or, in the case of future shamans and bewitched fetuses, to stillbirth, cf. pt. 7, pp. 331–339. It is also during this period that the fetus has those dreams that determine the course of its entire life.

The Mohave specify that whereas some infants react to forcible weaning by "just giving up, when they see that it is no use, and that no milk will come, no matter how hard they suckle," others react by causing a great deal of trouble. The—often fatal and allegedly suicidal—illness of this latter group was described in some detail by a shaman specializing in the cure of this ailment:

Hivsu: Tupo:ma's statement (1933): The suckling has the power to sense that its mother is pregnant once more, because her womb was formerly "its own place." It can, therefore, sense that someone else is now occupying it. This ability vanishes when the child reaches the age of three (which is the usual age at weaning). The 3-year-old child can therefore not be hurt by something that it can no longer sense. Until that age, however, the child is jealous of the intruder. It feels angry and hurt and makes itself sick from spite. [Would a nursing child be angry if its father impregnated another woman?] No, it only resents the presence of an intruder into its "own place," its mother's womb. [Does it matter whether the mother was impregnated by the child's own father, or by another man?] No—the child is only concerned over the intrusion of a new fetus into the place it formerly occupied and still considers its own. Of course, the mother's milk dries up during the sixth (lunar) month of pregnancy and the child resents not being given any more milk. Even if it wants to play away from its mother, it lacks "pep" and soon comes back to her, whining for milk and crying bitterly. Then, because there is no milk to be had, it will make itself sick and fade away, because it does not get what it wants. There are sometimes also other causes for the child's fretfulness. For example, the child may have been scolded or "corrected" [96] when its parents got all worked up over the fuss it made. A sensitive child, who is not only deprived of mother milk, but is also scolded or corrected, will resent this and will make itself sick. When it thinks of the intruder, it just lies there lethargically, with closed eyes. The food it receives does not agree with it and its bowels are loose and give trouble. Its feces are dark green in color and might even contain streaks of blood. Moreover, though it may not refuse a piece of candy offered by someone, eating the candy will only worsen its condition and it will end up by being

---

[95] The unborn fetus does, in fact, swallow some of the amniotic fluid, as is shown by the presence of meconium (fetal feces) in the intestines of neonates.

[96] In view of the Mohave Indian's reluctance to strike children (Devereux, 1950 h) it is interesting to note that the interpreter—an acculturated woman who did, in fact, spank her son—used the euphemism "to correct" rather than the straightforward term "spank" or "hit." (For a discussion of such evasive euphemisms, cf. Devereux, 1956 a.)

really ill. It will cry and cry and will make everyone wait on it. All such infants are likely to feel sufficiently hurt to make themselves die, in order to spite their parents, but twins, if they happen to be jealous of heart, will be even more affected by their mother's new pregnancy than other children.[97] This does not mean that adult twins are more envious, or meaner, than other adults. It only means that they are more sensitive than other children, whose souls are not immortal and who do not come from heaven.[98] Moreover, twins are not thought to be each other's rivals for the maternal breast.

I must take all of these circumstances into account whenever I intend to treat such a sick child.

I obtained by power to cure this and other illnesses from Pahotcatc. When he made them (the people) and divided them into different groups, he also explained the different diseases, including this one. If such a sick child is well taken care of, and is taken to a competent shaman, to whom power was given to cure this illness, it will recover, unless its parents dream of losing it.[99]

I impose neither food nor other types of taboos on anyone, and expect to cure this illness without singing curing songs. I press the child's stomach with my left hand, blow my breath on it, and smear my spittle on its belly. My breath, spittle, and massage arouse the sick child from its drowsy state. While I do all this, I do not sing songs, but simply tell about the origin of this illness and mention everything related to its treatment. But it is a hard sickness to cure! Above all, I urge the child to have a good disposition and tell it not to be jealous and resentful of the new baby's existence." (In other words, the psychologically still infantile nursing child is invited to mature psychologically and to display the culturally highly valued virtue of generosity.)

The manner in which the preceding account—presented here in the first person singular—was obtained, sheds some light upon the psychology of Mohave shamanism.

When asked to discuss the diseases of children, Hivsu: Tupo: ma described tàvàknyi: k, its treatment and the powers needed for effecting a cure with scrupulous honesty, simply failing to mention that he, himself, was a tàvàknyi: k specialist. Some weeks later, after we had become friends, he spontaneously told me that he, himself, had these powers and had reported them to me in the third person only because he thought that I—who was at that time still a stranger—might bewitch him if he discussed his powers too openly (Devereux, 1957 b). He then spontaneously repeated his entire account, as well as the relevant case history (Case 84), in the first person, the two accounts matching in every respect.

The key pathogenic factor in tàvàknyi: k appears to be the strong bond between the small child and the maternal womb. Indeed it is said that the Mohave child is not wholly detached from the womb until after it is weaned. Moreover, as long as it sleeps in its cradle,

---

[97] Twins inevitably get less milk than other infants.

[98] For a less honorific explanation of the origin of twins, cf. pt. 7, pp. 348–356.

[99] This specification has two important implications. In cultural terms, it proves that ordinary Mohave dreams are not the causes of future events, but simply omens (Devereux, 1956 c). On the psychological level, death dreams usually reflect primary or secondary hostility toward the person of whose death one dreams. Since such a sick child is quite troublesome to begin with and since, moreover, the parents can blame only themselves for the mother's new pregnancy, both primary and derivative (projected) hostilities toward the child are bound to arise and to elicit dreams of death.

its real home is the cradle—i.e., a uterus substitute [1]—and not the parental dwelling. In brief, the assumption of a full human and social status—characterized by a loss of interest in the womb—does not occur until the Mohave child is weaned and ceases to sleep in its cradle. This delayed assumption of full human status is probably related to a high infant mortality, since, should an as yet incompletely humanized child die, the parents are not obliged to burn down the house, as they must do when a completely humanized person dies (Kroeber, 1925 a; Devereux, 1942 a, and pt. 7, pp. 431–459).

The treatment of tàvàknyi: k calls for the following comments:

(*1*) *Manipulations.*—The use of the left hand suggests that Hivsu: Tupo: ma's relevant curing powers were obtained from the gods rather than from the "Ancient Ones," whose identity is far from certain (Devereux, MS., 1935). He used both his breath and his spittle, because these substances are the means whereby the shaman transmits his powers—be it for good or evil purposes (Kroeber, 1925 a; Devereux, 1937 c)—to those whom he wishes to cure, or else to bewitch. In this context brief mention may also be made of Róheim's interpretation of these technical aspects of therapy among the Yuma. Róheim (1932) viewed rubbing and massage as masturbation equivalents, and the use of saliva as a substitute for fellatio. He also specified that, during the treatment, the shaman's curing hand must sweat. This last point may be of some significance, since it suggests that the shaman is under tension while treating a patient.[2] If this hypothesis is correct, the presence of salivation presents a real problem, because in certain states of anxiety and tension—for example, when one is lying— the saliva tends to dry up.[3]

Salivation and sweating occur simultaneously only in relatively high specific states of tension. Hence, their occurrence in Mohave therapeutic activities defines rather clearly the affective state of the shaman who is treating a patient. Indeed, in some individuals, one act which causes salivation and sweating to occur simultaneously is eating; a finding which supports Róheim's (1932) thesis that the shaman's healing activities are related to oral impulses.

(*2*) *The lack of songs* in nowise diminishes the effectiveness of the treatment, since, as stressed elsewhere (Devereux, 1957 b), curing songs are simply "telegraphic" allusions to a myth and derive their

---

[1] The psychological equating of the uterus with the cradle is shown by the fact that a woman can make herself sterile by burning the cradle of her dead child (Devereux, 1948 c), to prevent its return to earth. The house of the adult dead is burned for the same reason (pt. 7, pp. 431–459).

[2] Compare in this context the fact that the lie detector measures the psychogalvanic skin reflex, i.e., the intensity of the current which is determined by the amount of skin moisture, i.e., of sweating.

[3] Cf. the primitive form of lie detection, which consists in causing the suspects to lick a hot iron. The guilty party will suffer a burn, because, due to tension and anxiety, his saliva dries up.

therapeutic effectiveness from that myth.   The last person who knew the songs in question is said to have been Takpa:rà Nyàma: (Bat's breast), also called Kuoto:và (meaning unknown; erroneously translated (Devereux, 1947 a) as "like a clown").[4]

(*3*) *Appeals.*—As the Mohave see this treatment, the intrusion of the shaman's healing power into the small patient is supplemented by the shaman's attempt to mobilize in the child a higher type of motivation than the one which had caused it to become ill: the suckling is urged to be generous and not to resent the birth of another Mohave, since only in that manner can the perpetuation of the tribe be insured.

From the ethnopsychiatric point of view, the single most important aspect of tàvàknyi:k is the belief that it is a form of suicide, caused by resentment over the mother's new pregnancy and over the weaning which it necessitates. As stated above, the suckling is certain to have an adverse psychophysiological reaction to the inferior and increasingly scanty milk of the mother.   Moreover, a 2- or 3-year-old child is far from incapable of understanding the allusions of adults to its mother's new pregnancy, because—as both parents and child analysts have discovered—little jugs often have surprisingly big ears.   It is therefore permissible to suppose that the frustration-aggression-self-aggression etiological theory of this disease was first evolved by a shaman who had experienced considerable oral conflicts in his childhood, and that tàvàknyi:k specialists are shamans who have marked oral problems.   (Cf. Hivsu: Tupo:ma's voraciousness.)

This process explains why the Mohave define tàvàknyi:k as an attempt to commit suicide, and react to it in terms of the generalized Mohave attitude toward atypical behavior: "It is their nature; they cannot help it."

In conclusion, regardless of whether the psychic reactions which the adult Mohave ascribe to traumatically weaned children correctly reflect what really takes place in the weaned child's psyche, or are simply a projection of adult feelings into the child, the Mohave theory of this illness is clearly compatible with current psychoanalytic theory and reflect the Mohave Indian's singular ability to understand the language of the unconscious, including even the unconscious of the psychiatrically or psychosomatically ill individual (pt. 8, pp. 485–504).

CASE 84 (Informants: Hivsu: Tupo:ma and Hama: Utce:):

Kunyii:th, of the Kunyii:th gens, the (half?) sister of two men who had committed suicide (Cases 116 and 117), was married to Hamce: of the O:otc gens. They had a little daughter, named O:otc, of the O:otc gens, who, though already 3 or 4 years old, was still nursing. When her mother became pregnant once more, O:otc became quite sick and her mother called me in to treat the

---

[4] Although the Mohave clown at some rituals (Devereux, 1937 b), they have no ritual clowns.

little girl. I looked at the child and said: 'She acts as though she were jealous of your unborn baby. That is why she is making herself sick.' Strange to say, Kunyii:th denied that she was pregnant once more. When she told me this lie, I replied: 'Do not deny it, because if you do, I will not be able to cure your child entirely.' Despite this, Kunyii:th kept on pretending that she was not pregnant, though in due time she gave birth to a second daughter, also named O:otc. The older daughter did recover, however. You met her only the other day.

Comment

Two points call for special comment. The first of these is that little O:otc's mother was the sister of two men (Cases 116 and 117) who had committed suicide. If these suicides occurred before little O:otc became ill—which can no longer be ascertained at this late date—it is quite likely that the diagnostician, Hivsu: Tupo:ma— who was keenly aware of the tendency of suicides to occur in clusters (pt. 7, pp. 460–478)—may have felt inclined to impute to his little patient the tàvàknyi:k type of suicidalness, no matter what ailed her, simply because he would have *expected* her to have it. As for Kunyii:th's refusal to admit that she was pregnant, it suggests that she felt at least unconsciously responsible for her daughter's illness, even though she expressed this guilt in a manner which was compatible with the Mohave Indian woman's notorious tendency to deny that she is pregnant (Devereux, 1948 b).[5]

SUICIDE OF TWINS

The Mohave have two logically incompatible, but psychologically perfectly complementary and well-articulated, sets of beliefs concerning twins. These two patterns are so complex and elaborate (Devereux, 1941) that only those traits which have a direct bearing upon the problem of the "suicide" of twins can be considered in the present context.

The official or primary belief, according to Kroeber (1925 a) and others, is that twins are eternal heavenly beings, who were not created and have no parents. When twins—who are closely associated with rain and thunder—decide to visit the earth, they descend into a woman's womb during a rainstorm, at the precise moment when she is being impregnated by a man. Their purpose in assuming a human shape is to visit the earth, in order to become acquainted with earthly conditions. Hence, even though they possess the mature minds of old persons from the moment of their birth—and, presumably, even while still in utero—they behave like other babies, but understand everything that is said around them. This means that persons consorting with infant twins must "watch their tongues," lest these wise babies should be offended by some careless remark. These heavenly visitors are

---

[5] Thus, after translating the case history given above, Hama: Utce: ridiculed the tendency of Mohave women to deny that they are pregnant, even going so far as to drape their shawls in a manner likely to conceal their pregnant state. She also mentioned that this latter custom may be alluded to in the personal name Humar Tudhu:lyk=baby hidden. Note in this context that two women (Cases 45 and 46) denied, even to themselves, that they were pregnant and therefore erroneously believed themselves to be suffering from hiwey lak (pt. 4, pp. 150–175). Humar Tudhu:lyk had suicidal wishes. (Supplementary Case A.)

welcomed to the earth with formal speeches, are told of life on earth, and are given absolutely identical presents.[6] The parents of twins feel honored to have been chosen by these heavenly beings to be their parents on earth, and will have very good crops afterwards, as will persons visiting the babies. Twins must be given preferential treatment, and children are "told to be especially kind to twins."

The secondary pattern presents twins in a very different light. According to this second set of beliefs, twins are the reincarnated, acquisitive ghosts of deceased persons, who return to earth from the land of the dead, in order to accumulate additional property, which will eventually be burned on their funeral pyres, so that it can be transferred to the land of the dead (Case 87). The parents of twins are less happy than are the parents of ordinary children, since they do not feel that the twins truly belong to them, the way ordinary children belong to their parents. Moreover, in returning to earth for additional property, twins prove themselves to be acquisitive, which is a serious violation of Mohave ethics. Finally—and even though no informant actually described such an attitude—it seems reasonable to assume that at least some Mohave may feel uncomfortable about associating with "reincarnated ghosts," since contact with the dead is, by definition, harmful (pt. 4, pp. 128–186). Yet, despite the existence of this secondary set of beliefs, the actual treatment of twins conforms in every respect to the rules laid down in the primary pattern, which defines twins as honored heavenly visitors.

The one real convergence between these two patterns is the belief that twins have adult minds from birth, either because they are eternal beings, or else because they are ghosts who had already lived on earth.

Although these two patterns seem mutually contradictory, they are psychologically complementary, in that each of these two sets of beliefs elaborates one aspect of Mohave ambivalence toward twins. In fact, the primary pattern itself contains at least two explicit allusions to this ambivalence. The first of these is the specification that people approaching twins must "watch their tongues" lest they should make remarks which the twins may resent. Clearly, there is no need to watch one's tongue in the presence of a person whom one loves and admires unambivalently. The second fact which reveals the presence of an ambivalence is that children are *told* to be especially nice to twins, which would not be necessary if the adults themselves were unambivalently enthusiastic over the birth of twins. In brief, it is precisely the elaborateness of the precautions taken to avoid giving

---

[6] Thus, should each of two persons prepare an absorbent cradle pad for the twins, the two pads will be presented to them by one person only, since, despite the identity of the presents, the twin who did receive a pad from one person, but not from the other, will feel disliked and discriminated against.

offense to twins which reveals the presence of an intense ambivalence. Otherwise expressed, the Mohave do seem to "protest too much" and to overprotect twins precisely because they feel hostile to them.[7]

This finding calls for certain methodological considerations, which are of fundamental importance for an understanding of the structure of culture, especially in relation to the cultural implementation of basic attitudes.

The existence of hostility toward twins, reflected by a second set of beliefs, in terms of which they are not honored heavenly visitors but contemptibly acquisitive ghosts, was not discovered until 1938, although its existence could have been predicted solely on the basis of cultural considerations. Indeed, most tribes either heap honors on twins, the way the Mohave and other Yuman tribes do, or else they consider them as a calamity and therefore kill either one or both twins (Thomas, 1937). Now, whenever the same social stimulus elicits in various groups one of two extreme and mutually contradictory patterns of reaction, it is almost certain that the reaction type which is emphatically excluded from, and negated by, the strongly formalized and emphasized "mainstream" (Devereux, 1954 a) of a given culture will manifest itself, in one way or the other, in the "latent" (Chapin, 1934, 1935) or subsidiary portion of that culture (Devereux, 1957 a).[8]

One possible cause of the Mohave Indians' ambivalence toward twins is the fact that, in aboriginal times, the life expectancy of twins was quite low, so that the birth of twins usually meant that the family would soon have to mourn the loss of one or both twins. This inference is materially strengthened by the finding that the Mohave themselves are, in a roundabout way, quite aware of the fact that twin mortality was rather high in aboriginal times, and state this insight in two ways:

(1) A culturally rather unimportant expression of the insight is the belief that, due to a (purely imaginary) change in the climate the number of twin births has increased in recent years, although, in reality, it is survival rate of twins which has increased.[9]

---

[7] It is a well-established fact that maternal overprotection is invariably rooted in hostility toward the child (Levy, 1943).

[8] Thus, the mere fact that there exist cultures—such as Islam—in which dogs are despised and considered unclean, makes it certain that even officially cynophilic cultures—such as our own—will have a secondary attitudinal pattern toward dogs, in which the word "dog" is an opprobrious epithet. Conversely, the existence of a highly cynophilic pattern in certain cultures, such as ours or that of certain Australian tribes, suffices to make us expect that even the markedly cynophobic Arabs would have a secondary, cynophilic pattern. This expectation is confirmed by the finding that the purebred Arab greyhound is so highly esteemed that his pedigree—like that of the purebred Arab horse—is sometimes recorded in the family Koran (Devereux, 1957 a).

[9] Twins who, under aboriginal conditions, died in infancy were soon forgotten, partly because of the general taboo on mentioning the dead (Kroeber 1925 a) and partly because they did not live long enough to do anything worthy of remembrance.

(2) The culturally important phrasing of the Mohave Indians' awareness of the prevalence of twin mortality in aboriginal times is their belief that twins are abnormally susceptible to both real and imagined slights, and are therefore prone to "make themselves sick and die." It is this belief which is to be analyzed in the present chapter.

The pivot of Mohave beliefs concerning the "suicide" of twins is that all twins who plan to visit the earth know in advance that, until they contract a marriage on earth, they are not fully committed to human existence and can return to heaven any time they wish to do so, simply by making themselves fatally ill, i.e., by committing psychosomatic suicide.

The suicidal impulses of twins may be aroused by a large variety of events:

(1) Twins *in utero* may suddenly reach the conclusion that a visit to earth does not appeal to them, after all, and may therefore decide to be stillborn (Case 86).

(2) After being born alive, the twins may simply decide that they do not like the earth, or their family. This decision need not have a rational basis, since the Mohave themselves say that twins sometimes take an unreasonable dislike to an inoffensive person and avert their faces whenever that person approaches them.[10]

(3) Twins who feel that they are not treated absolutely equally become resentful, sicken and die. Their insistence on equal treatment is so great that they must not only receive identical gifts and be dressed alike (Devereux, 1941), but must even paint their faces alike. If this does not happen, at least one of the twins will sicken and die (Taylor and Wallace, 1947).

(4) The twins may feel that the treatment accorded to them is not preferential and favorable enough.

(5) Twins die if each person visiting them does not give both of them equal presents, or, what is worse, gives them no present at all.

(6) Should the mother of twins become pregnant once more before she had a chance to wean them, and should her twins happen to have a "jealous disposition," they make themselves develop an unusually virulent case of the "suicidal" tàvàknyi:k illness (pt. 7, pp. 340–348) which, needless to say, is actually due to the fact that the milk of a pregnant woman deteriorates quite rapidly and does not even suffice to feed one child adequately.

(7) Twins, one of whom is a boy and the other a girl, were spouses in heaven and therefore sometimes quarrel, the way married couples

---

[10] Actually, it is psychologically quite possible that such "irrational dislikes" may be due to the infants' extraordinary ability to sense a seemingly benevolent person's basic hostility or ambivalence. This sensitivity is, of necessity, very great, since hypersensitivity and hyper-reactivity are among the infant's most important homeostatic mechanisms (Devereux, 1951 e).

do. If this happens, the offended twin will sicken and die, and the surviving twin will soon follow it back to heaven.[11]

(8) If a twin dies for any of the seven reasons cited above, the surviving twin usually also makes itself sick, so as to join the deceased in heaven, as soon as possible.

(9) There are also some—never formally stated—indications (Case 87) that a twin may also follow her mother, or her son, into death.

The ability of twins to sicken and die at will supposedly ceases when they marry, thereby signifying their willingness to live out man's normal span of life on earth. Nonetheless, even adult twins are treated in an exceptionally considerate manner, and are never asked to discuss their memories of heaven. Thus, when I asked Hama: Utce: to arrange for me an interview with her adult half-sister, who was the surviving half of a pair of twins, Hama: Utce: asked me as a favor to abandon this project, lest questions about her heavenly home should offend her half-sister.

Seen from the psychiatric point of view, the hypersensitiveness of twins, which even the Mohave consider to be more or less irrational and extreme, has a marked paranoid tinge, as is shown by their proneness to take offense, their irrational dislikes for unoffending persons, their atypical (pt. 5, pp. 219–221) obsession with receiving absolutely equal treatment, and their insistence on being treated better than other children and adults. This diagnostic impression is further substantiated by the Mohave belief that twins are clairvoyant (Kroeber, 1925 a),[12] the point being that both actual feats (?) of clairvoyance and claims of being clairvoyant have clearly paranoid psychic components (Devereux, 1953 a).

In addition to being paranoid, twins also appear to have a markedly infantile character structure, even in adult life. According to the Mohave, twins are not fully committed to life on earth until they marry, although, once they are married they are—unlike other Mohave—exceptionally faithful spouses. Moreover, Case 87 shows that they can become overly involved emotionally also with their mothers and their children. This is quite unusual in some respects, since the average Mohave's affective economy is characterized by the fact that he is very fond of a fairly large number of friends and relatives, but—except in early infancy, when he still thinks of the mother's womb as "his place" (Devereux, 1947 a; and pt. 7, pp. 340–348)—is not likely to become passionately devoted to any single person and quite unlikely to "fall in love" (pt. 3, pp. 91–106). By contrast, due to the special

---

[11] Although such twins were spouses in heaven and will, after their return to heaven, be spouses again, on earth they do not marry each other, since "they came to earth to live like people." There are, however, tribes in which twins born to persons of certain classes do marry each other (Loeb, 1958).

[12] Pulyi:k, who is something of a skeptic, was not quite certain that twins were necessarily clairvoyant.

treatment accorded to twins and also because of the, partly "natural" and partly culturally fostered, intense bond obtaining between twins, the Mohave twin is conditioned, from childhood on, to form only a very small number of emotional relationships, whose exclusivenes and intensity is at variance with the prevailing pattern of affective commitments (Devereux, 1939 a, 1942 d). This, in turn, makes it probable that the Mohave are at least psychologically correct in their belief that twins are not fully committed to life on earth until they marry, i.e., until they transfer their intense affections from their twin to a spouse who is, of necessity, not related to them.[13]

Interestingly enough, twins are not said to engage in rivalry for the maternal breast. For reasons of expository convenience, this belief was discussed in connection with tàvàknyi:k (pt. 7, pp. 340–348). It suffices to say that the Mohave seem to have denied the existence of such a rivalry—chiefly because there was nothing that could be done about the situation—and displaced the whole rivalry for the breast to the outer world, by professing to believe that twins insist on being treated better than anyone else. On the other hand we must mention, at least in passing, that the Mohave defines the twins' situation at the breast not so much in infantile, competitive nursing terms as in terms of adult, generous cooperativeness. This Mohave theory of the nursing twins' psychic state is presumably determined partly by the belief that twins are adult persons in an infantile body and partly by the tenet that there exists a deep and indissoluble bond between twins, which causes them to insist only on being treated exactly alike, instead of demanding exclusive access to the breast, the way a real child does, whose mother also has to wetnurse an orphaned relative (pt. 3, p. 115; pt. 7, pp. 340–348).

Summing up, when one or both twins die before being married—and sometimes even if they die after being married (Case 87)—the Mohave usually assume that they had decided to sicken and die. Hence, most illnesses of twins, especially in early childhood, are likely to be diagnosed as attempts to commit psychosomatic suicide.

The Mohave seem to have no special techniques for inducing twins, who have fallen sick because they wish to die, to stay on earth. In fact, the whole Mohave approach to the problem of twin mortality is prophylactic rather than therapeutic, and consists in solemnly welcoming them to earth, in speaking to them as though they were respectable older persons, and in making life as attractive to them as possible. It is permissible to assume that this prophylactic approach does not

---

[13] It is worth noting in this context that deaths from psychosomatic causes in occidental children appear to become less prevalent after the children are old enough to make friends outside the family—i.e., after the oedipal conflicts have been more or less successfully outgrown. Moreover, deaths from psychosomatic causes—and possibly even simple psychosomatic illnesses—seem to occur predominantly in adults who have few adult emotional attachments and are emotionally still committed primarily to their parents and siblings.

exclude the possibility that a shaman treating twins for tàvàknyi:k, or for some other ailment, may, in addition to other techniques, also resort to exhortations, urging twins to stay on earth and pointing out to them how well they are being treated by everyone. While I recorded no clearcut statements to this effect, the supposition seems valid in terms of what is known of Mohave therapeutic techniques.

If the treatment failed, and one or both twins died, they supposedly returned to the place they had come from—i. e., to heaven, or else to the land of the dead—and never again revisited the earth. Their death was defined as suicide due to walae:(y)k (grieving).

Brief mention should also be made of the fact that a twin's immortality could come to an end if the twin became a witch, and was killed, or else fell victim to witchcraft.

Hivsu: Tupo:ma's statement (1936): If a twin became a witch, and was killed for his deeds, his soul went to the land of the dead, because he wished to stay with the ghosts of his non-twin victims, whom he could not take to heaven. He therefore gave up his immortality and, in the company of his victims, went through the four metamorphoses which follow death and lead to final extinction. As for bewitched twins, they also lost their immortality, since they had to follow the witch's ghost to the land of the dead and then through the metamorphoses which lead to final extinction.

Tcatc's statement (1938): Bewitched twins return to heaven, when they came. [Hivsu: Tupo:ma told me.they went with the witch to the land of the uead.] I disagree. My old friend Kunyii:th, who was a twin, told me that "whatever sickness may have been put on us twins (by witchcraft), it leaves us when we are cremated."

These two statements are admittedly irreconcilable, perhaps because the whole question is largely academic, since—though twins are supposed to be extremely powerful shamans whose powers are derived from heaven—no informant remembered any twin who was a witch, or who had been killed by witchcraft.

The implicit attitude of the Mohave toward the psychosomatic suicide of twins is revealed by the fact that they have two sets of beliefs concerning twins. Their more explicit attitudes can be stated somewhat as follows. Twins are hypersensitive (because they are heavenly beings) and sometimes also have a jealous and mean disposition (presumably because they are reincarnated, acquisitive ghosts). If they do not like what is happening to them on earth, they make themselves sick and die, secure in the knowledge that they will return to heaven, to live there forever.[14] While their suicidal sickness and death causes much grief to their parents and relatives, it is recognized that they acted in accordance with the inevitable dic-

---

[14] The alternative, that they will return to the land of ghosts, from which they temporarily emerged to acquire further funeral property, was also mentioned, though less explicitly and with very few details. This is not surprising, since the twins=ghosts pattern is a secondary one and is therefore less fully elaborated than the twins=heavenly beings belief.

tates of their nature.   At the same time the Mohave's resentment over this uncalled for and inconsiderate behavior finds expression in the secondary pattern, which views twins as acquisitive ghosts.   All of this proves that one is not dealing here with a superficial difference between "priestly" and "lay" knowledge, but with certain basic problems of the place of attitudes in culture.   This is also proved by the syncretism evident in Case 87.

CASE 85 (Informants: Hivsu: Tupo:ma and Hama: Utce:) (1936):

Mah, of the Mah gens, bore her lover Kalowe: twin boys, who were 4 months old in November 1936. One of the boys allegedly had a "hydrocephalus" (sic!). "This boy intended to die that way. He does not like the family. He just makes himself and everyone else miserable that way, before he dies."

Comment

The most striking part of this account is the remark that the child "makes himself and everyone else miserable." Hivsu: Tupo: ma used almost the same words in characterizing the fretful behavior of children suffering from táváknyi:k. (pt. 7, pp. 340–348). Although the cause of this boy's dislike for his parents was not explained, it is possible to infer that the Mohave felt that he had good reasons for being displeased with them, since Kalowe:, not being married to Mah, apparently did not contribute to their support.

CASE 86 (Informants: Hivsu: Tupo:ma and Hama: Utce:) (1936):

Mu: th, of the Mu: th gens, a 24- to 27-year-old Mohave woman, bore her Chemehuevi husband A. P. twins, who were stillborn "because they decided already in the womb that they did not care for the family into which they were about to be born."

Comment

Although the informants did not specifically explain why these twins disliked their prospective family, they did hint in a roundabout way that the children simply did not wish to be born half Chemehuevi. It should be remembered in this context that, in 1936, the *older* Mohave were far more contemptuous of the Chemehuevi than was the *much younger* E. S. in 1938 (Case 76).

CASE 87 (Informants: Tcatc and Hama: Utce:):

Once I (Tcatc) asked an old woman named Kunyii:th, of the Kunyii:th gens, just why she disliked certain people. She told me that if a person whom she disliked came to eat her food, and if she then ate of that self-same food afterwards, she would hemorrhage from the mouth and would lose her appetite. I also asked her whether her home was really in heaven (ama:y) and she replied that she and other heavenly twins lived there just like any other Mohave, but that sometimes they were out of clothing and even hungry. When that happened, they would ask someone to come to earth for these things.[15] I did not quite believe her, but Kunyii: th insisted that she was telling me the truth. She had lost a son (on earth) and was downhearted. She told me that she was leaving (the earth) and she did die (fairly soon afterwards). This old woman's twin sister had died when her mother died, because she did not feel like living.

---

[15] This is clearly syncretistic in that it seeks to reconcile the two different patterns.

Comment

Kunyii:th's wish to die was apparently caused by a prolonged mourning reaction for her son, and was therefore part of a death "cluster." The fact that her death wish was elicited by her son's death is in line with the belief that, after twins get married, they are no longer attached to their twins, becoming attached instead to their own families. The same "clustering pattern" is also present in the case of Kunyii:th's sister, who died at the same time as her mother (because she did not wish to be separated from her?). In this instance the pattern of one twin following the other twin into death is replaced by the pattern of a twin following her mother into death. One presumes that this must have occurred before this twin could marry, since otherwise her death would not fit the traditional pattern. It is also interesting to note that, immediately after stating that Kunyii:th did die, Tcatc suddenly referred to the death of Kunyii:th's twin sister. This juxtaposition is probably due to Tcatc's tacit assumption that—in accordance with the pattern that twin follows twin into death—these two deaths were also somehow connected. (Cf. pt. 7, pp. 459–478.)

The one atypical feature of this case history is that old Kunyii:th, who had been married and had borne at least one son who had died, was, despite the Mohave belief that married twins lose their capacity to die at will, credited with the ability to cause her own death, simply by wishing to die. Leaving out of consideration the naturalistic explanation that a grieving, weak, and old woman is quite likely to die because she hasn't anything left to live for, the most likely explanation of Tcatc's statement is that the informant must have felt that even a married twin had a greater capacity than other people to cause herself to die when she no longer wished to live. Finally, Tcatc's statement "she was leaving the earth" is, in a way, somewhat ambiguous, since it can be interpreted either as a wish to die, or else as a preconscious awareness of the proximity of death.[16]

SOCIAL SUICIDE

The concept of total or partial social death, without any impairment of the organism itself, is present in many societies. In early modern times, when commerce was incompatible with the status of nobleman, in at least one part of France an impoverished nobleman could appear before the parliament of his province, place his nobility temporarily in escrow, engage in commerce until he reestablished his fortune, and then, after renouncing commerce, resume his noble status. Simulated social death was a common judicial procedure in the feudal age. When a suitably gagged recreant knight failed to answer the herald's three-times-repeated shout: "Sir X. Y., knight!" the court declared him dead and caused his knightly regalia to be broken. When a Jew becomes an apostate, he is declared dead; his father rends his clothes and utters the prayer for the dead, as though his son had actually died.

---

[16] It is interesting to note in this context that, even though Tcatc was not a twin, she, too, appears to have sensed somewhat later that death was not far away, although she was at that time apparently in good health, as is shown by the fact that she put on all her finery and asked a young Mohave friend of ours to take her picture and to send me a print, so that I would not forget her. In so doing, she violated the Mohave taboo against being photographed, which she had observed all her life so conscientiously that she always refused my repeated requests to allow me to photograph her (Devereux, 1951 b). (Pl. 9, b, c.)

It is important to stress that in certain forms of social death the "dead" person himself is felt to have contrived his "demise"; i.e. he is held to have committed "social suicide." Thus, the nobleman who renounced his nobility in order to engage in commerce was thought to have destroyed—at least temporarily—his real social identity and self. He *put himself* beyond the pale, instead of *being sent* to Coventry, like an ordinary social reject.

The practical implications and penalties of social death, be it self-inflicted or imposed by society, are variable. The orthodox Jewish father actually denies that his son is still alive, just as medieval society denied that the gagged recreant knight was still alive. In other instances the outlaw is held to have become an animal. If an incestuous Sedang (Devereux, MS., 1933–34, 1937 e) is unable to pay a suitable fine, he is forced to live alone in the forest and is said to have become a wild boar. The same is also said of young men who, having enlisted in the gendarmerie, are not in a position to participate in regular collective rituals. Likewise, medieval German law called the outlaw "vogelfrei," which meant that, like a bird, he could be shot and killed by anyone who chose to do so. In other instances the outlaw is treated as a quasi-alien. When an Australian war party approached a smaller camp in order to take revenge for some real or fancied hostile act, the attacked camp often simply handed over to the assailant certain quasi-outlawed (iturka) men to serve as scapegoats for the community. In other instances—as when a Mohave marries his cousin—the bridegroom's "social suicide" involves nothing more than a purely pro forma dissolution of the kinship tie between himself and his bride-to-be.

The sole purpose of the preceding paragraphs was to emphasize that the idea of social death—or of social suicide—was not invented either by the Mohave or by the present writer, in order to account for a specifically Mohave custom. As the preceding data indicate, the concept of social death (or suicide) is quite widespread, and occurs in a large variety of cultures and at various stages of cultural development. A systematic study of social death—with special reference to outlawry—is, however, beyond the scope of the present work.

SYMBOLIC SOCIAL SUICIDE

The type of suicide to be discussed in this chapter appears to be a purely symbolic rite, consisting originally of the alienation of a piece of farmland, and, after the introduction of horses, of the killing of a horse belonging to the bridegroom who has contracted an "incestuous" marriage with a kinswoman—usually a second cousin. Unlike other types of illness and death which the Mohave define as "suicides," the "suicide" in question does not even involve actual illness or death, except insofar as it is believed that such incestuous marriages—like extramarital incest (Devereux 1939 a)—ultimately cause the extinction of the "entire family."

Most informants—with the exception of Tcatc—felt that the rite in question represented a kind of partial and symbolic social suicide, which amounted to nothing more than a change in the bridegroom's social identity. Whether this putative "change" in the bridegroom's social identity was actually implemented by a change in the behavior of his "former" kinsmen toward him, or whether it was a more or less empty and formal gesture, without practical consequences of any kind, could not be ascertained, since this rite is, and has been for some decades, wholly obsolete.

The first—and, in a sense, most important—point to be discussed is one which the Mohave themselves did not even mention. Mohave marriages are, and have always been, highly informal arrangements, entirely devoid of ritual aspects. After a rather desultory courtship in the case of virgins—or at least of girls who had not been married previously—or after a brief and casual affair in the case of widows, divorcées, and married women, the couple simply began to live in the same house, thereby signifying that they were married (Devereux, MS., 1935). By contrast, "incestuous" marriages were validated by means of a public feast at which, previous to the introduction of the horse, a piece of the groom's farmland was alienated, while after the acquisition of horses, a horse belonging to the bridegroom was killed, and, according to most informants, eaten. The avowed purpose of this practice was the dissolution of the kinship tie between the spouses, or, according to some informants, also between the girl's and the boy's immediate families. Otherwise stated, the chief objective of this rite—*which was the only "real" marriage ceremony in Mohave culture*—was the lifting of a taboo, or, if one prefers, the formal "modification" of the existing situation, in which the incest taboo would have to be observed.

When the rite is described in such terms, it does not automatically create the impression that it is primarily a true wedding rite. Yet, a moment of reflection will show that, in the last resort, every wedding rite represents, in one way or the other, a lifting of taboos obtaining until that moment [17] and a regularization of a situation which, without this rite, would be wholly objectionable or deplorable. In fact, it is even possible to suggest that almost every rite consists in

---

[17] The taboo which is lifted in the course of wedding ceremonies need not be a sexual one. Thus, in the Trobriand Islands (Malinowski, 1932), where complete premarital freedom—or, rather an obligation to be promiscuous (Devereux, 1955 a)—obtains, the marriage lifts the taboo on the couple eating together and on having children. Among the Sedang Moi (Devereux, MS., 1933–34), the wedding ceremony lifts the taboo only on *normal* (vaginal) coitus and on having children together, *perverted* coitus being tolerated both premaritally and extramaritally.

making something normally forbidden permissible, and in the performance of an act which, in the wrong context, or when performed by an unauthorized person, is sacrilege pure and simple. The finding that the Mohave deem a wedding ceremony necessary *only* where, without this rite, the relationship would be an incestuous one, is therefore readily understandable in terms of the fact that premarital coitus is a normal and accepted occurrence in Mohave society. Indeed, if one views Mohave marriage solely from the sexual point of view and disregards its procreative, economic, and other functions, it is nothing more than an assumption of a common domicile, so as to enable the partners to engage in sexual relations over a longer period, with the least possible inconvenience. Such a view of marriage would, quite obviously, not call for a lifting of any taboo, be it sexual or not, and would therefore not necessitate a marriage ceremony. By contrast, an incestuous "engagement," or affair, does stand in need of being regularized, through a lifting of taboos, before it can become a real marriage. Hence, a wedding rite is, in such cases, quite necessary.

In brief, this particular Mohave marriage custom—which is still primitive and rudimentary enough to reveal its real and basic nature— probably sheds a great deal of light upon the origin of wedding rites which transform what without these rites would be simply a public concubinage into formal relationship, explicitly recognized by society.

In this context it is extremely important to note that, according to Hivsu: Tupo:ma, one of the chief purposes of this rite was to compel the incestuously engaged couple to "remain together forever, since they wanted to marry each other so much." This objective may not seem unusual to occidental man, who takes it for granted that marriage is, at least in principle, a permanent commitment. It is quite unusual, however, in Mohave society, where marriage does not imply a priori and by definition a permanent commitment, since it can be—and often is—dissolved simply by packing up one's things and leaving (Kroeber, 1925 b).

Thus, it is not a great exaggeration to say that the only "real" wedding in Mohave society is the rite which is performed at the marriage of an incestuously "engaged" couple, and that the only "real" marriage, in the western sense, which obtains in the Mohave tribe is the marriage of such a couple, because *only* in the case of such a couple does the tribe seem to *demand a permanent commitment.* The fact that this demand is not always and necessarily complied with does not impair the validity of the point just made, any more than the prevalence of divorce in American society impairs the validity of the thesis that occidental society does demand, at least in principle, that marriages should be entered into with the intention of making them last forever.

Hivsu: Tupo:ma's remark, that such couples are expected to stay married forever, since they were headstrong enough to insist upon contracting an incestuous marriage, also implies that the *permanency* of such marriages is, for all practical purposes, viewed by the Mohave as a kind of *penalty*. This aspect of the very rudimentary Mohave marriage rite for incestuous couples probably sheds some light also upon the origins of marriage rites and upon the obligations which the married state carries with it everywhere.[18] Further aspects of this finding can best be discussed in connection with the mythical precedent for incestuous marriages.

The mythical precedent for incest, and especially for incestuous marriages, is the Tuma: np'à Utàu: t myth (Kroeber, 1925 a, and M.S., n.d.; Devereux, 1939 a). Briefly stated, the prototypal incest was not a casual affair, but a formal marriage. This point is of great importance since, so far as can be ascertained, no one has ever pointed out that all truly basic incest myths almost invariably pertain to incestuous *marriages*, rather than to casual incestuous affairs.

For the purposes of the present discussion it suffices to present this myth in the form of a synopsis.

After Matavilye's death, the people, among whom were Tuma: np'à and his sister Kuakwicavepon, left the death house. At a certain place, now called St. George, this pair turned back and once more passed Matavilye's death house. Then, wandering around, they entered Chemehuevi Valley and reached the southern edge of a camp inhabited by various tribes. There the brother and sister danced and sang all night the Tuma: np'à song cycle.[19] That night the girl left her brother and "married" a young man, but at daybreak Tuma: np'à went to her house and took her away from her husband, because he did not favor this marriage. Having persuaded his sister to follow him, Tuma: np'à once more proceeded southward with her. After they had covered some four or five miles, Tuma: np'à somehow acquired certain magical powers, through the fact that the sun shone on him.[20] This magic enabled the brother and sister to travel underground. Finally, after emerging from the ground at Hakutcip

---

[18] The preceding considerations are based solely on sociocultural facts and upon anthropological reasoning. Exactly the same conclusions could have been reached also through psychoanalytic reasoning, in terms of Freud's views on the origins of marriage and the incest taboo. Indeed, even though the "cyclopean family" (Freud, 1952) is certainly a fiction, which condenses into a single event a development lasting many millennia, Freud's critics have perhaps been overly hasty in refusing to see something which Freud himself *did without realizing that he was doing it:* The single "critical occurrence" in the "cyclopean family" postulated by Freud can be quite effectively thought of as a scientifically productive "as if" conceptual device, comparable to the theoretical physicist's nonexistent "frictionless surfaces," "unbendable levers," "perfectly elastic bodies" and the like. This is shown, inter alia, by the existence of a Fan myth (Trilles, 1912) which is, almost word for word, identical with Freud's convenient fiction of the cyclopean family and with his theory of the origin of the incest taboo. One might almost say that in this instance, *in seeming to perpetrate a scientific monstrosity, Freud—with the unerring instinct of genius—wrought better than he himself knew.* In advancing a theory which he believed to be factually correct, he actually rose to great heights of methodological imaginativeness, and formulated a scientific "fiction" comparable in legitimacy and usefulness to the fictions used by theoretical physicists, day after day.

[19] Despite this detail, the cycle in question is not a dancing song in Mohave culture.

[20] The activation of a magical object by the rays of the sun is also mentioned by McNichols (1944).

(Bill Williams River) they married and lived together, saying that they did this so as to establish the custom of marriage. However, at that time the dead Matavilye transformed various people into rocks and beasts, and this couple too was turned into a strangely shaped rock formation called Hamasem Kutco : yva.[21] The Mohave say that this rock shows the couple kissing. "The girl sits erect, proud of what she had done, but the man is bowed down by shame. That is why no Mohave will marry his sister." [22]

The rocks just mentioned are approximately 30 miles from Parker and about a quarter of a mile from the Bill Williams River. Although these rocks are quite famous, they are neither respected nor dreaded. Thus, Kohovan Kura :u, a halfbreed who was a firm believer in the old ways, had some of his fields at the very foot of this rock formation. He eventually sold these fields to a Mexican, who farmed them without let or hindrance from the tribe. The rocks themselves are rather striking in appearance, since they rise from the very rim of a low mesa. Their top portion is black, while their lower portion is a slightly yellow-hued reddish brown. The photographing of these rocks was not objected to by anyone and the pictures which I had taken were examined by many Mohave with considerable interest and approval (pl. 3).

The significance of this myth was explained by Tcatc and Hama: Utce: as follows: "This incest story is just like a prophecy. It shows that this kind of thing was going to happen also to (ordinary) people. 'That is the way it was meant to be,' the Mohave say, 'one cannot control fate.' It is fate that wipes out families, not the gods. [Do you mean this in the sense that lightning is not the cause of thunder, but simply a sign that thunder is about to be heard?] Yes—people commit incest because they are going to die out. Their extinction is not even due to witchcraft. It was just meant to be that way." "This cycle is not a dance song. It is sung in the house by a man who sits on his upturned soles" (i.e., in the traditional Mohave manner, cf. Kroeber, 1925 a).

A discussion of the latent content of this myth is not necessary in the present context, particularly since such an analysis has been made available elsewhere (Devereux, 1939 a).

On the other hand, the myth in question does contain one explicit statement which has a direct bearing on our thesis that the only true Mohave wedding ritual is that which takes place on the occasion of incestuous marriages.

The myth just summarized states that Tuma :np'à and his sister contracted an incestuous marriage *so as to establish, and to set a precedent for, the custom of getting married.* This specification is quite striking, since it implies that the sister's one-night relationship with a stranger did not constitute a real marriage, *even though it parallels in every respect both modern practice and the marriage patterns outlined in the Mastamho myth.* What is more, this finding is

<hr/>

[21] Kroeber (1925 a) calls it Chimusam kuchoiva. Hivsu : Tupo : ma called it Tcamosem Kutcoyv; Mohovan Kura : u called it Tcumusem Kutco : va :; and Pulyi : k, the linguistic informant, called it Hamasem Kutco yva.

[22] This specification fully dovetails with the fact that even Mohave women concede that women are looser than men.

completely confirmed by the fact that sexual life, promiscuousness, and nonincestuous "marriages" were established earlier by Thrasher and Mockingbird, in accordance with Mastamho's instructions (Kroeber, 1948), and were—according to another version (Devereux, 1948 f)—first taught *practically* by Matavilye's daughter Bull- frog, who cohabited promiscuously with all living creatures. It is, moreover, of great interest to note that the myth instituting sexual life devotes far more space to promiscuousness than to marriage, un- derscores the desultory nature of courtship and the lability of ordinary marriages, and stresses the venereal diseases which are contracted through sexual relationships. One particularly illuminating passage (Kroeber, 1948, p. 65, paragraph 91) shows that the woman's simple willingness to allow a man to take her hand is labeled "marriage," in a casual, amused way. The actual text runs: "Then they said: 'That man has her; he is married to her.' And all *laughed*." (My italics.)

By contrast, unlike Bullfrog, who set a precedent for mere co- habitation, and unlike the personages mentioned in the Mastamho cycle (Kroeber, 1948), who set a precedent chiefly for courtship and also for promiscuousness, the brother-sister couple of the Tuma: np'ā myth set a precedent for actual marriage, which is even "immortal- ized," since the incestuous spouses were turned into rocks for all times, in the very act of "kissing," though kissing among the Mohave may be a practice acquired through acculturation.

In brief, Mohave mythology accounts separately for the origins of mere sex life and for the origins of "real" marriage. The Mastamho myth discusses primarily courtship, promiscuousness and—almost as an afterthought—ordinary, casual, nonincestuous marriages, con- tracted without any formality and lasting only until one wearies of them, or decides to contract another marriage. Likewise, the related story of Bullfrog's promiscuousness sets a precedent only for sexual intercourse. Finally, the Mastamho myth does *not* state *in so many words* that the actual "marriages" it mentions were contracted *for the purpose of setting a precedent;* or, if one wishes, these marriages constitute precedents only because they happened at the time of creation. By contrast, the brother and sister couple married *specifically* in order to establish the custom of marriage; their own being a marriage which endures in stone to this very day, exactly as incestuous marriages—and the marriages of heavenly twins—are sup- posed to last forever.

In brief, nonincestuous sexuality, promiscuousness, and casual mar- riages, at which "all laugh," are accounted for by one myth, while real and lasting (i.e., incestuous) marriages are accounted for by an- other myth.

The final point to be made is that casual incest appears to be mentioned only in ribald Coyote tales (Devereux, 1939 a), and not in myths.

The rite.—The Mohave man was not allowed to marry a woman of his own gens, nor a woman of another gens whose grandparents or great-grandparents were also his forebears. If two cousins absolutely insisted upon getting married, they could do so only after the performance of a certain ritual, which dissolved the kinship between the future spouses. This rite, like the incest taboos, was established by Matavilye.

Before the introduction of the horse, a piece of the bridegroom's farmland was alienated. According to Drucker (1941) the couple's relatives also cut their hair (like mourners) and burned down the house (of the groom?). Pulyi:k said, however, that the couple's relatives only destroyed his property, but neither burned down the house nor cut their hair. Since the alienation of farmland, the burning of the house, and the cutting of one's hair (or, if Pulyi:k's alternative is accepted, the destruction of property) are all mourning observances, the precise minutiae of what was, and what was not, done at such weddings are relatively unimportant, as long as it is made evident that *the rite resembled certain basic funeral customs*, thus indicating that in such marriages someone was supposed to have "died."

After the introduction of horses, the alienation of farmland was replaced, both in funeral practices and at incestuous marriages, by the killing of a horse. According to Hivsu: Tupo:ma, when an incestuous marriage was finally decided upon, the father—or, sometimes, the grandfather (Case 89)—of one of the spouses, but preferably the father of the bridegroom, went around, announcing to people that the two cousins had decided to marry on a certain day. He also told people that a feast would be given, at which a horse would be killed, so that the cousins, who wanted to get married so badly that they were willing to disregard even the incest taboo, would have to stay married as long as they lived. Then, on the appointed day, the bridegroom's family gave a feast at which a horse belonging to the bridegroom—or, if he had none, to his family—was killed and, according to most informants, eaten.[23] The killing of the horse "broke off the kinship ties" between the two spouses and, possibly, also between their immediate families.

Most informants insisted that people cried over the horse, either because it "was" a dead kinsman, or else because the killing of the horse was part of a symbolic funeral. Hivsu: Tupo: ma at first declared that people simply cried because such marriages dissolved the

---

[23] This was apparently also done at funerals.

kinship tie between two families. However, as he went into further details, he spontaneously concluded that the dead horse was, after all, "sort of considered as a dead relative."

According to one informant, both the occurrence of incest and the rites consolidating incestuous marriages were established by Matavilye at the time of creation.

Since the rite in question is—and has been for some decades— wholly obsolete, informants disagreed on a number of minor points, or even on mere nuances. The points on which there was some disagreement fall into three broad categories:

I. Disposal of the horse:

(1) A horse of either sex was killed, mourned for, and cremated, as though a Mohave—and, specifically, as though the bridegroom—had died (Hivsu: Tupo: ma and other informants). (Case 89.)

(2) The horse was killed and eaten by the bride's kin at the bride's camp, where the relatives and guests had assembled. (Tcatc.)

(3) The horse meat was eaten, but the scraps and bones were cremated and the family "held a cry" (wake, mourning) as though a relative had died.

(4) A complete mock funeral, which even included the erection of a pyre, was conducted at such wedding (cf. Drucker, 1941).

(5) The horse was killed, but not eaten.

(6) Sometimes two horses were killed (Case 89). (This may possibly have symbolized the death of both bride and groom, unless, of course, it was mere ostentation.)

The only important divergence between these various statements concerning the disposal of the horse is whether or not the horse was eaten after being killed. On the whole, informants who stressed the "funeral" aspect of the custom held that the horse was eaten, while the minority which felt that the slaying of the horse symbolized chiefly the "killing" of the bridegroom maintained that the horse was not eaten— an understandable conclusion, since the Mohave did not practice cannibalism, were horrified by cannibalistic actions occurring among their neighbors (Devereux, 1951 b; Dobyns et al., 1957), and considered cannibalism one of the most horrible traits of mythical monsters (Devereux, 1948 h). The one puzzling aspect of this problem is that, according to Tcatc, the flesh of the horse was consumed only by the girl's relatives, i.e., presumably by those who were more closely related to the girl than to the boy. Were cannibalism a Mohave practice, Tcatc's account of the disposal of the horse's meat would clearly signify that, the kinship bond having been dissolved, the horse representing the bridegroom could be eaten by those who were no longer related to him.[24] However, since the Mohave were not cannibals and did not have a system of fines, the real underlying meaning of Tcatc's remark remains a complete mystery.

II. Meaning or effect of the rite:

(1) The rite signifies that the bridegroom is "kind of dead." (Hivsu: Tupo:ma).

(2) It does not mean that the bridegroom is dead. It only means that the kinship tie between the boy and the girl is dissolved, so that a new boy marries the girl. (Tcatc.)

(3) The kinship tie between the boy's and the girl's immediate families is also dissolved. (Hivsu: Tupo:ma.) (This was vehemently denied both by Tcatc and by one or two other informants, who stressed that the young husband remained a member of his own gens and was capable of transmitting membership in his gens to his children. It should be noted, however, that this argument pertains only to the gens and not to the immediate family as such.)

(4) Since the groom consents to the killing of his horse, which represents him, it means that he is, in a sense, committing vicarious suicide.

(5) The killing of the horse does not represent symbolic suicide in any way. (This opinion was held only by a minor informant.)

(6) The chief purpose of this rite was to prevent a subsequent divorce. As Hivsu: Tupo:ma expressed it: "People felt that if cousins wanted to get married so badly, and did marry in spite of the fact that they were related, they had to remain married forever." The effectiveness of this rite in strengthening the very tenuous Mohave marriage bond could, unfortunately, not be ascertained.

III. Affective reactions:

(1) The tribe was angry when relatives married.

(2) People mourned at such rituals, because it was as though they had lost a relative, through the severing of kinship ties. "The boy was as good as dead."

(3) They mourned because the kinship tie between the two families was severed. The boy's and the girl's immediate families each "lost" a blood relative, which apparently outweighed the fact that—as a compensation—they "acquired" an affinal relative in the course of these events.

(4) They cried because an incestuous marriage means that the two families will probably die out. As for the incestuous couple itself, it

---

[24] To take—purely for illustrative purposes—an example more or less at random, the Sedang Moi sharply differentiate between three classes of persons: (1) Those with whom one can cohabit; (2) those whose milk one drinks actually or symbolically; and (3) those whose flesh may be eaten either actually, or else symbolically (Devereux, 1958 b). Relatives belong to category (2).

was said that "incestuous marriages cause the sickness and death of one of the spouses, the surviving spouse usually following the deceased within a year" (Case 90). (Compare, in this context, the belief that the death of one twin is usually followed by the death of the other twin, especially if the two were husband and wife in heaven (pt. 7, pp. 348–356). Also, the children of such couples were likely to be born mute, which was considered a form of "insanity" (yamomk) (pt. 5, pp. 248–251). A minor, additional calamity was that the children of such couples usually had some unpigmented spots, which the Mohave find quite repulsive (Devereux, 1948 b).

(5) Incestuous marriages, unlike the impulsive incestuous acts of shamans, were not dismissed with vague references to temperamental compulsion. Moreover, when such a family died out, the tribe reacted, at least in theory, by saying that it served them right. Whether the Mohave did, in fact, react in this way to the extinction of a family is, of course, open to debate, especially since one notes in connection with various other types of suicide that the *expected* condemnatory reaction to a given *act* is often very different from the Mohave's compassionate *actual* reaction to the *people* who perpetrated that act.

In summary, if one disregards the differences of opinion between informants on points of minor significance, it is quite clear that the alienation of farmland or the killing of a horse at incestuous marriages represented a kind of symbolic or social vicarious suicide of the bridegroom. The fact that only the groom was so penalized was explained by Hivsu: Tupo:ma as follows: "Since the boy transmits the gentile name, they consider him the guiltier of the two. Hence, it is he who is deprived of some farmland or of a horse." [25]

The last point to be mentioned is that the occurrence of incestuous marriages among the Mohave became known to the adjoining tribes, one such marriage being explicitly referred to by Gifford's (1931) Kamia informants.

The real meaning of the rite in question was far from clear even to the best informants. In seeking to elucidate its significance, the informants repeatedly referred to two other practices which, in their estimate, were related to the rite under consideration. In other words, they treated these two related practices as "free associations," likely to cast light upon the latent meaning of the incestuous wedding rite; a procedure which is methodologically quite sound (Devereux, 1955 a).

The eye-loss ceremony.—When a young person loses an eye, the maimed individual's family gives a special feast, at which a horse is killed. The purpose of this rite is to "accustom" the tribe to that person's changed appearance.

---

[25] A possible alternative explanation, in terms of a hypothetical matrilineal survival, is wholly unacceptable.

Hivsu: Tupo:ma's statement (1936).—In aboriginal times, before the Mohave had horses, if someone lost an eye the maimed person's family would harvest everything and store the crops. Then they called in the people and told them to help themeselves to their crops. After the Mohave acquired horses, the killing of a horse at a feast was substituted for the distribution of crops. Suppose that a young woman, while gathering mesquite beans, was hit by a twig and lost an eye. When that happened, her father went and announced that a horse would be killed and eaten. Then they (apparently the guests, cf. below) foregathered and killed the horse, as though the girl had died.[26] This horse then waited for the girl in the land of the dead. People who attended such a feast were supposed to get accustomed to the girl's changed appearance.

CASE 88 (informants: Hivsu: Tupo: ma and Hama: Utce:.) :

I myself (Hivsu: Tupo :ma) once ate a horse killed at a feast given by Mashatcem Anya: ye,[27] whose nephew Nyail Kwaiki: yo (Case 123)—the father of M. S. and a relative of Sumurâmurâ—lost an eye when a stick poked him in the eye. His uncle called in the people and the guests killed the horse and saw the man whose eye had been poked out. [Hama: Utce: then said that this man now has a glass eye and that makes him look all right.] (This accident may have been self-punitive, since he so neglected his mother that she killed herself.) (Case 123.)

Sometimes, in giving such a feast, the Mohave combined the killing of a horse was a kind of special harvest feast: If a person loses an eye, he waits until harvest time and then makes a big feast with all his crops, also killing a horse. People come to such feasts to get accustomed to the maimed man's appearance. The horse killed at this rite waited for the maimed person in the land of ghosts.[28]

The fact that such an issue was made of a relatively limited kind of accident was explained by the informant as follows:

Hivsu: Tupo:ma's statement (1936): If a young person loses an eye, it is almost as bad as being dead. As a matter of fact, it *is* a little like being dead.

Precisely why the loss of one eye should be such a calamity, when complete blindness, due, e.g., to trachoma, does not call for a similar ceremony and does not seem to be compared to being almost dead, is problematic. The only clue is the specification that the loss of an eye is especially calamitous when the person is still young, presumably because he is likely to be handicapped in amorous pursuits by his uninviting appearance.[29]

---

[26] Kroeber (1925 a) mentions that old women sometimes keep a horse, so that there would be something to kill at their funeral or "cry" (wake).

[27] This man's name was usually abbreviated to Hatcem Anya :ye or even to Tcemenya :ye. His picture was published by Kroeber (1925 a).

[28] This last remark may point to a hitherto unexplored aspect of Mohave eschatology, since it is the only known example of a creature waiting for its owner in the land of ghosts. (The souls of a witch's victims wait for him in a "special place" and do not enter the land of the dead until the witch also dies.) (Pt. 7, pp. 383–426.)

[29] It is, conceivably, not without interest to note that the only known Mohave puritan was the half Cocopa old Hi :dho (=eyes), so called because he became *blind* in his old age. Significantly, he spoke of sexual relationships as acts which "smell up the bed-cloths"—a remark which suggests that he became a puritan when, after losing his eyesight, he became more keenly aware of odors.

Culturally, the most interesting feature of this practice is that it seems somehow "un-Mohave" to seek to regain public esteem, after sustaining some accidental injury, by a distribution of property (crops), or by giving a lavish feast. Such a practice would seem more compatible with the basic pattern of Northwest Coast cultures, where a man, who accidentally lost prestige—be it but by slipping and falling down—gave a feast and distributed property (potlatch) so as to regain "face" (Benedict, 1934). In view of the fact that no comparable customs seem to exist in Mohave society, it is probably incorrect to compare the eye-losing rite to Northwest Coast face-saving potlatches, especially since a more convincing parallel may be drawn between the eye-losing rite and the spiteful giving of funeral goods, which are purchased expressly in order to be thrown on the funeral pyre (pt. 7, pp. 431–459). In both instances the grieved and provoked Mohave seem to "throw good money after bad," reacting to an unavoidable loss by a frantically, and probably spitefully, contrived further loss: the loss of a kinsman through death leading to the giving of funeral gifts and the loss of an eye leading to the sacrificing of a horse and of crops.

Equally interesting, from the cultural point of view, is the spontaneous, or seemingly spontaneous, development of an animal sacrifice pattern after the introduction of the horse into Mohave country, which suggests that the idea of animal sacrifices readily presents itself to any group, once it possesses domestic animals. Indeed, prior to the introduction of the horse, the Mohave do not seem to have sacrificed and eaten either their few prisoners of war or their dogs, which were the only "livestock" they kept in aboriginal times. Game was, likewise, never used sacrificially.[30]

The interesting psychocultural aspects of this practice will be discussed in conjunction with certain related aspects of boundary disputes, which are about to be described.

Boundary disputes were usually settled by formal fights (Kroeber, 1925 a). According to Hivsu: Tupo: ma and Tcatc:

Boundary quarrels arose when a vine grew across a boundary line and the man into whose field the vine had crept took the pumpkins, squashes, or melons growing on it. Verbal quarrels over the exact location of the boundary went on until the harvest. Then each of the contending parties took his crops, killed a horse, and gave a feast for his potential supporters. The two groups then began to push against each other (Kroeber, 1925 a: "thupirvik;" Pulyi:k: "thupirvåk") and also engaged in formal stick fights (Kroeber, 1925 a: "chetmana'ak;" Pulyi:k: "ai: matatekwatk"). In such fights not only the boundary strip, but the whole tract adjoining that strip was at stake. Usually the man who had the most guests at his feast won and occupied the whole tract

---

[30] The "sacrificing" of game does not seem to be prevalent in truly primitive societies.

of land. Puzzlingly enough, one of the informants then added that "after winning, the lot of them fight with each other." [31]

Comment

The informants, in seeking to elucidate the meaning of the wedding rite for cousins, conjoined that rite with the eye-losing ceremony and with boundary disputes. The nexus between these three observances was especially stressed by shamans, perhaps because they are more sensitive to unconscious meanings and connections than are laymen, who are less preoccupied with preconscious and unconscious psychic materials and processes than shamans are.

The following points deserve special notice:

(1) The functional equivalence of "farmland" and "horse" is established quite specifically by the incestuous wedding ritual. The equivalence of crops and of the horse is established by all three observances.

(2) The unpublished full-length version of the Yellak-Halyeku:p cycle (Kroeber, MS., n.d.) makes it quite clear that land tenure is an integral and important aspect of the human estate. Indeed, according to this myth, certain birds, who were originally "persons" (ipa:), but not yet human beings, became genuine humans after acquiring land. This implies that the loss of farmland at incestuous weddings necessarily represents an impairment of the bridegroom's social identity. The same interpretation also fits the slaying of the bridegroom's horse, since this custom is, quite explicitly, the modern equivalent of the alienation of farmland in earlier times.

(3) Since, in aboriginal times, the farmland of a deceased person was either alienated or else left fallow for some years, and since funeral observances usually included the killing of a horse, the wedding rite for incestuous couples necessarily symbolizes the partial social death of the bridegroom. Moreover, since, in order to be permitted to contract such a marriage, the bridegroom voluntarily surrendered a horse and agreed to have it killed, it is clear that his partial social death was viewed as a form of vicarious suicide. This point was made quite explicitly by some of the best informants.

(4) The state of being "almost like the dead" was explicitly mentioned both in conjunction with the wedding rite for incestuous couples and in connection with the loss of an eye.[32]

---

[31] Unfortunately, the complex implications of this last remark were not noticed in time, and were therefore not investigated more in detail.

[32] Whether or not this juxtaposition of the two occurrences is rooted in an unconscious need to equate the loss of an eye with self-punishment for incest (cf. Sophocles: Oedipus trilogy) cannot be determined with any degree of certainty.

(5) All three observances seek to regularize an unpleasant and threatening situation, by publicizing both the occurrence itself and its final social acceptance by means of a feast.

(6) All situations which must be regularized in this manner represent fundamental threats: Incest threatens the survival of the kin group, the loss of farmland threatens the group's basic food supply, while the loss of an eye radically impairs the subject's body image.

(7) In all three contexts a feast is given, so as to assemble a large gathering, presumably in order to minimize the psychological, social and practical threat by means of an intensification of one's social ties.

CASE 89 (Informants: Hivsu: Tupo:ma and Hama: Utce:):

Altonio and Aoo:rà (from Spanish "oro"=gold) were full brothers and members of the O:otc gens. Altonio's 30-year-old daughter Oo:tc and Aoo:rà's daughter's 25-year-old son Humar Atcem, whose gens was not remembered by the informants, decided to get married. Both were fullblood Mohave Indians. At the wedding the groom's grandfather, Aoo:rà, killed two horses, although the rite was not accompanied by mourning. This wedding took place at Parker, Ariz., "about 40 years ago" (1892?) and appears to have been the last, and already somewhat atrophied and simplified, performance of this rite.

Comment

Although this case history contains no explicit reference to suicide, it was narrated in the course of a discussion of symbolically suicidal wedding observances.

CASE 90 (Informants: Hivsu: Tupo:ma and Hama: Utce:): [33]

One of two girls, who were first cousins since their fathers were full brothers, married Atci: Akw(o)ath, a "good shaman who specialized in the treatment of diseases of the eye, and had never bewitched anyone." The Mohave considered the couple the embodiment of all old-fashioned Mohave virtues, partly because of their staunch adherence to the old way of life and their consistently antiwhite attitude, but chiefly because they had lived together all their lives, in exemplary fidelity and harmony. The son of this conservative couple, Sudhu:rà (Case 44) of the Mah gens, eventually married Tcatc (N) who was not only a member of his own gens, but also his second cousin, being the daughter of his mother's first cousin. Their marriage took place after the girl went to Yuma for a visit and came back pregnant. At first she claimed that her unborn child had been fathered by a Yuma Indian, but, in the end, admitted that Sudhu:rà claimed to be the baby's father. As soon as the girl admitted her child's real paternity, Mrs. Atci: Akw(o)ath made her son marry her, even though they were second cousins. The extent to which the wedding rite for cousins was obsolete already in the third decade of the present century is best shown by the fact that even Atci: Akw(o)ath, the outstanding champion of the old way of life, did not kill a horse at this wedding. Despite this omission, the validity of Sudhu:rà's marriage to Tcatc (N) was generally recognized, though people were critical of them for having married within the family.

According to some informants, Tcatc (N) worried so much over what she had done, and over being a "social outcast" (sic!), that she came down with

---

[33] A great debt of gratitude is owed to Prof. George H. Fathauer, who kindly unraveled, and checked in the field, an extremely complicated genealogy. The present account supersedes an earlier, incorrect, version (Devereux, 1939 a).

tuberculosis, and possibly also with an abscess of the lung. Other informants felt, however, that her tuberculosis had been simply aggravated by her constant anxiety. Later on, an informant said that Tcatc (N) finally died of tuberculosis and worry, predeceasing her husband.

Around 1932 Sudhu:râ also came down with tuberculosis, and was in such pain that he begged his family to shoot him. The details of his illness and death are recorded elsewhere in this work (Case 44).

Comment

Although at Sudhu:râ's marriage the traditional wedding rite for cousins was not performed, it was accepted as a bona fide, albeit objectionable, marriage. Its most significant aspect is the fact that it was cited as a proof that cousin marriages do, in fact, lead to the extinction of entire families. A relatively unsatisfactory informant even added that Atci: Akw(o)ath's granddaughter lost a child—apparently because of this marriage." This clue was not followed up, and may be erroneous, since my field notes contain no other indication that Atci: Akw(o)ath ever had a granddaughter, and especially not one old enough to lose a child in the early 1930's. This entire—and presumably erroneous—detail is mentioned here only in order to show the extent to which the Mohave are convinced that incestuous marriages decimate the extended family.

CASE 91 (Informant: Tcatc):

X. Y., whose family is supposedly riddled with witchcraft and incest (Devereux, 1939 a), married his second cousin Nyoltc, without the proper ritual. The bridegroom's paternal grandfather and the bride's maternal grandfather were siblings.

Comment

Informants cited this case in support of the thesis that incest and witchcraft recur in the same family. It is therefore more than a coincidence that Sudhu:râ, who supposedly died because he, too, had married his second cousin, was also believed by some people to have been bewitched by two of X. Y.'s sisters, E. and W., one of whom had actually been caught in the act of committing incest (Devereux, 1939 a). A juvenile delinquent (by Western standards) (Case 77) also belonged to this family.

SUMMARY

At incestuous marriages the Mohave performed a rite which appears to have symbolized the partial social death of the groom. Since the groom freely submitted to this observance and since, moreover, in contracting an incestuous marriage, he exposed himself to death, both symbolically and also through running the risk of dying as a result of his incestuous act, the rite may be viewed as an attenuated and symbolic form of vicarious suicide, and was so viewed by several reliable informants.

VICARIOUS SUICIDE

PSYCHOSOCIAL DYNAMICS OF VICARIOUS SUICIDE

The Mohave define as vicarious suicide any procedure whereby a person who wishes to die, but does not choose to be his own executioner, maneuvers someone else into killing him, or at least consents to become the victim of a witch, or of a foe. In fact, in some instances even an undue delay in consulting a shaman (McNichols, 1944) may indicate the presence of a self-destructive impulse, since it is a basic tenet of Mohave therapeutics that the sooner a shaman is called in, the better will be the chances of recovery. This inference is strongly, albeit indirectly, supported by the Mohave belief that death from witchcraft is usually due to the victim's failure to cooperate with his therapist (pt. 7, pp. 383–386).

The Mohave themselves gave many hints that, in numerous instances, the victim is intentionally uncooperative. Thus, if the witch chooses to appear to his victim in a dream, in a disguised form, but does not actually "seal his lips," there are quite clear-cut indications that the witch's disguise is not wholly impenetrable. Indeed, if the dream lasts long enough the disguised shaman—especially if he adopts an animal disguise—usually ends up by changing his shape and revealing his true identity (pt. 2, pp. 40–42). Since "waking up" is clearly an ego function, the Mohave are, psychologically at least, quite right in more or less blaming the victim for not "knowing" who his magical assailant is. Moreover, the Mohave not only define the victim's failure to name his bewitcher as willful uncooperativeness, but even provide a dynamic explanation for such behavior, by saying that the victim loves his killer, though, needless to say, in this context the word "love" actually means "psychological thralldom" (Hörigkeit).[34] It is exemplified by Pi:it Hi:dho Kwa-ahwat's frantic obsession with Kumádhi: Atat (Case 49), as well as by Tcatc's belief that two persons, who were deeply involved with each other, but could neither get together nor separate, had "bewitched" each other (pt. 3, pp. 91–106).

An understanding of vicarious suicide calls, first of all, for a differentiation between the *need*, or *wish*, to become someone's victim, and the psychocultural *process* whereby this goal is attained.

The wish to be a victim is clearly described in at least one tale ("Deer"), which also provides many useful insights into the process whereby this objective is realized (Kroeber, 1948).

A *mythological model*, besides the death of Matavilye, is that of two deer, that, though aware of their doom—i.e., "fey" in the old Anglo-Saxon sense of this term—stoically, and almost somnambulistically, drift toward the place where Mountain Lion, specifically described as their "maker," waits to kill them. Since the designation of the Mountain Lion as his victims' "maker" is certainly not derived from the English expression "to meet one's Maker," it must be presumed to reflect some basic unconscious fantasy of a type that can arise independently, and in various forms, in historically and geographically

[34] Outstanding literacy characterizations of this scientifically little-studied state are W. Somerset Maugham's "Of Human Bondage" and Heinrich von Kleist's "Das Käthchen von Heilbronn."

widely separated cultures. Be that as it may, the designation of the deer's killer as their "maker" calls for a careful scrutiny of Mohave data which may clarify this seemingly paradoxical designation.[35]

The notion that parents may harm and destroy their children is deeply embedded in Mohave culture, and, presumably, also in other cultures. The following are the principal Mohave beliefs that reflect this conviction.

(1) The Mohave account of the origins of agriculture specifies that in preagricultural days starving parents sometimes had to kill their children (Devereux, 1948 d).

(2) The Mohave woman sometimes aborts her child, either by mechanical means (ibid.) or with the help of a witch (pt. 7, pp. 331–339).

(3) The child in utero may be damaged if the man cohabits too violently or abnormally with the pregnant woman (Devereux, 1948 b).

(4) The fetus can also be damaged by the failure of its parents to observe certain pregnancy taboos (ibid., and pt. 5, pp. 248–251).

(5) The evil shaman bewitches preferably his own family or else people he loves. If a witch starts an epidemic, most of his victims tend to be children (Devereux, 1937 c). Moreover, Kumádhi: Atat's children openly accused her of having bewitched them (Case 49), while Anyay Ha:m allegedly bewitched his own son (Case 104).

(6) The ghosts of dead parents and relatives seek to lure their surviving kin to the land of the dead, thereby causing them to contract a type of illness that is almost identical with the illness resulting from contact with enemies and aliens (pt. 4, pp. 128–186). For this and other reasons both Fathauer (1951) and the present writer (pt. 4, pp. 128–186) concluded that the Mohave unconsciously equate the ghosts of their dead relatives with enemies and aliens.

---

[35] It is desirable to stress that in many primitive religions the originator of death—and therefore the one responsible for man's death—is usually not the creator and giver of life, but a so-called "marplot." In somewhat higher religions, however, man's killers are usually the deities, or at least their supernatural messengers : a belief that forces man to accept death with submission and good grace. Thus, the Greeks referred to Artemis' lethal missiles as her "gentle arrows." The deeper significance of this murderous conception of Artemis becomes understandable only if one realizes that originally Artemis was not exclusively the slender and virginal huntress of classical sculpture. Artemis the Maiden was but one aspect of a triple Goddess, whose two other—and originally far more important— aspects were a many-breasted, maternal Earth Goddess (protectress of the wild animals who were Artemis the Huntress' natural prey), and the death Goddess Hecate. These three together represent the virgin, mother, and hag aspects of the same female deity ; the giver of love, the bearer of life, and the ultimate destroyer. The equating of man's maker with his destroyer is also present in many of the higher religions, the transition from the one aspect of the deity to the other being usually triggered by man's sexuality. Thus, Matavilye decided to bring death into being because, by reproducing itself, mankind would have multiplied to such an extent that living conditions would soon become quite intolerable. It is also not without interest that, in a way, the "individual" protozoa do not die of old age. The death of the individual organism from old age first occurs at a stage of evolution where sexual reproduction replaces more primitive forms of nonsexual multiplication.

(7) The heart of a bewitched person, unless seized and drowned in time by the witch, turns into a kind of owl which calls the witch "father" (pt. 7, pp. 387–426).[36]

These data, and especially the fact that the victim of witchcraft calls his killer "father," suggests that Mountain Lion is called the "maker" of the two deer whom he kills, *precisely because he kills them.* This interpretation is strongly supported by the Mohave belief that a shaman can cure *because* he can kill, and vice versa of course. Thus, it seems legitimate to conclude that the person who commits vicarious suicide unconsciously equates his slayer with his parent(s).

The psychological roots of the parent=enemy equation.—It is hardly necessary to stress that no emotionally mature and balanced person equates his kind parents with his enemies, at least on the conscious level. This psychic equation must therefore be rooted in early childhood fantasies, which disturbed persons, such as suicidal individuals, never quite give up and from which they derive their own symptomatic fantasies and imageries.

The chief point to be stressed is that the infant is neither neurally nor intellectually developed to the point of being fully reality-oriented, and is therefore unable to classify the various components of reality in terms of their *objective* and inherent characteristics. Instead, it classifies the various parts of reality in terms of its reactions to reality, i.e., in terms of its own passing, uninhibited, and vehement subjective moods. Hence, the child *does not* and *cannot* realize that the mother who nurses him one minute and the next minute frustrates him is actually one and the same person all the time. He cannot realize this because he intensely loves the gratifying mother and sees her as a kind of all-bountiful Earth-Mother, but bitterly hates the frustrating mother, whom in his hatred and despair he visualizes as a kind of monster. In brief, the small child sees the mother alternatingly as Dr. Jekyll and as Mr. Hyde, though—being both vaguely aware of and very much confused by the fact that these two, emotionally incompatible, persons form a single continuum in time—he craves the love, or least the presence and the attentions, of the "evil" mother quite as much as he craves that of the "good" mother

A great deal of further neural and intellectual development must take place before the child is capable of perceiving that the different modes of behavior exhibited by the mother do not impair or destroy her continuity and self-identity in the time dimension, even though he, himself, alternatingly experiences her as gratifying and worthy of love, or else as frustrating and loathsome. In brief, a certain degree of organic maturation must occur before the child can cease to classify outer reality solely in terms of its own reactions to it; before it learns

---

[36] Needless to say, there are also beliefs concerning the murderous impulses of children toward their parents. Thus, Matavilye was bewitched by his own daughter, etc.

that whereas the "good" breast, the tasty baby bottle, and the warming sun are three different things, the nursing and gratifying mother and the scolding and frustrating mother are one and the same person. In brief, time must elapse and maturation must take place before the segments of reality are classified in terms of their objective characteristics, instead of solely in terms of the child's emotional reactions ("good and gratifying" vs. "bad and frustrating") to them.

There is perfectly conclusive psychiatric evidence that severely disturbed children—and also many psychotic adults—can only love their parents by clinging, on the one hand, to the illusion that they are absolutely perfect, and, on the other hand, by projecting their infantile image of the monstrous "bad" parent(s) upon some external foe. This mechanism is often present in an almost undisguised form in suicidal depressions and also in certain other severe psychic derangements.

In brief, formal Mohave beliefs which implicitly equate the parent(s) with the enemy are, thus, nothing more than cultural phrasings of the psychologically archaic-infantile tendency to view one's frustrating parents as threatening enemy monsters.

Traditional cultural phrasings of these archaic-infantile attitudes appear to possess considerable motivating force for depressed and suicidal Mohave Indians, who seem to regress to an infantile psychic state and to revive certain early infantile ways of experiencing or fantasying their parents as murderous monsters.

The desire to be killed is, according to modern psychoanalytic findings, closely related to the small child's efforts to blend into a unified whole the image of the bad, monstrous, frustrating parent(s) and the image of the inexhaustibly bountiful, loving, and gratifying parent(s). In seeking to develop a unified image of the parent(s) and a coherent attitude toward this unified image, the small child—who deals with problems by means of fantasies, rather than by means of logic—may develop the idea that it will be devoured by its parent(s). This idea is both thrilling and anxiety-arousing, since it reflects both the wish to be cannibalized and the fear of being cannibalized.

The fantasy of becoming the victim of one's parents is first formulated in terms of cannibalism, since the voracious child appears to feel that it is *attacking* its mother's beloved breast with its teeth, seeking to cannibalize her and therefore expects her to retaliate in kind, animated by the same love-hate which he, himself, feels. There is incontrovertible evidence that this fantasy occurs among the Mohave, who believe that future shamans are prone to bite the nipple (Devereux, 1947 a), and who refuse to nurse snake-headed monsters, because their bite is thought to be poisonous (pt. 6, pp. 257–259). Gradually the idea of being eaten by the parent(s) becomes highly pleasurable, without ever ceasing to arouse also a great deal of anxiety

(Lewin, 1950).[37] This interpretation is indispensable for an understanding of the process whereby the person who wishes to become a victim manipulates others into destroying him.

The wish to be killed is implemented on two levels: the psychological level and the cultural one.

The urge to live is a very basic and universal impulse. Hence, any intrapsychic urge or motive powerful enough to overcome it must be potent indeed and must, moreover, bring about an affective state or mood which is quite abnormal. In fact, the wish to die is, of necessity, so ego-alien, that it is often first projected upon the outer world, so as to enable the depressed person to experience it as external to his self. This, in turn, implies that in every real suicide there occurs a so-called "splitting of the ego," one part of the ego becoming the killer and the other part the victim. The depressed person who seeks to become the victim of a killer manages to avoid this destructively anxiety-arousing splitting of the ego by maintaining his psychic unity (as a victim) and by maneuvering another person into the role of the killer. This process is exceptionally obvious in the case of Sahaykwisa: (Case 105).

So extreme a form of behavior cannot occur without a correspondingly atypical psychic state, which enables the prospective victim to drift to his doom with an almost somnambulistically assured goal-directedness. This psychic state appears to have been sufficiently common in early, semitribal Anglo-Saxon—and perhaps also other Indo-European—societies to have brought into being the concept of being "fey," which Webster's "New Collegiate Dictionary" defines as "having the air of one under a doom or spell"; a definition which fails to stress, however, that the "fey" person is usually aware of his doom and more or less accepts it.[38] Now, this term is perfectly applicable to the behavior of the two deer (Kroeber, 1948) who go to meet Mountain Lion, their "maker," and slayer. The two deer seem to live only from one moment to the next, without a shadow of a purpose other than to meet their slayer at the appointed place and time. Their behavior is so nearly somnambulistic ("under a spell") that the entire atmosphere of this mythical episode borders on the uncanny, because

---

[37] The arousing of pleasurable (and often markedly eroticized) anxiety is an important form of "entertainment." It is present in dangerous sports, big game hunting, listening to ghost stories, gambling for disastrously high stakes—like the mythical Mohave personage whose gambling stake was his own body (Kroeber, 1948)—etc. Likewise, in seeking to "clean up" the shocking story of Pelops, who was killed and cooked by his father and was partly eaten by the mother-goddess Demeter, Pindar (First Olympian Ode) simply transposed the story from the oral-cannibalistic to the oedipal-homosexual level. He asserted that Pelops was not *eaten* by a *mother-goddess,* but was abducted by a *father-god* Poseidon, who had *fallen in love* with the handsome boy. In "cleaning up" this story—at least by Greek standards—Pindar simply succeeded in stressing even more clearly the erotic thrill which the child derives from its passive submission to parental "aggression" (Devereux, 1953 c).

[38] The manic counterpart of feyness is the conviction that one is a man of destiny, who cannot fail.

the very aimlessness of their behavior from moment to moment only serves to increase one's sense of the uncanny goal-directedness and self-destructiveness of their total action pattern.   In brief, the entire narrative reflects a markedly regressive and archaic-infantile psychic state.

The "feyness" of these two deer is, however, not at all unique in Mohave mythology, where mythical heroes and deities go through their appointed motions—with hardly a hint of motivation, or even of a causal sequence of the "because-therefore" type (Kroeber, 1948)—only to be turned into rocks, for no better reason than that the tale must be ended.   Nor is this mood of aimlessness limited to Mohave myth· ology.   In analyzing the extraordinary story of the Oatman girls' captivity, Kroeber (1951 a) very perceptively stressed the utter lack of intelligible motivation in the purchase of the Oatman girls, their treatment during their captivity, and their ultimate surrender to American authorities.

In brief, so perceptive a student of the Mohave as Kroeber felt that the entire affair of the Oatman girls, which involved travel, expense, effort, risk, and long negotiations, was, in the last resort, utterly pointless.   It is therefore nearly impossible not to gain the impression that it represents a typical "acte gratuit," as this term is defined by French sociologists; that it was simply a means of spending time and effort for its own sake,[39] in a futile attempt to give meaning to life, even though such gratuitous acts usually end in tragedy.

Once this point is grasped, the myth of the fey deer, the "gratuitous act" quality of the entire Oatman girls incident and the manner in which Sahaykwisa: (Case 105) managed to engineer her own destruction, while seemingly seeking to escape it, are seen as a single continuum, showing the manifestations of "feyness" in all major aspects of Mohave life: in myth, in concrete and historically verifiable group activities, and in the life history of a neurotic, perverted, and suicidal witch.

In such a cultural setting it is not the presence of vicarious suicide, but rather its absence which would call for both anthropological and psychoanalytic explanations.   Its presence, even in nonshamans, is also to be expected and is, in fact, known to occur.   Thus, when Mah Wenawen's two sons, who were shamans and braves, either tried to rape her, or did, actually, rape her, she told her relatives what had taken place and begged them to kill her (vicarious suicide).   Her relatives refused, however, to do so and comforted her instead, so that, in the end, Mah Wenawen died a natural death (Devereux, 1939 a). For a sick man's request to be shot, so as to end his sufferings, see Cases 44 and 90.

---

[39] A classical literary treatment of the "acte gratuit" is André Gide's novel, "Les Caves du Vatican."

INTERPLAY OF CULTURAL AND SUBJECTIVE FACTORS IN VICARIOUS SUICIDE

Anthropologists as well as historians possess incontrovertible evidence that standard cultural beliefs, functioning as motives, are strong enough to neutralize even so basic a drive as the instinct of self-preservation. Hence, from the cultural point of view, the Mohave belief that a witch must get himself killed, if he is to retain forever his hold over his victims, is as satisfactory an explanation of the Mohave witch's suicidalness as the Manichaean belief that apostasy means eternal damnation is a satisfactory explanation of the Albigensians' readiness to be burned at the stake rather than accept the religion of their conquerors.

Evidence of this nature is so massive and so irresistible that one tends to lose sight of the very important implications of the fact that some Mohave shamans did *not* seek to be killed [40] and that some Albigensians *did* become converted in order not to be burned at the stake.

As a rule, students of society and culture explain such "derelictions of duty" in terms of the insufficient socialization and ethnicization of, e.g., the individual Mohave witch who does not try to get himself killed, or of the individual Albigensian who preferred conversion to a martyr's death. In less extreme cases even students of psychodynamics ascribe the individual's failure to neutralize some basic impulse by pitting against it some social ideal—or, more often, dogma—as evidence of a defective superego development.[41]

Partially true though this explanation may be, it has the disadvantage of completely obscuring an aspect of compliance with social standards which may be of paramount importance for the correct understanding of effective socialization and ethnicization. Indeed, it seems likely that compliance with social demands is only possible for persons whose personality makeup—be it sick or healthy—happens to be compatible with these demands. Where the demands are rational and constructive, compliance is made possible by the individual's healthy ego and ego ideal. Where the demands are irrational and destructive, compliance is possible only for superego-ridden individuals, who happen to have the proper kind of psychopathology (Devereux, 1939 c).

It is felt that the cultural beliefs which motivate the vicarious suicide of certain witches are irrational and destructive and therefore become effectively operative only in the case of witches who also have marked

---

[40] Compare Hivsu: Tupo: ma's insistent pleas that his confession of witchcraft, made while intoxicated, be kept confidential (Devereux, 1948 1).

[41] This is the "official" view, which, as was shown elsewhere in detail (Devereux, 1956 a), utterly fails to differentiate between superego and ego ideal and also between rational and irrational demands regarding the proper management of the impulses. Compliance with irrational demands is made possible by the superego. Compliance with rational and creative demands is made possible by the ego ideal.

idiosyncratic self-destructive impulses. Where these idiosyncratic self-destructive, or self-punitive, impulses are less intense, the person who believes himself to be a witch may not always deliberately maneuver others into killing him, as a "proper" Mohave witch should, but may simply contrive "accidentally on purpose," i.e., quite unconsciously, to kill himself by taking foolish risks. This latter type of self-destructiveness was clearly present in the case of Hivsu:Tupo:ma, who, some time after confessing to me that he, too, was a witch, managed to sleep off his drunkenness outdoors, in a cold winter night, thus contracting a fatal pneumonia (Appendix, pp. 505–548).

The manner in which individual psychopathology may dovetail with cultural motivation in bringing about a culturally standardized catastrophe is strikingly demonstrated by the case of the witch Sahaykwisa: (Case 105). From the moment when Haq'au raped her, thereby causing this lesbian to become an alcoholic nymphomaniac, everything she did to gratify her neurotic needs and to escape her old and new difficulties only served to hasten her doom, by involving her more and more in a downward spiraling vicious circle, or quicksand, which is characteristic of almost every kind of functional psychiatric illness (Devereux, 1955 b).[42] Otherwise expressed, it is certain that even if Mohave culture did not expect witches to cause themselves to be killed, Sahaykwisa: would, nonetheless, have managed to maneuver someone into killing her. In brief, in Sahaykwisa:'s case, purely idiosyncratic psychological factors provide a satisfactory (i.e., *psychologically complete*) explanation of her need to be murdered, without making it necessary to refer also to culturally determined motivation in order to make her actions understandable. This, however, is but half of the picture. Purely cultural factors *also* provide a satisfactory (i.e., *culturally complete*) explanation of her need to be murdered. Indeed, she bewitched a man whom she loved but also hated for rejecting her advances with insulting references to her former status as a homosexual, and was culturally expected and prepared to long so much for the constant company of her victim that it was socioculturally mandatory for her to contrive her own murder.

Thus, we are confronted with the seeming anomaly of possessing *two equally satisfactory and sufficient explanations* of Sahaykwisa:'s vicarious suicide, *in terms of two radically different sets of concepts:* the psychological frame of reference and the cultural frame of reference.

It is of utmost importance to stress that the existence of two sets of explanations has logically nothing in common with the well-known

---

[42] A step-by-step discussion of the dynamics of Sahaykwisa:'s drift toward becoming the victim of a killer will be found at the end of her case history (Case 105).

psychological "overdetermination" of all human actions. The multiple motives subsumed in psychoanalysis under the heading "overdetermination" are all psychological ones and none of these motives, taken by itself, is necessarily expected to explain adequately the entire action under scrutiny. In fact, in many instances the action must subjectively be heavily overdetermined to occur at all.[43] By contrast, where both cultural and psychological explanations are available, in most cases either of the two suffices to make the occurrence understandable.

Before we discuss the relationship between these two explanations, formulated in terms of two different frames of references, it is necessary to distinguish, first of all, between a satisfactory and sufficient explanation and a complete (reductionistic) explanation.

It is logically possible, and indeed necessary, to explain a phenomenon whose reality one does not wish to deny by providing an explanation which accounts satisfactorily, *but not completely*, for its occurrence. As Meyerson (1921) pointed out, in fully explaining a given phenomenon X, one reduces it to a set of "more basic" phenomena A, B, C, etc., thereby logically denying the existence of that phenomenon as an entity *sui generis*. Hence, any explanation, causal or otherwise, of a given phenomenon which does not seek to deny the existence and reality of that phenomenon by *wholly* reducing it to other phenomena must, of necessity, be a partial one and, *at the same time*, must be *sufficient* to make that phenomenon understandable and necessary in terms of *one* frame of reference. This, in turn, inevitably implies that a different, equally partial and yet *also* sufficient explanation of the same phenomenon can be offered also in terms of *another* frame of reference.[44] This finding has certain extremely important implications, which can best be discussed with direct reference to the case of Sahaykwisa:. It was noted that, in explaining her death entirely satisfactorily in *psychodynamic* terms, one left the door open for an equally satisfactory explanation of this occurrence in *cultural* terms. Yet, neither of these explanations makes the other one false, inconclusive or supererogatory, because, while each of these explanations is entirely sufficient to make Sahaykwisa:'s death seem inevitable, either psychologically or else culturally, neither of the two explanations is *complete in the sense of being reductionistic*. Moreover, neither the psychological nor the cultural explanation, no matter

---

[43] I.e., an American may kill himself because he is old, ill, broke, and widowed, though possibly none of these motives, taken separately, could have caused him to commit suicide. Moreover, no matter how much we may sympathize with his plight, we recognize that his entire motivation was subjective, since our culture does not expect a man to kill himself for any one of these four reasons, nor even for all four of them in conjunction.

[44] Compare in this context Poincaré's (1901) thesis, that if a phenomenon admits of one explanation, it will also admit of any number of other explanations accounting equally well for the characteristics of that phenomenon.

how satisfactory it may be and no matter how inevitable it may make Sahaykwisa :'s murder seem in terms of its own frame of reference, can possibly be either complete or reductionistic.[45]

The finding that the psychological explanation of a cultural fact can be *sufficient, without necessarily reducing* that fact to psychology pure and simple—and vice versa, of course—once and for all disposes of Kroeber's (1952) recurrent fear that a supposedly reductionistic psychology may seek to supersede the science of culture, anthropology. Psychology simply cannot do so, because even its most satisfactory and sufficient explanations are incomplete. Conversely, anthropology cannot swallow psychology, because its most satisfactory and sufficient explanations are also incomplete. A failure to grasp this point is responsible for Kroeber's lifelong (1952) and freely admitted perplexity over how psychology could be fitted into his theory of culture.

Having now clarified the difference between satisfactory psychological and satisfactory cultural explanations of a phenomenon, both of which, though partial, are capable of making that phenomenon seem inevitable and necessary within the respective frames of reference to which they pertain, we may now briefly discuss the logical relationship between the psychological and the sociocultural explanation of a given phenomenon. As stated elsewhere (Devereux, 1945 a), there exists a typical complementarity relationship between the psychological and the cultural understanding of a given phenomenon, such as Sahaykwisa :'s maneuvers to cause herself to be killed. The more fully one understands it *at a given moment* in terms of her individual psychology (neuroticism), the less one understands *simultaneously* (at that *same* instant) that her maneuvers were also inevitable in cultural terms (vicarious suicide of witches)—and vice versa, of course. When one realizes how absolutely inevitable it was *psychologically* for Sahaykwisa: to contrive her own death by murder, *at that moment* any *cultural* explanation seems extraneous and unnecessary— and vice versa, of course.[46]

This being said, the significance of Sahaykwisa :'s case for an understanding of other *actual cases* of vicarious suicide among witches and

---

[45] An analogy may help one to understand this point. One can unmistakably identify a given car either in terms of its *mechanical* properties—no two cars being mechanically absolutely identical—or else in terms of its license plate, which denotes the car's *legal* "properties." Both identifications are absolutely satisfactory, even though neither of the two is complete.

[46] The thesis proposed elsewhere (Devereux, 1955 a) that the same inferences regarding the meaning of a human act can be made either by studying one individual in depth, by psychoanalysis, or one culture in depth, by something like the functional method, or by studying the forms in which that trait occurs in a large number of cultures is a direct consequence of the complementarity relationship between the psychological and the cultural understanding of a given trait, in addition to being related to the ergodic hypothesis. Unfortunately, a discussion of this point would take us beyond the legitimate boundaries of the present study.

for the understanding of the relevant Mohave *beliefs* as well, may be stated as follows:

(1) Either psychological (neurotic) motives or cultural beliefs can provide a sufficient and convincing explanation of the vicarious suicide of witches in Mohave society.

(2) Seen psychologically, a Mohave witch unconsciously contrived her own murder by maneuvering herself into a position in which someone was subjectively motivated to kill her. Thus, her lover was angered by her infidelity, and by his awareness that he was but a substitute for his own dead father; moreover, he wished to avenge his father, whom Sahaykwisa: admitted having killed. All these are basic, "culturally neutral" human reactions.

(3) Seen culturally, Sahaykwisa: wished to be killed in order to join forever the ghost of her loved and hated victim. Hence, in accordance with the Mohave pattern, she confessed her misdeed to her victim's son, thereby culturally motivating him to murder her, who, being a witch, was, by definition, likely to bewitch him next. Thus, seen culturally, Sahaykwisa:'s killer simply implemented a major and basic Mohave cultural rule.

(4) Sahaykwisa: also used *psychologically* (i.e., neurotically) determined maneuvers to elicit a *culturally* determined response in her killer. Thus, precisely by becoming her killer's mistress, she unconsciously made certain that the latter would—in accordance with Mohave belief—fear that he was destined to be her next victim, since witches often kill entire families. Moreover, he was also obliged to avenge his father.

(5) Sahaykwisa: also used *cultural* means for eliciting in her killer certain *psychological* (subjective) murderous impulses. She made a confession in due form, but unconsciously managed to do so while drunk, thereby giving it a certain personalized, involuntary quality. Moreover, she made herself exceptionally available for a culturally prescribed aggression, by being helplessly drunk.[47]

Summing up, the complex interplay of cultural and psychological factors is one of the most characteristic features of the vicarious suicide of witches—as well as of all human actions—which can, however, be satisfactorily explained either in purely psychological or in purely cultural terms. The subtle convergence of psychological goals and cultural mandates in bringing about the final catastrophe is not only the best proof of the complexity of processes whereby the ethnic character comes into being, but also the most convincing demonstration of the complementarity and the mutual irreducibility of "the psychological" and "the sociocultural."

---

[47] For a discussion of the psychodynamics of this aspect of her confession, compare the Comments appended to Case 105.

THE WILLING VICTIMS OF WITCHES

The simplest form of vicarious suicide is that of bewitched persons, who refuse to cooperate with the shaman called in to treat them and do not reveal to him the name of the witch, even though they know that, unless they do so, they are doomed to die, which is, of course, precisely what they wish to happen. Startling as this may seem to naturalistically oriented men, the notion that the bewitched person may be a willing victim is by no means limited to the Mohave, and appears even in higher cultures. Thus, reliable French historians pointed out that quite a few of the victims of the satanistic poisoning epidemic, which swept through the French upper classes during the reign of Louis XIV, were the willing victims of witches and poisoners and refused to reveal the names of the satanists who had harmed them. Moreover, according to these selfsame authorities, the refusal of these victims to betray those who harmed them actually seems "inexplicable," since not all of the victims were themselves so deeply involved with satanism as to have had to dread religious and/or secular punishment, nor were all simply too proud to act as informers. Today, as one reads the eager self-accusations of brainwashed defendants in Communist treason trials and as one obtains a deeper insight into the experience of being brainwashed by fanatics, the determination of both Mohave and 17th century French bewitched persons to conceal the identity of the witch and to become the victims of witchcraft becomes more understandable.

Before discussing this point in detail, it is necessary to stress that, according to the Mohave, the bewitched person usually loves the witch whose victim he (or she) wishes to become, and is, both in waking life and in dream, constantly thinking of the witch. Moreover, even though the victim may profess to be physically and/or morally repelled by the witch, there is, allegedly, often a marked, though not wholly conscious, sexual—and often incestuously sexual— attraction present (Case 105). Now, even though it seems unreasonable to love one's magical killer, solid scientific evidence shows that the prisoners of the Communists, who are ceaselessly tormented and interrogated by some official, eventually become extremely attached to the interrogator and are genuinely eager to submit to him and to satisfy him. It is extremely important to stress in this context that the prisoner's eagerness to please the interrogator is not due primarily to fear, since the only way the prisoner can please his interrogator is by incriminating himself, feeling guilty, and demanding "deserved" punishment. This masochistic eagerness for punishment is so strongly developed in the properly brainwashed person, that he does not retract his confession even in court, where neutral newspapermen are present and ready to let the whole world know that the extorted confession was repudiated by the defendant.

According to Hinkle and Wolff (1956) this is primarily due to the fact that the prisoner's life pattern is so systematically disorganized and impoverished, that finally the interrogator becomes the one and only person with whom the prisoner is permitted to have anything resembling a close and meaningful relationship, which—we assume—gratifies the prisoner's otherwise completely frustrated "primary affect hunger" (Levy, 1937). Thus, the prisoner actually comes to love the interrogator, who is the only person with whom he is permitted to interact. Hence, in order to keep the relationship with this one person unimpaired, the prisoner will confess anything and everything, will accept the interrogator's ideology, will persuade himself that he is guilty as charged and will literally clamor for punishment in order to alleviate his induced guilt feelings. In other words, like the willing victim of the Mohave witch, the brainwashed prisoner comes to love his tormentor and craves to become his victim.

It will be objected, of course, that the brainwashed prisoner responds in this manner only because he is systematically isolated from others and because his life pattern is systematically disorganized and impoverished by his jailers,[48] whereas the victim of the Mohave witch is not isolated from human contacts and is not, at least at the start, in fear of his life. This objection disregards several important matters.

(1) A primitive who falls ill, *for no obvious reason*, tends to become quite panicky. Thus, Kroeber (1952) rightly contrasts the matter-of-fact manner in which a primitive bandages a minor wound with his panic when the cause of his illness is not obvious to him.[49]

(2) The belief that one is bewitched sometimes does not precede illness, but follows it (e.g., Case 44). Likewise, even though the Sedang Moi believe that it is very risky to visit the Reungao lowlanders, who are great witches,[50] they do not begin to think that they were bewitched in the course of their last visit to that tribe until they begin to feel ill. Now, while it is possible to assume that they often begin to feel ill simply because the thought that they might be bewitched was present in the back of their minds all along, in one case at least it seems probable that this thought did not occur to a Sedang, who had recently visited the Reungao, until he developed an earache—perhaps because of the change of altitude, and the temporary blocking of his

---

[48] Current research shows that perfectly normal subjects placed in a tank of warm water, and cut off from most external stimuli, rapidly begin to hallucinate (Bexton et al., 1954; Heron et al., 1953; Lilly, 1956 a, 1956 b). For the relevance of this finding to brainwashing, see Group for the Advancement of Psychiatry, 1956.

[49] A Sedang Moi girl went into shock—her lips blue, her pulse threadlike, etc.—when she realized that she was constipated . . . a condition rare in that area (Devereux, MS., 1933–34).

[50] Needless to add, the Reungao say the same thing about the Sedang.

Eustachian tubes. This is a fairly plausible supposition, since earaches were frequently mentioned as a proof that one was magically shot (bewitched) during one's last visit to the Reungao lowlands.

(3) Once the ailing person becomes convinced that he was bewitched, it is quite understandable that all his thoughts and dreams should be focused on the witch.

(4) This preoccupation, combined with the culturally fostered conviction that the witch obsessively loves his victim (pt. 7, pp. 387–426), presumably suffices to cause the victim to love his magical assailant. This inference dovetails perfectly with the Mohave Indians' tendency to marry those who want them, rather than those whom they want (Devereux, 1951 f).[51]

(5) The fact that the witch is often a relative of the victim—i.e., the fact that he is a tabooed incestuous love object—in itself suffices to explain why the victim is sexually so attracted in fantasy to his (or her) supposed killer, and so eager to meet all his demands.

(6) Illness, the conviction of being bewitched, and a constant obsession with the witch suffice to bring about a state of *psychic isolation* or withdrawal, in which an attachment to the powerful witch, who supposedly loves one (usually incestuously), can come into being in a manner which is relatively similar to the way in which the prisoner subjected to brainwashing comes to love his interrogator in a masochistic and self-destructive manner.

While the preceding remarks are admittedly inferential, they are greatly strengthened by the fact that not only laymen but even confessed witches are convinced that their victims are passionately devoted to, and enthralled by them.

CASE 92 (Informant: Hivsu: Tupo:ma.):

While intoxicated, Hivsu: Tupo:ma spontaneously confessed to me that he had bewitched two of his close relatives: his uterine half brother ("because he was my mother's favorite, because he once broke my arm and because he interfered with my affair with his daughter") and his uterine half brother's daughter, who had been his mistress. (Cf. Case 139.)

Hivsu: Tupo:ma's description of his relations with this girl, both while she was alive and after she became his ghostly captive, differed significantly from the way in which he usually described both his own sexual adventures and those of others. While leaving nothing to the imagination, as usual, his account of this affair was very different from his usual rabelaisian anecdotes; his narrative was tenderly sensual rather than humorously coarse. Moreover, he gave the impression that his dream relations with this captive ghost were, if possible, even

---

[51] This tendency explains in part why older Mohave persons often manage to marry very young spouses and why the lesbian Sahaykwisa: (Case 105) was able to marry at least three times.

more thrilling than the real affair had been. Thus, after describing his ghostly sex partner's charms in considerable detail, he wistfully concluded: "Ghosts stay young." [52] Finally—and this is the point which is of the greatest importance in the present context—Hivsu: Tupo:ma made it quite clear that his ghostly mistress enjoyed their dream intercourse as much as he did and was as enamored of him as he was of her. He himself yelled in dream with delight, but when his wife asked him why he yelled he said: "I dreamed that someone came to *kill* me." [53] This lie is probably an unconscious allusion to the fatal enticements of the dead (pt. 4, pp. 128–186).

In some instances the Mohave actually take it for granted that if the victim does not reveal his magical killer's name, this proves that the bewitched person is a willing victim. Thus, even though Tcuhum contemptuously rejected the advances of Sahaykwisa:, because she had been formerly a lesbian, the fact that he did not reveal her name when she bewitched him was said to prove that he did love her after all and wished to become her victim (Devereux, 1937 b, and Case 105).

The next point to stress is that the witch's victim knows that, sooner or later, the witch will succumb to the temptation of being forever with his beloved victims, and will therefore commit vicarious suicide (pt. 7, pp. 387–426). Hence, the linked "suicides" of the victim and of the witch resemble in many respects the suicide pacts of lovers,[54] in which the stronger of the two first kills the more timid partner and then commits suicide. The similarity between such suicide pacts and the linked voluntary deaths of the victim and the witch is further increased by the fact that, just as suicide pacts are made by frustrated lovers, so these linked witch-and-victim "suicides" usually involve persons who—being related to each other, or at least of the same gens (Case 105)—cannot marry, nor even have an affair, without being socially penalized for it.

As regards the real cause of the willing victim's death, it is more likely to fit the "vagus death" pattern (Richter, 1957) than the fear-and-rage type of psychic death described by Cannon (1942).

Given the intimate link between the death of the willing victim and the vicarious suicide of the witch, the latter form of "suicide" will be discussed in the next section.

---

[52] Presumably the witch's captive ghosts are meant, since ordinary ghosts are supposed to grow old and to die in the land of the dead (Devereux, 1937 a). It is permissible to suppose that captive ghosts stay young precisely because their killers *remember* them as they were. By contrast, all other deceased persons are supposed to be *forgotten* as soon as possible (Kroeber, 1925 a), which explains why the survivors can believe that they do not remain forever as they were when they died. In fact, one may even suggest that beliefs concerning the aging and ultimate "second death" of ghosts can occur only in societies where the survivors seek to forget the deceased as soon as possible.

[53] A complete account of Hivsu: Tupo:ma's confession was published elsewhere (Devereux, 1948 i; and Appendix, pp. 505–548).

[54] Suicide pacts were cogently discussed by Jones (1951).

VICARIOUS SUICIDE OF WITCHES

The present chapter is strictly limited to a discussion of the vicarious suicide of practicing witches, since the "innate" suicidal impulses of shamans, which cause some to be stillborn (Devereux, 1948 e and pt. 7, pp. 331–339) and the evolution of an initially good shaman into a witch (Devereux, 1937 c; and pt. 2, pp. 54–71, 83–89) are discussed elsewhere in this work.

The first point to be stressed is that the concept of "vicarious suicide" was not invented by the present writer to account for strictly Mohave phenomena. To take an example at random, already Krafft-Ebing's (1875) textbook of forensic psychiatry mentions suicidal persons who commit capital crimes in order to be executed. Likewise, whenever some spectacular crime is committed, the police usually receive voluntary "confessions" from supposedly self-dramatizing, but actually suicidal, persons who, were their confessions believed, would be executed. These data suggest that the suicidal Mohave shaman may not only boast of having bewitched persons whom he actually *tried* to kill by magical means, but may also disdain to deny unjust accusations, or may even persuade himself, by a retroactive self-deception of the "opportune confabulation" type, that he had actually bewitched someone who just happened to die at a time when this shaman experienced especially strong suicidal impulses. This latter hypothesis is strongly supported by the fact that certain types of psychotics feel responsible for tragedies which they could not possibly have caused.

In brief, the urge to commit vicarious suicide is not a distinctively Mohave phenomenon. It is a human, rather than a specifically Mohave, impulse. It is a product of human culture per se, rather than of the Mohave culture pattern. Hence, what is ethnologically relevant is simply the extent to which Mohave culture has elaborated and implemented this urge, by means of complex beliefs and practices which, in turn, provide the opportunities, channels, justificatory rationalizations, and means for the final activation of the individual's subjective, and often partly unconscious, suicidal impulses. In fact, it is even permissible to suppose that the great "cultural mass" of the concept of vicarious suicide may play a decisive role in causing some Mohave Indians to commit vicarious suicide, instead of simply killing themselves.

The basic pattern.—According to Kroeber (1925 a):

Doctors are despatched for blighting the crops; for repeatedly attending a patient but killing instead of curing him; for having said about a sick person: "I wish you would die"; and for admitting responsibility for deaths. There is a doctor now [early 1900's] who stands at funerals and says aloud: "I killed him." Doctors and brave men are alike. The latter say: "I do not wish to live long." The doctor says: "I shall not live a long time. I wish to die. That is why I kill people. Why do you not kill me?" Or he may hand a stick to a man and say: "I killed your father." Or he may come and tell a sick person: "Don't you know that it is I that am killing you? Must I grasp you and despatch you with my hands before you will try to kill me?"

Kroeber then notes that the Mohave speak of such utterances as being frequent, and expresses the belief that some shamans—convinced as they are of the reality of their powers—achieve a "delirium of provocation and hate" especially if they believe themselves to be suspected of witchcraft. My own informants fully confirmed Kroeber's characterization of the provocative behavior of witches: "The witch will say to someone: 'Why don't you kill me? Don't you know that I bewitched your relative, who is now dead?'" This is a doubly insulting thing to say, since one should not refer to a person's deceased relatives (Kroeber, 1925 a; Devereux, 1951 c). (See also Case 104.)

Various informants also stated that some shamans are killed simply because they lose several patients in a row. If this statement is taken literally, it may mean that such shamans are killed either because they are incompetent, or else because they fail to exert themselves to the utmost. Taken in a less literal sense, this statement may simply imply that the failure to cure a patient is viewed as prima facie evidence of malice. Indeed, it is well to remember in this context that, if a person is believed to have been bewitched by a certain shaman, the relatives of the patient may use threats to compel the alleged witch to treat his supposed victim. Then, if the treatment is unsuccessful, the shaman is killed, partly for having caused the illness and partly for having failed to cure it. Finally, the Mohave are so ready to blame the shaman who fails to cure a patient that they may behave threateningly (McNichols, 1944) toward a shaman who angers the sick person's relatives by saying that they waited too long before consulting him.

Hence, according to McNichols (1944), even a perfectly innocent and unjustly accused shaman was once goaded into suicidally defiant behavior. When this shaman blamed an old man's kin for not having called him in until it was too late to save the patient, the dying man's daughter hurled the worst possible insults (Krober, 1925 a, Devereux, 1951 c) at the shaman, telling him that his father, his mother and his paternal grandfather were all dead. The insulted shaman replied defiantly that these relatives of his were indeed dead, since they had the good sense not to live too long, adding that the dying man himself would readily agree that he had been unlucky to live as long as he did, because neither brave men, like the patient, nor shamans wish to live long. He concluded his challenging remarks by saying that he himself did not wish to live long and asked whether any man cared to kill him then and there.

Concealment vs. confession.—The Mohave are firmly convinced that every murdered witch committed vicarious suicide, even if he did not confess his crimes in so many words. It is therefore necessary to discuss in some detail the means whereby a witch—who is not, as yet, ready to let himself be killed—manages to conceal his identity. In fact, the confessions of the witch cannot be effectively discussed apart from the means he may use for disguising his identity.

(I) *Concealment* may take place either before or after the death of the victim.

(A) *Concealment before the victim dies:*

(1) A witch who has power over a disease which other shamans can also cause and cure, can inflict this illness upon his victims without thereby revealing his identity.

(2) The witch may appear to the victim in dream, in the guise of an animal, and especially of a bull (pt. 2, pp. 40–72).

(3) A very powerful witch can, by "using his breath," purloin the shadow (soul, image, appearance) of a less powerful shaman and appear to his victim in dream in that disguise, in order to divert suspicion to another shaman. It is said that Sudhu:râ (Case 44) accused Hivsu: Tupo:ma of having bewitched him, because a witch had purloined Hivsu: Tupo:ma's shadow and appeared to his victim in that disguise.

(4) He may "seal" his victim's lips, so that the bewitched patient will be either unable or unwilling to reveal the witch's identity to the therapist. This disguise is especially effective when the patient actually wishes to become the victim of the witch (pt. 7, pp. 371–386).

(5) The witch may use the type of witchcraft (Devereux, 1937 c) which fells the victim before he can reveal the name of the person who bewitched him.

These disguises and concealments are usually effective, except in cases where the victim's therapist is so powerful that he can overcome every obstacle the witch may place in the therapist's path.

(B) *Disposal of the post-mortem evidence.*—It is, in principle, quite possible for a bewitched person to die without anyone suspecting that the death was caused by witchcraft. However, the behavior of the bewitched corpse on the funeral pyre automatically proclaims that death was not due to natural causes, and there is nothing the witch himself can do to prevent the corpse from revealing this fact. Hence, shortly after the cremation, the witch must take special precautions to prevent his victim's "heart" from betraying him. For reasons of expository convenience we will describe first the atypical behavior of the corpses of bewitched persons, and will then proceed to discuss the witch's attempt to silence his victim's heart.

(1) *Behavior of the corpse:* According to Drucker (1941) the Mohave place all corpses face downward on the funeral pyre, to prevent them from rising to a "sitting position . . . frightening spectators out of their wits." While Drucker is certainly right in suggesting that such movements may be due to muscular contractions caused by the heat, one must also envisage the possibility that some of these moving "corpses" were placed on the funeral pyre before actual death had occurred. Thus, according to McNichols (1944), the Indian Agency formerly sometimes sent a native policeman to the home of a dying person, in order to prevent premature cremation. Moreover, by placing the corpse face downward on the pyre one can prevent the corpse from "sitting up," but cannot prevent it from writhing, or from slipping as various burnt logs collapse. Be that as it may, the fact that some corpses "move" while being cremated is known to the Mohave, who believe such movements to occur only when a person died of witchcraft.

Tcatc's statement (1938): When a victim of witchcraft is being cremated, toward the end of the cremation the corpse rises up on the pyre. That is how people know that this person died of witchcraft; it happens every time they cremate a bewitched person. Hivsu: Tupo:ma's corpse did not rise up, but when they cremated Tcatc (J.H.), Kari Vaha:'s (=basket guts) 50-year-old wife, who had been bewitched by Kwathany Hi:wa and died of a hemorrhage from the mouth, a woman named T. S., as well as others, saw her corpse rise up on the pyre. This happened about 2 years ago (1936?).

(2) *Killing the victim's heart:* Since the movements of the corpse on the funeral pyre once more remind the mourners that there is a witch at large, the evil shaman must make special efforts to silence the victim's heart which, after assuming the shape of an owllike being,[55] calls the witch "father" and names his name for all to hear. The fact that the heart of the deceased victim calls his killer "father" is of special interest. It dovetails with the belief that witches kill chiefly their own relatives and also yields some insight into the possible motivation of the victim of witchcraft, who refuses to cooperate with his therapist by naming the person who bewitched him (pt. 7, pp. 383–386). Finally, it explains, at least in part (pt. 7, pp. 372–377), why Mountain Lion, who kills two mythical deer, is specifically referred to as their "maker" (Kroeber, 1948).

Tcatc's and E. S.'s statement (1938): When a person dies (of witchcraft) and, 4 days later (sic!), is cremated, there comes from the hole or pit in which they cremated the corpse an owl that is like a person (ipa:).[56] It has a face and ears like a human being, but has the feet of an owl. It has, however, no feathers. This creature is called hamu:ly kat-pa:tc (= ashes came out). The way it comes out, it seems to be blown out of that hole. The evil shaman who be-

---

[55] Bourke (1889) says that the heart of every corpse turns into a special kind of owl. This is not incompatible with the data given above. Some Mohave say that it is a ball of fire which emerges from the burnt corpse and then turns into an owl.

[56] Bourke (1889) says that the "poison" of the witch, not an owl, emerges from the ashes.

witched that person must be there to grab this creature before an owl, who is said to be there at the same time, can get hold of it, and must throw it into the river. If, however, the owl gets hold of this creature before the witch does, the owl takes it to its nest in a cottonwood tree. Then, at night, it takes this creature on its back and teaches it to call out the name of the witch. The witch does not like that at all and that is why he tries to kill this owllike being before an owl can get hold of it. If the owl gets hold of this creature before the witch does, after a while this being turns into an owl. Then it goes about calling out the witch's name and saying ku:t, ku:t, which is the last syllable of naku:tk (= father). In other words, this creature calls the witch "father." [What does this creature say if the witch is a woman?] It says ku:t all the same. In the old days there were few female shamans, but now there are a lot of them. However, if the shaman can get hold of this creature, he throws it in the water, where it drowns. Then the shaman bathes and abstains from salt for 4 days. [Does the shaman bathe in water in which arrow weed has been steeped, the way people do when they seek to purify themselves?] No one knows—the witch does these things in secret. This being is the heart of the victim and it is alive. [What happens to the heart of a person who did not die of witchcraft?] Nothing—it burns like all the rest." [56a] At this point the interpreter, E. S. said: "When I was acting as an interpreter for Dr. Ruth Underhill, Big Dick, a Mohave who lives at Yuma, told us that the unburned parts of the body turn into various other kinds of birds; only the heart became an owl." Tcatc shrugged her shoulder and said: "Perhaps so—Big Dick knows more about these matters than I do. Anyhow, the owls are Mohave, since they are the hearts of the Mohave. This owl-being appears (emerges from underneath the pyre) at an indeterminate time of the day. Only the shamans know when it appears . . . I think it probably appears at night. [When someone's corpse rises on the pyre, showing thereby that he died of witchcraft, do his relatives lie in wait for the witch who may try to get hold of this owllike creature?] Yes, sometimes they do that; at least, they did it formerly. They don't do it now, because now witch killing is considered murder (by the whites). The braves used to do the witch killing. Anyhow, this owl-being not only calls out the name of the witch, and does not only say ku:t, ku:t, as I just told you, but it also says kidhi: khi:yu = come and see. [Does it say what one is supposed to come and see?] No. The Mohave believe that if an owl of this kind visits a home, one may expect bad news, such as news of the death of a relative." At this point, E. S. the interpreter, said: "Not all owls are that way. Once I killed an owl and it had tattoo marks on its chin: One line down the middle of its chin and two rows of dots. [That is the way men tattoo their chins, isn't it?] Yes. (Kroeber, 1925 a, Taylor and Wallace, 1947, fig. 1 j.) That owl—it was a bewitched man's heart. Even the ears of these owls look something like the ears of human beings. Thus, only one kind of owl is the heart of a bewitched person. These owls are big ones—they are about a foot and a half high and gray in color. Only this kind of owl comes out of the cremation pit. All witches who grab and drown these owl-beings are bad people. Not only do they cause epidemics, but, when they bewitch a particular person directly, they kill that person twice, first by killing him and then by killing also his heart."

CASE 93 (Informant E. S.):

"Once I had a very strange experience with an owl. I was living with my brother who, at that time, was married to D. T. My sister-in-law had been ill for some 6 months, so we told her to go to the hospital. She agreed to do so and stayed in the hospital for 2 months. Then she came back and stayed

---

[56a] The bewitched Matavilye's heart was stolen by Coyote (Kroeber, 1948).

home for 3 months. Two nights after she came home an owl came to our corral; it alighted on one of the mesquite trees and began to hoot. My brother's wife got out of bed, went to the mesquite tree and began shooing away the owl. When she came back into the house we told her that this was a sign that there would be a death in our family, because this was the first time an owl ever came there at night. After a while my sister-in-law returned to the hospital and died there within a short time. Almost the same thing happened when a woman called Vi:mak died. After our father's death we stayed away from our home for a while. The first night we returned to our house, four or five owls were around and kept on hooting and screeching in the mesquite trees . . . and, sure enough, this girl died in less than 3 weeks.

(II) *Confession.*—The prototype of all confessions made by witches is the means whereby a young shaman first advertises his powers to the community. A person who feels that he received the necessary powers to treat some illness will attend a gathering and will mildly bewitch—using a minor form of love magic—a young person of the opposite sex, who will immediately be treated by one of the shamans who are routinely asked to see to it that no one is bewitched during a gathering or feast. Since the young witch is actually eager to make his powers known, he allows his "victim" to reveal his name to her therapist, thus making an almost instantaneous cure possible. Needless to say, this incident immediately becomes known to the tribe as a whole, and even though people may, at first, minimize the young shaman's powers,[57] in due time they will consult him for minor ailment, and, if he is successful, his reputation as a therapist becomes firmly established. It is important to stress that even shamans who will never really bewitch anyone first advertise their powers in this manner. Thus, at least once in his life every shaman publicly displays his powers by bewitching someone.

Turning now to genuine witches, their evil deeds can become known to the community in several ways:

(1) Some witches, who specialize in an illness which only they are competent to cure, betray their identity by causing their victims to contract this particular disease. In such cases the very nature of the victim's illness is, in itself, a kind of trademark or confession (Case 100).

(2) A witch who needs money very badly—perhaps because he is an epileptic cripple (Case 103) who barely manages to eke out a living—may start an epidemic, usually affecting children, of a type which he is qualified to cure, in the hope of earning money by treating his victims. In such instances the witch partly betrays himself by being one of those who benefit by the epidemic.

(3) A witch starting an epidemic may betray himself by visiting various people who will subsequently sicken, or else by simply stroll-

---

[57] According to Ahma Huma:re, "At first people thought my powers were something to laugh about." For other slighting remarks, see Devereux, 1937 c.

ing around on the reservation, without stopping at any particular home, spreading the epidemic everywhere.

(4) A witch may betray himself by bewitching a relative of someone whom he notoriously hates, so as to grieve his enemy (Case 102). He allegedly never bewitches anyone he dislikes, since he does not care to have such a person join his ghostly retinue.

(5) A witch may be known to be ambivalent about someone whom he loves, but is also angry with, at the same time. "In such cases the witch does not hate his victim—he really loves his victim." Such a witch reveals his identity by bewitching someone he is known both to love and to be angry with (Case 101).

(6) The witch may betray himself by bewitching several of his own relatives whom he loves but who have angered him. It does not matter in this context whether the victim is a spouse (Case 49) or a blood relative, since incestuous dream relations with one's blood kin are said to be especially thrilling (Devereux, 1939 a).

(7) A witch betrays himself by bewitching a professional rival, or a shaman who disparaged his powers (Case 50) or who explained his own powers in a different way (Devereux, 1957 b), or else one who bewitched one of his relatives.

(8) When bewitching a person, the witch may appear to that person without any disguise whatsoever.

(9) The witch may decide not to "seal the lips" of his victim, thus permitting his victim to reveal his identity. In so doing, he actually makes a kind of vicarious confession.

(10) The witch may be overly eager to be with his victim. If his victim dies too slowly, the witch sends his shadow to visit the ailing person. Only by haunting the victim in this manner can he keep himself from visiting his victim in person.

(11) The witch may refuse to deny accusations of witchcraft and may calmly wait for the killers to arrive (Case 99). Whether a shaman's denials are believed or not will, of course, depend on his general reputation. When Sudhu:râ (Case 44) unjustly accused Hivsu: Tupo:ma, who was actually trying to cure him, the deeply distressed old shaman's denials were generally believed. By contrast, even though Kwathany Hi:wa denies with tears in his eyes the repeated accusations of members of his own family that he is a witch, his denials are not believed by anyone. However, even an unjustly accused good shaman may become angry enough to refuse to deny accusations and may even behave in a provocative manner (McNichols, 1944).

(12) A witch who started an epidemic among children may learn that a child whom he liked died in the epidemic. This will upset him so much that he will decide to confess his guilt.

(13) The witch may openly confess his evil deeds, may boast of them and may deliberately incite others to kill him. He may do so either in response to an accusation, or else spontaneously and in a threatening way (Case 104). In still other instances the witch may make a confession while intoxicated (Devereux, 1937 b; 1948 i; cf. also pt. 7, pp. 383–386, and Cases 92 and 105).

(14) The witch may be seen killing his cremated victim's "owl" heart (Case 95).

Summing up, in the opinion of the Mohave a witch always commits vicarious suicide by allowing his identity to become known. At the same time, not all Mohave may be convinced that a particular murdered shaman was actually a witch (Case 100).

Motivation.—In seeking to understand the suicidal impulses of Mohave witches, and their decision to commit suicide by causing themselves to be killed, it is necessary to differentiate, first of all, between their allegedly innate (pt. 7, pp. 331–339) unconscious suicidal impulses on the one hand, and their culturally defined conscious motivation on the other hand. Only after this distinction is made is it possible to analyze the interplay between these two sets of motives in the causation of actual cases of vicarious suicide.

(*a*) *The unconscious suicidal impulses* of aging shamans were already discussed in some detail (pt. 7, pp. 331–339) and need not be repeated in the present context.

(*b*) *Mohave culture* postulates that it is advantageous for the witch to commit vicarious suicide. We will ignore here the (supposedly exceptional) bewitching of those whom the witch hates unambivalently, or whom he bewitched for a fee, on behalf of another person (Devereux, 1948 h), since he has no use for the souls of such persons and therefore allows them to enter the land of ghosts in the usual way. Such acts of witchcraft do not appear to elicit suicidal impulses in the witch. The usual victim of the witch—and the one whose death ultimately induces the witch to commit vicarious suicide—is, however, generally a person whom the witch both loves and is angry with, in a markedly ambivalent manner.[58] He therefore does not allow them to go to the land of ghosts until he himself dies. While the souls of his victims are confined to a certain special "place" belonging to him, he dreams of them and has extremely satisfying dream intercourse with them (Devereux, 1939 a). In fact, his gratification is so intense (pt. 7, pp. 385–386) that he gradually develops an irresistible desire to join his victims permanently, instead of communicating and cohabit-

---

[58] In stating that the Mohave witch seems to be ambivalent about his victims, we do not impute to the Mohave an attitude of which they, themselves, are ignorant. Thus, according to the Mohave, if a young man hears that a girl speaks ill of him and mentions his dead relatives, he exclaims: "She is as good as mine," and proceeds to her house in order to cohabit with her. Moreover, when I explained to Hama: Utce: the meaning of the word "ambivalence," she replied: "If someone says that he hates a certain person, the Mohave tell him that he must love that person very much."

ing with them only in dream. Moreover, even if such dreams are incestuous, they will not cause the witch to become insane. By contrast some truly incestuous witches "act goofy" as Tharavi:yo (Hukthar Havi:yo) did (Devereux, 1939 a).

An equally strong motivating factor is the belief that only if the witch is killed can he maintain forever his hold over the souls of his victims, and go in their company through subsequent reincarnations. Indeed, should the witch die a natural death, or should he himself become a victim of witchcraft, his control over his victims automatically comes to an end; the souls of his victims are immediately liberated and proceed to the land of the dead, where they join the ghosts of their own relatives and spouses, instead of staying with the ghost of the witch who had killed them. Finally, if a witch waits too long before deciding to join his victims, they may be kidnaped by another witch, who incorporates them into his own retinue of ghosts.

In brief, a shaman who embarks on a career of witchcraft knows in advance that he will not be able to reap all the potential benefits of his evil deeds unless he sees to it that he is killed before anyone kidnaps his victims, and/or before he himself dies of illness, witchcraft or old age (Devereux, 1937 c).

(c) *Unconscious suicidal impulses and cultural motivation* form a structurally unified pattern in Mohave life and culture. From the psychological point of view, cultural specifications regarding the advantages to be derived from committing vicarious suicide perfectly dovetail with the subjective aggressivity, guilt feelings, and reactive self-punitiveness of the Mohave witch. Moreover, the longing of the shaman for the company of his victims not only dovetails with the generalized Mohave belief that ghosts seek to lure the living to the land of the dead (pt. 4, pp. 128–186), but also helps one to visualize the degree of ambivalence which actuates such "indirect" or imaginary forms of aggression as witchcraft. It is therefore entirely reasonable to assume that, given the Mohave shaman's firm belief in his own powers (Kroeber, 1925 a), the existence of the beliefs just mentioned actually enables the shaman to rationalize and to justify his suicidal impulses. From the cultural point of view the imputation of suicidal wishes to the witch alleviates the witch killer's guilt feelings, since, in killing a witch, one supposedly does him a favor which he himself is said to crave. In fact, it is possible to suggest, at least tentatively, that one of the chief functions of these cultural reasons for committing vicarious suicide is to make possible the actualization of subjective unconscious suicidal wishes in a socially approved manner. Indeed, it is quite probable that if the Mohave witch were not culturally encouraged to believe that it is to his advantage to be killed, he might, instead of causing himself to be killed, simply become psychotic or else commit actual suicide. This interpretation is quite compatible with the well-established fact that a certain proportion of suicides represent a flight from psychosis.[59] The general theoretical point to be made in this context is that accepted cultural beliefs often serve to rationalize and justify unconscious impulses, thereby making possible their actualization in overt behavior. This finding applies quite as much to the acting out of neurotic or psychotic conflicts or impulses as to the cultural reinforcement or activation of defenses against such conflicts or impulses.

The strength of cultural motivations in the vicarious suicide of witches must be discussed both in terms of the shaman's intense belief in shamanistic powers, and in terms of the reality of his affective reactions to the culturally postulated disadvantages of dying a natural death.

The reality of the Mohave shaman's belief in his own powers was cogently emphasized by Kroeber (1925 a). The following incident is cited simply in order to show that this belief is strong enough to effect a cure even in the absence of the actual therapist.

CASE 94 (Informant Hivsu: Tupo:ma; interpreter, Hama: Utce:) (1933):

Once I had a bad cold and pain in my throat; there seemed to be a swelling where my Adam's apple is. I stayed in bed, feeling very sick and finally decided to go for help to a certain crippled shaman, who is one of Hama: Utce:'s uncles. There was a fire in his house and I lay down in front of the fire and dreamed. Something came to me in my dream and said: "Well, you are here. What is the matter?" I answered in my dream and explained what was wrong with me: "I came here because this is the place where that shaman lives, but he is not at home." Then this thing said to me: "Get up and go home; you are all right." At that moment someone woke me up, because I was saying "a-a-a" in my dream.[60] However, when I woke up, I felt much better and, after one night's sleep, I was even able to eat some solid food. After that I went to see the reservation physician, who swabbed my throat with iodine. Then I made a complete recovery.

Comment

Apart from the fact that this account demonstrates the faith of shamans in each other's powers, Hivsu: Tupo:ma's narrative is also interesting in that it not only indicates that the subjective experience of being healed may be a dream experience (cf. also Case 29), but actually suggests that he was healed by means of an Aesculapian "incubation" (Tempelschlaf) experience, and in the absence of any human therapist. This point is of some importance, since therapeutic incubation has not been previously reported from the Mohave.

As regards the witch's affective acceptance of the belief that he has nothing to gain and everything to lose by allowing himself to die a natural death, it is sufficient to state that, according to Tcatc, "a witch

---

[59] Thus, an American psychotic in remission committed suicide when he felt that he was about to become acutely psychotic once more.

[60] Hivsu: Tupo:ma also made sounds when dreaming of intercourse with one of his victims (Devereux, 1939 a).

dying a natural death cries on his deathbed, because he regrets losing his retinue of beloved ghosts."

If one views the witch's motivation against a much broader background, it is striking to note that his attempt to delay the normal metamorphoses of his victims is quite atypical in terms of the normal objectives of Mohave shamanism. Indeed, as Fathauer (1951) rightly stresses, the Mohave shaman does not seek to interfere with the basic processes of nature, or with the basic order of things. In curing, he simply restores that which "should be" (Devereux, 1957 b). Hence, in delaying the metamorphoses of his victims, as well as in other respects, the Mohave witch appears to actualize socially disapproved and culturally dystonic aggressive wishes and fantasies of omnipotence, which set him apart from the average man and doom him to a violent death if he externalizes these fantasies by becoming a shaman and a witch, and cause him to become psychotic if he does not (pt. 2, pp. 57-71). Thus, we can visualize the Mohave witch's vicarious suicide as the final act of his lifelong struggle against the stream of time. The witch first seeks to prevent his separation from his mother by refusing to be born. Next, he attempts to postpone the inevitable separation of the dead from the living and when he fails to do so he hastens his own demise, in order to enjoy a perpetual reunion with his deceased victims in one of the small imaginary eddies which cultural fictions create for the benefit of those who refuse to become reconciled to the passage of time, to change, and to death. (Devereux, 1954 a)

In conclusion, we must ask why only some Mohave shamans become suicidal witches and why no shaman—except one, who was wrongly accused of witchcraft (Case 106)—seems to have committed actual suicide. It is tentatively suggested that, since the witch is believed to be suicidal and believes himself to be suicidal, the actual implementation of this suicidalness by means of overt acts may not be an absolute psychological necessity. This, admittedly speculative, statement is indirectly supported by the fact that, according to the Mohave, there are people who admit that they have shamanistic powers but make no effort to function either as healers or as witches. In such cases the social acceptance of the individual's self-definition, as a person endowed with shamanistic powers, apparently gratifies this person's narcissism to a sufficient extent to protect him both from the psychosis of those who refuse to actualize their shamanistic powers and from the suicidalness of those who drift from healing into witchcraft.

Preparation for the killing.—Even defiantly provocative witches were apparently seldom killed on the spot. Thus, even though Anay Ha:m repeatedly threatened a couple and boasted of having killed their relatives, they did not kill him on the spot, but made relatively careful plans for killing him (Case 104). Sometimes groups of people plotted to kill a witch whom they held responsible for some current calamity. "At other times warriors, who were sitting together, making bows, arrows or war clubs, would say: 'Let us try our weapons on a witch.' [61] Then they would go and slay some witch who had been giving offense to the tribe for some time." It is even possible to infer that potential witch killers were more or less expected to receive public encouragement. Thus, in the case published by Kroeber (1925 a, 1925 b; cf. Case 96), when some warriors killed a witch, more or less on a sudden impulse, and then boasted of having done so, their audience thought they were simply announcing their intention to slay this witch and encouraged them to go ahead with their plans.

The killing.—The statement that witch killings were called "stealing" was unanimously denied by all of my informants. According to the Mohave, in aboriginal times shamans were killed by taking them to a mountain and stoning them to death.[62] Stratton's (1857) statement that the Mohave used to burn witches alive was unanimously denied by all informants. More recently, most witches were beaten to death with sticks. In this context it is noteworthy that even though witch killers were senior braves, whose official weapon is the short club, witches were beaten to death with mere sticks, which are the traditional weapons of apprentice warriors (Stewart, 1947 c; Fathauer, 1954). The reason for the use of such second-line weapons in the killing of witches could not be ascertained. In one instance the killers used a piece of metal, apparently picked up in the vicinity of the railroad shops (Case 103). The shaman whose killing was described by Kroeber (1925 a, cf. Case 96) was slain with a steel ax and so was the last witch to be killed (Case 104). Sahaykwisa: (=Masahay Matkwisa:) (Devereux, 1937 b; and Case 105) was drowned while intoxicated. Informants also spoke of plying a witch with drink and then laying him on the railroad tracks or else stabbing him to death, but could cite no concrete instances of such murders. One evil shaman was killed by means of witchcraft (Case 101).

At present witches are no longer killed, since it is against the law to do so. However, informants believe that even nowadays a person accused of witchcraft may be beaten up by his victim's relatives. Be that as it may, it is quite certain that Hivsu: Tupo:ma was deeply hurt when Sudhu:rà's relatives (Case 44) talked of beating him up, and felt convinced that they would carry out their plan. What seems to have prevented this attack was probably the more or less unanimous feeling in the tribe that Hivsu: Tupo:ma had been unjustly accused of having tried to harm his own patient. It is also worth noting that,

---

[61] Although this statement suggests that witches were slain with arrows, or with clubs, the recorded slayings involved the use of less warlike means. Cf. immediately below.

[62] On the road from Parker to the rock into which the incestuous couple mentioned in the Tuma :np'a Utàu :t cycle (Devereux, 1939 a ; and pt. 7, pp. 356-371) was transformed, there is a small pile of stones to which, for some unknown reason, each passer-by is supposed to add a stone. Whether this was a witch killing place could not be ascertained at this late date.

when Hivsu: Tupo:ma confessed to me that he, himself, had bewitched certain persons—though not Sudhu:râ—he begged me not to
tell this to anyone, lest he should suffer bodily harm.

In theory, witch killing is now obsolete—but it is well to recall that
it was stated to be obsolete already in the middle thirties (Case 100),
i.e., only 2 years or so before a new witch killing took place (Case 104).
Thus, since Mohave shamanism is still very much alive, it would be
hazardous indeed to predict that no further witch killings will occur
among the Mohave.

Attitudes toward witch killings cannot be fully understood unless
one discusses also the Mohave attitude toward the shaman, the witch
and toward the general misbehavior of shamans and witches, which
was described elsewhere (pt. 6, pp. 282–285) in some detail and may be
briefly summed up by saying that the possession of shamanistic powers
is not viewed as a localized and circumscribed function, but one which
affects the shaman's entire psychic makeup and behavior pattern.
Hence, all objectionable actions performed by shamans are accounted
for by the remark: "It is their nature, they cannot help it." The
Mohave Indian's view of the shaman's destructive impulses, implemented by means of witchcraft, was described as follows:

Tcatc's statement (1938): Shamans cannot control themselves. They will
do anything. Their power makes them act that way. It makes them crazy.
Nothing is too low for them. Others sometimes marry their cousins (Devereux,
1939 a; and pt. 7, pp. 356–371), but shamans commit incest with their nearest kin.
They also like to bewitch their own relatives. [Are they incestuous because they
have intrauterine memories and shamanistic dreams?] No. They just want to
do awful things. When they begin to cure, they quiet down. They become almost
human.[63]

Similar views are voiced even by such highly educated persons as
Hama: Utce:, who occasionally seemed almost obsessed with the idea
that Kwathany Hi:wa—who was perhaps married for a time
to a relative of hers—was trying to bewitch her entire family. Hence,
whenever this fear was present in her mind, she spoke angrily and
contemptuously of all shamans, calling them "cowards at heart," and
gloating over the death of a certain witch who had been slain several
decades earlier (Case 101).

Turning now to attitudes toward witch killings, as a rule both the
victim's own relatives and the tribe as a whole felt that the killing of
witches was a socially beneficial action, so that, in aboriginal times,
braves were openly encouraged to kill witches who threatened the welfare of the community (Kroeber, 1925 a). Even as late as the 1930's,
the tribe as a whole made considerable efforts to save two persons who
had killed a witch, by sending some "good shamans" to testify in court
that the murdered witch was a public menace (Case 104).

---

[63] Note the clipped, "preaching" style of the Mohave orator, which is often used also in
making especially emphatic statements.

The Mohave as a whole are undecided whether American interference with the slaying of witches—a "meddling" which they resent on principle—increased or decreased the number of deaths due to witchcraft. The following discussion between Tcatc and Hama: Utce: reflects clearly the extent to which the Mohave are of two minds about the current status of witchcraft.

Tcatc: Nowadays they don't kill witches anymore. They are afraid of the American law. That is why, nowadays, whole families are wiped out by witches. Witches have become bolder than ever before.

Hama: Utce: As far as I can see, now that witches no longer manage to get themselves killed, the number of deaths due to witchcraft has fallen off. Moreover, nowadays there are fewer shamans than there were formerly. In the past, there were many shamans. In aboriginal times, when someone bewitched a shaman's relative,[64] the bereaved shaman retaliated by bewitching the witch. Anyhow, I can't see why a witch, who knows in advance that he will die a natural death, and will therefore inevitably lose his hold over his victims, should bother to bewitch anyone nowadays.[65]

Tcatc: They continue to bewitch people because, until they themselves die, they can at least dream of their victims and can have intercourse with them in dream.

The reactions of the witch's own relatives were variable. If they were convinced of the murdered shaman's guilt, and especially if they felt that he had bewitched his own relatives, they were the first to condemn him, refused to protect him from his assailants, and did not seek to punish the killers afterward. If, however, they believed the accused witch to be innocent, they tried to prevent his slaying and, if they could not prevent it, they subsequently fought with the witch-killing braves with sticks (Kroeber, 1925 a, 1925 b), sometimes even donning war paint for this purpose.

It is interesting to note in this context that the contemporary Mohave continue to have strong opinions and feelings about the guilt or innocence of witches slain several decades ago. Thus, Hama: Utce: gloated over the slaying of one alleged witch (Case 101), but angrily condemned the murder of another, who, according to some, was a relative of hers, and whom she believed to have been innocent (Case 100). The point to be stressed here is that both of these slayings occurred so long ago that she probably had no personal memories of either of these men.

The attitude of shamans toward the slaying of witches deserves special mention. It was repeatedly stated that all shamans—and not only witches—are reluctant to live very long (Kroeber, 1925 a; Devereux, 1937 c; McNichols, 1944). Thus, when Hivsu: Tupo:ma discussed the obsolescence of witchcraft he said: "In times of old I would

---

[64] Compare, above, the custom of bewitching the relative of someone whom one hates, so as to grieve the hated person.

[65] It is probable that Hama: Utce: emphasized the decline of witchcraft because she tried to reassure herself that her fear that Kwathany Hi:wa might bewitch her entire family was unwarranted.

not have lived this long (56 years). They would have killed me long before this. Shamans seldom lived to a ripe old age. But I would have become a shaman all the same. I could not have helped it." [66] The most striking thing about this statement was the markedly wistful manner in which Hivsu: Tupo :ma spoke of the good old days when he would have been killed in a manner befitting a shaman. This tallies with the fact, known even to laymen, that shamans are far from happy over the disappearance of witch slayings. Thus, as stated before, according to Tcatc: "A witch who dies a natural death cries on his deathbed, saddened by the knowledge that he is about to lose his hold over his retinue of beloved ghosts." It is also significant that at the trial of Anyay Ha :m's murderers several shamans testified in court in favor of the defendants (Case 104).

In view of this general attitude, it is not at all surprising that, soon after confessing to me in strict confidence that he had bewitched several people, Hivsu: Tupo :ma managed to kill himself in a typical "accidentally on purpose" way. He became intoxicated, slept off his drunkenness outdoors, in the middle of the winter, and contracted a fatal case of pneumonia (Devereux, 1948 i).

Further light is shed upon the attitude of witches toward witch killings by the fact that several known witch killers were, themselves, shamans and witches, who, had they lived earlier, would themselves have been killed in due time. It is also necessary to recall in this context that witch killers run the risk of becoming psychotic, as a result of their murderous activities (pt. 2, pp. 45–46).

In brief, the entire witchcraft and witch-killing pattern is characterized by countless ambivalences, ambiguities, and paradoxes, both on the psychological and on the cultural level. It is therefore almost mandatory to conclude that both witchcraft and the killing of witches are largely expressions of individual psychopathology reinforced and canalized by what is usually called "social pathology." (See below.)

CASE MATERIAL

The case material about to be presented is uniform neither in scope nor in quality. Some cases shed light chiefly on Mohave custom or on the psychology of witch killers, while others enable us to get at least a glimpse of the purely subjective factors which cause the witch to seek death. In view of the fact that our chief topic is the vicarious *suicide* of the witches, rather than the formal *killing* of witches, the cases are arranged in a sequence of increasing insight into the subjective motivation of the witch who courts death. The first case (Case 95) makes no mention of any wish to die right away. The second (Case 96), recorded and published by Kroeber (1925 a),

---

[66] This statement was made before he confessed to me in private that he, too, had bewitched some of his relatives (Devereux, 1948 i).

provides excellent insight into the psychology of the witch killers; as for the witch, he is asleep and plays a purely passive role. The next to last case (Case 105)[67] casts a vivid light on the manner in which a sorceress manipulated herself into a position where her victim's son simply had to kill her. Indeed, from the moment when Haq'au raped Sahaykwisa: everything this lesbian-turned-nymphomaniac did to gratify her neurotic needs and to escape her difficulties only served to hasten her doom. Such perfect convergences between neurotically idiosyncratic psychological processes and culturally mandatory behavioral sequences, both leading to, and culminating in, the same "solution," are far from rare in primitive society [68] and, presumably, also in our culture, though in the latter case our automatic scotomization of cultural factors familiar to us tends to create the impression that the decisive forces are the purely psychological ones.

The last case in this series (Case 106) is, strictly speaking, not a vicarious but an actual suicide. It was, however, decided to include it in the present series, instead of in the series of cases illustrating types of actual suicide (pt. 7, pp. 465–484)[69] because it demonstrates that accusations of witchcraft can enrage a shaman to the point of becoming suicidal.[70]

CASE 95 (Bourke, 1889; information he obtained from Merryman, a Mohave.) :

"Once a witch was paid seventeen dollars by a Mohave to kill another Indian whom he disliked. She watched and followed in the trail of the victim, stepping carefully in his foot-prints. 'Tis well,' she said, 'say nothing: he dies in four days: say nothing. I don't want to be killed just yet. I've killed only two, and when I die, I want to rule a bigger band than that.'

"But the spirit doctors consulted the spirits and knew that the victim had been murdered.

" 'We can't tell who killed him,' they said to the relatives, 'but watch near the spot where his body was burned. The poison which the witch put in his body must come out from the ashes in four days, and if the witch don't be on hand to gather it up, it will do her great harm.' So they watched, and, sure enough, they saw tracks and they caught the witch, and they killed her with rocks and then burnt her, and I was a very small boy at the time and saw them do it over there on that spit of land next the sand-bar."

Comment

The hiring of a witch to kill an enemy is mentioned also in mythology (pt. 3, pp. 91–106, and Devereux, 1948 h). However, according to my informants, the witch does not recruit the ghosts of those she or he killed for pay for

---

[67] Originally published as an instance of Mohave female homosexuality (Devereux, 1937 b).

[68] Compare, to take an example at random, the incest and suicide of a Mnong Gar named Tieng, which Condominas (1957) only analyzed from the cultural and "behavioral sequence" point of view.

[69] It is, however, also briefly summarized in part 7, page 478, as Supplementary Case C.

[70] The possibility that this shaman may have been drowned by others and that the killing was successfully misrepresented to the tribe as a suicide is wholly incompatible with the Mohave tendency to gossip.

his or her own band of retainers, since that band is supposedly composed only of the souls of those whom the witch liked. Be that as it may, the wording of the preceding case is not specific enough to permit one to decide whether or not the witch included this particular victim of hers into her ghostly retinue. The method used by this witch for slaying her victim was not mentioned either by my own informants, or by the informants of other contemporary anthropologists. The statement that the witch must be on hand to collect the "poison" she had put into her victim superficially contradicts both Bourke's own statement that the heart turns into an owl and the data provided by my informants. However, if we bear in mind that the power of a witch or of some other supernatural slayer kills the victim by "going to his heart," it is probable that Bourke's informant, Merryman, had in mind the poison-laden heart of the victim,[71] and not simply the "poisonous"(?) power which the bewitcher put into the victim's heart. The watch for the witch near the funeral pyre clearly confirms the data provided by Tcatc and E. S. concerning the disposal of the evidence. Merryman's typically Mohave concluding reference to the burning of the witch's *corpse* explains why Stratton (1857) mistakenly assumed that witches were killed by burning them alive. This assumption is also supported by Hama: Utce:'s gloating references to the final cremation of the witch Kwitcia:r (Case 101). Otherwise stated, Stratton must have reached the conclusion that witches were burned *alive* because his informant, Olive Oatman, the captive white girl, had (perhaps) told him of a witch slaying and had, *in the Mohave manner*, concluded her account of the slaying with a mention of the cremation of the (*slain*) witch.

CASE 96 (Kroeber, 1925 a. Name of informant not recorded):

"When I was young, I was once with a friend at a shaman's house. My friend proposed that we kill him. I took my bow and four arrows and said to the shaman: 'I am going to shoot doves.' He assented. When I returned, the shaman seemed to be asleep under the shade before his house. My friend was indoors, and said: 'He is sleeping.' I took a (steel) ax and swung at the shaman's head. I struck him in the cheek. As he sat up, no blood came from the wound. Then suddenly a torrent gushed out. My companion became frightened, ran off, returned, struck at the shaman's head, but hit only his legs, and ran off, hardly able to drag his own. Two women had been sitting near, lousing each other, and at first had not seen what we did. Then they began to cry and wail. I crossed the river, and found some men gambling, and sat with them. In the afternoon I said: 'I have killed so-and-so.' They thought I was boasting. 'Yes, do it,' they said. 'That will be good. Too many people are dying.' 'I have done it already,' I answered. Soon the dead man's relatives came, and it seemed that we should fight with sticks. But on the next day the shaman's son announced that he would not fight, and nothing further happened." [72]

Comment

The preceding account sheds more light on the psychology of the witch killer than on the vicarious suicide of shamans. The idea of killing the shaman arises in an almost casual manner. The impulse does not seem to be either well motivated or particularly strong, since the prospective murderer calmly goes off to hunt doves for a while. The same casualness is reflected also by the fact that the narrator does not even trouble to mention at first that he believed this shaman to be a witch. Only the reactions of the people, who are told that the sha-

---

[71] See above and also Kroeber, 1925 a, and Devereux, 1937 c.
[72] Certain passages of Kroeber's "Earth Tongue, a Mohave" seem to be a fictionalized version of this killing (Kroeber, 1925 b).

man was killed, indicate that the victim had been suspected of witchcraft, possibly even by his own son, since the latter announced that he decided not to fight his father's slayers. The almost incredible casualness of the killers' impulse and plotting vividly illustrates Kroeber's (1951) analysis of the Mohave tendency to behave in an aimlessly impulsive manner—seemingly motivated by boredom—even in situations of some magnitude which would seem to call for careful planning and systematically goal-directed behavior.

Psychologically as well as culturally the most interesting part of this narrative is, however, the incredibly clumsy and panicky manner in which this sleeping shaman was slain. A determined man, fully convinced that his deed was righteous, could have killed the sleeping witch with a single blow of his steel ax. The fact that it took two men to butcher the witch piecemeal suggests, at the lowest estimate, that they were quite ambivalent about slaying a fellow Mohave. It is, moreover, extremely probable that the clumsiness was also due to the fact that the slayers were almost paralyzed with fright, presumably because the slaying of witches is thought of as an inherently dangerous act, as is shown by the belief that witch killers may become psychotic (pt. 2, pp. 45–46). The whole incident forcibly reminds one of the fact that, according to the Malay national epic "Hikayat Hang Tuah" (Anonymous n.d.), armed warriors often scatter in panic—some men even defecating from fright—when attacked by a single amok runner.[73] This explains why the Mohave are convinced that witch killers usually are not only noted braves but also shamans and witches.[74]

CASE 97 (Informants: Hivsu: Tupo:ma and Hama: Utce:):

Hi:wa Maa:ma, of Fort Mohave, whose vital statistics are no longer remembered, had the power to cause as well as to cure the types of convulsive seizures ("fits") which are believed to result from excessive masturbation (pt. 2, pp. 71–81).

Hi:wa Maa:ma bewitched several women between the ages of 35 and 40, as well as some men and children, causing them to develop convulsive seizures. My informants specified that this witch "gave his victims fits" without having to compel them, by means of witchcraft, to engage in masturbation.

"Eventually he was killed. We do not know who did it, or how it happened. They just sent word that he had been killed."

Comment

The fact that Hi:wa Maa:ma's victims also included men and children makes it quite certain that his evil powers did not cause the type of sexual insanity which results from witchcraft of a certain type (pt. 2, pp. 87–89). Hence, from the Mohave point of view, his acts of witchcraft had no explicit and specific sexual component; he sent these "fits" not because he was sexually interested in his victims, but because he could only cause an illness which he was also qualified to cure. Needless to say, his choice of this particular specialty must have had

---

[73] Some of the fantastic-seeming feats ascribed to "battle mad" warriors in medieval stories become quite credible if one assumes—as one is entitled to do—that their battle madness paralyzed their opponents with fright. Compare in this context the seemingly inexplicable flight of Hector, when attacked by a thoroughly aroused Achilles ("Iliad") or the puzzling fact that one of Harald Hardraade's berserkers was able to hold Stamford bridge against whole units of the army of Harold of England.

[74] The entire plot of the "Hikayat Hang Tuah" (Anonymous n.d.) shows that slaying an amok runner is considered more heroic than defeating a large body of pirates or warriors.

at its root a rather intense preoccupation with—and conflict over—normal sexuality.[75]

The most puzzling feature of this case history is, however, the fact that informants knew nothing about the circumstances under which Hi:wa Maa:ma was killed. The nescience was certainly genuine, since the Mohave would not have suppressed information in speaking with me; they would have simply asked me to keep certain data confidential.

CASE 98 (Informants: Hivsu: Tupo:ma and Hama: Utce:) :

Tcemupa:và, of the Tcatc gens, a 40-year-old fullblood Mohave shaman, specialized in the treatment of rheumatism and aching joints. Although he had begun to practice around 1880, when he was about 20 years old, it was not until some 20 years later (1900?) that people began to say that he was a witch. Roughly a year after these rumors had begun to circulate, Tcemupa:và bewitched Nyortc, of the Nyoltc gens, a 25-year-old fullblood Mohave married woman, who had been quarreling with Tcemupa:và's relatives. Since the witch did not wish to live any longer, he made no attempt to "seal her lips." Consequently, as soon as the ailing Nyortc began to relate her dreams, it became obvious that she had been bewitched by Tcemupa:và. This did not surprise Nyortc's relatives who had suspected Tcemupa:và all along and had therefore questioned the ailing woman rather carefully. However, for the time being, they made no overt move against the witch, and merely "kept the matter in mind."

Eventually Nyortc—who seems to have been Tcemupa:và's only known victim—died and was immediately cremated. One night after the cremation, Nyortc's two brothers of the Nyoltc gens, Atceyer Thume:, a 50-year-old man and Ampot Tcàvudho:, a 45-year-old shaman, both of whom were fullblood Mohave Indians, decided to kill Tcemupa:và, even though he had never claimed to have bewitched Nyortc.

Since these brothers were both kwanàmi:hye (braves) and since, moreover, Ampot Tcàvudho: was also a "good" shaman who cured arrow wounds and bewitched no one, the two brothers went quite openly to Tcemupa:và's winter house at Parker, Ariz., where they found the witch asleep in the midst of his relatives, none of whom tried to interfere with the killers. According to one version, Atceyer Thume: held Tcemupa:và down, while Ampot Tcàvudho: slashed open his throat and belly. According to another and more reliable account, they beat him to death with sticks. Not even the victim's own wife and children tried to save him, nor did they subsequently attempt to take revenge on the killers. "The killing took place in accordance with Indian law, and was therefore kept secret from the whites. For this reason, no official action was ever taken against the killers."

Comment

The cross-questioning of Nyortc by her relatives may have suggested to her the idea that she may have been bewitched by Tcemupa:và. It is also noteworthy that, even though this woman's brothers were famous braves, they did not try to force Tcemupa:và to cure his victim, and made no move against him

---

[75] Compare the personal experiences which caused Ahma Huma:re to become an obstetrical specialist (Devereux, 1948 e). It is, moreover, a psychoanalytic truism that the choice of an occupation is determined not only by objective considerations, but also by certain unconscious factors.

until after their sister had died. Hence, it is perhaps permissible to suspect that this was the first time the two brothers came face to face with witchcraft and that it took them some time to decide to become witch-killers. Once they decided to function as public executioners, they must have found it easy to slay O:otc, who is supposed to have killed some of their nephews and nieces and to have harmed the tribe as a whole (Case 99). Be that as it may, the two brothers managed to acquire the reputation of having been, in their time, the tribe's chief protectors against witches, and were praised for it as late as 1938, i.e., several decades after their death.

CASE 99 (Informants: Hivsu: Tupo:ma and Hama: Utce:) :

O:otc, of the O:otc gens, a 40-year-old fullblood Mohave woman, specialized in the cure of "colds," and especially of "epidemic colds." In addition, she was also a noted eye specialist. Although O:otc had never married, she was not a virgin, and appears to have led a fairly normal and active sex life. She became a practicing shaman at the age of 30, and was first accused of witchcraft at the age of 40, during an epidemic of severe colds which occurred approximately in the year 1902. "O:otc liked to kill adults. In addition, she also wanted to earn some money, by treating the people whom she had bewitched." This epidemic killed so many people, including even her own brother's two daughters, that the Mohave were beginning to get restless. Finally two fullblood Mohave Indian brothers of the Nyoltc gens, who had also lost several nephews and nieces during the epidemic, decided to kill her. These noted braves (kwanámi:hye), witch killers and "real persons" (ipa: taha:ná) were the 50-year-old Atceyer Thume: and the 45-year-old Ampot Tcávudho: (dust wind), who was also a "good shaman" specializing in the cure of arrow wounds.[76] These brothers belonged to the Nyoltc gens.[77]

The two braves and witch killers made no attempt to keep their plan a secret. Hence, when, one afternoon, they set out for O:otc's house, which stood on the sandy stretch of ground now occupied by the Parker, Ariz., church, a well-meaning person hurried ahead, to warn O:otc that two braves were coming to kill her. O:otc, who was parching corn at that time, took the news quite casually, however, and merely said: "Let them come!" "She herself was just like a kwanámi:hye—very brave, because she had this (shamanistic?) power." She kept on parching her corn until the two killers arrived and beat her to death with sticks. This happened in the presence of O:otc's relatives, who, apparently, did not try to defend her. These two braves also killed another witch (Case 98).

Comment

The preceding case history illustrates the similarity between witch and witch killer in two ways. One of the two witch killers was himself a shaman, and O:otc's stoical attitude in the face of certain death caused the informants to compare her to a brave. It is also noteworthy that, in this particular instance, the informants did not specify that the witch's relatives failed to defend her

---

[76] The name of this man was first mistakenly recorded as Apot Tcimmátha: and one informant said that he was the father of my old informant Tcatc. This is absolutely impossible, chiefly because at a time when Ampot Tcávudho: was said to have been 45 years old, Tcatc herself must have already been a middle-aged woman.

[77] This gentile affiliation was questioned later on by Pulyi:k, who added that he could not recall their gentile affiliation. Since the name of their sister (Case 98) was Nyortc, it is necessary to assume that Pulyi:k was mistaken in saying they were not of the Nyoltc gens. The gens of these men could not have been anything but Nyoltc, if their sister's name was Nyortc, unless all informants forgot to specify that Nyortc was not a full, but only a half, sister of these men, which seems unlikely.

because they too believed in her guilt. This omission, when taken in conjunction with the fact that someone actually tried to warn O :otc, suggests that only the great prestige of the witch killers persuaded O :otc's relatives that she was guilty— or else caused them to pretend that they too believed her to be guilty, in order not to have to fight two famous braves and witch killers. The fact that O :otc was never married, as well as her extraordinary stoical courage, suggest that this shamaness was a relatively masculine type of personality.

CASE 100 (Informants: Hivsu : Tupo :ma and Hama : Utce :) :

Ah'a Kupa :m (cottonwood fallen) of the Tcatc gens, a 45-year-old fullblood Mohave shaman, began to treat upper respiratory tract infections (colds, pneumonia, and influenza), as well as a certain disease of children which resembles the tåvåknyi :k ailment (Devereux, 1947 a ; and pt. 7, pp. 340–348, at the age of 20. He was, at first, a "good shaman," but, around 1890, he decided to increase his income by treating people whom he, himself, had bewitched. He therefore started an epidemic of a kind which he—and only he—could cure. When people began to sicken and to die, Ah'a Kupa :m's own relatives were the first to accuse him of witchcraft, because the epidemic had started at his camp. Despite the curative efforts of several shamans, some 15 children died in the epidemic, because Ah'a Kupa :m's power (suma :tc) was so different from that of the would-be healers that they did not know how to counteract it.

The bereaved families finally made common cause, four men banding together to kill the witch. These men were:

(1) Tcuva :r(h), of the Syuly gens, a 35-year-old fullblood Mohave, who had lost a brother and a sister in the epidemic.

(2) Tenyamoek, of the O :otc gens, a 40-year-old fullblood Mohave, who had lost a brother and a sister.

(3) Kåva :r(h)e, of the Mah gens, a 25-year-old fullblood Mohave, who had lost his mother.

(4) Amo: Me (sheep hoof) of the O :otc gens, a 30-year-old fullblood Mohave, who had lost an uncle.[78]

Ah'a Kupa :m did not confess his guilt in so many words. However, the nature of the epidemic which he had caused was, in itself, revealing enough to amount to a confession. Hence, one afternoon, the four bereaved men went to his house at Parker, Ariz., and, in the presence of his indifferent relatives, who did nothing to protect him, beat him to death. This happened about 45 years ago (1890). "Ah'a Kupa :m was the last (?) witch killed by the Mohave." (But cf. Case 104, etc.)

Comment

Although the epidemic supposedly affected mostly children, it is noteworthy that the killers were men who had lost adult, or presumably adult, relatives in the epidemic. This suggests that child mortality was so great at that time, that the loss of a child was less traumatic than the death of an adult relative. This inference is supported by the fact that in all "clustered" suicides (pt. 7, pp. 465–478) the person who died first was an adult. The only indirect exception to this rule is the belief that if a witch starts a pediatric epidemic which also carries away some child he loves, he will become (vicariously) suicidal. In all other cases, the triggering, or precedent-setting, death is that of an adult ; neither parents nor relatives seem to become suicidal when a baby dies at birth, or of tåvåknyi :k, or if one or both twins die in infancy.

---

[78] The fact that the killers were men who had lost *adult* relatives in this epidemic which supposedly affected primarily *children,* will be discussed further below.

Although Ah'a Kupa:m's story is a rather commonplace one, the attitudes and opinions expressed in connection with his death shed an interesting side-light upon the problem of witch killing.

When the informant had completed his story, the highly educated Hama: Utce:, who may or may not have been related to Ah'a Kupa:m,[79] exclaimed rather sarcastically: "And *that* brought all the dead back to life! Ah'a Kupa:m was a pretty good man!" This statement is worthy of detailed scrutiny. It is certainly not simply an expression of the interpreter's very real humaneness, which also found an expression in her comments on the death of the unjustly accused Táma:ráhue (Case 106) since, in another instance, she expressed satisfaction over the death of a witch (Case 101). Nor did her remark seem motivated by the fact that she may have been related to this witch, partly because Ah'a Kupa:m was killed before the interpreter was born, and partly because this witch's own kin were, indirectly at least, responsible for his death. Finally, her remark does not simply reflect an educated person's contempt for those who believe in witchcraft, since Hama: Utce: was never quite certain of just where she stood on the subject of witchcraft. In other words, her remark cannot be viewed as an assertion of Ah'a Kupa:m's innocence. If, however, it is viewed as a form of gloating over the death of Ah'a Kupa:m's victims, some of whom were related to him, the interpreter's comment can be viewed as an expression of her identification with the aggressor. This interpretation is the most probable one, since, at that time, Hama: Utce: harbored conscious death wishes toward her aunt, and also professed not to care whether she, herself, lived or died (Case 115).

Equally noteworthy was Hivsu: Tupo:ma's concluding remark: "Ah'a Kupa:m was the last witch to be killed among the Mohave." The manner in which this statement was made, when taken in conjunction with the fact that several decades had elapsed since Ah'a Kupa:m's murder without a single further witch killing, suggested that, in this informant's opinion, the custom of killing witches had become entirely obsolete. At the same time, the informant was not too sure of this, since, when he confessed to me that he, too, had bewitched some people, he begged me not to mention this to anyone, lest he be assaulted as a witch. Oddly enough, the informant's *drunken* fears turned out to be more realistic than his *sober* predictions, since, less than 2 years after this conversation, a Mohave couple killed a "witch" who was threatening them (Case 104). The fact that this witch-killing couple was rather young and relatively "progressive" shows how tenaciously certain basic attitudes and behavior patterns resist acculturation (Hallowell, 1955 [1945]; Thompson, 1948; Devereux, 1951 a; A. F. C. Wallace, 1951). Hence, it is unwise to call a custom obsolete until it is entirely forgotten and until even the basic attitudes related to it have been superseded by different ones.

CASE 101 (Informants: Hivsu: Tupo:ma and Hama: Utce:):

Kwitcia:r, of the Mah gens, a 45-year-old fullblood Mohave, lived in a house located on the Arizona bank of the Colorado River, just opposite Needles, Calif. He specialized in the treatment of bewitched people and of respiratory diseases (colds, influenza, pneumonia, etc.). This "very powerful" shaman, "who seemed to know everything," was killed around 1893.

Kwitcia:r became a practicing shaman at the age of 30 and was soon afterward accused of being also a witch, though informants could not agree as to whether Kwitcia:r himself ever admitted being a witch. It is known, however, that he bewitched Ma:tas, of the Hualy gens, a fullblood Mohave male, 25

---

[79] Opinions differ on this point. The relationship was affirmed in 1936 and denied at a later date.

years of age, and not related to him in any way, partly because he was angry
with Ma:tas for having failed to return an ax, a shovel, and a shotgun which
he had borrowed, and partly because Kwitcia:r "liked people." "He liked his
relatives so much that he killed them all by means of witchcraft." Since
Kwitcia:r specialized in the cure of respiratory disorders, he bewitched Ma:tas
by "taking away his breath." His victim gasped, "had a short breath" and,
being on the verge of death, begged the witch to cure him. Although Kwitcia:r
professed to know nothing about this illness, he finally agreed to treat Ma:tas.
However, Ma:tas soon died "still gasping for breath," because Kwitcia:r
"either could not or would not cure him." Although Kwitcia:r was blamed
for Ma:tas' death, the victim's relatives did not attack him and he was
eventually killed by witchcraft, for a wholly different reason, and therefore his
bewitcher was not punished the way some shaman killers are—supposedly—
punished by the indignant relatives of the slain witch.

Kua:lyec, of the Nyoltc gens, a fullblood Mohave shaman about 50 years
of age, could ("like Ahma Huma:re") cure various diseases caused by eating
certain (alien?) foods. This shaman was not related to Kwitcia:r, whom he
disliked for some unspecified reason. He therefore "put some power" into the
horsemeat Kwitcia:r was eating and "poisoned" him. Though Kwitcia:r, who
was a shaman, must have known who had bewitched him, no attempt was made
to induce Kua:lyec to treat his victim, who died that very night, at midnight.

No one tried to punish Kua:lyec for having bewitched Kwitcia:r, presumably
because "Kwitcia:r's relatives were convinced that he had been a witch and
therefore felt that he deserved to die of witchcraft." The Mohave were so convinced of Kwitcia:r's guilt that Hama:Utce:—who was not even born yet
when Kwitcia:r died—concluded her translation of Hivsu:Tupo:ma's account
with the gloating remark: "They cremated Kwitcia:r the next day, and then this
witch was nothing but charcoal and ashes." In order to grasp the extraordinary hostility of this remark, it is necessary to stress that Hama:Utce: did more
than just gloat over the fact that this man's *body* was now simply a small pile
of ashes. Had she meant nothing more than that, she would have specified in
some way that she was speaking of the man's *corpse*, as distinct from his "total
personality" (souls). In failing to differentiate between the two—which the
Mohave nearly always do when discussing death and cremation—she not only
expressed pleasure over the destruction of Kwitcia:r's *corpse*; she also more or
less "jumped the gun," by implying that *all* of Kwitcia:r had become charcoal and
ashes the next day, even though the soul of a dead person is reincarnated four
times before it turns into charcoal and ashes (Devereux, 1937 a). In other
words, in seeming to gloat over the destruction of Kwitcia:r's body, Hama:
Utce: also prematurely "annihilated" his soul, the way a witch annihilates the
owl heart of his victim.

Comment

Although, strictly speaking, Kwitcia:r did not commit vicarious suicide, the
Mohave felt that he may not have wanted to be cured, since, even though he
supposedly knew who had bewitched him, he made no attempt to persuade
Kua:lyec to treat him.[80] It is also interesting to note that, just as braves
who kill a recognized witch are not molested by the victim's relatives, so
Kua:lyec, who killed the witch Kwitcia:r by witchcraft, was not punished by
his victim's relatives. As regards Hama:Utce:'s gloating over the death of
Kwitcia:r, it is almost inexplicable, since she herself was not even born until
after Kwitcia:r's death. Moreover this witch does not seem to have killed any

---

[80] Since Kwitcia:r died shortly after eating horse meat, possibly from a horse slaughtered
several days before, he may have died of some kind of acute food poisoning.

of Hama: Utce:'s relatives. By contrast, in discussing the slaying of Ah'a Kupa:m, the same Hama: Utce: vehemently condemned the killers and asserted, without giving reasons, that Ah'a Kupa:m had not been a witch. (Case 100.) There is an obvious contrast between these two reactions, but its causes could not be definitely ascertained. One reason seems to be that when she first interpreted for me the case of Ah'a Kupa:m, she was under the impression that this witch was somehow related to her. Whether or not this (mistaken?) belief suffices to account for the extreme contrast between her two reactions is a moot question.

CASE 102 (Informants: Hivsu: Tupo:ma and Hama: Utce:):

Kamaye:hue, of the Nyoltc gens, a 35-year-old fullblood Mohave, specialized in the cure of slow witchcraft—thatnyume:(u)k—(Devereux, 1937 c) and became a practicing shaman at the age of 15. About 3 years before he was killed, people began to say that he had bewitched four or five people he was known to have liked, because he was supposed to be one of those witches who kill only people they are fond of.

His slaying occurred in connection with the death of Nyoltc, of the Nyoltc gens, a 30-year-old fullblood married Mohave woman. Kamaye:hue is said to have bewitched Nyoltc partly because he was fond of her and partly because he hated her relatives. In other words, the witch harmed those he hated by killing one of their relatives, thus causing them grief and distress. Since Nyoltc's relatives suspected that she had been bewitched by Kamaye:hue, they told her: "We will bring Kamaye:hue here, to cure you." The sick woman was, however, frightened and protested vigorously: "No, don't bring him here! If you do, I shall die!" Her relatives were, however, determined to force the witch to cure his victim and therefore said: "We will bring him here to cure you, and then we shall see what is to be done next. If you die, he too shall die!" Then they went to Kamaye:hue's house and tried to persuade him to treat Nyoltc but, even though they frankly told him that they suspected him of having bewitched her, Kamaye:hue absolutely refused to treat her. In fact, according to some informants, he even confessed to Nyoltc's relatives that he had bewitched her. Soon after this fruitless discussion Nyoltc's condition began to deteriorate quite rapidly. When, shortly afterwards, Nyoltc died, two of her maternal uncles, Hukthar Humthuvi:ny, of the Mu:th gens, a 40-year-old fullblood Mohave, and his half brother, Tceha:tce, of the Mah gens, a 35-year-old fullblood Mohave shaman specializing in the cure of spider bites, decided to kill the witch. One afternoon they went to Kamaye:hue's house, which was located opposite Avi: Vata:y (Riverside Mountains) and, in the presence of Kamaye:hue's relatives, beat him to death with sticks. The witch's relatives, believing him to be guilty, did nothing to protect him and did not even try to take revenge on the killers. In fact, "the matter was hushed up so effectively that Mr. Clark, who succeeded Colonel Hugh as superintendent of the Mohave Reservation, never even heard of this murder."

Comment

Several informants said that the victim, Nyoltc, was Kamaye:hue's sister's daughter, while informant Pulyi:k insisted that she was not related to him in any way. This denial is entirely credible for several reasons:

(1) Had Kamaye:hue been Nyoltc's maternal uncle, his killers, who were also the victim's maternal uncles, would have had to be Kamaye:hue's brothers or at least half-brothers, which would have made the murder a particularly horrible affair. Since not even those informants who said that Kamaye:hue was Nyoltc's maternal uncle said anything about Kamaye:hue's murderers

being his own brothers or half-brothers, it is likely that Nyolic was not Ka-maye :hue's niece.

(2) Kamaye :hue is said to have been a member of the Nyoltc gens, while Nyoltc's "other" maternal uncles were said to have belonged to the Mu :th and to the Mah gens respectively. This could have happened only if the mother of these men had had three sons by three different men, which, given the instability of Mohave marriages, is not impossible, but also not very probable. The only alternative explanation would be that the informants were mistaken in saying that Kamaye :hue was of the Nyoltc gens—a hypothesis which is not altogether unlikely, for the following reasons : If Kamaye :hue was a full brother of Nyoltc's mother, then the mother too must have been Nyoltc, and must therefore have married a man of her own gens, in order to have a daughter also named Nyoltc. This is not impossible, but somewhat improbable, since marriages within the gens were still extremely rare during the period under consideration.

In brief, it is simpler to assume that Pulyi :k was right in saying that Ka-maye :hue simply belonged to the same gens as his victim, but was not directly related to her.

Kamaye :hue's suicidalness is not interpretable in subjective (psychological) terms, since we have no strictly personal data which would explain why he chose to boast of being a witch at this particular time. The only clue is provided by the fact that Kamaye :hue must have been an unusually disturbed person, very eager for tribal limelight, to have become a practicing shaman while still in his middle teens. Moreover, the very fact that he specialized in the cure of witchcraft automatically implied that he could also bewitch people, since one can only cure those diseases which one is also able to cause. Hence, by deciding, consciously or unconsciously, to specialize in this type of shamanism, he prac-tically made certain from the start that he would sooner or later be accused of witchcraft and killed.

CASE 103 (Informants: Hivsu: Tupo :ma and Tcatc) :

Tcávákong, of the O :otc gens, a 40-year-old fullblood Mohave, had acquired in 1900, at the age of 35, the power to cure dysentery. Tcávákong was, moreover, an epileptic, who during one of his atcoo :r hanyienk seizures (pt. 2, pp. 72–76) had fallen into the fire and had burned his hand so badly that it was useless ever after. "He did not seem to have any feelings (sensitivity) when he burned himself." He concealed his crippled hand in a tobacco bag attached to a spoon which hung from a cord tied around his neck. For some reason the informants specified that Tcávákong was an epileptic but not an alcoholic.[81]

Tcávákong was so poor that he had to earn his living chiefly by singing and dancing for tourists at the Harvey House in Needles.[82]

In 1905 an epidemic killed a number of children and people began to suspect Tcávákong of having caused it. Tcávákong himself confirmed these suspicions, by saying that he had started the epidemic because he needed the money which he would earn by treating the ailing children. "He was that mean !"

Hikoc Hmaykuta :vá, of the Nyoltc gens, a 40-year-old fullblood Mohave em-ployed in the Santa Fe Railroad roundhouse, had lost a daughter and, according

---

[81] This specification is rather interesting, since even people who are not epileptics can have convulsive seizures while in a state of severe intoxication. Whether or not the Mohave realize that severe intoxication can cause seizures is unfortunately not known.

[82] McNichols (1944) states that a crippled Mohave, named Dancing Dick, used to dance at the Harvey House. This man was said to have been crippled when—believing him to be dead—people tried to cremate him prematurely, which suggests that he may have been an epileptic. It is therefore likely that Tcávákong and Dancing Dick are one and the same person.

to one informant, also a son in this epidemic and therefore felt very bitter toward Tcàvàkong, who openly claimed to have caused the epidemic. Hence, the bereaved Hikoc Hmaykuta:và and certain other railroad workers, who, according to Pulyi:k at least, were Kaveltcadhom Indians, and who had also lost children in this epidemic, decided to kill the witch. They waylaid him one evening near the roundhouse, which Tcàvàkong had to pass on his way home, and asked him point blank whether he was actually responsible for the epidemic. When Tcàvàkong once more admitted having caused it, Hikoc Hmaykuta:và wounded him mortally by hitting him over the head with a piece of metal. The attackers then departed, leaving Tcàvàkong lying in a pool of blood. The witch died the same night and his corpse was discovered next morning by some Mohave beadwork sellers on their way to the station. His relatives took possession of his corpse and cremated it, but did nothing to avenge his death "because they could not find the murderers." (Presumably the identity of the killers did not become known until some time later.)

Comment

Tcàvàkong was one of the few witches actually known to have boasted of having caused an epidemic. It is not hard to see why a wretchedly poor and crippled epileptic, who had little enough to live for and enjoyed almost no prestige, should have persuaded himself that he had caused an epidemic and should have sought notoriety by advertising this fact, in order to become—at least temporarily—an important personage. His steadfastness in telling his assailants that he had started the epidemic—even though he must have known that in so doing he sealed his own fate—can likewise be understood in simple human terms. Tcàvàkong's final defiance was apparently the one great moment in the life of a crippled, epileptic, and neglected pauper, who had to clown day after day for the despised whites in order to eke out a meager living. It was an "operatic" gesture, but an understandable one, especially on the part of an epileptic, whose neurological disability is always aggravated by a great deal of impulsive and reactive hostility.

CASE 104 (Informants: Tcatc and E. S. also O:otc herself.) :

The following case history is presented here in an abridged form, the entire occurrence, together with a detailed account of an interview with O:otc, having been published elsewhere (Devereux, 1948 f).

Anyay Ha:m—whose various other names, gentile affiliation, and vital statistics are given in part 4 (pp. 184–186)—was a witch who cured the hikwi:r disease (pt. 4, pp. 117–128), body sores, colds and pneumonia and the moua:v hahnok illness (pt. 4, pp. 184–186). He was, moreover, a well-known witch, who made no secret of his activities. Thus, he openly admitted that, for some unknown reason, he had bewitched his own son, R. E. L., whose Indian name could not be recalled. He also boasted both to people in general and to Huau Husek', the maternal uncle of his bewitched son's widow, that he had bewitched the parents of Huau Husek' some 18 or 20 years earlier, and then threatened to bewitch also Huau Husek' and his wife O:otc. Moreover, adding insult to injury, Anyay Ha:m had an affair with O:otc, which became known, either because, according to one report, Anyay Ha:m and O:otc were caught in the act by Huau Husek's sister Mu:th Nyemsuthkha:v (=to pick out), who reported the matter to Huau Husek' (Case 42 and 43), or, according to another account, because Anyay Ha:m himself openly boasted of the affair to Mu:th Nyemsutkha:v, or, more probably, because, after being caught in the act, Anyay Ha:m chose to boast of his conquest, as lewd men are prone to do (Devereux, 1950 a).

No one knew why Anyay Ha:m chose to bewitch his 23-year-old married son. Tcatc simply said: "If a shaman's close relatives are good to him, he may bewitch them—he will just take them (to the place where he keeps his ghostly victims)." Likewise, no one knows why he had bewitched Huau Husek's parents, or why he threatened to bewitch Huau Husek' and his wife, although (or is it perhaps because?) he had an affair with the latter.

It is said that Huau Husek' and O:otc finally waylaid Anyay Ha:m, killed him with an ax and left his corpse in a ditch, where it was eventually found. When the matter came to the attention of the reservation authorities and Huau Husek' was tried for murder, the Mohave tried to save him by sending shamans to testify that the Mohave believed in witchcraft, and that Huau Husek' and his wife were therefore genuinely afraid of being killed. Unfortunately for the accused, the court, for some unknown reason, did not allow either the shamans or anyone else to testify regarding this matter, which greatly embittered the Mohave. Huau Husek' was sentenced to a long term in prison, while O:otc went scot free. After the imprisonment of her husband O:otc professed to suffer from hi:wa itck (pt. 3, pp. 91–106) as a result of losing her husband, but this claim was not accepted by the tribe, probably because her subsequent conduct caused most Mohave to think of her as a kamalo:y and not as a person suffering from kamalo:y táminyk (pt. 2, pp. 81–83).

Comment

The present case history fits every Mohave specification regarding the vicarious suicide of witches. Anyay Ha:m bewitched his own son, who—as Tcatc said—was good to him, and whom he must therefore have loved. While it is not known why he bewitched the parents of Huau Husek', in threatening to bewitch also Huau Husek' himself, Anyay Ha:m acted in accordance with the belief that witches destroy entire families.[83] His threat to bewitch O:otc, his adulterous mistress, also fits Mohave cultural expectations. He must have liked her, since he had an affair with her,[84] but, once the affair became known, he must have been angry with her, since she apparently had no intention of leaving her husband, whom she shortly afterward allegedly helped to kill Anyay Ha:m.

It is also noteworthy that this witch—who would not have boasted and threatened unless he wished to be killed—must have experienced a great deal of longing for the ghosts of his beloved victims, which probably explains why he specialized all along in the cure of moua:v hahnok (pt. 4, pp. 184–186)—a disease which is a *delayed mourning reaction* for a close relative, whom one repeatedly sees in dream. The unconscious connection between Anyay Ha:m's acquisition of the power to cure moua:v hahnok and his own suicidal longings for his deceased relatives, whom he, himself, had bewitched, was discussed in part 4 (pp. 184–186) and therefore need not be reexamined in the present context.

Given the culturally predicated, psychologically established and objectively verifiable "contagiousness" of suicide in Mohave society, which is responsible for the clustering of suicides (pt. 7, pp. 460–478), it seems worth mentioning that,

---

[83] Although it may be nothing more than an interesting coincidence, it is worth pointing out that men especially are believed to be prone to marry repeatedly into the same family. Both the bewitching and the marrying of several members of a kin group is called in English "going through the entire family." The occurrence of incest is also believed to destroy the entire family (Devereux, 1939 a).

[84] As stressed elsewhere (Devereux, 1950 a), except for the raping of drunken women and the punitive raping of the habitual kamalo :y, the Mohave cohabit with people whom they like.

in somewhat remote and complex ways, Anyay Ha :m had personal connections with a man who had been involved in a suicide.

Tcematcem(å), of the O :otc gens, had, apparently rather early in his life, seduced the wife of a man who thereupon killed himself (Case 125).[85] Later on—perhaps because he had caused one woman to lose her husband—he married Nyoltc, the widow of Anyay Ha :m's bewitched son, thus stepping into a dead man's shoes. Later on, when O :otc—a woman of his own gens!—was doubly bereaved, by the killing of her lover Anyay Ha :m and the imprisonment of her husband Huau Husek',[86] he took *two* "dead" men's places at a single stroke, by allegedly becoming one of O :otc's lovers. Tcematcem(å)'s psychological need to become connected with the two "widows" of three men is culturally quite atypical, since the Mohave is somewhat reluctant to marry a woman who has lost one or more husbands, for fear that his wife's bad luck will affect him, too, and cause him to die like his predecessors. Hence Tcematcem(å)'s readiness to become connected sexually first with a simple widow and then with a "double widow" suggests that his repeated choices of widowed partners must represent a restitution, presumably because he had caused one woman to become a widow.[87]

This, however, is only one side of the problem. The more interesting aspect of Tcematcem(å)'s early adulterous affair which led to a suicide, his subsequent marriage to the widowed Nyoltc, and his later affair with the doubly "widowed" O'otc, is the complex, though somewhat indirect, connection between Nyoltc and O :otc.

Anyay Ha :m was Nyoltc's father-in-law and, later on, the lover of O :otc, who was his daughter-in-law's maternal aunt by marriage. If, for the sake of simplicity, we ignore in the following discussion the difference between affairs and marriages—which is quite minimal in Mohave society—Tcematcem(å) first replaced Anyay Ha :m's son and then Anyay Ha :m himself. He first married a woman of his own generation and then a woman who, though belonging, in terms of actual age, to his generation, was connected sexually with Anyay Ha :m, a man of the parent generation. Indeed, had O :otc married Anyay Ha :m, she would have not only become the stepmother of R.E.L., whose aunt-in-law (by marriage) she already was, but, in a loose way, she would also have become the stepmother-in-law of Tcematcem(å) who married R.E.L.'s widow, whose aunt by marriage she already was. Hence, it was almost as improper for Tcematcem(å) to have connections with O :otc, as it would have been for R.E.L., whom he replaced by marrying his widow. These connections may seem loose and far-

---

[85] He seems to have been related also to another suicidal man (Case 118).

[86] It is quite certain that the long imprisonment of Huau Husek' was equated by the Mohave with death. Thus, O :otc complained that, when she wished to marry a certain man shortly after her husband was imprisoned, her mother prevented the marriage by insisting that, like a proper "widow," O :otc should not remarry for at least a year (Devereux, 1948 f).

[87] The substitution of the murderer for the murdered man is a formally institutionalized practice in numerous societies (Devereux, 1942 d). What is less obvious is that even where this substitution is defined as an act of triumph, the underlying psychic mechanism is still that of a restitution, although it is disguised as an act of triumphant hostility, whose oedipal sources are not hard to see. Thus, Genghis Khan is quoted as listing among the greatest pleasures of life, holding in one's arms the wives of one's foes, whom one had just slain (Grousset, 1941). Such an utterance, coming from Genghis Khan, is of great significance. Indeed, his father Yesukai had many years before, kidnaped Hö'elum, Genghis Khan's mother, from her Merkit husband. Therefore, Genghis Khan's own Empress, Börte, was kidnaped by his deceased father's Merkit enemies so early in their married life, that no one ever knew whether Börte's oldest son, Djötchi, was fathered by Genghis Khan or by the kidnaper. Moreover, on at least two other occasions Genghis Khan—who was not noted for clemency—proved himself to be singularly tolerant of real or alleged sexual rivals, even surrendering to a poor boy a girl who had just been presented to him, and whom the boy loved.

fetched to the occidental mind, but are quite real relationships in the small Mohave tribe.

In one way, however, Tcematcem(å) did, in contracting these relationships, follow a genuine, though subsidiary Mohave marriage pattern, in that he first married Nyoltc, who, by every standard, belonged to his own generation, and then established connections with O :otc, who, by her association with Anyay Ha :m, "technically" belonged to a parent generation, since in a loosely informal way O :otc was Nyoltc's stepmother-in-law as well as her aunt by marriage. The statement that "technically" O :otc belonged, through her affair with Anyay Ha :m, to an older generation, is, moreover, perfectly in accordance with the Mohave habit of considering someone formerly married to an older person sexually repulsive, because "the smell of the old person still clings to them." (I.e., they, too, smell like old people, and are therefore sexually as ineligible as though they were, in fact, old.)

Now, there exists a minor Mohave marriage pattern which permits a man, disgusted with the flightiness and bad housekeeping of his young wife, to desert her and to marry his hardworking mother-in-law instead (Devereux, 1951 f). This, in a very roundabout way, is precisely what Tcematcem(å) did when, after being Nyoltc's husband, he allegedly became O :otc's lover.

Now, it is a well-established psychological and anthropological fact that the idea of having relations with two women connected with a given man has a certain perverse appeal for some people. To take an anthropological example first, a Naga (Fürer-Haimendorf, 1946), who manages to have an affair simultaneously with two sisters,[88] or has seduced a married woman, is entitled to sew an extra row of shells on his breechcloth, as a "badge of merit" for his "feat." The infantile source of this wish is the incomplete displacement of oedipal interests from the mother to the sister, in early childhood. This displacement is, of course, a healthy—albeit transitory—component of psycho-sexual maturation, in that it leads up to the permanent displacement of affect from the sister to a suitable unrelated love object. This displacement pattern is relatively clearly implemented in a number of tribes which practice stepdaughter marriage (Kroeber, 1940). Compared to the stepdaughter marriage pattern, the Mohave pattern of marrying one's mother-in-law is, however, regressive rather than progressive, in that it represents a shift of interest from women of one's own generation to women of the parent generation.[89]

While too much should not be made of Tcematcem(å)'s successive neurotic choices of widowed partners, the matter seemed worth mentioning at least in passing, both because he was first involved in a suicide and then came uncomfortably close to incest, which is characteristically related to witchcraft in Mohave society.

Two objections must be met before concluding the present discussion:

(1) It will be stressed that no explicit connection has been shown to exist between Anyay Ha :m and Tcematcem(å). This objection is invalid, since even though Tcematcem(å) only married Anyay Ha :m's widowed daughter-in-law, given the smallness of the tribe and the extensiveness of Mohave social relationships, such a connection is a genuine one by Mohave standards. Moreover, it is extremely unlikely that Tcematcem(å) would have gone out of his way to establish a connection with O :otc, had he been socially isolated from her murdered lover Anyay Ha :m, and had O :otc not been his wife Nyoltc's aunt by marriage.

(2) It will be pointed out that the preceding comments are overly speculative, in that affairs are equated with marriages and all kinds of kinship ties are equated with each other.

---

[88] Sororal polygyny is, of course, routine in many cultures.
[89] The psychodynamics of this shift are related to the dynamics of gerontophilia.

(a) As regards the equating of marriages and affairs, the difference between the two is quite minimal in Mohave society. As reported elsewhere (Devereux, 1950 a), Melyikha: could not get credit at the Parker stores for quite a while, because no one quite knew whether, on any given day, Hivsu: Tupo:ma was her husband and Ahma Huma:re her lover, or vice versa. Even the criterion of living under one roof is not always readily usable, since in many instances a married woman has an affair with a man who lives in the same house, as a relative or as a long-term boarder who has no other home.[90]

(b) As regards the equating of assorted kinship ties with each other, not only do classificatory kinship systems equate with each other kinship bonds which are considered quite different in our own kinship system, but it is also important to realize that the unconscious is not an anthropological expert on kinship, and therefore readily confuses not only mother and mother's sisters, but also mother, mother's sister, father's sister, mother-in-law and aunt by marriage.[91]

CASE 105 (Informant: Hivsu: Tupo:ma, Interpreter: Hama: Utce:):

Sahaykwisa: (i.e., Masahay Matkwisa: = girl's shadow or soul), a fullblood Mohave woman of the Nyoltc gens, was born around the middle of the 19th century and was killed toward the end of that century, at the approximate age of 45. She was a lesbian transvestite, formally referred to as a hwame:, which suggests that she may actually have undergone the initiation rite for female transvestites (Devereux, 1937 b). Even her personal name appears to have been of the masculine type, since Mohave men often select names referring to women—usually in a derogatory manner—just as some women select names which are a slur on men (Devereux, 1947 a).

Sahaykwisa: was apparently not a hermaphrodite, since all informants agreed that she was feminine in appearance and had large breasts. On the other hand she allegedly never menstruated in her life. How credible this last statement may be is hard to decide in retrospect. Since Sahaykwisa: professed to be a man, she would certainly not have discussed her menses with anyone. On the other hand, given the fact that the Mohave had no menstrual pads at that time, had she menstruated people could have noticed traces of her menses on her skirts and thighs, although they may have chosen to ignore these telltale stains which were incompatible with her socially accepted "masculinity."

Her dress, too, was described in somewhat puzzling terms. She is said to have worn short skirts "like a man." Taken literally, this statement is self-contradictory, since Mohave men originally wore breechcloths (Drucker, 1941). Perhaps the informant simply meant to suggest that, unlike most of her female contemporaries, Sahaykwisa: did not wear a Mother Hubbard. Moreover, since she occasionally prostituted herself to whites, it seems necessary to assume that her attire—though unconventional in terms of Mohave standards prevailing at that time—was a predominantly feminine one.[92] Finally, all inform-

---

[90] This is an important specification, since, if such a relative or boarder dies, the house must apparently be burned down, exactly as though he had a proprietary right to, or equity in, the house.

[91] Thus, just as we are puzzled by the habit of some primitives of applying the term "mother" also to the mother's sister, so these primitives would no doubt be puzzled by our "illogical" and "incomprehensible" tendency to call both the father's and the mother's sister "aunt," while reserving the term "mother" both for the real mother and the stepmother. The unconscious simply goes one step further and equates all women of the mother's generation with the mother.

[92] In the old frontier days white prostitutes wore relatively short skirts in saloons and dance halls. The tendency of primitives to consider white women masculine is well known, and is further supported by evidence from the psychoanalysis of a Plains Indian woman (Devereux 1953 b). The unconscious tendency to consider prostitutes "masculine" is a well documented psychoanalytic fact.

ants stressed that she was "rich enough to wear real shoes," and not just Mohave sandals (Drucker, 1941), because she occasionally prostituted herself to whites,[93] though part of her relative prosperity was due to her being an industrious farmer and hunter, as well as a practicing shaman specializing in the treatment of venereal diseases. Since such specialists are, by definition, lucky in love, it is likely that her striking ability to find wives was only partly due to her well-deserved reputation of being a good provider. The principal reason for her marked success in obtaining wives was probably the belief that, being a specialist in venereal diseases, she was necessarily lucky in love.[94]

In addition to functioning as a healer, Sahaykwisa: also began to practice witchcraft in her middle twenties, but was not accused of being a witch until some 5 years later.

The first of Sahaykwisa:'s wives to be mentioned by the chief informant was a very pretty girl, whom many men tried to lure away from her "husband" by ridiculing the lesbian. Thus, one suitor said: "Why do you want hwame: for a husband? Hwame: mutonem non habet et mero digito fodicat." Sahaykwisa:'s wife was, however, not impressed by this argument, and replied: "That is all right for me, if I wish to remain with her," whereupon her suitor gave up and left her alone. However, shortly thereafter another suitor appeared on the scene and also tried to persuade her to leave her "husband," saying: "Mentula ei non est; est sicut tu ipsa. If you remain with her, no 'other' man [95] will want you afterwards." [96] Finally, even though Sahaykwisa: was an excellent provider, who cultivated her fields well and did all the work a husband is supposed to do,[97] her wife liked the second suitor well enough to elope with him. After her wife left her, Sahaykwisa: began to attend dances and flirted with girls who were present, which caused a man, who noticed this, to say sneeringly: "Why don't you leave those women alone? You can't do anything with them anyway!" Behind her back people even called her Hispan Kudha:pe (=vagina scissa), id quod tribadis schema significat.[98] However, since this is a bad insult, no one dared to call her Hispan Kudha:pe to her face.

Before Sahaykwisa: could induce another girl to marry her, her former wife, who had eloped with a man, decided to return to her. "Despite his boasts, she found him less satisfying than Sahaykwisa: had been." The male husband let her go and did nothing further about it.

After regaining her wife, Sahaykwisa: often took her to dances. At such gatherings the hwame: sat with the men and, boasting in a typically masculine manner, described to them the pudenda of "his" wife. However, while Sahaykwisa: was busy boasting, people teased her wife, saying: " 'Viro' tuo

---

[93] Lesbianism is far from rare among prostitutes.

[94] It is a well-known fact that a reputation of irresistibility enables even homely men and women to make amorous conquests. Thus, the hunchbacked François de Montmorency-Boutteville, Duc de Luxembourg (known as the Maréchal de Luxembourg), was a notoriously successful amorist.

[95] When ridiculing a transvestite, the Mohave refer to a transvestite's anatomical sex; otherwise they refer to the transvestite's adopted sex. In this instance, however, in order to make his point, the sarcastic suitor had to refer to Sahaykwisa: as a "man."

[96] Arguments of this type are also used in order to shame people married to persons much older than themselves. Thus, a man may be told by a girl that he smells of the old woman whom he married (Devereux, 1951 f).

[97] The only men who did women's work were older men who married prepubescent children (Devereux, 1951 f) and famous warriors who voluntarily did household chores for sick families (Stewart, 1947 c), presumably because they were quite certain of their masculinity (Devereux and Weiner, 1950).

[98] Tribades quae schema quod hispan kudha:pe vocatur usurpare cupiunt, capitibus aversis decumbunt, altera in dorso, altera in latere recubans; ambaeque ita intertextae sunt, ut utraque truncum alterius prenset inter femura sua, volvam fricans contra volvam sociae.

nec mentula nec colei sunt." One man even exclaimed: "(Di me perdant) ni concumbam et tecum et cum 'viro' tuo! Est isti feminae id quod habes et tu!" But don't tell your husband I said so, because your husband will be angry with me." [99] However, the girl was getting so tired of being teased that she ended up by complaining of all these sneers to Sahaykwisa:, who became so angry that she told her wife to leave. The girl replied: "If you tell me to go, I shall go," [1] and left Sahaykwisa: forthwith.

After a while Sahaykwisa: found herself another wife, who also had to endure a great deal of teasing and ridicule. In addition, people also jeered both at Sahaykwisa:'s former wife and at her new husband, who, be it noted, was not the man she had married after first running away from Sahaykwisa:. People would tell this man: "Age, fodita eam digito: hoc est quod amat; utere digito: hoc solita est. Ne perdideris mentulam tuam in illa!" [2] To make matters worse, Sahaykwisa:'s former wife took it upon herself to tease the hwame:'s current wife: "Non ignoro quid tibi contingat! Digito volvam tuam fodicat; adhuc dolet mea, ubi ista unguibus rasit." Sahaykwisa:'s current wife resented all this teasing and complained to her "husband" who, this time, instead of getting angry, haughtily repiled: "Never mind what my former wife tells you! She wants to come back to me—that is all!" Sahaykwisa:'s wife insisted that this was not true, but the hwame: retorted: "I know better," and let it go at that. [3]

Eventually Sahaykwisa: and her current wife met the former wife and the latter's husband at a dance. When the former wife once more heaped ridicule on Sahaykwisa:'s current wife, the latter felt that she had stood more than enough and decided to have it out with the former wife. At first the two women only hurled insults at each other, but when the men who were present began to egg them on, they actually began to fight. As for Sahaykwisa: and the former wife's current husband, they remained seated, and maintained the dignified bearing befitting men when women are fighting over them. The rest of the crowd behaved, however, in a quite undignified manner and began to jeer at the transvestite: "The hwame: is proud now! Fingit, puto, sibi mentulam esse!" Finally a practical joker pushed the fighting women on top of Sahaykwisa:, so that all three rolled around in the dust. Soon after this incident Sahaykwisa:'s current wife also decided that she could not bear the insults any longer and deserted the hwame:.

The desertion of her second wife disappointed Sahaykwisa: a great deal and made her so resentful that she painted her face black, the way a warrior on the warpath, or a man going to fight his wife's seducer does, picked up her bow and arrows and went away (apparently giving people the impression that she was going to fight her eloping wife's paramour.) [4] We think, however, that she must

---

[99] It is impossible to decide whether this man ironically pretended to be physically afraid of a pseudo-man, or whether he was actually afraid that Sahaykwisa: would bewitch him.

[1] Compare this wording to the typical Crow expression: "You told me to do it—now I did it," (Lowie, 1935) or to Molière's celebrated: "Tu l'as voulu, Georges Dandin!"

[2] Quod maxime concinnum videtur esse cum Mohaviorum mentis ratione, quippe qui dignitatem quandam mentulae inesse existiment. Itaque cum mulier quaedam coitum ab ano posceret, vir indignabundus: "Pudor," inquit, "est mentulae meae." Hoc quoque demonstrat Mohavios fastidire quin pudenda muliebra manu tractent, "quia male olentes hoc facit manus."

[3] It seems reasonable to assume that Sahaykwisa: was not only voicing the traditional Mohave belief that a woman who wantonly insults a man is in love with him, but was also objectively right in assuming that her previous wife still struggled with the desire to renew their former relationship.

[4] It is noteworthy that Sahaykwisa:—though professing to be a man—took only her bow and arrows and not the war club, which is reserved for senior braves, nor even a straight club or stick of the type which the Mohave use to settle formal fights within the tribe (pt. 7, pp. 356–371).

already have had some other girl in mind, since, instead of going to the home of the eloped wife, she went to another camp, where she was very badly received. The married woman she wished to visit jeered at her and insultingly spoke to her the way one woman speaks to another woman: "She thinks maybe that the bow and arrows suit her. She thinks she is a man." These remarks did not appear to ruffle Sahaykwisa:. She calmly replied: "Yes, I can shoot game for you," and then left. We think she must have felt encouraged, because we say that if a girl or woman insults her suitor, he can be pretty certain of winning her in the end. A few days later Sahaykwisa: visited this woman once more and asked her to grind corn for her, which is precisely what a bride is supposed to do the moment she reaches her new husband's camp. Surprisingly enough, the woman complied and ground corn for the hwame:. The news of this spread like wildfire all over the reservation, and people said: "I bet she will get herself another wife. What can be the matter with all these women who fall for a hwame:?" The third time Sahaykwisa: visited this camp, the woman left her husband and eloped with the hwame:. The husband, a 35-year-old man named Haq'au, did nothing about it at that time; "He could not very well fight with a transvestite."

Actually, Sahaykwisa:'s ability to obtain one wife after another surprised no one; she was a venereal disease specialist and was therefore automatically expected to be lucky in love. Moreover, she was a good provider, who earned a living not only by practicing shamanism, but also by farming and hunting and, according to some, also by prostituting herself occasionally to whites. In brief, she earned enough to give her successive wives quantities of beads and pretty clothes.

Yet, in the end, Sahaykwisa:'s third wife also deserted her and returned to Haq'au, who took her back, though not without some hesitation, "since she had lowered herself by becoming the wife of a hwame:," and perhaps also because people warned him that Sahaykwisa:—who, by this time, was a recognized healer and a practioner of witchcraft—might bewitch him. "She will get even with you," people said, but Haq'au took back his former wife all the same.

When Sahaykwisa: heard that her wife had gone back to Haq'au she once more picked up her bow and arrows and went from her house, which was on the southern outskirts of Needles. Calif., to Haq'au's camp, which was on the northern edge of that town. She did not actually go to Haq'au's house, but stood at a certain distance from it, looking at the camp. She did this several times, "thinking of how she could bewitch this woman." People who noticed what she was doing warned Haq'au, but he was not afraid and jestingly replied: "Let her come! The next time she comes, I will show her what verus muto can do." The next time Sahaykwisa: approached his camp, he waylaid her in the bushes which surrounded his camp, tore off her clothes, and assaulted her. Then he left her in the bushes and returned to his camp. As for Sahaykwisa:, she picked herself up and left the scene without saying a word to anyone.

After this occurrence Sahaykwisa: ceased to court women. Of course, by that time she had already bewitched quite a few women, put their captive souls in a place of her own, and cohabited with these souls in dream. Moreover, after being raped she became a regular drunkard and developed a craving for men.[5] Nonnumquam, cum temulenta sensu careret, quidam in locum secretum illam trahebant et pro pecunia eam a pluribus—ab albis quoque—stuprari sinebant.[6]

---

[5] A discussion of this changeover from lesbianism to alcoholism will be found at the end of this case history.

[6] While group intercourse with drunken women was fairly common (Devereux, 1948 1), as a rule the Mohave did not invite whites to participate in it and no one paid anything to anyone.

Of course, by this time she was on the downgrade and, like any wanton kamalo :y, was considered fair game (Devereux, 1948 f).

It was at this time that Sahaykwisa: fell in love with an elderly man named Tcuhum, who, like herself, was of the Nyoltc gens.[7] Tcuhum refused to cohabit with her, however, telling her: "You are a man." The spited and angry Sahaykwisa: thereupon bewitched him, in order to have intercourse at least with his ghost in dream. Yet, despite his refusal to cohabit with her, Tcuhum died without revealing to anyone that she had bewitched him, which led people to believe that he must have wanted to become her victim—i.e., because, in a way, he loved her (pt. 7, pp. 383–386).

After Tcuhum's death Sahaykwisa: started an affair with Tcuhum's son Suhura :ye, of the Nyoltc gens, who was at that time about 40 or 45 years of age.[8] At the same time she also had an affair with Suhura :ye's friend Ilykutcemidho :, of the O :otc gens, who was about 50 years old. These three traveled together to a certain place, some 30 miles north of Needles, where all three intended to work for a living.[9] However, by this time, Sahaykwisa: longed so much for the company of those whom she had bewitched that she began to look for a chance to be killed, so as to be able to join her retinue of ghosts forever. Hence, during that trip—i.e., either while traveling north, or else after reaching her destination—she became drunk once more and openly told her lovers that she had bewitched Tcuhum and boasted of it until the two baited men picked her up and threw her into the Colorado River, where she drowned.

I (Hivsu: Tupo :ma) was living at that time in Needles and, some two weeks after Sahaykwisa :'s murder, I heard that people had noticed some buzzards circling over a sandbank. When they investigated, they found Sahaykwisa :'s partly decomposed body, which had run aground there. I and some others then picked up the corpse and carried it back to the Mohave settlement, where it was cremated in the usual manner. At first people thought that she had jumped into the river while drunk (suicide 1), but later learned that she had been murdered. They did nothing about it, because witches *should* be killed and *wish* to be killed. It is said that, except for Tcuhum, who, though of her own gens, was not really related to her, Sahaykwisa: had not bewitched any one of her relatives.[10]

[What happened to Sahaykwisa :'s former wives?] One of them, a woman named Nyoltc, of Sahaykwisa :'s own gens, is still alive. [Could I see her?] You should not even try to talk to her about her life with Sahaykwisa :—she is still quite touchy about that episode and does not like to be reminded of it.

Comment

A meaningful interpretation of the preceding case history is impossible unless one can bring oneself to ignore its scabrous and grotesque features, so as to perceive the human being behind the anecdote. Only then can one realize that,

---

[7] Since prostitutes and promiscuous women have strong oedipal fixations, the fact that Sahaykwisa: fell in love with an elderly man of her own gens could almost have been predicted on psychoanalytic grounds only.

[8] This, too, is typical oedipal behavior, corresponding to a transfer of one's affections from an older father figure to that man's son, who represents a brother.

[9] It is hard to escape the inference that Suhura :ye knew of Sahaykwisa :'s relations with Ilykutcemidho :.

[10] This detail, when taken in conjuction with the fact that there is no mention whatsoever of Sahaykwisa :'s own relatives in this case history, has important implications. It suggests that Sahaykwisa: had not simply been *rejected* by her family because of her lesbianism, but had also *withdrawn* from them, so as to escape potentially unmanageable oedipal-incestuous temptations. Moreover, she was *never* referred to as "Nyoltc."

at least from the moment when she was raped, Sahaykwisa:'s ultimate tragedy was a foregone conclusion, in that, with an almost somnambulistic assurance, she unerringly gravitated toward death and destruction. Every one of her attempts to extricate herself from her difficulties and to allay her anxieties only involved her more and more irreversibly in the typical vicious circle, or downward spiral, of psychiatric illness (Devereux, 1955 b). From the psychiatric point of view she was as truly "fey"—doomed to death—as the two deer of Mohave mythology (Kroeber, 1948).

One may be able to look beyond the grotesque features of this case history if one compares Sahaykwisa:'s progress toward her doom to the manner in which the heroes and heroines of Greek tragedy meet theirs. The harder these tragic personages struggle against their character, which is also destiny,[11] the deeper they sink into the quicksand of their fate. Those who would challenge the validity of this comparison would do well to remember that the greatest of Greek tragedies deal with topics which are fundamentally quite as scabrous as the incidents of Sahaykwisa:'s life. Only the greatness of the dramatic poetry which these outrageous scandals inspired obscures the fact that Greek tragic destinies have as their pivot such criminal or police-court matters as incest and parricide (Sophocles: Oedipus trilogy), adultery, husband killing, and matricide (Aeschylus: "Oresteia"), collective psychosis, orgiastic behavior, murder of a kinsman, the devouring of human flesh torn from the living body (Euripides: "Bacchae"), and the like. Were the heroes and heroines of these great tragedies insignificant Mohave lesbian witches, instead of kings and queens, and had great poetry not thrown its magical mantle over their locker-room scandals, one would more readily apprehend that Sahaykwisa:'s fate is the stuff of which Sophocles, Aeschylus, and Euripides fashioned their masterpieces,[12] which, to this day, do, as Aristotle expressed it, purify men by filling them with terror and pity.

Perhaps the most extraordinary and theoretically also most enlightening feature of Sahaykwisa:'s destiny is the *double* inevitability of her doom. which can be satisfactorily explained either in purely psychological terms, as the inescapable consequence of her neurosis, or in purely cultural terms, as the foreordained fate of a witch. What, in terms of her personality structure and psychopathology, can be viewed as a neurotically self-destructive *goal* is, in terms of the cultural frame of reference, a sociocultural *mandate* to commit vicarious suicide. Both are inescapable, and both are equally satisfactory as explanatory devices. In brief, Sahaykwisa:'s case is an almost classical illustration of the principle (Devereux, 1945 a; and pt. 7, pp. 378–382) that the sociocultural and the psychological explanations of a given act are perfectly complementary and lead to identical conclusions (Devereux, 1955 a).

In view of the detailed discussion of the sociocultural dynamics of the vicarious suicide of Mohave witches, which is presented in the introductory sections of this chapter, the following comments will be limited to a scrutiny of the neurotic elements which made Sahaykwisa:'s murder inevitable.

Although neurosis—like every other psychic state or process—is overdetermined, one of the main unconscious sources of female homosexuality is the desire to escape an oedipal involvement with the father, which the girl child desires, but also dreads, because she imagines that its actual implementation would physically destroy her. In order to escape this fate, and also in order not to compete with her mother for her father's love, she competes instead with

---

[11] A demonstration that the fate of Greek dramatists was a poetic allusion to character structure was given elsewhere (Devereux, 1953 c).

[12] The stimulus for Stendhal's immortal novel "The Red and the Black" was provided by nothing more than a newspaper account of a cheap and tawdry murder, committed by an insignificant social climber.

the father for the mother's love and becomes masculine in her interests and deportment.

Sahaykwisa :'s life history illustrates this defensive maneuver to perfection. In order to allay her anxieties, she became an almost ideal "husband," and was therefore able to compete with men and to win at least three wives. Yet, even though the Mohave institutionalize transvestitism (Devereux, 1937 b), she was not rewarded either for being a good provider or for being "one of the boys." [13] This, of course, is the characteristic self-defeatingness of neurotic defenses, which also makes it extremely unlikely that she would have been able to maintain indefinitely her precarious psychic balance, even if Haq'au had not assaulted her.

Given her unrewarded attempts to be a real man, it is easy to see why she should have wished to bewitch a woman she had not been able to hold in the first place, so as to reaffirm her maleness by capturing her for life in the other world. There is, thus, a certain tragic but inescapable grotesqueness in the fact that it was at this precise moment that Haq'au proved to her, once and for all, that she was a woman and not a man. It is, moreover, reasonably certain that she, herself, made it—"accidentally on purpose"—possible for Haq'au to attack her at the precise moment when she tried to take away his wife a second time. Indeed, since she knew that Haq'au had openly threatened to assault her, it is hard to escape the conclusion that she chose to hang around his camp, not only for the purpose of bewitching her ex-wife, but also in order to expose herself to the very type of assault which she both craved and dreaded all her life. Moreover, she competed with a man for that man's wife for a *second* time—just as the little girl, after having successfully monopolized the mother during her nursing period, may, as her lesbian tendencies develop, once more—this time fruitlessly—enter into competition with her father. Otherwise stated, for a neurotic like Sahaykwisa: the whole assault episode was an almost perfect gratification of her infantile oedipal wishes and fears, which she had warded off all her life by being a female transvestite. The fact that she managed to have her oedipal wishes gratified by means of an act of violence, rather than through seduction is, likewise, a necessary psychological component of the total occurrence, since it enabled her to pretend to herself that she was not "really" responsible for the occurrence.[14] The legitimacy of this last inference will be demonstrated further below, by means of an analysis of Sahaykwisa :'s subsequent alcoholism. The last point to be made at this juncture is that it was psychologically necessary for Sahaykwisa: to subject herself to violence, since that is precisely the small girl's conception of the oedipal act.

Having once experienced that which she desired and dreaded all her life, without being destroyed by it, Sahaykwisa :'s earlier defense (lesbianism) became automatically obsolete.[15] Her first experience of heterosexuality—even though she managed to make it appear as an "unprovoked" assault—permanently undermined her transvestite defense against her femininity and its oedipal components—something which her earlier prostitution to whites was unable

---

[13] Compare the ridiculing of her sexual adequacy, the humbling of her "masculine" pride precisely when women fought for her, her futile attempts to boast in a masculine way, which resulted in her being called a kamalo :y (=promiscuous woman), etc.

[14] Similarly, one reason why one can "do" in dream deeds one dares not do in a waking state is that one feels much less responsible for one's dreams than for one's actions (Freud, 1943; Devereux, 1951 a).

[15] A discussion of the way in which defenses become obsolete will be found in part 2, pages 54–56. It should also be noted that some neurotics can change over to entirely new sets of symptoms either as a result of some important traumatic occurrence, or else in the course of psychotherapy.

to accomplish.[16] From that moment on, she was permanently committed to an, admittedly infantile, pseudo-heterosexuality, whose analysis is our next task.

Before we can investigate in detail Sahaykwisa :'s subsequent relationship to men, we must briefly discuss the fact that she became not only promiscuous, but also alcoholic, which she could certainly not have been at a time when she was, in her own way, a "model husband." In brief, alcoholism was one of the new symptoms she substituted for her earlier, now inoperative and pointless, homosexual symptom. The clue to her choice of this symptom is provided by the Mohave practice of subjecting drunken women to serial assault, supposedly without any feeling of guilt, since—as the Mohave put it—"A drunken woman has it coming to her. She knows what happens to a woman who gets dead drunk" (Devereux, 1948 i). By becoming repeatedly drunk, even though she had been repeatedly attacked on similar occasions, Sahaykwisa : achieved two major neurotic objectives:

(1) Actuated by the characteristic repetition compulsion of neurotics, she contrived frequent repetitions of her experience with Haq'au, as well as of her previous "impersonal" experiences as a prostitute, both of which unconsciously gratified her infantile oedipal fantasies.

(2) By allowing such things to happen to her while intoxicated, she could consciously pretend to herself that she was not responsible for these occurrences,[17] exactly in the way in which, while functioning as a prostitute, she could use her "economic motivation" and subjective lack of involvement as intrapsychic alibis.[18]

Unfortunately for Sahaykwisa :, even the dual substitute symptoms of intoxication and repeated subjection to assault did not suffice to appease the anxieties mobilized by her (psychologically infantile) pseudo-heterosexuality. Once forcibly feminized,[19] it was inevitable that she should fall in love with an oedipal substitute, i.e., with a man of her own gens, much older than herself. Even the fact that she loved this man with such intensity is culturally atypical, since the Mohave seldom fall "romantically" in love (Devereux, 1950 a and pt. 3, pp. 91–106). The intensity of her love for Tcuhum is shown by the fact that when he rejected her, she bewitched him so as to be able to possess him forever, first in dream and then in the land of the dead.

At this crucial point Sahaykwisa :'s ultimate vicarious suicide, which had previously been unavoidable only in the *psychological* sense, also became a certainty in the *cultural* sense. What one observes, from this moment onward, is the subtle but unerring goal-directedness of the process whereby seemingly strictly idiosyncratic maneuvers were made to implement also the cultural mandate requiring witches to cause themselves to be killed.

---

[16] Prostitutes, many of whom are privately homosexual, are also oedipally fixated. They are able to ply their trade only because they do not participate in the act psychologically and therefore can view it as an economic (Davis, 1937) rather than as an amorous or "familial" action. This, in turn, enables them not to feel conscious guilt over their infidelity to their oedipal love object, or over their violation of society's moral code. Compare in this context the insightful witticism: "A gentleman can do anything he pleases, as long as he does *not* enjoy it." (For the equation white alien=oedipal love object, cf. Devereux, 1950 a.)

[17] La Barre (1939) discussed, at least in passing, the "alibi" and self-exculpating function of intoxication. It is quite likely that the traditional maxim: "The superego is soluble in alcohol" should actually read: "The superego can be placated by using intoxication as an alibi."

[18] The well-known psychic equation "oedipal love object=many anonymous men" also operates in such situations. Its detailed discussion would, however, take us too far afield.

[19] Assault was a common means for feminizing an aggressive female in Mohave society (Devereux, 1948 f).

The first decisive step was Sahaykwisa:'s culturally atypical maneuver of selecting the bewitched man's son as his substitute and successor. In other words, Sahaykwisa:'s next love object was a man who—had Tcuhum married her—would have been her stepson. Now, if one views Sahaykwisa: as a "woman," her choice of this love object was atypical, since stepson marriages are unknown among the Mohave, though marriage to a former son-in-law is a minor pattern (Devereux, 1951 f). Her choice is, however, equally atypical if one views Sahaykwisa: as a "man," since in the same marginal marriage pattern the man, after marrying a woman of his own generation, proceeds to marry a woman of the parent generation.[20] As for the polyandrous arrangement of living simultaneously with two men—and a ghost—more or less under the same roof, it is absolutely deviant and unique, and differs even from the case of Melyikha:, who lived alternatingly with Mivsu: Tupo:ma and with Ahma Huma:re (Devereux, 1950 a).

We must therefore examine carefully the hidden purpose of this extraordinary arrangement which, be it said, was possible only because both Suhura:ye and his friend were presumably deviant personalities. It is suggested that this arrangement had a very definite, though unconscious, self-destructive purpose. By living constantly with a man whose father she bewitched, Sahaykwisa: made (accidentally on purpose) absolutely certain that he would be present when, sooner or later, she got drunk enough to confess her misdeed. Moreover, by giving Suhura:ye a rival, she saw to it that his filial anger would be reinforced by latent jealousy and resentment over this abnormal polyandrous arrangement, which placed him in a position of rivalry not only with his friend, *but also with the ghost of his own father, with whom Sahaykwisa: supposedly cohabited in dream.*

Once this arrangement came into being, Sahaykwisa: was irrevocably doomed to die. Indeed, it would have doomed her to death also in almost any other society, though it is obvious that the Mohave cultural mandate, which requires witches to court death and the surviving relatives of bewitched persons to exact revenge, greatly reinforced both Sahaykwisa:'s self-destructiveness and Suhura:ye's vengefulness. This explains why they first thought that her death was a suicide.

In brief, from the psychoanalytic point of view, Sahaykwisa:'s self-destructiveness would have led to her being murdered even in the absence of a highly specific cultural mandate. Moreover, she would have developed such self-destructive urges even if she had not been conditioned by Mohave culture to become suicidal. Conversely, given her self-destructive and provocative maneuvers, Suhura:ye would have murdered Sahaykwisa: even if he had not been culturally conditioned to exact revenge for the death of his father. In this instance these cultural mandates probably did little more than reinforce the subjective motivations of these persons, by neutralizing their remaining scruples and reticences.

Even the actual conditions of Sahaykwisa:'s death fit the above pattern perfectly. She was murdered by her lover and his friend, who was also her lover, so as to avenge her third, invisible and ghostly, dream lover, Tcuhu:m. This setup corresponds perfectly to the small girl's infantile-masochistic fantasies, in which she visualizes herself as simultaneously loved and destroyed by her oedipal love object. The fact that she managed to confess her guilt while drunk [21]—and therefore to be killed while drunk—also fits the infantile pattern, since infantile fantasies are liberated by alcoholic intoxication which, as pointed out above, also serves as an alibi for normally prohibited and ego-dystonic types

---

[20] For an indirect sample of this pattern, see Case 104.

[21] Similarly, Hivsu: Tupo:ma was drunk both when he confessed to me that he was a witch, and when he exposed himself to a fatal chilling (Devereux, 1948 i).

of "acting out." Indeed, just as she had previously exposed herself to the *unconscious gratifications* to be derived from assaults, without being able to enjoy them *actually* and therefore without having to feel guilty for them, so now she intoxicated herself in order *not* to be able to flee her murderers.

The pattern of Sahaykwisa :'s life is, thus, a highly coherent one and fits perfectly also basic psychoanalytic theories of transvestitism and suicide.[22]

In brief, Sahaykwisa :'s detailed case history reveals with great clarity the subjective factors which make the actual implementation of cultural mandates possible, while the briefer witch-killing reports highlight primarily the effects of the cultural mandate which forces the witch to have himself killed. In this case, however, the ultimate killing appears to be inevitable even in purely psychological terms. Sahaykwisa :'s life history enables one to witness the gradual unfolding of certain inner forces, which made her vicarious suicide absolutely inevitable. One notes the perfect identity of her neurotic goal and of the cultural mandate to commit vicarious suicide. One can trace, step by step, the convergence of the psychic process and of the cultural process toward this unified, though Janus-faced, goal. The actual convergence was, no doubt, made possible by the fact that Sahaykwisa : was a *Mohave*, in the same sense in which the cultural mandate she had to obey was a *Mohave* mandate. Both she and this mandate were products of the same cultural pattern.

The one element which still eludes one is the exact way in which seemingly idiosyncratic psychic processes and random external occurrences are subtly, and almost imperceptibly, patterned by cultural expectations, so that the evolution of a neurosis and a series of culturally prescribed responses are forced to converge irresistibly toward the same climax. It is one thing to note this fact and to consider it the basis of all culture and personality studies. It is another thing to grasp the essence of this convergence. The nearest one can come to an understanding of the real causes of this convergence is the essentially metacultural and metapsychological conclusion that human culture and the human psyche are complementary coemergents. Technically, they admittedly belong to different disciplines and are understandable in terms of different frames of reference. However, and in the last resort, both are but different phrasings of man's basic and essential humanness. Were it otherwise, it would be inconceivable to speak of a cultural patterning of the personality, when it is evident that, on the one hand, Sahaykwisa : was the kind of neurotic who would have caused herself to be killed even if she had not lived in a culture in which it is mandatory for witches to commit vicarious suicide, and that, on the other hand, being a *Mohave* witch, Sahaykwisa : would have managed to manipulate someone into killing her even if her life—like that of some other suicidal witches—had been infinitely less traumatic than it actually was.[23]

In the last resort, Sahaykwisa :'s story illustrates both the basic unity of man's bio-psycho-social humanness and the methodological complexities of analyzing the interaction between these constantly converging aspects of man.

CASE 106 (Informants: Hivsu: Tupo :ma and Hama: Utce :) :

Tàma: ràhue, a 40-year-old, fullblood Mohave of the Mu :th gens, without any formal education, was both a farmer and a shaman, who "like Kwathany Hi :wa" (a notorious witch!), specialized in the treatment of colds, "pneu-

---

[22] This last argument is far weightier than is usually realized. In an earlier publication (Devereux, 1955 a) I estimated the number of persons in whose therapy psychoanalytic theory had been tested at approximately 10,000. A more systematic second estimate is that, to date, some 50,000 to 60,000 persons have had psychoanalyses. There can be few psychological theories which have been so extensively tested and validated.

[23] A technical discussion of the nexus between psychopathological processes and cultural mandates will be found in part 7, pp. 378–382.

monia," and "rheumatism." He was single, and, at the time of his suicide, which occurred around 1896, both of his parents were still alive.

The case of Táma:ráhue is a rather puzzling one. According to Hama: Utce., "he was a good man, who never bewitched anyone." My other informants were likewise unable to say precisely why various people, including even his own relatives, kept on accusing him of witchcraft. According to Pulyi: k, Táma:-ráhue's chief accuser appears to have been Ahwe: Tcukiev Hinok (enemy together human-spider),[24] a warrior and a witch killer. Another of his accusers was Pakutce (="brainy," a wise person).

Táma:ráhue "was getting tired of it, although he was not afraid (of being killed)." One afternoon he therefore dug up some ismaly katuh (Jimson weed, or datura), soaked it in water for a while, and then drank almost a gallon of this liquid. Then he headed for the Colorado River, intending to drown himself. Some people, who found out what he was planning to do, promptly pursued him, hoping to prevent him from killing himself. However, Táma:ráhue had so much of a headstart over his pursuers, that he reached the river at around 6:00 p.m., and, before anyone could catch up with him, jumped into the water and drowned almost immediately. His corpse floated from Parker, Ariz., all the way to Avi: Vata:y (Riverside Mountains) where it ran aground. Eventually some people found his body and brought it back to Parker for cremation.

Comment

Táma:ráhue's suicide is remarkable in several respects. Since the Mohave are not malicious people, it is unusual for them to accuse anyone of witchcraft, unless the witch practically confesses his misdeeds (Devereux, 1937 c). The use of Jimson weed is also atypical, partly because, unlike the Diegueño (Toffelmier and Luomala, 1936), the Mohave do not use Jimson weed in shamanistic practices (pt. 4, pp. 208–212), and partly because this is the only recorded Mohave instance of acute Jimson weed poisoning. The drowning is also noteworthy, partly because most Mohave are competent swimmers (Devereux, 1950 e) and partly because this is the only recorded case of suicide by drowning.[25] These unusual details suggest that Táma: ráhue must have been so deviant a personality that he aroused suspicion even in Mohave society, which is notoriously tolerant of personal eccentricities.

The main importance of this case history is, however, the fact that Táma:-ráhue's behavior can best be described as jumping from the frying pan into the fire. He committed suicide, in order to avoid being killed, whereas other witches cause themselves to be killed in order *not* to have to commit suicide. It is for this reason that his case history is included in the chapter on vicarious suicide, and is only briefly referred to in the case material on actual suicide. (See Supplementary Case C.)

VICARIOUS SUICIDE OF BRAVES

The Mohave warrior's vicarious suicide appears to be a link connecting the suicide of relatively ordinary persons with the vicarious suicide of witches (pt. 7, pp. 387–426). According to various informants, suicidal braves sometimes deliberately strayed into enemy territory in order to be killed.[26] Since warfare is now obsolete, the in-

---

[24] The word "hinok" was also translated as "human-animal" meaning presumably a mythical spider, animal, or creature which is a person (ipa:).

[25] Sahaykwisa:'s death was at first mistakenly believed to be due to accidental drowning (i.e., perhaps to suicide). (Case 105.)

[26] The existence of this practice was first brought to my attention by Dr. A. M. Halpern (1938).

formants were unfortunately unable to give further details about this seemingly marginal practice and could not recall any concrete example of this type of suicide. They were, however, quite certain that such a custom did exist in aboriginal times and definitely felt that it should be viewed as a form of suicide.

In the absence of more detailed data, this custom can be discussed only in terms of its general cultural setting.

Death wishes of warriors.—The Mohave explicitly state (Kroeber, 1925 a) that braves and shamans are alike, in that neither of them wishes to live long. McNichols (1944) adds that a really brave man who lived a long life considered himself unfortunate.

In order to understand the suicidalness imputed to the Mohave brave, it is important to understand that the Mohave concept of courage is based upon the ideal of stoical steadfastness. According to Hama: Utce: "Braves are like Spartans (sic!). You could stand and kill them and they will not budge. They take it standing. Only such braves can and will kill witches." This definition of courage is clearly formulated in terms of a man's willingness and ability to endure punishment and to be steadfast in adversity,[27] rather than in terms of reckless, berserker aggressivity. Steadfast courage appears to be essentially a *military* virtue, possibly associated with sedentary life and infantry, while reckless aggressivity is apparently a *warrior* virtue, perhaps associated with nomadism and cavalry. The pattern of Mohave warfare clearly emphasized the virtue of steadfastness, even—and perhaps especially—in the face of impossible odds. This steadfastness was extremely conspicuous at the disastrous battle of Avi:-vava, where of 142 Mohave and Yuma infantry only two men—left for dead on the battlefield—escaped alive (Kroeber, 1925 a; 1925 b).[28] The point to be made in connection with this battle is that, even though hopelessly outnumbered from the start, the Mohave and the Yuma refused to escape without a fight to the finish. "They felt that even though they had not expected to fight against a foe who greatly outnumbered them, they had come to fight and that it was therefore up to them to give battle, no matter what the odds were." This statement, made by one of my informants, clearly underscores the place of stoicism in the Mohave conception of courage.

Travel.—The brave's tendency to commit suicide by straying into enemy territory cannot be understood unless it is discussed in terms of the role of traveling in Mohave society.

---

[27] Compare the Hungarian adage: "The real man (legény = bachelor) is not the one who can dish it out, but the one who can take it."

[28] According to Kroeber (1925 b), part of the Mohave broke and fled. According to my informants, however, the senior Mohave warriors (who wield short mallet-shaped clubs), ordered the adolescents and young men (who wield straight clubs) to retire, while they and the Yuma stood fast and were wiped out.

(1) *Mythology* is replete with lengthy accounts of—frequently aimless—traveling. The outstanding characteristic of these mythical accounts of travel is the extreme elaborateness of geographical details (Kroeber, 1948).[29]

(2) *Name traveling* was undertaken by young men who set out on foot, looking for an occasion to perform some feat which would establish them as men and warriors (McNichols, 1944; Stewart, 1947 c; Fathauer, 1954). While such young knights errant were expected to look for and meet danger, they did not deliberately court death.

(3) *Aimless traveling*—simply for the sake of experience, or to escape that sense of aimlessness which, according to Kroeber (1951), explains much of the Mohave tribe's actions in connection with the captivity of the Oatman girls—appears to have been fairly common in aboriginal times. According to some informants, single Mohave men could travel as far as the Hopi country in relative safety, since it was generally known that, were a Mohave molested or harmed, he would be promptly avenged. People who traveled for pleasure avoided enemy country, and did not try to get themselves killed.

(4) *Business trips:* Groups seeking to obtain certain types of shells, etc. (Devereux, 1949 a) generally took no unnecessary risks.

(5) *Scouts* entering enemy territory ahead of a war party were not expected to risk their lives, but to return to the war party with the needed information.

(6) *Trips into enemy territory* for the purpose of being killed were apparently made only by senior warriors who, like witches, no longer wished to live.

A mythical precedent for traveling to one's doom appears to be the eerie narrative concerning two deer—doomed and conscious of their doom, i.e., "fey" in the old Anglo-Saxon sense of that term—who stoically, and yet somewhat aimlessly, proceeded to the spot where they were to meet Mountain Lion, described as their "maker," whose task it was to slay them (Kroeber, 1948). Numerous other mythical accounts also describe, though in less specific terms, how more or less explicitly fey personages traveled to their place of doom, or to a place where they were transformed into rocks or into some other landmark.

A detailed discussion of the impulse to go to one's doom, by deliberately exposing oneself to one's enemies, need not be undertaken in this context, since the matter is adequately covered in our general discussion of the dynamics of vicarious suicide (pt. 7, pp. 372–377).

Aftermath.—Even though senior warriors who deliberately exposed themselves to death at the hands of the enemy were held to have com-

---

[29] The psychological basis of this Mohave interest in geography is far from clear; it may, conceivably, be related to their tendency to establish a nexus between land tenure and human status (cf. Devereux, MS., 1935, and pt. 7, pp. 356–371).

mitted vicarious suicide, the Mohave felt compelled to avenge these deaths exactly as though these braves had not been suicidal to begin with.   In a personal letter, Fathauer (1952) described the organization of a retaliatory raid as follows:

I think one of my informants may have told me something which adds to your material, in the realm of warfare. Revenge appears to have been one of the main motives for warfare among the tribes. Frequently a young man would attempt to interest the kwanami:hye in leading a war party to avenge the death of a dead brother or father of whom he had been very fond while a boy. The youth would carry this in his mind until he was able to go on the warpath, and would think frequently of the dead brother or father. When such a young man went to war he would be very brave, taking unusual risks and acting beyond and above the call of duty. The informant did not think it was a matter of trying to get himself killed consciously, but there was the feeling that if he was killed he would be compensated by the fact that he would go to join the dead warrior whom he loved. Since warriors went to a special place in the spirit world, one had to be killed in battle in order to join a relative who had been killed in battle and there was also the matter of catching up before the final metamorphosis, which you have described (Devereux, 1937 a). This is probably not to be considered suicide, but it is another facet of the lure of the dead which you have discussed.

The preceding account—with which one cannot but agree, except for the final suggestion that such deaths are not suicides—is extremely important for an understanding of the fact that, in Mohave society at least, there is a marked tendency to view many forms of death— and almost every form of suicide—as directly due to a previous death, or at least as related to it in some significant manner.   This "clustering" is especially striking in the case of active suicides, since, in these instances, we do not deal simply with generalized beliefs, but with actual and known connections between the various persons who killed themselves (pt. 7, pp. 459–478).   At the same time, there are indications that, in some cases at least, the survivors of a vicariously suicidal warrior were disinclined to undertake a risky war party only because the slain brave had wished to die.   This explains why attempts to discover the whereabouts of a lost warrior by means of a spiritistic seance were sometimes deliberately frustrated by the brave's own kinsmen.[30]

The seance.—The following data regarding the use of mediums in tracing the whereabouts of lost persons were obtained from Pulyi:k, who volunteered them in 1950 in reply to a question which had nothing to do with war, mediums, or trance.

If someone was lost in battle and therefore could not be brought home, or if a person was missing and people wished to find him, or to know where he was, they went to a shaman who had tcehami:ytc suma:tc (power) and asked him to help them locate the lost person. The shaman would then get hold of some-

---

[30] The role which the knowledge that he would be avenged played in the motivation of a suicidal brave can no longer be reconstructed at this late date.

one (apparently of a person capable of going into a trance) and organized a seance in the ava: hatcor (winter house). He would take the medium and lay him down on the floor of the house, with his head pointing southward (i.e., toward the land of the dead). On each side of this medium, I mean at each side of his head and feet—in the four corners—there would be a pile of sand. The shaman then sat down and picked up four handfuls of sand. Most shamans did not take these handfuls of sand from the four piles, although a few did. He then put these four handfuls of sand into the mouth of the medium. Then the shaman got up and sang. After he sang four songs, the spirit of the lost person—or his ghost, if he was already dead—came and entered (took possession of) the medium, who was lying there on the ground. If the lost person was still alive, he would say so, and would tell where he was held captive. If he was already dead, he would state this fact and tell people where his corpse was to be found. Sometimes it was hard to understand these utterances because the spirit or ghost did not speak clearly. At the end of the performance people seized the prone medium's legs, and shook him until the sand poured out of his mouth. Then the medium sat up, joined the rest of the group, and listened while the shaman interpreted the medium's earlier utterances.

These seances were not always successful. Sometimes a relative of the lost person felt that it would be best to leave things as they were, because the Mohave dislike speaking of the dead (and it was, obviously, impossible to know before the seance whether the lost person was alive or dead). If a relative felt that way, he would attend the seance, but would prevent it from succeeding by retracting his foreskin and baring his glans; he did this either surreptitiously or else quite openly. The spirit of the lost person would then smell the stench of the exposed glans, exclaim: "Pukcah(m)!" (phew!) and go away, without saying anything else.

A similar ceremony was also resorted to when one wished to find a lost object, by locating the thief. [Who came to take possession of the medium in such instances?] The soul of the thief.[81] (1950.)

As regards self-suffocation, it was first mentioned by the Mohave as an obsolete means of committing suicide (Case 123). Only much later was it mentioned as a means for inducing a trance state. The technique of inducing a trance by self-suffocation appears to be both ancient and widespread (Courville, 1950). In fact, certain Eskimo sometimes practice self-suffocation as a substitute for intoxication (Freuchen, 1957). As regards the Yuma, Róheim (1932) reports a reference to self-suffocation, but appears to imply that it pertained to a shamanistic dream experience, rather than to the inducing of a trance state. As regards the Maricopa, Spier (1933) states that shamans "sucked up four piles of dirt" to obtain, through clairvoyance, knowledge of the enemy's whereabouts. This differs from the Mohave seance both in that the Mohave tried to obtain information regarding a fellow Mohave's whereabouts, rather than knowledge about the enemy and also in that the interpreter of the medium's utterances, rather than the medium himself, was a shaman. Other Yuman data are cited by Gifford, 1936, Kroeber (ed.), 1935, and

---

[81] This is the only reference to adult thieving in my field notes.

Stewart (1946). After the present work went to press, Kroeber (1957) published data on such seances which he had obtained in 1953 and 1954 and which he correlated with a previously puzzling passage of the Hipahipa epic (Kroeber, 1925 a). The chief differences between Kroeber's accounts and the present one are that not the shaman himself, but a medium supervised by a shaman, went into a trance, and that the medium was possessed not by the spirit of the sacred mountain, but by the soul or ghost of the lost person. The other differences concern minor technicalities only.

The most important comment to be made pertains, however, to the fact that, contrary to most statements in the literature (Stewart, 1946), spirit possession did, apparently, occur in Mohave society and could be brought about by ritual means. This finding suggests that it is rather risky to deny the occurrence of some major cultural trait in any culture whatsoever, until that culture has been most exhaustively studied, since traits which are extremely conspicuous in some cultures have a way of turning up in some relatively marginal and subordinate segment of another culture, when one least expects it. At other times such items can turn up simply in the form of idiosyncratic beliefs held by individual neurotics (cf. especially Devereux, 1955 a, 1957 a).[32] In brief, it seems probable that students of trait distributions would be well advised to leave traits reported to be absent entirely out of consideration, especially if these traits are widely distributed in other areas, have important psychological connotations, and do not require an advanced technology. Moreover, the integration of these seances with the broad vicarious suicide pattern suggests that it was far more fully integrated with the mainstream of Mohave culture than Kroeber (1957) claims it was.

FUNERAL SUICIDE

Introduction.—The proper evaluation of Mohave funeral suicide is quite difficult, especially since, in the last resort, psychoanalytically all real suicides are more or less also funeral suicides, in the sense of being mourning reactions involving an identification with someone consciously known or unconsciously fantasied to be dead.

The culturally most important aspect of Mohave funeral suicide is its extraordinarily ambiguous position in Mohave culture. On the one hand, funeral suicide was so closely related to major eschatological beliefs, and—though theoretically "disapproved" of—seems to have been so common in aboriginal times that people attending a funeral practically expected such attempts and therefore kept a watch-

---

[32] After Gayton (1935) stated that the Orpheus myth was absent among the Yuman tribes, I published a Mohave legend, collected in 1932, which was unmistakably of the Orpheus type (Devereux, 1948 h).

ful eye on persons likely to jump on the funeral pyre. Partly because of this watchfulness, no recorded attempt to commit funeral suicide ever proved successful. Since this was known to the chief mourners, the certainty that they would be stopped in time apparently simply served to encourage them to make such a gesture. It is extremely interesting in this context that the one person who was apparently *not* caught in time managed to "fall down" *beside*, and *not on*, the funeral pyre, and only burned his hair, which he, as the chief mourner, would have had to cut short anyhow.[33]

In brief, funeral suicide was largely a special kind of ritual gesture—disapproved of and yet expected and almost demanded by certain conventions. It is only a slight exaggeration to say that the mourner was expected to try to commit funeral suicide, while society was expected to frustrate the attempt, the whole representing a kind of tacit "contract."[34] It is, in fact, highly probable that this tacit contract encouraged the chief mourners to make an exaggerated display of their grief, since they knew that the more loudly they announced their "intention" to commit funeral suicide, and the more dramatically they "attempted" to carry it out, the more certain they could be that measures would be taken to prevent them from actually harming themselves. This, in turn, enabled them to abreact a maximum of grief and tension, while forcing their environment to give them a maximum of gratifying attention and support, thereby stealing the limelight from the corpse.[35] As for those who restrained the would-be suicide and comforted him, they not only basked in the glory of having had a share in some spectacular occurrence, but also derived satisfaction from the fact that in Mohave society—as in many others—comforting the bereaved is almost as respectable as being a real mourner.

This type of tacit contract to do the expected—though theoretically "wrong"—thing is not quite the same as Linton's (1936) concept of a "pattern of misconduct," which simply specifies the *manner* in which

---

[33] It is of great interest that the only nonfuneral cutting of the hair occurred when a man, depressed by the desertion of his wife, contracted hi :wa itck (pt. 3, pp. 91–106) and cut his hair short, as though he were mourning a dead spouse. When the depression dissipated, he tried to remedy the situation by tying back his braids to his remaining hair (Case 21).

[34] A strong display of grief at funerals was mandatory. Thus, a relatively modern version of Matavilye's funeral, obtained from Hivsu : Tupo :ma, specified that the whites forever disgraced themselves by their indifference to the death of this deity. Impious behavior at this divine funeral is also mentioned in more archaic versions, which report that Coyote shamelessly stole Matavilye's heart from the pyre and therefore became "crazy" (Kroeber, 1948). Coyote's "craziness" is so generally accepted that the word "hukthar" (=coyote) also means "crazy" (Case 79), in the colloquial sense of that word.

[35] The fact that voluminous widow's weeds and other extreme outward mourning reactions represent a kind of social blackmail was demonstrated elsewhere (Devereux, 1956 a).

a penalized or forbidden act should be committed.[36] Indeed, in this instance it is the *act* itself, rather than a particular *way* of committing some act, which is both prescribed and forbidden. This type of ambiguousness appears to arise chiefly in connection with once highly prized, but increasingly obsolescent, patterns.[37]

A clear grasp of the ambiguous position of funeral suicide in Mohave culture is indispensable for a real understanding of the fundamentally ritual character of this grand but empty gesture, of the predictable failure of nearly every attempted funeral suicide and, finally, of the frequent lack of a true and generally understandable subjective and specific motivation. Moreover, only if these points are clearly understood is it possible to perceive the fundamental connection between funeral suicide and the throwing of property on the funeral pyre.

The act or gesture.—At the cremation of a spouse or member of the immediate family, the chief mourner sometimes tried to kill himself by jumping on the funeral pyre of the deceased. According to the Mohave, women were more prone than men to attempt this form of suicide—possibly because women are less ready than men are to accept irreversible losses with dignified stoicism. This statement, if taken literally, is not supported by the four available case histories, half of which pertain to men. Nor do the case histories seem to support the further assertion that women are more prone than men to attempt suicide by leaping on the pyre of a deceased *spouse*, since one of the two persons who tried to do so was a man, though his attempt was obviously far less resolute than that of the suicidal widow.[38] It

[36] The binding character of such specifications is quite definite (Devereux, 1940 a). Such patterns are markedly present in criminal activities which Tannenbaum (1938) rightly views as institutional. Moreover, the ritual nature of patterns of misconduct is especially apparent in the activities of the Thugs, whose murderous activities had a religious character, derived from a special justificatory myth. The same is true, albeit to a somewhat lesser extent, of the so-called criminal tribes of India (Cox, 1911; Cressey, 1936; Hasanat, n. d.; Owens, 1941; M. Taylor, 1839; etc.).

[37] In early 20th century Hungary the duel had a similarly ambiguous position. Women were proud of having a duel fought over them, though they trembled for their men and knew that having a duel fought over them could impair their reputation, while making them, at the same time, the envy of other women. Society despised the man who did not fight a duel when it seemed proper to do so, but, at the same time, enacted laws against duels. The law itself was equally ambiguous. It defined dueling as a crime, but specified that it was not a "dishonorable" crime. Convicted duelists were imprisoned in a "fortress" (run like a country club), rather than in an ordinary jail. They were confined to the fortress, but it was forbidden to lock them in their cells, which they were permitted to redecorate before being imprisoned, just as they could order their food and beverages from the outside. The law was, moreover, administered by judges and prosecutors who were quite as ready to duel as everyone else, and who, after prosecuting and convicting a duelist in strictest accordance with the law, visited him in the fortress with basketfuls of roast fowl and wine, and played cards with him day after day.

[38] Insofar as one can discuss "statistics" in connection with only four cases, the only significant differences between men and women are that: (*a*) the only would-be suicide who had an understandable subjective motive was a man, and (*b*) that whereas a father attempted funeral suicide when his son (child of the *same sex*) died (identification), a mother tried to leap on the funeral pyre of her son (child of the *opposite sex*) who had just died (counter-oedipal impulse).

will be possible to show, however, that, if the Mohave statement concerning the ratio between men and women trying to jump on the funeral pyre is not interpreted *numerically* but *psychologically* (characterologically), the Mohave are right in viewing funeral suicide as a markedly female reaction pattern. (See below.)

The technique.—Suicide by fire in the course of a funeral is, strictly speaking, the only ritual form of *actual* self-destruction in Mohave society. This finding is strongly supported by the fact that the only other type of ritual "suicide" in Mohave culture occurs at incestuous weddings, which closely resemble funeral rites (pt. 7, pp. 356–371). By contrast, even though witch killing is an important Mohave *custom*, the actual murder is a *nonritual act*, performed in whatever way seems most practical under the circumstances (pt. 7, pp. 387–426).

On the whole, suicide by fire is a ritual act in nearly all cultures where it occurs and appears to be characteristic especially of societies where corpses are cremated—presumably because suicide by fire condenses into a single act both death and cremation. As regards the Mohave, it is almost certain that suicide by fire represents such a condensation, since they are markedly inclined to indulge in condensations (Devereux, 1957 b). Moreover, a Mohave, who actually manages to kill himself by jumping on the funeral pyre of a spouse or relative, is sure to enter the land of the dead at the same time as the deceased and to go through all future metamorphoses in the company of the person from whom he does not wish to be separated. This, needless to say, is precisely the real objective of funeral suicide.

In this context, it seems important to mention the possibly highly significant fact that the Mohave were formerly so markedly overhasty in cremating people that the Indian Agency sometimes sent a native policeman to the camp of a person known to be on the verge of death, to make sure that the ailing person was actually dead before being placed on the funeral pyre (McNichols, 1944). Whether there was some cultural or psychological connection between this rush to cremate the dead and the custom of trying to commit suicide by fire can probably no longer be ascertained at this late date.

It is also quite likely that even if suicide by fire were not frequently associated with the cremation of corpses, it would still tend to be viewed as a ritual act, simply because it is a singularly dramatic gesture, which not only puts an end to life, but also utterly destroys the body.[39]

---

[39] The dramatic character of suicide by fire may explain why Herakles—whom Greek mythology describes as an emotionally immature, inordinately vain, exhibitionistic, bisexual, and even manic-depressive personality—chose to commit suicide by fire precisely while Nessus' shirt was already burning into his flesh. To the best of my knowledge it has not yet been pointed out that Herakles' suicide by fire implies—if Herakles was a real Dorian chieftain—that he lived at a time when the Greeks practiced funeral cremation, or else, if he is a purely imaginary mythical personage, that at least the story of his suicide came into being during the period when the Greeks still practiced cremation.

Be that as it may, all remembered Mohave attempts to commit suicide by fire occurred at funerals, though Hivsu: Tupo:ma did mention that a—presumably non-Mohave—transvestite "might" jump into the fire, if people teased him too much. This may possibly be significant, since Herakles, who committed suicide by fire, dressed as a woman at least twice in his life: once when hiding from his enemies and once to please Omphale [40] and had several homosexual relations in the course of his agitated life.

A minor, but quite interesting, sidelight upon suicide by fire is provided by the Mohave belief that convulsives who become incontinent during their seizures are markedly prone to fall into the fire (pt. 2, pp. 72–76). This belief may very well correspond to actual facts, since there exists a statistically significant correlation between urinary incontinence and neurotic fire setting (Michaels, 1955). This fact should be noted, even though its psychoanalytic elucidation is beyond the scope of the present work.

Finally, there is at least a hint that the departing ghost of the deceased seeks to seize the living. This is suggested by the belief that all small whirlwinds, such as are often seen in the desert, contain ghosts and that the small whirlwinds rising from beneath the funeral pyre carry away the dead person's ghost—presumably to the land of the dead. All these whirlwinds—but especially those arising from beneath the pyre—are so greatly dreaded, that even elderly Mohave nimbly jump out of the path of these tiny, funnel-shaped whirling masses of dust or ashes.

The motivation of funeral suicide provides an extraordinarily interesting object lesson in the interplay of cultural, characterological, and (temporary) conflictual determinants.

Cultural factors in the motivation of funeral suicide are chiefly related to Mohave eschatology. The soul of the deceased first lingers for 4 days on earth, revisiting familiar places and persons, and then proceeds to the land of the dead, where it recapitulates its life on earth and dies a second time. Then, after undergoing three more metamorphoses, it ceases to exist entirely. Hence, unless the mourner dies soon after the demise of the beloved person, he runs the risk of never again being able to catch up with the one who predeceased him.

This danger has a great deal of motivating force for the Mohave. (Devereux, 1937 a.) The only ones who can temporarily neutralize this risk are witches, who segregate the souls of their victims in a place of their own, until they, too, are ready to die. Then they join their victims, lead them to the land of the dead and go through all subsequent metamorphoses in their company (pt. 7, pp. 387–426). The unborn shaman achieves the same objective even more simply, by

---

[40] On this latter occasion the phallic god Pan—who mistook (?) burly Herakles for a woman—actually tried to rape him in his sleep.

killing both himself and his mother at birth (pt. 7, pp. 331–339). Any other person who does not wish to be separated forever from an individual who predeceases him, must die as soon as possible, in order to catch up with the ghost of the deceased in the land of the dead.[41]

The most effective way in which a mourner can make sure that he will not be forever separated from the deceased is to commit funeral suicide.

When the matter is viewed in this light, it becomes quite evident that funeral suicide is a ritual and not an impulsive act, and that it is motivated primarily by eschatological considerations and social expectatons, rather than by an acute mourning depression. This finding is crucial for an understanding of the funeral-suicide pattern, as well as of the relevant case material.

The most effective way of demonstrating the scope of this insight is to apply it to the problem of the unsuccessfulness of all known attempts to commit funeral suicide. As stressed in the introductory section, the Mohave attitude toward this custom is a rather ambiguous one. The Mohave both expected—and, by expecting them, almost encouraged—such attempts and, at the same time, took effective measures to frustrate them. Hence, as soon as the chief mourner made the expected—and more or less desultory—gesture of attempting funeral suicide—which, as he well knew, was bound to be frustrated— the conventional proprieties of the latent culture pattern were held to have been complied with, which is all the situation called for. Hence, anyone who actually managed to sustain severe burns, as Syuly (Case 109) did, was thought to have behaved in an almost incomprehensible, and possibly even ridiculous, manner.[42]

The inference that most Mohave attempts to commit funeral suicide were primarily conventional "gestures," which lacked the reinforcement of a more subjective motivation, is supported by the finding that only one of four recorded attempts had an explicitly stated and psychologically understandable subjective background (Case 111), and that only one would-be suicide (Case 109) actually sustained serious bodily harm. This almost means that one should eliminate from the series of *ritual* attempts to commit funeral suicide the case of Anyanyema:m (Case 111), since this man had valid *subjective*

---

[41] A moment of reflection will show that this belief could probably have arisen only in a tribe where people seldom reached old age. Otherwise a person dying 20 years after the relative predeceasing him would still have a chance to spend at least a few years in the company of the predeceased relative, who fully recapitulates his earthly life—and lives out his earthly life span a second time—in the land of the dead. Such cultural clues to unrecorded aboriginal conditions are usually ignored.

[42] An illuminating parallel is the post-World War I dueling pattern in Hungary. Although the offended person felt obliged to send his seconds to the one who had insulted him, it was often a foregone conclusion that his seconds would contrive to obtain an apology and effect a reconciliation. The empty gesture of sending one's seconds to the offending person satisfied the superannuated conventions of chivalry, while preventing many actual duels, which were increasingly incompatible with modern customs.

reasons for seeking to kill himself and did not simply indulge in a culturally expected "gesture." Otherwise expressed, precisely because his act is understandable primarily in psychological, and only secondarily in cultural, terms, it cannot be viewed *chiefly* as a "ritual gesture." This finding has a direct bearing upon the problem of characterological factors in funeral suicide.

Characterological factors.—According to the Mohave, funeral suicide is a typically feminine reaction pattern, in the same sense in which hi :wa itck (pt. 3, pp. 91–106) is supposed to be a typically masculine reaction. This Mohave belief is supported by the fact that— after eliminating the case of Anyanyema :m (Case 111) from the series of cases, on the grounds that it was primarily a subjectively and not a culturally determined act—women who tried to commit (ritual) funeral suicide outnumbered men two to one.

However, even if one does not eliminate Anyanyema :m's attempt from the case-history series, this does not impair the validity of the Mohave thesis that funeral suicide is a sex-linked reaction. Indeed, the Mohave simply claim that funeral suicide is a *typically feminine* reaction pattern, which is not the same as claiming that *only women* do, in fact, commit funeral suicide. Indeed, the thesis that a given reaction pattern or character structure is more feminine than masculine does not imply that neurotic men cannot manifest a similar reaction pattern, nor have a passive-feminine ("effeminate") character structure.[43]

The relevant characterological difference between Mohave men and women appears to be related to their culturally conditioned reaction to the loss of a beloved person, and especially of a spouse or close relative.

Although even Mohave women concede that women are less stable in their affections than are men, it is the male who is expected to accept emotional losses in a steadfast and stoical manner. Even where the loss is potentially still reversible—for example, before the runaway wife settles down with another man—the deserted husband is not supposed to do anything to win back his unfaithful wife's affections, nor is he even permitted to display his grief. A man who was not strong enough to shrug off so "trifling" an incident as the loss of an unfaithful wife, had only one permissible alternative, which did not enhance, however, his reputation for true masculinity, since it represented at best a masculine type of patterned misconduct: he could paint his face black and arm himself as though preparing to go on the warpath, and then meet his rival in a more or less formal duel, about which no further details could be obtained in 1932, since, by

---

[43] A grotesquely naïve inability to grasp this simple point caused one of Freud's early critics to remark that men could not possibly have hysteria, since they had no uterus (hystera=uterus). This critic apparently did not realize that, in uttering this remark, he accepted uncritically the classical Greek belief that the locus of hysteria was the uterus.

then, the custom was completely obsolete and all but forgotten.[44] As regards the semicomical display of grief of a certain deserted Mohave husband, or the altogether exceptional behavior of another deserted husband who killed his ex-wife's new husband, these incidents were viewed by the Mohave solely as breaches of decorum and not as neurotic or psychotic symptoms.

Men who were neither stoical enough to shrug off such losses, nor exhibitionistic enough to fight their rivals, sometimes developed hi:wa itck. Although this was a supposedly masculine reaction [45] it was also clearly a pattern of misconduct, which revealed the man's essential lack of stoicism. Hence, even though they comforted him while he was acutely depressed, after his recovery they openly laughed at his past antics (Case 21).

Summing up, the Mohave man was trained and expected to accept both potentially reversible losses—such as the desertion of his wife— and completely irreversible losses—such as the death of a wife, or of a member of his family—in a steadfast and stoical manner. Hence, even though an occasional man did attempt funeral suicide, the Mohave Indian's conception of what constitutes a masculine reaction to an emotional loss forced them to define funeral suicide as a typically feminine reaction pattern.

This sex-linked conception of funeral suicide was further reinforced by the fact that the woman was expected to display stoicism only in a purely sexual context.[46] Her usually calm acceptance of a husband's or sweetheart's desertion, the fact that no woman ever tried to kill herself because she was deserted, and the overwhelming preponderance of male cases of hi:wa itck, was, probably rightly, viewed by the Mohave simply as further evidence that women are less involved with those whom they love or marry than are men. Moreover—and perhaps precisely because women did not, *as a rule*, overreact to disappointments in love—the Mohave woman was free to seek to win back her runaway husband, even after he settled down with

<hr/>

[44] Significantly, the last person who tried to revive this custom was the transvestite Sahaykwisa :, presumably because she was always looking for an opportunity to reaffirm her "masculinity." Partly because this practice was outmoded, partly because it represented only a tolerated masculine pattern of misconduct, rather than an ideal masculine pattern and chiefly because such pretensions on the part of a female transvestite seemed grotesque, her grand gesture was universally ridiculed. Hence, when seeking to win back her third eloped wife, she behaved in a more restrained—i.e., "ideally masculine"—manner, by not approaching the runaway wife directly; she was simply hanging around in the vicinity of Haq'au's camp. However, even this relatively restrained behavior only led to further humiliations, partly because her desire to win back her ex-wife, or to bewitch her, was a feminine, rather than masculine, impulse, and partly because she went about it in an informal way, instead of seeking, as before, to "fight" the man with whom her former wife was now living (Case 105). This series of incidents sheds a great deal of light upon the neurotic sources of certain forms of extreme traditionalism.

[45] O :ote's claim of suffering from hi:wa itck, was unanimously rejected by the tribe (Case 104).

[46] She was not expected to cry out either during defloration or during childbirth, and was ridiculed if she did (Devereux, 1950 g).

another woman, and could even engage in physical combat with her rival (Case 105). Moreover, apparently only female shamans (Case 49) and one female transvestite shaman (Case 105) ever tried to bewitch the spouse or lover who rejected or deserted them. In brief, only Mohave women appear to have reacted to emotional frustration with overt (real or magical) aggression. This more or less tolerated aggressive reaction to an emotional loss was so closely identified with femininity that even male transvestites were permitted to fight their (female) rivals (Devereux, 1937 b). In brief, it was the Mohave woman's privilege to give free rein to her jealousy and resentment when a beloved person deserted her. Hence, unlike men, she was poorly prepared to react to the death of a beloved person with stoical resignation. Given this—definitely Mohave—conception of a "typically" feminine reaction to an irreversible emotional loss, it was inevitable that funeral suicide should be thought of as a typically feminine reaction pattern. It is, in fact, quite probable that even if men attempting funeral suicide had actually outnumbered women 10 to 1, the Mohave would nonetheless have continued to define funeral suicide as a *characterologically* feminine reaction.

The last point to be made in this context is that Mohave attempts to commit funeral suicide seem to be largely dramatic, i.e., more or less hysterical, gestures. Since hysteria is nearly everywhere more common among women than among men, given a ritual opportunity for a grand, and perfectly safe, hysterical gesture, women rather than men would be tempted to make the most of it. This may explain why, in most societies, including even the Mohave, whose women are not noted for their loyalty, the principal—i.e., the most ostentatious and noisy—mourners are usually the women.[47] The one fact which best highlights the validity of these conclusions is that the most serious burns were sustained by a woman, whose subjective reasons, if any, for wishing to leap on her husband's funeral pyre were incomprehensible even to the Mohave (Case 109), although members of this tribe are often startlingly perceptive (pt. 8, pp. 485–504).

Subjective motivation, related to understandable current conflicts, was mentioned only in the case of Anyanyema:m (Case 111). While not even the most innocuous cultural mandates can be implemented behaviorally without at least some subjective motivation (pt. 7, pp. 371–431), it is extremely probable that the failure of all remembered attempts to commit funeral suicide is directly attributable to the lack of an effective subjective motivation. In fact, funeral suicide may have so completely deteriorated into a hollow ritual gesture that it is not even suitable any more for the implementation of genuine

---

[47] Needless to say, there are many other reasons, in addition to those just mentioned, why women tend to react to such losses more violently than men. However, an enumeration of these additional reasons is not necessary in the present context.

suicidal mourning reactions. This inference is strongly supported by
the fact that adequately motivated people would manage to commit
funeral suicide successfully, no matter what precautions the secondary
mourners may take to prevent it.[48]

The most telling argument in support of the thesis that funeral
suicide is simply a ritual gesture is, however, that Mohave Indians
whose suicidal mourning reaction is genuine nearly always manage to
put an end to their lives. Those who have *conscious*, but purely *subjective*, mourning depressions kill themselves in private (pt. 7,
pp. 459–484), those whose *conscious* subjective suicidal urges are reinforced by certain *eschatological beliefs* maneuver others into killing
them (pt. 7, pp. 387–426), while those whose suicidal mourning reactions are more or less *unconscious* allow the ghosts of their deceased
spouses or relatives to lure them in dream to the land of the dead, and
develop one of several potentially "fatal" ghost diseases (pt. 4, pp.
128–186) which represent "psychic suicides" (Brill, 1934; Mauss, 1926;
Yawger, 1936). All of these three types of suicide are usually successful, presumably because they are subjectively motivated and because
the person wishing to kill himself does not indulge in a grandiose public gesture, but kills himself, or causes himself to be killed, in private,
and in the most efficient manner possible.

The conspicuous absence of a subjective motivation in most Mohave
funeral "suicides" can be readily correlated with the type of affective
involvement ("libidinal bond") approved of by Mohave society. The
traditional pattern of such commitments (pt. 3, pp. 91–106, pt. 7, pp.
298–326) was a broad network of moderately intense involvements.
Hence, in aboriginal times, all strong *subjective* reactions to the loss
of a spouse or sweetheart were considered extreme, those exceeding a
certain limit being defined as hi :wa itck (pt. 3, pp. 91–106). Although
this pattern has changed somewhat in modern times (pt. 7, pp. 308–
326), the ideal type of emotional involvement continues to be the amiable, helpful, and affectionate, but not excessive, devotion of a person
to his spouse, his kin, his friends, and the tribe as a whole. At first
blush, the atypical pattern of excessive emotional involvement appears
to be present also in funeral suicides. This, however, is an entirely
misleading impression. For example, the real motivating factor in
Anyanyema :m's attempt (Case 111) was not so much tenderness and
love, as guilt over having driven his son to suicide. Utu :rå's gesture
(Case 110) was so conspicuously halfhearted that it can barely rate
as a sucidal attempt, and therefore does not suggest that he was too
intensely involved with his deceased wife. Mu :th (Case 108) did
seem to be very devoted to her son, but her devotion represented a type

---

[48] Every psychiatrist knows that really determined people manage to commit suicide
even while physically restrained and constantly watched.

of asexual love no Mohave would call excessive, which may explain why no one ridiculed her unsuccessful attempt to kill herself. Psychologically, the most revealing case is that of Syuly (Case 109), who did seem to have loved her husband with more than average intensity, which may explain why she managed to burn herself more severely than any other would-be funeral suicide. The unusual intensity of her wifely devotion may also explain why, of all attempted funeral suicides, her case was considered to be the least comprehensible and the most ridiculous.

Actually, it is not even necessary to assume the presence of an abnormally strong emotional involvement with the deceased to understand the impulse actuating attempted funeral suicides, especially since it is known that such attempts are always frustrated. The fact is that, like everyone else, the Mohave Indians tend to become disturbed by the loss of someone close to them, and this emotional upset is further intensified by the culturally determined practice of the wake or "cry," during which—despite the ideal of steadfast resignation—extreme emotionality is actually encouraged, as well as by the frantic destruction of property during the cremation (Hall, 1903). It is true, of course, that, due to the instability of Mohave marriages, many a Mohave child learns, quite early in life, to move from home to home and to expect changes in the personnel of his immediate family, so that he realizes quite early that whereas the *attitude* of his human emotional environment is constant, the *personnel* of this environment is not constant (Devereux, 1939 b). While this may accustom the Mohave to the disappearance of persons from his intimate environment and may persuade him that the lost love object will soon be replaced by an equivalent one, the emotional intensity of the funeral rites intensifies, if not his actual sense of loss, then at least his tendency to display his grief. Hence, except for Anyanyema :m (Case 111), the persons who tried to commit funeral suicide were probably hysterically exhibitionistic, rather than truly depressed and suicidal.[49]

The formal, traditional and even ritualistic element in funeral suicides—as distinct from a genuine grief and sense of loss—is further underscored by the fact that every single recorded case of attempted funeral suicide took place in connection with the death of a member of the immediate family or of a spouse, i.e., of persons who had definite primary social obligations toward the survivor. No Mohave appears to have attempted to commit *funeral* suicide at the pyre of a brother, distant cousin, affinal relative, sweetheart, or friend, since such persons have no *important*, primary and formal obligations toward the

---

[49] Compare the widespread custom of scarification and self-mutilation at funerals, or the rending of clothes, all of which, while promoting the abreaction of genuine grief, also serve exhibitionistic and self-dramatizing impulses, and, in some instances, help to protect the survivors against the dead, who become incensed when not mourned adequately.

mourner.[50] The few nonfuneral suicides triggered by the death of a person not a member of the mourner's immediate family were, moreover, preceded by a long period of brooding and led to informal, nonritual attempts to commit suicide in private (pt. 7, pp. 459–484). It is therefore this latter type of suicide—actuated by a subjective delayed mourning reaction—rather than funeral suicide which reflects an exceptionally intense emotional involvement, and, significantly, it is this type of suicide which the Mohave themselves explain, in case after case, in strictly psychological terms.

This being said, it is perhaps desirable to stress that the ready availability of some relatively "respectable" social motivation may partly inhibit the development of a more subjective motivation, or else encourage a partial repression of an effective subjective motivation. This thesis is not incompatible with the view expressed elsewhere in this work that all action results from the interplay of sociocultural and subjective motives.

Funeral suicide and the cremation of property.—Funeral suicide is closely articulated with the total cremation pattern, which involves not only the burning of the corpse, but also of the deceased person's entire estate and dwelling.[51] The prospect of being suddenly left without a roof and of having to burn even (some of?) their personal property which the dwelling inhabited by the deceased contains, induces many young couples to leave their aged parents and to seek another shelter which, while possibly less comfortable, is less likely to have to be burned down in the foreseeable future. In brief, the severance of the child's bonds with its prenatal—or prehuman—existence is stressed quite as consistently as the severance of the relationship between the living and the dead.

The bonds which tie the dead to the land of the living are severed through the cremation of his corpse, his dwelling, and his property, since, if this is not done, the ghost will return to earth to get what belongs to him.[52] The dead man's corpse and his property are piled on one and the same pyre and are cremated so as to insure that the "soul" or "essence" of his property will go with him to the land of ghosts. Hence, many otherwise generous persons even begin to hoard

---

[50] Kinsmen and friends were expected to help a needy person, but only if his immediate family was unable to provide assistance.

[51] The only death which does not make the burning of the dwelling and all it contains mandatory is that of a child whose "house" is still the cradle (Devereux, 1948 c) and whose soul does not go to the land of the dead, but into a rat hole, since the child did not live long enough to have its chin tattooed. In such cases the cradle is broken and thrown into the Colorado River.

[52] When there is a scarcity of goods or crops in the land of the dead, two ghosts, who will be born as twins, are sent to earth to obtain additional funeral property (pt. 7, pp. 348–356).

in their old age things which would be useful to them in the land of ghosts. The Mohave—

are careless of property and spend money freely . . . Only the old women evince some disposition to hoard for their funeral . . . The destroying of property with the dead is the subject of much concern to most Mohave and is frequently discussed . . . Old women with difficulty keep a horse alive on gathered mesquite ([53]) in order that it may be killed and eaten at their funeral . . . When a man has sung for his dying or dead son, he throws away and gives him—chupilyk (tcupilyk)—his songs. An old woman had saved some odds and ends of property for *chupilyk* for herself. When she sold them, she declared her intention of buying food which would pass into her body and thus be destroyed with her. She was perhaps humorous in her remarks, but at the same time evidently explaining to her conscience. (Kroeber, 1925 a.)

It is obvious that the wholesale destruction of a dead man's home and property, which was heretofore also available to his family and friends, is bound to elicit some anxiously, but ineffectually, concealed regret, even in notoriously generous people, as the following observation will show.

CASE 107 (Personal observation) :

In July 1935 I arrived unannounced at Parker, Ariz., and immediately learned that a certain fine old gentleman—the father of Sumurámurá and the father-in-law of Hama: Utce:—had just died, and that a wake ("cry") was being held for him.[54] Though it was already late in the evening, I immediately drove down to the reservation to comfort my friends, but, due to the fact that during my 2½ years of absence new roads had been built, I was unable to find Hama: Utce:'s house. Finally I stopped a passing car and asked the Mohave who were in it to tell me where I could find the bereaved family. Since it was dark, I was not recognized, and since I was perhaps not personally acquainted with these persons, a man told me rather brusquely that I could not see that family since they were at the "cry" for the deceased. I replied that I understood that no outsider could be present at a cry and that I had only meant to let the bereaved couple know that I deeply shared their grief.

As soon as I gave him my name the man made a complete about face and insistently asked me to follow his car, since they were themselves on their way to the cry and felt perfectly certain that the mourners would want very much to see me. I agreed to follow them to the house where the cry was held, but, despite the urging of my new friends, remained outside, for fear of intruding, and simply asked my guide to inform Hama: Utce: of my presence and to convey to her my sympathy, which he agreed to do. However, in less than a minute Hama: Utce: came running through the courtyard, and, taking my hand, led me indoors, saying: "If anything could comfort me at this time, it would be your being here with us, my friend." After expressing in a few words my genuinely felt sympathy and sorrow, I quietly entered the house, where I was warmly welcomed by Sumurámurá and others, and was asked to sit at the same table with the chief mourners and to share their meal. I imagine that this was done not only because the bereaved couple was as fond of me

---

[53] Mohave women hardly ever ride (Case 24) or drive a wagon and therefore seldom own horses. (Present writer's note.)

[54] This "cry" was held in a private home and not in a certain tribal building usually spoken of as the "cry house" (pl. 4, *b*).

as I was of them, and because they had never expected to see me again after I left them in 1933 to go to Indochina, but also because they knew that I was genuinely devoted to the admirable old gentleman whose death all of us were mourning.

Shortly before her father-in-law's death Hama:Utce: had made for him an exceptionally fine Mohave bead belt [55] of a type which, even during the depression, commanded a good price from tourists and which takes many scores of hours to make. During the entire cry Sumurámurà, an extraordinarily gentle and generous man, most of the time either examined regretfully, or else actually wore his father's fine bead belt. These acts probably meant that, quite apart from its keepsake value, Sumurámurà, in his own gentle and wistful way, was manifesting not only his carefully controlled, and perhaps unconscious, resentment over having to destroy so beautiful and valuable an object, but also a certain amount of identification with his dead father.

If a man so incredibly generous that his own generous wife sometimes teased him for being too good-natured (Devereux, 1937 b) showed some reluctance to destroy an object made by his wife and given to his dead father, it seems reasonable to assume that less generous mourners would experience a great deal of unverbalized resentment over the obligatory cremation of property. This, presumably, explains why the cremation of the corpse and of property elicits a great deal of emotionality, which is often whipped up to a veritable frenzy (Hall, 1903; Burbank, 1944; McNichols, 1944; Pickerell, 1957) by the eerie sight of the flaming pyre, the occasional movements of the burning corpse (Drucker, 1941, and pt. 7, pp. 389–392), the shrill wailing of mourning women, the impassioned oratory of funeral officials, and the exhaustion induced by a prolonged vigil and real grief. Such a state of exaltation can—at least occasionally—crystalize into one of two—diametrically opposite—reactions: on the one hand one meets with cases of attempted suicide and, on the other hand, with brazenly scandalous sexual behavior which, in one instance at least, involved the attempt to rape a woman who had offended one of the men present with certain highly improper taunts (Devereux, 1947 a).

In some cases the destruction is not limited to the objects which actually belonged to the deceased. At certain important funerals the mourners even tear off their own clothes and hurl them, together with some of their other possessions, into the flames, while in at least one instance (Hall, 1903), when there was nothing left to destroy, the Mohave went to town and bought additional things to be cast into the flames. The frenzied nature of such acts clearly indicates that they represent an "aggressive overcompliance" with cultural demands—a type of reaction which automatically implies the presence of strong, but strenuously inhibited, wishes to preserve all of the property for those who had been permitted to use it while its owner was still alive.

---

[55] In 1933 Hama : Utce : had made a similar belt for me, as a farewell present.

Indeed, due to the Mohave pattern of generosity, not only those who live under the same roof, but also relatives and friends are free to borrow each other's property whenever they need it.[56] Hence, those who use another person's property consistently come to rely on its availability to the point where they almost consider it (psychologically) "their" property,[57] i. e., as part of their social integrity (Pareto, 1935), and possibly even of their "body image."[58] Thus, when the mourners were forced to burn a man's property, which they were accustomed to use, they necessarily felt that the deceased had suddenly become avaricious[59] and was forcing them to destroy what, through prolonged use, they had begun to regard as at least partly their property. Their conviction that the dead are strongly property-minded is also reflected in the belief that if the property of the deceased is not destroyed, he will return to get it. Needless to say, the sudden change in character attributed to the dead[60] is simply a projection of the mourners' own changed attitude toward the person who just died, and who, after a life-long display of generosity, suddenly forces them to destroy badly needed property.

---

[56] A Mohave who wishes to borrow something and does not find the prospective lender at home, may even take the needed item in the absence of its owner, but will return it as soon as he no longer needs it. By contrast, theft was practically unheard of among the Mohave (Case 76). This was fully understood by the late M. A. I. Nettle, M.D. When a hospitalized Mohave woman, who was given scissors to enable her to do some sewing, took them home after being discharged, Dr. Nettle refused to call this a theft, rightly stressing that the woman felt that the scissors had been given to her, or, if they had only been lent to her, that the hospital only had to ask for their return in order to get them back immediately. The Mohave are so baffled by theft, that when a white man stole and gelded the finest stallion of the reservation, its owner did manage to get it back, but took no steps to punish the thief either legally or extralegally.

[57] The owners of property actually encourage this attitude. When Hivsu: Tupo :ma and Hama: Utce: learned in 1938 that I had had some very hard sledding in recent years, Hivsu: Tupo :ma declared with tears in his eyes that I should have come to Parker, so that he could have slaughtered a horse to feed me. As for Hama :Utce:, she angrily reprimanded me for my "unfriendly" failure to let her know of my plight: "Don't you know that as long as there is a dollar in my house, half—or even all—of it is *yours*? Don't ever let it happen again!"

[58] Teitelbaum (1941) discovered that clothes were parts of the body image when his hypnotized subjects, instructed to develop agnosia for the parts of the body, developed agnosia also with regard to their clothing.

[59] The acquisitiveness of ghosts is explicitly referred to in one of the two theories accounting for the origin of twins (Devereux, 1941, and pt. 7, pp. 348–356).

[60] Note an earlier reference to the fact that old women approaching death suddenly begin to hoard property for their funeral (Kroeber, 1925 a). At the same time Tcatc, when she felt certain that she would not live much longer, gave me a gift which she had refused to give me all her life: She had herself photographed, so that I would not forget her. Both the fact that she allowed herself to be photographed and her desire not to be forgotten by me violated basic Mohave tenets and may therefore have represented not only the wish to leave me a memento, but—unconsciously at least—also an attempt to induce me—whom she often called her "favorite grandson"—to join her in the beyond (Devereux, 1951 b). The fact that she implemented her psychologically human, but culturally un-Mohave wish not to die entirely, i.e., to be remembered, through the medium of a non-Mohave—myself—is a culturally and psychologically important fact. Indeed, in all societies there seems to exist a tendency to actualize culturally forbidden impulses through cooperation with aliens. This tendency is probably to be thought of as an important motivating factor underlying acculturation processes.

In brief, it is extremely probable, and, in fact, almost certain, that not only the bonds of affection—which must be severed by never again mentioning the name of the deceased (Kroeber, 1925 a)—but also a more or less "shared" ownership of property link the living to the dead. This latter bond must also be severed before the dead can become fully detached from the living.

When seen in this light, the frantic destruction of all of the deceased man's property, of parts of the mourners' own property (which was probably used formerly also by the deceased) and, finally, the occasional destruction of additional goods bought for this specific purpose, must represent more than simple piety. It is, probably, also a taunt to the suddenly possessive and acquisitive dead, which seems to say: "Having deprived me of the things which were, in a way, also mine, because I used them, you might as well take what is wholly mine—and more!" [61]

It seems probable that the frenzied destruction of the dead person's property, and, especially, the—presumably even more exalted—heaping of additional goods on the pyre, is, subjectively, the emotional equivalent of self-immolation, while "objectively" it represents a compensation to the dead for the mourners' failure to follow him into death, which—as the efforts of ghosts to lure the survivors to the land of the dead (pt. 4, pp. 128–186) indicate—may be something the dead desire.

Needless to say, this interpretation presupposes a ritual and psychological equivalence between man and his property. The genuineness of this equivalence was demonstrated sociologically by Pareto (1935), who viewed property as part of a person's "integrity" and clinically by a large number of psychoanalysts. As regards the Mohave in particular, a major myth (Kroeber, MS., n.d.) specifically shows (Devereux, MS., 1935) that true human status is acquired through the ownership of land, and that in at least one rite (pt. 7,

---

[61] Such an attitude is far from rare in primitive society, as two—almost ritual—examples will indicate.

(1) In 1906 the Dutch, who had been looking for a pretext to occupy Bali, invaded that island, under the pretense of recovering silver allegedly pilfered from a shipwrecked Chinese junk. When the Dutch troops landed in Bali, the King and his concubines marched into the rifle fire of the Dutch, flinging coins at them and shouting: "This is what you came for—now get it."

(2) In 1933 I asked a Sedang friend, who was also one of my informants and a relative-by-adoption, to make a tour of the neighboring villages and buy me as many chickens as possible. He returned from this tour with a large number of chickens, for which he had paid more than they were worth. When I pointed this out to him in a quite friendly manner, he became angry, rushed to his house and returned with a pig worth far more than the difference between the actual value of the chickens and the price he had paid for them. He insisted that I had to accept this pig as a fine and as a compensation, and I had quite a bit of trouble persuading him that I desired no fine, did not expect him to make up the difference between the actual value of the chickens and the price he had paid for them and that I had not suspected him of dishonesty, but simply of inefficient bargaining (Devereux, MS., 1933–1934).

pp. 356–371) a horse represents its owner. This explains why, when someone dies, his farmland is either left fallow for several years, or else is alienated, not only among the Mohave, but also among the Yuma (Forde, 1931). Hence, what stood in need of a discussion was not so much the tendency to equate a man with his property, as the mourners' attitude toward the property which is being destroyed. In other words, we had to examine "whose" property is really destroyed, even when only the legal property of the deceased is cremated. It was found that, even though—when seen from the viewpoint of the suddenly legalistically minded and possessive dead—most of the property destroyed was his and his alone, the mourners viewed the matter in terms of the more generous and flexible social realities of Mohave life, where the difference between the ownership and the use of property is minimal and almost negligible.

Summing up, since the mourner cannot but feel that in cremating the dead person's property he is depriving himself of goods which, through prolonged use, he views as being partly his, and since, moreover, the Mohave condemn the sudden possessiveness and acquisitiveness of the dead, one is practically forced to conclude that the mourner who jumps on the funeral pyre throws himself quite as much after "his own" property, as after that of the dead man and after the deceased himself. This conclusion leads directly to the problem of a subjective latent hostility to the deceased.

Hostility to the dead.—In many instances the Mohave mourner controls his unconscious hostility toward the dead by projecting his death wishes upon a witch, who supposedly killed the deceased by witchcraft. It is a psychological truism that such an—objectively unrealistic—accusation would be made only by someone who tries hard to deny his own hostilities and does so by projecting them upon someone else.[62]

The fact that the mourner actually impoverishes himself at the funeral [63] definitely suggests the presence of self-aggression and masochism, since not only the dead man's actual property, but also that of the mourners is sometimes cast on the funeral pyre. It is psychologically necessary to assume that this self-aggression and/or self-impoverishment occur in response to the supposed hostility and sudden

---

[62] Many Australians typically seek to assuage their grief over the death of a fellow member of the tribe by attacking another tribe—apparently *not invariably* because they believe that the attacked tribe had actually killed the deceased by witchcraft. This is the well-kown defense of "handing on the trauma," which occurs also in other primitive societies. Thus, when Queen Kauna of Nukuoro lost her infant son, she first ordered all small boys to be killed and then made all pregnant women abort, so as to force her subjects to share her mourning (Eilers, 1934).

[63] Compare also the fact that a father, whose son is about to die, often throws away (= tcupilyk) (Kroeber, 1925 a) the songs which he learned in dream, and which represent psychologically valuable "incorporeal property."

possessiveness of the dead, whose very death is—at least uncon-sciously—apparently apprehended as an aggression against the living, who lose not only a kinsman but also the use of his property.[64] Since it would be highly improper to respond to possessiveness with counter-possessiveness, the masochistic and self-impoverishing excessive de-struction of property represents an overly vehement denial of counter-hostilities, whose very intensity renders them suspect, since the mourners seem to "protest too much."

This, however, is not a complete explanation of the phenomena under consideration. Psychoanalytic theory as well as clinical experience suggest that such a taunting masochism probably also seeks to mask even more deeply repressed and ego-dystonic primary hostilities to-ward the deceased. There is nothing contrary to common sense in such an assumption, since even the most normal and warmhearted people are sometimes startled by the sudden and frighteningly incomprehen-sible emergence of fleeting death wishes toward those whom they love most.[65] Hence the unconscious self-accusation: "You died because I wanted you to die" [66] is inverted and appears in the guise of the (uncon-scious) accusation: "You died in order to desert and impoverish me. If so, I hope you are satisfied, now that I have destroyed not only your property, but also my own. Take it all, do not appear to me in dream to lure me to the land of the dead and do not return as a twin for further property." This almost paranoid attitude is culturally implemented by means of the frenzied destruction of property and also by the am-biguous ritual of attempting funeral suicide. Though culturally im-plemented, both of these activities represent, on the subjective level, symptomatic behavior, whose purpose—like that of other symptoms—is to disguise a strongly ego-dystonic impulse—in this instance the mourner's primary hostility to the deceased—by bribing and concili-ating the neurotic conscience [67] through a hostile and mocking self-impoverishment and through an empty and ritual suicidal gesture.

There is strong indirect evidence that death wishes have to be minimized even among the warmhearted and generous Mohave.

[64] Compare the belief that "suicidal" sucklings and twins (pt. 7, pp. 340–356) "make everyone miserable" before they actually die. Compare also the Hopi belief (Kennard, 1937) that people die in order to grieve their relatives.

[65] Genuine and creative love does not imply the *absence* of death wishes; it implies that these wishes are *sublimated* into unconstricting and realistic protectiveness against illness, accidents, etc. When the death wishes are not sublimated, but are only suppressed by means of a reaction formation, protectiveness becomes hostile and crippling over-protectiveness.

[66] Compare the suicidal self-accusations of witches (pt. 7, pp. 387–426), which are highly relevant in this context, since the inner conflicts of shamans and witches differ from those of other members of the tribe only by their greater intensity (Devereux, 1956 b).

[67] Regressive and neurotic mechanisms can be observed even in basically normal persons subjected to extreme stress. The neurotic conscience is represented by the archaic and infantile *superego*, whereas the healthy conscience is represented by the mature and creative *ego ideal* (Devereux, 1956 a).

Indeed, as Kelly (1949) points out, the Cocopa—and obviously also the Mohave—practice of completely destroying the dead person's property prevents the accumulation of capital and therefore also impedes material and social progress. Unfortunately, this sociologically and economically very penetrating comment disregards certain important psychological consequences of this practice. In societies where the survivors inherit, death wishes toward older relatives are often strengthened by practical considerations, whereas in societies where not only the entire estate of the deceased but also additional property is destroyed, acquisitiveness does not intensify unconscious death wishes. Hence, psychologically speaking, the custom of destroying the dead person's property helps the relatives of elderly people to control their death wishes. This is of some importance in Mohave society, where the care of the aged was sometimes a genuine burden for the young, as is shown by the fact that at least one son shamefully neglected his old mother (Case 123). In fact, it is probable that many societies suspect the old of witchcraft chiefly because the young are forced to support them. Hence, the absence of inheritances and the massive destruction of additional property in Mohave society presumably helped the young to repress their hostility toward those whom they had to support, because their unconscious primary death wishes were not intensified by the prospect of deriving tangible benefits ("secondary gain") from the death of aged dependents. Otherwise stated, even though many a Mohave had to support an old person, the aged relative was less of an economic problem alive than dead.[68]

The effectiveness of the destruction of property in reducing hostility toward the aged in Mohave society is suggested by two facts:

(1) On the whole, the Mohave seem somewhat less inclined than many other groups to view the old more or less *indiscriminately* as witches, though they did believe that the singers of certain song cycles became shamans—albeit not necessarily also witches—in old age (Kroeber, 1925 a) and that some aging shamans became suicidal witches (pt. 7, pp. 387–426). On the other hand, the *average* old person was not suspected of witchcraft *simply because of his age.*

(2) The Mohave were unaware of the existence of senile psychoses and possibly even of certain minor psychological symptoms of old age (pt. 5, pp. 254–255). This striking gap in their otherwise compendious nosology suggests either a marked lack of hostility toward the old, or—more probably—a fairly effective sublimation of, or at least control over, such hostilities.[69]

This finding explains why, even though the cremation of property prevents the accumulation of capital and impedes progress (Kelly,

---

[68] The same is even more true of a spouse, or of a son or daughter.

[69] Another factor was probably the shorter life span characteristic of aboriginal life conditions.

1949), the Mohave continued to impoverish themselves periodically. Like everyone else, they apparently felt that it was more important to alleviate anxieties and inner conflicts than to obtain practical benefits at the cost of an intensification of inner turmoil. A more systematic application of this insight to the study of irrational-seeming traditionalisms and obstacles to progress would probably clarify many puzzling aspects of the dynamics of social change.[70]

The preceding considerations strongly suggest the presence of certain ego-dystonic and "unavowable" impulses in the mourners, which are liberated in the course of funerals in the form of semiritualized regressive behavior consisting of a frantic destruction of property[71] and suicidal attempts. From the strictly anthropological point of view the fact that culture encourages such regressive behavior is a sufficient explanation of its occurrence at funerals. However, if one accepts the view that man is not a cultural robot and that at least a minimal subjective motivation is necessary for the behavioral implementation of even the most trifling social mandate (pt. 7, pp. 371–431), it is necessary to do more than just prove the presence of ego-dystonic impulses or to demonstrate that, during funerals, their manifestation, in the form of regressive behavior, is encouraged by culture; it is also necessary to prove that no other outlet or "safety valve" is available to Mohave mourners.

One of the Mohave Indian's principal safety valves seems to be a conspicuous sexual laxity, which appears to be largely compensatory in character, since it seems to provide substitute gratifications for a variety of frustrations, at least some of which are economical, and also serves to alleviate tensions of various kinds (Devereux, 1939 b). However, the Mohave prohibit all sexual activity during funerals (pt. 4, pp. 186–195), though, due to the mobilization of a variety of ordinarily repressed impulses, the mourner badly needs an outlet for the tensions and explosive anxieties which he normally controls through sexual activity.

Denied the use of this habitual technique for the alleviation of his tensions, the mourner is forced to seek relief by means of safety valves "built into" Mohave funeral rites, but strictly forbidden in daily routine. Hence, the *individual mourner*, unaccustomed to frenzied destructiveness and suicidalness in daily routine,[72] *experiences* these unfamiliar, though culturally sanctioned, funeral safety valves as "improvised" or "idiosyncratic" symptoms of a markedly regressive

---

[70] A brilliant application of this principle to the history of technology was published by Sachs (1933).

[71] Frenzied destructiveness is so archaic a trait that it occurs even in the lower primates.

[72] For a description of a destructive tantrum during the breaking up of a marriage, compare Kroeber, 1925 b. Behavior of this type is not common among the Mohave.

kind,[73] which probably explains why the Mohave are so ambivalent about the custom of funeral suicide. The unfamiliarity of the safety valves built into special rites, such as funerals, also explains why they are less satisfactory than are the routine defenses built into daily practices.

Another important aspect of ritual regressive behavior during funerals is that not all members of the crowd assembled near the pyre are entitled or expected to behave in an equally destructive manner. Close relatives of the deceased will throw more property, in a more frenetic manner, on the pyre than will others and usually only the chief mourner is expected to dramatize his grief by making a suicidal gesture. Funeral ritualists, secondary mourners, and the rest of the crowd are denied even this type of emotional outlet. It is therefore not in the least surprising to note that, in some cases, funeral orators and secondary mourners, who are denied both the special outlet of exalted funeral behavior and the normal outlet of sexual activity, not only violate the taboo on sexual intercourse (Case 48), but sometimes even engage in behavior which would be considered outrageous even at an uninhibited party (Devereux, 1947 a). It is hardly necessary to add that the *extreme* scandalousness of such behavior, especially at a funeral, is, in itself, proof positive both of the compensatory nature of Mohave sexual activity and evidence that funerals elicit regressive ("extreme") behavior, precisely because they mobilize ordinarily well-controlled ego-dystonic impulses under circumstances in which recourse to normal, routine outlets (sexual activity) is forbidden. In brief, the destructive and self-destructive behavior of the chief mourners, and the conduct of persons who behave scandalously at funerals are equally regressive, because both are the inevitable byproducts of the "psychological climate" of funerals, which mobilizes ordinarily well-controlled objectionable impulses. Hence, these two extreme patterns differ only in that the regressive behavior of the chief mourners is culturally more or less sanctioned, whereas that of the sexually misbehaving members of funeral crowds is contrary to all rules and conventions.

It is therefore safe to say that one function of Mohave funerals is to promote regressive (symptomatic) behavior at funerals. This, however, is not an unmitigated evil. Indeed, even though the Mohave are ambivalent about excessive mourning reactions and certainly do not condone sexual misconduct at funerals, the regressive behavior encouraged at funerals has, in the long run, at least one important beneficial effect: it permits the massive and instantaneous abreaction

---

[73] A detailed discussion of the functional difference between routine (culturally provided) defenses and improvised idiosyncratic symptoms will be found in part 2 (pp. 57–71) and in Devereux, 1956 b and 1957 b.

of grief as well as of ordinarily repressed destructive, hostile and self-destructive impulses, and therefore, by intensifying mourning behavior during the funeral, tends to abridge intrapsychic mourning, which the Mohave seek to limit to 4 days.[74]

It may, conceivably, be objected that we imputed to the Mohave a hostility toward the dead and an acquisitiveness which are not confirmed by their ordinary behavior. This objection is both anthropologically and psychologically untenable. The Mohave Indian's hostility to the dead is revealed by his habit of wailing before the patient is actually dead, his former proneness to place the body on the pyre before the sick person was actually dead (McNichols, 1944; see also Case 6), and his fear of ghosts, who seek to lure the living to the land of the dead and whose very name he intends to forget. The repressed acquisitiveness of the Mohave Indian, though perfectly controlled, and even sublimated into generosity, in his daily life, is revealed by the fact that he imputes a marked acquisitiveness to ghosts, and especially to those ghosts who return to earth for additional property in the shape of twins (pt. 7, pp. 348–356). This sudden "change of character"—for the worse—which the Mohave impute to the dead is the perfect psychological equivalent of the process which requires occidental man to impute a change of character—for the better—to the dead, and which he voices by means of such expressions as "my *sainted* grandmother" or "de mortuis nil, nisi *bonum*." In fact, the characteristics ascribed to ghosts are usually those which people have to inhibit—or have markedly failed to manifest—in life.[75]

The most telling argument in favor of the legitimacy of imputing even to the warmhearted and generous Mohave certain hostilities and some acquisitive and hoarding impulses is that such impulses are universal human characteristics. The Mohave are not kind and generous because they *lack* all hostility and acquisitiveness, but because a series of historical accidents led them to evolve a culture which facilitates the *control* and *sublimation* of these impulses to an unusual extent. The fact that their finest traits represent sublimations of less desirable ones does not cancel their good qualities any more than the manure used to fertilize a flower garden impairs the scent of roses.

Acculturation.—The dates of the case histories, recorded in 1936, indicate that, already two decades ago, funeral suicide was rapidly be-

---

[74] During the 4 days which follow a death, the name of the deceased can apparently be mentioned, and one may even dream of sexual relations with the deceased without contracting a ghost illness (pt. 4, pp. 128–186). The parents of a dead child must, however, refrain from coitus, lest the woman should become sterile (Devereux, 148 b). After the 4 days have elapsed, the name of the deceased may no longer be mentioned, his property and dwelling are destroyed, and dreams about the deceased cause a ghost illness, since, at the end of the 4 days, the deceased ceases to revisit his old haunts and proceeds to the land of the dead.

[75] The same is, of course, true of the characteristics imputed to "the enemy," which further proves that the Mohave equate the dead with enemies (Fathauer, 1951; and pt. 4, pp. 128–150).

coming obsolete. This impression is further confirmed by Hama: Utce:'s ironical remarks about Syuly (Case 109), since, despite her efforts to be a good Mohave, Hama: Utce: no longer shares all of the traditional outlook of her tribe. The wholesale destruction of property is also increasingly interfered with, since, to take but one example, in the 1930's the Government refused to lend money to the Mohave for the building of houses, unless they guaranteed not to burn them down. However, in the 1930's any house owned outright—with the possible exception of some American-style frame houses (pl. 5, a)—was still burned down at the death of an adult inhabitant. Last of all, the impact of American culture led—without seriously impairing the old pattern of generosity—to an increasing awareness of legal title to property, at the expense of the psychological sense of coownership rooted in the regularly shared usufruct of the property in questiton.[76] On the other hand the Mohave Indians' awareness of the existence of inheritances among whites does not appear to have influenced their funeral practices even as late as the 1930's, and at least some valuable property apparently continues to be burned even at present.

Attitudes toward funeral suicide can be summarized in a few sentences. The attempted funeral suicide of a bereaved father or mother was considered less silly than a similar attempt made by a bereaved spouse. Moreover, whereas the Mohave were more critical of a widower than of a widow who tried to leap on the funeral pyre of a deceased spouse, simply because men are supposed to accept the loss of a love object more stoically than women, a bereaved and "suicidal" father was not held to have shown more weakness than a bereaved mother who tried to leap on her child's funeral pyre. This finding once more underscores the extent to which the Mohave differentiate affectively between mere sexual relations and matters related to procreation and to the perpetuation of the tribe (Devereux, 1950 a).[77] At the same time it is of great interest that apparently no one ever tried to jump on the funeral pyre of an infant or young child, presumably because the Mohave were so accustomed to a high rate of child mortality that they reacted to the loss of a young child less vehemently than to the loss of a grown son or daughter.

Although extreme emotionality at funerals was expected and practically extorted from the mourners, because it abridged their period of mourning—thereby enabling them to observe the taboo on the names of the dead—the Mohave felt that such hyperemotionality was incompatible with their tribal ego ideal of stoical strength, which, as

---

[76] It should be stressed that the Mohave were simply generous rather than "communistic," a distinction which, as Herskovits (1940) has shown, is of some importance for the understanding of primitive economic processes.

[77] Anyanyema :m (Case 111) was criticized not because he tried to commit funeral suicide on his son's pyre, but because he had driven his son to suicide.

stressed elsewhere (pt. 7, pp. 298–308), was one of the cherished self-deceptions of this highly emotional tribe.

Yet, as usual, the Mohave condemned the act more than the person who performed it, and—except in the case of Anyanyema:m, who was condemned for entirely different reasons (Case 111)—they did not actually tease people who had attempted funeral suicide the way they ridiculed those who tried and failed to kill themselves in a private and nonritual manner. At the same time, they seem to have clearly understood the temporary nature of such emotional upheavals at funerals, since, unlike, e.g., the vicarious suicide of witches (pt. 7, pp. 387–426), funeral suicide was not explained—or explained away—by saying: "It is their nature, they cannot help it." Instead, they react to such occurrences by saying: "One feels sorry for them—but, all the same, it is a crazy (yamomk) thing to do."

The fact that would-be funeral suicides are not taunted about their dramatic gesture afterward as well as Hivsu: Tupo:ma's disapproval of Hama: Utce:'s sarcastic comments about Syuly (Case 109), indicates that the ritual nature of the gesture is well understood and fully empathized with by the tribe as a whole. In fact, in the absence of an appreciable subjective motivation, the cultural impetus and characteristic "type conflicts" (Devereux, 1956 b) underlying such suicidal gestures must, of necessity, be both exceptionally strong and generally understandable, since otherwise no one would ever attempt to leap on the funeral pyre during the cremation itself, which is usually the high point of the "spectacle" [78] side of Mohave funerals.

CONCLUSIONS

Mohave funeral suicide is primarily a ritual gesture, forming a part of a broader pattern which, in its totality, is, when seen *only culturally*, a somewhat antisocial and dysfunctional one. This essentially negative cultural behavior was, however, effectively integrated into the structure of Mohave society and culture, by assigning to it the role of a psychological safety valve in a type of crisis which tends to bring to a head some of the major basic conflicts of the Mohave. It is, in fact, quite likely that *culturally destructive* patterns can be integrated with the total culture pattern only if they provide—or *seem* to provide—*psychologically necessary* gratifications and special means for alleviating tensions usually relieved by other means.

CASE MATERIAL

CASE 108 (Informants: Hivsu: Tupo:ma and Hama: Utce:) :

Mu:th, of the Mu:th gens, an approximately 40-year-old fullblood Mohave woman, tried to jump on the funeral pyre of her 20-year-old son, Câlea Hi:wa

---

[78] This "spectacle" aspect is so marked that even whites make considerable efforts to be admitted to the cremation grounds—where they often behave in a highly objectionable manner (Burbank, 1944; Pickerell, 1957).

(Sand Heart), of the Nyoltc gens. Her suicidal attempt was frustrated by
Hivsu: Tupo:ma and others, who dragged her away and poured cold water on
her until she quieted down. This incident took place on the Needles, Calif.,
cremation ground, at about 1:00 p.m., "some twenty years ago" (1916?). At
that time both of Mu:th's parents were already dead, but her husband was still
alive.

Comment

Mu:th's suicidal attempt was the only one of the four recorded cases of
attempted funeral suicide which was not criticized in one way or the other,
perhaps because devotion to a son is more "respectable" in terms of the Mohave
value system than is attachment to a husband (Case 109). Moreover, unlike
Anyanyema:m (Case 111), Mu:th was not responsible for her son's death, nor
did her suicidal attempt involve the kind of grotesque mishap which occurred
when Utu:râ (Case 110), in trying to commit funeral suicide, only managed to
burn his hair. The fact that she quieted down after cold water was poured on
her suggests that her attempt was made in a state of hysterical excitement.

CASE 109 (Informants: Hivsu: Tupo:ma and Hama: Utce:):

Syuly, of the Syuly gens, a 25-year-old fullblood Mohave woman, threw herself
on the funeral pyre of her husband, Hamo:ce Kwaki:yo (mo:ce carrier) [79] of
the Mu:th gens, a 30-year-old fullblood Mohave, who had died of hiku:pk
(syphilis). Just before the cremation Syuly repeatedly declared that she would
throw herself on her husband's pyre. When, around 4:00 or 5:00 p.m., the pyre
on the Needles, Calif., cremation ground started to burn, Syuly began to run
around the fire until, suffocated by the smoke, she fell into the flames. The
burns she sustained were so severe that, for a while, her life seemed in danger.
This incident took place during the first decade of this century, at a time when
both of Syuly's parents were already dead. Sometime later she remarried and
eventually also died of syphilis. After translating this statement, Hama: Utce:
said: "She wanted to go with her husband (to the land of the dead)—but, all the
same, she married again, later on. Why, then, did she get so excited?"—a jibe
which elicited a markedly disapproving reaction in Hivsu: Tupo:ma.

Comment

Syuly apparently did mean to kill herself, since, unlike Utu:râ (Case 110), she
actually sustained severe burns. On the other hand, the fact that she loudly
proclaimed her intention to commit funeral suicide casts some doubt upon her
sincerity, since she could not help knowing that the Mohave are always on the
alert to frustrate such attempts. By contrast, the fact that she remarried fairly
soon does not necessarily justify Hama: Utce:'s skepticism about the sincerity of
Syuly's love for her deceased husband, since the grief of a loving widow is often
evidence of a real inclination for domesticity. At the same time Hama: Utce:'s
sarcastic remark also seems to reflect a certain degree of puzzlement. Being
exceptionally devoted to her husband Sumurâmurâ, she apparently could not understand how a truly loving wife could remarry so soon after the death of her
husband.[80] It is, however, also possible that Hama: Utce:, who is not a fullblood
Mohave and is therefore especially anxious to proclaim her integral membership
in the Mohave tribe, simply voiced traditional Mohave attitudes more emphati-

---

[79] This man was so fond of the edible mo:ce plant, that he always carried some of it
on his person.

[80] Needless to say, precisely because Hama: Utce: had had a real taste of domestic
bliss, she herself remarried after being widowed.

cally than did Hivsu: Tupo:ma, who, being a fullblood Mohave, had no subjective reason for constantly emphasizing his allegiance to the Mohave way of life.

CASE 110 (Informants: Hivsu: Tupo:ma and Hama: Utce:):

Utu:rà, of the Tcatc gens, an approximately 40-year-old fullblood Mohave, tried to jump on the funeral pyre of his wife O:otc, of the O:otc gens, a fullblood Mohave woman approximately 30 years of age, who had died of "pneumonia." He ran toward the funeral pyre and (presumably because his courage failed him at the last moment) fell down just beside it, only managing to burn his long hair, which, since it had caught fire, had to be cut off. This incident took place at the Needles cremation grounds, around 2:00 or 3:00 p.m., some 30 years ago (1906?). At that time both of Utu:rà's parents were already dead. Later on, Utu:rà died of hiku:pk, which, in this case, was translated as syphilis. At this point Hama: Utce:, who was from Parker, Ariz., said rather tartly: "Syphilis is just about all they die of over at Needles.[81] Here, at Parker, they had no syphilis until, several decades ago, some Federal troops were stationed at La Paz." [82]

Comment

Since Utu:rà allegedly died from syphilis, it seems necessary to stress that his "suicidal" gesture was almost certainly only a dramatic bit of hysterical exhibitionism, rather than a symptom of mental derangement caused by paresis, since neurosyphilis is practically absent among Indians (Kraepelin, 1904). The fact that he "collapsed"(?) *just beside* the pyre, instead of falling *on it*, as did Syuly (Case 109), strongly suggests that, at the very last moment, his courage deserted him. Indeed, had he actually stumbled, or had he collapsed as a result of sheer exhaustion after a prolonged wake, he could just as easily have burned his hand or his face, instead of simply singeing his hair *which, as the chief mourner, he would have had to cut off anyhow*.[83] His dramatic gesture simply enabled him to get rid of his hair in a more obstentaious manner than if it had been clipped in the traditional, and relatively humdrum, way.

At the same time Ut:rà's gesture yields important insights into the emotional significance of funeral gifts and of the hair-cutting rite. Since the Mohave are very proud of their hair and take excellent care of it (Case 30), the clipping of the mourner's hair represents a real sacrifice,[84] as does the frantic—and spiteful—cremation of funeral gifts, which, as stated before, also seems to symbolize a partial self-immolation. In allowing his hair to catch fire Utu:rà simply condensed into a single act three, formally distinct but psychologically interconnected, matters: the clipping of the mourner's hair, the spiteful giving of funeral gifts, and the hollow gesture of attempted self-immolation.

---

[81] This specification may represent an indirect allusion to the fact that the Mohave at Parker had great confidence in "our doctor," M. A. I. Nettle, M.D., who took excellent care of them.

[82] According to Dr. Nettle (1933), several Mohave women had prostituted themselves to this unit of Federal Negro cavalry, contracting venereal diseases and bearing a few half-Negro and half-Mohave children. Most informants denied, however, that any Mohave had a Negro father or grandfather. This denial is relatively credible, since, in the 1930's, the Mohave had no prejudice against Negroes, and always had a kind word for a Negro handyman and his practical nurse wife, who were employed at the Agency Hospital. Moreover, the Mohave freely—though perhaps erroneously—conceded that a certain Mohave had a Chinese father (Devereux, 1937 d, 1949 c).

[83] Although the hair of the mourners does not seem to be thrown on the funeral pyre, the connection between the clipping of hair and death is so close that dreams of having one's hair cut short are believed to be omens of an impending bereavement.

[84] The man who, during an attack of hi:wa itck depression, cut off his hair as though he were in mourning, on getting over his depression carefully picked up his braids and tied them back to his remaining hair (Case 21).

The fact that Utu:râ seems to have been the only Mohave who managed, "accidentally on purpose," to condense [85] these three separate practices into a single dramatic gesture suggests that he must have been a relatively atypical individual, who experienced not only unusually strong guilt feelings, but also felt quite hostile to the wife who had "deserted" him by dying,[86] and therefore was punitive toward himself. This set of inferences is compatible both with Mohave cultural attitudes and practices and with Freud's (1925 d) characterization of the psychology of mourning.

CASE 111 (Informants: Hivsu: Tupo:ma and Hama: Utce:):

Anyanyema:m, a 45-year-old fullblood Mohave of the Nyoltc gens, had, by his fullblood Yuma wife, a 25-year-old son named Tunayva Kor, of the Nyoltc gens. Anyanyema:m, who lived at Parker, Ariz., owned a very fast horse, which Tunayva Kor took to Samtcevu:t—a locality near Needles, Calif., inhabited by several Mohave families—in order to enter it in some races. Tunayva Kor's base of operation as a jockey appears to have been the Mohave settlement just across the river from Needles, presumably because he had some relatives there. Anyanyema:m was quite put out by this—"perhaps he was proud of that horse"—and went to Needles after his son and his horse. For a week Anyanyema:m lived in the house of his son's hosts, constantly nagging him about the horse. One day, around 4:00 or 5:00 p.m., the son finally lost patience, went to get the horse, which was picketed near the house, led it up to his father and said: "I thought you were my father and liked me as I like you, but you seem to care more for the horse than for me and nag me all the time. The gun is in the house; I will shoot myself. Here is your horse; you were after me about it all the time." Tunayva Kor then went into the house, picked up a .32 caliber revolver right in front of his hosts, went to a shed near the house and shot himself in the heart. "He fell over dead then and there." His relatives picked up the gun and "got mad" at Anyanyema:m, who was "all broken up and cried." "You are the cause of all this," the family said, and, to this day, the Mohave feel that Anyanyema:m behaved toward his son in an incomprehensibly selfish [87] and improper way.

At his son's cremation Anyanyema:m tried to jump on the funeral pyre, but, even though they still blamed him, his relatives managed to restrain him in time. "Years later they still blamed him for his son's death." This happened some 15 years ago (1921?). After a while, Anyanyema:m returned to Parker, where he died a few years later. "He smoked an awful lot and therefore coughed a great deal." [88] [Did Anyanyema:m dream of his dead son?] "Even if he had dreamed of his son, he would not have told anyone about it." After a few moments of silence Hama: Utce: said: "It must be awful to have caused someone's death and then to go on living—on and on." (Cf. Case 115.)

Comment

Tunayva Kor's suicide is a perfect example of the Mohave Indian's tendency to react in a highly emotional way to rejection on the part of those from whom he is entitled to expect consistent support (pt. 7, pp. 457–484). Indeed,

---

[85] The tendency to condense, or to compress, things is a marked characteristic of Mohave cultural processes (Devereux, 1957 b).

[86] The Hopi explicitly justify their anger toward the recently dead, by saying that they died only in order to grieve the survivors (Kennard, 1937). The notion of hostility toward those whom one's death will grieve is implicitly present in Mohave beliefs concerning, e.g., the "suicide" of sucklings and twins (pt. 7, pp. 340–356).

[87] Note the completely unconvincing and even illogical "explanation" that Anyanyema:m may have objected to his son's racing his horse, because he was "proud of that horse."

[88] This was a friendly jibe at the anthropologist.

Anyanyema:m had not only proved to be stingy, but added insult to injury by displaying this strongly disapproved trait toward his own son. This may explain the extraordinary vindictiveness of the family, which blamed him for his son's death to the end of his life. In so doing, they rejected their kinsman Anyanyema:m, presumably in order to dissociate themselves from his heinous deed; the Mohave value system, backed up by public opinion, outweighing in this instance the ties of kinship. Such a breakdown of family loyalty is quite unusual, except in cases where the rejected relative is believed to be a witch.[89] At the same time, they did not reject him to the point of allowing him to commit funeral suicide.

One possible reason why Anyanyema:m tried to kill himself, whereas the Mohave father who nagged his son to divorce his unfaithful wife until the son killed himself (Case 116) did not, may be that Anyanyema:m was married to a Yuma woman among whom, according to A. M. Halpern (1938), funeral suicide was somewhat more common than among the Mohave. Of course, the other father violated only the relatively minor rule that one should not interfere with quarreling spouses (Devereux, MS., 1935), whereas Anyanyema:m violated one of the cardinal values of Mohave ethics.

It seems probable that, in attempting to leap on his son's pyre, Anyanyema:m not only tried to alleviate his own guilt feelings, but also sought to appease his indignant relatives. Since, unfortunately for him, such techniques of appeasement are completely at variance with Mohave culture and character, his grand gesture was, both psychologically and practically, a waste of effort. His thoroughly aroused kin group failed to respond to his gesture with sympathy and forgiveness and continued to blame him for his son's death to the bitter end. The fact that, despite their disapproval, they did prevent him from immolating himself was merely an automatic cultural response and not a token of their forgiveness.

A whole series of facts suggest that Anyanyema:m was an altogether atypical and deviant person:

(1) He was sufficiently familiar with whites to be known, even among the Mohave, by the English name "Slim Jim."

(2) He married an alien (Yuma) woman.

(3) He was, by Mohave standards, unduly interested in horses.[90]

(4) He was stingy, even toward his son, whom he nagged until the son committed suicide.

(5) Acting in a wholly un-Mohave manner, he apparently tried to obtain sympathy and forgiveness by a grandiose expiatory gesture.

(6) Unlike most Mohave, he smoked excessively, which suggests that, at least by Mohave standards, he was a somewhat tense person, though his tenseness and excessive smoking may, perhaps, have appeared only after his son's tragic death.

The last point which calls for a comment is Hama:Utce:'s grim concluding remark, that it must be dreadful to have to live on and on, after causing someone's death. While the remark itself simply mirrors a basic Mohave—and

---

[89] The Mohave would rather allow a brazenly exploitive atypical relative to take advantage of them, than deny support to a kinsman. Thus, when the very progressive Hama:Utce: and her husband Sumuràmurà complained that the husband's fairly well-to-do and able-bodied uncle exploited them quite openly, and I ventured to suggest that they let him fend for himself, this progressive couple was almost horrified by my suggestion, saying that they would rather allow themselves to be exploited, than refuse support to a close relative.

[90] The Mohave were neither enthusiastic, nor accomplished horsemen. They despised "unsportsmanlike" tribes that fought on horseback and ridiculed those younger men who went "name traveling" astride a horse (McNichols, 1944; cf. also Dobyns et al., 1957).

human—attitude, its emotional charge was probably derived from more subjective conflicts. Indeed, at this particular time Hama: Utce: herself had fantasies of punishing her stingy and nagging aunt Tanu:, by committing suicide (Case 115), the way her half brother had done when the selfsame aunt made his life miserable with her stingy selfishness and nagging (Case 114).[91]

In brief, Anyanyema:m appears to be the only Mohave who had clearly stated any understandable *subjective* reasons of some specificity for trying to commit funeral suicide. Otherwise expressed, whereas the other three Mohave known to have tried to throw themselves on a beloved person's funeral pyre *appear* to have done so in response to a (conditional) cultural mandate, best understandable in cultural terms, Anyanyema:m's attempt *appears* to have been motivated "primarily" by psychological factors. Needless to say, this impression is probably an erroneous one, since there are cogent reasons for assuming that even the implementation of the most basic cultural mandates requires a certain degree of supplementary subjective motivation and *vice versa* of course (pt. 7, pp. 371–431). Hence, an analysis of the (recorded) subjective factors in Anyanyema:m's suicidal attempt also enables one to obtain at least a glimpse of the (unrecorded) subjective motives which impelled three other Mohave Indians to throw themselves on a son's or on a spouse's funeral pyre. The plausibility of this assumption is greatly enhanced by the fact that Anyanyema:m's known and inferred personal motivation seems adequate both in the light of common sense and in terms of the psychoanalytic conception of the dynamics of mourning.

ACTIVE SUICIDE

Active suicide, as defined here, is either an actual attempt to kill oneself by one's own hand, or the wish to kill oneself. In terms of this definition one should—at least in principle—also view funeral suicides as active suicides. However, since the Mohave themselves differentiate both intellectually and attitudinally between ordinary active suicidal acts and attempts to throw oneself on the funeral pyre of a spouse or relative (Devereux, 1942 a; and pt. 7, pp. 431–459), the two are discussed separately. Apart from the fact that cultural tenets oblige us to differentiate between these two types of actual suicide, discussing them separately also has definite expository advantages. By demonstrating in this chapter the extent to which suicides tend to "cluster," even where the survivor does not seek to throw himself on someone's funeral pyre, we can underscore in an especially effective way the extent to which the Mohave view death as contagious. This point is discussed in some detail in the section on the clustering of suicides.

Any discussion of beliefs, both from the cultural and from the psychological point of view, inevitably entails a certain amount of repetitiousness, especially if they are supported by copious case material. In order to reduce repetitions to a minimum, it is not intended to discuss in this introductory section the motivation of active suicides in general, nor a number of other aspects of active suicide which are either already

---

[91] The foregoing paragraph once more demonstrates to what extent an informant's state of mind, current problems, and character structure can influence the wording and affective charge of his statements concerning genuine tribal attitudes and value systems.

covered in part 7 (pp. 286–329), or are best mentioned in the comments which follow the individual case histories.

The present section is therefore devoted primarily to a discussion of the single most characteristic feature of active suicides: their tendency to occur in clusters.

The clustering of Mohave suicides.—Perhaps the most striking way of showing that clustering is a basic characteristic of the Mohave suicide complex is to contrast clustered suicides as a group with unclustered suicides as a group.

(1) *Frequencies.*—Cases of suicide, of attempted suicide, and of suicidal preoccupations occurring in clusters, outnumber unclustered suicides 14 to 6. In fact, even the absolute number of *clusters* is greater than the absolute number of unclustered suicide *cases*, the former outnumbering the latter 7 to 6.

(2) *Typical vs. atypical motivation.*—Atypical or socially disapproved types of motivation are more frequently present in unclustered than in clustered suicides. Thus:

(*a*) The Mohave disapprove of extreme emotional reactions to adultery, divorce and desertion. Hence, only 2 out of 14 cases of clustered suicides are definitely due to the adultery of the wife (Cases 117 and 120)—Case 122 being ambiguous—whereas 3 of the 6 unclustered cases of suicide are attributable to infidelity (Cases 125, 126, 127). This statement disregards the case of a man (Case 116) whose father drove him to suicide by pestering him to divorce his adulterous wife.

(*b*) Not one of the 14 clustered cases, as against 3 of the 6 single suicides (Cases 106, 123, and 124), was actually due to a *real* isolation of the suicide, which is an altogether exceptional occurrence in Mohave society and must be sharply differentiated from mere resentment over being abused or nagged in a manner which does not involve actual isolation or total rejection.

(*c*) Not even one of the 14 clustered suicides, as against 2 of the 6 unclustered ones, was caught in a culturally wholly anomalous position. Táma:ráhue was the only shaman known to have been *wrongly* accused of witchcraft (Case 106), which may explain why he was the only accused witch who, instead of causing himself to be killed, or facing his killers with equanimity, took matters in his own hand and killed himself. Likewise, the situation of Nyortc (Case 123), whom her son refused to support and to cherish in her old age, was also altogether anomalous in Mohave society. It is true, of course, that Tanu:'s behavior toward her nephew (Case 114) and her niece (Case 115) was also atypical. However, in this instance both the Mohave as a group, and Tanu:'s niece herself emphasized that Tanau: was neither racially nor culturally a real Mohave.   (As regards Case 111, it is ambiguous in this respect.)

(3) *The means used to commit suicide* are conventional and aggressive ones in the case of clustered suicides, but often unconventional, passive (suffocation), or obsolete ones in the unclustered cases. All clustered suicides used ordinary and effective weapons, such as guns or knives, whereas 3 out of 6 unclustered suicides used such obsolete or unusual means as stuffing one's mouth with earth (Case 123), hanging oneself in a particularly gruesome way (Case 124), or else by using two simultaneous means—drowning and poisoning—in order to make doubly sure that one would actually die (Case 106).

A careful examination of the case material will also reveal other differences between the two groups.   However, the preceding data suffice to show that clustered suicides seem to be more typically Mohave than unclustered ones.

The causes of clustering seem to be both psychological and cultural.

(1) *Psychological factors* responsible for the clustering of suicides can best be formulated in psychoanalytic terms.   The more acceptable one of the two existing psychoanalytic theories of suicide postulates that self-destruction is due to an interplay of two mechanisms:

    (*a*) Aggression against an emotionally significant person is first inhibited and is then directed against oneself.

    (*b*) The survivor identifies himself with an emotionally significant deceased person to the point of incorporating him into his psychic economy.   This identification is then followed by suicide, which represents a combined mourning and self-punitive reaction.

One important point to be mentioned is that, in our own society, the deceased person with whom the suicide identifies himself is usually a parent.   A proper evaluation of this finding is impossible unless one stresses that the nuclear family plays a greater role in our society than it does among the Mohave, and that in our society, where life expectancy is higher than among the Mohave, fewer young adults tend to be orphans.   Nonetheless, an attempt was made to ascertain whether the parents of the suicides were dead or alive, and whether, in any given instance, the deceased person *identified with* was a parent.   Unfortunately the cases were not numerous enough to permit one to assert with any degree of confidence that orphaned Mohave adults are more prone to kill themselves than are nonorphaned ones.   Moreover, even if such a correlation had been found, it would not have been readily comparable to a similar correlation in our society, due to the different role of the parent in Mohave society, his smaller life expectancy and the emotionally healthier provisions made for orphans in Mohave society (Devereux, 1956 b).   We must hasten to add, however, that this finding in nowise undermines the validity of the psychoanalytic thesis that suicide is a pathological form of mourning. In Mohave society, too, suicide is a kind of mourning, though cultural conditions determine *whom* one mourns in so self-destructive a manner.[92] Thus, the finding that the mourned-for person is often a brother or a person of the suicide's own generation is satisfactorily explained by the fact that the Mohave child is educated primarily by its own age group (Devereux, 1950 h), instead of being chiefly under the tutelage of adults, as is the case in our society.

(2) *Cultural factors* responsible for the clustering of suicides are partly mythological and partly related to current patterns of belief.

    (*a*) The mythical precedent for death is the quasi-suicide of the god Matavilye (Bourke, 1889; Kroeber, 1925 a and 1948), who decided to die in order to set an example and a precedent for all future deaths. Thus, in accordance with the Mohave dogma, that every single contemporary occurrence, belief, and practice has a mythical prototype, every Mohave death is, basically, a replica of Matavilye's intentional death. Otherwise stated, every single death is—in theory at least— the second component of a cluster, the first of which is the supernatural precedent set by Matavilye. In this context the term "supernatural" pertains, *on the psychological level*, to the example or to the activities of the dead. In Mohave belief, the dead include all deities and mythological personages, with the possible exception of the—apparently catatonic (pt. 2, pp. 50–54)—culture hero Mastamho, who is today simply an osprey or fish eagle completely devoid of sense (Kroeber, 1948). They also include all deceased human beings, but more especially the ghosts of the recently dead, who are still in the first of the four stages through which men go after dying (Devereux, 1937 a), and are therefore still close enough to the living to influence them effectively.

    (*b*) Cultural tenets pertaining to life, as it is lived now, also tend to emphasize the contagiousness of death.

Types of clustered deaths:

(1) A family in which incest has taken place soon becomes extinct (Devereux, 1939, a, and pt. 7, pp. 357–371).

(2) The ghost of the dead seeks to lure the living to the land of the dead (pt. 4, pp. 128–186).

(3) The shamanistic or bewitched fetus, who refused to be born, kills both himself and his mother during parturition (Devereux, 1937c; and pt. 7, pp. 331–339).

---

[92] In the same sense, the child has oedipal conflicts even in a matrilineal society, though the actual personnel of the oedipal situation consists of four persons (father, mother, mother's brother, and child) rather than of three, as in the Western world.

(4) The voluntary death of one twin is usually followed by the voluntary death of the surviving twin (Devereux, 1941; and pt. 7, pp. 348–356).

(5) Some women are said to be unlucky, because they are widowed several times. Hence, prospective suitors are warned not to marry them (Devereux, MS., 1935).[93]

(6) It is believed that the victims of witchcraft often do not co-operate with the shamans who seek to heal them, so that, in a sense, they commit vicarious or passive suicide. Then, by cohabiting with their beloved killer—the witch—in dream, they elicit in him such a strong wish to die, that he too seeks to commit vicarious suicide (Devereux, 1937 c; and pt. 7, pp. 387–426).

(7) Braves who kill people in battle do not expect to live long (Kroeber, 1925 a; and pt. 7, pp. 426–431).

(8) Scalpers run the risk of becoming insane and/or of dying (pt. 2, pp. 43–45).

(9) Witch killers run the risk of becoming insane and/or of dying (pt. 2, pp. 45–46).

(10) Funeral ritualists and mourners who violate certain funeral taboos may become insane and/or die (pt. 4, pp. 186–145).

(11) Some mourners commit funeral suicide. In one instance a father threw himself on the pyre of his son whom his nagging drove to suicide (Devereux, 1942 a, and pt. 7, Case 111, pp. 431–459).

These *explicit* data suggest that the Mohave think of death as something "contagious." If *implicit* data are also taken into account, one notes that, of the six nonclustering suicides, one was committed by a man, all of whose relatives had died (Case 124), and a second by an old woman whose only surviving relative, a son, deserted her in a shameful manner (Case 123). In a third instance, the suicide of the husband (Case 127) was soon followed by the death of his—supposedly guilt-ridden—adulterous wife, from a seemingly psychosomatic illness possibly representing a psychic suicide. In a fourth instance (Case 126) two members of the suicide's gens behaved as though they were not of his gens; they committed adultery with his wife.[94] In a fifth case, that of the unjustly accused shaman (Case 106), society as a whole withdrew from him, so that he might as well have had no relatives or friends at all, nor even a membership in the tribe. In the sixth and last "unclustered" case (Case 125) the suicide had already lost his mother and was then actually deserted by his wife. It is not an exaggeration to say that even in these six, seemingly "single," suicides the social situation of the suicide was not unlike that of a

---

[93] Compare also the belief that marrying an alien may be fatal (pt. 4, pp. 128–150).

[94] The idea that the formal dissolution of kinship ties is a form of symbolic suicide is explicit in the Mohave explanation of the symbolic social "suicide" which precedes incestuous marriages (Devereux, 1939 a, and pt. 7, pp. 336–371).

"survivor," so that, psychoanalytically at least, even these "single suicides" belong, in a sense, to (real or social) "death clusters."

This insight enables us to reconcile Durkheim's (1897) theory of the motivating force of social isolation in suicide with the psychoanalytic theory of clustering suicides. It is sufficient to suggest that, *from the psychological point of view*, the physical death of a love object and the psychosocial withdrawal of one's associates have exactly the same effect and suicide-motivating force.

As regards clustered suicides, the fact that the successful first suicide of a given cluster is sometimes followed by a *bungled* second suicide is of special importance for the understanding of the basic importance of the Mohave tendency to commit suicides in clusters. Indeed, on closer scrutiny these bungled reactive suicides do not suggest that the "model" suicide lacks compellingness. On the contrary, they suggest that the "model" is so compelling that even the *subjectively inadequately motivated* survivor—who does not *really* want to die—feels impelled to make at least a suicidal gesture, be it only by clumsily attempting to cut his own throat (Case 117) or, more simply, by contemplating suicide, without actually doing anything about it (Case 115). Moreover, it is quite noteworthy that the imitative suicide usually tries to kill himself by the same means as his model. This is apparently recognized even by the Mohave themselves, since they specified that Pa:hay (Case 117) used a knife only because—unlike his brother (Case 116)—he had no gun at his disposal. A more indirect proof of this thesis is the fact that the "vicarious suicide" of victims of witchcraft leads up to the vicarious suicide of the witch, who incites his victims' relatives to kill him (Devereux, 1937 c; and pt. 7, pp. 387–426). Likewise, both the first and the second of a pair of twins who do not wish to live cause themselves to die by identical means, i.e., by making themselves ill (Devereux, 1941; and pt. 7, pp. 348–356).

The last argument showing the motivating force of the "model" suicide, as distinct from that of genuine *subjective* reasons, is that none of the six "single" suicides was bungled. By contrast, three of the clustering suicides (Cases 117, 121 and 122), and all four of the recorded funeral suicides were bungled. Moreover, two of the six single suicides were committed by rather gruesome means, such as self-suffocation by eating earth (Case 123) or hanging oneself from a low beam (Case 124), whereas all successful clustering suicides were committed by simple, rapid, and reliable means. It is also noteworthy that the "spectacular" funeral suicides by fire were invariably bungled, and that the would-be suicides knew in advance that they would be saved in ample time.

In brief, on the latent (Chapin, 1935) level of Mohave culture a suicide appears to be socially defined as a model even for those who do *not* have an *adequate subjective reason* for killing themselves. This explains why quite a few of these "imitative" or "derivative" suicides were either bungled, or else never got beyond the stage of suicidal ruminations.

In a very genuine sense, all societies seem to construe death as a "model" for the mourners, this being especially true of the Mohave, who believe that death came into being through Matavilye's deliberate attempt to die of witchcraft (Bourke, 1889; Kroeber, 1948), so that his (voluntary) death may serve as a model and as a precedent for all future deaths. In fact, nearly all funeral customs—from suttee to mere self-denials and taboos during mourning—symbolize, in one way or other, a total or partial death of the mourners and may be viewed as a kind of blackmail levied by the dead on the living (Devereux, 1956 a; and pt. 7, pp. 431–459).[95]

Thus, on the whole, we are led to agree with Mauss' (1925) view that suicide is, in a social sense, the "prestation suprême" demanded from the living. In the light of Mohave belief, suicide is, thus, simply the quickest and most dramatic means of achieving the reunion of the living with the dead and of doing homage to them.

CASE MATERIAL

Since the outstanding characteristic of Mohave suicides appears to be their tendency to cluster (14 cases, forming 7 clusters, contrast with 6 unclustered cases) it is proposed to present first the clustered cases and then the isolated ones.

The clustered cases are divided into three subgroups, depending on the degree of explicitness of the clustering mechanism involved. Within each cluster the cases are cited in chronological order.

As regards the single cases, they are grouped together according to the type of motivation involved.

CLUSTERED CASES

SUBGROUP I.—Cases illustrating the triggering role of the death (or suicide) of a relative, explicitly expressed by the depressed survivor.

Cluster A.—Suicide of O :olva, who was nagged by his kinsman P. N., followed by the suicide of his brother Amalyk Tumádha :p, who brooded over O :olva's death. (Cases 112 and 113.)

---

[95] Compare in this context Homer's description ("Odyssey," book 11) of Achilles' psychic state in the underworld, which is, strictly speaking, the psychic state of a *mourner,* here imputed to the *deceased.* Compare, also (ibid.) the belief that the dead become more lively if they drink the blood of freshly slaughtered sacrificial animals.

Cluster B.—Suicide of Taparevily, nagged by his aunt Tanu:, over a matter involving an automobile. Suicidal thoughts of his half-sister Hama: Utce:, who openly referred to Taparevily's suicide, when she, too, had troubles with Tanu: over a car. (Cases 114 and 115.)

Cluster C.—Accidental death of Amat Yavu :me followed by suicidal brooding on the part of his brother Humar Tudhu:lye. Supplementary Case A. See Case 138).

Subgroup II.—Cases in which the nexus between several suicides is inferential, the connection between the various successive suicides being of a *traditional type*. (Father and son, brothers, successive mates of the same woman.)

Cluster D.—J. A., pestered by his father to divorce his unfaithful wife, kills himself. Later on his brother Pa :hay tried to kill himself over the infidelity of his own wife. (Cases 116 and 117.)

Cluster E.—The wife of Pi :it (I) nags him to go to dances, until he kills himself. His brother Pi :it (II) commits suicide when Po :tâ terminates her adulterous and incestuous affair with him. Later on Po :tâ's infidelity drives her new husband, E. T., to suicide. (Cases 118, 119 and 120.)

Cluster F.—Tunayva Kor kills himself because his father nags him about a horse. The father then tries to commit funeral suicide. (Supplementary Case B. See Case 111.)

Subgroup III.—Case suggesting that a *modern* type of connection with a suicide may also trigger off a second suicide.

Cluster G.—Kamey He :ya tried to kill himself over a girl. Soon afterward Atci: Ahwat, the Indian sheriff who investigated this suicide, also tried to kill himself because of his wife's infidelty. (Cases 121, 122.)

SUBGROUP I

CLUSTER A:

CASE 112 (Informants: Hivsu: Tupo :ma and Hama: Utce:) :

Name: Oo :lva. Gens: Tcatc. Race: Father, Mohave; Mother, Yavapai. Sex: Male. Age at death: 50. Marital status: (?). Children: (?). Parents: It was not ascertained whether they were still alive. Education: None. Occupation: Farmer and shaman. Date of death: 1902 (?). Cause of death: Suicide. He shot himself in the heart with a .44 revolver. Motive: Abused by a cousin and weary of life.

Oo :lva was a shaman specializing in the cure of diseases caused by "poison plants," i.e., by magic plants which only those who received special supernatural powers in dream can habitually handle without danger to themselves. Yet, most of these "plants" bring their owner luck, especially in gambling and in love, regardless of whether or not the owner received the relevant supernatural powers in dream (pt. 4, pp. 202–212). Oo :lva was a "good" shaman, who never bewitched anyone.

Oo : lva had no relatives except his brother Amalyk Tumádha : p (cf. Case 113) and a half cousin, P. N. (Indian name not recalled). Gens: Tcatc. Race: Fullblood Mohave. Sex: Male. Age: 45–50. Relationship to Oo :lva: Their mothers were half sisters.

P. N. was "mean" to Oo:lva. (At this point Hama: Utce: remarked that: "P. N. could make anyone feel like shooting him, he was that mean.") Oo:lva was "tired of the earth; he was not happy." Hence, one noon he shot himself in the heart in a shed located near his house at Parker, Ariz.

A year or so later his brother, Amalyk Tumâdha: p, also killed himself (Case 113).

Comment

The preceding case exemplifies the Mohave tendency to react with suicide when a person from whom one expects love and support disappoints one. According to the Mohave, this suicide was not motivated by the suicidal urge of witches, since Oo:lva was said to be exclusively a healing shaman. The fact that he specialized in the cure of the deleterious effects of charms, which is apparently a somewhat unusual "speciality," may be due to his being half Yavapai—members of that tribe being believed to have power over some of these "charms" (pt. 4, pp. 202–212).

CASE 113 (Informants: Hivsu: Tupo:ma and Hama: Utce:):

Name: Amalyk Tumâdha:p. Gens: Tcatc. Race: Father, Mohave; Mother, Yavapai. Sex: Male. Age at Death: 45. Marital status: (?) (probably single). Children: (?). Parents: Not ascertained whether still alive. Education: None. Occupation: Farmer. Date of Death: 1903 (?). Cause of death: Suicide. He shot himself with a .32 revolver, either in the heart, or, more probably, in the forehead. Motive: He was brooding over the fact that his brother Oo:lva had been driven to suicide a year before (Case 112).

When Oo:lva (Case 112) killed himself, his brother, Amalyk Tumâdha: p, began to brood over it. He often spoke of his grief and of his distress over having to live alone and being alone in the world. He intensely resented P. N., whom he held responsible for Oo:lva's suicide. (For P. N.'s vital statistics, who at this time was 51 years old, cf. Case 112.) The fact that Oo:lva's and Amalyk Tumâdha:p's mother, and P. N.'s mother were half sisters probably aggravated the situation, since cousins are supposed to be good to each other.

Amalyk Tumâdha:p often spoke of this matter, saying darkly: "You just watch and see what I am going to do." One night he attended a gambling party at Parker. During the first part of the night he repeatedly said, "I may be brave enough to kill someone first and myself afterwards, but if I am not brave enough to do that, I will only kill myself." While waiting for P. N., who failed to turn up at the party, Amalyk Tumâdha:p kept on repeating: "I do not like the way he talks. He is mean." Toward 4:00 a.m., weary of waiting for P. N., he went to his host's hencoop and shot himself.

It was not possible to ascertain whether anyone had warned P. N. to stay away from the gambling party, because P. N. died some years after Amalyk Tumâdha: p committed suicide, and before 1936, when suicide was investigated in the field.

Comment

The preceding case history exemplifies the manner in which suicides tend to cluster among the Mohave. The transition from frustrated and partly inhibited anger ("I may be brave enough to kill someone first and myself afterwards, but if I am not brave enough to do that, I will only kill myself") to suicide is also quite obvious.

Amalyk Tumâdha :p's suicide resembles that of his brother Oo :lva, in that both killed themselves near an outlying building (shed, chicken coop), both used revolvers, and—though there is some disagreement about this point—both shot themselves in the heart. This suggests a considerable identification with the deceased brother, whose suicide Amalyk Tumádha:p imitated in at least two, and possibly three, respects.

CLUSTER B:

CASE 114 (Informants: Hama: Utce: and Hivsu: Tupo:ma):

Name: Taparevily. Claimed gens: Syuly. Race: Father's mother, Yavapai. The three other grandparents were predominantly Mohave, perhaps with some admixture of white. Sex: Male. Age at death: About 17. Marital status: Single. Children: None. Parents: Alive. Education: Indian Agency School, Parker, Ariz. Occupation: None. Date of death: 1924 (?). Cause of death: Suicide. He shot himself in the heart with a 12-gage shotgun. Motive: His aunt nagged him. (The complex racial ancestry of this family is discussed in the appended comments.)

Taparevily lived in Parker, in a tent erected in the yard of, or at least near to, his maternal aunt's house. Aunt's name: Tanu. Claimed gens: Kunyii:th, (Claim denied by her niece.) Claimed race: Fullblood Mohave. (Claim denied by her niece, who says that Tanu: is half Mohave and half white.) Sex: Female. Age: 50. Relationship: Uterine (?) half sister of Taparevily's mother.

Taparevily borrowed his aunt's new car, and then got drunk with another man. While intoxicated, he drove the car into a ditch and left it there overnight. Ever after, "as usual," (sic!) Tanu: pestered Taparevily about the car. A week later she was still nagging him. Eventually Taparevily "got so sick and tired" of being nagged that, around 11:00 a. m., he went into his tent and shot himself in the heart. According to Hama: Utce:, who is Taparevily's uterine half sister, the reservation physician—perhaps out of kindness—certified that his death had been an accidental one.

Comment on the racial origins of Taparevily and Tanu

"There have been halfbreeds in this Kunyii:th lineage as far back as anyone can remember. Hence, I cannot be entirely sure either of my racial origins, or of those of my uterine half brothers L. M. and Taparevily, or of those of my aunt Tanu:. My mother was mostly Mohave, though she probably had some white blood as well. One of my mother's half sisters was half Mohave and half Maricopa, and lived on the Maricopa Reservation. Once my mother went to visit her, and, while among the Maricopa, she had an affair with a man who was mostly white, but also had some Maricopa blood in him. I was born of this union. Then my mother lived with another man, who was 'mostly' Mohave (sic!) though his mother had been a Yavapai woman. This man was the father of my half brothers L. M. and Taparevily, who, like myself, were brought up mostly by our mother's half sister Tanu:.

"As regards my Aunt Tanu:, it is hard to say what she is. The Mohave can claim as their own the child of a woman who has been their wife for the greater part of the first 6 lunar months of her pregnancy (Devereux, 1949 c). Hence Tanu: claims to be a fullblood Mohave Indian, of the Kunyii:th gens, just because her mother's husband was kind enough to pretend that she had 'become' his child. My aunt was always snooty to me and my half brothers, because we were halfbreeds, though she herself is really half white, her real father having been a white man."

In summary, if Tanu:'s mother was indeed a fullblood Mohave woman, she herself was half Mohave and half white.

The considerations above are of some importance for the complete understanding of this suicide. The Mohave both fear and despise aliens and halfbreeds, whose "strong blood" tends to "hit the weaker blood" of those Mohave with whom they come in contact (pt. 4, pp. 128–150). Tanu:, though pretending to be a fullblood Mohave Indian, appears to have married a Mexican, and displayed a number of character traits, such as stinginess and quarrelsomeness, which the Mohave habitually associate with whites. Taparevily, on the other hand, lived like a Mohave Indian, just as Hama: Utce:, though very well educated, always tried to live up to Mohave standards of conduct. Hence, racial snobbishness, as well as a clash between Mohave and white ethics, played an important role in creating a fatal conflict between Tanu: and her nephew Taparevily, and in perpetuating a feud between Tanu: and her niece, who was very much embittered by Tanu:'s behavior toward Taparevily, so that, when she too had trouble over a car with Tanu:, she consciously identified with Taparevily and planned to kill herself the way he did (Case 115).

CASE 115 (Informant: Hama: Utce:) :

Name: Hama: Utce: (Testicles charcoal). Gens: Claims to be Kunyii:th, which is her mother's gens, but has no real gentile affiliation. Race: Probably half Mohave, three-eighths white, and one-eighth Maricopa. Sex: Female. Age: 35 (?). Marital status: Twice married. Children: One boy (half Pueblo Indian), living. One child died of "spinal meningitis." Parents: Dead. Education: Well educated even by American standards. Occupation: Occasional clerical work and housewife. Date of events 1936. Cause of suicidal wishes: Friction with mother's half sister Tanu:. (Most of the events herein described were personally observed by the writer.)

In 1935, Hama: Utce: borrowed $80.00 from her morther's half sister Tanu;, in order to buy a car, and promised to repay the money within a year. Two weeks after she borrowed the money, Tanu: dragged her to "court" before the Agency Superintendent, and asked for the immediate return of the money. The Superintendent, a sensible man who knew the defendant to be honest, believed her statement that the money was lent for a year, and dismissed the case. "After that I cried for days. I had an awful time keeping away from the gun and the bichloride of mercury tablets. Only the thought of my son kept me from doing it. I was thinking all the time of my (half) brother Taparevily (Case 114). I said to myself that he too went through it—also because of a car. Now I don't hate my aunt any longer. She is just dead to me. I don't know what I would do if she died now. I could not mourn her. My feelings toward the whole reservation have changed. People don't mean anything to me. I just force myself to go to funerals. In the past I could really mourn for the dead. My (half) brother must have felt the same way. He just sat and thought. Now I sit and think: 'This is how he must have felt.' " On another occasion she said: "My aunt can be nice, but mostly she is mean."

One day, while Hama: Utce: was working with me, a man called her to his car and spoke to her for a few minutes. When she came back she seemed very wrought up, and, in reply to my questions, said that her aunt had just gone to the Agency again, to make further trouble about the money. "My aunt—I hope she dies of a stroke. She said to my half sister T., who is a twin and should therefore be treated with special courtesy [Devereux, 1941]: 'On my deathbed I'll pick up a stick and beat you up—all of you.' After that my half-sister T. said to me, 'I hope she dies of a stroke—slowly. I hope she will be unconscious, so she won't talk.' That is how I feel too. I want to die because I feel so bitter. I like no one." Shortly afterward Hama: Utce: drove me uptown in her car and saw her aunt sitting in the street, which upset her again a great deal. She turned to me and said, "There she is again—I don't even want to look at her. To me she is dead. She causes us all this trouble. I don't like anyone anymore." Trying to quiet her down, I said, "Don't you even like me?" She forced herself to reply, "No one !", but her remark did not sound convincing either to me, or to herself.[96] I therefore began to tease her about the famous temper of the Kunyii:th gens, and that was the last I heard of her suicidal intentions.

It is of great psychological interest that Hama: Utce: expressed suicidal thoughts, hostile feelings toward Tanu:, and thoughts comparing her troubles with Tanu: to Taparevily's troubles with the same, chiefly *while riding in a car* with me, though there were no reasons why she should not discuss this matter also on other occasions, i.e., when not riding in a car.

Comment

The preceding case history illustrates two major aspects of Mohave suicide:

(1) If a person from whom one expects love and support frustrates these expectations, there is at first impotent anger, which, soon afterwards, turns into self-aggression.

(2) Frustrated and angry persons tend to identify with those who actually killed themselves, especially if the suicide was a relative or was in some other manner connected with the person who contemplates suicide, or was in a similar predicament. This factor may be responsible for the "clustering" of Mohave suicides, either in the same family, or else among the suitors of the same woman or, apparently, even in time, as exemplified by the fact that two *formally* unrelated suicides occurred in rapid succession in the spring of 1944 (Cases 121, 122). This problem is discussed in some detail in the introductory section of this chapter.

SUPPLEMENTARY CASE A (For a full account, see Case 138):

Syuly deserted her husband Humar Tudhu:lye, allegedly because he was an alcoholic, and married his brother, the equally alcoholic Amat Yavu:me, who, a year or so later, was hit and killed by a car while drunkenly walking at night on a reservation road. This death so depressed Humar Tudhu:lye, that he began to drink more than ever before, saying, when drunk: "I keep on thinking of my brother. I don't care if the same thing happens to me too. I too want to die. I don't care." It was ascertained that Humar Tudhu:lye had no thoughts of dying before his brother's fatal accident.

Comment

The "clustering" mechanism is clearly reflected by the present case. In fact, it is even legitimate to assume that the marked increase in Humar Tudhu:lye's alcoholism was partly a suicidal mechanism, not only because alcohol is inherently harmful, but chiefly because his brother was killed while too drunk to watch for approaching cars. This interpretation is supported by his statement: "I don't care if the same thing happens to me too." It is also significant that the basic nexus between the two brothers was further reinforced by their having been married successively to the same woman. The functional significance of this latter type of nexus is proved by Cluster E, Cases 119 and 120.

--SUBGROUP II

CASE 116 (Informants: Hivsu: Tupo:ma and Hama: Utce:):

Name: J.A. (Mohave name not recalled.) Gens: Kunyii:th. Race: Full-blood Mohave. Sex: Male. Age at death: 21. Marital status: Married.

---

[96] A few days earlier she was almost in tears when she heard what hard times I had had and scolded me because I did not write to her for help, saying, "As long as there is a dollar or a mouthful of food in this house, half of it is yours. What kind of friend are you anyway, if you don't ask your friends to help you when you need it?"

Children: One. Parents: Father alive. Education: Sherman Institute ("better than average"). Occupation: Santa Fe Railroad shops. Date of death: 1928 (?). Cause of death: Suicide. He shot himself in the stomach with a .32 revolver. Motive: His father nagged him, urging him to leave his adulterous wife. J. A.'s brother Pa:hay, tried to commit suicide 6 years later, probably in 1934.

J. A. was married to: Name: Nyortc Moråmor. Gens: Nyoltc. Race: Fullblood Mohave. Sex: Female. Age: 25. Marital status: Married. Children: One. (Her name indicates that she had lost at least one child.) J. A.'s wife was unfaithful to him and this fact was known both to himself and to his father. His father was: Name: Kuu:yteva. Gens: Kunyii:th. Race: Fullblood Mohave. Sex: Male. Age: 40. Marital status: Widowed. Children: Two sons. Kuu:yteva incessantly pestered his son to leave his wife, "before he did something desperate." This remark is a curious one, since there are no indications that J. A. was thinking of doing anything "desperate." The father's constant nagging so exasperated J. A., that he finally felt that "his father did not like him," presumably because any interference with the relationship between spouses is severely frowned on by the Mohave (Devereux, MS., 1935). One day, at 9:00 a.m., when his father was again nagging him and telling him to leave his wife, J. A. went into his house at Needles, Calif., and shot himself in the stomach. Since he did not die at once, the Santa Fe Railroad Co., for which he had been working, rushed him to its hospital at San Bernardino. According to some Mohave, he died on the train, while according to others he died in the hospital. The Mohave then subscribed a sum of money, to cover the expense of having him returned to Needles for cremation.

Soon after J. A.'s death his wife and child came to Parker. She then married Hakatoktare:(w)a, whose half brother was once allegedly "raped" (sic!) by a certain promiscuous woman in his own bed.

Comment

J. A.'s suicide has several features which seem extremely paradoxical to the American mind; he committed suicide not because his wife deceived him, but because his father pestered him to divorce the unfaithful woman.

Actually, J. A., like some other deceived Mohave husbands, seems to have accepted his wife's infidelity with considerable patience. This passivity is not at all unusual in Mohave society. Thus, the acculturated Hama: Utce: sarcastically remarked in another context: "Some fellows were awful nice about letting people sleep with their wives." A real understanding of this seemingly anomalous patience can only be obtained if one discards the occidental notion that marriage is primarily an exclusive love-and-sex relationship and views it instead as a multivalent, functionally multiple relationship, in which a variety of practical reciprocal services wholly overshadow the sexual reciprocity. Otherwise expressed, the core objective of a Mohave marriage is the creation of a home, rather than the establishing of an exclusive sexual relationship. It is to be noted in this context that the informants did not suggest that the adulterous Nyortc Moråmor was also hard to live with and/or neglected her housewifely duties. In fact, the Mohave definitely specify that some nymphomaniacs (Case 14) are kind persons and good housewives. It is also definitely known that more than one Mohave man is so desirous of finding a wife who takes her domestic work seriously, that he will go to the extreme of divorcing his young and irresponsible wife, in order to marry a better housekeeper, such as his former mother-in-law, or even a male transvestite who glories in performing his "wifely" duties properly (Devereux, 1937 b; Devereux, 1951 f). It is also probable that Nyortc Moråmor was not a wholly undesirable wife in terms of Mohave ideas, since, soon after being widowed, she found another husband in the person of Hakatoktare:(w)a. While these observations do not imply that J. A. was indifferent to his wife's infidelity, they force one to suppose that she must have had certain domestic assets, which, for a Mohave man anxious to have a well-run home, would have outweighed the drawback of her notorious infidelity. We might also add that occasionally a Mohave man gets indignant and violent over his wife's infidelities only after he has already "lined up" another, and seemingly more desirable, prospective wife.

It should also be noted that, in pestering his son to divorce his wife, the father, Kuu:yteva, violated the rule that one should not become involved in the matrimonial quarrels of other persons, lest the spouses should become reconciled and make a common front against the meddler. Hence, in an extreme instance, an unfaithful wife's mother did not interfere until the furious husband actually threatened to shoot his wife (Devereux, 1950 a).

Another point concerns the apparent inability of the Mohave Indian to cope effectively with real nagging. Since the cultural and personal aspects of this inability are discussed in connection with Case 118, we simply note in this context that Pi:it (I) (Case 118) killed himself because his wife nagged him, without being also unfaithful to him, while Tunayva Kor (Case 111) shot himself when his father nagged him for racing his swift horse without his permission. In all of these instances the suicide reacted with despair to what he felt to be as a violation of the cultural rule that one's father, relative, or wife should provide approval and moral support under any condition whatsoever. In the present instance it seems quite certain that the father had certain latently hostile feelings toward his son, since he *gratuitously* "worried" that his cuckolded son might "do something desperate," although there is no evidence whatsoever that J. A. was unusually depressed by his wife's misconduct.

In brief, while it seems likely that J. A. did not relish the role of a cuckold, he did not become suicidal until his father began to nag him and to make an issue of it. Even more important is the fact that the father, by needlessly seeking to *prevent* his son from doing something desperate, actually *caused* him to kill himself. Such sequences are quite common in cases of overtly oversolicitous but latently hostile overprotectiveness. It is well to recall in this context that Pi:it (II) (Case 119) also did not become suicidal simply because Po:tà ceased to have adulterous and incestuous relations with him; he became truly depressed only because their relatives made an issue of this affair.

Finally, mention should be made of the notorious "temper" of the Kunyii:th gens, to which both father and son belonged, though informants did not refer to this notorious "temper" in connection with J. A.'s suicide, but did mention it in connection with the suicide of J. A.'s brother Pa: hay (Case 117).

CASE 117 (Informant: Hivsu: Tupo:ma and Hama: Utce:):

Name: Pa:hay. Gens: Kunyii:th. Race: Fullblood Mohave. Sex: Male. Age when attempting suicide: 33. Marital status: Married. Children: Presumably none. Parents: Dead (?). Education: Sherman Institute. Occupation: Santa Fe Railroad shops. Date of attempt: 1934 (?). Nature of attempt: He tried to kill himself by slashing his throat with a small pocketknife. Motive: Wife's infidelity. Comment: Attempt unsuccessful.

Pa:hay knew that his wife (Name: Nyortc. Gens: Nyoltc. Race: Fullblood Mohave. Sex: Female. Age 33. Marital status: Married. Children: (?) (her name shows that she had lost at least one child) was deceiving him with his cousin, whose father was Pa:hay's father's full brother. The seducer was Akwep (Gens: Kunyii:th. Race: Fullblood Mohave. Sex: Male. Age: 28.)

Marital status: Presumably single). Pa:hay repeatedly said that he would commit suicide if the affair did not cease. One day he was looking for the adulterous couple and found them sleeping together in the house of one of his relatives, called Huyatc (Gens: Mah. Race: Fullblood Mohave. Sex: Male. Age: 55). Huyatc was Pa:hay's second cousin; their fathers' mothers were sisters. Pa:hay did not waken the couple, and left Huyatc's house as quietly as he had entered it, believing that no one had seen him. He then returned to his own house, without realizing that he was being followed by Huyatc, who feared that Pa:hay might try to kill himself. Huyatc saw Pa:hay go into his house, where, "not having a gun," he slashed at his throat with a pocketknife. Although this incident took place at night, immediate medical assistance was obtained from Needles, Calif., so that Pa:hay's life was saved. The Mohave still laugh about Pa:hay's abortive attempt to kill himself and joke about the proverbial temper of the Kunyii:th gens.

Pa:hay's brother J. A. (Case 116), with whom he was on excellent terms, committed suicide some 6 years earlier, because his father had been pestering him to divorce his adulterous wife.

Comments

Pa:hay's case is, in many respects, similar to that of his brother J. A. (Case 116). Both were relatively well educated, worked for the railroad, and were married to women of the Nyoltc gens, who deceived them. Both had reasons to be displeased with the behavior of their own kin: J. A.'s father nagged him to divorce his adulterous wife, while Pa:hay's relative Huyatc went to the other extreme, helping the wife to commit adultery by letting her use his home for that purpose.[97] In both instances, the meddling relative was worried that the deceived husband might do something desperate. The father made explicit statements of this nature, while Huyatc, realizing that Pa:hay had seen the adulterous couple asleep together, secretly followed the deceived husband to his home, thereby presumably saving his life by promptly calling for help.

In both cases the suicidal attempt was a rather clumsy one: Pa:hay, "having no gun," cut his throat with a small pocketknife and was saved, while his brother J. A. lived several hours after shooting himself in the abdomen, instead of in the head or heart, thereby revealing that his suicidal attempt was a relatively halfhearted one.

It is also permissible to suppose that Pa:hay reacted to his wife's infidelity with suicidalness, because—by Mohave standards—his brother J. A. had practically been forced to *overreact* to his wife's infidelity.

In brief, all available data indicate that Pa:hay's suicidal attempt—and even his suicidal threats [98]—appear to have been heavily influenced by the suicide of his brother and model J. A., and also by the expectations which his father Kuu:yteva voiced when J. A.'s wife committed adultery. The fact that he bungled the attempt, by using a mere pocketknife,[99] also suggests that his action did not express real resolution, but only a rather superficial compliance with motivationally inadequate internal and external expectations.

These factors, when taken together, clearly suggest that the suicides of these brothers are genuinely linked together and form a psychologically coherent "cluster."

---

[97] As a rule, the Mohave neither interfere with, nor encourage, extramarital relations.
[98] Compare the father's gratuitous fears that J. A. may do "something desperate" because of his wife's infidelity.
[99] Would-be suicides who try to cut their throats usually bungle the job. Even those who actually kill themselves in this manner do not, at first, inflict more than shallow wounds (called "hesitation marks") upon themselves.

CLUSTER E:

CASE 118 (Informants: Hivsu: Tupo:ma and Hama: Utce:):

Name: Pi:it (I). Gens: Nyoltc. Race: Fullblood Mohave. Sex: Male. Age at death: 25 (?). Marital status: Married. Children: None. Parents: Living. Education: Indian Agency School, Parker. Occupation: Farmer. Date of death: 1901 (?). Cause of death: Suicide. He shot himself in the heart with a .44 revolver. Motive: He was nagged by his wife.

Name of wife: Hidhi:k. Gens: Tcatc. Race: Fullblood Mohave. Sex: Female. Age: 30. Marital status: Married. Children: None. Occupation: Housewife.

Pi:it (I) was a "homebody," whereas his wife was extremely fond of attending Mohave dances. Although she did not misbehave at dances, she was so eager to participate in them that she constantly nagged her husband to go to the dances with her, ignoring his repeatedly expressed wish to stay home. One evening some Yuma Indians, on their way from Needles to Yuma, gave a dance at Parker. Hidhi:k again tried to induce her husband to take her to this dance, but, "even though the Mohave love to hear the Yuma sing," she could not persuade him to take her to the dance. She thereupon decided to go to it alone, while her husband went to sleep on the roof, which is a favorite sleeping place of the Mohave in warm weather. While tossing about, he kept thinking of his wife's incessant nagging. Eventually his wife came back from the dance and nagged him some more, trying to prevail on him to attend the rest of the all-night dance. When Pi:it (I) refused once more and said: "Very well! I am going to kill myself and then you will be free to go to dances," Hidhi:k became frightened and begged him not to kill himself. Unmoved by her pleas, he climbed off the roof before his wife could stop him, went into the house and shot himself in the heart, even though his wife, who had scrambled down after him, kept on begging him not to kill himself.

Comment

Pi:it (I) was the paternal half brother of a man (Case 119) who committed suicide some 27 years later. His sister, the wife of Ahma Huma:re, died in childbirth, which severely traumatized both her husband and her son (Devereux, 1948 e).

The present case is somewhat unusual, since the henpecked husband is quite exceptional in Mohave society, despite the fact that the Mohave man is anything but a domestic tyrant, and wife beating an almost unheard-of occurrence. On the other hand, extreme gentleness is far from being exceptional behavior in a Mohave husband.[1] It is also significant that the Mohave seems to be incapable of tolerating, or of coping with, nagging, be it that of a wife or that of a parent (Case 116), and may respond to it by killing himself. This may be due to the fact that, like theft (Case 76), tenacious nagging is an anal character trait, which is beyond the pale of the Mohave value system (Devereux, 1951 c), and therefore so unexpected, that cultural means for its control are apparently altogether lacking.

On the whole, this suicide belongs in the category of suicidal acts triggered by disappointment over the inappropriate conduct of a relative, even though, on the manifest level, it represents—technically at least—suicide motivated by marital discord.

As regards Hidhi:k's flightiness and thirst for amusement, it fits in every respect the Mohave thesis that women are much flightier than are men. It will

---

[1] Hama: Utce: told me that her husband's extreme gentleness sometimes exasperated her (Devereux, 1937 b).

be seen that the same flightiness, carried to even greater extremes, was a crucial motivating factor also in the other two suicides belonging to this cluster, while pressure (nagging) was markedly a motivating element in one of the other two related cases (Case 119).

CASE 119 (Informants: Hivsu: Tupo:ma and Hamma: Utce:) :

Name: Pi: it (II) (not to be confused with Case 118). Gens: Nyoltc. Race: Fullblood Mohave. Sex: Male. Age at death: About 27. Marital Status: Single. Children: Apparently none. Parents: Father dead. Education: Phoenix, Ariz. Occupation: None. Date of death: 1928 (?). Cause of death: Suicide. He shot himself in the heart with a .32 revolver. Motive: Family pressure put an end to an adulterous and "incestuous" relationship.

Pi: it (II) was living at Needles, Calif., with, and apparently off, some relatives of his. A man named Amaly Tamoo: rà (mentioned also in Case 120) and his wife Po: tà, a distant relative of Pi: it, lived in the same house. Po: tà's gens was Po: tà. Race: Father, Mohave; mother, Wanyume:. Sex: Female. Age: 33. Marital status: Married. Children: None. Parents: Thought to have been alive. Occupation: Housewife. Psychiatric status: Chronic alcoholic. She was first married to Amaly Tamoo:rà, whom she later deserted to marry Avunye Humar. However, she soon deserted the latter as well and married E. T., who was at that time about 19 to 22 years old (Case 120).

Soon after Pi: it (II) moved into this household, his kinswoman Po: tà became also his mistress. Although this relationship had been known, or at least suspected, for some time, nothing was done about it for quite a while. Then, suddenly, Po: tà's family began to accuse Pi: it (II) of incest, since the lovers were third cousins, so that Pi: it was "supposed" to address her as "older sister" (hintcienk). Po: tà, who, all along, had been fully aware of the fact that the relationship was both an adulterous and an "incestuous" one, thereupon ceased "going with him", and refused him all further sexual favors. It is interesting to note that the husband himself does not seem to have interfered, and that neither Po: tà's relatives nor my informants seem to have stressed the fact that this relationship was not only incestuous, but also adulterous.

Exasperated both by the cessation of the affair, and by the publicity given to its incestuous nature, Pi:it(II) went outdoors and, just before sunrise, shot himself in the breast, in the immediate vicinity of the house in which he was living.

Comment

Pi: it (II) was the paternal half-brother of another Pi: it (I) (Case 118), who committed suicide by identical means some 27 years earlier. Shortly after Pi: it (II)'s death Po :tà also drove E.T. (Case 120) to suicide, and then deserted her husband Avunye Humar, to whom she was married at that time.

It may perhaps be significant that the case of the other Pi :it (I) (Case 118) had to be interpreted not so much as a typical form of marital discord as an incident comparable to the type of frustration and disappointment likely to occur between relatives. If this interpretation is valid, it is just barely possible to consider as significant—*in so far as the mechanisms of "clustering" are concerned*—that Po :tà was related to this Pi :it (II), and also violated her kinship obligations (by having intercourse with him, at least for a while). While this parallel may seem farfetched in the light of available data, it is precisely the farfetched type of "logic" which characterizes the typical (unconscious) "primary thought processes," and therefore deserves mention at least as a tentative hypothesis. Be that as it may, it is a fact that some other incestuous relationships in Mohave society were "brazened out"—sometimes in a startingly cynical manner (Devereux, 1939 a)—and did not lead to suicide. We must therefore assume that this Pi:it(II)'s suicide was, at least in part, determined by his older paternal halfbrother's suicide (Case 118).

CASE 120 (Informants: Hivsu: Tupo:ma and Hama: Utce:) :

Name: E.T. (Indian name not recalled.) Gens: Nyoltc. Race: Fullblood Mohave. Sex: Male. Age at death: 22 (?). Marital Status: Married. Children: None. Parents: Dead. Education: Sherman Institute. Occupation: None. Date of death: 1928 (?). Cause of death: Suicide. He shot himself in the heart with a revolver. Motive: Resentment over the infidelity of his wife, exacerbated by alcoholic intoxication. (The wife herself was a chronic alcoholic.)

At that time E.T. was newly married to Po:tȧ (whose vital statistics are listed in Case 119) whom he appears to have but recently taken away from her most recent husband, Avunye Humar.

Shortly after marrying E.T., Po:tȧ began an affair with M.M. (Gens: Kumȧdhi:. Race: Fullblood Mohave. Sex: Male. Age: 27–30). Although she continued to live with E.T., she made no effort to keep her adulterous affair a secret. One day the exasperated E.T. went to the house of Po:tȧ's first husband, Amaly Tamoo:rȧ, and, not finding him at home simply took Amaly Tamoo:rȧ's revolver.[2] It could not be ascertained whether E.T. had called on Amaly Tamoo:rȧ for the sole purpose of gaining possession of a revolver. Next, E.T. proceeded to M.M.'s house and knocked at the door.[3] When M.M. came to the door, E.T. first fired two shots in the air, and then shot M.M. in the stomach, inflicting a severe, but not lethal, wound. He then turned around and went back to his own house. When a few deputy sheriffs from Needles, Calif., began to pursue him and came to his home, E.T. hid himself in the bushes, near his house. The deputies were afraid to follow him into the bushes because they knew that he was armed. Around midnight, while the deputies were still maneuvering around and looking for him, E.T. stealthily returned to his house and shot himself in the heart.

Comment

This was the second suicide caused by Po:tȧ within a year's time. The other one was that of Pi:it (II) (Case 119).

The firing of two shots in the air and the fact that even though E.T. fired at point-blank range at M.M. he only wounded him, suggested that E.T. shared the average Mohave Indian husband's reluctance to attack his wife's lover. The fact that he chose to purloin precisely a gun belonging to the man whose former wife he, himself, had but recently abducted—i.e., a gun which Amaly Tamoo:rȧ may well have used against him under similar circumstances—suggests that, as an avenger, he identified with the man whose divorced wife he had abducted from her next husband, and that, as a guilty person, he identified with the man who deceived him. The latter is shown by the fact that he failed to kill M.M. at point blank range, but shot and killed himself quite efficiently.

It is possible that E.T.'s act was also partly determined by Po:tȧ's record as a "femme fatale," already responsible for another suicide (Case 119) and irresistible to men because she (allegedly) owned a love charm, the lodestone (katc humu:kwa) (Case 55).

If, as we suppose, these three suicides constitute a cluster, it is noteworthy that the purely sexual factor is practically absent in the first case, which was motivated primarily by a more familial type of disappointment, but acquires

---

[2] Although theft is quite exceptional among the Mohave, they sometimes borrow an item in the absence of its owner, but make no secret of it and return it after using it.

[3] The Mohave seldom knock before entering.

a greater significance in the second suicide, where sexual and kinship types of relations are fused into an incestuous and adulterous relationship, while in the third case, the sexual element plays a decisive role.   Since these three cases are spread out over nearly three decades, in the course of which aboriginal Mohave society and values became increasingly disorganized, it is possible that the increasing importance of mere sexuality and of feminine looseness and the decreasing role of family cohesion during that period is paralleled by a similar shift in the motivation of these three successive suicides which appear to form a cluster.

CLUSTER F:

SUPPLEMENTARY CASE B (for a ful account, see Case 111).

The motivating power of nagging by a close relative, such as a father, is also shown by the fact that Tunayva Kor killed himself because his father Anya-nyema:m nagged him for having raced his father's horse without first obtaining his permission.   The griefstricken and remorseful father thereupon tried to commit funeral suicide by throwing himself on his son's funeral pyre.

SUBGROUP III

CLUSTER G:

Case 121 (Informant: Hitcu:y Kutask(w)elvȧ, in a letter dated April 27, 1944) : "I received a letter from mother (Hama: Utce:) today and they seem to be having a little trouble back home.   (Kamey He:ya = camel's mouth, of the Kat gens) a man about the age of 27 was staying with his relations and he got into trouble with this girl (O:otc), so he decided the only thing he could do was kill himself.   He shot himself through the right side of his chest but he missed his heart and they have him in the hospital.   The sheriff found a note by his body telling why he shot himself."

Comment

This case is atypical—or, perhaps, more properly, "modern"—in two respects.
   (1) The suicide was caused by some apparently minor trouble with a girl. (Had the trouble been a major one, Hitcu:y Kutask(w)elvȧ, who was an expert informant, as is shown by his having specified the age and residence of the man, would have provided relevant details.)
   (2) The suicide left a note.
   The nontraditional motivation may explain why the suicidal attempt was not successful.

CASE 122 (Informant: Hitcu:y Kutask(w)elvȧ, in a letter dated April 27, 1944) : "And the Sheriff (Ind.[ian]) (Atci: Ahwat, fish red, no gens) shot himself on account of his wife (Nyoltc) about a month ago to[o] but he is well and on the job, again.   He shot himself twice through the chest and he almost died. They operated on him about a month ago and he is doing well.   Mother (Hama: Utce:) stayed up day and night with him for four days and nights in the Ind[ian] Hospital in Phoenix."

Comment

Atci: Ahwat's suicidal attempt may—as the informant seems to have unconsciously sensed, since he started this paragraph with "and" [4]—have been stimulated or triggered by his investigation of Kamey He:ya's suicide (Case 121), which suggests that, here too, we are dealing with a "cluster," which is determined partly by an administrative nexus between the two cases, and partly by proximity in time.   Indeed, it would be highly unusual in terms of

---

[4] A careful examination of all of this man's letters yielded no other example of a paragraph starting with "And."

Mohave habits for Atci: Ahwat to kill himself the minute he began to have troubles with his wife. It is far more likely that these difficulties were of some duration and that the idea of suicide occurred to Atci: Ahwat as a result of his recent investigation of Kamey He:ya's suicide.

The fact that Atci: Ahwat, who, being a sheriff, must have had a lot of experience with firearms, was one of the few Mohave who bungled his suicide, is also noteworthy. It suggests an appreciable lack both of real resolution and of an effective identification with Kamey He:ya, due in part to the fact that the nexus between him and his "model" Kamey He:ya was outside the regular network of basic Mohave relationships, and belonged to the sphere of acculturation relationships (i.e., a sheriff investigating a suicide) which, as yet, are not sufficiently a part of the Mohave Indian's social personality to motivate him effectively, especially in so extreme an undertaking as suicide. This hypothesis is perfectly compatible with Durkheim's (1897) views concerning the basic role of anomie in suicide, though in this instance the lack of a traditionally affective bond between Kamey He:ya and the sheriff made the former an ineffective "model" which, while presumably triggering off the sheriff's suicidal attempt, also explains its ultimate ineffectiveness, which parallels the failure of Kamey He:ya's suicidal attempt.

It should also be specified that these unique examples of seemingly "serious" Mohave suicides being saved from death cannot be explained solely in terms of the fact that they are the *most recent* suicides of which I have a record, because, due to the competence of the late M. A. I. Nettle, M.D., the Mohave had excellent medical care ever since 1910 or thereabouts. Had it been possible to save any of the other (earlier) suicides, Dr. Nettle would have done so.

SINGE CASES

SUBGROUP I.—Suicides resulting from social isolation.

> (A) The shaman Tâma:râhue was unjustly accused of being a witch. (Supplementary Case C, see Case 106).
> (B) Nyortc was neglected by her son (Case 123).
> (C) Kwali: was old, ill, and had no relatives (Case 124).

SUBGROUP II.—Suicide caused by the wife's simple or aggravated infidelity.

> (D) Wilymawilyma's wife was first unfaithful and then left him (Case 125).
> (E) Hipily Tcukup was cuckolded by members of his gens (Case 126).
> (F) Atceyer Tcuva:u's wife deceived him with aliens (Case 127).

SUBGROUP I

SUPPLEMENTARY CASE C (for a full account see Case 106, pp. 425–426):

Tâma:râhue, embittered by unjust accusations of being a witch, first drank datura and then drowned himself in the Colorado River.

Comment

Tâma:râhue used atypical means to kill himself.

This motivation is, on the other hand, typical, since disappointment over society's unjust accusations is but a more generalized form of the individual's distress when his own kin persecutes or rejects him (Cases 111, 116, 118). Examples of shamans distressed when unjustly accused of witchcraft are given in pt. 4, pp. 150–175, and pt. 7, pp. 387–426.)

CASE 123:

Name: Nyortc. Gens: Nyoltc. Race: Fullblood Mohave. Sex: Female. Age at death: 40–50. Marital status: Widow (?). Children: The name shows that she lost at least one child. Surviving son, Nyail Kwaki:yo. (Gens: Nyolte according to some, O:otc according to others. Race: Fullblood Mohave. Age: 25.) Parents: Dead. Education: None. Occupation: None. Date of death: First decade of 20th century. Cause of death: Suicide. She suffocated herself by stuffing earth and sand into her mouth. Motives: Old age, illness, neglect, "tired of life."

Nyortc had been ill for several years and had no relatives, except a son who, unlike the average Mohave son, neglected her to such an extent that in the end she had to be given a home by a friend, Hispan Tåruu:ly (vagina fixed-up-good), of the O:otc gens, a fullblood Mohave approximately 40 years of age. In this context Hama: Utce: remarked, "That sounds just like old Pantåruuly (abridged form of the name). He is always kind to people."

One day Nyortc was dozing outside the house—a favorite resting place of the Mohave—and "as she tossed about, she felt that she did not wish to live any longer. Toward dawn she therefore stuffed dirt and sand into her mouth until she choked. She must have died early at dawn." In the morning, when Pantåruuly was bringing her breakfast, he found her dead.

Comment

It should be noted that, if her son's gentile affiliation was indeed Nyoltc, she and her husband (or lover) must have belonged to the same gens. Since the Mohave consider this to be a form of incest, it might just possibly explain why her son neglected her in so unusual a manner. The fact that she had no other living relatives was actually cited by those informants who said that her son was of the Nyoltc gens, in support of the belief that gentile endogamy and incest causes the extinction of entire families (Devereux, 1939 a).

Before the introduction of guns, suicides by means of self-suffocation were rather common, perhaps because, in addition to stillborn children, halfbreeds and unwanted puppies were, in the past, disposed of by burying them alive (Devereux, 1948 d). Nyortc, however, seems to have had neither illegitimate, nor halfbreed children. Be that as it may, it is interesting that Hama: Utce: felt impelled to add that Nyortc's son later on lost an eye. "Now he has a glass-eye and looks much better." (Case 88.) Recently the son had been in the Reservation Hospital with an ulcerated leg, which caused some unpleasant gossip on the reservation.

Whether Nyail Kwaki:yo lost his eye "accidentally on purpose" as a result of a need for self-punishment, and whether the loss of the eye, *rather than some other misfortune*, was caused by an unconscious need to "allude" in some manner to his, possibly incestuous, descent—in that the loss of an eye and an incestuous marriage call for similar types of feasts (pt. 7, pp. 356–371)—is something which only an actual psychonanalysis of this man would enable one to ascertain. Such a hypothesis is, inherently, quite plausible, since, unless we assume that his presumably incestuous descent troubled Nyail Kwaki:yo and caused him to neglect his mother, his altogether atypical lack of filial piety would be incomprehensible.

As regards the loss of Nyail Kwaki:yo's eye, the very fact that Hama: Utce: felt impelled to mention this (seemingly irrelevant) detail, suggests that she, at least, viewed it unconsciously as a retribution for Nyail Kwaki :yo's unfilial behavior.[5]

CASE 124 (Informants: Hivsu: Tupo :ma and Hama: Utce :) :

Name: Kwali :. Gens: Nyoltc. Race: Fullblood Mohave. Sex: Male. Age at death: According to Hivsu: Tupo :ma, 45; according to others, "old." Marital status: Presumably single. Children: None. Parents: Dead. Relatives: None. Education: None. Occupation: Formerly a laborer. Date of death: 1924 (?). Cause of death: Suicide by hanging. Motive: Ill and lonely. Psychiatric status: Chronic alcoholic. Medical status: He had an incurable cancer of the rectum, mistakenly believed by the Mohave to be due to hiku :pk, i.e., syphilis.

Kwali: had originally worked at Blythe, but, toward the end of his life, lived at Needles. He was a lonely man, having no relatives, and only a few friends, one of whom sheltered him in his home. One evening his hosts went to town to sell some Indian beadwork and other knickknacks, leaving Kwali: at home. Between 8:00 and 9:00 p.m., the lonely man slung a rope over a beam in the house and hanged himself. The beam was so low that he actually had to let his body sag in order to kill himself, a fact which may explain certain rumors that he had not committed suicide, but had been murdered. However, all competent informants disbelieved these allegations, and no one was prosecuted for murder.

Comment

The informants' denials of these rumors seem credible for five reasons:

(1) The only person who mentioned this gossip was a sincere but usually not too well informed person, who, for various reasons, could not have possessed any "inside" information about this case.

(2) A seemingly aimless murder of this type is entirely out of keeping with basic Mohave behavior patterns.

(3) Tested and proved informants, who never held back information of any kind, however damaging to anyone, flatly denied that there was any basis to this rumor.

(4) No one was even accused of having neglected or abused this ill and lonely old man.

(5) Cases of suicide by hanging oneself from a low point of suspension are less rare than one might think,[6] and may be a reflection of an unconsciously spiteful need to die as dramatically as possible, so as to make the survivors feel doubly guilty. On the other hand, a suicide by this means also gives the subject a chance to save his life, up to the very last minute. The fact that Kwali: failed to do so, and showed so much resoluteness, only increased the "awfulness" of his death and the guilt feelings of the survivors.

The fact that this ailing old man, who, though lacking relatives, was adequately cared for by friends, committed suicide may indicate the importance of having blood kin, and a primitive, culturally conditioned, inability to accept loyal friends as adequate substitutes for relatives. This view is supported also by the suicide of Nyortc, who was lovingly cared for by her old friend

---

[5] Compare in support of this view, Hama: Utce :'s spontaneous remark that the illness of Hilna Tumak, who drove her husband to suicide (Case 127), was not due to witchcraft but to pangs of conscience.

[6] Thus, while doing fieldwork in Indochina, I learned from official sources that a French civil servant had killed himself by hanging himself from so low a point of suspension that he actually died in a quasi-sitting position, with his buttocks almost touching the ground.

Hispan Târuu :ly, but was neglected by her unfilial son Nyail Kwaki :yo (Case 123). In fact, the ability to accept friends as adequate substitutes for kins-folk may be a trait occurring only in advanced societies and correlated with the breakdown of the truly functional aspects of kinship ties (Devereux, 1942 d).

It should also be specified that the pains of cancer are, in themselves, capable of motivating suicidal acts. It is, nonetheless, significant that Kwali: killed himself at a time when his friendly hosts had to be absent, so that he must have felt more than usually lonely and depressed, and also sorry to be a burden to these friends, who had to go out even in the evening to earn a living.

SUBGROUP II

CASE 125 (Informants: Hivsu: Tupo :ma and Hama: Utce:) (1932) :

Name: Wilymawilyma. Gens: Tcatc. Race: Three-quarters Mohave, one-quarter (father's mother) Cocopa. Sex: Male. Age at death: 29. Marital status: Remarried. Children: None. Parents: Father living. Education: Sherman Institute. Occupation: Sante Fe Railroad shops. Date of death: 1929 (?). Cause of death: Suicide. He shot himself in the chin with a shot-gun. Motive: Deserted by his wife.

Name of wife: Kat. Gens: Kat. Race: Fullblood Mohave. Sex: Female. Age: 23. Marital status: Married. Children: None.

Kat was promiscuous and had an adulterous affair with Tcematcem(à) (Gens: O :otc. Race: Fullblood Mohave. Sex: Male. Age: 17–19), who was not related to either of them. (See also Case 104.) Wilymawilyma was ap-parently aware of this situation, though at first he does not seem to have in-terfered with the lovers. However, 3 days after his wife left him and married (went to live with) her lover, between 8 :00–9 :00 a.m., Wilymawilyma retired to his house in Needles, took a 12-gage shotgun, and, working its trigger with his foot, shot himself in the chin. He did not die at once and was rushed to the Santa Fe Railroad hospital in San Bernardino, where he died of his wounds. The Mohave put up enough money to have his corpse returned to Needles for cremation.

This suicide disgusted Hama: Utce: a great deal: "We despise people who commit suicide. They show their emotions. They are weak. In olden times people did not commit suicide (for such reasons?)."

Comment

This case was first recorded in 1932, in connection with an inquiry into Mohave divorce. It was cited as an example of the decreased self-control of the younger Mohave, who throw away their lives even over so "trifling" a matter as a broken marriage. Actually, it is quite probable that this native interpretation is valid, the real cause of this new attitude being presumably, the gradual disintegra-tion of the functional kin group and the increasing need of the younger Mohave to stabilize themselves emotionally by relying primarily upon the love and com-pany of one spouse, instead of upon the collective affection and support of the kin group (Devereux, 1942 d). This does not mean, of course, that, even in aboriginal times, the Mohave did not experience distress when they were de-serted by a desirable spouse, especially if that spouse could not be readily re-placed with an equally desirable one (Devereux, 1942 d). When such a situ-ation arose, it was common enough e.g., for, an old man deserted by a young wife to develop the transitory hi :wa itck neurosis (pt. 3, pp. 91–106). By contrast all informants emphatically denied that, in aboriginal times, anyone was "crazy enough" to kill himself just because his wife left him. It is also quite noteworthy that, even during the period of gradual acculturation, only broken *marriages* led to suicide; the sole exception being a case of adultery combined with incest—and therefore indicative of an extremely atypical type (Devereux, 1939 a) of emotional involvement (Case 119). The first suicide caused by a stormy, but socially regular, love affair occurred as late as 1944 (Case 121), i.e., at a time when at least the younger generation was already appreciably acculturated and imbued with occidental romanticism.

CASE 126 (Informants: Hivsu: Tupo :ma and Hama: Utce:) :

Name: Hipily Tcukup. Gens: Nyoltc. Race: Fullblood Mohave. Sex: Male. Age at death: 41. Marital status: Married. Children: None. Parents: Mother living. Education: Indian Agency School, Parker, Ariz. Occupation: Odd jobs, selling wood, and ritual singing. Like every singer, Hipily Tcukup received in dream the power to sing. His particular song was the Tu :ma :np'å Utåu :t or short Tu :ma :np'å cycle (Devereux, 1939 a; and pt. 7, pp. 356–371), which is about a brother-sister incest. Persons who sing this song-cycle do not necessarily become shamans in their old age (Kroeber, 1925 a). Date of death: 1929 (?). Cause of death: Suicide. He fired a shotgun into his heart. Motive: Infidelity of his wife.

Name of wife: O :otc. Gens: O :otc. Race: Fullblood Mohave. Sex: Female. Age: 50. Marital status: Married. Children: None. Parents: Dead. Occupation: Housewife.

Hipily Tcukup and his wife lived opposite the town of Needles, Calif., on the Arizona side of the Colorado River, where the so-called Fort Mohave Reservation is located. Hipily Tcukup's wife had affairs simultaneously with two men, who, though of her husband's gens, were no blood-relatives of his. Her lovers were:

(1) Talyhia :ra. Gens: Nyoltc. Race: Fullblood Mohave. Sex: Male. Age: 43. Marital status: Single.

(2) Hamcukuenk. Gens: Nyoltc. Race: Fullblood Mohave. Sex: Male. Age: 45. Marital status: Single.

Hipily Tcukup was aware of his wife's infidelity. One day, just as she was about to leave for another tryst with one of her lovers, he said: "I shall shoot you, and myself as well," and then shot her in the stomach with a shotgun, just as she ran to hide in the bushes. Hama: Utce: felt that "if he had known that she was still alive, he would have finished her off." Thinking that he had killed her, he went back into the house and put on all his finery for his own funeral. He then lay down on his bed, stretched out on his back, and (presumably?) sang the Tu :ma :np'å Utåu :t cycle. Then, between 4 :00 and 5 :00 p.m., he got up and shot himself in the heart, by working the trigger of the shotgun with his foot.

After his death his wife married one of her lovers, Talyhia :ra. Her son, known both as Pi :it Hi :dho Kwa-ahwat (Pi :it eyes red) and as Kwakuy Tadhuk (oldwoman?) of the O :otc gens (?), was eventually bewitched by Kumådhi: Atat, of the Kumådhi: gens (Case 49).

Comment

As in several other instances, the husband's final aggressive and self-destructive behavior is preceded by a long period of purposeless patience and tolerance. It must be assumed that it is during this period of behavioral quiescence and self-control that emotional pressures accumulate to the point where they can find an adequate outlet only in suicide and/or a murderous assault.

CASE 127 (Informants: Hivsu: Tupo :ma and Hama: Utce:) :

Name: Atceyer Tcuva :u. Gens: Vahath. Race: Fullblood Mohave. Sex: Male. Age at death: 30. Marital status: Married. Children: Allegedly a son,

9 years of age. Parents: Mother living. Father died 15 years earlier. Education: Indian Agency School, Fort Mohave. Fairly well educated. Occupation: Santa Fe Railroad shops. Date of death: 1916 (?), around midnight. Cause of death: Suicide. Shot himself in the head with a .32 caliber revolver. Motive: Wife was promiscuous, even with racial aliens.

Name of wife: Hilna Tumak. Gens: None. Race: Mother, Mohave; father, White. Sex: Female. Age: 20. Marital status: Married. Children: Allegedly a (step?) son, 9 (sic!) years of age. Parents: No data recorded. Occupation: Housewife. Comment: Illegitimate, gensless, halfbreed daughter of a woman described as a thinyeak hiko-nyentc (i.e., woman whites-copulate-with; woman copulates with whites.)

Hilna Tumak married Atceyer Tcuva:u when she was about 18 or 19 years of age. He was an industrious man, who worked in the Santa Fe Railroad roundhouse at Needles. Husband and wife got along well with each other. "I know this to be a fact, having lived with them for a year." Hilna Tumak was, however, very promiscuous, not merely with Mohave men, but also with Americans and Mexicans, in fact, according to Hama: Utce:, "with anyone who would have intercourse with her." Although Hivsu: Tupo:ma denied it, he too may have been one of Hilna Tumak's lovers. Sometime after Hivsu: Tupo:ma returned to Parker, he heard that Atceyer Tcuva:u had become aware of Hilna Tumak's infidelities, and had even caught her several times with certain Mexicans. One day, after catching her again in the act, he decided that the situation had become intolerable. He went home and stopped en route for a drink. When he reached his home he said to his mother-in-law: "Your daughter misbehaves. I knew it. I never complained. But this is the end. I shall kill myself." [7] He then went into his house and, around midnight, killed himself by shooting himself in the head with a .32 caliber revolver.

Atceyer Tcuva:u was cremated next day at noon and his relatives felt so bitter toward Hilna Tumak that, 1 month later, they hired a shaman to bewitch her. When, as a result of witchcraft, she became ill, she ignored the admonitions of the shamans who treated her, and did not confess the bewitcher's name, even though she knew that nothing else could save her. "She could not utter the name of the witch because he had sealed her lips" (Devereux, 1937 c). Finally, they brought Hilna Tumak to Parker, where she lingered on for several months. A shaman specializing in the cure of witchcraft, as well as other shamans, tried to cure her, but without success. One of them, called Masahay Lyiva:u (i.e., girl stand-in), treated her at informant's house, but could not help her either. "She simply suffered from witchcraft. She had pains in her left side, under the arm, although there was neither a sore nor a swelling. The pain was just waiting to go to her heart." (Hama: Utce remarked, "I think that her conscience hurt her.") She died 2 months after her husband's death, and was cremated.

She left a son, allegedly "9 or 10 years old" (**which** seems improbable, since she herself was said to have been only 20 years old) who was brought up by relatives. This son is now a grown man, and lives alternately with two sisters, being married now to one, and now to the other of the two.

Comment

The above suicide was ultimately due to the average Mohave man's reluctance to behave aggressively toward his unfaithful wife and her lovers. As regards the lovers, the fact that they were Mexicans presumably increased the odious-

---

[7] The choppy style of the translation suggests that he uttered these remarks in the so-called "preaching" (i. e., formal, or ritual narrative) style.

ness of the wife's infidelity and may have further inhibited the husband's impulse to retaliate.

The hiring of a witch to kill an unfaithful wife is an ancient Mohave pattern, mentioned even in folklore (Devereux, 1948 h). Since the bewitching was done by request and for pay, the witch would, naturally, not allow his victim to utter his name.

The likelihood that the wife's fatal illness was motivated by guilt, and was therefore presumably psychosomatic, was spontaneously mentioned by Hama: Utce: herself.

Utce: herself. Moreover, Hilma Tumak's self-destructive silence perfectly fits the pattern ascribed to the willing victims of witches, except in that she had been bewitched for pay, instead of being (preconsciously) enthralled by the witch (pt. 7, pp. 383–386.)

PART 8. CONCLUSION

Πάντα θεῖα καὶ πάντα ἀνθρώπινα
—Hippocrates.

GENESIS AND VALIDITY OF MOHAVE PSYCHIATRY

The Introduction stressed the accuracy of Mohave clinical descriptions and the unsystematic, spotty but extensive compatibility of Mohave psychiatric thought with modern psychoanalytic theory and indicated that these two phenomena stood in need of explanation.

Neither of these two facts would surprise the Mohave themselves, since they ascribe universal validity to their psychiatric thories. Thus, the "highstrung" personality of an American was believed to have been due to premature sexual relations (Devereux, 1950 a), another was believed to have the hikwi:r illness, while still another is said to have had the atcoo:r hanyienk type of convulsions. In fact, whites are believed to be relatively immune only to foreign sickness. Yet, even in that connection one Mohave at least suggested that, despite the relative weakness of the Mohave Indian's "blood," contact with a Mohave may also have mildly deleterious effects on whites. In addition, Ahma Huma:re specified without any prompting on my part that he could cure even whites who had hiwey lak, while Tcatc spontaneously gave me "supportive psychotherapy" at a time when I was supposed to have hi:wa itck. Even Hivsu: Tupo:ma, who declared that he was not able to treat white patients, freely interpreted some of my dreams. Finally, even though some of the information which I provided about the symptoms of white and Sedang Moi neurotics or psychotics elicited consternation, and while the Mohave are always ready to draw invidious comparisons between their ethnic character and that of whites, the symptoms of alien patients did not seem to impress them as "non-human" and "beyond empathy."

Before we attempt to account for the presence of these extensive congruences, we must seek to explain why there is any Mohave folk psychiatry at all.

THE GENESIS OF MOHAVE PSYCHIATRY

Neither science nor pseudoscience comes into being for its own sake, but always in response to a socially significant challenge, which has an appreciable "social and/or cultural mass" (Devereux, 1940 b). Yet, even though the mentally deranged person possesses a great "social mass"—i. e., the capacity to trigger social action and to influence the behavior of others—this social mass need not necessarily serve as a challenge for the development of *psychiatry*. Thus, the psychiatric knowledge and curing rites of the Sedang Moi are quite rudimentary. Moreover, owing to the legalistic and punitive temper of that tribe, its "psychiatry" is, at times, indistinguishable from law. Yet there are quite as many insane among the Sedang as among the Mohave.

Apparently the genesis of psychiatry also presupposes more than just a therapeutic orientation, which is present in most cultures. Indeed, it is, at least in principle, possible to develop a respectable science of psychiatric diagnosis even in an imaginary society which postulates that insanity is the consequence of so great a sin and represents such a danger to society, that the psychotic must be executed as soon as he is diagnosed as such. We therefore suggest that the crucial factor responsible for the emergence of a science of psychiatry, however primitive, is the implicit assumption that the seemingly chaotic behavior of the insane *makes some kind of sense in terms of itself*, and not simply in terms of some *external* frame of reference such as possession, defective genes, or organic illness.

Needless to say, psychiatry is not the only trait whereby the "social mass" of the insane is made manifest. Laws, attitudes, social concern over insanity, etc., are also repercussions of the social mass of the insane person and of the social image ("collective representation") of insanity. Even psychiatry itself may acquire a semiautonomous "social mass" of its own; witness, to take a striking though unconventional example, the fantastically large current crop of sophisticated jokes, beloved by the intelligentsia, about psychiatrists, and especially psychoanalysts, which are not to be confused with jokes about morons and lunatics, favored chiefly by the unsophisticated. A discussion of this topic is, however, beyond the scope of the present essay, chiefly because my preliminary investigations of this field indicate that existing studies have barely scratched the surface of the problem, which has, so far, not even been recognized as a problem sui generis. It is therefore sufficient to give only one example of the complexities confronting the student who wishes to explore, e.g., the "social mass" of the *idea of suicide* in Mohave society.

Although the Mohave are not exceptionally prone to suicide, the idea of suicide has a great cultural mass and is a major reference point in Mohave theorizing about death. Thus, they consider as suicide:

(1) The prenatal deaths of bewitched fetuses and of potential future shamans (pt. 7, pp. 331–339).
(2) Certain types of pediatric illnesses of sucklings (pt. 7, pp. 340–348).
(3) The death of twins who have not yet married (pt. 7, pp. 348–356).
(4) The symbolic, ritual "suicide" of men who marry a female relative of theirs (pt. 7, pp. 356–371).
(5) The death of the willing victims of witches (pt. 7, pp. 383–386).
(6) The vicarious suicide of witches who incite others to kill them (Kroeber, 1925 a; and pt. 7, pp. 387–426).
(7) The death of isolated warriors, who deliberately stray into enemy territory (Halpern, personal communication, 1938; and pt. 7, pp. 426–431).

(8) Predictably frustrated suicidal attempts during funerals (pt. 7, pp. 431–459).

(9) Real suicides (pt. 7, pp. 459–484).

In one of the above instances (4) there is not even illness, let alone death. In four other instances (1, 2, 3, 5) we are confronted with organic, or, at most, psychosomatic illness, sometimes followed by death. In two instances (6, 7) the suicide is vicarious. In one instance (8) the suicidal attempt is a hollow gesture, since it is known in advance that it will be frustrated. Yet, precisely because most types of events defined by the Mohave as "suicides" are not suicides in any real sense, the preceding list reveals the great "social and cultural mass" possessed by the idea of suicide in Mohave culture.[8]

To a certain extent this great "mass"—and consequent great elaboration—of "psychiatry" itself accounts for some congruences between Mohave and modern psychodynamic theories, simply on the principle that even the blind hen finds an occasional grain of corn, if it pecks the ground long enough.[9] This, however, does not account either for the elaborateness of Mohave psychiatry when contrasted, e.g., with the meagerness of Sedang psychiatry—which is precisely the point we propose to discuss here—or for the great number of congruences between Mohave and scientific psychopathology, which will be analyzed further below.

It is suggested that the elaborateness of Mohave psychiatry is due to at least four major factors:

The first—though not necessarily the most important—of these is the Mohave Indian's preoccupation with dreams (Kroeber, 1925 a; Wallace, 1947; Devereux, 1956 c), which presumably sensitizes him to intrapsychic happenings and to the unfolding of the "primary process"[10] which manifests itself so strikingly in dream as well as in psychosis.

The second factor is a direct consequence of the first: the Mohave Indian's preoccupation with his own dreams enables him to empathize with the psychotic.

The third factor to be considered is the Mohave Indian's tendency to speculate about abstruse matters. This accounts for the elaborateness of his mythology and intellectual supernaturalism, which so strikingly contrasts with the meagerness of his ritual and the backward state of his technology (Kroeber, 1925 a). It is this tendency to speculate about unusual matters—and the behavior of the psychotic

---

[8] The "mass" of a conceptual point of reference can apparently be measured by the extent to which unrelated ideas and events are forcibly brought within its scope, in a relationship of artificial compendence (Devereux, 1957 a).

[9] Many historians of psychiatry (e.g., Zilboorg and Henry, 1941) have shown an inclination to assume that the rare psychiatric verities found in early authors were the products of carefully constructed inferences based upon sound data, instead of truths accidentally stumbled upon by their authors and completely unrelated to the untenable frame of reference in which they were placed. Historians of science would save themselves from similar pitfalls if they took care to remember that a correct noema may be the product of an utterly erroneous noesis.

[10] We may note in passing that the "primary process" follows the same rules of "logic" as Lévy-Bruhl's much maligned "prelogical" mentality.

is as peculiar a phenomenon as any—which accounts for the elaborateness, rather than for the existence, of Mohave psychiatry.

Precisely what role, if any, the Mohave Indian's humanity toward his fellow man—including at times even captives (Stratton 1857)—and his unwillingness to reject him in his distress, played in the genesis of Mohave psychiatry is hard to determine. Personally I cannot but believe that it did play an important motivating role, in the sense that concern over and helpfulness toward the insane, who continues to be defined as a fellow Mohave, was bound to lead to speculations about the nature of his distress. The principal argument in favor of this assumption is the infinite patience which the Mohave display toward monstrous babies, whose condition is due to the sins of their parents, and whom they seek to keep alive simply because they, too, are Mohave, and despite the fact that they are bound to become lifelong burdens on their sponsors. Since this point was discussed elsewhere in some detail (pt. 6, pp. 257–260), it is only mentioned here in passing.

All of these factors, except only the last one, will be given due consideration in the course of our attempt to account for the objective validity of Mohave psychiatry.

THE GENESIS OF MOHAVE PSYCHIATRY

In studying the congruence of Mohave psychiatric beliefs with modern theories of psychopathology, one is tempted to ascribe *all* of this overlap to the sound psychiatric insights of the Mohave shaman, and to ignore certain important factors which may, to a far from negligible extent, account for at least some of the congruences.

One of these is the already mentioned fact that even a generally irrational, but highly elaborate and rambling system will, simply because it is elaborate, be congruent with reality at least now and then. Yet, even though the validity of a few Mohave psychiatric notions may be "accidental," it is felt that mere chance accounts only for a negligible portion of objectively valid Mohave psychiatric theories.

The second cause of these numerous congruences is relatively obvious, though seldom formally expressed. Each culture has its basic themes and "type conflicts," as well as its "type defenses" against these very specific conflicts. Now, it is self-evident that these conflicts and defenses pervade and determine the pattern of each culture quite as much as they pervade and determine the etiology and symptomatology of the concrete clinical cases occurring in each cultural setting. In other words, the individual Mohave psychotic is quite as much a product of his culture as is Mohave psychiatric theory. This fact would, in itself, account for some degree of congruence between theory and clinical fact. A direct corollary of this thesis is that every system of psychiatry is a product of the cultural milieu in which it evolved, and will therefore fit persons belonging to that group better than it fits members of culturally alien groups. This is also suggested by the total lack of an acceptable modern psychodynamic interpretation of such descriptively rather well studied culture-specific "ethnic psychoses" (Devereux, 1956 b) as *amok*. In fact, it seems probable that it will prove impossible to evolve any kind of universally applicable, i.e., culturally neutral, system of psychiatry which is not solidly rooted in the concept of Culture *per se*—i.e., of Culture as a *generic human phenomenon*—as distinct from any particular culture, be it Occidental or Eskimo (Devereux, 1956 b).

The third factor to be taken into consideration in seeking to explain the objective validity of much Mohave theory and clinical observation is considerably less obvious. It stands to reason that any conflict-ridden person will seek to conform extensively to cultural *beliefs* concerning the *manner* in which the mentally deranged do, in fact, *behave*—or are at least *supposed to behave*, in order to be recognized as, and given the status of, psychotics or neurotics. Thus, cultural beliefs concerning the "standard" or "expected" behavior of "mental cases" often serve as models for the symptoms which the actually conflict-ridden persons must evolve. Otherwise stated, native psychiatric belief in itself seems to be a "model" or a "pattern of misconduct" (Linton, 1936) for the individual in conflict, who has reached the point where he begins to look for means of expressing, repressing, distorting, and disguising his conflicts and urges . . . i. e., who is *about* to evolve a neurosis or a psychosis (Devereux, 1956 d).

Of course, the degree to which the conflict-ridden person conforms to this culturally delineated pattern of misconduct, i. e., the extent to which he conforms to the type of behavior *expected in that culture* from any mentally deranged person, is inversely proportional to his rejection of society and of all its works; i. e., it is inversely proportional to the amount of his "social negativism" (Devereux, 1940 a; 1956 b). Thus, at least as regards the factor of social negativism, the conflict-ridden person who actualizes his difficulties in accordance with local psychiatric beliefs is "less sick" than one who is no longer capable of conforming even to the prevailing "pattern of misconduct," i.e., who refuses to "go crazy according to Hoyle" and evolves instead his own constellation of symptoms. This may explain why almost every reported case of ethnic psychosis (amok, windigo) and ethnic neurosis (latah, piblokto) is a "classical textbook case," even though the classical textbook case is a rarity in culturally nonstandardized forms of mental derangement (Devereux, 1956 b).[11]

---

[11] This conformism of the psychotic is sometimes obscured by diagnostic trends and fashions. Thus, at a time when "schizophrenia" is the fashionable diagnosis to make, more "atypical schizophrenias" (sic!) will be diagnosed than typical ones. Also, patients who do not have the "fashionable" neurosis or psychosis may attempt to develop at least some of its characteristic symptoms. The history of diagnostic fashions in psychiatry is still to be written !

In brief, we postulate that at least *part* of the congruence of Mohave (or any other) psychiatric theory with clinical data is not always *primarily* due to the basic realism of the theory, or to the fact that theory and individual psychosis alike are products of the same total cultural pattern. The congruence is, in some cases, due simply to a tendency of conflict-ridden persons to conform to cultural ideas of "how the insane should behave," i. e., they act the way their culture expects an insane person to act.

A fourth factor, of an altogether different order, is the tendency of historians of psychiatry to ascribe a meaning to an old theory which, in fact, it does not have. Thus, the historian of psychiatry often professes to find in a musty old tome indications that a medieval student of psychopathology somehow anticipated modern psychiatric insights. Such alleged findings must be subjected to very careful scrutiny. Leaving aside, for the sake of brevity, the imputation of modern meanings to medieval or renaissance psychiatric works, which would require an elaborate discussion, I propose to discuss instead briefly a recent attempt to suggest that Shakespeare's well-known remark: "There is method in his madness" somehow anticipates modern insights into psychic determinism and into the "logic" of the unconscious. A closer examination of the context of this utterance shows that the "method" which Shakespeare "discovered" in his character's madness pertains simply to pathological preoccupations on the one hand, and, on the other hand, provides a basis for *the imputation of a quasi-clairvoyant significance* to that character's rambling utterances. Neither of these two "methods in madness" has even the remotest connection with modern theories of the logic of the unconscious.

The preceding considerations are sufficiently weighty to induce one to exercise the greatest caution in evaluating certain Mohave psychiatric insights as genuine anticipations of modern psychiatric thought.

Having entered every possible *caveat* against overvaluing the realism of Mohave psychiatry, we must now take cognizance of the fact that, insofar as such matters can be judged impressionistically, the number of factual and theoretical congruences between modern and Mohave psychiatry is simply too great to be explainable in terms of any or all of the preceding considerations. Our next task will therefore be the presentation of factors responsible for these congruences.

The student of Mohave psychiatric ideas cannot fail to be struck, e.g., by the ability of this relatively primitive people to differentiate between neurosis and perversion, or between the psychiatric sequelae of organic illness and the organic sequelae of psychiatric illness (organisches Entgegenkommen).

Even more startling is the Mohave Indian's ability to differentiate between physiological and psychic orgasm, both in normal and in pathological sexuality. Thus, in discussing normal sexuality, all informants differentiated between real intercourse (love making) and mere fornication, while Hivsu: Tupo:ma explained in detail that, when a couple makes love, body cohabits with body and soul cohabits with soul, so that the sexual act takes place on two levels, the physiological and the psychic (Devereux, 1950 a). As regards psychopathology, the Mohave specify that only "disgusting" lechers (pi-ipa: ala:yk=people bad), who seek in vain to obtain release from psychosexual tensions by means of masturbation and/or fornication, have convulsions of the atcoo:r hanyienk type, which the Mohave rightly believe to be orgasm equivalents. This Mohave belief reflects real insight into the psychodynamics of various sexual activities, since it is a well-established fact that neither masturbation nor mere fornication ever culminates in a real psychic orgasm, because—as a Mohave might express it—in neither of these (predominantly physiological) activities is there also coitus between the *souls* of the partners. In fact, there are even indications that the Mohave ascribe a greater intensity to a psychic orgasm than to a merely physiological one, since they hold that psychic (dream) coitus with a beloved ghost has an irresistible appeal and motivating force, whereas mere fornication is something one takes in one's stride.

These and many other congruences between Mohave and modern psychiatric views cannot, obviously, be entirely due to chance, nor even to the various other factors discussed previously. We must therefore seek to account for the extensiveness of these congruences not only in terms of psychology and anthropology, but in terms of culture history as well.

Actually, this extensive overlap between modern and Mohave psychiatry is less puzzling than it may seem at first. Any psychologically sophisticated student of literature, such as Freud (1917), knows that poets and writers discovered certain important psychiatric truths long before the scientific psychiatrist did. One may, for example, think in this context of Catullus' famous description of ambivalence: "Odi et amo." "I hate and I love. Why, I do not know, but I am in agony." Many primitive myths, beliefs, and customs likewise mirror, in an almost undisguised form, psychological processes which, in our own daily life and culture, are buried in the deepest layers of the unconscious, and are only accessible to, and meaningful for, the well-analyzed person.

The congruence between Mohave and modern psychiatric ideas can be explained on several levels.

The validity of Mohave clinical observations.—The first factor to be discussed is the Mohave Indian's ability to observe and to remember accurately his dreams as well as the behavior and utterances of the psychotic.

A recent summary of studies on the relationship between personality structure and perception (Blake and Ramsey, 1951) shows that a segment of objective reality which is, in principle, accessible to direct observation by means of the senses, is often partially distorted and sometimes even actually negated (repressed) by the percipient. The history of science in general, and the history of psychiatry in particular, are likewise replete with instances in which supposedly trained observers simply did not "register" something which was fully accessible to their senses.

The classical culture-historical instance was the absolute refusal of occidental adults—including even scientists—to acknowledge in any manner whatsoever the existence of infantile sexuality, and this despite the fact that anyone who ever tended babies must have seen that male infants had so-called "tension erections." Moreover, the educated person's absolute "ignorance" of infantile sexuality existed side by side with his conscious awareness that peasant nursemaids masturbate fretful babies, in order to quiet them—a practice also obtaining, e.g., among the Navaho (Leighton and Kluckhohn, 1947; Bailey, 1950). The attitude that something which should not exist, should be ignored, was adhered to even by psychiatrists. It was, I believe, Ferenczi who reported that when an inmate of the principal Hungarian mental hospital tried to discuss his masturbation problems with the chief psychiatrist, the latter severely reprimanded him for mentioning such obscenities.

It is hardly necessary to argue that such a psychic scotoma—i. e., the tendency to notice only that which one can tolerate psychologically—is due to repression and to other defense mechanisms. In fact, the ultimate purpose of the training analyses of future psychoanalysts is precisely to render them capable of tolerating—and of being objective about—the "shocking" material which their future patients will inevitably produce in the course of their therapeutic analyses (Devereux, 1956 a).

The real problem which confronts us in this connection is, therefore, the Mohave "psychiatrist's" startling ability to notice what is before his eyes, and to remember it correctly. This ability is not a monopoly of the Mohave Indian. Indeed, Róheim (1933) rightly stressed that the primitive's superego is, in many ways, less pervasive than ours. Hence, where the manifestations of the instincts and the "logic of the emotions and of the unconscious" ("primary process") are concerned, he is bound to have fewer "blind spots" than the pre-Freudian psychiatrist. In fact, a fear of the "primary process" and of dereism is, itself, a cause of some distortions of perception, and, a fortiori, an obstacle to insight into the patient's—and one's own—unconscious. This matter will be discussed further in connection with difficulties experienced by rationalistic psychiatrists in assigning an internal meaning to the utterances and behavior of their patients.

The imputation of "a" meaning.—The next problem confronting us is the Mohave psychiatrist's startling ability not only to register what he sees, but to grasp these data insightfully, i. e., empathically. This implies, first and foremost, a willingness to assume that the seemingly chaotic and meaningless symptoms, actions, and utterances of the psychotic have—quite as much as the (supposedly) more intelligible reactions of normals [12]—an implicit or latent pattern, and are not simply a chaotic jumble of reflexes, etc., in the sense, e. g., in which some older students of dreams mentioned by Freud (1953) believed anxiety dreams to be caused by indigestible foods.

Now, it seems quite certain that the *willingness* to search for the pattern and meaning of psychotic behavior presupposes an affirmation of the normal man's kinship with the deviant, somewhat in the sense of the classical exclamation: "There, but for the grace of God, go I." It was an absolute refusal to recognize any kinship between man and animal which led a well-known 18th-century French savant to say that it was perfectly humane to kick an animal, since beasts did not "really" experience pain, but simply behaved "as if" they did. As for the unwillingness of normal man to admit his psychological kinship with the psychotic, it is at least partly responsible for some of the more extreme attempts to explain mental disorder exclusively in terms of such organic factors as defective genes, submicroscopic brain damage, or radically altered bodily biochemistry.

The first thing to be noted is that not only the Mohave "psychiatrist" but even the Mohave layman is able to observe psychotic behavior accurately, to sense its meaning and to empathize with it. This suggests that Mohave culture itself helps the normal individual to understand that—in a rather extreme way—his psychology is not altogether different from that of the psychotic. By contrast, few occidental laymen are willing to realize that every person, no matter how normal he may be, has a kind of "psychotic core," which finds expression, inter alia, in his dreams, in which he thinks, experiences, and behaves exactly as though he were a schizophrenic. In cat, making allowances for the inevitable oversimplification inherent in all "pithy" axioms, one may

---

[12] Since the psychotic is actually a "simplified" or "dedifferentiated" person, his behavior is actually more predictable than that of the normal, provided only that one uses the proper frame of reference for understanding it (Devereux, 1951 h, 1952 b).

say that a schizophrenic is simply someone who dreams even when he is awake.[13]

The best proof of our resistance against becoming aware of our "psychotic core" is, perhaps, the general tendency to forget our dreams. They are repressed not only because they are incompatible with our waking standards and aspirations, but also because they use a frame of reference, and operate in terms of a logic, greatly at variance with our waking reality orientation.

Now, it is a fact that—due to their culturally determined interests—the Mohave are singularly able to remember even quite complicated and disturbing dreams, such as those cited in this work. This characteristic also appears to be present in other groups—such as some Plains Indians—in which certain autistic experiences are culturally approved because both the dreamer and the community have a kind of "stake" in them (Devereux, 1951 a). Given the close relationship between dream and psychosis, it is not in the least surprising that people like the Mohave, who habitually *wish* to dream, *do* dream and *think over* their dreams in great detail, should gradually evolve a certain ability to tolerate at least some of the irrational core of their selves, i.e., their unconscious, by becoming, so to speak, immune to it.[14]

In brief, given the fact that Mohave culture is a "dream culture" (Kroeber, 1925 a), which tolerates even peculiar and extreme forms of sexual behavior, the Mohave are—almost by definition—capable of tolerating what they observe and can afford to recognize that the psychic processes of the neurotic or psychotic are simply more extreme manifestations of those psychic urges and happenings which are also expressed in their own dreams. In fact, given even the Mohave layman's preoccupation with dreams and his broadmindedness about sexual matters, it would have been psychologically inconceivable for him to be *incapable* of seeing, registering, remembering, and developing insight into the behavior of those psychiatric patients whom he has occasion to observe.

As regards the shaman, who is even more preoccupied with dreams, and even more extreme in his sexual behavior than the run-of-the-mill

---

[13] In 1939 I had occasion to see a paranoid schizophrenic in a colleague's office, which contained a big poster with the slogan: "Schizophrenia—a waking dream." When the patient noticed this poster, he was greatly startled and exclaimed: "That is exactly right. That is how it feels." There are even reasons to assume that this slogan materially advanced his recovery, since this long hospitalized patient was, some months later, discharged from the hospital and proved capable of supporting himself (Devereux, 1944 b).

[14] This immunization to certain types of anxieties is actually indispensable for the pursuit of certain professions. Thus, in defiance of the ordinary rules of psychotherapy, I felt free to interpret quite early his castration anxieties to an Indian cowboy, who had to castrate both bulls and stallions in reality (Devereux, 1951 a). By contrast, it is credibly reported that some U. S. combat infantrymen failed to fire their rifles, apparently because these scions of an essentially peaceful society could not bring themselves to fire shots in anger, and especially not at a *visible* enemy. In fact, it is permissible to suggest at least tentatively that—psychologically speaking—the invention of artillery, which kills invisible or distant foes, was partly motivated by the desire of people to "depersonalize" killing. The appeal of "pushbutton warfare" may also have a similar psychological source.

Mohave and who, furthermore, experienced extreme psychic turmoil—bordering on a temporary psychosis—in his youth, he is, by
definition, unusually well qualified to observe, to describe, and to
understand the behavior of mentally deranged individuals.[15]

Thus, both the perceptiveness and the insightfulness of the Mohave
are directly related to the dream orientation of his culture and its
broadmindedness about sexual matters. The culturally determined
excessive preoccupation of shamans with dreams and their—also culturally determined—transitory mental derangement in youth are,
in turn, responsible for the shaman's unusually great ability to observe and to understand neurotics and psychotics. In brief, instead
of having to suggest that there is something unusual—and, possibly
not culturally determined—about the Mohave Indian's "clinical"
acumen and capacity for empathy, it is actually clear that his "psychiatric" awareness is a direct, and practically inevitable, consequence
of some of the *most fundamental* characteristics of Mohave culture.
This, in turn, further supports the position taken elsewhere (Devereux, 1956 b) that psychiatric anthropology is not only "real"
anthropology, even in Kroeber's sense (1952), but is actually concerned primarily with the concept of "Culture," and with some of the
major "bedrock" problems and aspects of every particular culture.

Another, psychologically closely related but logically distinct, factor
in the Mohave Indian's willingness to impute a meaning to psychosis
is understandable in terms of Kroeber's (1952) suggestion that the
trend of culture is in the direction of greater realism, including, presumably, also rationality. Brief reference was already made to the
distinctive "logic of the unconscious" (primary process) by means
of which repressed urges and fantasies strive to express themselves.
Precisely because the emergence of such material is threatening to
the ego, the trend in the direction of greater rationality signifies,
in psychological terms, a progressive intensification of man's struggle
against his "primary processes," by means of an increasingly greater
overvaluation of, and allegiance to, the logical "secondary process."
This, in turn, deeply affects both his ability to perceive, and his
capacity to discover the meaning of psychotic behavior, which is
governed by the primary process. On the perceptual level the overly
or exclusively rationalistic observer can actually end up by noticing
only that which seems logical, because that is all he expects to see.
As a result, instead of becoming increasingly reality oriented, he
sometimes ends up by becoming incapable of observing that part of

---

[15] A psychoanalytic finding may help clarify this last point. It is well known that a
seemingly normal psychoanalytic candidate will, in the course of his training analysis,
develop at least a "transference neurosis." It is suggested that this experience of being
personally neurotic may, itself, appreciably help him later on to understand his neurotic
patients, again in terms of the feeling: "There, but for the grace of God, go I."

reality—dreams, psychotic behavior, etc.—which is governed by, and is a manifestation of, man's irrational component.

As regards the inhibiting effects of an exclusive allegiance to the logical "secondary process," it is also extremely important to understand that the "primary processes" of others cannot be understood *directly* by one's own "secondary processes." The "primary process" utterances of the psychotic must *first* set up reverberations in the clinical observer's own unconscious. This, in turn, mobilizes the observer's own "primary processes," which can then be subjected to the objective and logical scrutiny of the observer's rational ego, which operates in terms of the "secondary process." Any attempt to find the meaning of a psychotic's utterances directly and solely by means of logic, i.e., without first allowing these utterances to reverberate in one's own unconscious, only leads to pseudo-objective intellectual constructs, at variance with psychiatric realities.

This point will be referred to again in connection with the developmental history of psychiatry.

In brief, three factors are responsible for the Mohave Indian's clinical acumen, as reflected in his skillful observations and in his willingness to assume that even psychotic behavior has a discoverable meaning.

(1) The *inherent psychological ability* of the human unconscious to understand everyone else's unconscious perfectly (Ferenczi, 1926). The notorious difficulty of "fooling" children and dogs, whose intuitive awareness of the real feelings of others is not inhibited by culture, clearly demonstrates the inherent character of this ability. In fact, the inhibition of intuitiveness is incomplete even in adults, who often have certain hunches about people which are confirmed by subsequent experiences. Scientifically speaking, these hunches appear to be evolved on the basis of our preconscious appraisal of the expressive behavior (Allport and Vernon, 1933; Birdwhistell, 1952) of our interlocutors.[16]

(2) The characteristic *tendency of Mohave culture* not only not to inhibit, but actually to foster the development of this intuitiveness, by emphasizing the importance of dreams and by disinhibiting large portions of the instincts.

(3) The Mohave Indian's *readiness to utilize his own primary processes* in the course of his attempts to obtain insight into the meaning of psychotic behavior, dreams, etc.

The substantive meaning of psychopathological behavior.—It is not possible to evolve a psychiatry simply by assuming that abnormal behavior has a meaning. It is also necessary to define the *substantive*

---

[16] The Mohave Indian's characteristic tendency to react to people in terms of their individuality, rather than on the basis of their membership in some special unit, may have increased their understanding of expressive behavior.

nature of this meaning—i.e., whether it is psychological, organic, supernatural, etc.—and to select a *methodological* frame of reference for its systematization, e.g., either in supernaturalistic or in naturalistic terms.   It is proposed to discuss first the substantive meaning imputed by the Mohave to psychotic behavior.

So far we have only shown that, in the very act of empathizing with the psychiatric patient, the Mohave automatically assume that his behavior has an implicit meaning.   We now propose to show that this meaning is, broadly speaking, felt to be psychological in nature, even where the "pathogenic agent" is believed to be an exogenous one. Indeed, it is implicit in Mohave belief that even though aliens, ghosts, witches, etc., can trigger off mental disease, the actual psychosis is not created or "injected" by these external forces, but is a product of the reverberations and adjustments which the impact of these forces mobilizes in the patient's psyche.   There are countless references to this process in the descriptive passages of this work.   Health struggles against sickness, good dreams cancel bad ones, victims of witchcraft force themselves to reveal the name of the one who bewitched them, dreamers visited by ghosts seek to resist the blandishments of their deceased relatives, etc.   Thus, in a very genuine sense, the Mohave view mental disease as an essentially intrapsychic happening, even though it is often set in motion by supposedly external forces or by traumatic events.

The next objective is to show that the Mohave Indians' theories of psychopathology are greatly influenced by their experience of, and culturally determined preoccupation with, dreams (Kroeber, 1925 a; Wallace, 1947; Devereux, 1956 c).   We hasten to add, however, that even though dream theory is a good basis on which to build a theory of psychopathology, we are not, for the moment, concerned with the validity of the substantive meaning which the Mohave profess to find in abnormal behavior.   It suffices to stress that they do impute "a" meaning to such behavior, and that this meaning is related to their preoccupation with dreams.   This can be done without specifying for the moment whether their insights are valid or not.

The Mohave—like aesculapian priestly healers and medieval theological experts on mental disease—took as their point of departure certain objective observations and the assumption that these data had "an" (unspecified) implicit meaning, and then proceeded to formulate this meaning in *terms of traditional Mohave "thought models"* of a supernaturalistic type (Devereux, 1958 b).   What saved them from evolving a psychiatric system as unrealistic as that of the Middle Ages was the fact that dreams were practically the basis of their generalized "thought model."   This specific interest obliged them to derive their "theory of the universe" from the psychodynamics of dreams, instead of deriving a theory of dreams from a "theory of the universe" based upon (supposedly) different types of data and considerations. For example, where the Middle Ages formulated their conception of human nature in terms of a theological *imagery* whose dream sources were deliberately denied, the Mohave developed a theological imagery consciously correlated with dream experiences. In addition the Mohave also used "models" derived from the physical universe. Thus, as suggested elsewhere (pt. 2, pp. 72–76), their idea of the damming up of the libido, which then suddenly floods the organism, producing hysterical convulsions (atcoo:r hanyienk) may well have been inspired by the economically highly important (and therefore noteworthy) yearly floods of the Colorado River (Devereux, 1958 b).

The preceding considerations show that the substantive meaning which the Mohave professed to find in abnormal behavior was essentially a psychological one, inspired by, and derived from, their culturally determined preoccupation with dreams. This explains the existence of many segmental congruences between Mohave and modern psychiatric theories, but fails to account for the *overall incongruity* of Mohave psychopathological thought with modern psychiatric theory. This problem can best be tackled by recalling that, despite their interest in the abstruse and their tendency to speculate about it, the Mohave never evolved an explicit *general* theory of psychopathology.

The methodological frame of reference of Mohave psychiatry.— Broadly speaking, it is possible to view any phenomenon whatsoever—and this specifically includes both irrational behavior and alleged "spiritualistic phenomena" (Devereux, 1953 a)—either scientifically (naturalistically) or else nonscientifically (supernaturalistically). For example, such "natural" phenomena as sunrise and sunset, etc., were, once upon a time, placed into a methodologically supernaturalistic frame of reference and were thought to be actuated by divine will. By contrast, allegedly "spiritualistic phenomena" can—perhaps substantively wrongly, but methodologically correctly—be viewed not as "supernatural," but as natural manifestations of hitherto (supposedly) ignored "natural" human abilities. It should also be stressed that many scientifically valuable data and formulations were produced by supernaturalistically oriented individuals. Thus, Dodds (1951) rightly insists that, despite his great mathematical discoveries, Pythagoras was not primarily a scientist but a shaman, presumably because he made these discoveries in order to pursue more effectively certain mystical objectives and, furthermore, assigned a supernaturalistic meaning to his own discoveries.

Somewhat anticipating our conclusions, it is suggested that the inability of the Mohave to evolve a general theory of psychopathology and the extensive lack of congruence between their implicit "system" as a whole and the broad theoretical formulations of modern psychiatry are both due, first and foremost, to the fact that, even though they did impute a psychological meaning to dreams and psychoses, their basic orientation was, nonetheless, not a naturalistic-scientific one. Thus, even though they did "psychologize the universe," thereby causing many of their *specifically psychiatric* theories to seem highly realistic, their fundamental methodological position was, nonetheless, supernaturalistic. By contrast, the often grotesquely unpsychological "psychiatric" theories of the Age of Enlightenment were, despite their substantively erroneous content, scientific rather than supernaturalistic.

Now, it stands to reason that a sound dynamic psychiatry must, on the substantive level, assign an implicit psychological meaning to dreams and to abnormal behavior, and, on the methodological level, must formulate this substantive meaning in scientific-naturalistic, rather than in supernaturalistic, terms. The entire history of psychiatry can, in fact, be viewed as a blind groping toward this objective. This developmental process is so interesting, and so important for the proper understanding of the relationship between Mohave and modern psychiatry, that it deserves at least a summary discussion.

The development of modern psychiatry.—One need not be dedicated to the shibboleth of unilinear evolution to view the history of psychiatry as a gradual approximation of the objective of viewing the (substantively) irrational in (methodologically) rational ways. This problem is, in a limited sense, related to the mathematician's attempt to evolve the calculus of probabilities, so as to cope with problems where sheer technical difficulties make it necessary to deal with a complex whole, rather than with all the individual components of that whole. Now, even though, in this latter instance, the behavior of the individual components is not irrational, but simply technically hard to define, not until the 19th century did mathematicians succeed in evolving an effective calculus of probabilities and the science of statistical mechanics. Little wonder, then, that the psychiatrist, whose data are not simply too numerous to be managed comfortably, but definitely pertain to the irrational, should have needed so much time even to begin to master the problem of handling the irrational rationally.

Man's first attempt to understand the abnormal and irrational appears to have been both substantively and methodologically supernaturalistic. In fact, it is permissible to suppose that, precisely because supernaturalism can be both a substantive and a methodological position, myth-making is still a fashionable psychiatric pursuit.[17] Actually, little or nothing more can be said about the general charac-

---

[17] Few people are as conscious of this trend as was Freud, who openly referred to *some* of his specifically *metapsychological* concepts as "our mythology."

teristics of the "psychiatric thought" of true primitives, for the good and sufficient reason that very little is known about this matter. Anthropological literature is so barren on this topic that, to take an example at random, Wisse's (1933) tremendous monograph on primitive suicide hardly even mentions native ideas on that subject, so that his work is simply a study of primitive behavior, but not of primitive psychiatric thought, as it pertains to suicide. Little wonder then that histories of psychiatry either ignore primitive psychiatry altogether, or else contain only a sketchy first chapter on this topic, which is often "more poetry than truth."

Mohave psychiatry, which is substantively psychological, but methodologically still supernaturalistic, appears to represent a second step in the development of psychiatry.

The third step appears to be represented by certain early attempts to think naturalistically about the problem of mental disorder. An early representative of this new methodology was Hippocrates (n.d.), who insisted, e.g., that there was nothing "sacred" about the "sacred disease" (epilepsy) and therefore advocated treating it like any other illness. Unfortunately, though quite understandably, the lack of any effective method for dealing with the irrational rationally, caused Hippocrates to model his rationalistic conception of mental disease upon that branch of Greek medicine which already dealt fairly rationally with *organic* illness. In so doing, he initiated an "organicistic" trend, which remained associated with every rationalistic type of psychiatry up to and including even Freud, who felt impelled to postulate the existence of "Aktualneurosen" [18] and to hint that biochemistry may, in the end, provide the definitive answer to the problem of mental disorders.

Side by side with this methodologically scientific but substantively unpsychological (organicistic) conception of mental disorder there existed a second school of thought which was substantively more or less "psychological" but remained methodologically bound to supernaturalism. This point of view was represented by the aesculapian (nonhippocratic) healing priest, by the medieval exorcist, and by a number of medical and philosophical mavericks, who advanced psychiatry by stubbornly clinging to the position that mental disease had an implicit and inherent "meaning," but, at the same time, also retarded its progress by clinging to a variety of supernaturalistic methodological positions.

As for the few who did adhere to a more or less psychologistic position and, at the same time, also groped for a naturalistic methodology, their many misadventures with their contemporaries (Zilboorg and Henry, 1941) indicate that neither Western society nor Western

---

[18] One "Aktualneurose" is supposed to be caused by a kind of autointoxication of the sexually inactive organism.

medicine was prepared to tolerate, let alone encourage, the methodologically scientific but substantively psychological study and interpretation of mental disease.

In the end, this long see-sawing led to an irrevocable cleavage between the grotesquely unpsychological exponents of the doctrine of "man the machine," and the grotesquely supernaturalistic advocates of theological theories of mental illness, with a few eccentrics like Mesmer walking the tightrope above the chasm gaping between the two.

As is so often the case when things come to this pass, the struggle between these two seemingly irreconcilable points of view finally brought about a unification of the two philosophies on a level of abstraction higher than that of either of the two competing theories.

The supernaturalists preserved, in the teeth of the trend toward rationalism and naturalism, a more or less psychological point of view, and an awareness that there was some meaning and pattern even in seemingly chaotic irrational behavior. The rationalists, despite their grotesquely unpsychological organicism, contributed for their part the conviction that mental disease had to be studied naturalistically. Only after both points of view became crystallized could Charcot and then Freud take the decisive step of dealing rationally with the irrational. Substantively these two pioneers reached back to the shaman, and methodologically to Hippocrates, discarding the supernaturalistic commitments of the first and the organicistic ones of the second school of thought.

This was a considerable intellectual feat, since it cannot even be said that the shaman and his spiritual descendants actually "discovered" the unconscious, except in the sense in which some Ionian philosophers "invented" the atom. Indeed, neither the unconscious nor the atom were put to any scientific use for many centuries. Until recently they simply accumulated dust in the musty cubicles of the kind of philosophers whom Rabelais calls "abstractors of quintessence."

In brief, the "psychiatric revolution" followed in every respect the pattern of other scientific revolutions. The innovator took the factually sound data and partial insights of a "temple science," stripped them of their mystical husk and dealt with them in a relatively culture-free "naturalistic" manner (Devereux, 1957 a).[19]

Summing up, Mohave psychiatry is characterized by:

(1) An ability to tolerate and therefore to register observed clinical facts.
(2) A readiness to empathize with the psychotic and therefore to impute a (psychological) meaning to his behavior.
(3) A formulation of this meaning in essentially supernaturalistic terms, in accordance with the basic axioms of the Mohave culture pattern.

---

[19] The preceding position implies that even though the acceptance or rejection of naturalism and logic may be a cultural phenomenon, logic and naturalism per se are, in the last resort, culture-free, or at least culturally neutral phenomena, simply because two and two are conceded by all groups to add up to four.

(4) A limited validity of even this supernaturalistically oriented system, attributable to the Mohave tendency to "psychologize" the universe . . . which is slightly similar to, yet not *quite* the same as, the "animation of the universe" by animists.

(5) A lack of an explicit *general* theory of psychopathology (pt. 1, pp. 9–38), due primarily to the essentially nonscientific, supernaturalistic orientation of the Mohave.

These characteristics of Mohave psychiatric thought explain why so many of their data, as well as some—though not all—of their special etiological theories and therapeutic practices (e. g., the examination of dreams) are valid even in terms of modern dynamic psychiatry, despite many differences of detail and despite the fact that the implicit overall pattern of Mohave psychiatric thought—so far as one is able to infer it from their disjointed special theories—is essentially different from the basic psychoanalytic theory of psychopathology.

The last point to be examined is the *practical use* to which a knowledge of Mohave psychiatry may be put by the theoretically sophisticated clinical psychiatrist and psychoanalyst, who is ever on the lookout for better and more workable theoretical formulations.

The problem can be discussed from two angles:

(1) In terms of the possibility of reformulating, and then actually putting to use, the valid segmental insights of the Mohave "psychiatric shaman."

(2) In terms of the usefulness of becoming familiar with a different system of thinking about psychopathology, true or false though this system may be.

The relevance of Mohave psychiatry for the clinical psychiatrist.— It is implicit in the preceding paragraphs that the clinical psychiatrist, who wishes to derive substantive ideas from the primitive and from ancient authors, will benefit more from a study of Mohave, Tembu (Laubscher, 1937), aesculapian (Dodds, 1951), or inquisitorial (Zilboorg and Henry, 1941) psychiatry than from the perusal of the writings of Hippocrates, Galen, or Lombroso, since, after flowering in primitive and mystical cultures and groups, psychiatric insight gradually declined in quality and, above all, in prestige, perhaps precisely because it dealt with raw—and, in fact, very raw—material.[20]

By contrast the clinical psychiatrist looking for guidance in *naturalistic methodology* will find little that is new and stimulating in the works of the naturalistic ancient students of mental disorder. In brief, the unsophisticated but essentially psychologistic psychiatry of primitives, such as the Mohave, can provide many valuable stimuli for the clinical research psychiatrist, even if these naive psychiatric ideas seem only weird superstition to the undynamic psychiatrist whom, like the poor of the Gospel, we shall always have with us.

---

[20] Compare in this context the criticism to which Archimedes was subjected when he forsook the pursuit of pure, speculative, science in order to devise engines for the defense of his home city. This, to the Greek intelligentsia, was a disgraceful act, since applied and experimental science was worthy only of those who worked with their hands (cheir +ergon).

It is certainly not suggested, e. g., that the concept "nyevedhi: taha:na" is about to replace the concept of psychogenic depression, or that psychoanalysts are about to interpret psychogenic convulsion exactly the way the Mohave explain atcoo:r hanyienk. On the other hand certain suggestive ideas, such as the Mohave notion that an inhibited ability or ego function can cause quite as much psychic damage as the repression of instincts, may well deserve systematic study (Devereux, 1956 a).

The relevance of Mohave psychiatry for the theoretical psychiatrist.—It is proposed to show that Mohave psychiatric thought not only contains *substantive* ideas which merit attention, but may actually help train the theoretician in the art of "thinking through" familiar problems in unfamiliar ways. This task is far from simple and the difficulty of shifting one's frame of reference may well be partly responsible for the abysmal naiveté of much factually sound work, e. g., in the field of culture and personality studies (Devereux, 1957 c).

Major advances in science invariably presuppose changes in the frame of reference. This, in turn, causes a genuine psychic wrench, since men are wedded to their habitual frame of reference by almost unbreakable psychic bonds. Thus, E. T. Bell (1937) pointed out that even though Henri Poincaré—whom his peers called the prince of mathematicians—had at his fingertips all the data, techniques, and genius needed for the formulation of the theory of relativity, by the time he accumulated, or personally created, that knowledge he had grown old thinking in terms of a Newtonian universe. Hence, he was simply too accustomed to thinking in Newtonian terms to change his frame of reference overnight. By contrast, Einstein was able to divorce himself from the Newtonian system and evolve his own, because he was still young enough to have made no permanent commitment to any existing system. Other data also support this view. Thus, a Harvard University report stated that the student working in rapidly changing sciences, such as physics, gets his doctor of philosophy degree several years earlier than does the student in more staid fields. The same report, and other sources as well, also stress that, unlike, e. g., humanistic or social science luminaries, physicists make most of their great and truly innovating discoveries early in their careers, i. e., before they become intellectually committed to any particular system in a science in which the replacement rate of systems is, at present, quite high.

These considerations suggest the need for practice in periodically rethinking one's data in terms of unfamiliar frames of reference, if only in order to preserve a useful degree of intellectual flexibility. Since in the relatively slowly changing humanistic and behavioral sciences truly new frames of reference are few and far between, it is conceivable that a useful degree of intellectual flexibility may also be maintained by rethinking all one knows in terms of a totally unfamiliar old system. It is, in fact, quite possible that the great intellectual freedom and flexibility of Renaissance man was the direct outcome of the new habit of rethinking that which he had first learned in a *medieval* frame of reference, in terms of the *Greek* frame of reference which, though ancient, was new to Renaissance man. Today, due to the homogenization of occidental culture, neither the frame of reference of some other modern nation, nor the frame of reference of the occidental world's historical forebears, is sufficiently different from the present world view to require a radical reorientation when one seeks to think through familiar data in terms of Athenian, medieval, or French frames of reference.[21]

Given this state of affairs, the frame of reference most likely to produce a real shift in our way of thinking would be one borrowed from an alien culture, such as that of the Mohave. The study of, e.g., Mohave psychiatric thought is, thus, useful because it provides a new frame of reference for thinking through once more one's entire knowledge of psychopathology, in order not to become too indissolubly wedded to one's current thought habits and thought models. Even if, after thinking through one's storehouse of data in Mohave terms, one decides in the end that the Mohave system is entirely inadequate, one will have had the experience of seeing one's old data in a new light and might, in the end, either develop new insights in terms of one's existing frame of reference, or else modify that frame of reference in various useful ways. Speaking for myself, while writing the present work I was forced to rethink all of psychiatry in startlingly unfamiliar ways, which, in the end, appreciably deepened my understanding of the classical psychoanalytic frame of reference.

---

[21] It would be a profitable and revealing undertaking to demonstrate the extent to which both Fascist and Marxist totalitarian systems—once believed to represent "The Wave of the Future"—are actually pale and distorted copies of the basic occidental pattern. This is shown, e. g., both by Red China's difficulties in blending occidental Marxism into the old Chinese culture pattern, and by the repeated changes in official Marxist doctrine regarding the extent to which Occidental feudalism and Oriental despotism are similar, respectively dissimilar (Wittfogel, 1957).

APPENDIX

THE FUNCTION OF ALCOHOL

PREFATORY NOTE

As stated previously (pt. 4, p. 212), it was decided to discuss Mohave alcoholism in an Appendix, because the Mohave themselves view excessive drinking not as a type of neuroticism (yamomk), but simply as misconduct (ala:yk=bad.), though, needless to say, the psychiatrically informed anthropologist cannot concur with this Mohave evaluation of drinking behavior.

The material presented in this study pertains to conditions which prevailed at a time when the American Indian could not yet obtain alcohol lawfully.

Given the special position of alcoholism in Mohave psychiatric theory, it was deemed desirable to make the Appendix a self-contained unit. This explains why a few of the cases about to be presented are nothing more than abstracts—slanted so as to emphasize incidents involving alcoholic excesses—of cases already reported in full elsewhere in this work. Of these overlapping cases only Case 137—identical with Case 64—contains new material, because the inclusion of that material in the text of the already very long Case 64 would have interrupted the orderly presentation of those aspects of Case 64 which were directly relevant to its central theme.

INTRODUCTION

Glover's (1932) appeal for anthropological contributions to the psychoanalytic study of various forms of addiction has, so far, elicited only a meager response. This may be due in part to the difficulty anthropologists have experienced in deriving a systematic theory of alcohol addiction from the maze of the literature on alcohol; in spite of Horton's (1943) valuable attempt to test certain general propositions in cross-cultural terms, the comparative study of alcohol addiction is still in the fact-collecting stage. The anthropologist must therefore restrict his interpretations to the culture from which his own data have been drawn, and refer to existing—and by no means generally accepted—theoretical interpretations in the most tentative manner. Accordingly, the sole aim of this Appendix is a systematic presentation of concrete data, with a limited

505

and tentative interpretation thereof in terms of Mohave culture and of certain reasonably well-established psychological mechanisms.

HISTORY OF THE USE OF ALCOHOL

The Mohave Indians had no intoxicating beverages in aboriginal times. According to Kroeber (1931), the Gila River was the northwestern boundary of the area in which aboriginal types of alcohol were manufactured. It is characteristic of Mohave cultural ethnocentrism that, despite their passion for distant travel, they never learned the art of preparing fermented beverages from other tribes.

The first contact of the Mohave with European alcoholic beverages occurred presumably not before the middle of the 16th century, and probably not later than the end of the 17th. There is no evidence to suggest that European or Mexican alcoholic beverages played an important role in Mohave life during the period of Spanish contacts. Alcohol began to make appreciable inroads only during the second half of the 19th century, as a result of an influx of white Americans, who used alcohol in the economic and sexual exploitation of the Mohave (Devereux, 1948 f). According to Allen (1891), "Those who go to the railroad towns and mining camps soon become demoralized by whisky and contaminated by tramps."

During the last decades the advent of law and order in Arizona and in California has somewhat reduced the indiscriminate debauching of Indians by disreputable whites. Federal laws prohibiting the sale of alcohol to Indians, as well as other forms of liquor controls, had also decreased excessive drinking in the tribe, for the average Mohave could seldom afford to buy illegal, and therefore expensive, beverages. On the other hand, the fact that the Mohave woman was unable to purchase alcoholic drinks at a reasonable price tended to revive the use of alcohol for seduction and as an outright fee in informal and occasional prostitution, especially during the building of the Parker Dam, which necessitated the importation of many single white and Mexican workers. At the same time, the Mohave employed on that project began to earn enough money to purchase illegal and overpriced alcohol more frequently.

According to recent information, the current inflationary trend in wages and in the price of agricultural products, which appreciably increased the purchasing power of the Mohave, also led to an increase in drinking.

All things considered, the Mohave cannot be described as a tribe whose vitality and social structure have been appreciably impaired by alcoholism. Drinking remains a marginal phenomenon in Mohave life, and the fundamental drinking pattern is the one-night "spree," rather than the systematic excessive use of alcohol by even a small fraction of the population. This is probably due to the basic psychological health of the individual Mohave, which is rooted in the mature erotic satisfactions and in the psychological security which his culture affords him (Devereux, 1939 b).

Dealers in illegal alcohol.—Bootleggers are protected by the Mohave. A young Mohave man, who occasionally acted as my interpreter, described the situation as follows: "There were recently (1938?) a couple of convictions and several men were expelled from this area, but this did not put down the alcohol trade. I think that the bootleggers must have emissaries who arrange these things. You can't persuade a Mohave to tell you the names of the bootleggers and of their emissaries, because he is accustomed to alcohol."

Although the Mohave knew that bootleggers charged outrageous prices, their resentment was directed at the law prohibiting the sale of alcohol to Indians, and at whites in general, rather than at the illicit dealers as a class, or as individuals. The fact is that the discriminatory law actually increased, rather than decreased, the social cost of alcoholism. It is true that the average Mohave could not afford to buy illegal liquor frequently. However, the high cost of bootlegged alcohol lead to the exploitation of the Indian by unscrupulous dealers. Furthermore, when the Mohave did obtain alcohol, he felt impelled to drink it up all at once, partly because he did not know how to handle liquor rationally and partly because he wished to dispose of the incriminating evidence as quickly as possible. In brief, psychological problems do not seem to yield to legislative solutions among the Mohave any more than they do among other nations. Only a systematic strengthening of the fundamental values, satisfactions, and security systems of Mohave culture could counteract the spread of alcoholism. The forced acculturation and pauperization of the Mohave (Devereux, 1942 c, 1948 f) lead only to an increase in anomie—and therefore also in alcoholism.

Expectations of gifts of alcoholic beverages.—The Mohave do not expect the average white to give or sell them alcohol. Only one of my closest friends ever asked me to obtain alcohol for him (Case 139), and was not in the least offended when I declined to do so, since my policy of neither drinking, nor procuring drinks, was so well known that, when a certain disreputable woman alleged that I had offered her a drink, her statement was promptly challenged by several of her relatives, some of whom did not even know me personally (Devereux, 1948 f).

On the whole, the Mohave did not press their white friends to procure alcohol for them, perhaps because they could freely purchase it from certain notoriously unscrupulous individuals.

The integration of alcohol with the Mohave way of life will be discussed in terms of three frames of references: I, The Sociocultural; II, the Subjective-Psychological; and III, The Unconscious Factors.

I. THE SOCIOCULTURAL ROLE OF ALCOHOL

1. ETHICS

The Mohave drinking pattern is closely integrated with the pattern of compulsory generosity (Devereux, 1939 b), which is one of the cardinal virtues of the Mohave system of ethics. No Mohave would think of taking a drink in public without offering the bottle to his friends. Nevertheless, the excessive drinking of a certain individual (Case 138) caused his friends so much concern, that they more or less systematically attempted to prevent him from drinking and almost never produced a bottle in his presence. On the other hand, they pitied rather than condemned him for being so compulsive a drinker as to enter the houses of his friends in their absence and help himself to whatever drinks he could find.

While the Mohave expect their friends to share their drinks, habitual "drink-cadgers" are practically unknown. The Mohave pattern of generosity with drinks closely parallels their behavior with regard to cigarettes (Devereux, 1948 a).

2. SOCIAL DRINKING

Mohave drinking is mostly of the "social" type and does not usually culminate either in severe intoxication or in antisocial or objectionable behavior. According to the late M. A. I. Nettle, M.D., and several native informants, this is due in part to the Mohave tendency to "pass out" [1] very rapidly, and in part to the fact that there is seldom enough alcohol to intoxicate an appreciable number of persons. The Mohave usually manage to obtain liquor before they go to a gathering or dance. They drink a certain amount during the evening and then either go home quietly or else pass out and sleep it off. Mildly intoxicated persons behave, as a rule, in a fairly reasonable way and are easily managed. Hence, ordinary, more or less public, parties almost never end in fights, or in scandals. The average Mohave dance or gathering is, thus, a fairly orderly and quiet affair; those who wish to engage in sexual irregularities will generally withdraw from the party and perform the sex act either in private, or in small groups.

---

[1] The term "pass out" usually suggests a state of severe intoxication. In the case of the Mohave, however, it merely describes the behavior of falling asleep. The ease with which Mohave drinkers "pass out" after drinking relatively small amounts of liquor suggests a strong tendency to respond to alcohol intake with this behavior. This topic is discussed in detail below (see pp. 524–525).

3. ATTITUDES

Mohave attitudes toward excessive drinking must be differentiated from their attitudes toward excessive drinkers. On the whole, the Mohave do not feel that drinking is a manly act. It is simply a thing which some people do and others do not. Thus, although several of my Mohave friends chided me in 1932 for not inhaling my cigarettes "like a man" (Devereux, 1948 a), none of them ever bothered to comment on the fact that I did not drink. A moderate amount of "social drinking," especially if it does not lead to a sexual orgy or to aggressive behavior, is viewed as a normal and pleasurable form of relaxation. Excessive drinking is, however, freely criticized. Thus, one day, in the course of an inquiry into the Mohave conception of human status, I asked my octogenarian informant Tcatc to comment on the old adage, "The more I know people, the better I like dogs." She replied: "The things I saw in my youth, when I was old enough to remember what I saw, were better than . . . what one sees nowadays. People behaved differently. Take for example these constant rumors of incest . . . they would have been unthinkable in the old days. In my youth the Mohave did not even know what alcoholic intoxication meant." This comment reveals a severely condemnatory attitude toward alcoholic excesses, since Tcatc paired them with incest, which is one of the greatest crimes in Mohave society (Devereux, 1939 a), especially because it is frequently associated with witchcraft (Devereux, 1937 c). (The psychological significance of this "accidental" pairing of incest with intoxication will be discussed further below.) The Mohave therefore attempt to interfere with the propensities of severe drunkards (Case 138) and are not offended when known nondrinkers refuse a drink.

The Mohave Indian's condemnation of drunkenness is tempered by his regard for the human being who is unfortunate enough to be a drunkard. Yet, none of my informants ever defended inebriates by propounding the traditional plea of temperamental determinism (i.e., "it is his nature, he cannot help it") which, in Mohave society, serves to mitigate and to explain the offensive or antisocial conduct of some individuals (Devereux, 1939 b). On the whole, the intoxicated individual is usually treated like an ordinary person, and the habitual drunkard is pitied rather than blamed. Thus, even though Hama: Utce: abhorred drunkenness, she freely admitted that two alcoholic brothers were fundamentally kind and good people (Case 138).

Occasional drunkenness is not penalized and elicits relatively little gossip. Drunken misbehavior tends to be laughed at and gossiped about, but is condemned less severely than the disorderly behavior of sober persons. In this respect the Mohave pattern resembles not the French, but the American attitude, which condemns drunkenness less severely than disorderly acts committed in a state of intoxication.

Intoxicated persons are seldom if ever abused. The serial rape of intoxicated women is to be construed not as a conscious aggressive act but simply as a form of the sexual "humor" (Devereux, 1950 a) to which the Mohave are addicted. The retaliatory aggression of two women who, while intoxicated, had their pubic hair burned off by two drunken men, was likewise more or less in the nature of a practical joke (Case 139). I know of no instance in which an intoxicated person was intentionally and cold-bloodedly manhandled or robbed. Incident b of Case 139 cannot be construed as theft, since the highly acculturated halfbreed, Kohovan Kura :u (kicks-up-dirt fast) merely took advantage of his knowledge of American mores to obtain for himself Hivsu : Tupo :ma's job.

Summing up, the Mohave attitude toward inebriates is rooted in their basic creed that every human being deserves respect and that no person is to be denied a chance to regain the esteem of his fellow men, regardless of how drunken and dissolute that individual may have been in the past.

II. THE SUBJECTIVE-PSYCHOLOGICAL ROLE OF ALCOHOL

1. THE SEXUAL UTILIZATION OF ALCOHOL

Drinking in connection with sex activities must be sharply differentiated from the hospitality pattern. Whenever an unattached or adventurous man, attending a gathering or a dance, has some alcohol in his possession, it is more or less taken for granted that he will share his drinks with the woman with whom he wishes to have sexual relations, or with a group of men and women who happen to be footloose and fancy free. A woman who accepts several drinks from a man thereby implicitly indicates her consent to the probable sexual consequences of this transaction. (Cf. pt. 2, pp. 81–83.)

An overt or tacit invitation to join in an alcoholic spree must be differentiated, however, from a systematic and underhanded attempt to intoxicate a woman in order to seduce her. I know of only one instance in which an unscrupulous man deliberately plied with drink a woman whose reputation and behavior did not justify the assumption that she would consider these drinks as a tacit invitation to sexual intercourse (Devereux, 1950 a).

The invitation to go on a spree must, furthermore, not be confused with offers of liquor tendered as advance payment for sexual favors. Only one of the women whom an informant called promiscuous (kamalo :y) was known to require alcohol as a payment for her favors. Other women who were known to make themselves accessible after becoming intoxicated, were simply held to be less discriminating in the choice of lovers when drunk than when sober (Devereux, 1948 f; 1950a).

It should be added that apparently only the real kamalo:y ever accepts alcohol from Whites, Negroes, or Chinese, since women know that such offers are to be construed as advanced payments for sexual favors.

The function of alcohol in the sexual life of the Mohave is, thus, not identical with its function in American society, since the Mohave do not consider sexual relations to be either vile or antisocial and, therefore, need not "dissolve the superego in alcohol" in order to gratify their sex drive (Devereux, 1950 a).

As pointed out elsewhere (Devereux, 1950 a), the main sexual stimulus in Mohave society is opportunity, pure and simple. The role of alcohol in Mohave sexuality fits this pattern perfectly. The possession of a bottle of liquor almost irresistibly tempts a man to invite a woman to go on an alcoholic (and, implicitly, sexual) spree with him. It is, however, important to realize in this context that the woman thus invited need not necessarily be a paramour; she may actually be the man's own wife. In the latter instance, marital relations are often performed in some strikingly novel or droll manner.

The Mohave conception of intoxication as one type of sexual opportunity is also exemplified in their treatment of women discovered drunk. Any woman who becomes severely intoxicated knows that her escorts, among whom may be her own husband, or one or more men who happen to find her in that condition, may decide to "take turns on her." Intercourse with intoxicated women is frequently performed a tergo, in the prone position (Devereux, 1950 a.)

Some habitually drunken women are not deterred, however, by the risk of being serially raped. A pretty Walapai girl, who lived among the Mohave, as well as some other women, continued to drink to excess despite the fact that groups of men had abused them on previous occasions. Incidents of this kind are not taken too seriously, and public opinion blames the woman who became drunk, rather than the men who took advantage of her condition. In fact the husband of such a woman flatly declared: "I don't mind it! She had it coming to her!" (Devereux, 1950 a).

This—to us paradoxical—reaction of the husband stands in need of some comment. While few Mohave are indulgent enough to let others cohabit with their wives, it is generally felt that drunkenness mitigates the offense of adultery. For example, the drunken husband of an intoxicated woman, who joined his friends in cohabiting with her serially, objected only when his companions also attempted to have anal connections with her. At that point he rescued her and the two spouses staggered home hand in hand (Devereux, 1950 a).

A serially raped woman has no recourse, since "she knew what would happen to her if she got drunk." Thus, the Mohave made it

quite clear that the girls mentioned in Case 139 did not avenge the
fact that they had been serially abused, but merely retaliated for the
burning of their pubic hair, which, to the Mohave, was by far the
more grievous offense. Since psychoanalytic experience indicates
that the seducer or rapist may always count upon some cooperation
from the woman, whose masochistic unconscious craves rape, it is
plausible to assume that—as in our own culture—some women get
drunk "accidentally on purpose," in order to gratify unconscious rape
fantasies without being "responsible" for the coital act. It is, furthermore, important to realize in this context that some women who drink
to excess are "phallic"—i.e., disolute and hostile—kamalo:y (Devereux,
1948 f). Since such women are insatiable precisely because they are
orgastically frigid (Hitschmann and Bergler, 1936; Devereux, 1948
f), their recurrent intoxication should probably be interpreted as the
masochistic provocativeness of women who seek to alleviate their
penis envy by inviting many men to "give" them a penis and, at the
same time, also to force them to experience fully gratifying sexual
relations. The latter hope is hardly ever fulfilled, for three reasons:

(a) Large amounts of alcohol diminish the woman's orgastic potential.

(b) Alcoholic excesses decrease the erectile potency of the man.

(c) Intoxicated men sometimes subject drunken women to crude, and almost
cruel, practical jokes. Since an incident of this type was published in full elsewhere (Devereux, 1950 a), it will only be summarized in the present context
(Case 139, incident a).

It seems probable that these serial rapes satisfy the masochistic
cravings of alcoholic women precisely by frustrating their phallic and
orgastic ambitions. Since the particularly obnoxious kamalo:y is
subjected to punitive mass rape, followed by clitoridectomy and sometimes even by a laceration of the vulva (Devereux, 1948 f), it is
plausible to infer that alcoholic women of this type are caught in a
vicious circle, in which the gratification of one wish automatically
involves the frustration of another wish. In the case of ordinary
women, this vicious circle is often broken by marriage, whereas in
the case of the kamalo:y this is accomplished only by mass rape and
genital mutilation. In both instances the vicious circle is apparently
broken by the acceptance of the feminine role, which, in some cases,
was temporarily repudiated, because of a divorce, or of the loss of a
lover, or because of homosexuality (Case 140). This inference is supported by the fact that many deserted or divorced women drink to
excess. Thus, a women was deliberately plied with liquor by the
man whom she had asked to reconcile her with her husband, after the
man falsely asserted that his mission had failed (Devereux, 1950 a).
Another woman allegedly abetted her husband in killing a witch (believed to have been her adulterous lover) and, after her husband's
imprisonment, began to drink to excess (Devereux, 1948 f and Case

104).   This woman's half sister, O:otc, an attractive though crippled woman, who had a confusional episode after an accidental miscarriage, also drank to excess when she left her first husband, and ceased to drink only when she found a good second husband (Case 129; cf. Case 24).

2. MAUDLIN SENTIMENTALITY

This mood, defined here as a form of mawkish affectivity which contrasts with the individual's usual affective behavior, appears to be lacking among the Mohave.   Thus, Hama: Utce:, in describing the affectionate behavior of her somewhat intoxicated husband, specifically remarked that he was "as nice and sweet as he always is" (Case 136).   This remark is significant, since Hama: Utce: likes to affect a certain gruffness of manner and definitely dislikes mawkishness.

The above comments emphasize an outstanding characteristic of the Mohave drinking pattern.   The intoxicated person acts as he always does, and is what he always is—only more so.   The change is quantitative, rather than qualitative.   In Mohave society at least, intoxication merely exaggerates the individual's most obvious character traits, without suppressing his minor characteristics.   The drunken Mohave either becomes "bigger than life size" or passes out.   This continuity of behavior and affect, throughout the transition from sobriety to intoxication, is probably due partly to the slight intensity of some Mohave repressions, which is connected with the general patchiness and nonpervasiveness of their superego (Róheim, 1933), and partly to the high degree of continuity in cultural conditioning which is characteristic of many primitive societies (Benedict, 1938).

Some observers of human character believe that mawkish people have no genuine and deep feelings and merely develop reaction formations against their intense unconscious sadomasochistic impulses. Since the Mohave are capable of giving and receiving love (Devereux, 1939 b), and express their feelings rather freely (Kroeber, 1925 a; 1925 b), they do not have to get drunk in order to be affectionate.

The Mohave is not prone to indulge in wanton outbursts of sadism. Mohave courage, which is second to none, is of the steadfast (pt. 7, pp. 426–431) rather than of the spectacularly foolhardy (bravado) variety.   It lacks the dramatic, rhetorical, larmoyant and distinctly sadomasochistic background of Plains Indian valor (Lowie, 1935; Devereux, 1951 a), which is an almost classical instance of a type of moral masochism brilliantly characterized by Berliner (1947).   In Veblenian terms (Veblen, 1899), Mohave gallantry seems almost like drudgery when contrasted with Crow Indian exploits, for example. Hence, the Mohave does not feel that he has to purchase courage and social approval through self-inflicted suffering, in an essentially hostile universe.

Summing up, the absence of mawkishness in the behavior of the intoxicated Mohave is due to his seeming lack of the basic psychological requisites for maudlin sentimentality.

An instance of genuinely affectionate behavior in an intoxicated person noted for his kindliness is recorded further below (Case 136).

3. AGGRESSIVE BEHAVIOR

The average intoxicated Mohave is not aggressive, and drunken brawls are rare. It seems significant that, of the few drunken brawls known to me, two were initiated by intoxicated men attempting to protect drunken women against some slightly sadistic practical joke. Thus, the shaman Hivsu: Tupo:ma tried to interfere with men who wished to singe off the pubic hair of two intoxicated girls, while T. attempted to prevent a group of men who, with his approval, had had sex relations with his drunken wife, from abusing her also anally (Devereux, 1950 a). (Anal coitus is thought of as a sexual "joke.") Similarly, although Hivsu: Tupo:ma seemed slightly wild eyed while confessing to me that he had committed witchcraft and incest, his behavior toward me was as cordial as always (Case 139). The late Dr. M. A. I. Nettle's impression that the average drunken Mohave do not fight, but merely pass out, was confirmed independently by every reliable informant.

The extreme rarity of drunken aggressiveness among the Mohave, and their apparent lack of any psychic need to seek Dutch courage in the bottle, require some comment. The stoic courage (pt. 7, pp. 426–431) of these huge men (Kroeber, 1925, a; Hrdlička, 1908), which enabled them on occasion to accomplish dazzling feats of valor in the face of overwhelming odds (Kroeber, 1925 b; McNichols, 1944), is still a living force among them. Since courage is taken for granted, no Mohave feels impelled or compelled to validate his claims to bravery by constant displays of valor. In simplest terms, the Mohave despise the bully, because their ideal is the man who combines gentleness with stoic courage (Stewart, 1947 c). This ideal pattern also explains why Hivsu: Tupo:ma, a huge man weighing nearly 250 pounds, gave up his attempt to protect two drunken girls rather than start a fight (Case 139).

It goes without saying that all Mohave do not live up to this ideal of the brave and gentle man.

CASE 128. (Informants: Tcatc and E. S.):

In 1937, or thereabouts, an elderly woman, Nyortc Huhual (reputed to have been ya tcahaetk, i.e. "man crazy," in her youth was walking home from a party, when two men pulled a sack over her head and took her money; one man—a thickset youth—even raped her. Though this youth was never positively identified, he was believed to be a relative of the old woman, and to have been intoxicated at the time. No one is certain, however, whether the man in question was actually drunk, or whether intoxication was merely imputed to him in order to explain his conspicuously deviant behavior, the most atypical part of which was not the incest, but the robbery—an almost unheard-of thing in Mohave society.   (Cf. also Case 15.)

A systematic discussion of the motivation of drunken aggressiveness must emphasize primarily divergences between Mohave and white conceptions of what constitutes "adequate provocation" justifying aggression.

(*a*) The following excerpt from Case 24 illustrates the type of drunken aggressiveness which Mohave and white opinion alike would describe as "unprovoked brutality."

CASE 129.

O:otc, whose half-sister allegedly helped her husband kill a witch (Devereux, 1948 f, and Case 104), was faithful to her husband and behaved the way a good wife should.   However, she left him in the end, because he drank to excess and abused both her and their small son.   While separated from her husband, she too began to drink to excess, but denied having had affairs during that period.   Eventually she married a sober and kindly man and was, by 1938, simply a very moderate "social drinker."   (Cf. also Case 24.)

(*b*) The question whether, in the case history about to be cited, the provocation was sufficient to elicit extreme physical violence, will be answered in one way by the Mohave and in another way be a member of our own society.   White moralists, lawyers, and psychologists will hold that the provocation was more than adequate, since their basic frame of reference is the axiom that premeditated sexual infidelity, especially when "insult is added to injury," automatically justifies aggression.   The Mohave, on the other hand, feel that only an intoxicated or unreasonable person would degrade himself to the extent of fighting over a mere matter of infidelity, even though they too would unanimously characterize the wife's behavior as objectionable.[2]

CASE 130 (Informants: Hiusu: Tupo:ma and Hama: Utce:) :

P. lived "near the ball-place" with his wife G., who had formerly been J.'s mistress.   One day when P. had bought some liquor, J., who happened to be visiting them, winked at his former mistress, thereby asking her to help him get P. drunk.   J. even pretended to drink heavily himself, although he managed to stay more or less sober.   After a while P. became quite drunk and began to doze off.   "You go outside and wait for me," J. told G.   After her departure, he continued to force drinks on P., until he believed that the husband had "passed out" completely.   He then locked the door from the outside, imprisoning P. in the house, and went to join G.   The husband, less drunk than J. had supposed, became suspicious however, and managed to struggle to his feet in

---

[2] It is beyond the scope of this article to discuss the merits of the Mohave point of view regarding jealousy.   Yet, one cannot help being amazed by the tenacity with which modern psychologists—including even an extremist like Wilhelm Reich—cling to the view that jealousy is, in its entirety, a natural and innate sentiment, in the face of at least partly contradictory evidence furnished not only by anthropologists and historians, but even by students of primate zoology (Maslow, 1940).   Homines id quod volunt credunt!

time to see his wife and her former lover walk hand in hand toward the outhouse.[3] He also observed and heard J's attempts to have coitus per anum with G., who was bending over the toilet seat. These attempts were only partly successful, because J., due perhaps to his intoxication, found it difficult to become sufficiently tumescent. When P. heard J. exclaim prematurely, "It is all right now," he broke down the door of his house and began to creep toward the outhouse, intending to surprise his wife, who, being less drunk than the men, heard the noise and quickly pushed J. into a corner, trying to hide him from her husband. By that time P. had come close enough to grasp his wife's shawl, whereupon G. slipped out of her shawl and ran toward the house, while P. lost his balance and fell down. He rose immediately, however, and followed his wife into the house. He then accused her of various misdeeds and, despite her denials, threatened to thrash her. Next, P. decided to look for J., who, by then, had disappeared. This angered P. so much that he struck G. on the head with a blunt instrument, knocked her unconscious, and left her lying on the ground. G. was found next day, with a wound on her head, by the owner of the ball place, who notified the authorities. When G. was questioned, she pretended at first that she did not understand English, but eventually broke down and confessed that she had had sexual relations with J. In view of her confession, the case against P. appears to have been dismissed.

(*c*) In extreme instances—i.e., if a major component of the tribal value system appears to be threatened—an intoxicated Mohave may even commit murder. The case history about to be quoted is of great interest, because, in contradistinction to the previous case, the provocation is inadequate in terms of the American conception of justifiable homicide, whereas it would strike the average Mohave as a particularly grievous one, although even they felt that Mukoh's violence was altogether excessive. Yet, since the continuity of the tribe (Kroeber, 1925 a; Devereux, 1939 b) and of the family (Devereux, 1939 a) are among the basic values of Mohave culture, they did not seem surprised that the rivalry of two men, over which of them had fathered a certain infant, eventually led to murder. It should be pointed out, however, that the aggressor's wrath may have had some other sources as well. Indeed, the Mohave is not only not permitted to fight when his wife deserts him, but, once his former wife has settled down with another man, he is expected to show a great deal of indifference and self-restraint (pt. 2, pp. 91–106). It is therefore tempting to infer that Mukoh was glad to be able to claim—and perhaps even to persuade himself—that his resentment toward his wife's new husband was due *exclusively* to his culturally justifiable indignation over the latter's insistence that he, rather than Mukoh, was the legal father of an infant conceived by Mukoh's former wife. This interpretation is quite plausible, since some men are known to have arbitrarily repudiated the paternity of a child whose mother they had deserted (Devereux, 1948 d).

---

[3] This detail tends to support my thesis that the actual onset, depth and termination of the alcoholic stupor are more decisively influenced by psychodynamic than by physiological factors.

CASE 131 (Informants: Hivsu: Tupo:ma and Hama: Utce:):

Around 1900, the pregnant wife of Mukoh (to hit against; the name refers to a game), a resident of Needles, left him and married Vaha Munyu: (=guts fights-over). The latter, in conformity with Mohave beliefs concerning the possibility of changing the paternity of an unborn child (Devereux, 1937 d, 1949 c), thereupon claimed Mukoh's infant as his own. Mukoh, as the pro-creator, also had a culturally acceptable claim to the paternity of the child, and therefore did not cease to assert that it was his. Relations between Mukoh and Vaha Munyu: were therefore extremely strained, and over a period of 4 years the two men engaged in several drunken fights. One day, when both of them happened to be drunk, Mukoh went to Vaha Munyu:'s house and shouted that he would kill him. When Vaha Munyu: replied: "Come on then and kill me," Mukoh picked up an iron rod and hit his rival on the side of the head so hard that Vaha Munyu:'s "brains came out." "You said you would kill me, and now I am as good as dead!" Vaha Munyu: exclaimed as he fell. Mukoh was immediately arrested. When Vaha Munyu: died the next day, his stepfather went to the jail and asked that Mukoh be released, so that the Mohave could even up the score by killing him. However, the authorities trans-ferred Mukoh to the San Bernardino jail. After serving a term in prison, Mukoh settled down among the kindred Yuma Indians, not daring to return to the Mohave Reservation. Nonetheless, he did visit Parker several times, and, in 1930, even went to Needles, where the murder had taken place. He was, how-ever, still afraid that someone might wish to avenge Vaha Munyu:'s death, although most of his victim's relatives had died in the meantime. (Pulyi:k professed never to have heard of this incident, which had been reported in detail by Hivsu: Tupo:ma.)

Comment

Vaha Munyu:'s almost provocatively passive attitude in the face of certain death is of considerable interest, since it closely approxi-mates the behavior of witches who are about to be killed (pt. 7, pp. 387–426). It seems likely that his passivity was motivated by rela-tively intense guilt feelings. This inference does not explain, how-ever, why Vaha Munyu: should have chosen to imitate, out of context, a pattern of behavior which is characteristic of another segment of culture, since only witches, and, to a lesser extent, the kwanámi:hye heroes (Kroeber, 1925 a; Stewart, 1947 c), are expected to accept death stoically. The notorious grandiosity of some inebriates also fails to explain Vaha Munyu:'s pseudo-heroic pose, unless alcoholic intoxication were in some way unconsciously related to witchcraft. The possibility of such a nexus between alcoholism and witchcraft will be discussed further below.

Aggressive actions, committed while drunk, fall into several categories:

1. *Overt aggression.*

(*a*) Minor explosions of aggressivity due to intoxication pure and simple are exemplified by drunken scuffles.

(*b*) Aggression motivated entirely by threats to the individual's subjective security system is exemplified by P.'s wounding of his adulterous wife (Case 130).

(c) Aggression allegedly motivated entirely by a threat to a basic value of Mohave culture, but actually motivated in part by a factor which Mohave society does not consider a legitimate cause for aggression, is exemplified by the slaying of Vaha Munyu: (Case 131).

(d) Atypical aggression by a maladjusted person, whose alcoholism is symptomatic of his neurosis, is exemplified by the beatings O :otc received from her first husband (Case 129).

2. *Disguised aggression.*

(a) "Jocose" aggression against other men participating in the serial rape of women is typefied by the pushing of a drunken man's face against a woman's genitals (Devereux 1950 a).

(b) "Jocose" aggression against drunken women subjected to serial rape is exemplified in the burning of two women's pubic hair (Case 139).

(c) Aggressive impulses masked by incestuous ones are usually manifested by means of witchcraft (pt. 7, pp. 371–426).

3. *Aggression against the self.*

(a) Self-destruction due to aggressive impulses originally directed at other persons is exemplified by suicide (Case 135).

(b) Self-destructiveness due to guilt feelings caused by previous acts of witchcraft usually takes the form of a confession (Cases 139, 140).

(c) Self-destructiveness in individuals preoccupied with thoughts about lost love objects is exemplified by Cases 137 and 138.

Perhaps the most striking aspect of the aggressive behavior of intoxicated Mohave Indians is the almost total absence of attacks directed at individuals who do not belong to the Mohave tribe. This observation cannot be understood without a brief analysis of the history of Mohave aggressiveness.

In aboriginal times the Mohave Indian had ample opportunities to manifest his aggressions by making war on his neighbors. Warfare, undertaken in an almost sportive and yet doggedly obstinate frame of mind, was, at that time, an integral part of Mohave life (Kroeber, 1925 a, 1925 b; McNichols, 1944; Stewart, 1947 c). This outlet for aggressive impulses enabled the warlike Mohave to behave in a conspicuously peaceful manner within the tribe. Hence, despite belief in witchcraft, Mohave society was not steeped in the oppressive atmosphere of hag-ridden terror so characteristic of the allegedly Apollonian Hopi Indians (Simmons, 1942). The stubborn, individualistic and temperamental Mohave warriors did not have to press a lid of pseudo peaceful unassertiveness on a boiling witches' cauldron of hate, suspicion, and fear. Two men might, now and then, come to blows; families contending for the ownership of a piece of land might sometimes engage in highly formalized and rather harmless "battles" (pt. 7, pp. 356–371) ; a particularly obnoxious witch might be killed (pt. 7, pp. 307–426); a conspicuously offensive and dissolute kamalo:y might be raped and clitoridectomized (Devereux, 1948 f). Yet, on the whole, life within the Mohave tribe was singularly peaceful and free of violence and extreme suspiciousness. It was white conquest which brought in its train a radical modification in Mohave patterns of aggression.

The first decades of reservation life were characterized by a crisis in the management of aggressions, brought about by the forcible suppression of intertribal warfare. Since aggressivity could no longer find an outlet through traditional channels, the Mohave had to cast about for new outlets. The crisis was marked by a temporary flareup of internecine killings which, on closer investigation, appear to have been substitutes for aggression against the unconquerable whites. Thus, the Mohave murdered a Yuma Indian, although the culturally kindred Yuma were their traditional allies. Another Yuma, acting as an emissary for the U.S. Army in negotiations for the release of a white girl, was allegedly threatened with death (Stratton, 1857). Shamans were killed for starting "strange" (i.e., presumably, imported) epidemics (pt. 7, pp. 387–426). Some halfbreed infants were buried at birth (Devereux, 1948 d). Each of these incidents was complicated by the problem of escaping the punishment likely to be meted out by the reservation authorities. Yet, neither private strife with the Yuma, nor witch killings, nor infanticide, ever reached epidemic proportions, probably because the Mohave is not particularly prone to deflect his aggressivity from the strong to the weak.

The availability of large quantities of alcoholic beverages likewise failed to open up adequate new avenues for the manifestation of aggressions, perhaps because the stern warrior ideal was too deeply embedded in the Mohave group ideal to enable them to accept the drunken bully as an adequate substitute for, and as a reasonable facsimile of, the kwanàmi :hye hero.

In brief, precisely because the Mohave were traditionally unwilling to borrow the ideology of other groups, they had to grope for a new solution compatible with the basic themes of their own culture.

In concrete terms, the disappearance of traditional outlets for aggression and the multiplication of new frustrations appear to have been compensated for by the attrition of certain traditional frustrations and controls. In this manner the overall amount of frustration was maintained at a constant level and the frustrated warrior was permitted to gratify his thwarted ambitions through unlimited sexual conquests.

This reaction to externally imposed pressures can be analyzed in cultural as well as in psychological terms.

A cultural analysis of this reaction to white pressures must seek to discover why the attrition of almost all sexual controls did not turn the Mohave into an American equivalent of the detribalized, slum-dwelling African native (Carothers, 1947; W. Sachs, 1947), whose behavior is asocial both in African and in European terms, and why Mohave culture did not disintegrate as a result of the effective removal of almost all sexual inhibitions.

It is of some importance to find a correct answer to these questions, since, according to what I, for one, construe to be crypto-deviant psychoanalytic theory, instinctual frustration is an indispensable prerequisite of socialization and of educability. This untenable thesis is only partly supported by the observation that many *originally ritualistic and more or less puritanical societies* actually disintegrated as a result of excessive sexual laxity.

In Mohave society, however, sexual indulgence was always a major, and culturally approved, pattern of behavior (Devereux, 1950 a). Hence, the extreme attrition of the few traditional sexual controls did not constitute a radical modification of the basic themes of Mohave culture. It merely broadened the scope and exaggerated the value of a behavioral theme which was already an important component of the traditional Mohave way of life. Had sexual indulgence been alien to the Mohave way of life, its sudden efflorescence would perhaps have brought about a complete breakdown of the traditional way of life. However, since the Mohave had always been quite free in their sexual behavior, an increase in promiscuousness merely meant a relatively minor quantitative shift in basic interests, and not a qualitative innovation in the tribal way of life. It involved a moderate readjustment of the hierarchy of existing values, rather than an incorporation of new values into Mohave culture. In other words, the increasingly promiscuous acculturated Mohave was in the position of being able to be promiscuous in the traditional way.

Summing up, even after the Mohave were prevented by external pressures from pursuing aggressive goals, they still had ample opportunities to cultivate another set of socially determined ambitions. Hence, they did not become marginal men, or promiscuous and worthless loafers, lacking ties either with Mohave culture or with American society. They became, instead, Mohave sex specialists, i.e., persons consistently engaged in the pursuit of what was formerly a culturally accepted "alternate" (Linton, 1936) behavior pattern. This did not mean, however, a discarding of the warrior ideal—witness the Mohave's unwillingness to think of the drunken bully as a hero and the eagerness with which even middle-aged Mohave men served in both World Wars.

Psychological reactions to the suppression of intertribal warfare were somewhat complex, although they, too, can be suitably analyzed in terms of a shift in the goal structure of Mohave culture.

The first reaction was a somewhat chaotic one, and consisted of witch killings and infanticide. These aggressions differed from war-like activities in being relatively private undertakings, which lacked the framework and moral basis of an organized tribal activity, so important to the Mohave who are highly conscious of their tribal unity and identity (Kroeber, 1925 a; Devereux, 1939 b). These semiprivate types of aggression appear to have been subsequently abandoned, presumably because they did not provide the basic psychological satisfactions of organized warfare, which had formerly deflected aggressions *in a morale building manner* from members of the ingroup to members of the outgroup. Last, but not least, intratribal acts of violence inevitably elicited additional governmental interventions in Mohave affairs and were therefore contrary to tribal interests.

The second reaction consisted in the evolving of an attitude of utter contempt for the white man and his ways (Devereux, 1948 a). This relatively healthy defense mechanism still persists and serves to perpetuate many important values of Mohave life, and especially those patterns which contrast with white practices. In other words, the *defensive* persistence of many Mohave values is due not so much to mere inertia, as to "antagonistic acculturation" (Devereux and Loeb, 1943 a).

The third reaction is psychologically a rather complex one. Since genital sexuality was substituted for the gratification of (pregenital) aggressiveness, genital behavior became contaminated by certain aggressive impulses. The fact that the invasion of genitality by pregenital impulses is incompatible with Mohave tribal ideals is highlighted by one of Hama: Utce:'s remarks. On being asked about the occurrence of sadomasochistic behavior, she said, "Only whites do such things. We are not sufficiently civilized for that," but added that amorous biting was believed to be a sign of undesirable jealousy (Devereux, 1947 a). Hence, whenever aggressiveness appears in a genital context, it tends to be disguised either as humor, or as "legitimate" indignation, thus allowing it to escape the censorship of the superego, or, more probably, of the ego ideal.

The fourth reaction was a socially constructive one. On the one hand, external pressures compelled the Mohave to abandon organized intertribal aggressions, while their contacts with modern life, especially in schools and in hospitals, interfered so much with the survival of the ancient tribal interest in supernaturalistic (shamanistic) dreaming that, according to Wallace (1947), hardly any member of the younger generation has had such dreams in recent decades. On the other hand, the Mohave systematically rejected both the internecine, petty hostilities and the property-centered goals of white civilization. The final outcome of the process was a further increase in the compensatory cathecting of such traditional values as individualism, broad sociability, and rather uninhibited amorousness. Hence, the Mohave Indian's persistent decency toward his fellow man appears to be functionally connected with uninhibited and even somewhat indiscriminate amorousness.[4]

While the above comments clarify many of the main factors accounting for the limited aggressiveness of the Mohave, and also suggest that suppressed rage is relatively rare among them, due consideration must be given also to three additional facts: The absence of overt acts of aggressions against whites, the occurrence of self-destructive behavior in intoxicated persons, and the dynamics of the Mohave pattern of "passing out." The first of these problems can be discussed briefly in the present section; the other two will be analyzed under separate headings.

The absence of aggressions against whites by intoxicated Mohave Indians is probably connected with the suppressions of intertribal warfare by governmental authorities. The actual dynamics of this process were discussed with C. E. Prince, Jr., and led to the following tentative formulation: When the whites suppressed Mohave warfare, they provided the Mohave Indian with only one new outlet for his aggressions—alcohol. At the same time, the whites also became the representatives of the superego. Hence, the Mohave was constantly torn between the need to express aggression in the traditional manner and his fear of governmental intervention. The Mohave therefore evolved a compromise solution, which permitted a partial expression of aggressive impulses. This solution—the use of alcohol—was essentially a symptom formation, which, like all symptoms, failed to resolve the basic conflict in a lasting and effective manner.

However, a further analysis of this problem convinced me that, whereas there could be little doubt of the symptomatic nature of Mohave alcoholism, a somewhat different and perhaps more satisfactory interpretation—which adhered more closely to the traditional conception of the superego as a psychic instance whose ideology is subjectively evaluated as "good" and "right"—should be preferred to the interpretation first formulated.

In reformulating the dynamics of the process under study, a decisive importance was assigned to the fact that the white man and his ideol-

---

[4] This relationship appears to be more than a mere coincidence, since internecine peace and decency toward one's fellows frequently characterize tribes with few sexual inhibitions and a highly genital personality makeup. The nexus between anality, sadism, warfare, and the pursuit of wealth was cogently discussed by Jones (1923).

ogy are despised by the Mohave, and that this contempt seems to be more than a mere reaction formation, because the white man's ways are distinctly incompatible with Mohave ideology and are composed essentially of elements which the Mohave apprehend as ego alien. If the Mohave Indians could express their views in psychoanalytic terms, they would probably affirm that the white man's ideology has its roots in, and supports, pregenital urges. Now, the Mohave technique of handling whites is almost identical with their way of handling pregenital impulses: They despise and ignore them as best they can, and consider them unworthy even of open hostility. They are quite aware of pregenital impulses (Devereux, 1947 a), just as they are aware of whites, but repudiate both as being unworthy of notice by adults. When infants display behavior which is pregenital (i.e., when they are stingy, envious, etc.), the Mohave attempt to persuade them to behave like decent adults, but do not punish them (pt. 7, pp. 331–356). When adults behave in an objectionable manner, the Mohave first seek to encourage decent behavior, and, if they fail, tend to ignore the offender and the offense as long as possible. As for whites, the Mohave seem to feel that their behavior is beneath contempt, and therefore also beneath notice.

Summing up, white people and their ideology are apprehended by the Mohave as part of the id, rather than as part of the ego ideal. Since the Mohave do not expect anything good from whites, they are seldom disappointed, and therefore feel no strong urge to punish whites for their improper behavior. On the other hand they definitely expect at least some decency from a fellow Mohave, and even from enemy Indians—witness their contempt for the Maricopa, who refused to play fair and allied themselves with mounted Pima Indians armed with rifles (Kroeber, 1925 b). Thus, the Mohave do not behave aggressively toward whites any more than toward snakes or vermin, since none of these beings is felt to be capable of decent conduct. If, however, an individual white proves to be a decent person, the Mohave readily accept him as a human being, and expect him to conform to Mohave standards of decency (Devereux, 1948 a). Hence, the highest praise a Mohave can bestow on a white is the statement that "He is really a Mohave and not a white man at all."

Both the first scheme and the more complete second interpretation oblige one to view Mohave alcohol addiction as a symptom. The similarity between the two theories ends there, however. The initial scheme sought to explain primarily the marginal and rare phenomenon of aggression, whereas the more elaborate second scheme tried to interpret primarily the problem of the conspicuous rarity of drunken aggression. In the initial scheme the intrapsychic compromise presupposed an at least partial gratification of id impulses,

by means of intoxication and aggression, whereas in the second scheme
the compromise represents a victory for the ego ideal, which is incomplete only when, instead of engaging in sexual acts, or instead of passing out, the Mohave engages in overt acts of aggression. This point is
important enough to be discussed under a separate heading.

4. PASSING OUT

It is a psychoanalytic truism that the seemingly "accidental" pairing
of two ideas is never an "accident," but the unintentional revelation
of an unconsciously perceived nexus between two factors. It is, therefore, of the utmost significance that the late M. A. I. Nettle, M.D., as
well as several Mohave informants, remarked that "Drunken Mohave
Indians do not fight—they merely pass out." This formulation clearly
suggests a nexus between aggression and passing out, although it does
not disclose the nature of that relationship. Our next task, therefore,
is to investigate the nature of this connection.

In accordance with the fundamental principle of psychic determinism, it is proposed to start with the assumption that "passing out"
fulfills a wish and is a means to an end. This assumption is particularly convincing in the case of the Mohave, for several reasons:

(a) The average Mohave passes out after imbibing relatively small
quantities of alcohol.

(b) Hardly any male Mohave ever passes out before or during a
sexual orgy.

(c) Mohave women do frequently pass out before sexual orgies,
because, as was shown above, the psychodynamics of the drunken
woman's unconscious consent to serial rape must be understood in
terms of her aggressive frigidity and phallic pretensions (Devereux,
1948 f).

(d) An exceptionally gentle Mohave passed out during a very
mild altercation with his devoted, but also somewhat gruff, wife (Case
136).

It is my thesis that "passing out" is a defense against the eruption
of ego-dystonic impulses, or against the obligation to perform some
unwelcome task. This is true especially when the subject has imbibed
only moderate amounts of alcohol.[5]

The point of the above remark is a relatively simple one. Passing
out has a clearcut function in Mohave drunkenness. When, due to
drinking and to the concomitant relaxing of his inhibitions, the individual is in danger of performing some ego-dystonic action, the
superego, the ego ideal, and the ego forces as well, fall back upon their
last line of defense and bring about the phenomenon known as "pass-

---

[5] The following personal observation is pertinent: A moderately intoxicated white
habitual drinker looked at his watch, realized that he would have to perform an unpleasant task in exactly 90 seconds, and promptly passed out "cold."

ing out." In terms of this frame of reference, passing out is viewed here as a quasi-hysterical reaction, akin to fainting, or to hysterical paralysis. Similar flights from anxiety or tension into unconsciousness or sleep have been observed also among other primitive tribes (Bateson and Mead, 1942).

Since practically the only wholly ego-dystonic force that intoxication releases in the Mohave male is aggression, it seems probable that passing out is primarily a defense against aggression. This view is substantiated by the fact that Mohave individuals do not seem to pass out when aggression is disguised as humor (Case 139), or is bolstered by a "legitimate" cause (Case 130), or, finally, when the drunken act of aggression was soberly premeditated (Case 131). It is important to point out in this context that aggression against whites would not fit into any of these categories, since whites "don't know any better" and therefore cannot provide "legitimate" provocation.

As regards the Mohave woman, she seems to pass out so as to invite either sexual (Devereux 1948 f, 1950 a) or else murderous aggression, or both (Case 140, see also Case 105).

Although the above comments constitute, to a certain extent, a new approach to one aspect of alcoholism, they are wholly compatible with classical and time-tested psychoanalytic theories.

5. CHARACTERISTICS OF MOHAVE DRINKING HABITS

The preceding sections consistently emphasized that the conduct of the average intoxicated Mohave does not differ appreciably from his normal behavior. Unfortunately, it is almost impossible to illustrate normal and average patterns of behavior with case histories sufficiently striking to overshadow those which describe unique, marginal and sensational forms of misconduct. It is therefore to be feared that the accounts of spectacular murders or orgies, to be given below, will divert attention from the simple fact that the overwhelming majority of intoxicated Mohave Indians behave in a quiet and fairly reasonable manner.

The unique or spectacular event constitutes an ever present temptation to emphasize the marginal rather than the average, and to focus one's attention on climactic, rather than on routine, patterns of behavior. Even anthropologists have occasionally succumbed to the fallacy of misplaced emphasis, causing Róheim to exclaim ironically that the only "savage" in primitive society is the visiting anthropologist. Similarly, the strange notion—formerly so popular with armchair anthropologists—that the "primitive" devotes most of his time to magico-animistic pursuits, was severely criticized by Kroeber (1934), who rightly stressed that the primitive behaves most of the time in a perfectly rational and matter-of-fact manner, and acts alogically only in situations involving stress.

Unusual and spectacular details tend to distort the scientist's perception of the real relationship between the constituent elements of a broad phenomenon. It is not sufficient, however, to view this state of affairs solely as an obstacle impeding the proper analysis of the phenomenon to be studied. Like all difficulties arising in the course of scientific work, the one just mentioned is at once an obstacle and a challenge; a hindrance to glib generalizing and a signpost pointing toward an important new insight. It is therefore incumbent upon us to give further consideration to problems arising in connection with the scientific utilization of routine, as well as of climactic, events.

Anthropologists and psychoanalysts alike have been bedeviled by the lure of the unusual and by the fallacy of misplaced emphasis. Just as anthropologists have gradually abandoned their former obsession with ritual and belief, and have increasingly emphasized routine modes of behavior, so psychoanalysts have gradually developed also a psychology of the ego, after a long period of intensive—and almost exclusive—preoccupation with the more striking aspects of the unconscious. At the same time, many psychoanalysts have shifted their attention from id psychology to ego psychology, and from symptom neuroses to character neuroses.[6] The similarity between these two developments, which is not fortuitous, has a direct bearing on the proper interpretation of Mohave alcoholism.

Broadly speaking, the average behavior of the intoxicated Mohave Indian reveals important characteristics of Mohave ego psychology, whereas deviant and sensational forms of drunken conduct, or misconduct, tend to highlight chiefly the unconscious factors in Mohave alcoholism. It is therefore important to emphasize the unspectacular character of the average intoxicated Mohave's behavior, by means of an appropriately unimpressive example, before undertaking an analysis of the more or less unconscious mechanisms involved in spectacular drinking behavior.

CASE 132:

I returned to Parker, Ariz., in the summer of 1935. I reached the town in the evening and registered at the local hotel. As I emerged from the hotel and started to walk toward the restaurant, the first person I met was a young Mohave man, with whom I happened to be well acquainted. Since I had not informed my Mohave friends that I had returned from Asia, most of them believed me to be either in Indochina or in France, and, indeed, never expected to see me again. My friend was therefore surprised to see me and freely expressed his delight at my return. After an exchange of the usual amenities, he spontaneously mentioned that he was rather intoxicated, and distinctly pleased with his condition. After reminding him of our friendship, I took the liberty of gently rebuking him for drinking to excess and urged him to go home before he became involved in some trouble. He brushed my objections aside, however, and assured me that he would not get into any trouble. I then made some disparaging remarks about white bootleggers and asked him to name the person who had provided

---

[6] These lines were first published in 1948. Since then, the pendulum has sometimes swung so far to the other extreme, that a few psychoanalysts now practically ignore all that is not ego psychology.

him with liquor. Although he did not resent my question, he pretended that he did not know the bootlegger's name and added that there were plenty of whites willing to make some easy money by peddling liquor to the Indians. "The fact that there is a law against selling us liquor only means that we have to pay more for our drinks than the whites do. This gives white people an additional chance to exploit us." We then talked for a while about my experiences in Indochina and about the recent activities of our mutual friends. Throughout the conversation my Mohave friend behaved in a cordial and courteous manner, and, even though he was obviously delighted with my unexpected return, did not become either maudlin or overenthusiastic. After a while we bade each other good night and separated. I understand that he returned to his home unescorted and did not run into any diffculties.

It cannot be overstressed that this kind of amiable and quiet intoxication, rather than the spectacular orgy of murder, is the characteristic behavior of the intoxicated Mohave. If this fact is disregarded, it is impossible to understand a major component of Mohave personality structure, since many significant aspects of Mohave ego psychology will necessarily escape one's attention.

III. UNCONSCIOUS FACTORS IN MOHAVE ALCOHOLISM

Psychoanalytic conceptions of the dynamics of alcohol addiction are derived from the study of individuals belonging to our culture, in which alcoholic beverages have always played a significant role. An attempt to test directly the applicability of these theories to our Mohave data would be a meaningless exercise of mental agility, unless one proved first that alcohol is meaningfully integrated with contemporary Mohave life, both on the social and on the intrapsychic level.

1. It was shown above that drinking is fully integrated with Mohave social life, and that the alcoholic excesses of Mohave Indians must be thought of in terms of what Linton (1936) called culturally standardized "patterns of misconduct," rather than in terms of an atypical individual's purely marginal and idiosyncratic deviation from the social norm. However, though Linton himself did not do so, we must further refine the concept "pattern of misconduct" in terms of four Lintonian categories: universals, specialties, alternatives, and individual peculiarities. Universal misconduct patterns are available only to full members of the group: Only citizens can be traitors; aliens can only be spies. Specialty misconduct patterns are limited to members of a given subgroup: Prostitutes continue to be considered female; male prostitutes barely count as men. Alternative misconduct patterns are usually categorized without regard to their actual social harmlessness: Wastrels who pay their gambling debts, though not their tailors' bills, remain "gentlemen." Individual misconduct patterns highlight the repetitive core of neurosis: Habitual burglars are often readily identified by their "style." Mohave alcoholism is a universal misconduct pattern, available to all Mohave in situations of stress; moreover, they hold that a drunken Mohave misbehaves, while a drunken white simply acts like a typical white.

2. A rigorous proof of the thesis that alcohol and drinking are fully integrated with the psychic life of the Mohave Indian must satisfy several criteria. Specifically, it must be shown:

(*a*) That alcohol and drinking occur in the dreams of drinkers and nondrinkers alike, as part of the manifest content of dreams.

(*b*) That alcohol and drinking are susceptible of being utilized as "thought tokens" both by the primary and by the secondary psychic process. In particular, they must be susceptible of being utilized as symbols on a par with, and as fully equivalent substitutes for, standard aboriginal symbols.

(*c*) That alcohol and drinking are coordinated with existing symbolic equations; i.e., that they are susceptible of being added, as new terms, to existing symbolic equations.

(*d*) That alcohol and drinking are, in turn, susceptible of being represented by aboriginal symbols—i.e., they must sometimes be part of the latent content of dreams, and, conversely,

(*e*) That alcohol and drinking serve as symbols in dreams expressing both aboriginal types of conflicts and conflicts resulting from acculturation.

Only one configuration pertaining to items *b*, *c*, *d*, and *e* can be cited, and this configuration is, unfortunately, a rather elusive one, which will seem convincing to psychoanalysts, but may not satisfy a very conservative anthropologist. The Mohave believe that the ghosts of the deceased resort to one of two devices for luring their surviving relatives to the land of the dead. The first device is (incestuous) cohabitation with the surviving relatives in dream. The second is the feeding of the survivors in dream, i.e., the providing of oral gratifications. This belief, which explicitly equates the lure of incestuous relations with the lure of oral gratifications provided by relatives, is psychologically identical with Tcatc's and Harav He: ya's tendency to postulate an implicit nexus between incest and alcoholism. (See further below.) Now as stated in the preceding pages, heterosexual drinking is, in Mohave society, a common prelude to coitus, and the role of coital connections in cementing emotional bonds is explicitly recognized in the Mohave adage: "Do not interfere with quarrelling spouses. If you take sides, they will sneak out at night and cohabit with each other; then you will have two enemies instead of one" (Devereux, 1950 a). The same type of reasoning applies even more strongly to incest, which the Mohave themselves link with alcoholism. Indeed, incest is not only the acting out of an atypically intense attachment to another member of one's family (Devereux, 1939 a), but, in Mohave society, it so happens that the *only* type of marriage which actually involves an authentic "wedding" ritual, one defined as indissoluble and explicitly correlated with ideas of death by (symbolic) suicide (motivated by an incestuous attraction), is the marriage of cousins, between whom sexual relations are ordinarily taboo (pt. 7, pp. 356–371). It should also be stressed that, in at least one pathogenic dream (Case 47), the food provided by the deceased relative was the dead mother's own body—and this detail was actually a part of the manifest content of the pathogenic dream itself. Since clinical evidence concerning fantasies of devouring the mother indicates that the cannibalized maternal body is but an extension of the maternal breast, which is, in turn, simply an expanded symbol of maternal milk, ingested by the infant, one must conclude that the seductive food offered by the ghosts of deceased relatives is actually the mother's milk. Since it was previously pointed out that the Mohave equate milk (and semen as well, which is the food of the fetus, Devereux, 1949 c) with alcohol, the psychoanalyst at least will feel that alcohol (symbolically syncretized with milk and explicitly correlated with incest) does seem to be a part of the latent content of certain important and culturally emphasized types of Mohave dreams.

Further, psychoanalytically convincing, evidence bearing on this point is the marked proneness of the Mohave to "pass out" after drinking too much, since some psychoanalysts have cogently compared this type of "passing out" to the satiated suckling's sleep.

Other relevant cultural traits bearing on this problem are the Mohave taboo on playing erotically with a woman's breast, because such an act is reminiscent of incest, and the Mohave woman's tendency to ridicule a man by showing him her breasts, thereby explicitly reducing him to the status of an immature suckling (Devereux, 1947 a).

Despite these findings, it must be admitted that there is at least one relevant area of Mohave culture which is relatively non-integrated with alcohol. This segment of culture includes Mohave beliefs concerning magic substances and narcotics (pt. 4, pp. 202–212). As is well known, in many cultures alcohol is explicitly defined as a magic substance and alcoholic intoxication is viewed as more or less similar to a ritual trance state. Yet, even though the Mohave did occasionally exploit the narcotic properties of a decoction of datura for quasi-oracular purposes, they make no such use of alcoholic intoxication, probably because, by the time alcohol began to gain a real foothold in Mohave society, the ritual ingestion of datura was already largely obsolete. Nonetheless, it should be noted that the one shaman who actually committed suicide (Case 106) did so by first drinking datura and then drowning himself (suicide by means of a combination of two ingested fluids), while at least one non-shaman killed himself while more or less intoxicated (Case 120).

Actually, it seems desirable to indicate, though in the most tentative manner, that there appears to be at least one, ever so faint, connection between alcohol and magic substances. This connection has its roots in the fact that there exists not only the just mentioned equation: alcohol=milk (and semen), but also the equation: magic substances and narcotics=milk (pt. 4, pp. 202–212). Now, while it may be valid in pure logic to say: "If A resembles B and C resembles B in the same way, then A and C also resemble each other," this reasoning is not a sufficient basis for making convincing psychoanalytic-cultural demonstrations. Indeed, in a psycho-cultural context it is also necessary to show that these two discrete sets of equations, which have one term in common, are actually correlated with each other in the Mohave Indian's unconscious. Unfortunately, this correlation cannot be clearly demonstrated, at least not by evidence drawn directly from Mohave culture. The one indirect hint is the fact that, in some cultures, alcohol is a magical substance, formally defined as a part of a supernatural being's person—such as Dionysus—so that its ingestion is an act resembling nursing (fantasied as cannibalism of the breast). It is tempting, and not unreasonable, to speculate that, had alcohol gained a real foothold in Mohave society before the oracular use of datura became obsolete, and/or had the drinking of a decoction of datura played a major, rather than marginal, role in aboriginal Mohave culture, a similar conception of alcohol may have been evolved also by the Mohave.

Be that as it may, the data cited suffice to prove, at least to the psychoanalyst and probably also to the dynamically oriented student of personality-in-culture, that alcohol is a constituent element of the latent content of some Mohave dreams—and especially of pathogenic dreams about ghosts who seek to lure their surviving relatives to the land of the dead—though, in the last resort, among the Mohave as well as among ourselves, alcohol is, in turn, only one of the many symbols pertaining to the basic referent, milk.

(f) That dreams about alcohol and drinking, as well as alcoholic hallucinations, are consciously treated as the equivalents of dreams whose manifest content is composed entirely of aboriginal culture elements.

CASE 133 (Informant Hama: Utce:):

This dream was dreamed around 1910 by Hama: Utce:, who was, at that time, approximately a 10-year-old nondrinking girl. It was reported in 1932 by the dreamer herself, who, at that time, strongly disapproved of alcoholic excesses. "I dreamed that I held a bottle of whiskey in my hands, and was walking along happily, when an elderly man, whom I did not know, came up to me and tried to take it away from me. I jumped into the Colorado River and swam to the opposite shore. Then I woke up."

This dream satisfies several of our criteria. It is the dream of a nondrinker (criterion *a*). The whiskey bottle is both a phallic and a breast symbol, and the attempted theft is a threat of oral

deprivation and castration (criterion *b*). Whiskey is coordinated
with the symbolic equations milk=saliva=semen (criterion *c*). It
is used to express both certain aboriginal conflicts—phallic and oral
aspirations—and a conflict arising from acculturation: Because of
her mixed blood, the girl in question had had a harsh childhood, and
grew up to be a very positive, "phallic" sort of person (criterion *e*)
who is also a good provider. This dream, like other important
dreams in Mohave society, was remembered for more than 20 years
(criterion *f*).

CASE 134. (Informant Modhar Taa :p.) :

The following incident was related by a young adult man, Modhar Taa :p (Penis
cover=foreskin=condom), who had frequent anxiety dreams and quasi hallucinatory experiences. "I was drunk one day and was walking homeward
through the brush, when I saw something that looked like a white snake. I
almost collapsed from fright. People believed that this vision was an ominous
one; that it was, in some way, connected with someone's death." (This man's
younger sibling died in utero when his mother died in labor (Devereux, 1948 e).
This trauma is reflected in several of his dreams.) The informant, as well as his
friends, treated this alcoholic hallucination on a par with nonalcoholic dreams
and hallucinations (criterion f).

This alcoholic quasi-hallucination is mentioned also in Case 26.

The dream (Case 133) and the hallucinatory experience (Case 134)
just reported satisfy all criteria except (*d*). In view of the fact that
the material satisfies five of the six criteria, it seems reasonable to
assume that a more extensive collection of Mohave dreams would contain items in which alcohol and drinking are part of the latent dream-
content (criterion d). This is all the more likely, since Wallace's
recent study (1947) reveals an appreciable degree of acculturation
both in the manifest content of Mohave dreams and in the attitude of
the Mohave toward dreams.

(*g*) That alcohol should be referred to by at least one Mohave self-
given name. This point is of some significance, since such Mohave
names tend to emphasize the affectively significant elements of Mohave
culture, and to highlight the Mohave value system, especially by derid-
ing undesirable traits. In brief, Mohave names straddle the spheres of
culture and of psychology.

Two Mohave names pertaining to drinking were recorded: The first
is Yakapetk' Hapa :r(=when-drunk hollers), which is the self-given
name of a person who disapproves of this type of intoxicated behavior.
The fact that this critic of intoxication did not call himself, e.g.,
"when-drunk fights," strongly highlights the fact that most intoxicated Mohave Indians are only vocally aggressive. This interpretation is supported by the fact that fighting over food distributed by a
white, who butchered a steer and gave the Mohave the offal of the car-
cass, is explicitly referred to in the personal name: Vaha Munyu:=
guts fights-over. The second name referring to alcohol is of even

greater significance. A conservative Mohave shaman, of the Mah gens, who disapproved of drunkenness, called himself: Harav He :ya= whiskey mouth. What is of the greatest importance in this context is that this shaman *also* had a *second* self-given name: Mowa :va Kwanye :na=his-relatives coitizes (commit incest).

The fact that this champion of resistance to acculturation chose for himself two names, one of which condemns alcoholism and the other incest, strictly parallels Tcatc's already cited spontaneous juxtaposition of alcoholism and incest, in connection with her disapproval of acculturated behavior. This observation provides the best starting point for an analysis of the role of alcoholism in the Mohave unconscious, especially in relation to acculturation. The fact that acculturation often permits the acculturated individual to express behaviorally certain impulses, which were strongly inhibited by his aboriginal culture, explains why the first persons to be acculturated are so often either the subjectively maladjusted, or else those who are most consistently victimized by the aboriginal culture. The latter frequently behave as though they were idiosyncratically neurotic, simply because their culture denies them access to, and the use of, certain culturally standardized defense mechanisms, thereby infantilizing them and rendering them comparable to neurotics (Devereux, 1956 b).

It is hardly necessary to stress that whether acculturation is used by a given individual primarily as a means for the uncreative, self-destructive and sterile "acting out" of previously inhibited urges— for example, by becoming a dissolute alcoholic—or whether the previously inhibited impulses, freed by acculturation from their aboriginal cultural shackles, are immediately transformed into subjectively productive and culturally valuable sublimations, depends primarily on the acculturated person's pre-existing degree of psychic health or illness. The already maladjusted person will put his acculturation to neurotic uses. The emotionally healthy person will systematically attempt to use acculturation creatively. Instead of "acting out" his newly disinhibited impulses neurotically, he will sublimate them, thereby increasing both his own psychic security and the sociocultural security and productiveness of his own group.

It is quite evident that, during the historical period to which the data presented in this Appendix belong, the Mohave did use creatively a number of cultural items which they obtained in the course of their acculturation. It is, however, equally evident that they used the borrowed item "alcohol" primarily in a way which must be described as symptomatic acting out. This is proved both by Tcatc's statement and by Harav He : ya's two names: "Whiskey mouth" and "Commits incest," and is exemplified by Sahaykwisa :'s (Case 140) and Amat Yavu :me's (Case 138) self-destructive alcoholism. The use of acculturation as a means for evolving new and creative sublimations related to the newly disinhibited acquisitive impulses is exemplified by Hivsu: Tupo: ma's industriousness as a farmer using modern plows, and by Hama: Utce: 's marked ability to put her good education and striking energy to a creative use in connection with important tribal affairs. A third type of acculturation can best be described as "antagonistic acculturation" (Devereux and Loeb, 1943 a) and consists, for example, in adopting the dominant culture's means (tools, techniques, etc.), the better to resist its ends. Though primarily a sublimatory process, antagonistic acculturation nearly always brings in its train also certain types of symptomatic "acting out." Thus, when the Plains Indians obtained rifles, they used these weapons more often in intertribal warfare, than in resisting the encroachments of whites upon Indian territories, and thereby hastened the decline and fall of the Plains Indian way of life.

The manner in which acculturation releases previously inhibited impulses is strikingly highlighted by Tcatc's and Harav He: ya's preconscious awareness of the nexus between incest and alcoholism. If one recalls that the intoxicated Mohave is not aggressive—witness the fact that the only other recorded name pertaining to alcoholism is Yakapetk' Hapa: r (intoxicated hollers), which refers to a relatively mild form of aggressivity—one is obliged to conclude that the type of impulse which alcohol *first* and most strikingly releases in a person and in a group not accustomed to alcohol and having no traditional model for behaving in a particular way when drunk [7] is the impulse which was most consistently inhibited by the aboriginal culture.

The preceding considerations indicate that alcohol and drinking are sufficiently integrated with the social and psychic life of the Mohave to warrant an investigation of the unconscious mechanisms in terms of existing psychoanalytic theories of alcohol addiction.

---

[7] Such a model is the well-known Hungarian adage: "The Hungarian rejoices—(when drunk)—by crying" (Sírva vigad a magyar). It is important to stress in this context that, to the Hungarian, this type of tearful alcoholic "fun" seems an admirable, praiseworthy, and characteristic national trait. Even the type of particular drink which he ingests may provide the drinker with a specific model for drunken behavior. Thus, whenever a certain young American woman got drunk on champagne, she insisted on speaking French—though she knew little French—and behaved in an artificially gay (American style), "Parisian" and flirtatious manner. By contrast, when she got drunk on whiskey, she behaved like an average drunken college girl. Culture itself sanctions these variations of drunken behavior in terms of the type of alcohol ingested. In Germany, to get drunk on wine is elegant; to get drunk on beer is to be either a solid citizen, or else an admirable college student. An Englishwoman who gets drunk on gin is felt to behave like a member of the "lower class" since only charwomen are supposed to get drunk on gin. Getting drunk on California red wine stamps one as a "vino"—as a drunken bum—while getting drunk on imported Burgundy vintage wine is the mark of a gentleman. A girl who asks her escort to order sweet champagne might as well admit openly that she is a simple shopgirl; a lady drinks only "dry" or "extra dry" or "brut" champagne. Comparable nuances also exist with respect to the smoking of cigars, cigarettes, and pipes. A young woman analysand, who, in the transference, visualized me as a very tall, solidly built, slow moving, and tweed-clad invidual—though I am of medium height, slender and move rather quickly—completed this stereotype by saying that I smoked a pipe, though in reality I smoke only cigarettes.

1. PREOCCUPATION WITH THE DEAD

The intoxicated Mohave Indian shows a significant tendency to be preoccupied with the dead. Intoxicated witches refer to their victims (Cases 139, 140) with intense longing, while lay individuals consciously think and speak of their dead relatives (Cases 137, 138), in spite of the tribal taboo on mentioning the names of the dead (Kroeber, 1925 a; Devereux, 1937 a). Conversely, obsessive thoughts and anxieties connected with the beloved dead can apparently lead to alcoholic excesses (Cases 137, 138). The fact that the loss of realistic object cathexes often plays a major role in intoxication is also underscored by the observation that deserted and divorced women are especially prone to drink to excess, thereby inviting rape.

It is important to realize in this context that there are certain clearly formulated Mohave rules concerning the manifestation of emotions on the occasion of the severing of affective bonds. The Mohave condone—but do not admire—female displays of emotion both before and after separations and divorces (Devereux, 1937 b and pt. 3, pp. 91–106), and also before, during, and after funerals (pt. 7, pp. 431–459). By contrast, male displays of emotion are expected to cease once the separation or divorce is final and also when the cremation ceremony is finished. Hence, if a man continues to fret over the desertion and remarriage of his wife, his behavior will elicit ridicule rather than sympathy (pt. 3, pp. 91–106).

Furthermore, it is specifically believed that obsessive preoccupation with dead or lost love objects causes certain ailments (pt. 4, passim), that the dead attempt to lure the living to the land of the dead, and that witches seek to be killed in order to join the ghosts of their beloved victims (pt. 7, pp. 387–426).

These data suggest that the rule prescribing dignified self-restraint and the taboo on the names of dead represent a culturally standardized attempt to suppress intense preoccupation with lost love objects, in order to reduce anxiety and feelings of guilt to a minimum.

Intoxicated persons tend, however, to violate these rules and taboos. It is tempting to dispose of this entire problem in the traditional manner and to explain these violations of taboos in terms of the theory that "alcohol dissolves the superego." However, inasmuch as the "dissolving of the superego" is supposed to abolish anxiety, the traditional explanation appears to be inadequate, for in this instance the purpose of the rules and taboos in question is precisely the reduction of anxiety.

The actual psychodynamics of the situation are somewhat different. Paradoxically, intoxication can bring about noncompliance with these beneficial taboos only because it substitutes itself to the latter and achieves the goal of reducing anxiety by idiosyncratic, rather than by culturally standardized, means (Devereux, 1956 b). In fact, it must be suspected that certain individuals are impelled to substitute drunkenness for compliance with tribal taboos precisely because, in their case, the taboos failed to reduce anxiety to a tolerable level. The tribal taboos in question attempt to cope with anxiety by bringing about a conscious and deliberate suppression of all thoughts about the lost love objects. Alcohol, on the other hand, by providing compensatory infantile gratifications, tends to diminish the overall level of anxiety, and thus renders tolerable the reemergence of these thoughts into the field of consciousness.[8] In fact, intoxication seems to have certain advantages over the process of suppression. By permitting the reemergence of the tabooed thought, it partially enables the individual to "work through" (*durcharbeiten*) his grief. This interpretation seems to be supported by the observation that many individuals are relatively successful in their attempts to cope with the trauma of losing a love object by resorting to intoxication—witness the fact that indulgence in alcoholic sprees is usually abandoned spontaneously when the deserted woman finds a new spouse (Case 129).

On the other hand, when the conflict is complicated by incest, witchcraft, or an appreciable amount of latent homosexuality—and perhaps by certain other factors as well—the individual's attempt to "work through" his problem while intoxicated fails, and a vicious circle is established. In such cases the intoxicated person deliberately courts disaster, for example, by making damaging confessions (Cases 139, 140). Otherwise expressed, his attempt to cope with his problem psychologically fails and his attempt to "work it through" degenerates into mere "acting out." Nonetheless the above observations clearly indicate that in some instances it is—within limits—possible to think of alcohol addiction as a spontaneous, unconscious, and seldom successful attempt at psychological self-healing.

This view is entirely compatible with Gross' (1935) thesis that toxic and toxoid substances simply accelerate or slow down psychic processes.

Whatever the correct interpretation of these phenomena may be, the available case histories clearly indicate that intoxication may be used by the drinker as a means of fleeing obsessive thoughts about the dead, or of thinking of the dead without undue anxiety, or both (Case 137). The fact that the second aim is sometimes not achieved is shown by the self-destructive intoxicated behavior of those whose relationship with the love object was complicated by homosexual, incestuous, and aggressive (witchcraft) elements (Cases 138, 139, 140).

---

[8] Benzedrine is reported to have somewhat similar effects (Agoston, 1944).

The following case history reveals with great clarity the significance of the dead in alcoholic behavior:

CASE 135 (Informant: Hama: Utce:):

Hama: Utce: and her half brother, Taparevily, were raised by a very "bossy" aunt, whom both of them disliked exceedingly. One day the young man borrowed his aunt's car, became intoxicated, and wrecked it, whereupon his aunt nagged him so much that he shot and killed himself. It is interesting that the informant complained about her aunt mostly when she was riding in a car. The accidental wrecking of the aunt's car (car=phallus) was perhaps not entirely fortuitous, in terms of the logic of the unconscious, since the young man in question intensely disliked his aggressive and "phallic" aunt (cf. also Case 114).

Taparevily's suicide over a car may explain why Hama: Utce: was so ambiguously afraid of automobile accidents. Thus, in 1932–33, she professed to be afraid of my driving, because I was, at that time, a relatively novice driver. Yet, at the same time, she, herself, drove so fast over rutted roads on at least one occasion, that Hivsu: Tupo:ma and I, who were bouncing up and down on the open platform of the ramshackle truck, were quite afraid of falling off and laughingly encouraged each other by exchanging shouts of "alyha:" (=homosexual=coward). Hama: Utce's fear of automobile accidents also played a role when her intoxicated husband drove a car she had purchased with money lent to her by the same aunt, Tanu: (see also Case 136).

CASE 136 (Informant: Hama: Utce:):

My husband Sumurâmurâ is a very kindly person. He seldom drinks, and when he does drink he simply passes out. He was angry with me only once. One day he got drunk somewhere, and it was quite late before we managed to drive home. Since he drove in a zigzag line, I began to fear that he would have an accident, and asked him to let me drive the car. He refused to listen to me, however, and seemed to be somewhat annoyed because I was afraid of his driving. Yet he drove so badly that every other minute I had to grab the steering wheel, to prevent him from driving us into a ditch. Finally he fell asleep at the wheel, which enabled me to take his place in the driver's seat. While I was driving the car, he sat by my side, leaned his head against my shoulder, and kept mumbling, "Don't be angry, sweetheart, I do love you so!" He was just like a little baby—as nice and sweet as he always is. When we reached our house, I put him to bed and we went to sleep. That is about as angry as my husband will ever get. He is a good man.

The intoxicated behavior just described is precisely what one would expect from someone as gentle, kindly, and affectionate as Sumurâmurâ.

CASE 137 (For full details see Case 64).

(The present abstract of certain sections of Case 64 highlights problems connected with "John Smith's" transitory alcohol addiction.)

John Smith's principal, and emotionally highly important, father image died under tragic circumstances at a time when, for the most creditable reasons, John Smith had to spend many months away from the reservation. Shortly thereafter, John Smith repeatedly communicated with a substitute father image, indicating that, even though he did not feel happy and at ease in the position which he occupied away from the reservation, he intended to remain with the organization to which he belonged until he had fulfilled his deceased principal father image's expectations, which were closely related to a modernized version of a major and traditional Mohave interest. One striking aspect of these communications was John Smith's sudden insistence on addressing this substitute father image in terms of great respect, though he had formerly always addressed him in a manner which implied an affectionate relationship between equals. Although this sudden expression of respect was partly due to the special position which this substitute father image occupied at that time, on a deeper, and psychodynamically more significant level, John Smith's use of terms of respect probably indicated his acute need for a substitute father image, functioning as a paternal adviser.

At about the same time, John Smith's mother asked this substitute father image to urge John Smith to stop drinking to excess and to resume his correspondence with her and also with his relatives and friends. The substitute father image promptly wrote a supportive and encouraging letter to John Smith and his intervention was so successful that, in the course of a very few days, John Smith communicated not only with his mother, but also with 15 other relatives and friends. Moreover, he appears to have stopped drinking to excess, since his mother's subsequent communications with the substitute father image made no further mention of excessive drinking on the part of John Smith.

John Smith's own statement about his excessive drinking strongly highlights the nexus between his intoxication and his mourning reaction:

"Well as far as drinking goes, I don't care much about it, but when I go to bed at nights I keep dreaming of [the principal father image]. I keep seeing him and try to reach him but as soon as I get my hands on him he disappears and I wake up crying. If he had died of sickness I guess it wouldn't hurt me as much as it does now. But I keep thinking of him lying out there suffering and nobody to help him. That's when I get drunk, just to forget about that. I've been losing weight and lots of sleep," etc.

The obsessive preoccupation with the deceased, the reaching out for the deceased without being able to hold him—a theme also mentioned in the Mohave legend "Halyec Matcoo:tâ "(Devereux, 1948 h)—the crying on awakening, as well as the loss of weight and of sleep clearly fit the Mohave conception of pathogenic dreams which cause ghost diseases (pt. 4, pp. 128–186). Even more striking is the intrusion of oral elements into John Smith's concious plans. Although, as a child, John Smith hated to have to do his own cooking, at this precise moment he suddenly declared that he liked to cook when he was a child and began to make plans for getting, with the same organization, a new position, directly related to the preparation of food. This detail forcibly brings to one's mind the cannibalistic cooking dream mentioned in Case 47. The symbolic significance of these plans is highlighted by the fact that, immediately after mentioning them, John Smith stated that he intended to remain with this organization until he had fulfilled his deceased father image's expectations. He also added that, even though the deceased father image's request to fulfill these expectations "didn't mean much" to him at the time it was made, "now I know what he meant by that."

Comment

(1) John Smith responded to the tragic death of his principal father image with a mourning depression, which involved anxiety dreams, loss of sleep and anorexia, and with excessive drinking, which partially alleviated his obsessive preoccupation with the deceased.

(2) Simultaneously, he stopped communicating with his mother and with his friends and relatives. (Withdrawal.)

(3) When a suitable father substitute intervened, John Smith—still longing for a father—maneuvered this father substitute into an effectively paternal position, by suddenly ceasing to call him by his first name, and addressing him instead in terms of formal respect.

(4) The substitute father image responded to this tacit plea by providing encouragement, by explicitly agreeing to function as a father substitute, and by encouraging John Smith to identify himself with this substitute father image.

(5) John Smith responded to this acquisition of a father substitute by:

(a) Ceasing to drink to excess.

(b) Writing letters to his mother, his relatives, and his friends.

(c) Substituting for alcoholic gratifications (of a passive-ingestive type) an interest in work related to the preparation of food for others (active giving), and also by indulging in a retroactive falsification of his real reactions to having had to prepare much of his own food during his childhood. This process can, perhaps, best be understood in terms of a process which Kris (1952) called "regression in the service of the ego."

John Smith's subsequent difficulties, arising from his reactions to his principal father image's tragic death, are discussed in Case 64.

The nexus between alcoholism, mourning, and suicidal thoughts are also highlighted by Case 138.

CASE 138 (Informants Hivsu: Tupa:ma and Hama: Utce:):

It is convenient to describe first the dramatis personae of this case history before presenting the narrative proper.

(a) Humar Tudhu:lye (hidden baby, i.e., "concealed pregnancy," or else "child hidden from the Agency, so that it would not be taken away to go to school"). Gens, Nyoltc. Race, fullblood Mohave. Sex, male. Age, at time of events, about 36," "but looking only about 26 years old." Marital status, married, then divorced. Children, none. Education, unknown. Occupation, probably a farmer. Heavy drinker. Younger brother of (b); husband of (f); younger uterine half brother of (c); half uncle of (d); younger uterine brother of (e).

(b) Yavu:me (earth whiskers). Gens, Nyoltc. Race, fullblood Mohave. Sex, male. Age at death, about 40. Marital status, married to the former wife of (a). Children, one daughter. Education, unknown. Occupation, probably farmer. Date of death, 1931 or 1932. Cause of death, run over by a car. Heavy drinker. Older brother of (a); second husband of (f); younger uterine half brother of (c); half uncle of (d); younger uterine brother of (e).

(c) E. Gens. Po:tà. Race, fullblood Mohave. Sex, male. Father of (d); brother of (e); older uterine brother of (a) and (b), both of whom assumed his English family name.

(d) S. Gens. Po:tà. Race, fullblood Mohave. Sex, male. Age at time of events, 17. Son of (c); third husband of (f); nephew of (d); half nephew of (a) and (b).

(e) Po:tà. Gens, Po:tà. Race, fullblood Mohave. Sex, female. Sister of (c); aunt of (d); older uterine half sister of (a) and (b).

(f) Syuly. Gens, Syuly. Race, fullblood Mohave. Sex, female. Age at time of events, about 26. Marital status, married in succession to (a), (b), (d) and (g). Children, one daughter by (b) and one by (g).

(g) Hilkáyam Aa:u. Gens, Tcatc. Race, fullblood Mohave. Sex, male. Age, 21. Marital status, fourth husband of (f).

Syuly (f) was married to Humar Tudhu:lye (a) for quite some time—perhaps as long as 2 or 3 years. She ran away from him several times, allegedly because he was a very heavy drinker, but always returned to him. One day, however, she left him permanently and married his brother Amat Yavu:me (*b*). She was married to the latter for about a year and a half, and bore him a daughter. Since Amat Yavu:me (*b*) was a heavy drinker, too, informants suspect that she deserted Humar Tudhu:lye (*a*) not so much because he drank, as because she wished to marry his brother. This divorce and remarriage did not interfere in the least with the extremely warm and friendly relationship between the two brothers.

One day, when his daughter was about 3 or 4 months old, Amat Yavu:me (*b*), while very drunk, was run over at dawn by a car on the highway which passes through the Colorado River Indian Reservation near Parker, Ariz. It was assumed that the car belonged to a tourist, since its driver was never caught. Amat Yavu:me (*b*) was fatally injured. His legs and ribs were smashed, and "there was only mush inside his body." He was found lying on the highway by a white tourist, who promptly reported the accident to the Agency. Amat Yavu:me was thereupon taken to the Agency hospital by a group consisting of the white constable of Parker, the halfbreed Indian reservation policeman Kohovan Kura:u, the colored Agency truck driver, and Hama: Utce:'s husband, Sumurámurá. At the hospital Hama: Utce: tried to question the dying man about his accident, but could not obtain an answer. Amat Yavu:me (*b*) did, however, recognize Sumurámurá and asked him to take him home. Next, Hama: Utce: dispatched her husband, Sumurámurá, to the reservation, to inform Po:tá (*e*), the victim's half sister, of the accident, since Amat Yavu:me (*b*) had been found so early in the morning that no one knew about the accident. Consequently, although he did not die until about 10 a.m., Po:tá was at that time still on her way to the hospital.

Syuly (*f*), now a widow, lived alone for some time, and then married S. (*d*), half nephew of her two former husbands. "She sure must have liked that family," Hama: Utce: commented. "When a person marries two members of the same family in succession, they say that she will eventually run through the rest of the family as well." Eventually she bore a daughter also to her third husband. He, however, deserted her after a while. Sometime later she married Hilkáyam Aa:u (*g*)

Amat Yavu:me's (*b*) death greatly affected his family, as well as his friends. Thus, even Hama: Utce:, who loathes drunkenness and is not related to this family in any way, stated, "Neither I, nor Hivsu: Tupo:ma, who is not related to this family either, ever got over Amat Yavu:me's (*b*) death. Those two brothers are very good people—especially Amat Yavu:me."

Humar Tudhu:lye (*a*) was especially deeply affected by his brother's death. Although the two brothers did not live together—Humar Tudhu:lye lived in the house of his older uterine brother, E. (*c*)—they were so fond of each other that even my Mohave informants (who tend to take brotherly love for granted) made a point of stressing the intensity of their mutual devotion. Humar Tudhu:lye (*a*) kept on thinking of his brother's death. Although he had always drunk a lot, after his brother's death he became such a drunkard that even the Mohave tried to keep him from getting drunk, which was quite unusual, since the Mohave like to share their drinks. Finally Humar Tudhu:lye's (*a*) craving for alcohol became so great that he would even walk into the houses of his friends in their absence and drink up their liquor. When drunk, he often talked about his dead brother: "I keep on thinking of my brother. I don't care if the same thing happens to me too. I too want to die. I don't care." It was ascertained that thoughts of death did not preoccupy Humar Tudhu:lye (*a*) prior to his brother's death.

2. THE NEXUS BETWEEN THOUGHTS ABOUT THE DEAD AND ORALITY

The case histories just cited reveal the strong tendency of drinkers to identify with the dead. The same tendency is evident also in certain other atypical modes of behavior in Mohave society: Two men may kill themselves over the same woman; several persons connected with each other may commit suicide in succession; a brother or a father may imitate the suicide of a member of the family (pt. 7, passim); shamanism and witchcraft are said to "run in certain families" (Devereux, 1937 c). Finally, if a person marries in succession two members of the same family, it is said that, in the course of subsequent marital ventures, that person will "run through the whole family."

Since identification is the prototype of object relationships obtaining during the oral stage (Fenichel, 1945), a few words may now be said about the oral factors which play a role in the suicide clusters referred to in the preceding paragraph. In the case histories reported above, the oral element is represented chiefly by alcohol, though other oral factors also appear to be present. The oral element in Mohave jealousy was described elsewhere (Devereux, 1947 a and pt. 7, pp. 340–356). Saliva, or sucking, or both play an important role in shamanistic therapy, as well as in the technique of witchcraft (Róheim, 1932, Devereux, 1937 c). On the other hand, the oral component is less evident in the clustered suicides of relatives and in the tendency of certain persons to marry repeatedly into the same family.

These findings will now be examined in the light of Federn's (1929) and Friedländer's (1940) statement that the suicide longs for something lost, while the addict desires something he cannot obtain.

The fact that the Mohave alcoholic sometimes imitates the self-destructive behavior of, e.g., a brother who predeceased him, does not make this sound distinction inapplicable to Mohave data. It simply calls for a careful scrutiny of the manner in which the Mohave alcoholic manages to combine a longing for a concrete lost love object with the wish for something unattainable. And this inquiry must, in turn, be preceded by the demonstration that Mohave beliefs do, in fact, reflect a tendency to introject, or even to incorporate, lost love objects.

The Mohave believe that dreams about dead adults induce in the living a desire to join them in the land of the ghosts and cause the dreamer to contract either the hiwey lak nyevedhi:(anus pain ghostly), or the nyevedhi: taha:na (ghost real) ailment (pt. 4, pp. 175–184). Dreams about dead infants, on the other hand, cause pseudocyesis, which is likewise called hiwey lak nyevedhi:. The terminological identification of pseudocyesis with gastrointestinal ailments, both of which the Mohave believe to be "venereal diseases," need not surprise us, partly because the most dreaded dreams about dead relatives are either incestuous or else feeding (cannibalistic) dreams, and partly because the Mohave have a variety of obvious fantasies of oral impregnation (Devereux, 1937 b, 1947 a, 1948 f). It may therefore be considered as proved that the Mohave tend to incorporate dead love objects, thereby appeasing their longing for something lost. The guilt feelings resulting from such fantasied acts of incorporation are probably responsible for the subsequent illness, or self-destructive behavior, of the bereaved.

At the same time, the beliefs just cited also reflect a longing for something unattainable, i.e., for reunion with the lost love object. Mohave culture provides a fantasied gratification of this wish, by means of the belief that one can be either temporarily, or else permanently, reunited with the dead. Thus, "ghost doctors" (Fathauer, 1951), such as Kunyoo:r of Needles, and, according to some, also (Hispan Himith) Tcilyetcilye (vulva hair curly, or stick up), of the Masipa: gens, are believed to be able to lead the souls of the living to the land of ghosts, so that they may visit their deceased relatives, and then lead them back again to the land of the living. On the other hand, if the living desire to be permanently reunited with the dead, they must hasten their own death, since dead souls, after going through several metamorphoses, cease to exist altogether. According to the Mohave, this belief is responsible for funeral suicides, for the vicarious suicide of witches (pt. 7, passim), and for the fact that some people, who dream of their dead relatives, die shortly after the death of the lost love object (pt. 4, passim).

The manifest death wishes of certain alcoholics (Case 138), the self-destructive behavior of other heavy drinkers (Case 137), and the damaging confessions of intoxicated witches (Cases 139, 140), alike suggest that, in a state of intoxication, the Mohave manage to blend the wish for something lost with the wish for something unattainable; they do so by identifying the lost love object with its ghost and then, by means of incorporation, identifying themselves with both the love object and its ghost.

Since the Mohave are not, as a rule, oral dependent personalities, but psychosexually mature givers, who tend to control and to sublimate their oral desires (Devereux, 1947 a) and to translate them into genital terms, it is easy to understand why incestuous dreams about the dead should be deemed especially dangerous to the living and particularly likely to induce an intense longing for the dead. The tendency to express the oral component genitally is made evident by the fact that the Mohave equate gastrointestinal disorders with pseudocyesis and consider both these ailments to be "venereal diseases." This tendency to "genitalize" oral elements may be partly responsible for the tendency to blend the wish for the lost love object with the wish for the unattainable (incestuous) love object.

The above considerations, together with our earlier discussion of oral elements and of incest in relation to all forms of alcoholism, form a connecting link between obsessive preoccupations with the dead and the regressive oral component in Mohave alcohol addiction.

3. ORAL SADISM, WITCHCRAFT, AND INCEST

The relationship between oral conflicts and alcohol addiction was first suggested by Freud (1930). This nexus is reasonably obvious in the case of the Mohave, whose orality was described elsewhere in some detail (Devereux, 1947 a). It was found that the Mohave:

(*a*) Are aware of the existence of an oral sadistic stage, and credit future shamans and witches with the tendency to bite the nipple.

(*b*) Believe in an intense sibling rivalry for the maternal breast.

(*c*) Are conscious of the traumatic effects of weaning.

(*d*) Tend to equate milk with saliva and with semen.

(*e*) Prohibit the oral stimulation of the woman's breasts during sexual intimacies, because it seems quasi-incestuous to them.

(*f*) Practice fellatio, which they seem to equate unconsciously with nursing the "bad" mother, but refrain from cunnilingus.

(*g*) Assign an important role to saliva, both in shamanistic therapy and in witchcraft.

(*h*) Assert that witches are prone to commit incest and tend to bewitch principally their own relatives.

(*i*) Implicitly believe that witches experience severe guilt feelings. The Mohave are convinced that all witches wish to be killed, since, should they die a natural death, they would lose their hold on the ghosts of their victims. Kwanámi:hye heroes (Stewart, 1947 c), who are also professional witch killers (Devereux, 1937 c) even though they themselves are sometimes incestuous witches (Devereux 1939 a), likewise prefer to die a violent death (Kroeber, 1925 a).

In view of these facts, it is worthwhile to attempt to discover whether the behavior of Mohave witches addicted to alcohol includes significant oral mechanisms occuring in combination with self-destructive actions.

CASE 139

The shaman Hivsu: Tupo:ma was an exceptionally voracious eater, even for a man of his enormous bulk. He specialized, among other things, in the treatment of the weaning trauma (which is believed to be caused by a rivalry with an unborn sibling, whose impending birth brings about a cessation of the flow of milk) (pt. 7, pp. 340–348). This is highly significant, especially since one of his victims was his elder uterine half-brother, who was his mother's favorite and whose daughter was one of the women with whom he had had incestuous relations. Six incidents of his life illustrate certain self-destructive mechanisms in the drinking history of an older Mohave shaman:

(*a*) On the occasion of a trip to Los Angeles, a group of Mohave shinney-players had intercourse serially with the two intoxicated Mohave concubines who had accompanied them. Eventually, despite Hivsu: Tupo: ma's objections, some wags decided to set fire to the pubic hair of these women. Even though Hivsu: Tupo: ma's pleas and moderate show of force did not deter the group from perpetrating this practical joke, it caused them at least to protect the girls from burns, by rubbing wet sand into their pubic hair.[9] After their return to Needles, the girls found an opportunity to avenge this outrage, when they discovered two of the culprits in a state of intoxication. They bared and painted the glans of their penes red, and the shaft yellow and black, and left them exposed in this humiliating condition. A detailed account of this incident was published elsewhere (Devereux, 1950 a).

(*b*) In the 1920's, Hivsu: Tupo: ma was the policeman and ditchrider of the Colorado River Indian Agency. Although he knew that Kohovan Kurau coveted his job, he became intoxicated one day and fell asleep in a ditch. Kohovan Kurau, who happened (?) to discover him in this condition, took Hivsu: Tupo: ma's gun to the Agency and managed to have himself appointed reservation policeman. This incident was reported in detail elsewhere (Devereux, 1948 d).

(*c*) In 1933 a white friend, who stopped to talk to me while I was working with Hivsu: Tupo: ma, offered him a drink from a pint bottle containing ethyl alcohol sweetened with apricot-flavored syrup. Hivsu: Tupo: ma drank about 2 fluid ounces, returned the bottle to our mutual friend, and thanked him. Although the latter did not depart immediately, Hivsu: Tupo: ma did not ask for a second drink.

(*d*) In 1936 Hivsu: Tupo: ma asked me to get him some liquor, but did not resent my refusal to comply with his request.

(*e*) On Thanksgiving Eve, 1936, Hivsu: Tupo: ma told me that he would not be able to work with me the following afternoon. I was therefore in my hotel room when, toward the middle of the afternoon, Hivsu: Tupo: ma unexpectedly visited me. He was in an advanced state of intoxication, and spontaneously admitted having bewitched two persons: his older uterine half brother Hamuly Huk'ye :rà (=ashes makes-a-line, reputed to have been a witch) who had been his mother's favorite, and Hamuly Huk'yè :ra's daughter, with whom he had had an affair which, by Mohave standards, was an incestuous one, adding that he continued to have dream intercourse with the ghost of his bewitched half niece. He denied, however, having been responsible for the death of Sudhu: rà, who was the only person ever to accuse him of witchcraft (Case 44). This confession came as a great surprise to me, since Hivsu: Tupo: ma was believed to be the prototype of the benevolent shaman. Throughout the interview Hivsu: Tupo: ma's manner toward me was a friendly one, despite the facts that his usually smiling face was distorted into a fierce scowl and that he seemed to be somewhat confused and uncertain in his movements. It is also noteworthy that, even though he usually insisted on the presence of an interpreter, he revealed on this occasion that he spoke fair English. At the end of the interview he asked for his pay and departed. In order to understand the timing of this confession, it should be added that we were working at that time on the problem of witchcraft and of the vicarious suicide of witches (Devereux, 1937 c). The next day he confirmed his confession in every detail and readily provided data concerning the age and gentile affiliation of each person mentioned in his story, but asked me not to repeat his confession to anyone, lest he should be killed for practicing witchcraft.

---

[9] La Barre (1939) cites a limerick about a young man from St. James, who set fire to his sweetheart's pubic hair.

(*f*) In the winter of 1937 my interpreter informed me by mail that Hivsu: Tupo:ma had become intoxicated, spent a cold night sleeping outdoors, and died of pneumonia resulting from this exposure.

Comment

Self-destructive mechanisms are obvious in incidents (*b*), (*e*), and (*f*). Incident (*e*) closely resembles the suicidal confession of the lesbian witch Sahaykwisa:, which caused her lovers to drown her (Case 140). Incident (*f*) was obviously the culmination of a long quest for death by violence, which nowadays is seldom meted out to shamans who also practice witchcraft (pt. 7, pp. 387–426). The self-destructive use of alcohol by an incestuous witch throws into sharp relief the psychological significance of Tcatc's "accidental" pairing of incest and drunkenness in her condemnation of the present generation.

By contrast, incidents (*a*), (*b*), and (*d*) illustrate the fundamentally kindly and courteous disposition of my old friend Hivsu: Tupo:ma, as well as certain important aspects of Mohave ethics and etiquette.

In brief, it may be stated tentatively that the oral sadistic element in shamanism (and especially in witchcraft), the psychodynamics of the fellatio pattern in Mohave society, and the self-destructive confessions of witches, as well as the close nexus between oral eroticism, witchcraft, and incest, tend to support Freud's interpretations of the oral-erotic aspect of alcohol addiction. Within certain limits, Bergler's (1944, 1946) analysis of the role of the "oral triad" in alcohol addiction is also supported by some of our Mohave data.

A more detailed inquiry into the nexus between orality and witchcraft is obviously beyond the scope of the present study. The above considerations do reveal, however, certain important implications of Mohave alcoholism. It is apparent, first of all, that alcohol tends to be equated with milk, which, in turn, is equated with saliva and semen (Devereux, 1947 a). Thus, alcohol appears to be unconsciously endowed with some of the properties of these prototypal "magic" substances. It is, therefore, interesting to mention in this context that, according to Mohave belief, magic substances are highly dangerous to the uninitiated—and even to the initiated, since they eventually get "out of hand" and injure or destroy their owner (pt. 4, pp. 202–212). The same is true of shamanistic powers, which often get out of hand (Kroeber, 1925 a) and cause the shaman to become a witch, who, in the end, seeks to be killed, in order to remain the leader and owner of his beloved ghostly victims,. Since it has been shown above that there are good reasons for assuming that the beloved dead tend to be introjected, and even incorporated, it may be assumed, at least tentatively, that, in some remote and probably unconscious manner, alcohol, too, is equated with the dead. This last interpretation is, however, quite explicitly a highly tentative hypothesis, whose verification must remain in abeyance until further data can be obtained.

4. HOMOSEXUALITY

Mohave data tend to substantiate also the theory that latent or repressed homosexuality plays a certain role in alcohol addiction.

CASE 140. (Informants: Hivsu: Tupo: ma and Hama: Utce:):

The notorious lesbian transvestite and heterosexual prostitute Sahaykwisa: spontaneously accepted noncommercial heterosexuality after she was punitively raped by a man whose wife she had tried to seduce. [The phallic kamalo:y (Devereux, 1948 f) are, likewise, "feminized" by group rape.] Her conversion to heterosexuality appears to have been a conflict-laden and traumatic event, however. First, she "fell in love" with an oldish male kinsman of hers (father image?), whom she bewitched when he spurned her advances. Next, she had an (unconsciously incestuous?) affair with this man's son, and with a friend of the latter as well. While drunk, she confessed to her two lovers that she had bewitched the father of one of them; whereupon, they drowned her (see Case 105).

Comment

An analysis of the oedipal fixations of the Mohave kamalo:y (Devereux, 1948 f) and of Mohave lesbians suggests that Sahaykwisa:'s self-destructive intoxicated behavior may have been a manifestation of her oedipal guilt feelings, which were reactivated by her conversion to heterosexuality.

If one accepts the theory that men who deliberately share a woman sexually are frequently motivated by unconscious homosexuality, then homosexual factors may also be suspected in certain other episodes:

(1) A man participated in the serial sexual abuse of his wife and only protested when his friends attempted to have *anal* intercourse with her (Devereux, 1950 a).

(2) A jealous husband discovered his wife's misbehavior, took a drink and shot himself (Case 120). Several details of this incident suggest the presence of homosexual factors. Suicide by shooting is often motivated by passive homosexual impulses. A Mohave husband, dissatisfied with his dissolute young wife, frequently marries either his hard-working mother-in-law, or else a male homosexual who takes pride in being a good "wife" (Devereux, 1951 f). Drinking before committing suicide is indirectly illustrated also by the behavior of the shaman Tâma:râhue who, after being unjustly accused of witchcraft, drank a decoction of datura, before drowning himself in the Colorado River (Case 106). Finally, since jealousy is not an approved form of Mohave behavior, and since intense jealousy is often rooted in homosexual impulses (Freud, 1923), the suicide of a jealous husband is sometimes due to the onset of a homosexual panic.

The most striking aspect of the above incidents is that, even under the influence of alcohol, the Mohave do not appear to engage in overt homosexual acts. On the other hand, intoxicated individuals sometimes engage in heterosexual anal coitus, or in incest, or else confess former incestuous activities, or deeds of witchcraft. This observation confronts us with the most difficult problem in the analysis of Mohave alcoholism.

A brief preliminary review of the relevant facts will aid in this analysis:

1. Hivsu: Tupo:ma (Case 139) committed incest and killed his mistress and her father by means of witchcraft while sober, and then confessed these acts while drunk.

2. Sahaykwisa: (Case 140), a former lesbian, committed witchcraft, and also what may have been unconsciously an incest equivalent, while sober, and confessed her act of witchcraft while drunk.

3. In a number of other instances (Devereux, 1939 a), incestuous acts occurred when one or both partners were intoxicated, and usually involved persons who engaged in witchcraft, or witch killing, or both.

The occurrence of an alcohol-incest-witchcraft cluster and the near absence of an overt alcohol-homosexuality cluster require explanation, since, at least superficially, these facts appear to contradict the theory that alcoholism is intimately connected with homosexuality. In view of Lynd's (1939) defense of "outrageous hypotheses," it might be worthwhile to consider whether or not the intoxicated Mohave might, conceivably, substitute incestuous or excessive heterosexual activities for homosexual behavior.

It is a widely accepted psychoanalytic theory that homosexuality is related to a failure to come to terms with castration anxieties elicited by oedipal impulses. Specifically, many psychoanalysts hold that homosexuality is sometimes evolved as a defense against the incestuous and aggressive wishes, and against fears of castration, which arise in connection with oedipal impulses.

The occurrence of permanent transvestitism and overt homosexuality during sobriety, the absence of casual homosexuality during intoxication, and the performing of incestuous acts by persons who are witches, or intoxicated, or both, suggest that, in certain cases, alcohol may, in some manner, retranslate homosexual impulses into those heterosexual-incestuous impulses which originally served as a point of departure for the development of defensive homosexual impulses. This tentative hypothesis is compatible with the well-established fact that alcohol tends to promote regression by "dissolving the superego," which was originally responsible for the genesis of homosexual impulses. It is quite possible that this regression may also be fostered by the presence of massive oral elements in alcohol addiction, which gratifies oral wishes and hence leads the male at least, back to a heterosexual love object: the nursing mother. As regards women, it should be recalled in this context that the actively lesbian Sahaykwisa: became acquainted with the effects of alcohol in connection with her acts of heterosexual prostitution to white men, and turned into a consistently heavy drinker when, as a result of being raped, she was "converted" to a rather immature kind of heterosexuality. The inescapable inference appears to be that she was unable to accept heterosexuality without the regression induced by alcohol (Case 105). Since the woman's first heterosexual oral objective is the father's penis, and since Mohave mythology explicity calls Bullfrog's swallowing of her father's feces (anal penis) the "first act of witchcraft" (Devereux, 1948 f), it seems permissible to assume that female homosexuality can likewise be overcome by means of an oral regression induced by alcohol.

Summing up, regression from the homosexual line of defense to incestuous acts and wishes, usually involving also oral sadistic acts of witchcraft, often appears to be facilitated by the ingestion of alcohol. This implies, perhaps, that the drinker regresses to the early developmental stage in which oedipal problems are still closely intertwined with oral impulses.

Finally, it is important to stress once more that the preceding paragraphs are highly tentative in character, and that they represent an "outrageous hypothesis" (Lynd, 1939) rather than a genuine theory, in the traditional sense of that term. This hypothesis was formulated only because the construction of an outrageous—and possibly invalid—hypothesis is at least open to refutation and tends to suggest better formulations, whereas the mere statement of a difficulty is simply the sterile evasion of a genuine problem.

5. THE RETURN OF THE REPRESSED

Throughout the preceding pages it was suggested that, in alcoholic intoxication, there is a return of the repressed, and that climactic or unusual modes of behavior occurring in a state of intoxication should be interpreted as eruptions of repressed material. It is therefore interesting to observe that the Mohave themselves are by no means unaware of the fact that the ingestion of alcohol tends to liberate repressed material. This fact was demonstrated in a striking, because indirect, manner by Tcatc's previously cited statement, which deserves to be repeated in this context. When asked to comment on the Greek adage, "The more I see of people, the better I like dogs," Tcatc replied: "The things I saw in my youth, *when I was old enough to remember what I saw*, were better than, and different from, what one sees nowadays. These constant rumors of incest, for example—they would have been unthinkable in the old days. In my youth the Mohave did not even know what alcoholic intoxication meant."

Tcatc's spontaneous and elaborate reference to infantile amnesia, and her "accidental" pairing of incest and alcoholism, are psychologically too significant to be considered fortuitous. Regardless, therefore, of how accurate or inaccurate the special formulations and interpretations proposed in this Appendix may be, the general thesis that the strikingly atypical acts of certain intoxicated persons are due to a return of the repressed may be thought of as reasonably well proved.

It is likewise, characteristic of the Mohave that the repressed material erupting during drunkenness should be aggressive and orally incestuous or aggressively sexual rather than maturely genital, since, on the whole, the average Mohave appears to have attained a reasonably high degree of psychosexual maturity.

SUMMARY

The historical, sociocultural, ego-psychological and unconscious aspects of Mohave alcoholism have been described and discussed. It was found that drinking has become fairly fully integrated with present-day Mohave culture and with Mohave psychology as well. The absence of a high level of anxiety and the preservation of certain basic cultural attitudes probably explain why, on the whole, the intoxicated Mohave is not aggressively antisocial, and why Mohave society has fairly successfully withstood the ravages of alcoholism observed in many other American Indian tribes.

ADDENDUM

A NOTE ON GENTILE AFFILIATIONS AND NAMES

Due primarily to the taboo on the names of the dead and also to other factors discussed below, absolute certainty and precision could not be achieved with regard to gentile affiliations and names. For example, as regards gentile affiliations, Pulyi :k, an excellent and meticulous informant, stated that Apen Ismalyk's gens was Mat-ha, while Apen Ismalyk himself said that he belonged to the Melyikha gens.

The gentile affiliations of the following are known to be dubious:

Amalyk Tumádha :p (Tcatc or Syuly)
Amily Nyunye : (Nyoltc or Mah)
Anyay Ha :m (Hi :pa or O :otc)
Apen Ismalyk (Melyikha, or perhaps Mat-ha). Doubts exists because he is psychotic, because his mother's gens was Melyikha, and because some details of his genealogy are questionable (Case 4).
Hamcukuenk (Nyoltc or Mu :th)
Hikye :t (O :otc or Nyoltc)
Huau Husek' (Mu :th or Hualy)
Hu :kyev Anyay (Mu :th or O :otc)
Huyatc (Mah, but if identical with Huyatc Humar, then Hualy)
Kwitcia :r (Mah or Melyikha)
Nyail Kwaki :yo (Nyoltc or O :otc)
O :olva (Tcatc or Mu :th)
Pa :hay (Kunyii :th or Mo :the)
Suhuraye (Nyoltc or, doubtfully, Kunyii :th)
Sukat (Nyoltc or Mu :ha)
Tcakwar Alaye (Kat or Mat-ha)
Tcávákye : (Hualy or Tcatc)

Other gentile affiliations may also have been misreported. Thus, Amat Hu :dhap (earth rent or torn, Hi :pa) and Amay Tudha :pa (sky rent or torn, Syuly) may perhaps be the same person, for reasons explained further below, in connection with similar sounding, plural names, which may belong either to one person or else to two people, one of whom has imitated the name of the other, and adopted this imitated name for himself.

These observations make it necessary to discuss briefly the difficulties met with in recording Mohave names.

Few Mohave have names made up of one word only. On closer inquiry it often turns out that a routinely used one-word name is but a fragment of a name made up of several words (Tcilyetcilye

vs. Hispan Himith Tcilyetcilye) or is a compression of several fragmentary words into one word.   Indeed, the great length of the average Mohave name automatically leads to the gradual erosion of that
name.   Thus, the habitually used name Sahaykwisa turned out to
be a compression of Masahay Matkwisa Mànye: while the full name
of the person always spoken of as Toskinyil is actually Kamtoskà
Huanyeily.   During this process of erosion, syllables and even words
are dropped, stresses and vowel lengths are displayed, vowels are
changed (Hispan Tàruu:ly becoming Pantàràuly), consonants are
modified (s turns into th, especially in the case of toothless informants,
but also vice versa; h, k and t are used interchangeably, etc.) and
words, or fragments of words, are run together.

The position taken here is that the effective and functional "real"
name of, e.g., Kamtoskà Huanyeily is actually "Toskinyil," precisely
the way the "real" (spoken) name of Cholmondeley is Chumley.
When this problem was discussed with Prof. John Lotz, of Columbia
University, he suggested that these abbreviated names be designated
as allonoms, a term patterned upon such linguistic terms as allophons
and allologs.

Unfortunately for the etymologist, the exclusive use of an allonom
tends to obliterate the full name whose contraction it represents.   As
a result, especially in the case of deceased persons, the reconstruction
of the (forgotten) full name from the abbreviated allonom is sometimes entirely impossible.   In other instances two equally competent
informants reconstruct the full form of an allonom in two different
ways, which sometimes causes one to assume that the two differently
reconstructed full names are the names of two different persons.

The situation is further aggravated by the fact that the new and
striking name of individual A may cause individual B to select for
himself a similar name.   Moreover, when both of such paired names
are quite long, the process of erosion to which both are subjected sometimes causes the final (abridged) allonoms to resemble each other
even more than the two full paired names did.

A further source of doubt as to whether one is dealing with one
individual having several names or else with two distinct individuals,
each of whom has one name, is the fact that one and the same individual may, successively or else simultaneously, have more than one
name, two of which may actually resemble each other.

A curious, but not unique, variety of the latter type of double names
is a certain man's name which means "elephant's anus."   In Mohave,
this name is used in two forms.   One is Elefant Hiwey.   In the other
form the borrowed word "elefant" is replaced by the made-up Mohave
name for the elephant: "strong enough to stop a train."   In this
instance, a special inquiry was needed in order to ascertain that these
paired names were those of one person, rather than the names of two

people, one of whom had imitated the other, and both of whom had followed the Mohave fashion in self-naming which prevailed in the 1920's, when more than a dozen men had names which contained such words as "anus" and "feces."

Sometimes one also discovers in one's field notes two almost identical appearing allonoms. In some cases these similarities are due to the fact that two informants—one of whom may have been toothless, or else given to running words together in a particular way—simply pronounced the same allonom somewhat differently. In other cases, however, one wonders whether one is actually dealing with two different though similar sounding abridged names, and whether these two names are the paired names of two different persons, or else the similar sounding and simultaneously valid names of one individual, who happens to be fond of certain words and uses them in several of his names.

In Mohave society such difficulties cannot be disposed of by recourse to the genealogical method, because of such factors as the taboo on the names of the dead, unstable marriages, illegitimacy, alleged changes of social identity while still in utero, and the added confusion created by the introduction of English family names. As for the direct questioning of the individuals concerned, it is, in some cases, simply a further source of confusion. For example, it is almost certain that Tcatc did not know that she had several nicknames—some of them in English—all of which involved allusions to her bent back. Also, some individuals resent any mention of their early baby-names, discarded personal names, or offensive nicknames; in addition, unless they know the anthropologist personally, they may not be willing to admit that an especially obscene name is one of their currently valid multiple names.

Still more confusion is created by the fact that different informants may call a given person by different names. In 1932, when Hivsu: Tupo:ma had just discarded the name Siwi:, many people still referred to him by that name, though by 1938 most people called him by his new name. Moreover, when a person has simultaneously a neutral and an obscene name, there is a slight tendency to use this neutral ("decent") name when discussing his nonsexual behavior, and to call him by his obscene name when reporting some of his more grotesque sexual exploits. The ultimate in idiosyncratic naming was reached by Hivsu: Tupo:ma, who personally gave a certain man an obscene nickname and habitually referred to him by that name even though no one else did so.

The Mohave themselves seem keenly aware of the difficulties resulting from this proliferation of names. As a result, they increasingly use Agency-given English names, or else—unless they are quite certain that their interlocutor knows whom they are discussing—use both the Mohave and the English name of the person who is being discussed; e.g., they may say: "Hivsu: Tupo:ma—Dan Lamont," even when speaking Mohave with each other.

Despite these difficulties, it is almost certain that 90 to 95 percent of the names and gentile affiliations recorded in this book are correct, and involve neither the treating of one person as two individuals, nor of two persons as one individual. Of the remainder, many are the names of dead persons, which means that weeks would have had to be spent in order to ascertain beyond question the gentile affiliations and correct names of the deceased. This was not done, since it was felt that the time in the field could be more profitably spent in other ways, especially since it seemed obvious that the validity of the anthropological and psychiatric data reported in this work would not be materially increased by making quite certain that individual X was a member of the Kat rather than of the Hualy gens—except, of course, in connection with alleged cases of incest, where every effort was made to clarify these relevant details. In brief, it is felt that the degree of precision achieved in regard to names, multiple names, and gens affiliations is entirely adequate for the purposes of the present work.

ADDENDA TO THE REPRINT EDITION

page 77, note 54, line 2
insert after parenthesis (see Case 19)
page 125, Case 29
Mrs. Hilyera Anyay's name is Melyikha; her father was a shaman, whose specialty is no longer remembered.
page 146
insert after last line Some other informants held that Le:va was not bewitched, but simply suffered from itcema:v hahnok (food-caused disease); this, however, happens to be precisely the disease which his uterine half-brother could cure and could, therefore, cause the victims of his witchcraft to contract. These informants, too, said that itcema:v hahnok is a kind of ahwe: hahnok illness, or at least very similar to it.
page 175, Case 46
Some say G. A. is Ave: Pu:ly's daughter (see Case 60), but this is extremely unlikely.
page 176
insert after paragraph 3 Given the capacity of ghosts to cause insanity, it is of special interest that, in reply both to direct questions and to the citing of relevant Sedang beliefs, both Tcatc and Pulyi:k denied that the ghosts of those who died insane were inclined or able to cause the living to become insane. Tcatc added, however, that the ghost of a person who dies insane remains insane also in Calya:yt, the land of the dead, since ghosts repeat their life on earth in four different metamorphoses (Devereux, 1937 a). Asked which of man's four souls becomes insane, Tcatc said: "Different persons would give different answers; a lay person might not give the same answer as a shaman. The soul that goes insane

is the fourth soul—the one that goes to the land of the dead; it is the 'real shadow'—the makwisa: taha:na. That is the soul that gets people into trouble, because it is always on the go'' (i.e., hyperactive, see Pt. 2, pp. 46–54).

page 220

insert 3 lines from bottom of text Pulyi:k said that ''some people'' were compulsive but could cite no example. His statement may be due to a misunderstanding of my explanation.

pages 222ff., additional discussion

Pages 222ff. and 303ff. seem to contradict each other only if one fails to differentiate sharply between schizophrenia (a psychosis) and schizoidness (a character disorder). Actually, the views expressed on pp. 222ff. are strongly reinforced by two findings: (1) In pre-contemporary Mohave society apparently even the schizoid (pp. 303ff.) did not develop a genuine (''nuclear'' or ''process'') schizophrenia. (2) Even if one supposes that, under aboriginal (and early Reservation) conditions, there were no schizophrenics only because those who sensed the onset of a (schizophrenic?) psychosis committed genuine or vicarious suicide (p. 301), the generally admitted recent increase in Mohave suicide rates (p. 316) makes it even more certain that genuine schizophrenia was absent in aboriginal and even in early Reservation times.

Recent, and often excellent, field studies in Africa (M. J. Field, *Search for Security*, London, 1960; A. H. Leighton et al., *Psychiatric Disorder among the Yoruba*, Ithaca, N. Y., 1963, etc.) and elsewhere simply cannot disprove my basic thesis.

Indeed, by now, every ''primitive'' tribe is simply too acculturated to be free of schizophrenia. Also, it was far less stressful and disorienting for the mid 19th-century Mohave to become acculturated to a world of rationally used firearms and plows than it is for mid 20th-century New Guinea highlanders to become acculturated to a world of helicopters and atom bombs, brought to them by conquerors or acculturators who are, themselves, almost schizophrenically disoriented (Devereux, 1939 d) in the hallucinatory, and hallucinatorily used, mytho-technology and mytho-society they have created.

Last, but not least, even the culturally most negativistic (Devereux, 1940 a) mid 19th-century prairie man or beachcomber probably had more self-confidence and a deeper commitment to the civilization he was—at times unwittingly—mediating to the ''primitive'' than has the most ''virtuous'' mid 20th-century Occidental acculturator, who unjustifiably doubts and despises the civilization he purports to represent.

Given this state of affairs, schizophrenia cannot but be present in every society which comes in contact with such acculturators, and the mid 20th-century field ethnopsychiatrist can therefore no longer hope to find a tribe sufficiently intact to be entirely free of schizophrenia.

page 243

insert 4 lines from bottom of page

MANIA OF PERSECUTION

According to Tcatc, persecution mania is unknown. She may well be right, though some witchcraft panics resemble that condition in some respects.

page 245

insert after line 3

KLEPTOMANIA

Pulyi:k claims that C.B. (Hualy gens, ''Moon'') is a kleptomaniac. This is almost certainly wrong.

page 283, Case 79

This girl is almost certainly Nyoltc Hukthar (Case 13).

page 284

insert 5 lines from bottom of text For the Mohave's interest in the hissing sound of urination, cf. Case 26.

page 303

see addendum to p. 222

page 478

insert 10 lines from bottom after "Subgroup I"

It is striking that the three individuals about to be discussed, who committed suicide because of their social rejection or isolation: (1) used traditional means (see pp. 322–323), (2) suffocated themselves as (socially unwanted) halfbreed babies and also puppies were suffocated (buried alive), and (3) two of them (cases 106 and 123) reacted to their deprivation by recourse to oral-incorporative means of suicide (poison and drowning, geophagy), the third by oral-respiratory frustrative means (hanging).

Given the Mohave tendency to view oral deprivation as a token of lack of love (pp. 340–347), the facts just cited seem at least suggestive and are probably significant.

BIBLIOGRAPHY

ABRAHAM, KARL.
  1927. Selected papers of. London.
ACKERKNECHT, ERWIN H.
  1943. Psychopathology, primitive medicine and primitive culture. Bull.
    Hist. Medicine, vol. 14, pp. 30–67.
AGOSTON, TIBOR.
  1944. Experimental administration of benzedrine sulfate and other central
    stimulants in psychoanalyses and psychotherapies. Psychoanal.
    Rev., vol. 31, pp. 438–452.
ALLEE, CLYDE WARDER, and BOWEN, EDITH STEELE.
  1932. Studies in animal aggregations. Mass protection against colloidal
    silver among goldfishes. Journ. Exper. Zool., vol. 61, No. 2, pp. 185–
    207.
ALLEN, G. A.
  1891. Manners and customs of the Mohaves. Ann. Rep. Smithsonian In-
    stitution for 1890, pp. 615–616.
ALLPORT, G. W.
  1937. Personality: a psychological interpretation. New York.
ALLPORT, GORDON W., and VERNON, P. E.
  1933. Studies in expressive movement. New York.
ANONYMOUS.
  [n.d.] Hikayat Hang Toeah. Batavia, Java, Balei Poestaka, 1930 [Ro-
    manized edition in 3 fascicules.]
ARISTOTLE.
  [n.d.] De divinatione per somnum.
BAILEY, FLORA L.
  1950. Some sex beliefs and practices in a Navaho community. Pap. pea-
    body Mus. Amer. Archeol. and Ethnol., vol. 40, No. 2.
BARTEMEIER, L. H.
  1950. Illness following dreams. Internat. Journ. Psychoanalysis, vol. 31,
    pp. 8–11.
BARTON, R. F.
  1938. Philippine pagans. London.
BATESON, GREGORY, and MEAD, MARGARET.
  1942. Balinese character: A photographic analysis. New York Academy of
    Sciences, New York.
BATESON, GREGORY; JACKSON, D. D.; HALEY, JAY; and WEAKLAND, JOHN.
  1956. Toward a theory of schizophrenia. Behavioral Science, vol. 1, No. 4,
    pp. 251–264.
BELL, ERIC TEMPLE.
  1937. Men of mathematics. New York.
BENEDICT, RUTH.
  1934. Patterns of culture. Boston.
  1938. Continuities and discontinuities in cultural conditioning. Psychiatry,
    vol. 1, pp. 161–167.

BERGLER, EDMUND.
    1943. The gambler: a misunderstood neurotic. Journ. Criminal Psycho-
        pathology, vol. 4, pp. 379–393.
    1944. Contributions to the psychogenesis of alcohol addiction. Quart.
        Journ. Stud. Alcohol, vol. 5, pp. 434–439.
    1946. Personality traits of alcohol addicts. Quart. Journ. Stud. Alcohol,
        vol. 7, pp. 356–359.
BERLINER, BERNHARD.
    1947. On some psychodynamics of masochism. Psychoanal. Quart., vol.
        16, pp. 459–471.
BERNDT, RONALD M., and BERNDT, CATHERINE H.
    1951. Sexual behavior in Western Arnheim Land. Viking Fund Publ.
        Anthrop. No. 16. New York.
BEXTON, W. H.; HERON, W.; and SCOTT, T. H.
    1954. Effects of decreased variation in the sensory environment. Canadian
        Journ. Psychol., vol. 8, pp. 70–76.
BIRD, BRIAN.
    1958. A study of the bisexual meaning of the foreskin. Journ. Amer.
        Psychoanalytic Assoc., vol. 6, pp. 287–304.
BIRDWHISTELL, RAY L.
    1952. Introduction to kinesics. Louisville, Ky.
BLAKE, R. R., AND RAMSEY, G. V.
    1951. Perception: an approach to personality. New York.
BOGORAS, WALDEMAR.
    1904. The Chukchee; I. Material culture. Amer. Mus. Nat. Hist., Mem.,
        vol. 11. Leiden.
BOURKE, JOHN G.
    1889. Notes on the cosmogony and theogony of the Mojave Indians of the
        Rio Colorado, Arizona. Journ. Amer. Folklore, vol. 2, pp. 169–189.
BRILL, A. A.
    1934. Psychic suicide. Journ. Nervous and Mental Diseases, vol. 80, pp. 63–
        64.
BRODY, SYLVIA.
    1956. Patterns of mothering. New York.
BURBANK, E. A. (with ROYCE, E., and TAYLOR, J. F.).
    1944. Burbank among the Indians. Caldwell, Idaho.
CANNON, W. B.
    1942. Voodoo death. Amer. Anthrop., n.s., vol. 44, pp. 169–181.
CAROTHERS, J. C.
    1947. A study of mental derangement in Africans, and an attempt to ex-
        plain its peculiarities, more especially in relation to the African
        attitude to life. Journ. Mental Sci., vol. 93, pp. 548–597.
CHAPIN, F. S.
    1934. Latent culture patterns of the unseen world of social reality. Amer.
        Journ. Sociol., vol. 40, pp. 61–68.
    1935. Contemporary American institutions. New York.
CLEMENTS, F. E.
    1932. Primitive concepts of disease. Univ. California Publ. Amer. Archaeol.
        and Ethnol., vol. 32, pp. 185–252.
CONDOMINAS, GEORGES.
    1957. Nous avons mangé la forêt. Paris.
COURVILLE, C. B.
    1950. A contribution to the study of cerebral anoxia. Bull. Los Angeles
        Neurological Soc., vol. 15, pp. 99–195.

Cox, Sir E.
    1911. Police and crime in India. London.
Cressey, P. F.
    1936. The criminal tribes of India. Sociol. and Soc. Res., vol. 20, pp.
        503–511; vol. 21, pp. 18–25.
Czaplicka, Marie Antoinette.
    1914. Aboriginal Siberia. Oxford.
Davis, Kingsley.
    1936. Jealousy and sexual property. Social Forces, vol. 14, No. 3, pp.
        395–405.
    1937. The sociology of prostitution. Amer. Sociol. Rev., vol. 2, pp. 744–755.
Deutsch, Helene.
    1944–45. The psychology of women. 2 vols. New York.
Devereux, George.
    MS., 1933–34. Sedang Moi field notes.
    MS., 1935. Sexual life of the Mohave Indians. (Doctoral dissertation, type-
        script.) University of California Library, Berkeley.
    1937 a. Mohave soul concepts. Amer. Anthrop., n.s. vol. 39, pp. 417–422.
    1937 b. Institutionalized homosexuality of the Mohave Indians. Human
        Biol., vol. 9, pp. 498–527.
    1937 c. L'envoûtement chez les Indiens Mohave. Journ. Soc. des Améri-
        canistes de Paris, n.s., vol. 29, pp. 405–412.
    1937 d. Der Begriff der Vaterschaft bei den Mohave Indianern. Zeitschrift
        für Ethnologie, vol. 69, pp. 72–78.
    1937 e. Functioning units in Há(rhn) de:a(ng) society. Primitive Man,
        vol. 10, pp. 1–7.
    1939 a. The social and cultural implications of incest among the Mohave
        Indians. Psychoanalytic Quart., vol. 8, pp. 510–533.
    1939 b. Mohave culture and personality. Character and Personality, vol.
        8, pp. 91–109.
    1939 c. Maladjustment and social neurosis. Amer. Sociol. Rev., vol. 4,
        pp. 844–851.
    1939 d. A sociological theory of schizophrenia. Psychoanalytic Rev., vol.
        26, pp. 315–342.
    1940 a. Social negativism and criminal psychopathology. Journ. Criminal
        Psychopathology, vol. 1, pp. 325–338.
    1940 b. A conceptual scheme of society. Amer. Journ. Sociol., vol. 54,
        pp. 687–706.
    1940 c. Religious attitudes of the Sedang. In Sociology, by Ogburn, W. F.,
        and Nimkoff, M. F., Cambridge, Mass.
    1940 d. Primitive psychiatry. Part 1: Hi:wa itck. Bull. Hist. Medicine,
        vol. 8, pp. 1194–1213.
    1941. Mohave beliefs concerning twins. Amer Anthrop., n.s., vol. 43, pp.
        573–592.
    1942 a. Primitive psychiatry. Part 2: Funeral suicide. Bull. Hist. Medi-
        cine, vol. 11, pp. 522–542.
    1942 b. Motivation and control of crime. Journ. Criminal Psychopathology,
        vol. 3, pp. 553–584.
    1942 c. The mental hygiene of the American Indian. Mental Hygiene,
        vol. 26, pp. 71–84.
    1942 d. Social structure and the economy of affective bonds. Psycho-
        analytic Rev., vol. 29, pp. 303–314.
    1942 e. Review of Drucker (1941) Amer. Anthrop., n.s., vol. 44, pp. 480–481.

DEVEREUX, GEORGE—Continued

1944 a. A note on classical Chinese penological thought. Journ. Criminal Psychopathology, vol. 5, pp. 735–744.

1944 b. The social structure of a schizophrenia ward and its therapeutic fitness. Journ. Clinical Psychopathology, vol. 6, pp. 231–265.

1945 a. The logical foundations of culture and personality studies. Trans. New York Acad. Sci., ser. 2, vol. 7, pp. 110–130.

1945 b. The convergence between delusion and motor behavior in schizophrenia. Journ. Clinical Psychopathology, vol. 7, pp. 89–96.

1946.   La chasse collective au lapin chez les Hopi, Oraibi, Arizona. Journ. Soc. des Américanistes de Paris, n.s., vol. 33, pp. 63–90.

1947 a. Mohave orality: An analysis of nursing and weaning customs. Psychoanalytic Quart., vol. 16, pp. 519–546.

1947 b. The potential contributions of the Moi to the cultural landscape of Indochina. Far Eastern Quart., vol. 6, pp. 390–395.

1948 a. Mohave etiquette. Southwest Mus. Leaflets No. 22.

1948 b. Mohave pregnancy. Acta Americana, vol. 6, pp. 89–116.

1948 c. The Mohave neonate and its cradle. Primitive Man, vol. 21, pp. 1–18.

1948 d. Mohave Indian infanticide. Psychoanalytic Rev., vol. 35, pp. 126–139.

1948 e. Mohave Indian obstetrics. American Imago, vol. 5, pp. 95–139.

1948 f. The Mohave Indian kamalo: y. Journ. Clinical Psychopathology, vol. 9, pp. 433–457.

1948. g. Mohave zoophilia. Samīkṣā, Journ. Indian Psycho-Analytical Soc., vol. 2, pp. 227–245.

1948 h. Mohave coyote tales. Journ. Amer. Folklore, vol. 61, pp. 233–255.

1948 i. The function of alcohol in Mohave society. Quart. Journ. Stud. Alcohol, vol. 9, pp. 207–251.

1948 j. See Menninger, Karl Augustus, and Devereux, George.

1949 a. The Mohave male puberty rite. Samīkṣā, Journ. Indian Psycho-Analytical Soc., vol. 3, pp. 11–25.

1949 b. Some Mohave gestures. Amer. Anthrop., n.s., vol. 51, pp. 325–326.

1949 c. Mohave paternity. Samīksā, Journ. Indian Psycho-Analytical Soc., vol. 3, pp. 162–194.

1949 d. Post-partum parental observances of the Mohave Indians. Trans. Kansas Acad. Sci., vol. 52, pp. 458–465.

1949 e. Mohave voice and speech mannerisms. Word, vol. 5, pp. 268–272.

1949 f. Magic substances and narcotics of the Mohave Indians. British Journ. Med. Psychol., vol 22, pp. 110–116.

1950 a. Heterosexual behavior of the Mohave Indians. In Psychoanalysis and the Social Sciences, Róheim, Géza (ed.) vol. 2. New York.

1950 b. Notes on the developmental pattern and organic needs of Mohave Indian children. Trans. Kansas Acad. Sci., vol. 53, pp. 178–185.

1950 c. Mohave Indian autoerotic behavior. Psychoanalytic Rev., vol. 37, pp. 201–220.

1950 d. Psychodynamics of Mohave gambling. American Imago, vol. 7, pp. 55–65.

1950 e. Amusements and sports of Mohave children. The Masterkey, vol. 24, pp. 143–152.

1950 f. Status, socialization and interpersonal relations of Mohave children. Psychiatry, vol. 13, pp. 489–502.

DEVEREUX, GEORGE—Continued

1950 g. The psychology of feminine genital bleeding: An analysis of Mohave Indian puberty and menstrual rites. Internat. Journ. Psychoanalysis, vol. 31, pp. 237–257.

1950 h. Education and discipline in Mohave society. Primitive Man, vol. 23, pp. 85–102.

1951 a. Reality and dream: The psychotherapy of a Plains Indian. New York.

1951 b. Mohave chieftainship in action. Plateau, vol. 23, pp. 33–43.

1951 c. Mohave Indian verbal and motor profanity. In Róheim, Géza (ed): Psychoanalysis and the Social Sciences, vol. 3. New York.

1951 d. The primal scene and juvenile heterosexuality in Mohave society. In Psychoanalysis and Culture (Róheim Festschrift). Wilbur, G. B., and Muensterberger, Warner, editors. New York.

1951 e. Cultural and characterological traits of the Mohave related to the anal stage of psychosexual development. Psychoanalytic Quart., vol. 20, pp. 398–422.

1951 f. Atypical and deviant Mohave marriages. Samīkṣā, Journ. Indian Psycho-Analytical Soc., vol. 4, pp. 200–215.

1951 g. Neurotic crime vs. criminal behavior. Psychiatric Quart., vol. 25, pp. 73–80.

1951 h. Logical status and methodological problems of research in clinical psychiatry. Psychiatry, vol. 14, pp. 327–330.

1951 i. Three technical problems in the psychotherapy of Plains Indian patients. Amer. Journ. Psychotherapy, vol. 5, pp. 411–423.

1952 a. Psychiatry and anthropology: Some research objectives. Bull. Menninger Clinic, vol. 16, pp. 167–177.

1952 b. Practical problems of conceptual psychiatric research. Psychiatry, vol. 15, pp. 189–192.

1953 a. (ed.) Psychoanalysis and the occult. New York.

1953 b. Cultural factors in psychoanalytic therapy. Journ. American Psychoanalytic Assoc., vol. 1, pp. 629–655.

1953 c. Why Oedipus killed Laius. Internat. Journ. Psycho-Analysis, vol. 34, pp. 132–141.

1954 a. Belief, superstition and symptom. Samīkṣā, Journ. Indian Psycho-Analytical Soc., vol. 8, pp. 210–215.

1954 b. Primitive genital mutilations in a neurotic's dream. Journ. American Psychoanalytic Assoc., vol. 2, pp. 484–492.

1954 c. The denial of the anus in neurosis and culture. Bull. Philadelphia Assoc. for Psychoanalysis, vol. 4, pp. 24–27.

1955 a. A study of abortion in primitive societies. New York.

1955 b. Charismatic leadership and crisis. In Psychoanalysis and the Social Sciences, Muensterberger, Warner (ed.), vol. 4. New York.

1956 a. Therapeutic education. New York.

1956 b. Normal and abnormal: The key problem of psychiatric anthropology. In Some uses of anthropology, theoretical and applied. Anthrop. Soc. Washington. Washington, D.C.

1956 c. Mohave dreams of omen and power. Tomorrow, vol. 4, No. 3, pp. 17–24.

1956 d. The origin of shamanistic powers as reflected in a neurosis. Revue Internationale d'Ethnopsychologie Normale et Pathologique, vol. 1, pp. 19–29.

DEVEREUX, GEORGE—Continued

1957 a. Psychoanalysis as anthropological field work: Data and theoretical implications. Trans. New York Acad. Sci. Series 2, vol. 19, No. 5, pp. 457–472.

1957 b. Dream learning and individual ritual differences in Mohave shamanism. Amer. Anthrop., n.s. vol. 59, pp. 1036–1045.

1957 c. The criteria of dual competence in psychiatric anthropological studies. Journ. Hillside Hospital, vol. 6, No. 2, pp. 87–90.

1958 a. The significance of the external female genitalia and of female orgasm for the male. Journ. Amer. Psychoanalytic Assoc., vol. 6, No. 2, pp. 278–286.

1958 b. Cultural thought models in primitive and modern psychiatric theories. Psychiatry, vol. 21, No. 4, pp. 359–374.

1958 c. The cultural implementation of defense mechanisms. Lecture before the Philadelphia Association for Psychoanalysis.

DEVEREUX, GEORGE, and LOEB, EDWIN M.

1943 a. Antagonistic acculturation. Amer. Sociol. Rev., vol. 7, pp. 133–147.

1943 b. Some notes on Apache criminality. Journ. Criminal Psychopathology, vol. 4, pp. 424–430.

DEVEREUX, GEORGE, and MOOS, M. C.

1942. The social structure of prisons and the organic tensions. Journ. Criminal Psychopathology, vol. 4, pp. 306–324.

DEVEREUX, GEORGE, and WEINER, F. R.

1950. The occupational status of nurses. Amer. Sociol. Rev., vol. 15, pp. 628–634.

DOBYNS, H.F., ET AL.

1957. Thematic changes in Yuman warfare. In Cultural stability and cultural change. Ray, V. F. (ed.) Amer. Ethnol. Soc., Proc. Ann. Spring Meeting.

DODDS, E. R.

1951. The Greeks and the irrational. Berkeley.

DRUCKER, PHILIP.

1941. Culture element distributions: XVII Yuman-Piman. Anthrop. Rec., vol. 6, No. 3.

DURKHEIM, ÉMILE.

1897. Le suicide. Paris.

DURKHEIM, ÉMILE, and MAUSS, MARCEL.

1903. De quelques formes primitives de classification. Année Sociologique, vol. 6, pp. 1–72 (1901–2). Paris.

1912. Les formes élémentaires de la vie religieuse. Paris.

EILERS, ANNELIESE.

1934. Inseln um Ponape (Kapingamarangi, Nukuor, Ngatik, Mokil, Pingelap). In Ergebnisse der Südsee-Expedition 1908–1910. Thilenius, Georg (ed.). II.B., vol. 8, pp. 1–464. Hamburg.

ELIADE, MIRCEA.

1951. Le chamanisme et les techniques archaïques de l'extase. Paris.

ELLIS, FLORENCE HAWLEY.

1951. Patterns of aggression and the war cult in Southwestern Pueblos. Southwestern Journ. Anthrop., vol. 7, No. 2, pp. 177–201.

ERIKSON, ERIK H.

1943. Observations on the Yurok: Childhood and world image. Univ. California Publ. Amer. Archaeol. and Ethnol., vol. 35, No. 10.

FATHAUER, GEORGE H.
    1951. The Mohave "ghost doctor." Amer. Anthrop., n.s., vol. 53, pp. 605–607.
    1954. The structure and causation of Mohave warfare. Southwestern Journ.
        Anthrop., vol. 10, No. 1, pp. 97–118.
FEDERN, PAUL.
    1929. Selbstmordprophylaxe in der Analyse. Z. psychoanal. Pädag., vol.
        3, pp. 379–389.
FENICHEL, OTTO.
    1945. The psychoanalytic theory of neurosis. New York.
    1953. The collected papers of. Vol. 1. New York.
    1954. The collected papers of. Vol. 2. New York.
FENTON, WILLIAM N.
    1941. Iroquois suicide: A study in the stability of a culture pattern. Bur.
        Amer. Ethnol. Bull. 128, Anthrop. Pap. No. 14, pp. 79–136.
FERENCZI, SÁNDOR.
    1926. Further contributions to the theory and technique of psychoanalysis.
        London.
FINSCH, OTTO.
    1880. Über die Bewohner von Ponape (östl. Carolinen). Zeitschrift für
        Ethnologie, vol. 12, pp. 301–332.
FORDE, C. D.
    1931. Ethnography of the Yuma Indians. Univ. California Publ. Amer.
        Archaeol. and Ethnol., vol. 28, No. 4.
FORTUNE, REO F.
    1932. Sorcerers of Dobu. London.
FREUD, ANNA.
    1946. The ego and the mechanisms of defense. New York.
FREUD, SIGMUND.
    1917. Delusion and dream. New York.
    1922. Beyond the pleasure principle. London.
    1923. Certain neurotic mechanisms in jealousy, paranoia and homosexuality.
        Int. Journ. Psycho-Anal., vol. 4, pp. 1–10.
    1924 a. Obsessive acts and religious practices. Collected papers II. London.
    1924 b. Fausse Reconnaissance. Collected papers, II. London.
    1925 a. Repression. Collected papers, IV. London.
    1925 b. A note on the unconscious in psycho-analysis. Collected papers IV.
        London.
    1925 c. The occurrence in dreams of material from fairy tales. Collected
        papers, IV. London.
    1925 d. Mourning and melancholia. Collected papers, IV. London.
    1930. Three contributions to the theory of sex. Nervous and Mental Disease
        Monographs (4th rev. ed.). New York.
    1938. Wit and its relation to the unconscious. The Basic Writings of Sig-
        mund Freud. New York.
    1943. Moral responsibility for the content of dreams. Internat. Journ.
        Psycho-Analysis, vol. 24, pp. 72–73.
    1950. A premonitory dream fulfilled. Collected papers, V. London.
    1952. Totem and taboo. New York.
    1953. The interpretation of dreams. Vols. 4 and 5. Standard Edition of
        the Complete Psychological Works of Sigmund Freud. London.
FRIEDLÄNDER, KÄTE.
    1940. On the "longing to die." Int. Journ. Psycho-Anal., vol. 21, pp. 416–426.
FÜRER-HAIMENDORF, CHRISTOPH VON.
    1946. The naked Nagas. Calcutta.

GARCÉS, FRANCISCO.
  1900. *In* On the trail of a Spanish pioneer. Coues, Elliot (ed.). 2 vols.
    New York.

GAYTON, A. H.
  1935. The Orpheus myth in North America. Journ. Amer. Folklore, vol. 48,
    pp. 263–293.

GERŐ, GEORGE.
  1953. An equivalent of depression: anorexia. *In* Affective Disorders.
    Greenacre, Phyllis (ed.). New York.

GIFFORD, EDWARD WINSLOW.
  1918. Clans and moieties in Southern California. Univ. California Publ.
    Amer. Archaeol. and Ethnol., vol. 14, No. 2.
  1922. California kinship terminologies. Univ. California Publ. Amer.
    Archaeol. and Ethnol., vol. 18, No. 1.
  1931. The Kamia of Imperial Valley. Bur. Amer. Ethnol. Bull. 97.
  1932. The southeastern Yavapai. Univ. Calif. Publ. Amer. Archaeol. and
    Ethnol., vol 29, No. 3.
  1936. Northeastern and western Yavapai. Univ. Calif. Publ. Amer. Archaeol.
    and Ethnol., vol. 34, No. 4.

GLADWIN, THOMAS, and SARASON, SEYMOUR B.
  1953. Truk: Man in paradise. Viking Fund Publ. Anthrop. No. 20. New
    York.

GLOVER, EDWARD.
  1932. Common problems in psycho-analysis and anthropology: drug ritual
    and addiction. Brit. Journ. Med. Psychol., vol. 12, pp. 109–131.

GROSS, ALFRED.
  1935. The psychic effects of toxic and toxoid substances. Int. Journ. Psy-
    cho-Anal., vol. 16, pp. 425–438.

GROUP FOR THE ADVANCEMENT OF PSYCHIATRY.
  1956. Factors used to increase the susceptibility of individuals to forceful
    indoctrination: Observations and experiments. Group for the Ad-
    vancement of Psychiatry, Symposium 3. New York.

GROUSSET, RENÉ.
  1941. L'empire Mongol (1ʳᵉ phase). *In* Historie du Monde, Cavaignac, E.
    (ed.), vol. 8, pt. 3. Paris.

HALL, SHARLOT.
  1903. The burning of a Mojave chief. Out West, vol. 18, pp. 60–65.

HALLOWELL, A. IRVING.
  1939. Sin, sex and sickness in Saulteaux belief. British Journ. Med.
    Psychol., vol. 18, pp. 191–197.
  1955. Culture and experience. Philadelphia.

HARRINGTON, JOHN PEABODY.
  1908. A Yuma account of origins. Journ. Amer. Folklore, vol. 21, No. 82,
    pp. 324–348.

HASANAT, ABUL.
  n.d. Crime and criminal justice. Standard Library, Dacca, Bengal, India.
    See Owens, C. D., 1941.

HERON, W., BEXTON, W. H., and HEBB, D. O.
  1953. Cognitive effects of decreased variation in the sensory environment.
    Amer. Psychologist, vol. 8, p. 366.

HERSKOVITS, M. J.
  1940. The economic life of primitive people. New York.

HINKLE, L. E., JR., ET AL.
  1957. Studies in human ecology. Amer. Journ. Psychiatry, vol. 114, pp.
       212–220.
HINKLE, L. E., JR., and WOLFF, H. G.
  1956. Communist interrogation and indoctrination of "enemies of the
       state." Archives of Neurology and Psychiatry, vol. 76, pp. 115–174.
  1957. The nature of man's adaptation to his total environment and the rela-
       tion of this to illness. Archives of Internal Medicine, vol. 99, pp.
       442–460.
HIPPOCRATES.
  [n.d.] De morbo sacro.
  [n.d.] Prognosticon.
HITSCHMANN, EDWARD, and BERGLER, EDMUND.
  1936. Frigidity in women. Nervous and Mental Disease Publ. Co., New
       York.
HONIGMANN, JOHN J.
  1954. Culture and personality. New York.
HORTON, DONALD.
  1943. The function of alcohol in primitive societies: a cross-cultural survey.
       Quart. Journ. Stud. Alcohol, vol. 4, pp. 199–320.
HRDLIČKA, ALEŠ
  1908. Physiological and medical observations among the Indians of South-
       western United States and Northern Mexico. Bur. Amer. Ethnol.
       Bull. 34.
HRDLIČKA, ALEŠ
  1953. Conceptions of the soul among North American Indians. Ethnograph-
       ical Mus. Sweden. Monogr. Ser. Publ. No. 1. Stockholm.
HUNDT, JOACHIM.
  1935. Der Traumglaube bei Homer. Greifswald.
HURLEY, VIC.
  1936. The swish of the kris. New York.
HUTTON, J. S.
  1921 a. The Sema Nagas. London.
  1921 b. The Angami Nagas. London.
JOKL, ROBERT HANS.
  1950. Psychic determinism and preservation of sublimation in classical
       psychoanalytic procedure. Bull. Menninger Clinic, vol. 14, pp.
       207–219.
JONES, ERNEST.
  1923. Papers on psychoanalysis. New York.
  1931. On the nightmare. London.
  1951. Essays in applied psychoanalysis. 2 vols. London.
KARDINER, ABRAM, and LINTON, RALPH.
  1939. The individual and his society. New York.
KELLY, WILLIAM H.
  1942. Cocopa gentes. Amer. Anthrop., n.s., vol. 44, No. 4, pp. 675–691.
  1949. Cocopa attitudes and practices with respect to death and mourning.
       Southwestern Journ. Anthrop., vol. 5, No. 2, pp. 151–164.
KENNARD, EDWARD A.
  1937. Hopi reactions to death. American Anthrop., n.s., vol. 39, pp. 491–496.
KRAEPELIN, EMIL.
  1904. Vergleichende Psychiatrie. Centralblatt für Nervenheilkunde und
       Psychiatrie, n.s., vol. 15, pp. 433–437.
  1919. Dementia praecox and paraphrenia. Edinburgh.

KRAFFT-EBING, R. VON.
　1875. Lehrbuch der gerichtlichen Psychopathologie. Stuttgart.
KRIS, ERNEST.
　1952. Psychoanalytic explorations in art. New York.
KROEBER, ALFRED LOUIS.
　n. d. (MS.). Unpublished Mohave myths.
　1902. Preliminary sketch of the Mohave Indians. Amer. Anthrop., n.s. vol.
　　　4, pp. 276–285.
　1920. Yuman tribes of the lower Colorado. Univ. California, Publ. Amer.
　　　Archaeol. and Ethnol., vol. 16, No. 8.
　1925 a. Handbook of the Indians of California. Bur. Amer. Ethnol. Bull.
　　　78.
　1925 b. Earth Tongue, a Mohave. In Parsons, Elsie Clews (ed.), American
　　　Indian Life. New York.
　1931. The Seri. Southwest Mus. Pap. No. 6. Los Angeles.
　1932. The Patwin and their neighbors. Univ. California Publ. Amer.
　　　Archaeol. and Ethnol., vol. 29, No. 4.
　1934. Cultural anthropology. In The problem of mental disorder. Bentley,
　　　Madison, and Cowdry, E. W., editors. New York.
　1940. Stepdaughter marriage. Amer. Anthrop., n.s., vol. 42, 562–570.
　1944. Review of McNichols, C.L.: Crazy weather. Amer. Anthrop., n.s.,
　　　vol. 46, p. 394.
　1948. Seven Mohave myths. Anthrop. Rec., vol. 11, No. 1, Berkeley, Calif.
　1950. Personal communication.
　1951 a. Olive Oatman's return. Kroeber Anthrop. Soc. Pap. No. 4, pp. 1–18.
　1951 b. A Mohave historical epic. Anthrop. Rec., vol. 11, No. 2. Berkeley,
　　　Calif.
　1952. The nature of culture. Chicago.
　1957. Ethnographic interpretations (#6). Univ. California Publ. Amer.
　　　Archaeol. and Ethnol., vol. 47, No. 2.
KROEBER, ALFRED LOUIS, EDITOR.
　1935. Walapai ethnography. American Anthrop. Assoc. Mem. 42.
KUBIE, LAWRENCE S.
　1943. Manual of emergency treatment for acute war neuroses. War Medi-
　　　cine, vol. 4, pp. 582–598.
KUBIE, LAWRENCE S., and ISRAEL, H. A.
　1955. "Say you're sorry." The Psychoanalytic Study of the Child, vol. 10,
　　　pp. 289–299.
LA BARRE, WESTON.
　1939. The psychopathology of drinking songs. Psychiatry, vol. 2, pp.
　　　203–212.
　1946. Social cynosure and social structure. Journ. Abnormal and Social
　　　Psychol., vol. 14, No. 3, pp. 169–183.
　1954. The human animal. Chicago.
LANDES, RUTH.
　1938. The Ojibwa woman. New York.
LAUBSCHER, B. J. F.
　1937. Sex, custom and psychopathology. London.
LEIGHTON, DOROTHEA, and KLUCKHOHN, CLYDE.
　1947. Children of the people. Cambridge, Mass.
LÉVI-STRAUSS, CLAUDE.
　1944. The social and psychological aspects of chieftainship in a primitive
　　　tribe: The Nambikuara of Northwestern Mato Grosso, Brasil.
　　　Trans. New York Acad. Sci., Ser. 2, vol. 7, No. 1, pp. 16–32.

LEVY, DAVID M.
1937. Primary affect hunger. Amer. Journ. Psychiatry, vol. 94, No. 3, pp. 643–652.
1943. Maternal overprotection. New York.
LEWIN, BERTRAM D.
1946. Sleep, the mouth and the dream screen. Psychoanalytic Quart., vol. 15, pp. 419–434.
1950. The psychoanalysis of elation. New York.
1958. Dreams and the uses of regression. New York.
LILLY, J. C.
1956 a. Effects of physical restraint and of reduction of ordinary levels of physical stimuli on intact, healthy persons. Illustrative Strategies for Research on Psychopathology and Mental Health. Group for the Advancement of Psychiatry. Symposium 2, pp. 13–20, 44.
1956 b. Mental effects of reduction of ordinary levels of physical stimulation intact, healthy persons. Amer. Psychiatric Assoc., Psychiatric Research Rep., vol. 5, pp. 1–28.
LINTON, RALPH.
1922. The sacrifice to the morning star by the Skidi Pawnee. Field Museum. Chicago.
1936. The study of man. New York.
1945. The cultural background of personality. New York.
1956. Culture and mental disorders. Springfield, Ill.
LOEB, E. M.
1958. The twin cult in the Old and the New World. In Miscellanea Paul Rivet. Mexico City, D.F.
LOWELL, A. L.
1932. Conflicts of principle. Cambridge.
LOWIE, ROBERT HARRY.
1924. Primitive religion. New York.
1929. Are we civilized? New York.
1935. The Crow Indians. New York.
LYND, R. S.
1939. Knowledge for what? Princeton University Press, Princeton, N.J.
MALINOWSKI, BRONISLAW.
1932. The sexual life of savages in North Western Melanesia. 3d ed. London.
MASLOW, A. H.
1940. Dominance-quality and social behavior in infra-human primates. Journ. Soc. Psychol., vol. 11, pp. 313–324.
MAUSS, MARCEL.
1925. Sur un texte de Posidonius. Le suicide, contreprestation supreme. Revue Celtique, vol. 42, pp. 324–329.
1926. Effet physique chez l'individu de l'idée de mort suggerée par la collectivité. Journ. Psychologie Normale et Pathologique, vol. 23, pp. 653–669. (Reprinted in: Sociologie et Anthropologie. Paris, 1950.)
MAY, L. CARLYLE.
1956. A survey of glossolalia and related phenomena in non-Christian religions. Amer. Anthrop., n.s., vol. 58, No. 1, pp. 75–96.
McNICHOLS, CHARLES L.
1944. Crazy weather. New York.

MEAD, MARGARET.
1928. Coming of age in Samoa.   New York.
1932. The changing culture of an Indian tribe.   New York.
MENNINGER, KARL AUGUSTUS.
1938. Man against himself.   New York.
1940. An anthropological note on the theory of prenatal instinctual conflict.   Bull. Menninger Clinic, vol. 4, pp. 51–55.
MENNINGER, KARL AUGUSTUS, and DEVEREUX, GEORGE.
1948. Smith Ely Jelliffe: Father of psychosomatic medicine in America.
Psychoanalytic Rev., vol. 35, pp. 350–363.
MEYERSON, ÉMILE.
1921. De l'explication dans les sciences.   Paris.
MICHAELS, J. J.
1955. Disorders of character.   Springfield, Ill.
MONTAGU, M. F. ASHLEY.
1953. The sensory influences of the skin.   Texas Reports on Biology and
Medicine, vol. 11, No. 2, pp. 291–301.
MURRAY, GILBERT.
1955. Five stages of Greek religion.   Garden City, N.Y.
NETTLE, MARY ANNA ISRAEL.
n. d. (MS.) Lecture on the Mohave before a Women's Club.   Parker, Ariz
NORBECK, EDWARD.
1955. Trans-Pacific similarities in folklore: a research lead.   Kroeber Anthrop. Soc. Pap., vol. 12, pp. 62–69.
OWENS, C. D.
1941. Review of Hasanat, Abul, r.d.   Journ. Criminal Psychopathology,
vol. 3, p. 169.
PARETO, VILFREDO.
1935. The mind and society.   4 vols.   New York.
PARSONS, ANNE.
1956. Expressive symbolism in witchcraft and delusion: A comparative
study.   Revue Internationale d'Ethno-psychologie, vol. 1, no. 2,
pp. 99–119.
PARSONS, DENY S.
1957. Cloud busting: a claim investigated.   Journ. Amer. Soc. Psychical
Research, vol. 51, pp. 136–148.
PICKERELL, A. R.
1957. Death of Órawthomá.   The Masterkey, vol. 31, pp. 166–169.
POINCARÉ, HENRI.
1901. Electricité et optique.   Paris.
1946. The foundations of science.   Lancaster, Pa.
PÖTZL, OTTO.
1917. Experimental erregte Traumbilder in ihrer Beziehung zum direkten
Sehen.   Zeitschrift für die gesamte Neurologie und Psychiatrie,
vol. 37, pp. 278–349.
RICHTER, C. P.
1957. On the phenomenon of sudden death in animals and man.   Psychosomatic Medicine, vol. 19, pp. 191–198.
RIVERS, W. H. R.
1926. Psychology and ethnology.   London.

RÓHEIM, GÉZA.
  1932. Psychoanalysis of primitive cultural types. Internat. Journ. Psycho-Analysis, vol. 13, Nos. 1 and 2, pp. 1–224.
  1933. A primitiv ember [Primitive man.] (in Hungarian) [in] Magyarországi Pszichoanalitikai Egyesület Tagjai [eds.] : Lélek-elemzési tanulmányok [Ferenczi memorial volume]. Budapest.
SACHS, HANNS.
  1933. The delay of the machine age. Psychoanalytic Quart., vol. 2, pp. 404–424.
SACHS, WULF.
  1947. Black anger. Boston.
SCHILDER, PAUL.
  1936. The analysis of ideologies as a psychotherapeutic method, especially in group treatment. Amer. Journ. Psychiatry, vol. 93, No. 3, pp. 601–615.
SIMMONS, L. W., EDITOR.
  1942. Sun Chief. Yale University Press, New Haven.
SPIER, LESLIE.
  1933. Yuman tribes of the Gila River. Chicago.
  1936. Cultural relations of the Gila River and Lower Colorado tribes. Yale Univ. Publ. Anthrop., No. 3. New Haven.
  1953. Some observations of Mohave clans. Southwestern Journ. Anthrop., vol. 9, pp. 324–342.
SPITZ, RENÉ ÁRPÁD.
  1945. Hospitalism. The Psychoanalytic Study of the Child, vol. 1, pp. 53–74.
  1946. Hospitalism, a follow-up report. The Psychoanalytic Study of the Child, vol. 2, pp. 113–117.
SPITZ, RENÉ ÁRPÁD, and WOLF, K. M.
  1946. Anaclitic depression. Psychoanalytic Study of the Child, vol. 2, pp. 313–342.
STEWART, KENNETH M.
  1946. Spirit possession in native America. Southwestern Journ. Anthrop., vol. 2, pp. 323–339.
  1947 a. Mohave hunting. The Masterkey, vol. 21, No. 4, pp. 80–84.
  1947 b. The Mohave mourning ceremony. Amer. Anthrop., n.s., vol. 49, pp. 146–148.
  1947 c. Mohave warfare. Southwestern Journ. Anthrop., vol. 3, No. 3, pp. 257–278.
STOLL, OTTO.
  1904. Suggestion und Hypnotismus in der Völkerpsychologie. Leipzig.
STRATTON, R. B.
  1857. The captivity of the Oatman girls. New York.
SVERDRUP, HARALD ULRICH.
  1938. Hos Tundrafolket [With the people of the Tundra]. (In Norwegian.) Gyldenal Norsk Forlag, Oslo.
TANNENBAUM, FRANK.
  1938. Crime and the community. Boston.
TAYLOR, E. S., and WALLACE, W. J.
  1947. Mohave tattooing and face-painting. Southwest Mus. Leaflets No. 20.
TAYLOR, MEADOWS.
  1839. Confessions of a thug. (Reprinted as No. 207 of "The World's Classics," Oxford University Press, London, 1933).

TEICHER, MORTON I.
  1960. Windigo psychosis: A study of a relationship between belief and behavior among the Indians of northeastern Canada, ed. by Verne F. Ray. *In* Proc. 1960 Ann. Spring Meeting Amer. Ethnol. Soc. Seattle, Wash.

TEITELBAUM, H. A.
  1941. Psychogenic body image disturbances associated with psychogenic asphasis and agnosia. Journ. Nervous and Mental Diseases, vol. 93, pp. 581–612.

THOMAS, W. I.
  1937. Primitive behavior. New York.

THOMPSON, LAURA.
  1948. Attitudes and acculturation. Amer. Anthrop., n.s., vol. 50, pp. 200–215.

TINKLEPAUGH, O. L.
  1928. The self-mutilation of a male Macacus rhesus monkey. Journ. Mammalogy, vol. 9, pp. 293–300.

TOFFELMIER, GERTRUDE, and LUOMALA, KATHERINE.
  1936. Dreams and dream interpretations of the Diegueño Indians of Southern California. Psychoanalytic Quart., vol. No. 2, pp. 195–225.

TÖNNIES, FERDINAND.
  1887. Gemeinschaft und Gesellschaft. Leipzig.

TRILLES, FATHER H.
  1912. Le totemisme chez les Fan. Collection Internationale de Monographies Ethnographiques. Bibliothèque Anthropos, vol. 1, No. 4.

UCHIMURA, Y.; AKIMOTO, H.; and ISHIBASHI, T.
  1938. On the imu of the Ainu race I: Communication on the psychiatric investigation of the Ainu race. [In Japanese.] Psychiatria et Neurologia Japonica, vol. 42, pp. 1–69, 1–3.

UNITED STATES SENATE.
  1955. Hearings before the Subcommittee to investigate juvenile delinquency of the Committee on the Judiciary. U.S. 84th C⁝ng., 1st sess., S.R. 62. Washington, D.C.

USENER, HERMANN.
  1896. Götternamen. (3d unchanged ed. 1948. Frankfurt am Main.)

VEBLEN, THORSTEIN.
  1899. The theory of the leisure class. New York.

VESTAL, STANLEY.
  1932. Sitting Bull, Boston.

WALLACE, A. F. C.
  1951. Some psychological determinants of culture change in an Iroquoian community. Bur. Amer. Ethnol. Bull. 149, pp. 55–76.

WALLACE, WILLIAM J.
  1947. The dream in Mohave life. Journ. Amer. Folklore, vol. 60, pp. 252–258.
  1948. Infancy and childhood among the Mohave Indians. Primitive Man, vol. 21, pp. 19–38.

WILSON, MONICA.
  1954. Nayakyusa ritual and symbolism. Amer. Anthrop., n.s., vol. 56, No. 2, pp. 228–241.

WISSE, JAKOB.
  1933. Selbstmord und Todesfurcht bei den Naturvölkern. Zutphen.

WISSLER, CLARK.
  1932. *Preface to* The changing culture of an Indian tribe, by Mead, Margaret, 1932. New York.

WITTFOGEL, KARL A.
    1957. Oriental despotism. New Haven.
WULFFTEN-PALTHE, P. VAN.
    1936. Psychiatry and neurology in the tropics. *In* A clinical texbook of
        tropical medicine, by A. Liechtenstein. Batavia.
YAP, P. M.
    1952. The Latah reaction. Journ. Mental Science, vol. 98, pp. 515–564.
YAWGER, N. S.
    1936. Emotions as the cause of rapid and sudden death. Archives of
        Neurology and Psychiatry, vol. 36, pp. 875–879.
YERKES, ROBERT M.
    1939. Social dominance and sexual status in the chimpanzee. Quart. Rev.
        Biol., vol. 14, No. 2, pp. 115–136.
ZEIGARNIK, B. W.
    1927. Das Behalten erledigter und unerledigter Handlungen. Psycho-
        logische Forschungen, vol. 9, pp. 1–85.
ZILBOORG, GREGORY, and HENRY, G. W.
    1941. A history of medical psychology. New York.
ZILAHY, LAJOS.
    1949. The Dukays. New York.
ZUCKERMAN, SOLLY.
    1932. The social life of monkeys and apes. New York.

CORRIGENDA

page 40, line 10
    for TCEVA :RAM   *read* TCEVA :RÁM
page 40, line 26
    for tceva:råm   *read* tceva:ràm
page 80, line 17
    for someone present   *read* I
page 88, note 73, line 2
    for *Hippolytus*   read *Phaedra*
page 146, lines 16 and 27
    for Huk' yè:rà   *read* Huk'yè:rà
page 173, line 2
    for Mah   *read* Tcatc
page 201, 4 lines from bottom
    for Bohave   *read* Mohave
page 267, 14 lines from bottom
    for bride   *read* American bride
page 280, 10 lines from bottom of text
    for hoe   *read* hoc
page 280, 4 lines from bottom of text
    for coil   *read* coii
page 283, 15 lines from bottom of text
    for Nabant   *read* Natabant
page 370, 15 lines from bottom of text
    for Mah   *read* Tcatc
page 419, 9 lines from bottom of text
    for assaulted   *read* raped
page 420, note 10, last line
    for Nyoltic   *read* Nyoltc

page 421, line 19
  for trilogy   *read* the King
page 424, line 13
  for Mivsu: *read* Hivsu:
page 424, line 25
  for *supposedly*   read *presumably*
page 477, line 11
  for ful   *read* full
page 484, line 9
  delete entire line
page 493, 2 lines from bottom of text
  for cat   *read* fact
page 514, 6 lines from bottom
  close parentheses after youth
page 561, line 25
  for HRDLIČKA, ALEŠ   *read* HULTKRANTZ, ÅKE
page 564, 8 lines from bottom
  for ihrer Beziehung zum direkten   *read* ihren Beziehungen zum indirekten

ENGLISH TRANSLATION OF LATIN PASSAGES

page 138, note 35

At the peak of sexual excitement the woman sometimes urinates on the man. A drunken woman, whose pubic hair some youths had set on fire, extinguished the flames by urinating. A sexually excited Mohave woman sometimes relaxes her various bodily openings: in normal coitus her vagina may emit gurgling sounds; when penetrated anally she may fart, or defecate on her partner's penis; when performing fellatio, saliva mixed with semen may bubble from her mouth.

page 170, line 29

I am nude and carry my nude beloved in my arms.

page 273, line 4

Do you ever dream of coitus with girls?—No.—Did you ever see anyone copulate?—No.—Did you ever copulate?—No.—Do boys your age copulate with girls?—No.—Do you masturbate?—No.—. . . Do you have wet dreams?—No.

page 274, line 22

Have you seen dogs copulate?—Yes.—Do you get a kick out of it?—No.—Do you have erections?—No. . . .—Do you ever have an erection on awakening?—No. Case 78's penis is always erect. . . . He also masturbates, but I don't.—Does anything come to your mind when you have an erection?—No.—One day I saw Nepe:he with an erection. We were at a gathering and he was going to urinate. I was talking with him when suddenly I heard him exclaim: "Gee!" When I looked at him, I saw that he had an erection. I told him that maybe he wanted a girl, but he said he didn't.

page 277, line 12

I have no wet dreams. [H.K. spontaneously admits that he does have wet dreams.]

page 277, line 16

No boy ever tried to manipulate my penis. Sometimes I masturbate by myself. I do not ejaculate, but there is a tickling which I enjoy. I never saw adults copulate. E. S., a 13-year-old boy, showed me how to copulate; he copulated in my presence with a girl about 13 years of age (E. W.). I had never seen anyone copulate before that; it did not frighten me, but I was ashamed. This happened the same summer that I copulated with R.; it happened about a week before I copulated with her.

I copulated in the summer of 1937 (actually 1936) with R., an 11- (actually 9) year-old Mohave girl. That is how I caught a sore. We did it only once; it happened at her place; she asked to be copulated. In copulating with this girl, I ejaculated. She is the only one I ever copulated with, and only once at that. Now I don't do it—I am afraid of being scolded and am also ashamed.

R. also copulates with other boys, but since I do not care for her, it makes me neither angry nor jealous. She copulates with some Mexican boys who live near her. [. . . Some schoolgirls copulate with grown men.]

I had a sore after copulating with R., but not on my penis. . . . In the hospital I did not say that I had had intercourse, because I was ashamed.

. . . . Some people—both men and women—told my mother that I had copulated, but at first she did not believe it.

page 277, note 8

He does not ejaculate when he masturbates; see above.

page 280, line 37

I have never had intercourse. [Since H. K., Case 78's friend, did not believe this statement, he spontaneously questioned his playmate, mentioning various young girls. Case 78 continued to deny sexual experiences but his furtive giggling contradicted his assertions.]

I do have wet dreams—about big girls over 14 years old. I do not masturbate. [Interpreter once again spontaneously questions him, manifestly doubting his statements.] The fact is (he said) I do masturbate occasionally. To tell you the truth, I copulated with a 13-year-old girl named Mah. . . . I copulated with her frequently. The first time I copulated with her by force. W. H. and I raped her; she yelled loudly, but we did not stop even when some other boys unexpectedly arrived on the scene. I enjoy coitus but do not ejaculate.

page 281, line 9

[Did you ever see anyone copulate?] I saw F. St. copulate, but did not see Hamteya:u (Case 77) nor any adult copulate. . . . [Yet you deny seeing adults copulate?] I do.

page 281, line 25

[Who taught you to copulate?] No one. [And to masturbate?] No one—I learned it by myself. [Do you ejaculate now?] I don't—I do. Much stuff comes out and my penis hurts when I urinate. Also, my testicles became swollen, but I was not taken to the hospital. Also, some pus came out. [Did this happen after you copulated with Mah?] It happened before that. [Does the pus still come out?] Only sometimes. . . .

[Did you ever see animals copulate?] I did—yesterday I saw dogs copulating. I liked watching it; I got an erection but did not masturbate.

I never saw a girl masturbate.

. . . [Did you ever see a girl do this?] I haven't—to tell you the truth, I saw F. W. do it. She does it habitually and I like watching it; it gives me an erection.

page 281, note 21

It is not unusual even for adult Mohaves to engage in group coitus and not to allow themselves to be stopped by unexpected intruders.

page 281, note 29

Sometimes a neurotic girl masturbates in public.

page 283, line 9

Such a girl throws girls her own age or younger on the ground and, lying on top of them rubs her body against theirs. At the same time she constantly manipulates both her own genitals and those of her playmates and masturbates incessantly. Not even boys are safe from her; she throws the boy down the same way and, lying on top of him, grasps his penis and rubs it against her vulva—often violently enough to injure his penis and foreskin. Such a girl once manipulated a boy's penis so violently that she broke his urethra. The girl's relatives at first denied that she had done this, but another girl, who had seen her do it, betrayed her. . . . Later on, such a girl will ask boys to put their fingers into her vagina and even to examine her genitals closely—an action which is extremely abhorrent to normal Mohave women, since they do not allow this to be done to them, except when they are suspected of adultery.

page 283, line 21

Case 79. I recall such a girl, who later on became a great shaman and who did all these things before she was 11 years old. At that time a certain old man used to take her to the river—supposedly to swim. Though this man was old, his penis was not old—the two copulated often. She liked this so much that she repeatedly saw the old man in his home, and he certainly managed to satisfy the girl's desires. You heard Harav He:ya say that in former times men were potent until they died. Their affair became so well known that the old man's wife got suspicious; but, though greatly angered, she wanted to be sure before doing anything about it.

On one occasion this old man took the girl to the river to swim. They swam in the pond, which remained full of water even after the annual flood. The old woman, who had seen both of them leave, hid in the bushes. She saw the girl, bent over the bank, having her anus lubricated by the old man both internally and externally, with slippery clay of the kind that is sometimes used instead of saliva. The old man was trying to insert his penis into the girl's anus, but, just as he was on the point of succeeding, the girl, because of the pain this caused her, threw herself forward, thus causing his penis to slip out again. At that point the angry old woman grabbed a stick and rushed toward them. The old man immediately pushed the girl into the water, urging her to swim to the farther bank of the pond while his angry wife was beating him up with her stick. When she had sufficiently vented her anger on him she said: "It isn't worth the trouble. You can have her now. You don't want me—it is best that I leave you." So she left him and it was she who told me all this later on.

Next summer—at the time when the Colorado River has flooded, when the food is all eaten up and we are planting the fields—we heard that this old couple was once more living together in matrimony. This old couple had a son who was a friend and schoolmate of mine. One day, when the old woman was out, gathering mesquite beans, this girl took advantage of her absence to pay another visit to the old man. I and this old man's son went from school to his house to get some melons. When we reached his house we were amazed by what we saw. The old man had made the girl lean with spread legs and raised skirt against the center pole of the house, while he himself was squatting at her feet, trying to insert his fingers into her vagina. When I saw this, I said to my friend: "There is your father, back at his old tricks! Let us sneak up to them and catch them at it." When he agreed, we lay down on the river bank, some 20 steps from the house. Lying flat and hidden by the dike, we peeked over the bank. The old man was carefully trying to insert his finger, but whenever he pushed it in deeper, a spastic contraction of the girl forced his finger out again. After repeated attempts he finally managed to insert four fingers, while the girl was wriggling her buttocks to help him masturbate her. Suddenly we noticed some liquid dripping from the old man's elbow. I noticed it first and said: "Look— it drips!" The girl had become so aroused that she urinated on the old man's hand. (Hivsu: Tupo:ma denied that this liquid could have been the secretion of the Bartholinic glands. He said it was urine, because the girl "was full of the devil.") In the end, just as we decided to go back to school, because the bell had rung, we saw the girl grab the old man's head, bring it close to her vulva, and wet it with her urine.

page 283, note 32

Among both the Patwin and the Mohave, little girls tend to be penetrated anally at first.

page 284, line 40

After that I called the old man "Siup pip siup"—that being the sound of spurting urine.

page 284, note 33

The Mohave consider female coital hip-wriggling extremely salacious and disgusting.

page 284, note 34

In various parts of Micronesia the men stimulate the women until they urinate. Post-orgasmic urination is also reported from that area.

page 284, note 35

All Mohave deny cunnilingus and claim that a man goes blind if his face comes in contact with the moist vulva.

page 285, line 25

. . . whose most scandalous trick is that, in the presence of women, he [claps his penis between his thighs], pretends to have no penis, and urinates [backwards] like a mare.

page 417, line 16

"A hwame: has no penis. She only pokes you with her finger."

page 417, line 20

"He has no penis; he is just like you."

page 417, line 28

. . . (= split vagina), which describes the coital position of lesbians.

page 417, last line of text

Your "husband" has neither a penis nor testicles.

page 417, note 98

Lesbians who assume the hispan kudha:pe position lie with their heads in opposite directions, one on her back and the other on her side. Their legs are locked scissor-wise, each holding the pelvis of the other between her thighs. In this posture they rub their vulvae against each other.

page 418, line 1

"I'll be damned if I don't copulate with both you and your 'husband.' He is a woman and has what you have!"

page 418, line 12

"Just poke her with your finger, that is what she likes; use your finger, that is what she is accustomed to. Don't waste your penis on her." . . . "Well do I know what you are getting! She pokes her finger into your vagina. Mine still hurts because her fingernails scratched it."

page 418, line 30

"She thinks maybe that she has a penis!"

page 418, note 2

This remark perfectly fits the Mohave opinion that the penis has an inherent dignity. Thus, when a certain woman asked him to penetrate her anally, the man replied indignantly: "My penis has feelings!" It also shows why the Mohave are squeamish about manipulating the female genitals: "it makes the hand smell bad."

page 419, line 39

. . . a real penis. . . .

page 419, line 48

Not seldom, when she was blind drunk, some men would drag her to a hidden spot and farm her out to various men—some of them whites—at so much per intercourse.

CASE INDEX

41. Anonymous old woman, hiwey lak, p. 172.
42. Huau Husek, hiwey lak, incest dream (see Case 103), p. 172.
43. Mu:th Nyemsutkha:v (w) (subject of Case 42 dream), hiwey lak (see Case 103), p. 172.
44. Sudhu:rà, hiwey lak, incest (see Cases 1 and 90), p. 173.
45. N. (w), late pregnancy mistaken for hiwey lak, p. 175.
46. G. A. (w), whom some call a halfbreed (see Case 60), pregnancy mistaken for hiwey lak, p. 175.
47. Tcatc (w) (not the informant), nyevedhi: taha:na, "cannibalistic" dream, p. 182.
48. C. S., paralyzed, violated funeral coitus taboo, p. 191.
49. Pi:it Hi:dho Kwa-ahwat, bewitched by a kinswoman whose love he scorned (Case 75), p. 196.
50. Kanvotce (w) (also others), death from love magic, p. 199.
51. Anonymous victims of Hi:wa Maa:ma's sexual witchcraft, which causes masturbation and atcoo:r hanyienk convulsions (see Case 97), p. 201.
52. Anonymous old man, paralyzed by his magical tcapany root, p. 203.
53. Anonymous Yuma Indian, his hunyavre itcerk magical substance caused fratricide at his wake, p. 205.
54. Hulymànyo:va, made delirious and ill by his "jealous" lodestone (see Case 55), p. 206.
55. Po:tà (w), first wife of Case 54, crippled by her lodestone, p. 206.
56. Ma:le (w), a Chemehuevi, believed to own lodestone, p. 206.
57. People, (perhaps informant Tcatc [w]), dream of lodestones, p. 206.
58. Nyaipatcem, shaman, repeatedly harmed by his magic substances, p. 207.
59. Indian schoolgirls of various tribes drink datura and become intoxicated, p. 209.
60. G. A. (w), anxiety neurosis (?) (see Case 46), p. 216.
61. Nyortc Kupu:yha (w) (see Case 30), hysterical laughter, p. 218.
62. Anonymous Pueblo girl, hysterical laughter, p. 218.
63. Anonymous, hypochondria (?), pellagra psychosis (?), toxic psychosis (?), p. 222.
64. "John Smith," ahwe: (?) (see Case 137), p. 223.
65. Anonymous Havasupai man, dementia praecox, hebephrenic type, p. 243.
66. A. B., Yuma man, hospitalized psychotic, p. 243.
67. A.H.M., Yuma woman, hospitalized psychotic, p. 243.
68. Tànyo, facial tic (?), p. 247.
69. Anonymous Yuma man, chorea, p. 248.
70. Anonymous girl, mute, p. 249.
71. Anonymous girl, almost mute and (allegedly) feebleminded, p. 249.
72. Hu:piny, mute, p. 249.
73. Tuhum Hiwey, tcakwar itu:r (stammer), p. 250.
74. Hispan Tcàliyak, speechless from shock, p. 250.
75. Kumadhi: Atat, neurosyphilis (see Case 49), p. 255.
76. Nepe:he, truancy and stealing, p. 268.
77. Hamteya:u, neurotic negativism following severe ridiculing for contracting gonorrhea at the age of 10 from R. (whose medical record is given on p. 279) (also reference, p. 278, to E., a silent and withdrawn little girl), p. 275.
78. Anonymous boy, aggressivity, problem child, p. 280.
79. [Nyoltc hukthar] (w) (Case 13), precociously promiscuous future shaman, p. 283.
80. Anonymous Yuma berdache, suicide, p. 313.

81. Anonymous Yavapai female transvestite, suicide, p. 313.

82. Anonymous white lovers, double suicide, p. 313.

83. Hualy Hore:e's unborn baby, suicide and murder of mother, refusal to be born, p. 339.

84. O:otc (w), still nursing, contracts tàvàknyi:k, p. 347.

85. ''Hydrocephalous'' twin baby boy's ''suicide,'' p. 355.

86. Stillborn twins' ''suicide,'' p. 355.

87. Kunyii:th (w), an old twin, ''suicide,'' p. 355.

88. Nyail Kwaiki:yo loses eye, feast given, p. 367.

89. O:otc (w), marries her girl cousin's son Humar Atcem, last symbolic suicide feast given, p. 370.

90. Sudhu:rà (Cases 1 and 44) married Tcatc (w) (not the informant), his first cousin once removed, no symbolic suicide rite; both spouses die, p. 370.

91. X. Y. married his second cousin Nyoltc, no ritual, p. 371.

92. Hivsu: Tupo:ma, shaman, intoxicated (Case 139), confesses to incest and witchcraft, p. 385.

93. E. S.'s sister-in-law and Vi:mak (w), owls herald their deaths, p. 392.

94. Hivsu: Tupo:ma, shaman, ill, healed in dream by shaman he planned to consult, p. 396.

95. Anonymous female witch kills for hire, is killed with rocks when detected, p. 402.

96. Anonymous male witch hacked to death in his sleep, p. 403.

97. Hi:wa Maa:ma, causes convulsions, killed (see Case 51), p. 404.

98. Tcemupa:và, weary of life, permits victim to identify him; he is slashed or beaten to death, p. 405.

99. O:otc (w), caused epidemics so as to be paid for curing, awaited her killers stoically, p. 406.

100. Ah'a Kupa:m, caused epidemics so as to be paid for curing and is thereby identified; beaten to death, p. 407.

101. Kwitcia:r, bewitched both his enemies and beloved relatives; bewitched by Kua:lyec, p. 408.

102. Kamaye:hue, suspected of witchcraft, refused to treat his victim; on her death he was beaten to death, p. 410.

103. Tcàvàkong, a crippled, epileptic witch (Case 6), caused epidemics so as to be paid for curing, and admitted it; beaten to death, p. 411.

104. Anyay Ha:m, kills by witchcraft, boasts of it, and threatens his victims' relatives; killed with an ax, p. 412.

105. Sahaykwisa: (w), lesbian, transvestite, prostitute, then ''heterosexual,'' boasted while drunk of having bewitched one of her two current lovers' father, who had rejected her advances; her two lovers drowned her, p. 416.

106. Tàma:ràhue, a shaman (and witch?), drank datura and drowned himself, p. 425 (cf. p. 478).

107. Hama: Utce: (w), regrets cremation of property, p. 443.

108. Mu:th (w), attempts suicide at son's cremation, p. 454.

109. Syuly (w), attempts suicide at husband's cremation but subsequently remarries, p. 455.

110. Utu:rà, attempts suicide at wife's funeral, p. 456.

111. Anyanyema:m, attempts suicide at funeral of son who his nagging and selfishness caused to shoot himself, p. 457 (cf. p. 477).

112. Oo:lva, shaman, owner of magic plants, abused by male cousin, shoots himself, p. 466.

113. Amalyk Tumádha:p, broods over his brother's suicide (Case 112), shoots himself, p. 467.
114. Taparevily, one fourth Yavapai, nagged by Aunt Tanu:, shoots himself, p. 468.
115. Hama: Utce: (w), partly white, also partly Maricopa, nagged by Aunt Tanu:, recalls her brother's suicide (Case 114), thinks of suicide, p. 469.
Supplementary Case A (cf. Case 138). Humar Tudhu:lye, an alcoholic, broods over his brother's accidental death, wants to die, p. 470.
116. J. A., nagged by father to leave his adulterous wife, shoots himself, p. 470.
117. Pa:hay, wife adulterous, slashes his throat but recovers, p. 472.
118. Pi:it (I), nagged by wife, shoots himself, p. 474.
119. Pi:it (II), his family interferes with his "incestuous" and adulterous affair, shoots himself, p. 475.
120. E. T., drunk, wife adulterous, shoots himself, p. 476.
Supplementary Case B (cf. Case 111). Tunayva Kor, nagged by father, shoots himself, p. 477.
121. Kamey He:ya, in trouble with girl, shoots himself but recovers, p. 477.
122. Atci: Ahwat, Indian sheriff, wife unfaithful, shoots himself, recovers, p. 477.
Supplementary Case C. Táma:ráhue (Case 106), unjustly accused of witchcraft, drinks datura and drowns himself, p. 478.
123. Nyortc (w), old, neglected by son (Case 88), suffocates herself, stuffing earth and sand in her mouth, p. 479.
124. Kwali:, alcoholic, cancer of rectum, hangs himself (false rumors of murder), p. 480.
125. Wilymawilyma, deserted by wife, shoots himself, p. 481.
126. Hipily Tcukup, singer, first wounds adulterous wife then shoots himself, p. 482.
127. Atceyer Tcuva:u, wife adulterous, shoots himself; his relatives hire a shaman who fatally bewitches her, p. 482.
128. Allegedly drunk youth rapes and robs his elderly relative, Nyortc Huhual (w) (Case 15), p. 514.
129. Oo:tc (w), a good wife, leaves abusive alcoholic husband and then also drinks excessively for a while, p. 515.
130. P., though made drunk by his wife G. and by J., catches them committing adultery and wounds G., p. 515.
131. Mukoh, drunk, kills Vaha Munyu: in brawl over paternity of "their" child, p. 517.
132. Amiability of an intoxicated Mohave, p. 526.
133. Hama: Utce: (w), as a child, dreams of whiskey, p. 530.
134. Modhar Taa:p, drunk, thinks he sees white snake, p. 531.
135. Taparevily, drunk, wrecks Aunt Tanu:'s car; nagged, he shoots himself (Case 114), p. 536.
136. Sumurámurá, scolded by wife for drunken driving, reacts lovingly and gently, p. 536.
137. "John Smith" (Case 64), becomes temporarily alcoholic because of dreams about a tragically deceased father image, p. 536.
138. Amat Yavu:me, drunk, killed by hit-and-run driver; his equally alcoholic brother, Humar Tudhu:lye, depressed by this, wants to die (Supplementary Case A), p. 538.
139. Hivsu: Tupo:ma, shaman, while drunk, confesses to me his deeds of incest and witchcraft; subsequently, while drunk, sleeps outdoors during a winter night and dies from exposure, p. 542.

140. Sahaykwisa: (w), lesbian, witch, prostitute (Case 105), confesses to witch-craft while drunk and is killed, p. 545.

INDEX OF DREAMS NOT IN CASE HISTORIES

A. Author, running on all fours, p. 170.
B. Author, nudity, self-pursuit, p. 170.
C. Tcatc (w) (not the informant), attacked by lesbians, p. 171.
D. Hama: Utce: (w), cannibalism, p. 183.
E. E. S., cannibalism, p. 183.

INDEX